# DAVID BUSCH'S NIKON® D3S/D3X

## GUIDE TO DIGITAL SLR PHOTOGRAPHY



David D. Busch

**Course Technology PTR**
*A part of Cengage Learning*

COURSE TECHNOLOGY
CENGAGE Learning™

Australia, Brazil, Japan, Korea, Mexico, Singapore, Spain, United Kingdom, United States

COURSE TECHNOLOGY
CENGAGE Learning™

**David Busch's Nikon® D3s/D3x Guide to Digital SLR Photography**
**David D. Busch**

**Publisher and General Manager, Course Technology PTR:**
Stacy L. Hiquet

**Associate Director of Marketing:**
Sarah Panella

**Manager of Editorial Services:**
Heather Talbot

**Marketing Manager:**
Jordan Castellani

**Executive Editor:**
Kevin Harreld

**Project Editor:**
Jenny Davidson

**Technical Reviewer:**
Michael D. Sullivan

**Interior Layout Tech:**
Bill Hartman

**Cover Designer:**
Mike Tanamachi

**Indexer:**
Katherine Stimson

**Proofreader:**
Sara Gullion



Library of Congress Control Number: 2009924524

ISBN-13: 978-1-4354-5434-7

ISBN-10: 1-4354-5434-0

**Course Technology, a part of Cengage Learning**
20 Channel Center Street
Boston, MA 02210
USA

Cengage Learning is a leading provider of customized learning solutions with office locations around the globe, including Singapore, the United Kingdom, Australia, Mexico, Brazil, and Japan. Locate your local office at: **international.cengage.com/region**.

Cengage Learning products are represented in Canada by Nelson Education, Ltd.

For your lifelong learning solutions, visit **courseptr.com**.

Visit our corporate Web site at **cengage.com**.

Printed in the United States of America
1 2 3 4 5 6 7 12 11 10

*For Cathy*

# Acknowledgments

Once again thanks to the folks at Course Technology PTR, who recognize that cameras as sophisticated as the Nikon D3s and D3x deserve in-depth, full-color coverage at a price anyone can afford. Special thanks to executive editor Kevin Harreld, who always gives me the freedom to let my imagination run free with a topic, as well as my veteran production team, including project editor Jenny Davidson and technical editor Mike Sullivan. Also thanks to Bill Hartman, layout; Katherine Stimson, indexing; Sara Gullion, proofreading; Mike Tanamachi, cover design; and my agent, Carole Jelen, who has the amazing ability to keep both publishers and authors happy.

# About the Author

With more than a million books in print, **David D. Busch** is the world's #1 selling digital camera guide author, and the originator of popular digital photography series like *David Busch's Pro Secrets* and *David Busch's Quick Snap Guides.* He has written more than a dozen hugely successful guidebooks for Nikon digital SLR models, and a dozen additional user guides for other camera models, as well as many popular books devoted to dSLRs, including *Mastering Digital SLR Photography, Second Edition* and *Digital SLR Pro Secrets.* As a roving photojournalist for more than 20 years, he illustrated his books, magazine articles, and newspaper reports with award-winning images. He's operated his own commercial studio, suffocated in formal dress while shooting weddings-for-hire, and shot sports for a daily newspaper and upstate New York college. His photos have been published in magazines as diverse as *Scientific American* and *Petersen's PhotoGraphic*, and his articles have appeared in *Popular Photography & Imaging, The Rangefinder, The Professional Photographer*, and hundreds of other publications. He's also reviewed dozens of digital cameras for CNet and *Computer Shopper*, and his advice has been featured in National Public Radio's *All Tech Considered.*

When About.com named its top five books on Beginning Digital Photography, debuting at the #1 and #2 slots were Busch's *Digital Photography All-In-One Desk Reference for Dummies* and *Mastering Digital Photography.* During the past year, he's had as many as five of his books listed in the Top 20 of Amazon.com's Digital Photography Bestseller list—simultaneously! Busch's 120-plus other books published since 1983 include bestsellers like *David Busch's Quick Snap Guide to Using Digital SLR Lenses.*

Busch earned top category honors in the Computer Press Awards the first two years they were given (for *Sorry About The Explosion* and *Secrets of MacWrite, MacPaint and MacDraw*), and he later served as Master of Ceremonies for the awards. Visit his website at http://www.nikonguides.com.

# Contents

## Chapter 2
## Nikon D3s/D3x Roadmap 43



## Chapter 3
## Setup: Playback and Shooting Menus 93

## Chapter 9
## Working with Lenses 353

## Chapter 10
## Making Light Work for You 399

## Chapter 11
## Useful Software for the Nikon D3s/D3x 443



## Chapter 12
## Nikon D3s/D3x: Troubleshooting and Prevention 461

# Preface

The Nikon D3s and D3x digital SLRs are the most advanced full-frame (FX) format digital SLR cameras that Nikon has ever offered for the professional or avid amateur photographer. Yet, the 400-plus page black-and-white manuals packed in the boxes with these cameras are almost impossible to wade through. Everything is in there, but how do you find it? And what does it all *mean?* What you really need is a comprehensive guide that explains the purpose and function of every one of the controls of the D3-series cameras, how you should use them in specific situations, and why.

You don't simply want to learn how to use live view; you want to know how the ability to preview your picture on the D3s/D3x's huge LCD can help you compose or take better photos, and how you can use it when shooting your own motion clips with the video-capable D3s. Before you spend a chunk of change on the Nikon GP-1 global positioning system (GPS) accessory, you'd like to know the exact benefits of this device. What's Active D-Lighting, and when can using it actually *degrade* the quality of your images? You know that you can use certain older lenses with your D3s or D3x—but why would you want to? This is the book that provides those answers.

If you want a quick introduction to the D3-series focus controls, flash synchronization options, how to choose lenses, or which exposure modes are best, this book is for you. If you can't decide on what basic settings to use with your camera because you can't figure out how changing ISO or white balance or focus defaults will affect your pictures, you need this guide. I won't talk down to you, either; this book isn't padded with dozens of pages of checklists telling you how to take a travel picture, a sports photo, or how to take a snapshot of your kids in overly simplistic terms. There are no special sections devoted to "real world" recipes here. All of us do 100 percent of our shooting in the real world! So, I give you all the information you need to cook up great photos on your own!

# Introduction

My goal for this book is simple: to make this the best introductory guide for the Nikon D3-series cameras—especially the Nikon D3s and D3x—that has ever been written. I'm going to cover every aspect of these full-featured professional cameras, and share with you the experience and insight I've accumulated since I began using one of the first Nikon D3 cameras introduced in 2007. I'm going to avoid the limitations of those 300-page pocket-sized guides that summarize everything, yet fully explain nothing, while filling as many pages as I need to with the information you must have to use these cameras successfully. It's an ambitious undertaking, but I've never been quite as enthusiastic about any cameras as I am about the Nikon D3s and D3x.

So, I'll start off with, welcome back! Or, pleased to meet you!—as the case may be. My e-mails tell me that many of you have been looking forward to this book because you benefited from one of my previous guides to using Nikon digital SLRs. Every one of them has been the bestselling book available for their respective Nikon models. But if this is the first time you've given me the opportunity to introduce you to a Nikon dSLR, welcome aboard!

This is my most ambitious camera guide, yet, written for two of the most ambitious cameras Nikon has ever introduced. My original Nikon D3 became my mainstay digital camera body from the day I received it late in 2007; the new D3s supplanted it two years later as my go-to camera for the majority of my sports, action, concert, and travel shooting. I've owned a Nikon D3x since the first day they were available in the United States, too, and it quickly became my second-most-used camera, and my #1 choice for portraits, studio and location fashion photography, landscapes, and product photography of any type. So, when I undertook to produce a book about these cameras, I was writing about two of the best cameras I've ever owned. Although I relish using and documenting a variety of different camera models, this book about the D3-series models has been a labor of love in more ways than one.

Indeed, I've been using Nikon-based digital single lens reflex (SLR) cameras since before they had Nikon's name on them. That happy experience dates back to the previous millennium, when the wizards at Kodak began melding Nikon F3 film SLRs with 1.3-megapixel CCD sensors and a tethered 200MB *external* hard drive. After working with the Nikon-platform Kodak DCS dSLRs, right up through the final Kodak DCS SLR

14/n model, I've owned every single one of the Nikon-branded digital SLRs since the D70, and an alarming number of the company's lenses and accessories.

Although it's difficult to peg two cameras that had introductory manufacturers' suggested retail prices of $5,200 and $7,995 affordable, over the long term they can be called bargains of a sort, when compared to $30,000 1.3-megapixel cameras of the distant past, and even the $3,500 4.1-megapixel Nikon D2Hs, which was available new as recently as four years ago. People may blanch at the cost of these cameras, but for the professionals they are aimed at (and the avid non-professionals for whom price is no object), the D3s and D3x are good deals. (I know I've made far more money from each than I paid for either camera.)

The Nikon D3s and D3x are also more *expandable* than any previous Nikon dSLRs in this price range, although most of the accessories for these cameras (other than, say, viewfinder focus screens) are also available for less pricey cameras. You can add the Nikon GP-1 global positioning system adapter to embed location data in your images, or the WT-4a wireless transmitter for WiFi remote operation and direct transfer of your photos to a laptop or other computer. Want hi-res viewing? Your high definition television can be used to savor the output of your camera, with only an HDMI cable required.

You'll find that the Nikon D3s/D3x also include tons of *very cool features*, many of which they share with other models. These shared capabilities include a live view capability that allows previewing the actual image on the camera's LCD screen before you snap a picture; a super-speedy 51-point autofocus system; a metering system that works well with virtually every Nikon lens ever made, dating back to 1959 (although some require a $35 modification for compatibility); and, with the D3s, built-in sensor cleaning and HDTV movie-making capabilities (which were not included with the original D3 or D3x). If you can't outfit your D3s or D3x to handle a particular task, it probably can't be done with any camera.

## Which Cameras Are Covered?

This was written specifically for the Nikon D3s and Nikon D3x cameras, which are quite similar in layout and function, with a few exceptions, which I detail in more depth in Appendix A. Each camera has slight differences in control layout and menu navigation, and I'll point these differences out as we go along. For example, the D3x has a live view position on the release mode dial, and cannot shoot movies. The D3s includes a quiet shutter release mode on that dial, and uses a dedicated Live view button to activate sensor-based image and video clip preview. As I was writing this book, I found that the similarities between the two cameras and their functions were so numerous that it was entirely practical to write a guide that covered both, with only a minimal amount of differentiation. If you own a Nikon D3s or D3x, you can use this book as if it were written just for your camera.

I believe that owners of the original Nikon D3 will find *David Busch's Nikon D3s/D3x Guide to Digital SLR Photography* useful as well. After all, a great deal of the advice I supply within these pages was compiled from two years' use and tens of thousands of exposures with the "old" D3 model. (I've been using the D3x all along, as well, but, as a non-sports camera; the tendency has been to use it at slower frame rates for some thousands of fewer exposures in the time that I've owned it.) So, you'll find that most of the descriptions in this book apply to the D3 as well as the D3s and D3x. The only reason I didn't formally include that model in the coverage is that I wanted to avoid the complications of the few (but tricky) exceptions where the D3 is slightly different from *both* the D3s and D3x. And who wouldn't wonder if a book labeled as a "D3/D3s/D3x" guide weren't a bit too generic for their taste?

Nikon D3, Nikon D3s, Nikon D3x: I love all three of you, and this is the book I wish I'd had when I first moved up to a full-frame camera from my original 2005-era D2x.

**NAMING CONVENTIONS**

Throughout most of this book, I will refer to the two cameras covered in several different ways. When talking about aspects that are, more or less, identical between the cameras, I'll refer to them collectively as the Nikon D3s/D3x. I'll use both terms interchangeably, with the longer form helping to remind you that I am talking about both the D3s and D3x as if they were a single camera. (But you know that they aren't.) I may also refer to the Nikon D3s and D3x, either collectively or individually. When a feature or control or other aspect applies *only* to one camera or the other, I'll point that out explicitly, either with a sentence or paragraph describing the difference or, if the difference is minor, with a parenthetical note. For example, the No memory card? function in the Custom Setting menu is specified by using Custom Setting f9 (D3x) or Custom Setting f10 (D3s). The goal is to provide the most concise information, while avoiding confusion.

## Why the Nikon D3s/D3x Deserves a Book Like This One

Whether you're a veteran of my previous books or a new convert, I think you'll find this introduction to the D3s/D3x quite different from the other books on the market. It's bigger, more comprehensive, and has only color illustrations, unlike other books that are smaller, cover only the basics, and concentrate more on generalities than how to use your Nikon camera. When I first saw the first of the D3-series cameras, I scanned its list of features and realized that it deserved an entirely different approach than that offered by most so-called "guidebooks."

Feedback from readers of my previous books has convinced me that a compact "field guide" doesn't really provide all the information needed to become proficient with a digital single lens reflex (dSLR) camera. Don't let anyone convince you that what you need is a book you can tuck in a pocket and take with you everywhere. Nikon packs one of those in the box with the camera. My goal is to provide easy-to-understand, but comprehensive, information about this advanced camera.

Although many shrewd, if very ambitious, beginners will be buying the D3s/D3x as a first digital SLR, the vast majority of you will be advanced amateurs or professional photographers—or those who aspire to join those ranks as quickly as possible. You don't need a book that devotes almost a third of its pages to little sections that provide the rudiments of shooting the most basic types of pictures. You don't need to be told that you ought to use a fast shutter speed when shooting sports—you probably already know a dozen different kinds of action situations when *slower* shutter speeds are superior (such as motor sports with spinning tires, or when panning to capture a long jumper speeding towards the pit).

There's a good chance that telling you to use a large aperture when shooting a portrait is a bit simplistic for your skill level, too. If not, don't worry, I provide this kind of information, too. I just don't waste dozens of pages on these basic techniques when they can be covered in a few pages before jumping into the truly cool stuff. Instead, I'm going to emphasize the exciting things you can do with the Nikon D3s/D3x digital SLR. After a couple introductory chapters that help you get your bearings with this innovative camera, we're going to explore dSLR photography using a significant new tool.

I sincerely believe that this book is your best bet for learning how to use your new camera, and for learning how to use it well. If you're a Nikon D3s/D3x owner who's looking to learn more about how to use this great camera, you've probably already explored your options. There are DVDs and online tutorials—but who can learn how to use a camera by sitting in front of a television or computer screen? Do you want to watch a movie or click on HTML links, or do you want to go out and take photos with your camera? Videos and web pages are fun, but not the best answer.

Of course, there's always the 400-plus page manual furnished with the camera. It's compact and filled with information, but there's really very little in there about *why* you should use particular settings or features, and its organization may make it difficult to find what you need. Multiple cross-references may send you flipping back and forth between two or three sections of the book to find what you need. The basic manual is also hobbled by black-and-white line drawings and tiny monochrome pictures that aren't very good examples of what you can do.

As I mentioned earlier, I haven't been happy with the third-party guidebooks to Nikon cameras, either, especially those written for advanced models like the D3s/D3x. The existing books range from skimpy and illustrated by black-and-white photos to lushly illustrated in full color but too generic to do much good. Photography instruction is useful, but it needs to be related directly to the Nikon D3s/D3x as much as possible.

I've tried to make *David Busch's Nikon D3s/D3x Guide to Digital SLR Photography* different from your other D3s/D3x learn-up options. The roadmap sections use larger, color pictures to show you where all the buttons and dials are, and the explanations of what they do are longer and more comprehensive. Instead of the checklists devoted to general topics like "architectural photography" or "landscape photography," you'll find tips and techniques for using all the features of your Nikon D3s/D3x to take *any kind of picture* you want.

Nor is this book a lame rewriting of the manual that came with the camera. Some folks spend five minutes with a book like this one, spot some information that also appears in the original manual, and decide "Rehash!" without really understanding the differences. Yes, you'll find information here that is also in the owner's manual, such as the parameters you can enter when changing your D3s/D3x's operation in the various menus. Basic descriptions—before I dig in and start providing in-depth tips and information—may also be vaguely similar. There are only so many ways you can say, for example, "Hold the shutter release down halfway to lock in exposure and focus."

But not *everything* in the manual is included in this book. I don't include a table of error messages, for instance, because their appearance is fairly rare to begin with, and I'd expect you to go grab the manual to look one up if an error occurs. Nor do I provide advice on how to store your camera, or a complete list of memory card capacities for various file formats. I want you to *use* your D3s/D3x, not store it, and you can easily figure out the capacity of any freshly formatted memory card you own from the figure displayed on the top-panel LCD. Thinking of buying a card with twice as many gigabytes as your current memory card? Multiply the figure you get with the old card by two; that will be close enough. Not *everything* should be included in a guidebook like this one.

*David Busch's Nikon D3s/D3x Guide to Digital SLR Photography* is aimed at both Nikon and dSLR veterans as well as newcomers to digital photography and digital SLRs. Both groups can be overwhelmed by the options the D3s/D3x offers, while underwhelmed by the explanations they receive in their user's manual. The manuals are great if you already know what you don't know, and you can find an answer somewhere in a booklet arranged by menu listings and written by a camera vendor employee who last threw together instructions on how to operate a point-and-shoot digital camera.

Once you've read this book and are ready to learn more, I hope you pick up one of my other guides to digital SLR photography. All but one are aimed at photographers who are less advanced than you are likely to be. However, if you've jumped right into the pool with the Nikon D3s/D3x as your first digital SLR, one of them may provide the kind of introductory material you need to get up to speed. Several of these dSLR guides are offered by Course Technology PTR, and each approaches topics from a different perspective.

They include:

***David Busch's Quick Snap Guide to Using Digital SLR Lenses***

A bit overwhelmed by the features and controls of digital SLR lenses, and not quite sure when to use each type? This book explains lenses, their use, and lens technology in easy-to-access two- and four-page spreads, each devoted to a different topic, such as depth-of-field, lens aberrations, or using zoom lenses. If you have a friend or significant other who is less versed in photography, but who wants to borrow and use your Nikon D3s/D3x from time to time, this book can save you a ton of explanation.

***David Busch's Quick Snap Guide to Lighting***

This book tells you everything you need to know about using light to create the kind of images you'll be proud of. It's not Nikon-specific, and doesn't include any details on using any of the Nikon dedicated flash units, but the information you'll find applies to any digital SLR photography.

***David Busch's Quick Snap Guide to Photo Gear***

Here, you'll find tips on adding the best gadgets and gear to your shooting arsenal, from tripods and ballheads, to lighting equipment, GPS devices, and even camera bags. Like the other *Quick Snap* books, it's not Nikon-specific, but serves as a type of buying guide that tells you everything you need to know about accessories and equipment before you make an investment.

***Quick Snap Guide to Digital SLR Photography***

Consider this a prequel to the book you're holding in your hands. It, too, might make a good gift for a spouse or friend who may be using your D3s/D3x, but who lacks even basic knowledge about digital photography, digital SLR photography, and Nikon photography. It serves as an introduction that summarizes the basic features of digital SLR cameras in general (not just the D3s/D3x), and what settings to use and when, such as continuous autofocus/single autofocus, aperture/shutter priority, EV settings, and so forth. The guide also includes recipes for shooting the most common kinds of pictures, with step-by-step instructions for capturing effective sports photos, portraits, landscapes, and other types of images. (Here is where you will find those bullet-point checklists I've left out of *this* book.)

***Mastering Digital SLR Photography, Second Edition***

This book is an introduction to digital SLR photography, with nuts-and-bolts explanations of the technology, more in-depth coverage of settings, and whole chapters on the most common types of photography. While not specific to the Nikon D3s/D3x, this book can show you how to get more from its capabilities.

***Digital SLR Pro Secrets***

This is my more advanced guide to dSLR photography with greater depth and detail about the topics you're most interested in. If you've already mastered the basics in *Mastering Digital SLR Photography*, this book will take you to the next level.

## Family Resemblance

If you've owned previous models in the Nikon digital camera line, and copies of my books for those cameras, you're bound to notice a certain family resemblance. Nikon has been very crafty in introducing upgraded cameras that share the best features of the models they replace, while adding new capabilities and options. You benefit in two ways. If you used a previous Nikon dSLR prior to switching to the latest D3s or D3x model, you'll find that the parts that haven't changed have a certain familiarity for you, making it easy to make the transition to the newest model. There are lots of features and menu choices of this camera that are exactly the same as those in the most recent models, such as the Nikon D300s. This family resemblance will help level the learning curve for you.

Similarly, when writing books for each new model, I don't start completely from scratch. In that respect, you'll find the content of this book to be similar in some ways to my books on the Nikon D300s and D700. Rather than re-invent the wheel, I try to retain the easy-to-understand explanations that worked for the earlier cameras, and concentrate on expanded descriptions of things readers have told me they want to know more about, a solid helping of fresh sample photos, and lots of details about the latest and greatest new features. Rest assured, this book was written expressly for you, and tailored especially for the D3s/D3x. If you own one of my other guides, you'll find that descriptions of the features that haven't changed are very similar, but that I've updated this revision with lots of new material (on features like geotagging and HDTV movie-making) and expanded my tips and recommendations. This is my biggest and most complete Nikon guide yet.

## How This Book Is Organized

One of the most lively debates I have with my readers is how my books are organized. You're probably (painfully) familiar with how Nikon organizes the books that come with the camera. Nikon's tendency is to lay everything out, in terms of controls and functions, in the beginning of the book, then supply numerous cross-references for nearly everything to multiple locations in the guidebook. For example, if you look up the BKT (bracketing) button in the Getting to Know the Camera section at the front of the manual, you'll discover cross-references to no fewer than five locations in the book. Using the D3s as an example, you'd have to jump to pages 137, 141, 145, 204, and 322 to learn about bracketing (and *which* of those parts of the book have the information you need). When you jump to a cross-reference, you're just as likely to find another pointer to a *different* part of the manual.

Of course, some cross-references are a necessary evil. It's simply not possible to explain *everything* about a particular feature in one location. If I tried that, this book would consist of four 150-page chapters, and would be impossible to wade through. And, even then, it would *still* be necessary to have either repetition or cross-references, because you can't really understand something like, say, bracketing, without first grasping the essentials of correct exposure and things like histograms. And, to understand exposure, those of you who are newer to photography than the typical D3-series owner may benefit from a primer on f/stops and shutter speeds.

But not everyone needs every explanation. Some of you have a good grasp of many topics and just want to read the basics right now, and leave the in-depth explanations until later. So, that's the approach I've taken in my guidebooks. The first half covers basic information that you may need. Chapter 1 includes "quick start" setup and pre-flight checklist-type information. Chapter 2 provides a roadmap of every control and dial on the D3s and D3x, but *unlike* the Nikon manual, it also includes some basics on how to use those controls. You won't need to jump to another part of the book if all you need are the basics. Chapters 3, 4, and 5 go into more detail, outlining most of what you need to know about every single menu choice and option—and devoting roughly 150 pages just to that information.

Each of those first five chapters may include some cross-references to later chapters in the book, where things like exposure, using lenses, working with the movie features of the D3s, and so forth, can all be organized around like topics. I know there are some who would like to have comprehensive 150-page chapters, but I know this organization really works best for a sophisticated camera like the Nikon D3s or D3x. Dividing the book into two parts gives me the opportunity to first introduce you to the camera in the beginning chapters, and then relate its features to *photography* in the latter half.

## Who Are You?

I started my own guidebook series when I saw other publishers trying to use the exact same approach when preparing a book about cameras like the Nikon D3-series as for an entry-level model like the Nikon D3000. While there is always some overlap, individual camera models have specific types of photographers that they appeal to. So, when preparing a guidebook for an individual camera, I always consider it wise to consider exactly who will be reading the book. Indeed, thinking about the potential audience for *David Busch's Nikon D3s/D3x Guide to Digital SLR Photography* is what led me to taking the exact approach and format I use for this book and those intended for other "high end" cameras like the Nikon D700 and D300s. I realized that the needs of readers like you had to be addressed both from a functional level (what you will use the D3s/D3x for) as well as from a skill level (how much experience you may have with digital photography, dSLRs, or Nikon cameras specifically).

From a functional level, you probably fall into one of these categories:

- Professional photographers who will be taking photos for events, publication, portrait, or product photography studio work, or to meet other client needs.
- Individuals who want to get better pictures, or perhaps transform their growing interest in photography into a full-fledged hobby or artistic outlet with a Nikon D3s/D3x and advanced techniques.
- Those who want to produce more professional-looking images for their personal or business website, and feel that the Nikon D3s/D3x will give them more control and capabilities.
- Small business owners with more advanced graphics capabilities who want to use the Nikon D3s/D3x to document or promote their business.
- Corporate workers who may or may not have photographic skills in their job descriptions, but who work regularly with graphics and need to learn how to use digital images taken with a Nikon D3s/D3x for reports, presentations, or other applications.
- Professional webmasters with strong skills in programming (including Java, JavaScript, HTML, Perl, etc.) but little background in photography, but who realize that the D3s/D3x can be used for sophisticated photography.
- Graphic artists and others who already may be adept in image editing with Photoshop or another program, and who need to learn more about digital photography and the special capabilities of the D3s/D3x dSLR.

Addressing your needs from a skills level can be a little trickier, because the D3s/D3x is such a great camera that a full spectrum of photographers will be buying it, from absolute beginners who have never owned a digital camera before up to professionals with years of shooting experience who will be using the Nikon D3s/D3x as their main camera. While, I hope, true beginners won't bite off more than they can chew with a D3-series camera, I recognize that some the readers of this book will be at that level.

If so, before tackling this book, it would be helpful for you to understand the following:

- **What a digital SLR is:** It's a camera that generally shows an optical (not LCD) view of the picture that's being taken through the (interchangeable) lens that actually takes the photo, thanks to a mirror that reflects an image to a viewfinder, but flips up out of the way to allow the sensor to be exposed. Some dSLRs, like the D3s/D3x, also have a *live view* option that flips up the mirror to allow a real-time display on the LCD.
- **How digital photography differs from film:** The image is stored not on film (which I call the *first* write-once optical media), but on a memory card as pixels that can be transferred to your computer, and then edited, corrected, and printed without the need for chemical processing.
- **What the basic tools of correct exposure are:** Shutter speed determines the amount of time the sensor is exposed to incoming light; the f/stop or aperture is like a valve that governs the quantity of light that can flow through the lens; the sensor's sensitivity (ISO setting) controls how easily the sensor responds to light. All three factors can be varied individually and proportionately to produce a picture that is properly exposed (neither too light nor too dark).

If you have a good understanding of those points, and, if you purchased a super-advanced model like the D3s or D3x, I hope you do, then you're ready to go. I'm not going to explain those fundamentals in a lot of detail in this book. After some introductory material that lays out a roadmap of the D3s/D3x and its controls and settings, we're going to move quite quickly into more advanced topics. It's tough to provide something for everybody, so here is my advice for each group at typical skill levels:

- **Digital photography newbies:** If you've used only point-and-shoot digital cameras, or have worked only with non-SLR film cameras, you're to be congratulated for selecting one of the very best digital SLRs available as your first advanced model. (You're also very brave: these cameras are a lot for a beginner to handle, although they *can* be mastered with hard work.) This book can help you understand the controls and features of your D3s/D3x, and lead you down the path to better photography with your camera, but it doesn't spend a lot of time with the basic-basics, including what shutter speeds are, or how to compose a photo. You'll need to work extra hard to get up to speed. I don't want to seem like I am hawking my other books relentlessly, but you actually could benefit from other resources in addition to this guide, whether written by me or another author. Once you've absorbed the fundamentals, however, you'll find that the D3s/D3x will allow you to take your best photos ever.

- **Advanced point-and-shooters moving on up:** There are some quite sophisticated pocket-sized digital cameras available, including those with many user-definable options and settings, so it's possible you are already a knowledgeable photographer, even though you're new to the world of the digital SLR. You've recognized the limitations of the point-and-shoot camera: even the best of them have more noise at higher sensitivity (ISO) settings than a camera like the Nikon D3s/D3x; the speediest still have an unacceptable delay between the time you press the shutter and the photo is actually taken; even a non-interchangeable super-zoom camera with 12X to 20X magnification often won't focus close enough, include an aperture suitable for low-light photography, or take in the really wide view you must have. Interchangeable lenses and other accessories available for the Nikon D3s/D3x are another one of the reasons you moved up. Because you're an avid photographer already, you should pick up the finer points of using the D3s/D3x from this book with no trouble.
- **Film SLR veterans new to the digital world:** You may be a hold-out, but you do understand photography. You know about f/stops and shutter speeds, and thrive on interchangeable lenses. If you own a recent film SLR, particularly the Nikon F6, it probably has lots of electronic features already, including autofocus and sophisticated exposure metering. Perhaps you've even been using a Nikon film SLR and understand many of the available accessories that work with both film and digital cameras. All you need is information on using digital-specific features, working with the D3s/D3x itself, and how to match—and exceed—the capabilities of your film camera with your new Nikon D3s/D3x.
- **Experienced dSLR users upgrading to the D3s/D3x:** Perhaps you started out with the Nikon D70 back in 2004, a D100 before that, or have been working extensively with a more recent model, like the Nikon D90 or D300s. It's very likely that a large number of you used the Nikon D200 before the bug to advance to more megapixels and more advanced features bit you. You may have used a digital SLR from Canon or another vendor and are making the switch. You understand basic photography, and want to learn more. And, most of all, you want to transfer the skills you already have to the Nikon D3s/D3x, as quickly and seamlessly as possible.
- **Pro photographers and other advanced shooters:** I expect my most discerning readers will be those who already have extensive experience with Nikon intermediate and pro-level cameras. An amazing number of D3s/D3x cameras have been purchased by those who feel it is superior, in some respects, to their previous "favorite" camera, the ancient, but still serviceable Nikon D2x or D2xs. Others (like myself) owned the D3 and find that the D3s/D3x fills a specific niche incredibly well. You pros and semi-pros, despite your depth of knowledge, should find this book useful for learning about the features the D3s/D3x has that your previous cameras lacked.

# Who Am I?

After spending years as the world's most successful unknown author, I've become slightly less obscure in the past few years, thanks to a horde of camera guidebooks and other photographically oriented tomes. You may have seen my photography articles in *Popular Photography & Imaging* magazine. I've also written about 2,000 articles for magazines like *Petersen's PhotoGraphic* (which is now defunct through no fault of my own), plus *The Rangefinder, Professional Photographer,* and dozens of other photographic publications. But, first, and foremost, I'm a photojournalist and made my living in the field until I began devoting most of my time to writing books. Although I love writing, I'm happiest when I'm out taking pictures, which is why I took off several times in the year leading up to this book to visit Major League Baseball Spring Training; the Sedona Red Rocks and Grand Canyon areas of Arizona; Prague, in the Czech Republic; and, in October 2009, my biennial visit to Spain. My D3x got a real workout in January 2010, when it traveled with me to Florida to shoot flora and fauna in the Everglades.

Like all my digital photography books, this one was written by a Nikon devotee with an incurable photography bug. My first Nikon SLR was a venerable Nikon F back in the 1960s, and I've owned most of the newer digital models since then. Over the years, I've worked as a sports photographer for an Ohio newspaper and for an upstate New York college. I've operated my own commercial studio and photo lab, cranking out product shots on demand and then printing a few hundred glossy 8 × 10s on a tight deadline for a press kit. I've served as a photo-posing instructor for a modeling agency. People have actually paid me to shoot their weddings and immortalize them with portraits. I even prepared press kits and articles on photography as a PR consultant for a large Rochester, N.Y., company, which shall remain nameless. My trials and travails with imaging and computer technology have made their way into print in book form an alarming number of times, including a few dozen on scanners and photography.

Like you, I love photography for its own merits, and I view technology as just another tool to help me get the images I see in my mind's eye. But, also like you, I had to master this technology before I could apply it to my work. This book is the result of what I've learned, and I hope it will help you master your Nikon D3s or D3x digital SLR, too.

As I write this, I'm currently in the throes of upgrading my website, which you can find at www.dslrguides.com/blog/, adding tutorials and information about my other books. There's a lot of information about several Nikon models right now, but I'll be adding tips and recommendations about the Nikon D3s/D3x (including a list of equipment and accessories that I can't live without) in the next few months. I hope you'll stop by for a visit. I've also set up a wish list of Nikon cameras, lenses, and accessories on Amazon.com for those who want to begin shopping now. I hope you'll stop by for a visit to http://astore.amazon.com/nikonphoto-20.

# 1

# Getting Started with Your Nikon D3s/D3x

Whether you subscribe to the "my camera is just a tool" theory, or belong to the "an exquisite camera adds new capabilities to my shooting arsenal" camp, picking up a new Nikon D3x or D3s camera is a special experience. Those who simply wield tools will find either camera as comforting as an old friend, a solid piece of fine machinery ready and able to do their bidding as part of the creative process.

Other photographers see the low-light capabilities, the rapid-fire continuous shooting, and anvil-like ruggedness of the D3s, or the ultra-high resolution of the D3x, and gain a sense of empowerment. *Here* is a camera with fewer limitations and more capabilities for exercising renewed creative vision. In either case, using less mawkish terms, the D3s/D3x is one of the coolest cameras Nikon has ever offered. Whether you're upgrading from another brand, from another Nikon full-frame model (like the D700), from a DX model like the D2xs or D300-series, or (O brave one!) your D3s/D3x is your first digital camera and/or SLR, welcome to the club.

But, now that you've unwrapped and recharged the beast, mounted a lens, and fueled it with a memory card or two, what do you *do* with it? That's where this chapter—and the chapters that follow—should come in handy. Like many of you, I am a D*x* (single-digit, D1, D2, or D3 series) user of long standing. And, like other members of our club, I had to learn at least some aspects of my D3s and D3x cameras for the very first time at some point. Experienced pro, or D*x*-class newbie, you bought this book because you wanted to get the most from a very powerful tool, and I'm here to help.

The Nikon D3s and D3x are Nikon's unabashed "professional" cameras, a distinction that I find almost meaningless in the greater scheme of things. I know consummate professionals who produce amazing images with a Nikon D70; experienced wedding photographers who evoke the most romantic photos from a Nikon D80. The Nikon D3s/D3x is a professional camera in all the traditional senses: built like a tank, reliable for hundreds of thousands of exposures, capable of lightning-fast autofocusing and superb image quality, whether you're shooting in a studio or drenched in driving rain. But whether your *images* are of professional quality, both technically and inspirationally, depends on what's between your ears, and how you apply it. The goal of this book is to provide you with the information you need to put your brain cells and your Nikon's electro-mechanical components to work productively.

I have no doubt that you've already been out shooting a few hundred (or thousand) photographs with your pride and joy. After all, inserting a memory card, mounting a lens, stuffing a charged battery into the base, and removing the lens cap to fire off a shot or two isn't rocket science. Even the rawest neophyte can hold down the Mode button (located just southwest of the shutter release), and rotate the command dial at the upper-right edge of the back of the camera until a P (programmed auto) indicator appears in the monochrome LCD on top. Point the D3s/D3x at something interesting and press the shutter release. Presto! A pretty good picture will pop up on the color LCD on the back of the camera. It's easy!

But in digital photography, there is such a thing as *too* easy. If you bought a Nikon D3s/D3x, you certainly had no intention of using the camera as a point-and-shoot snap-shooter. After all, the D3s/D3x is a tool suitable for the most advanced photographic pursuits, with an extensive array of customization possibilities. As such, you don't want the camera's operation to be brainless; you want *access* to the advanced features to be easy.

You get that easy access with the Nikon D3s/D3x. However, you'll still need to take the time to learn how to use these features, and I'm going to provide everything you need to know in three parts. The first part will cover what you absolutely *need* to know just to get started using the camera (you'll find that information in this chapter). This chapter was written for those who have no previous experience with a Nikon D3-series camera, with earlier pro models like the Nikon D2xs, or with "semi-pro" cameras like the full-frame D700 or D300/D300s DX models.

The second part offers a more comprehensive look at what you *should* know about the camera and its controls (the buttons, dials, and switches) to use its features effectively. You'll find that information in Chapter 2. D3-series newbies will want to read that chapter carefully, and those of you with previous pro/semi-pro camera experience will want to go through the basics you'll find there.

Finally, all of you will want to learn how to make key settings using the menu system, so you'll be able to fine-tune and tweak the D3s/D3x to operate exactly the way you want. I'll show you every setting and option, and, more importantly, *why* you might want to use each of the choices available to you, in Chapters 3, 4, and 5.

That's a lot of material, but you don't have to learn everything all at once. Some of the other camera guides I've seen winnow this information down to about one-third as many pages. Indeed, I find it odd that those guidebooks use the same basic template for the D3-series cameras as for a resolutely amateur-level model like the Nikon D90. A professional/semi-professional camera like the D3s/D3x has a lot more depth than that, and deserves the in-depth coverage you'll find here.

Now that you've got that initial urge to punch the shutter and twirl the dials out of your system, you'll want to take a more considered approach to operating the camera. The next few pages are designed to get your camera fired up and ready for shooting as quickly as possible. After all, the Nikon D3s and D3x are not point-and-shoot cameras. There are no "scene mode" options with icons on a handy dial representing a person (for portraits), flower (close-ups), mountain scene (landscapes), or runner (sports activity). Instead, there are only the dials and buttons and settings that you might expect to find on a top-tier camera like this one. So I'm going to provide a basic pre-flight checklist that you need to complete before you really spread your wings and take off. You won't find a lot of detail in this chapter. Indeed, I'm going to tell you just what you absolutely *must* understand, accompanied by some interesting tidbits that will help you become acclimated to your D3s/D3x. I'll go into more depth and even repeat some of what I explain here in later chapters, so you don't have to memorize everything you see. Just relax, follow a few easy steps, and then go out and begin taking your best shots—ever.

Because I realize that some of you may already have experience with Nikon cameras similar to the D3s/D3x, each of the major sections in this chapter will begin with a brief description of what is covered in that section, so you can easily jump ahead to the next if you are in a hurry to get started.

## First Things First

> This section helps get you oriented with all the things that come in the box with your Nikon D3s/D3x, including what they do. I'll also describe some optional equipment you might want to have. If you want to get started immediately, skim through this section and jump ahead to "Initial Setup" later in the chapter.

The Nikon D3s/D3x comes in an impressive gold box filled with stuff, including connecting cords, booklets, a CD, and lots of paperwork. The most important components are the camera and lens (if you purchased your camera with a lens, it will be in a separate box, as neither camera is sold in a "kit"), battery, battery charger, and, if you're the nervous type, the neck strap. You'll also need a memory card or two, as one is not included. If you purchased your D3s/D3x from a camera shop, as I did, the store personnel probably attached the neck strap for you, ran through some basic operational advice that you've already forgotten, tried to sell you another memory card, and then, after they'd given you all the help you could absorb, sent you on your way with a handshake.

It's unlikely that you purchased your D3s/D3x from one of those mass merchandisers that also sell washing machines and vacuum cleaners, because few of them stock such an advanced camera. But, if you did, you might have been sent on your way with only the handshake, or, maybe, not even that if you resisted the hard-sell efforts to sell you an extended warranty. You save a few bucks at the big box stores, but you don't get the personal service a professional photo retailer provides. It's your choice. There's a third alternative, of course. You might have purchased your camera from a mail order or Internet source, and your D3s/D3x arrived in a big brown (or purple/red/white) truck. Your only interaction when you took possession of your camera was to scrawl your signature on an electronic clipboard.

In all three cases, the first thing to do is to carefully unpack the camera and double-check the contents with the checklist on one end of the box, helpfully designated under the [Supplied Accessories] bracketed heading. While this level of setup detail may seem as superfluous as the instructions on a bottle of shampoo, checking the contents *first* is always a good idea. No matter who sells a camera, it's common to open boxes, use a particular camera for a demonstration, and then repack the box without replacing all the pieces and parts afterwards. Someone might actually have helpfully checked out your camera on your behalf—and then mispacked the box. It's better to know *now* that something is missing so you can seek redress immediately, rather than discover two months from now that the video cable you thought you'd never use (but now *must* have) was never in the box. I once purchased a brand new Nikon D2x that was supposed to include a second focusing screen; it wasn't in the box, but because I discovered the deficiency right away, the dealer ordered a replacement for me post haste.

At a minimum, the box should have the following:

- **Nikon D3s or D3x digital camera.** It almost goes without saying that you should check out the camera immediately, making sure the back- and top-panel LCDs aren't scratched or cracked, the memory and battery doors open properly, and, when a charged battery is inserted and lens mounted, the camera powers up and reports for duty. Out-of-the-box defects like these are rare, but they can happen. It's probably more common that your dealer played with the camera or, perhaps, it was a customer return. That's why it's best to buy your D3s/D3x from a retailer you trust to supply a factory-fresh camera.
- **Rechargeable Li-ion battery EN-EL4a.** You'll need to charge this 7.4V, 2500mAh (milliampere hour) battery before use, and then navigate immediately to the Setup menu's Battery info entry to make sure the battery accepted the juice and is showing a 100% charge. (You'll find more on accessing this menu item in Chapter 5.) You'll want a second EN-EL4a battery as a spare (trust me), so buy one as soon as possible. It's the same battery as the one used in some earlier models, such as the

Nikon D2x/D2xs, so you may already own one. Your battery will be equipped with a terminal cover to protect the contacts. Don't lose it, as you'll want to replace it when transporting a battery (or spare battery) outside the camera itself, to avoid shorting out the contacts.

- **Quick charger MH-22.** This dual-battery charger is functionally similar to the earlier MH-21 unit supplied with cameras like the D2xs, so, if you have the earlier model, too, you already own a (slightly) more compact spare charger. The MH-22's advantage over the MH-21 is marginal; it doesn't recharge two batteries simultaneously: when you mount a pair in its dual wells, the MH-22 recharges one of the batteries, and then the other.
- **EG-D2 video cable.** Use this cable to connect your D3s/D3x to a standard definition (analog) television through the set's yellow RCA video jack when you want to view the camera's output on a larger screen. Although the D3s/D3x can be connected to a high-definition television, you'll need to buy a high-definition multimedia interface (HDMI) cable to do that. No HDMI cable is included with the camera.
- **USB Cable UC-E4.** You can use this cable to transfer photos from the camera to your computer (I don't recommend that because direct transfer uses a lot of battery power), to upload and download settings between the camera and your computer (highly recommended), and to operate your camera remotely using Nikon Camera Control Pro software (not included in the box). This cable is a standard one that works with the majority of digital cameras—Nikon and otherwise—so if you already own one, you now have a spare.
- **USB cable clip.** This component can be snapped over the mini-plug at the camera end of the USB cable, and used to provide a more secure connection that is not easily dislodged. The cable clip is moderately useful if you're using the USB cord to download images from the camera to your computer (which I don't recommend as a routine procedure—the process uses too much power), or to upload settings (such as Picture Controls) to the D3x/D3s. However, this clip *really* comes in handy when shooting in tethered mode, typically with a longer USB cable or extension, using Nikon Camera Control Pro or Breeze Systems' NK Remote software. It helps prevent the cable from being disconnected inadvertently.
- **AN-DC5 Neck strap (D3s)/AN-D3X Neck strap (D3x).** Nikon provides you with a neck strap emblazoned with your camera model. It's not very adjustable, and, while useful for showing off to your friends exactly which nifty new camera you bought, the Nikon strap also can serve to alert observant unsavory types that you're sporting a higher-end model that's worthy of their attention. I never attach the Nikon strap to my cameras (although once I put a D3x strap on a Nikon D40 as a jest), and instead opt for a more serviceable strap from Op-Tech (www.optechusa.com) or, best of all, an UPstrap (www.upstrap-pro.com). An UPstrap is shown in

Figure 1.1, with its patented non-slip pad that keeps your D3s/D3x on your shoulder, and not crashing to the ground. The straps best suited for the D3s/D3x feature a quick disconnect feature that allows you to use your camera on a tripod without a strap getting in your way. If you order one of these, tell inventor-photographer Al Stegmeyer that I sent you.

- **BF-1A body cap (D3x)/BF-1B body cap (D3s).** The body cap keeps dust from infiltrating your camera when a lens is not mounted. Always carry a body cap (and rear lens cap) in your camera bag for those times when you need to have the camera bare of optics for more than a minute or two. (That usually happens when repacking a bag efficiently for transport, or when you are carrying an extra body or two for backup.) The body cap/lens cap nest together for compact storage.

**Note**

If you happen to have one of the earlier BF-1 body caps for older film cameras, do not use it, as it may damage the lens mount's protruding autofocus screw, which focuses lenses that don't have an autofocus motor built in.

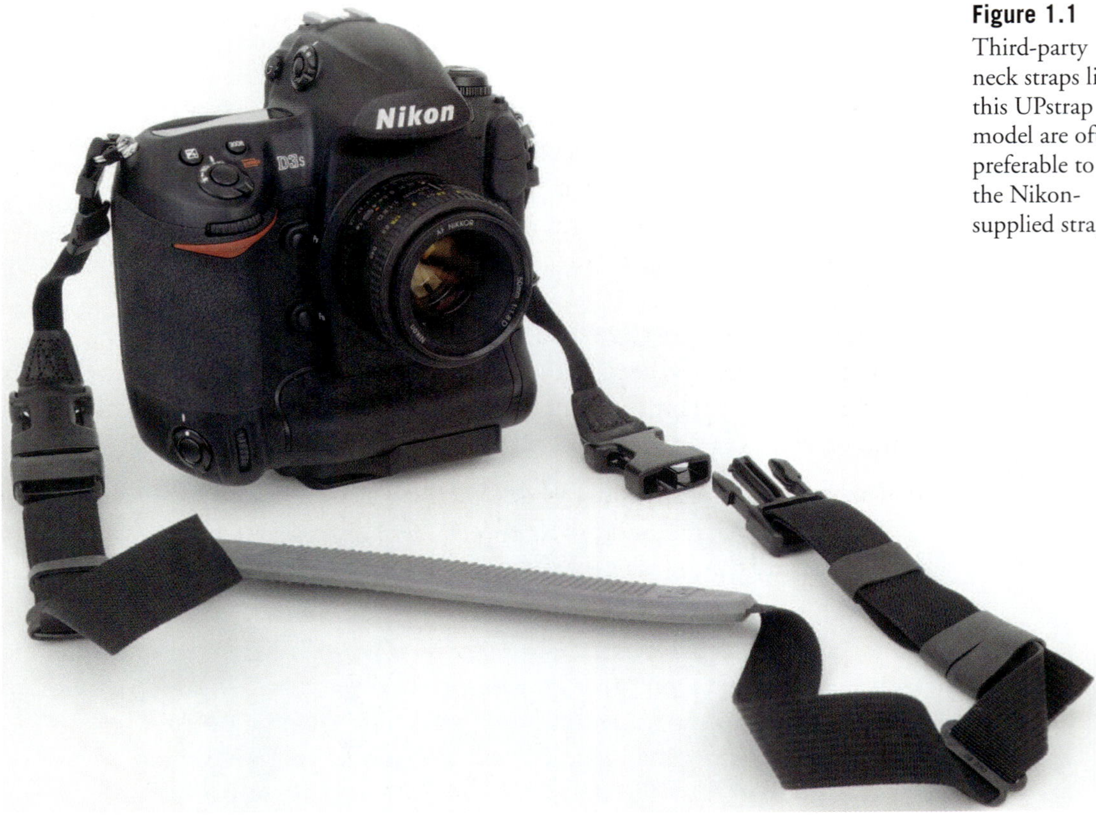


**Figure 1.1**
Third-party neck straps like this UPstrap model are often preferable to the Nikon-supplied strap.

- **BS-1 accessory shoe cover.** It slides into the "hot" shoe on top of the D3s/D3x to protect the electrical contacts until you need to attach an accessory like the Nikon SB-900 electronic flash or Nikon GP-1 GPS device. I confess that I leave this cover off most of the time, and have never damaged my accessory shoe. It's easily lost, too. But Nikon starts you out with one, and if you misplace it, you can order more for a few dollars from Boca Photo (www.bocaphoto.com).
- **User's manuals.** Even if you have this book, you'll probably want to check the user's guide that Nikon provides, if only to check the actual nomenclature for some obscure accessory, or to double-check an error code. Google "Nikon D3s/D3x manual PDF" to find a downloadable, non-printable version that you can store on your laptop, a CD-ROM, or other media in case you want to access this reference when the paper version isn't handy. If you have an old memory card that's too small to be usable on a modern dSLR (I still have some 128MB and 256MB cards), you can store the PDF on that. But an even better choice is to put the manual on a low-capacity USB "thumb" drive, which you can buy for less than $10. You'll then be able to access the reference anywhere you are, because you can always find someone with a computer that has a USB port and Adobe Acrobat Reader available. You might not be lucky enough to locate a computer with a memory reader. Nikon also offers a printable version for download if you supply the serial number of your camera, but I've never had a need to print mine, and so have never bothered to get the printable file.
- **Quick guide.** This little booklet tucked away in the camera's paperwork offers a reasonable summary of the Nikon D3s/D3x's basic commands and settings, and can be stowed in your camera bag more easily than a "field guide" or even this book.
- **Software CD-ROM.** Here you'll find the Nikon Software Suite, which includes various drivers required by some operating systems; Nikon Transfer (to move your files from camera or memory card to your computer); Nikon ViewNX (a useful image management program); as well as various third-party utilities (some of which you may already have installed on your computer), such as DirectX9, QuickTime, and Kodak EasyShare software. I'll cover all the Nikon software offerings later in this book.
- **Warranty and registration card.** Don't lose these! You can register your Nikon D3s/D3x by mail or online (in the USA, the URL is www.nikonusa.com/register), and you may need the information in this paperwork (plus the purchase receipt/invoice from your retailer) should you require Nikon service support.

Don't bother rooting around in the box for anything beyond what I've listed previously. There are a few things Nikon classifies as optional accessories, even though you (and I) might consider some of them essential. Here's a list of what you *don't* get in the box, but might want to think about as an impending purchase. I'll list them roughly in the order of importance:

- **Compact Flash cards (two, minimum).** First-time digital camera buyers are sometimes shocked that their new tool doesn't come with a memory card. Why should it? The manufacturer doesn't have the slightest idea of what capacity or speed card you prefer, so why should they pack one in the box and charge you for it? That's especially true for the Nikon D3s/D3x, which is likely to be purchased by photographers who have quite definite ideas about their ideal memory card. Perhaps you want to use tiny 2GB cards—and lots of them. I've met many paranoid wedding photographers who like to work with a horde of smaller cards (and then watch over them *very* protectively), on the theory that they are reducing their chances of losing a significant chunk of the event or reception at one time (of course, that's why you hire a second shooter as backup). Others, especially sports photographers, instead prefer an 8GB or 16GB card with room to spare. If you are shooting fast action at high frame rates, or transfer lots of photos to your computer with a speedy card reader, you might opt for the speediest possible memory card. Buy one (or two, or three) of your own and have your flash memory ready when you unpack your D3s/D3x.

### Note

The important thing to remember with the Nikon D3s, compared to the D3x, is that the D3s uses only the thinner (3.3mm) Type 1 Compact Flash card, and not the thicker (5 mm) Type 2 cards that you may sometimes encounter. In this respect, the newer D3s matches the specifications of recent CF-card using Nikon cameras, including the D700 and D300s, which also use only Type 1 cards. The D3x is the only current Nikon camera that can accept Type 2 cards.

As a practical matter, this restriction will affect you only if you want to use a CF-to-SD card adapter (available only in the Type 2 form factor) to insert a Secure Digital memory card in the camera. The most common reason for wanting to use an SD card with a CF-only camera like the D3x is to add cheap-o WiFi capabilities with an Eye-Fi Secure Digital memory card/wireless device (about $50 to $150). The least common need for Type 2 cards is for working with antique MicroDrive storage devices, which are mini-hard drives that were available only in the Type 2 form factor. True Type 2 flash memory cards are very rare, and Nikon is phasing out the ability to use them in its cameras, particularly as it adds dual memory card capabilities to various models. My guess is that Nikon expects anyone who can afford a high-end digital SLR will be willing to spring for an extra $700 or so for the Nikon WT-4a wireless transmitter. The unit is potentially more useful but is also a lot bulkier than the quick-and-dirty (and fun) Eye-Fi SD card.

- **Extra EN-EL4a battery.** I mentioned the need for an extra battery earlier, and I'll mention it here, again. Even though you might get 1,000 or more shots from a single battery, it's easy to exceed that figure in a few hours of shooting sports at 5 to 9 to 11 fps (depending on whether you're using the slower, but higher res D3x or the faster D3s). Batteries can unexpectedly fail, too, or simply lose their charge from sitting around unused for a week or two. Buy an extra (I own four, in total), keep it charged, and free your mind from worry.
- **Nikon Capture NX 2 software.** Although Nikon has sometimes offered free copies of Capture NX 1 with the purchase of a camera (the D3 or D300, back in 2007), there are no Capture NX 2 freebies this time around, so if you want to use this software after the free try-out period expires, you'll need to buy it.
- **Camera Control Pro 2 software.** This is the utility you'll use to operate your camera remotely from your computer. Nikon charges extra for this software, but you'll find it invaluable if you're hiding near a tethered, tripod-mounted camera while shooting, say, close-ups of hummingbirds. There are lots of applications for remote shooting, and you'll need Camera Control Pro to operate your camera. Buy a suitably longer USB cable, too, unless you plan to use the Nikon WT4a wireless transmitter (described below).
- **Add-on speedlight.** As a pro camera, your Nikon D3s/D3x does not sport a built-in electronic flash, and thus can't provide fill illumination, main flash illumination, or serve as a remote trigger for an off-camera speedlight such as the Nikon SB-900. You'll have to own one or two (or more) external flash units to gain that flexibility, and a Nikon SU-800 (flashless) wireless slave trigger. If you do much flash photography at all, consider an add-on speedlight as an important accessory.
- **Remote control cable MC-30.** You can plug this accessory electronic release into the 10-pin socket hidden behind the rubber cover on the front of the D3s/D3x, and then fire off the camera without the need to touch the camera itself. In a pinch, you can use the D3s/D3x's self-timer to minimize vibration when triggering the camera, or even take advantage of the mirror up (Mup) and delayed release features to reduce camera shake. (These are all described later in this book.) But when you want to take a photo at the exact moment you desire (and not when the self-timer happens to trip), or need to eliminate all possibility of human-induced camera shake, you need this release cord.

**Note**

The Nikon MC-30 can be tricky to find in stock. I've had excellent luck using the Phottix Remote N1 and Phottix Cleon II wireless remote at a fraction of the cost. I buy them from reliable Hong Kong dealer HKSupplies, which deals in the USA as eBay seller etefore-usacs. Check out www.ebay.com and www.phottix.com.

- **MC-21 extension cable.** This is a three-meter extension cord for the 10-pin terminal connector, allowing the use of the MC-30 remote cable and other accessories at greater distances.
- **MC-36 remote shutter release.** This is a pricey ($140) 33-inch remote shutter release that plugs into the 10-pin terminal connector and allows timed long exposures and interval shooting (time-lapse photography) of up to 999 shots with up to 99 hours, 99 minutes, and 99 seconds between shots.
- **ML-3 remote control.** An even more expensive ($175) remote release for the D3s/D3x, but this one operates wirelessly by infrared. I prefer the much cheaper Phottix wireless remote mentioned earlier, which uses radio control and has a much longer range (up to 320 feet instead of 26 feet).
- **Nikon GP-1 global positioning system (GPS) device.** This accessory attaches to the accessory shoe on top of the camera and captures latitude, longitude, and altitude information, which is imprinted in a special data area of your image files. The "geotagging" data can be plotted on a map in Nikon ViewNX or other software programs. I'll explain more about this feature in Chapter 7.
- **AC Adapter EH-6.** There are several typical situations where this AC adapter for your D3s/D3x can come in handy: when you're cleaning the sensor manually and want to totally eliminate the possibility that a lack of juice will cause the fragile shutter and mirror to spring to life during the process; when in the studio shooting product photos, portraits, class pictures, and so forth for hours on end; when using your D3s/D3x for remote shooting as well as time-lapse photography; for extensive review of images on your standard definition or high-definition television; or for file transfer to your computer. These all use prodigious amounts of power, which can be provided by this AC adapter. (Beware of power outages and blackouts when cleaning your sensor, however!)
- **DR-4/DR-5 right-angle viewer.** Fastens in place of the standard rubber eyecup and provides a 90-degree view for framing and composing your image at right angles to the original viewfinder, useful for low-level (or high-level) shooting. (Or, maybe, shooting around corners!) It's expensive at around $200, but worthwhile if you need it. The DR-5 viewer has 2X magnification.
- **DK-17M magnifying eyepiece.** Provides a 1.17X magnification factor of the entire viewing area (unlike the 2X DG-2 eyepiece, which enlarges the center of the image), making it easier to check focus. You might have to move your eye around a little to see all the indicators outside the image frame, but this magnifier is still suitable for everyday use. This eyepiece fits the D3s/D3x directly; if you opt for the DG-2 magnifier instead, you'll also need the DK-18 eyepiece adapter.

- **Wireless transmitter WT-4a.** This is the gadget for wireless remote control operation with Nikon Camera Control Pro 2 software. Wedding and event photographers can get a lot of use out of this accessory, and studio photographers can benefit from it, too. Not only can you back up all your photos to a laptop or desktop computer as they are taken, you or an assistant can be viewing, editing, and displaying them virtually simultaneously to clients, art directors, or anyone else.
- **GPS adapter cord MC-35.** Use this accessory to record location information such as latitude, longitude, altitude, and UTC (Coordinated Universal Time) at which a shot is taken. You don't need to be a National Geographic photographer to find this capability useful. The adapter cord plugs into the 10-pin connector beneath the rubber cover on the front of the D3s/D3x, and then plugs into your compatible GPS unit.
- **SC-28 TTL flash cord.** Allows using Nikon speedlights off-camera, while retaining all the automated features.
- **SC-29 TTL flash cord.** Similar to the SC-28, this unit has its own AF-assist lamp, which can provide extra illumination for the D3s/D3x's autofocus system in dim light (which, not coincidentally, is when you'll probably be using an electronic flash).

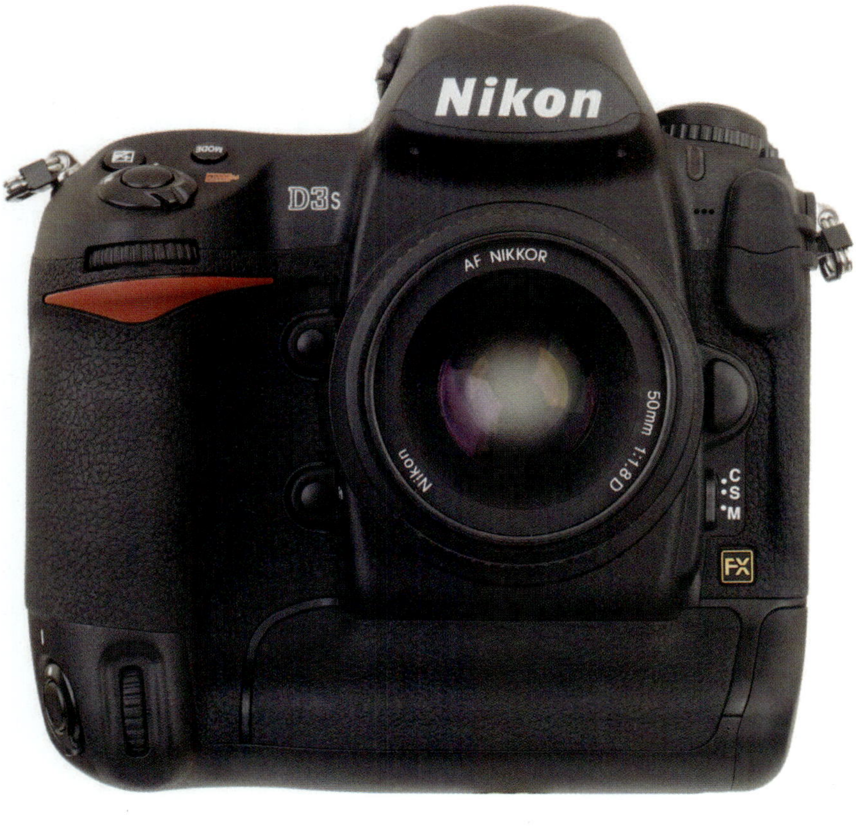


**Figure 1.2**
The Nikon D3s/D3x's built-in vertical grip offers more convenience when shooting vertically oriented photos.

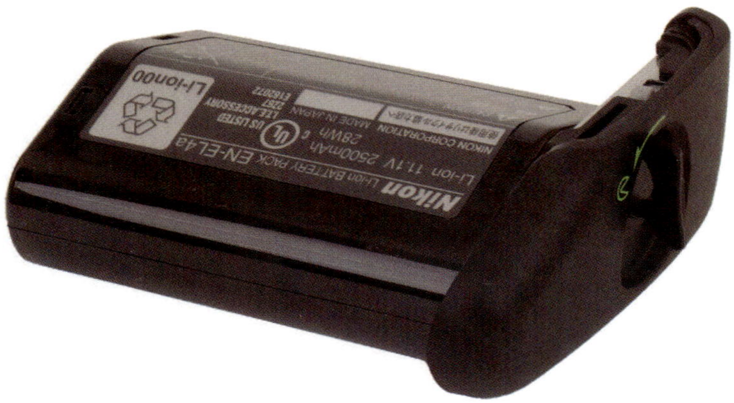


**Figure 1.3**
The key to the long shooting life of the D3s/D3x is the 2500 mAh Nikon EN-EL4a battery.

# Initial Setup

> This section helps you familiarize yourself with the three important controls most used to make adjustments: the multi selector and the main and sub-command dials. You'll also find information on charging the battery, setting the clock, mounting a lens, and making diopter vision adjustments. If you're comfortable with all these things, skim through and skip ahead to "Changing Default Settings" in the next section.

Once you've unpacked and inspected your camera, the initial setup of your Nikon D3s/D3x is fast and easy. Basically, you just need to charge the battery, attach a lens, and insert a memory card. I'll address each of these steps separately, but if you already are confident you can manage these setup tasks without further instructions, feel free to skip this section entirely. While most buyers of a D3s/D3x tend to be experienced photographers, I realize that some readers are ambitious, if inexperienced, and should, at the minimum, skim the contents of the next section, because I'm going to list a few options that you might not be aware of.

## Mastering the Multi Selector and Command Dials

I'll be saving descriptions of most of the controls used with the Nikon D3s/D3x until Chapter 2, which provides a complete "roadmap" of the camera's buttons and dials and switches. However, you may need to perform a few tasks during this initial setup process, and most of them will require the Menu button and the multi selector pad. The Menu button is easy to find: it's located to the left of the LCD, the first button in the series of four located to the left of the LCD. It requires almost no explanation; when you want to access a menu, press it. To exit most menus, press it again.

The multi selector pad may remind you of the similar control found on many point-and-shoot cameras, and other digital SLRs. It consists of a thumbpad-sized button with indentations at the North, South, East, and West positions, plus a button in the center.

It can also be pushed in diagonal directions to give you Northeast, Southeast, Southwest, and Northwest orientations. (See Figure 1.4.)

The multi selector on the D3s/D3x functions slightly differently than its counterpart on some other cameras. For example, some point-and-shoot models assign a function, such as white balance or ISO setting, to one of the directional buttons (usually in conjunction with a function key of some sort). The use of the multi selector varies, even within the Nikon dSLR line up. For example, many Nikon digital SLRs, such as the Nikon D50/D70/D80 have no center button in the multi selector at all. Other Nikon cameras, including the D3s/D3x allow assigning a function of your choice to the multi selector center button.

With the D3s/D3x, the multi selector is used extensively for navigation, for example, to navigate among menus on the LCD or to choose one of the 51 focus points, to advance or reverse display of a series of images during picture review, or to change the kind of photo information displayed on the screen. The center button is used to select a highlighted item from a menu, and also to enter movie-shooting mode when using live view on the D3s.

So, from time to time in this chapter (and throughout this book) I'll be referring to the multi selector and its left/right/up/down buttons, and center button.

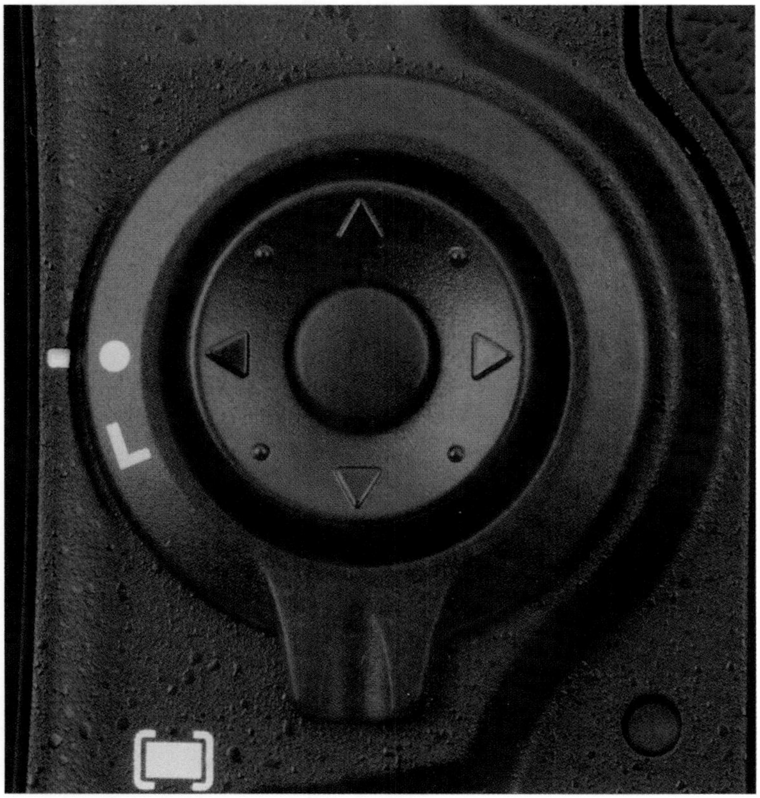

**Figure 1.4**
The multi selector pad has four directional buttons for navigating up/down/left/right, and a center button to confirm your selection.

The main command dial and sub-command dial are located on the rear and front of the D3s/D3x, respectively. The main command dial is used to change settings such as shutter speed, while the sub-command dial adjusts an alternate or secondary setting. For example, in manual exposure mode, you'd use the sub-command dial to change the aperture, while the main command dial is used to change the shutter speed. (In both cases, the dial is "active" for these adjustments only when the D3s/D3x's exposure meter is On.) The meter will automatically go to sleep after an interval (you'll learn how to specify the length of time in Chapter 4), and you must waken the camera (just tap the shutter release button) to switch the meter back on and activate the main and sub-command dials.

## Setting the Clock

It's likely that your Nikon D3s/D3x's internal clock hasn't been set to your local time, so you may need to do that first. If so, the flashing CLOCK indicator on the top-panel LCD will be the giveaway. You'll find complete instructions for setting the four options for the date/time (time zone, actual date and time, the date format, and whether you want the D3s/D3x to conform to Daylight Savings Time) in Chapter 5. However, if you think you can handle this step without instruction, press the Menu button, use the multi selector (that thumb-friendly button I just described, located to the immediate right of the back-panel LCD) to scroll down to the Setup menu, press the multi selector button to the right, and scroll down to Time Zone and Date (D3s) or World Time (D3x) choice, and press right again. The options will appear on the screen that appears next. Keep in mind that you'll need to reset your camera's internal clock from time to time, as it is not 100-percent accurate.

## Battery Included

Your Nikon D3s/D3x is a sophisticated hunk of machinery and electronics, but it needs a charged battery to function, so rejuvenating the EN-EL4a lithium-ion battery pack furnished with the camera should be your first step. A fully charged power source should be good for approximately 1,000 shots, based on standard tests defined by the Camera & Imaging Products Association (CIPA) document DC-002. Nikon's own standards are quite a bit more optimistic (it predicts as many as 3,000 shots from a single charge). In the real world, of course, the life of the battery will depend on how much image review you do, how many shots you take with the built-in flash, and many other factors. You'll want to keep track of how many pictures *you* are able to take in your own typical circumstances, and use that figure as a guideline, instead.

All rechargeable batteries undergo some degree of self discharge just sitting idle in the camera or in the original packaging. Lithium-ion power packs of this type typically lose a few percent of their charge every few days, even when the camera isn't turned on. The small amount of juice used to provide the "shots remaining" figure on the top-panel monochrome LCD when the D3s/D3x is turned off isn't the culprit; Li-ion cells lose their power through a chemical reaction that continues when the camera is switched off. So, it's very likely that the battery purchased with your camera is at least partially pooped out, so you'll want to revive it before going out for some serious shooting.

## A BATTERY AND A SPARE

I always recommend purchasing Nikon brand batteries (for about $110) over less-expensive third-party packs, even though the $80 (or less) saves you a little money. My reasoning is that it doesn't make sense to save $30 on a component for a $5000-$8000 camera, especially since batteries have been known to fail in potentially harmful ways. You need only look as far as Nikon's own recall of its earlier EN-EL3 batteries, which forced the company to ship out thousands of free replacement cells. You're unlikely to get the same support from a third-party battery supplier that sells under a half-dozen or more different product labels and brands, and may not even have an easy way to get the word out that a recall has been issued.

If your pictures are important to you, always have at least one spare battery available, and make sure it is an authentic Nikon product.

### Charging the Battery

When the battery is inserted into the MH-22 charger properly (it's impossible to insert it incorrectly), one or more of three Charge lights (arranged at the 50 percent, 80 percent, and 100 percent levels) begin flashing, and remain flashing until the 100 percent status lamp glows steadily and the battery cools to room temperature, indicating that charging is finished. If you've mounted a battery in each well, the indicators will begin showing the status of the charging process for the second battery after the first one is replenished. (See Figure 1.5, which shows the charger without its power cord.)

At intervals, you may need to calibrate your battery, which restores its ability to accurately report to the camera its remaining capacity level. The Battery Info. choice in the Setup menu will indicate *CAL when calibration is needed. This may happen every dozen or so charge/recharge cycles. However, when I received my new D3s, Battery info already reported Battery Age with a value of 1, but after recalibration, the indicator was restored to its proper level of 0. Press the Calibration button adjacent to each of the charging wells if you want to calibrate a particular battery.

The charger will first completely discharge the battery. Caution: in this mode, the charge lamps illuminate on beginning with the top lamp, using the time scale on the right side of the charger lights to indicate how long it will take to finish discharging the battery: 6 hours or more, 4 to 6 hours, or 2 to 4 hours; when the final lamp on the right side is extinguished, less than two hours of discharging remain. Then, the recharging cycle begins, and the lamps begin to illuminate again, and you should use the scale on the left side of the lamps to see that the battery has been 50 percent, 80 percent, and 100 percent recharged.

The entire calibration process can take 10-12 hours. I seriously goofed when I first received my D3s with its uncalibrated battery, and plugged it in for calibration the evening before a shoot. The next morning, I took the battery out and left for the shoot, not realizing that only the *discharge* cycle had been completed. The battery hadn't been recharged yet, and soon pooped out. I had to finish the shoot with my spare battery. The lesson here is that once you begin to calibrate your battery, let the process continue long enough to complete.

When the battery is charged, slide the battery in, as shown in Figure 1.6. Check the Setup menu's Battery info entry as I recommended earlier to make sure the battery is fully charged. If not, try putting it in the charger again. One of three things may be the culprit: a.) the actual charging cycle sometimes takes longer than you (or the charger) expected; b.) the battery is new and needs to be "seasoned" for a few charging cycles, after which it will accept a full charge and deliver more shots; c.) the battery needs to be calibrated, as mine did; or d.) you've got a defective battery. The final situation is fairly rare, but before you start counting on getting a particular number of exposures from a battery, it's best to make sure it's fully charged, seasoned, calibrated, and ready to deliver.

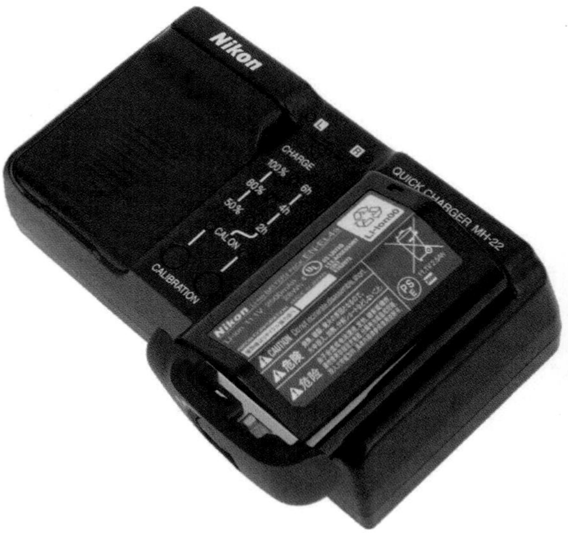


**Figure 1.5** Charge the battery before use.

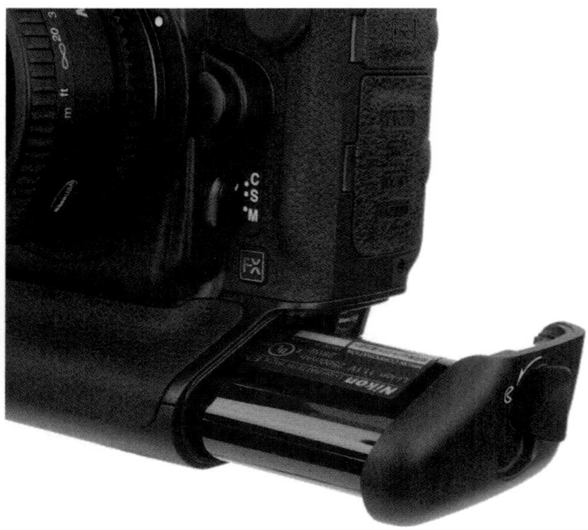


**Figure 1.6** Insert the battery in the camera; it only fits one way.

## Final Steps

Your Nikon D3s/D3x is almost ready to fire up and shoot. You'll need to select and mount a lens, adjust the viewfinder for your vision, and insert a memory card (or two). Each of these steps is easy, and if you've used any Nikon before, you already know exactly what to do. I'm going to provide a little extra detail for those of you who are new to the Nikon or SLR worlds.

### Mounting the Lens

As you'll see, my recommended lens mounting procedure emphasizes protecting your equipment from accidental damage and minimizing the intrusion of dust. If your D3s/D3x has no lens attached, select the lens you want to use and loosen (but do not remove) the rear lens cap. I generally place the lens I am planning to mount vertically in a slot in my camera bag, where it's protected from mishaps, but ready to pick up quickly. By loosening the rear lens cap, you'll be able to lift it off the back of the lens at the last instant, so the rear element of the lens is covered until then.

After that, remove the body cap by rotating the cap towards the release button. You should always mount the body cap when there is no lens on the camera, because it helps keep dust out of the interior of the camera, where it can settle on the mirror, focusing screen, interior mirror box, and potentially find its way past the shutter onto the sensor. (While the D3s sensor cleaning mechanism works fine, the less dust it has to contend with, the better.) The body cap also protects the vulnerable mirror from damage caused by intruding objects (including your fingers, if you're not cautious).

#### DEALING WITH ERRORS

After you've mounted your lens properly (or *think* you have), you might find various error codes appearing on the top-panel LCD, viewfinder, and back-panel color LCD. Here are the most common error codes, and what you should do next:

- **FE E.** This error code, with a smaller uppercase F followed by two Es indicates that you've mounted a lens that has an aperture ring, but haven't set the lens to its smallest f/stop (usually f/22 or f/32). Nikon autofocus lenses with an aperture ring have a lock lever that allows you to set the minimum aperture and lock it there so that this problem doesn't occur. However, you may have unlocked the aperture ring when you needed to set the aperture manually with the lens mounted on an older camera that didn't allow setting the aperture electronically. Or, you might have mounted the lens on a non-autoaperture extension tube, bellows, or other accessory.
- **E r r.** Some other error has taken place. Release the shutter, turn off the camera, remove the lens, and remount it. Try another lens. If the message persists, then there is a problem unrelated to your lens, and your D3s/D3x may need service.

Once the body cap has been removed, remove the rear lens cap from the lens, set it aside, and then mount the lens on the camera by matching the alignment indicator on the lens barrel with the white dot on the camera's lens mount. (See Figure 1.7.) Rotate the lens toward the shutter release until it seats securely. Some lenses are trickier to mount than others, particularly telephotos and telephoto zooms with swiveling collars that allow the lens to be fastened to a tripod. You might need to rotate the collar so the tripod foot doesn't bump into the front overhang of the D3s/D3x's prism.

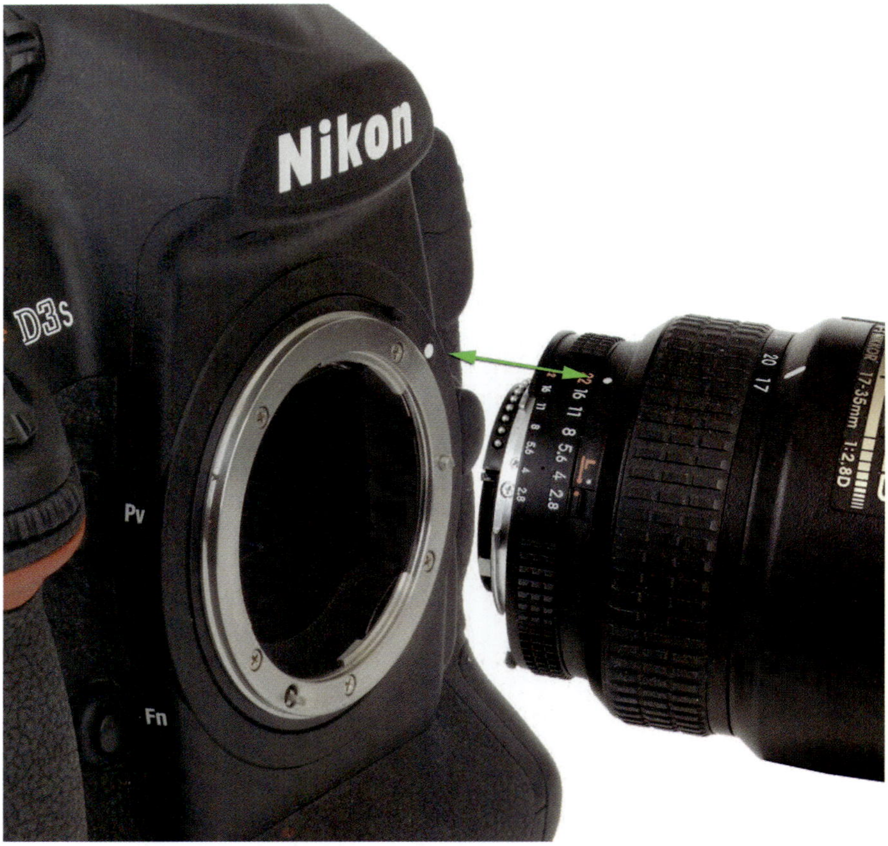


**Figure 1.7**
Match the indicator on the lens with the white dot on the camera mount to properly align the lens with the bayonet mount.

Set the focus mode switch on the lens to AF or M-AF (autofocus). If the lens hood is bayoneted on the lens in the reversed position (which makes the lens/hood combination more compact for transport), twist it off and remount with the "petals" (found on virtually all Nikon lens hoods) facing outward. (See Figure 1.8.) A lens hood protects the front of the lens from accidental bumps, and reduces flare caused by extraneous light arriving at the front element of the lens from outside the picture area.

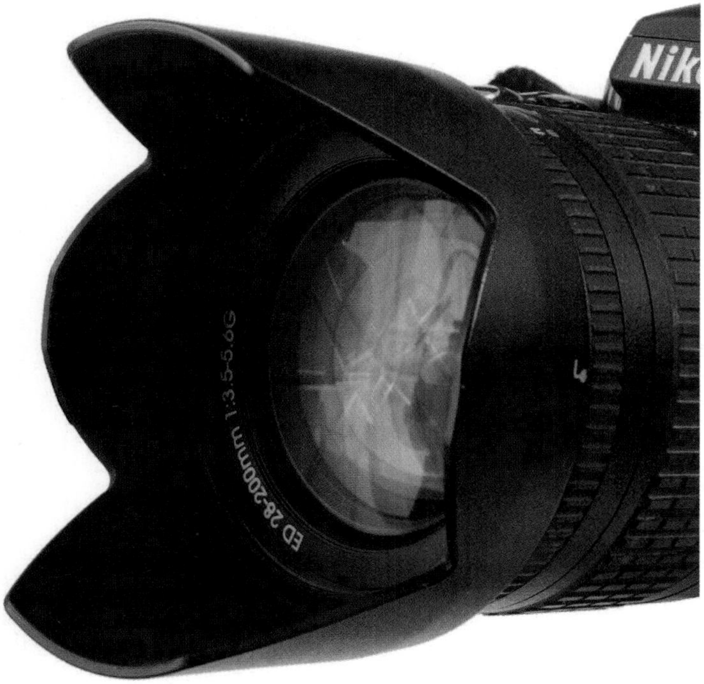


**Figure 1.8**
A lens hood protects the lens from extraneous light and accidental bumps.

## Adjusting Diopter Correction

Those of us with less than perfect eyesight can often benefit from a little optical correction in the viewfinder. Your contact lenses or glasses may provide all the correction you need, but if you are a glasses wearer and want to use the D3s/D3x without your glasses, you can take advantage of the camera's built-in diopter adjustment, which can be varied from –3 (nearsighted) to +1 (farsighted) correction. Note that the camera's viewfinder has a built-in diopter correction of –1, which is considered optimum for people with normal vision. Without further correction, the viewfinder produces a virtual image of the focusing screen as if it were viewed from a distance of one meter.

If you need additional correction, press the shutter release halfway to illuminate the indicators in the viewfinder, then pull out and rotate the diopter adjustment dial on the pentaprism to the right of he viewfinder (see Figure 1.9) while looking through the viewfinder until the indicators appear sharp. Snap the dial back in to lock your setting.

If more than one person uses your D3s/D3x, and each requires a different diopter setting on the camera itself, you can save a little time by noting the number of clicks and direction (clockwise to increase the diopter power; counterclockwise to decrease the diopter value) required to change from one user to the other. Should the available correction be insufficient, Nikon offers five different DK-17C Diopter-Adjustment Viewfinder Correction lenses for the viewfinder window, in values of –3, –2, 0, +1, and

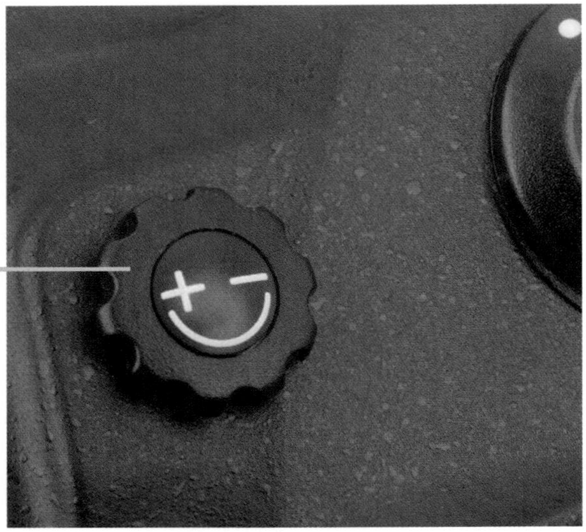


**Figure 1.9**
Viewfinder diopter correction from –3 to +1 can be dialed in.

+2 at a cost of about $18 each. These lenses actually have values that are one "less" than their marked value, to compensate for the D3s/D3x's built-in –1 diopter setting. That is, a DK-17C sold as a –3 diopter actually has a value of –2, while a +2 diopter is actually a +3 that is reduced to +2 by the viewfinder's built-in correction.

## Inserting a Memory Card

You've probably set up your D3s/D3x so you can't take photos without a memory card inserted. (There is a No memory card? entry, Custom Setting f9 [D3x] or f10 [D3s] that enables/disables shutter release functions when a memory card is absent—learn about that in Chapter 4.) So, your final step will be to insert a memory card. Release the memory card cover by pushing a finger under a spring-loaded flap located below the AF Mode selector and pressing the hidden release button which allows the slot cover door to spring open. (You should only remove a memory card when the camera is switched off, or, at the very least, the yellow-green memory access light that indicates the camera is writing to the card is not illuminated.)

Inside, you'll find a pair of slots, numbered 1 and 2. (See Figure 1.10.) Insert the memory card into one of the slots with the label facing the back of the camera oriented so the edge with the contacts (a double row of tiny holes) goes into the slot first.

**MORE ABOUT CSM OPTIONS IN CHAPTER 4**

The next section will suggest other "default" settings you might want to adjust before you get started. You'll find a complete list of Custom Setting menu options and parameters in Chapter 4.

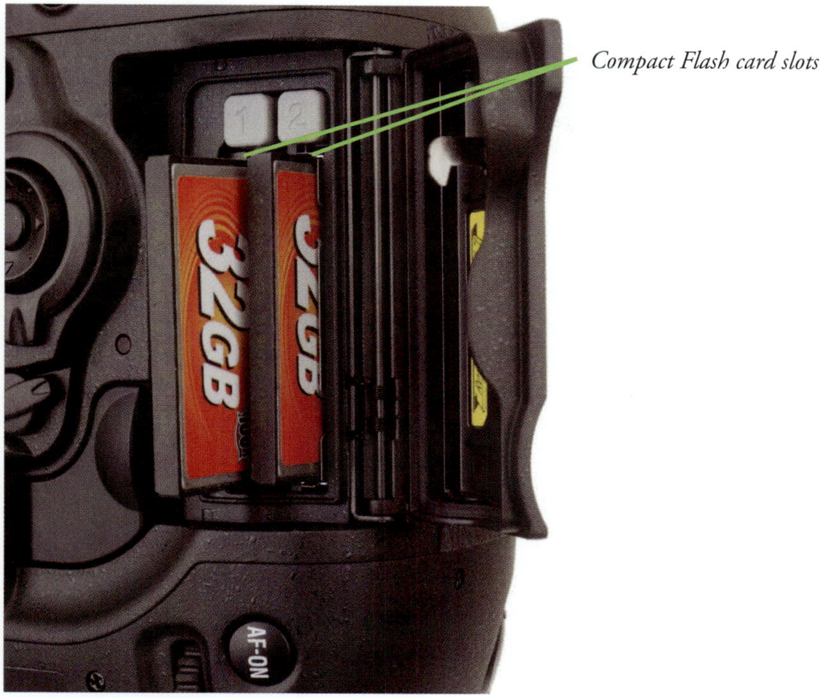


**Figure 1.10**
The memory card is always inserted with the label facing the right side of the camera.

Close the door, and, if necessary, format the card. When you want to remove a Compact Flash card later, press the gray buttons (shown at the top of Figure 1.10) to make the memory card pop out.

Slot 1 is the primary memory card slot, and Slot 2 is the secondary slot, and generally used either to store a backup of the image stored on the primary memory card; to store JPEG files when shooting RAW+JPEG, with the RAW files stored on the card in Slot 1; or as the overflow media, used only when the primary memory card is full. You can choose the role of the second memory card using the Slot 2 entry in the Setup menu, as described in Chapter 3.

Nikon explicitly states in the D3s and D3x manuals that Slot 2 should be used *only* if a card is already inserted in Slot 1. However, the camera functions just fine with a memory card only in Slot 2, or with only a card in Slot 1. If you have just one card available, you can use either slot interchangeably, with one exception: if the function of Slot 2 is set to store only the JPEG files of a RAW+JPEG set, then no RAW file will be saved (because it would normally be stored in the card in Slot 1, which is absent). However, I always put a card in Slot 1 if I have just one card. That's a rare occurrence, though; my more usual practice is to have a 32GB memory card in each slot, 1 and 2. The slot in use will be shown on the monochrome LCD display on top of the camera, and in the information display (when visible) on the color LCD on the back of the camera. (I'll explain these displays in more detail in Chapter 2.)

## Formatting a Memory Card

There are four ways to create a blank memory card for your D3s/D3x, and two of them are wrong. Here are your options, both correct and incorrect:

- **Transfer (move) files to your computer.** When you transfer (rather than copy) all the image files to your computer from the memory card (either using a direct cable transfer or with a card reader, as described later in this chapter), the old image files are erased from the card, leaving the card blank. Theoretically. Unfortunately, this method does *not* remove files that you've labeled as Protected (by pressing the Protect button to the left of the LCD while viewing the image on the LCD), nor does it identify and lock out parts of your memory card that have become corrupted or unusable since the last time you formatted the card. Therefore, I recommend always formatting the card, rather than simply moving the image files, each time you want to make a blank card. The only exception is when you *want* to leave the protected/unerased images on the card for awhile longer, say, to share with friends, family, and colleagues.
- **(Don't) Format in your computer.** With the memory card inserted in a card reader or card slot in your computer, you can use Windows or Mac OS to reformat the memory card. Don't! The operating system won't necessarily install the correct file system. The only way to ensure that the card has been properly formatted for your camera is to perform the format in the camera itself. The only exception to this rule is when you have a seriously munged memory card that your camera refuses to format. Sometimes it is possible to revive such a corrupted card by allowing the operating system to reformat it first, then trying again in the camera.
- **Setup menu format.** To use one of the recommended methods to format a memory card, press the Menu button, use the up/down buttons of the multi selector (that thumbpad-sized control to the right of the LCD) to choose the Setup menu (which is represented by a wrench icon), and navigate to the Format memory card entry with the up/down buttons of the multi selector. Select the Format function with the right button. Then, use the up/down buttons to select either Slot 1 or Slot 2, and press the right button again to begin the format step. Select Yes from the screen that appears. Press OK to activate the format process.
- **Two-button format.** The second recommended method requires no menus. Hold down the Mode button (on top of the camera, just southwest of the shutter release button) and the trash can button (on the upper-left corner of the back) simultaneously for about two seconds. (A Format label, color-coded with red printing, appears next to each button.) The characters For and the exposures remaining displays will blink in the viewfinder and top-panel LCD. Then press the pair of buttons again, and the D3s/D3x will format your card. To cancel the format, press any other button.

## How Many Shots?

The D3s and D3x provide a fairly accurate estimate of the number of shots remaining on the top-panel LCD at all times (even when the camera is turned off), as well as at the lower-right edge of the viewfinder display when the display is active. (Tap the shutter release button to activate it.)

It is only an estimate, because the actual number will vary, depending on the capacity of your memory card, the file format(s) you've selected, and the content of the image itself. (Some photos may contain large areas that can be more efficiently compressed to a smaller size.)

For example, using the D3s, an 8GB card can hold about 750 JPEG Fine shots in full resolution (Large) format; 1,500 shots using Normal JPEG compression; or 2,900 shots with Basic JPEG compression. (This is by actual count with one of my own memory cards.) When numbers exceed 1,000, the D3s/D3x displays a figure and decimal point, followed by a K superscript, so that 2,900 shots (or thereabouts) is represented by [2.9]$^{K}$ in the LCD and viewfinder. The D3s offers three different resolution settings that provide different numbers of exposures: Large (4288 × 2848; 12.2 megapixels), Medium (3216 × 2139; 6.8 megapixels), and Small (2144 × 1424; 3 megapixels). For example, JPEG Basic using the Small resolution setting yields 10.5K exposures on a single 8GB memory card! Using RAW/NEF format (more on that later) reduces the number of shots. An 8GB card has enough room for 400 RAW photos in Nikon's NEF format, or 261 pictures if you're shooting RAW+JPEG Fine pairs.

The higher resolution of the D3x provides fewer images per 8GB card, of course. Instead of 750 JPEG Fine images, the D3x can store just 377 of its 6048 × 4032 images on an 8GB card. You'll get 750 JPEG Normal, and 1,400 JPEG Basic images (these work out to about half the number for the 24.5-megapixel D3x camera compared to the 12.1-megapixel D3s, as you might expect).

Table 1.1 shows some typical capacities for an 8GB memory card. You should know that the D3s/D3x has various compression options for JPEG and RAW files, as well as 12-bit and 14-bit dynamic range settings for the RAW format; we'll look into those options in more detail in Chapter 3.

TIFF, a very memory-hungry format that the D3s/D3x records to the memory card at a snail's pace (a minimum of several seconds per photo) eats up so much space that you can fit a mere 215 images on an 8GB card with the D3s, and 107 with the D3x, with little discernable quality difference from RAW files (at the same time discarding the fine-tunability that you get from Nikon's NEF/RAW format). TIFF has seriously fallen from favor for most applications in the past few years.

Table 1.1 shows the typical number of shots you can expect with the D3s using 12-bit color depth and an 8GB memory card (which I expect will be a common size card among D3s/D3x users during the life of this book). Just divide these values in half to estimate the number of shots you can expect for the same size card when using the D3x. With either camera, hold down the Qual button on the lower back of the camera and rotate the main command dial to change the file/formats in column 1, and rotate the sub-command dial to change the image sizes in columns 2, 3, and 4. The current file format appears in the back-panel monochrome LCD and the number of exposures possible with the current memory card appears on the top-panel monochrome display.

**Table 1.1 File Capacity of 8GB Card with D3s (halve these for D3x)**

| | Large | Medium | Small |
|---|---|---|---|
| JPEG Fine | 750 | 1,300 | 2,900 |
| JPEG Normal | 1,400 | 2,500 | 5,700 |
| JPEG Basic | 2,900 | 5,000 | 10,500 |
| TIFF | 215 | 378 | 846 |
| RAW | 400 | N/A | N/A |
| RAW+JPEG Fine | 261 | 307 | 352 |
| RAW+JPEG Normal | 315 | 346 | 374 |
| RAW+JPEG Basic | 351 | 371 | 385 |

## Changing Default Settings

This section is purely optional, especially for those few true (but ambitious) beginners, who should skip it entirely for now, and return when they've gained some experience with this full-featured camera. This section is for the benefit of those who want to know *now* some of the most common changes I recommend to the settings that your D3s/D3x is set to when it comes from the factory. Nikon has excellent reasons for using these settings as a default; I have better reasons for changing them. If you think you'll be satisfied with the default options for now, jump ahead to "Choosing a Release Mode."

Even if this is your first experience with a Nikon digital SLR, you can easily make a few changes to the default settings that I'm going to recommend, and then take your time learning *why* I suggest these changes when they're explained in the more detailed chapters of this book. I'm not going to provide step-by-step instructions for changing settings here; I'll give you an overview of how to make any setting adjustment, and leave you to navigate through the fairly intuitive D3s/D3x menu system to make the changes yourself.

## Resetting the Nikon D3s or D3x

If you want to change from the factory default values, you might think that it would be a good idea to make sure that the Nikon D3s/D3x is set to the factory defaults in the first place. After all, even a brand-new camera might have had its settings changed at the retailer, or during a demo. Unfortunately, Nikon doesn't make it easy to reset *all* settings in the camera to their factory defaults. In fact, there are no fewer than *four* different ways to "reset" the D3s/D3x, each of which does slightly different things. Those ways include:

- **Two-button reset.** This type of "rebooting" changes a selection of the most basic settings in your camera (listed below), and is useful when you want to cancel the most common changes you make when adjusting your camera. It does not affect all Shooting menu settings, and affects *only* the currently selected Shooting menu (A, B, C, or D) settings listed in the bulleted list in the Two-Button Reset section following. Nor does it affect any of the four Custom Setting memory banks, described next. I'll show you how to perform the two-button reset shortly.
- **Shooting menu bank reset.** Your camera has four memory banks that store settings you've made in the Shooting menu. They are labeled A, B, C, and D by default, but can be renamed to a label of your choice (such as Sports, Landscapes, or Indoors), as explained in Chapter 3. The Shooting menu has a separate Reset Shooting menu option that zeroes out the changes you've made to the default options, for *the currently active shooting bank.* That is, if you want to reset all four banks, you'll need to perform the operation four times. A two-button reset does not wipe all the settings in any of the Shooting menu banks.
- **Custom Setting menu bank reset.** Your camera also has four memory banks that store settings you've made in any of the six individual Custom Setting menus. These banks are also labeled A, B, C, and D by default, and can be renamed to a label, as I'll show you in Chapter 3. The Custom Setting menu also has a separate Reset Custom Settings option that zeroes out most of the changes you've made to the default options, for *the currently active bank.* As with the Shooting menu banks, if you want to reset all four, you'll need to perform the operation four times. A two-button reset does not affect any of the settings in the Custom Setting menu banks.
- **Cold reset.** The only way to reset *all* of the D3s/D3x's internal settings is to remove the main and clock batteries and allow the internal backup battery to run down until the settings are lost, which can take as long as several weeks. You can remove the batteries and then turn on the camera briefly to reset *most* settings, but this won't zero out all settings to the factory defaults. You might want to try a cold reset if your camera is hopelessly locked up, and you'd like to make one last attempt at restoring it to factory operation before sending it in for service.

## Two-Button Reset

Just follow these steps to perform a two-button reset of the camera:

1. **Find reset buttons.** Locate the ISO and WB buttons on the back of the D3s/D3x, just below the back-panel monochrome LCD (which Nikon calls the back control panel). Each is marked with a green dot. Figure 1.11 shows the two buttons highlighted in yellow.
2. **Start reset.** Press and hold the two buttons for more than two seconds. The monochrome LCD control panels switch off momentarily while the settings are reset.
3. **Release the two buttons.** Your camera's key settings (listed next) have been returned to the factory default, but *not* Custom Setting f7, which assigns a function of your choice to the AE-L/AF-L button. (I'll explain this in Chapter 5.)

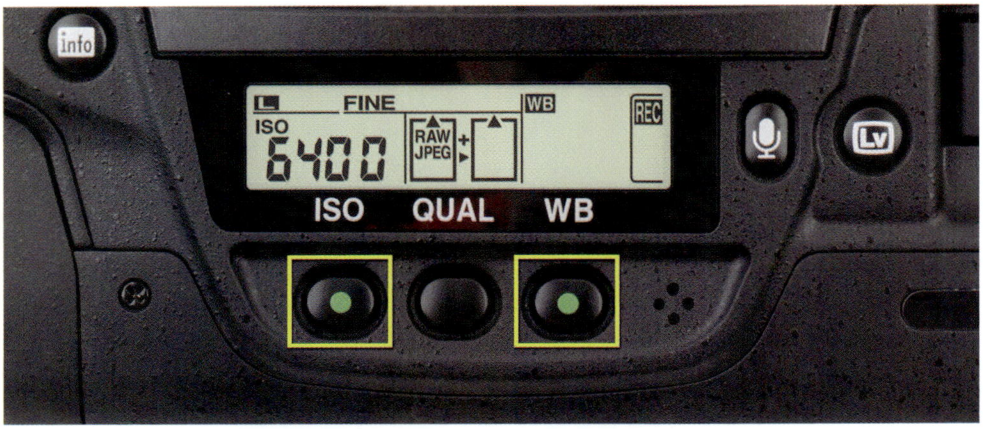


**Figure 1.11**
Perform a two-button reset by holding down the ISO and WB buttons for more than two seconds.

Once a two-button reset has been performed, the following settings in the *current* Shooting menu bank (A, B, C, or D) will be restored to their defaults (all these options are described individually in Chapters 2, 3, 4, and 5). You'll need to perform the two-button reset for each of the other Shooting menu banks (as described in Chapter 3) to return them to their factory values. If you want to reset *every* Shooting menu parameter, use the Shooting menu reset instructions that follow this section. The Shooting menu defaults that are reset with a two-button reset are as follows:

- **Image Quality:** JPEG Normal
- **Image Size:** L
- **ISO:** 200
- **Picture Controls:** Restored to factory settings, with your modifications removed
- **White balance:** Auto
- **White balance fine tuning:** Off

- **Choose color temperature:** 5000K
- **Focus point:** Centered
- **Exposure mode:** Programmed auto
- **Flexible program adjustments:** Off
- **Exposure compensation:** Off
- **Autoexposure lock hold:** Off
- **Aperture lock:** Off
- **Shutter-speed lock:** Off
- **Bracketing:** Off (Bracket set shots reset to 1; increment reset to 1)
- **Flash mode:** Front-curtain sync
- **Flash Value lock:** Off
- **Multiple exposure:** Off

## Shooting Menu/Custom Setting Menu Reset

If you'd like to go a step further and reset *all* the options in the Shooting menu and Custom Setting menu (bank by bank), follow these steps:

1. **Access menus.** Press the Menu button at the top of the array of five buttons located to the immediate left of the back-panel LCD.
2. **Choose Shooting menu or Custom Setting menu.** Press the multi selector down button to scroll down to either the Shooting menu (represented by a camera icon; the second icon from the top in the left-column of the menus) or the Custom Setting menu (represented by a pencil icon; the third icon from the top). Press the right multi selector button to reveal the Shooting or Custom Setting menus. (See Figure 1.12.)
3. **Select bank to reset.** If you want to reset the current bank, skip to Step 4. To change from the current bank, choose either Shooting menu bank or Custom Setting bank, which will be on the top lines of their respective menus. Press the right button on the multi selector to reveal the menu bank names, and use the down button to select the one you want to reset. Press OK to activate that bank.
4. **Reset menu.** Use the down button to scroll to the Reset Shooting menu or Reset Custom Setting choices, then press the right button to reveal a screen with Yes and No choices. Press the up button to highlight Yes, and press OK (or the center button of the multi selector) to reset the active bank.
5. **Reset additional banks.** If you'd like to reset additional named banks, repeat steps 3 and 4, or press Menu to exit.

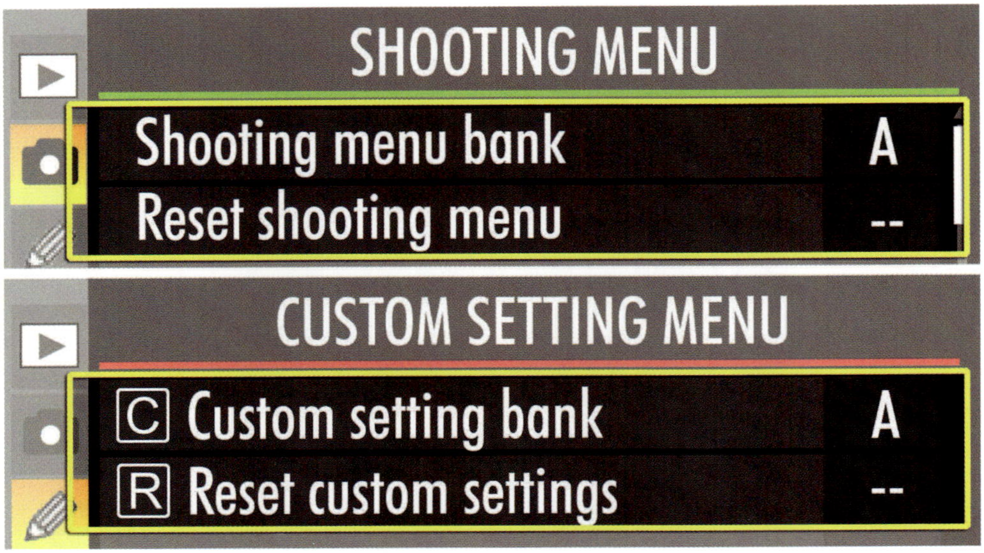


**Figure 1.12**
You can select a menu bank to modify, and then reset its entries to their factory defaults.

## Recommended Default Changes

Although I won't be explaining how to use the Nikon D3s/D3x's menu system in detail until Chapter 3, you can make some simple changes now. These general instructions will serve you to make any of the default setting changes I recommend next. To change any menu setting, follow these steps:

1. **Access menus.** Press the Menu button at the top of the array of four buttons located to the immediate left of the back-panel color LCD.
2. **Choose the main menu you need to access.** Press the multi selector down button to scroll down to the menu containing the entry you want to change. The available menus include (from top to bottom in the left column of the Menu screen): Playback menu (Right-pointing triangle icon); Shooting menu (camera icon); Custom Setting menu (pencil icon); Setup menu (wrench icon); Retouch menu (paintbrush icon); My Menu (text page/text page with checkmark icon).
3. **Select main menu.** Press the right multi selector button to choose the menu heading containing the submenu entry you want to change.
4. **Choose menu entry.** Press the down multi selector button to move within the main menu to the entry you want to change. A scroll bar at the right side shows your progress through the menu, as all the main menus have more items than can fit on a single screen, except for the Custom Setting menu and My Menu (if it contains fewer than five custom entries).

5. **Choose options.** Press the right multi selector button to choose the highlighted menu entry, and view a screen with options. Select the options you want, and press OK to confirm. Some menus allow you to confirm by pressing the right button again, or require you to move to a Done selection and choose that before exiting.
6. **Exit menus.** Usually you can exit the menu system by pressing the Menu button. If an option has variations, I'll explain them when I discuss each of the menu choices in Chapters 3, 4, and 5.

Here are some of the changes I recommend you make to the defaults that Nikon sets up for you. (I have no changes to recommend for the Playback, Setup, and My Menu settings, which are fine the way they are for most people, nor for the Retouch menu, which doesn't have parameters that can be stored.):

## Shooting Menu

Make these changes to the Shooting menu entries listed:

- **Image quality.** Change from RAW+JPEG Normal to RAW+JPEG Fine, to produce better image quality.
- **JPEG Compression.** Change from default Size Priority to Optimal Quality, again, to produce better quality with very little penalty in terms of memory card space consumed.
- **NEF (RAW) Compression.** Change from Compressed to Lossless compressed to get the best combination of image file size and quality.
- **Color space.** Change from default sRGB to Adobe RGB for a more useful range of colors, unless you plan to print directly from the D3s/D3x.
- **High ISO NR.** Change from default Normal to Off, until you've had a chance to evaluate whether the D3s/D3x performs to your liking at high sensitivity settings. Off produces the least amount of noise reduction, but also doesn't degrade the amount of detail as much as any of the On settings.

## Custom Setting Menu

Make these changes to the Custom Setting menu entries listed:

- **Custom Setting c2: Auto meter-off delay.** If you shoot sports or other events where you don't want the camera going to sleep and delaying your ability to snap off a shot *now*, change from the default 6 seconds to 30 seconds, 1 minute, 5 minutes, or 10 minutes. You'll use more power, but won't lose a shot from a split-second delay while the camera wakes up.
- **Custom Setting d1: Beep.** Turn it off to quiet the camera during self-timer countdowns and single-servo autofocus confirmation.

- **Custom Setting f9 (D3x)/f10 (D3s): No memory card?** This controls what happens when you press the shutter release while no memory card is loaded in the camera. Change from the default OK: Enable release to LOCK: Release locked. Why would you want to be able to take pictures with no memory card in the camera, other than to demonstrate the camera or a few other reasons? Even though a DEMO label appears on the LCD when you "take" pictures with no memory card inserted, it's easy to overlook. Turn this capability to LOCK.

# Choosing a Release Mode

> This section shows you how to choose from single frame, continuous mode, self-timer mode, "quiet" mode (D3s only), live view (D3x only), and a special vibration-damping Mirror Up (Mup) mode. Unless you have need of burst shooting or the self-timer, you can set your camera to single frame mode and skip ahead to "Selecting an Exposure Mode" (next). Just press the release mode dial lock release button at the 11 o'clock position on the release mode dial (at the top-left edge of the camera) and rotate to the first, or S position, if it's been changed to something else. (See Figure 1.13.)

The shooting mode determines factors such as when (and how often) the D3s/D3x makes an exposure. If you're coming to the dSLR world from a point-and-shoot camera, you might have used a model that labels these options as drive modes, dating back to the film era when cameras could be set for single shot or "motor drive" (continuous) shooting modes. Your D3s/D3x has six release (shooting) modes, which vary depending on which camera you own. The modes are single frame, two continuous shooting

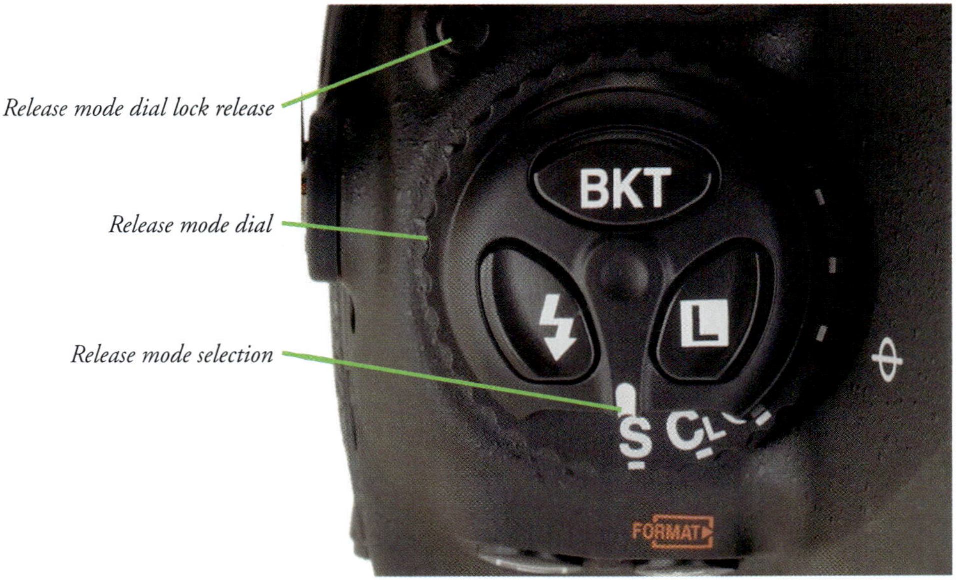


**Figure 1.13**
Hold down the lock release and rotate the dial to choose a release mode.

options, live view (on the D3x; the D3s has a dedicated Live View button on the back of the camera), quiet mode (on the D3s only), self-timer, and mirror up. I'll explain all these modes in more detail and provide tips for using them in particular situations in Chapter 8. The shooting modes are as follows:

- **Single frame.** In single frame mode, the D3s/D3x takes one picture each time you press the shutter release button down all the way. If you press the shutter and nothing happens (which is very frustrating!) you may be using a focus mode that requires sharp focus to be achieved before a picture can be taken. This is called focus priority, and is discussed in more detail under "Choosing a Focus Mode," later in this chapter.
- **Continuous low speed ($C_L$).** This "low speed" shooting mode can be set to produce bursts of 1 to 5 frames per second (D3x) or 1 to 9 fps (D3s) (the latter hardly qualifies as *low* speed). You can set the frame rate in Custom Setting d5. I use this setting when slicing a scene into tiny fragments of time isn't necessary or desirable (say, I'm bracketing in three shot bursts, or don't want a zillion versions of a scene that really isn't changing that fast).
- **Continuous high speed ($C_H$).** This mode fires off shots at up to 5/9 fps (D3x/D3s, respectively in full-frame mode). The frame rate can slow down as your D3s/D3x's memory buffer fills, which forces the camera to wait until some of the pictures you have already taken are written to the memory card, freeing up more space in the buffer. The frame rate may also decrease at shutter speeds slower than 1/250th second, or when operations like continuous-servo autofocus (described later in this chapter) force the D3s/D3x to work at a slightly slower interval.
- **Live view.** This setting activates the D3x's live view mode to preview the image through the LCD rather than optical viewfinder. When the dial is set to this position on the D3x, you can switch to live view mode by pressing the shutter release button all the way down (or an alternate button you've defined, as explained in Chapter 3). The D3s does not have this dial position; live view is activated by pressing the Live View button located just southeast of the back-panel color LCD.
- **Quiet shutter release.** This setting, found on the D3s (but not the D3x), is a single frame shooting mode that uncouples the rapid return mirror's action from the shutter release. When activated, the camera's beep is disabled (regardless of how you may have set Custom Setting d1), and when the shutter button is released halfway after a shot is taken, the mirror does not drop back down. All that is heard is the shutter opening and closing. The mirror slips back into viewing position only when you release the shutter button all the way. This delay produces a noticeably quieter picture-taking sequence.

- **Self-timer.** You can use the self-timer as a replacement for a remote release, to reduce the effects of camera/user shake when the D3s/D3x is mounted on a tripod or, say, set on a firm surface, or when you want to get in the picture yourself. Use Custom Setting menu choice Custom Setting c3 to specify delays of 2, 5, 10, or 20 seconds. Any time you use the camera on a tripod (with the self-timer or otherwise) make sure there is no bright light shining on the viewfinder window; if so, cover it or locate that DK-5 eyepiece cap and block the window.

**Note**

If you plan to dash in front of the camera to join the scene, consider using manual focus so the D3s/D3x won't refocus on your fleeing form and produce unintended results. (Nikon really needs to offer an option to autofocus at the *end* of the self-timer cycle.)

- **Mup (Mirror Up).** This mode delays the taking of the picture until after the mirror is flipped up out of the way (blanking the viewfinder), producing a short delay that also minimizes the effect of the mirror's movement on a picture taken using a long shutter speed. When shooting with telephoto lenses or during close-up photography, a "long" shutter speed can be anything from 1/125th seconds to several seconds. (Mirror movement has only an imperceptible effect on exposures longer than a second or two.) When Mup is activated, pressing the shutter release down all the way once lifts the mirror; pressing it a second time takes the picture and returns the mirror to its down position. To use Mup to take a picture after a delay, press the shutter just once. About 30 seconds after the mirror is raised, the camera will take the picture automatically, with no further action required on your part.

**Note**

The Mup facility is an offbeat way of producing a self-timer delay of 30 seconds, rather than the maximum 20 seconds that the D3s/D3x's self-timer feature provides.

## Selecting an Exposure Mode

This section shows you how to choose an exposure mode. If you'd rather have the D3s/D3x make most of the decisions for you, just hold down the Mode button (see Figure 1.14) and rotate the main command dial until P (Programmed) appears on the top-panel monochrome LCD. You can skip to "Choosing a Metering Mode" if you'd like to choose what areas of the frame the D3s/D3x interprets to calculate exposure.

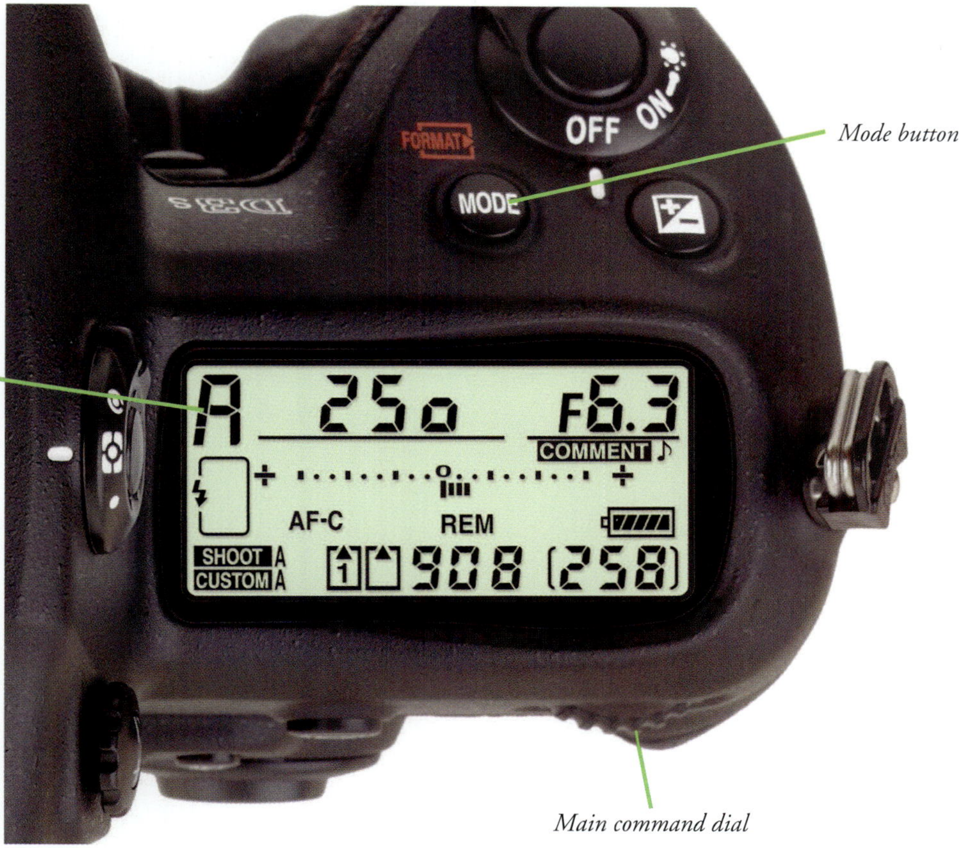


**Figure 1.14** Hold down the Mode button and rotate the main command dial to change shooting mode.

If you're very new to digital photography, you might want to set the camera to P (programmed auto mode) and start snapping away. That mode will make all the appropriate settings for you for many shooting situations. If you have more photographic experience, you might want to opt for one of the semi-automatic modes. These, too, are described in more detail in Chapter 6. These modes all let you apply a little more creativity to your camera's settings.

- **M (manual).** Select when you want full control over the shutter speed and lens opening, either for creative effects or because you are using a studio flash or other flash unit not compatible with the D3s/D3x's automatic flash metering. Use the main command dial and sub-command dial when the exposure meter is active to specify the shutter speed and f/stop (respectively).
- **A (aperture-priority).** Choose when you want to use a particular lens opening, especially to control sharpness or how much of your image is in focus. Specify the f/stop you want using the sub-command dial when the meter is "awake" (tap the shutter release to activate the meter, if necessary), and the D3s/D3x will select the appropriate shutter speed for you.

- **S (shutter-priority).** This mode is useful when you want to use a particular shutter speed to stop action or produce creative blur effects. Choose your preferred shutter speed by rotating the main command dial when the meter is active, and the D3s/D3x will select the appropriate f/stop for you.
- **P (programmed auto).** This mode allows the D3s/D3x to select the basic exposure settings, but you can still override the camera's choices to fine-tune your image, while maintaining metered exposure, as I'll explain in Chapter 6.

## Choosing a Metering Mode

This section shows you how to choose the area the D3s/D3x will use to measure exposure, giving emphasis to the center of the frame; evaluating many different areas of the frame; or measuring light from a small spot in the center of the frame.

The metering mode you select determines how the D3s/D3x calculates exposure. You might want to select a particular metering mode for your first shots, although the default matrix metering is probably the best choice as you get to know your camera. I'll explain when and how to use each of the three metering modes later. To change metering modes, rotate the metering button, located on the pentaprism just forward of the diopter correction knob (press the center button to release the lever lock), to select from among the choices shown in Figure 1.15.

- **Center-weighted metering.** The D3s/D3x meters the entire scene, but gives the most emphasis to the central area of the frame, measuring about 8mm.

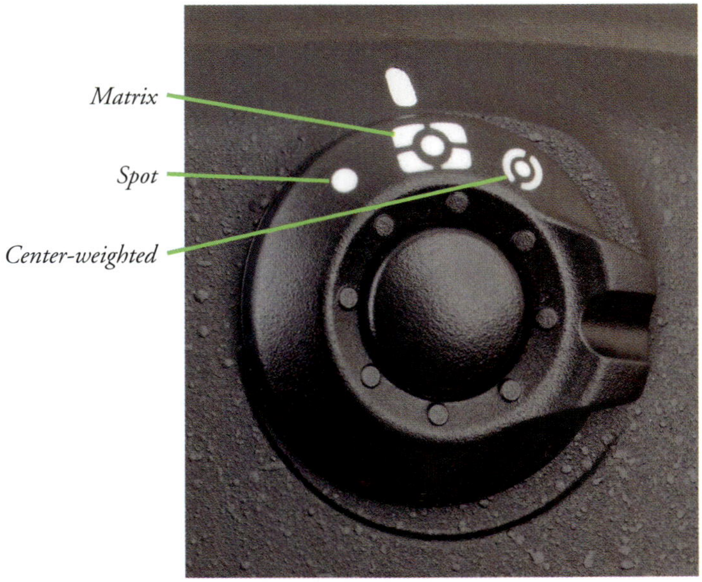


**Figure 1.15** Metering modes are selected using this dial.

- **Matrix metering.** The standard metering mode; the D3s/D3x attempts to intelligently classify your image and choose the best exposure based on readings from a 1005-segment color CCD sensor that interprets light reaching the viewfinder using a database of hundreds of thousands of patterns.
- **Spot metering.** Exposure is calculated from a smaller 3mm central spot, about 2 percent of the image area.

You'll find a detailed description of each of these modes in Chapter 6.

## Choosing a Focus Mode

This section shows how to select *when* the D3s/D3x calculates focus, either all the time (continuously), only once when you press a control like the shutter release button (single frame autofocus), or manually when you rotate a focus ring on the lens.

You can easily switch between automatic and manual focus by moving the AF/MF or M-AF/MF switch on the lens mounted on your camera. You must also set the focus switch on the camera body (located just under the lens release button) to either C (continuous-servo autofocus) or S (single-servo autofocus). When using autofocus, you have additional choices. You can select the autofocus mode (*when* the D3s/D3x measures and locks in focus) and autofocus pattern (*which* of the 51 available autofocus points or zones are used to interpret correct focus). The autofocus mode is chosen using a lever on the camera body, shown in Figure 1.16. Select from the following:

- **Continuous-servo autofocus.** This mode, sometimes called *continuous autofocus*, or AF-C, sets focus when you partially depress the shutter button (or other autofocus activation button), but continues to monitor the frame and refocuses if the camera or subject is moved. This is a useful mode for photographing sports and moving subjects. Focus or release priority can be specified for AF-C mode using Custom Setting a1.
- **Single-servo autofocus.** This mode, sometimes called *single autofocus*, or AF-S, locks in a focus point when the shutter button is pressed down halfway (there are other autofocus activation button options, described in Chapter 4), and the focus confirmation light glows at bottom left in the viewfinder. The focus will remain locked until you release the button or take the picture. This mode is best when your subject is relatively motionless. As you'll learn in Chapter 4, you can set your Nikon D3s/D3x using the Custom Setting menu (Custom Setting a2) so that the camera will not take a photo unless sharp focus is achieved (*focus priority*), or so that it will go ahead and snap a photo while still adjusting focus (*release priority*).

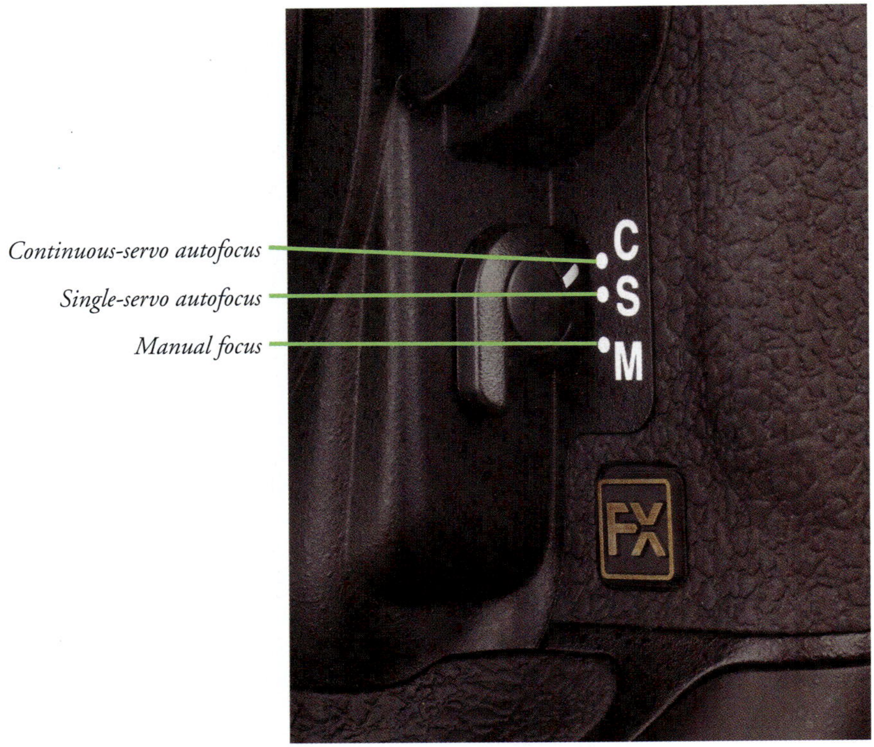


**Figure 1.16**
Set autofocus mode.

- **Manual focus.** With the lever set to this position, you always focus manually using the focus ring on the lens. The focus confirmation indicator in the viewfinder operates reliably, as long as the lens mounted has a maximum aperture of at least f/5.6.

> **Note**
>
> Note that the autofocus/manual focus switches on the lens and camera body must agree; if either is set to manual focus, then the D3s/D3x defaults to manual focus regardless of how the other switch is set.

The Nikon D3s/D3x uses up to 51 different focus points to calculate correct focus, using one or more points you can select yourself, or which the camera can choose. For your initial foray into shooting with the D3s/D3x, you can set the camera for single-point autofocus (you choose the focus point using the multi selector pad), dynamic-area autofocus (you select the focus point, but the camera can override in continuous-servo mode), or auto-area autofocus (the camera always chooses the autofocus point) using the selection switch shown in Figure 1.17. I'll elaborate on this (slight) oversimplification of the various point selection options in Chapter 2.

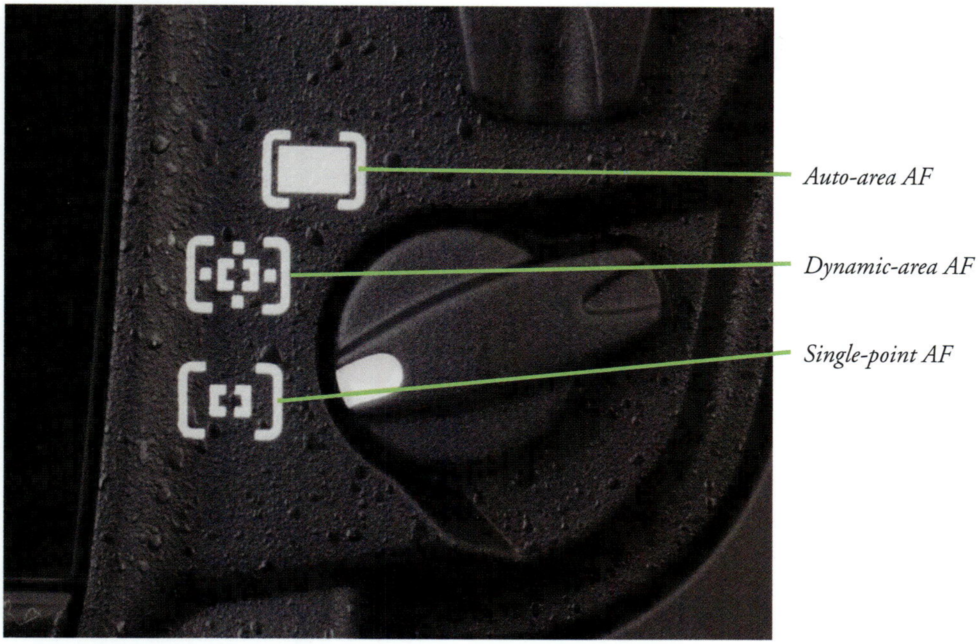


**Figure 1.17** Choose (top to bottom) auto-area autofocus, dynamic-area, or single-point autofocus point selection.

# Other Settings

This section describes some optional features you can select if you feel you need to choose the white balance, change the camera's sensitivity setting, or delay taking a picture with the self-timer.

There are a few other settings you can make if you're feeling ambitious, but don't feel ashamed if you postpone using these features until you've racked up a little more experience with your D3s/D3x.

## Adjusting White Balance and ISO

If you like, you can custom-tailor your white balance (color balance) and ISO sensitivity settings. To start out, it's best to set white balance (WB) to Auto, and ISO to ISO 200 for daylight photos, and ISO 400 for pictures in dimmer light. (Don't be afraid of ISO 1600 or even higher when using the D3s; it does a *much* better job of producing low-noise photos at higher ISOs. However, I find the D3x does its best work at ISO 1600 or lower.) You'll find complete recommendations for both these settings in Chapter 6. You can adjust either one now by pressing the WB (for white balance) or ISO buttons on the release mode dial (on the top-left side of the camera) and rotating the main command dial until the setting you want appears on the status LCD on top of the camera. Both buttons are shown in Figure 1.13, presented earlier.

### MAKING SETTINGS UNDER LOW LIGHT

When working under low light levels, you might experience some difficulty seeing the white balance, ISO, or other settings on the top-panel monochrome LCD as you make them. You can always rotate the ON-OFF switch an additional push in the clockwise direction to illuminate the LCD backlight, but there is a better way. Instead, press the Info button (it's to the left of the color LCD, the second button from the top, marked with a "key" icon) to show the much larger and easier-to-read shooting information display on the color LCD. Then press the WB or ISO button (or the button for whatever setting you're changing) and rotate the appropriate dial until the value you want appears on the shooting information display. Indeed, you can press the Info button at any time to pop up this information screen, which is especially helpful when working with the camera on a tripod, or under dim illumination.

## Using the Self-Timer

If you want to set a short delay before your picture is taken, you can use the self-timer. Press the lock release button to free the release mode dial, and rotate it four clicks clockwise until the self-timer icon appears next to the indicator line. Press the shutter release to lock focus and start the timer. The self-timer lamp on the front of the camera will blink and the beeper will sound (unless you've silenced it in the menus) until the final two seconds, when the lamp remains on and the beeper beeps more rapidly. The default delay is 10 seconds, but you can set it to 2, 5, 10, or 20 seconds using Custom Setting c3, as described in Chapter 3. As I mentioned earlier, you can also use the Mup release mode to get a 30-second delay.

# Reviewing the Images You've Taken

Read this section when you're ready to take a closer look at the images you've taken, and want to know how to review pictures and zoom in.

The Nikon D3s/D3x has a broad range of playback and image review options, and I'll cover them in more detail in Chapter 3. For now, you'll want to learn just the basics. Here is all you really need to know at this time, as shown in Figure 1.18:

- **View image.** Press the Playback button (marked with a white right-pointing triangle) at the upper-left corner of the back of the camera to display the most recent image on the LCD.
- **View additional images.** Press the multi selector left or right to review additional images. Press right to advance to the next image, or left to go back to a previous image.

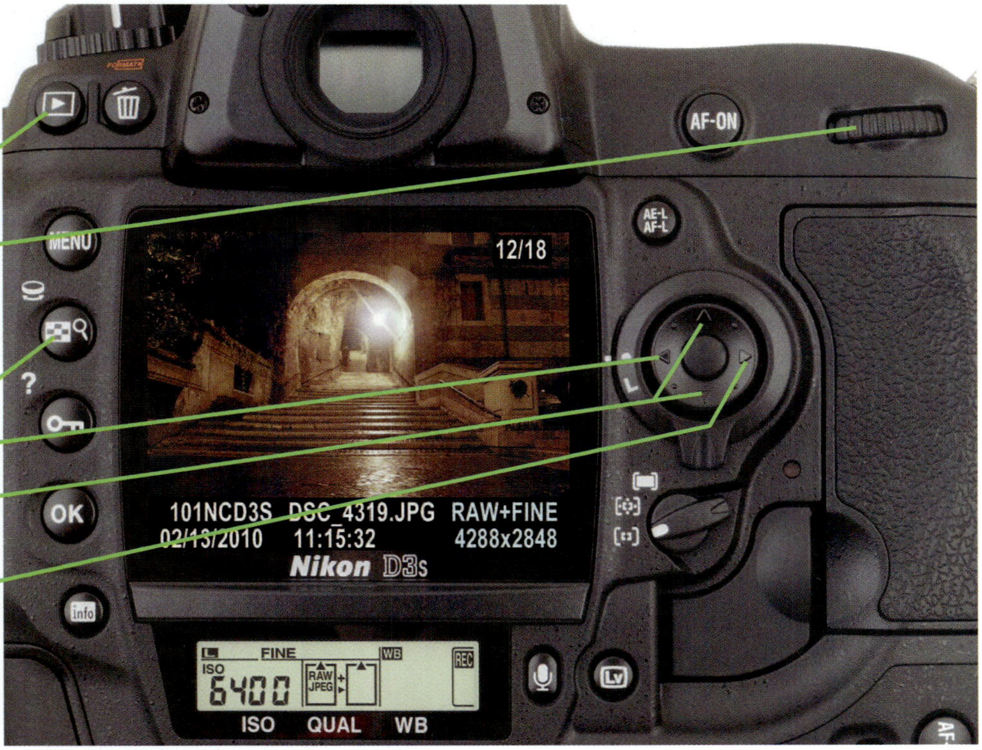


**Figure 1.18** Review your images.

- **Change information display.** Press the multi selector button up or down to change among overlays of basic image information or detailed shooting information.
- **Change magnification.** Press the Zoom button and rotate the main command dial to the right to zoom in on an image, or to the left to zoom out. A thumbnail representation of the whole image appears in the lower-right corner with a yellow rectangle showing the relative level of zoom. At intermediate zoom positions, the yellow rectangle can be moved around within the frame using the multi selector.

  With a full (non-zoomed) image on the LCD, holding the Zoom button while rotating the main command dial to the left shifts to thumbnail view, showing first four, then nine small-size images. Additional rotation with the D3s produces a 72-image thumbnail view (not available with the D3x) that displays truly minuscule versions of the images (and is useful for zipping through hundreds of pictures quickly). Press the multi selector's center button to toggle back and forth between a yellow-highlighted thumbnail version and a full-screen representation of that image.
- **Exit image review.** Press the Playback button again, or just tap the shutter release button to exit playback view.

You'll find information on viewing thumbnail indexes of images, automated playback, and other options in Chapter 3.

## Transferring Photos to Your Computer

The final step in your picture-taking session will be to transfer the photos you've taken to your computer for printing, further review, or image editing. Your D3s/D3x allows you to print directly to PictBridge-compatible printers and to create print orders right in the camera, plus you can select which images to transfer to your computer. I'll outline those options in Chapter 3.

I always recommend using a card reader attached to your computer to transfer files, because that process is generally a lot faster and doesn't drain the D3s/D3x's battery. However, you can also use a cable for direct transfer, which may be your only option when you have the cable and a computer, but no card reader (perhaps you're using the computer of a friend or colleague, or at an Internet café).

To transfer images from the camera to a Mac or PC computer using the USB cable:

1. Turn off the camera.
2. Pry back the rubber cover that protects the D3s/D3x's USB port, and plug the USB cable furnished with the camera into the USB port. (See Figure 1.19.)
3. Connect the other end of the USB cable to a USB port on your computer.
4. Turn on the camera. The operating system itself, or installed software such as Nikon Transfer or Adobe Photoshop Elements Transfer usually detects the camera and offers to copy or move the pictures. Or, the camera appears on your desktop as a mass storage device, enabling you to drag and drop the files to your computer.

To transfer images from a memory card to the computer using a card reader, such as the one shown in Figure 1.20:

1. Turn off the camera.
2. Open the memory card door and extract the Compact Flash card.
3. Insert the memory card into your memory card reader. Your installed software detects the files on the card and offers to transfer them. The card can also appear as a mass storage device on your desktop, which you can open and then drag and drop the files to your computer.

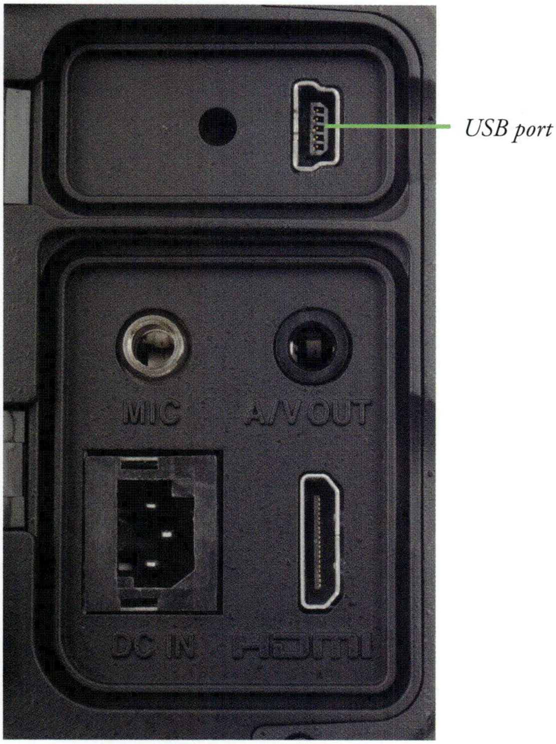


**Figure 1.19**
Images can be transferred to your computer using a USB cable connected to this port.

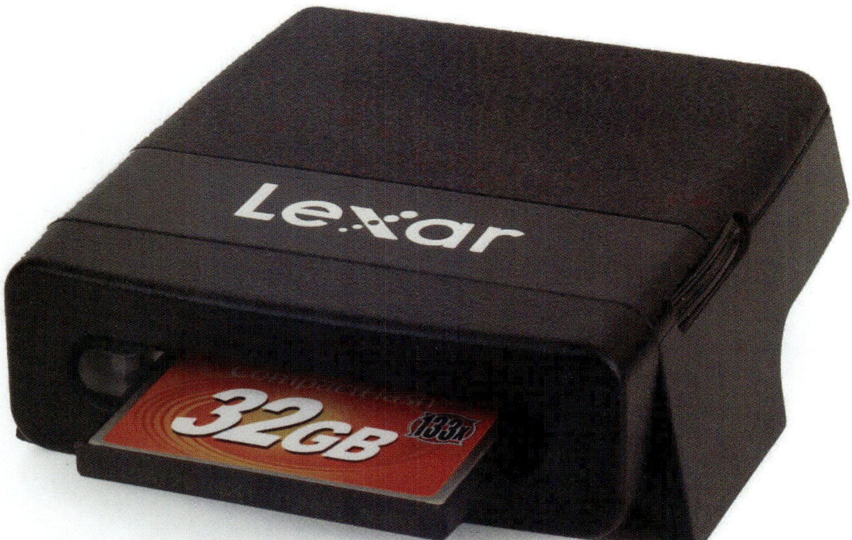


**Figure 1.20**
A card reader is the fastest way to transfer photos.

# 2

# Nikon D3s/D3x Roadmap

Most of the Nikon D3s/D3x's key functions and settings that are changed frequently can be accessed directly using the array of dials, buttons, and knobs that populate the camera's surface. With so many dedicated controls available, you'll find that the bulk of your shooting won't be slowed down by a visit to the vast thicket of text options called Menu-land. That's a distinct paradigm shift from some early digital cameras, which had only four or five buttons, and relied on menus to control virtually every setting you might want to make. With the D3s/D3x, you can press specific buttons dedicated to image quality, white balance, ISO sensitivity, shooting mode, exposure compensation, and playback options, and then spin a command dial or make adjustments using the multi selector.

While it might take some time to learn the position and function of each of these controls, once you've mastered them, the D3s/D3x camera is remarkably easy to use. That's because dedicated buttons with only one or two functions each are much faster to access than the alternative—a maze of menus that must be navigated every time you want to use a feature. The advantage of menu systems—dating back to early computer user interfaces of the 1980s—is that they are easy to *learn.* The ironic disadvantage of menus is that they are clumsy to *use.*

Imagine that you are familiar with digital SLRs in general, but know virtually nothing about the Nikon D3s/D3x. You've decided that you want to format the memory card. A-ha! There's a big 'ole Menu button on the left side of the camera. Press it, and you'll see a series of different menu icons, which, when you scroll through them, have titles like Playback menu, Shooting menu, Custom Setting menu, and Setup menu. You might guess that the Setup menu is the likely repository for a Format command, but even if you guess wrong, it takes only a minute or two to check out the other menus and discover the Format command tucked away within the Setup menu. A couple more button presses and you've successfully formatted your memory card.

You didn't really need instructions—the menu system itself led you to the right command. If you don't format another card for weeks and weeks, you can come back to the menus and discover how to perform the task all over again. The main cost to you was the time required to negotiate through all the menus to carry out the function; while menus are easy to learn, the multiple steps they call for (10 or more button presses may be required) can be cumbersome to use. Direct access buttons are the exact opposite: you have to teach yourself how to use them, and then remember what you've learned over time, but once learned, buttons are much faster to use.

For example, simple direct button presses can also format your memory card, as I pointed out in the last chapter. Recall how easy it is to just hold down the Mode button and the trash can button simultaneously for about two seconds. When the characters For and the exposures remaining displays blink in the viewfinder and top-panel LCD, select the slot containing the memory card you want to format (rotate the main command dial), press the pair of buttons again, and the D3s/D3x formats your card. To cancel the format, press any other button. The sequence may be tricky to learn or remember (although red Format labels appear next to the pair of buttons), but it's much faster to use than threading through a series of menu options.

If you want to operate your D3s/D3x efficiently, you'll need to learn the location, function, and application of all these controls. What you really need is a street-level roadmap that shows where everything is, and how it's used. But what Nikon gives you in the users manual is akin to a world globe with an overall view and many cross-references to the pages that will tell you what you really need to know. Check out the Getting to Know the Camera pages in Nikon's manual, which offers five tiny black-and-white line drawings, plus a couple insets, of the camera body that show front (see Figure 2.1), back, two sides, and the top and bottom of the D3s/D3x. There are nearly 70 callouts pointing to various buttons and dials. If you can find the control you want in this cramped layout, you'll still need to flip back and forth among multiple pages (individual buttons can have several different cross-references!) to locate the information.

Most other third-party books follow this format, featuring black-and-white photos or line drawings of front, back, and top views, and many labels. I originated the up-close-and-personal full-color, street-level roadmap (rather than a satellite view) that I use in this book and my previous camera guidebooks. I provide you with many different views and lots of explanation accompanying each zone of the camera, so that by the time you finish this chapter, you'll have a basic understanding of every control and what it does. I'm not going to delve into menu functions here—you'll find a discussion of your Setup, Shooting, and Playback menu options in Chapter 3. Everything here is devoted to the button pusher and dial twirler in you.

Figure 2.1

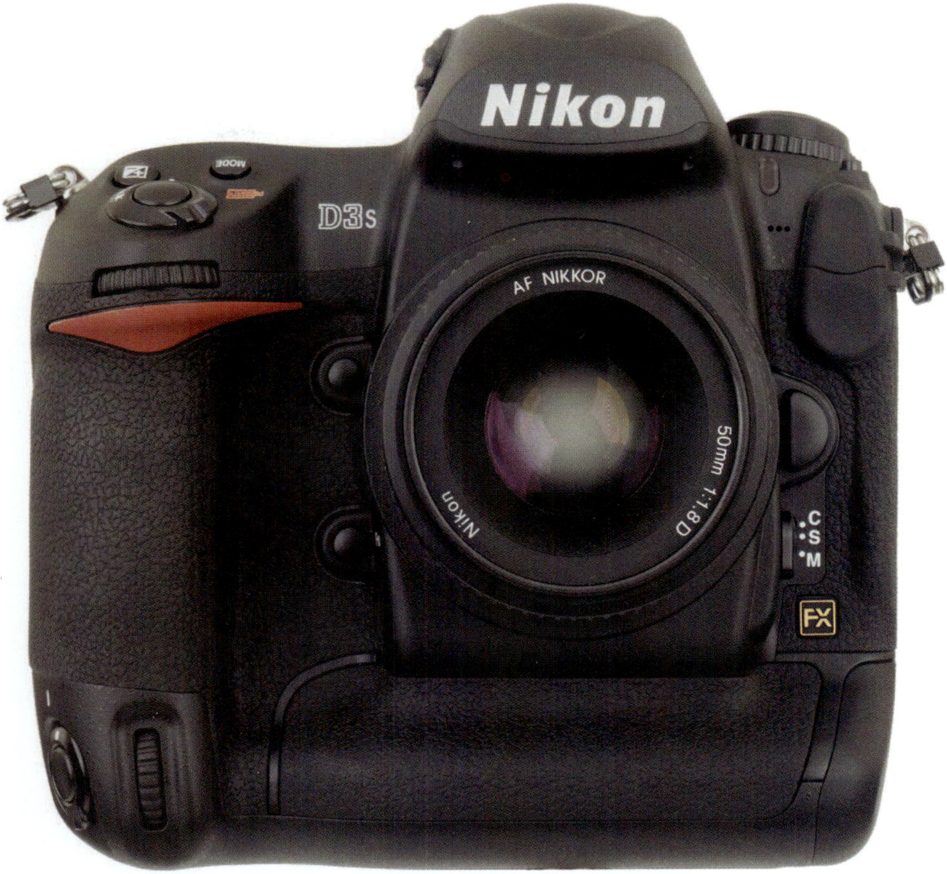


## NIKON D3s/D3/D3x DIFFERENCES

Counting the discontinued original D3, there are three different versions of the D3-series available. The control locations and most features and menus of the original D3 and the D3x are virtually identical, so for the purposes of this chapter you can consider them one model, differing only in their resolutions (12.1 megapixels vs. 24.5 megapixels). All the descriptions I use for the D3x apply to the original D3 as well.

The D3s *does* have slightly different controls and layout from the D3/D3x. For most of this book, I will use the D3s as the basis for the illustrations and point out (as in Figures 2.6 and 2.7, which you'll find later in the chapter) the key differences. Most of those, except for the video-mode microphone on the front of the D3s, are found on the back panel. Where the control layout and (later in the book) the menu layouts differ, I'll explicitly point out the variations in the text. The differences are so small that they make almost no difference.

You'll also find this "roadmap" chapter a good guide to the rest of the book, as well. I'll try to provide as much detail here about the use of the main controls as I can, but some topics (such as autofocus and exposure) are too complex to address in depth right away. So, I'll point you to the relevant chapters that discuss things like setup options, exposure, use of electronic flash, and working with lenses with the occasional cross-reference.

## Nikon D3s/D3x: Full Frontal

This is the side seen by your victims as you snap away. For the photographer, though, the front is the surface your fingers curl around as you hold the camera, and there are really only a few buttons to press, all within easy reach of the fingers of your left and right hands. There are additional controls on the lens itself. You'll need to look at several different views to see everything.

Figure 2.2 shows a view of the left side Nikon D3s/D3x, as seen from the front. The main components you need to know about are as follows:

- **Shutter release.** Angled on top of the handgrip is the shutter release button, which has multiple functions. Press this button down halfway to lock exposure and focus. (That is, unless you've redefined the functions of this control, or that of the AF-ON, and AE/AF Lock buttons on the back panel of the camera using Custom Setting f6, as explained in Chapter 4). Press it down all the way to actually take a photo or sequence of photos if you've changed the mode dial to either of the continuous shooting modes, $C_L$ or $C_H$ (continuous shooting low speed and continuous shooting high speed). Tapping the shutter button when the D3s/D3x's exposure meters have turned themselves off reactivates them, and a tap can be used to remove the display of a menu or image from the rear color LCD.
- **Sub-command dial.** This dial is used to change shooting settings. When settings are available in pairs (such as shutter speed/aperture), this dial will be used to make one type of setting, such as aperture, while the main command dial (on the back of the camera) will be used to make the other, such as aperture setting. Using the Custom Setting menu adjustments in Custom Setting f12, you can reverse the default rotational direction, swap the functions of the sub-command and main command dials, control how the sub-command dial is used to set aperture, and tell the D3s/D3x that you want to use the main command dial to scroll through menus and images. All these options are discussed in more detail in Chapter 4.
- **Hand grip.** This provides a comfortable hand-hold.
- **Fn (Function button).** This conveniently located button has no function by default, but can be programmed to perform any one of several different actions, ranging from metering modes (matrix, center-weighted, spot) to flash off or bracketing bursts. The Fn button can be given a different function for when you press it

or press it while spinning a command dial. I'll explain how to define a function using Custom Setting f4 in Chapter 4.

- **Depth-of-Field (Preview) button.** By default, this button closes down the lens aperture to the opening that will be used to take the picture, as set by the D3s/D3x's light meters or by you (when in manual or aperture-priority modes). The DOF button can be redefined using the same functions offered for the Fn button, with both solo button presses and presses while spinning a command dial, so two different functions can be assigned. I'll explain how to define a function using Custom Setting f5 in Chapter 4.
- **Vertical grip shutter release.** When the camera is rotated 90 degrees to shoot vertically oriented images, this shutter release falls naturally under the index finger, allowing a more natural position for the right hand.

**Figure 2.2**

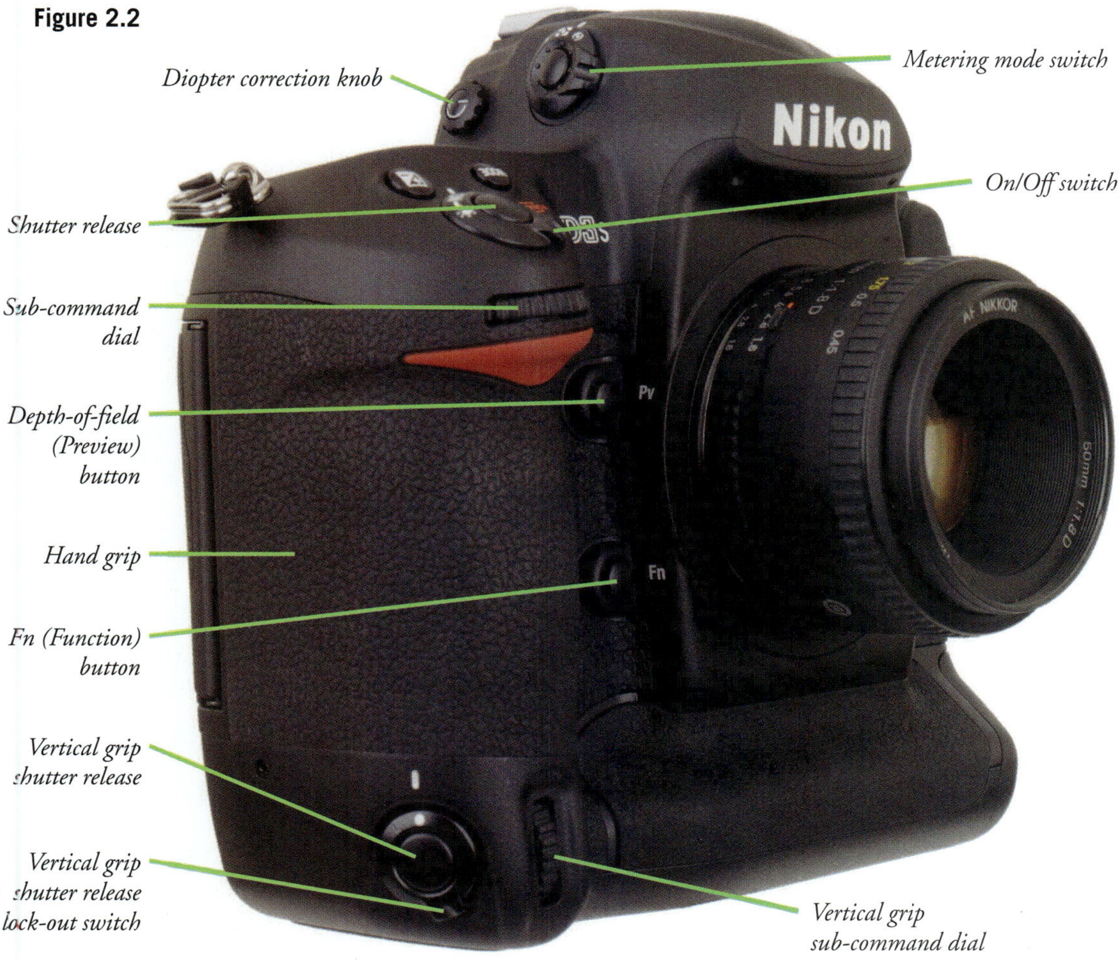

- **Vertical grip shutter release lock-out switch.** Deactivates the vertical grip shutter release, which is easy to trigger by accident with the palm of the right hand when holding the camera in its normal landscape orientation.
- **Diopter adjustment knob.** Pull out and rotate this knob to adjust the diopter correction for your eyesight, as described in Chapter 1. Snap it back in to lock the setting.
- **Metering mode switch.** This rotating switch chooses from among center-weighted (top), matrix (middle), or spot metering. If you'd like to switch back and forth between one metering mode and another rapidly, set your default mode, such as matrix metering, with this switch, then program the Fn or DOF preview button to provide your alternate mode (say, spot metering) with a simple press.

You'll find more controls on the other side of the D3s/D3x, shown in Figure 2.3. In the illustration, you can see the mode dial on top, and the rubber cover on the side that protects the camera's USB, TV, HDMI, external microphone, and DC power ports. The main points of interest shown include:

- **Lens release button.** Press this button to unlock the lens, then rotate the lens away from the shutter release button to dismount your optics.
- **Neck strap lug.** It comes with a split-ring attached that can be used to fasten a neck strap to the D3s/D3x.
- **Port covers.** These rubber covers protect the video, HDMI, DC power, external microphone, and USB port connectors when not in use.
- **Focus mode selector.** Use this switch to change from continuous-servo autofocus (AF-C) to single-servo autofocus (AF-S) or manual focus (M). I'll explain the focusing modes in more detail in Chapter 6, but you should remember that the modes selected with this switch and the autofocus/manual focus switch on the lens must agree. If you've chosen A (or M/A, which allows for manual fine-tuning of autofocus) on the lens, then the camera body switch must be set to either AF-C or AF-S. If either the lens or body switch (or both) are set to M, then the lens must be focused manually.
- **Flash sync connector.** This connector hides beneath a rubber cover, along with the 10-pin remote terminal. You can see the two connectors uncovered in Figure 2.4. Connect a standard PC/X-contact cable or other accessory to this connector. If you are connecting a non-dedicated flash unit to your Nikon D3s/D3x (say, a studio strobe or some other non-automatic non-Nikon flash), it would plug in here.

Figure 2.3

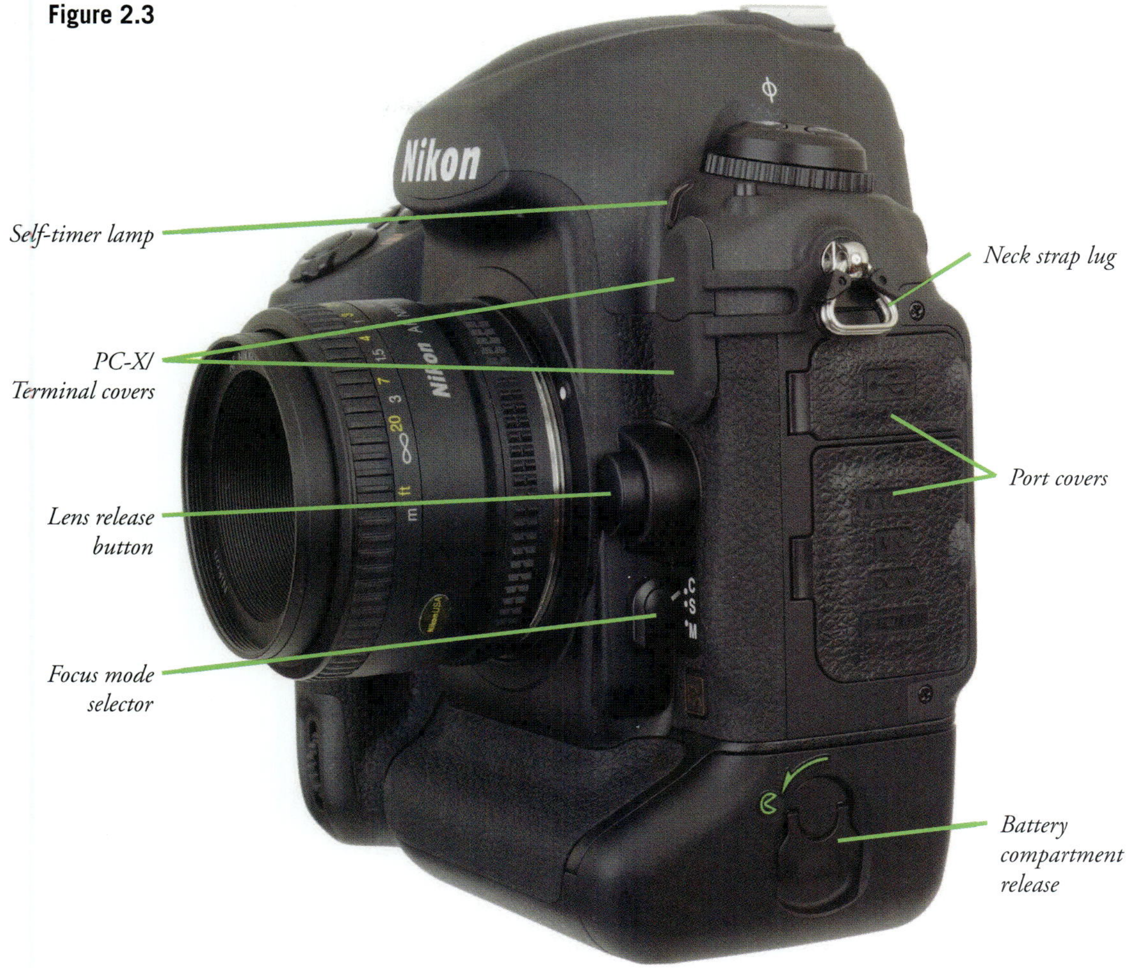


- **10-pin remote terminal.** This connector is used for a variety of accessories, including cable release cords, remote releases of other types (including radio/IR receivers), GPS links, and so forth.
- **Self-timer lamp.** This LED flashes to mark the countdown until the photo is taken.
- **Built-in microphone for movies (D3s only).** While the D3x has only a single microphone, used for voice memos and located on the back of the camera (as described later), the D3s can use any of three microphones: the voice memo mic on the back of the camera; an external microphone for recording sound when shooting movies, plugged into a port located under the rubber cover on the side of the camera; and this internal microphone, dedicated for movie use only.

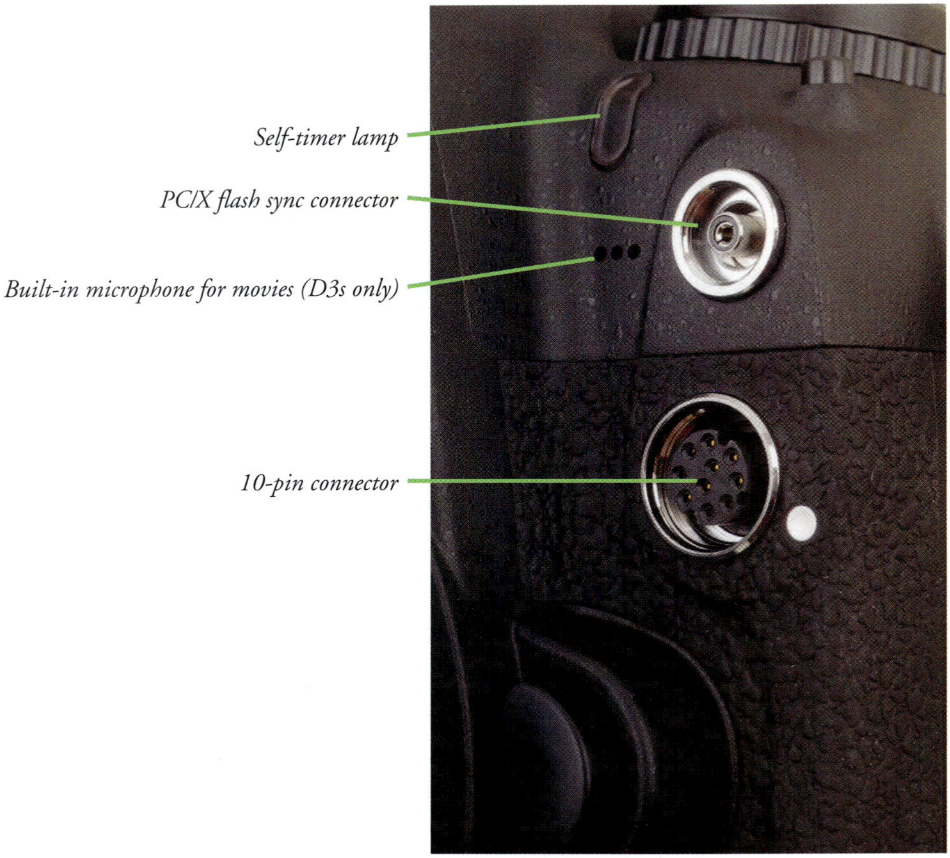


**Figure 2.4**

## LOSE THE RUBBER COVER

I don't like the rubber cover over the flash sync and 10-pin remote connectors. I use studio flash and remote devices so often that the cover ends up dangling at the side of the camera 90 percent of the time. If you're in the same boat, help is on the way. The rubber cover fastens to the D3s/D3x around the neck strap lug, so you can carefully remove it (it's easier to do this when no neck strap is attached, obviously) and store the cover away for re-installation when you sell your D3s/D3x. If you'd rather not leave your connectors "naked" (or just want to protect them when shooting in rain and other harsh conditions), the plastic PC connector and 10-pin terminal covers provided for earlier Nikon pro cameras screw into the connectors just fine. They can be purchased for a few dollars each from www.bocaphoto.com, which offers many other inexpensive Nikon replacement parts. I buy a bunch of them at a time, because the tiny connectors are easy to lose, but I find the inconvenience of screwing one of these connectors on and off from time to time, or replacing a lost one is much less of a hassle than dealing with that floppy rubber cover installed at the factory.

The main feature on the side of the Nikon D3s/D3x is a rubber cover that protects the five connector ports underneath from dust and moisture. The five connectors (four with the D3x), shown in Figure 2.5, with the rubber cover removed, are as follows:

- **USB port.** Plug in the USB cable furnished with your Nikon D3s/D3x and connect the other end to a USB port in your computer to transfer photos, to upload Picture Control settings, or to upload/download other settings between your camera and computer.
- **Microphone (D3s only).** Plug in an external microphone, either a mono or stereo mic (requires a stereo mini plug) to get better sound than is available with the camera-front monophonic microphone.
- **Video port.** You can link this connector with a television to view your photos on a large screen.
- **HDMI port.** You need to buy an accessory cable to connect your D3s/D3x to an HDTV, as one to fit this port is not provided with the camera. If you have a high-resolution television, it's worth the expenditure to be able to view your camera's output in all its glory.
- **DC power port.** Connect the Nikon EH6 AC adapter to provide DC power to your D3s/D3x for long periods when shooting in the studio, displaying slide shows, or doing interval/remote photography.

**Figure 2.5**

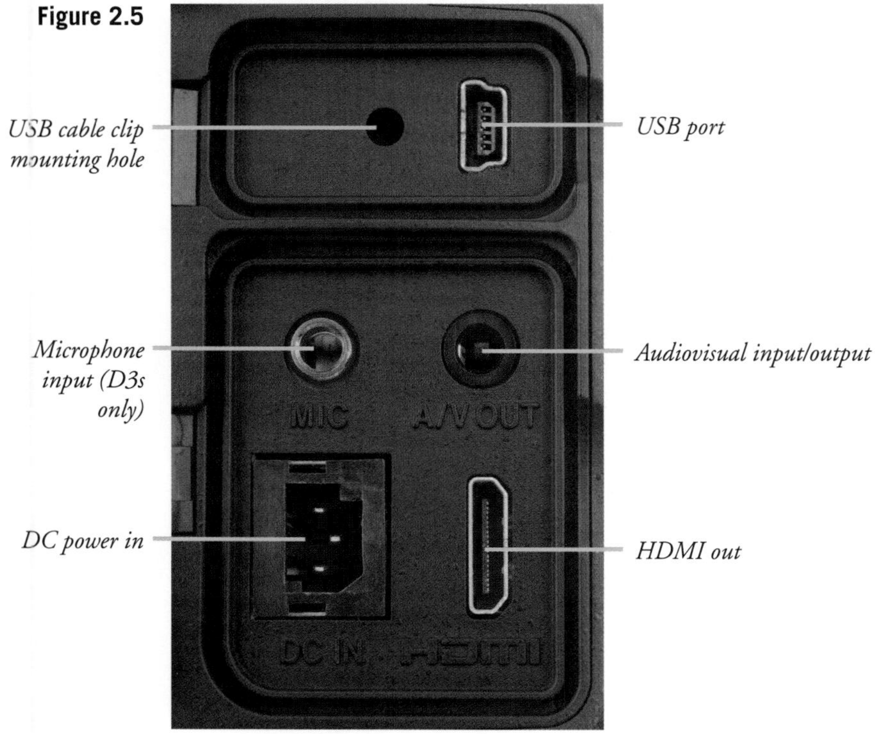

**ALTERED STATES**

I'm presenting a photo of the D3s port layout in Figure 2.5; the location of the connectors on the D3x (and original D3) is slightly different, and there is no microphone jack.

## The Nikon D3s/D3x's Business End

The back panel of the Nikon D3s and D3x (and original D3) is shown in Figures 2.6 and 2.7. I'll show you the modified location of some of the controls first, and then explain what those controls do in the paragraphs that follow. Figure 2.6 shows the back panel of the Nikon D3s; Figure 2.7 shows the back panel of the D3x/D3.

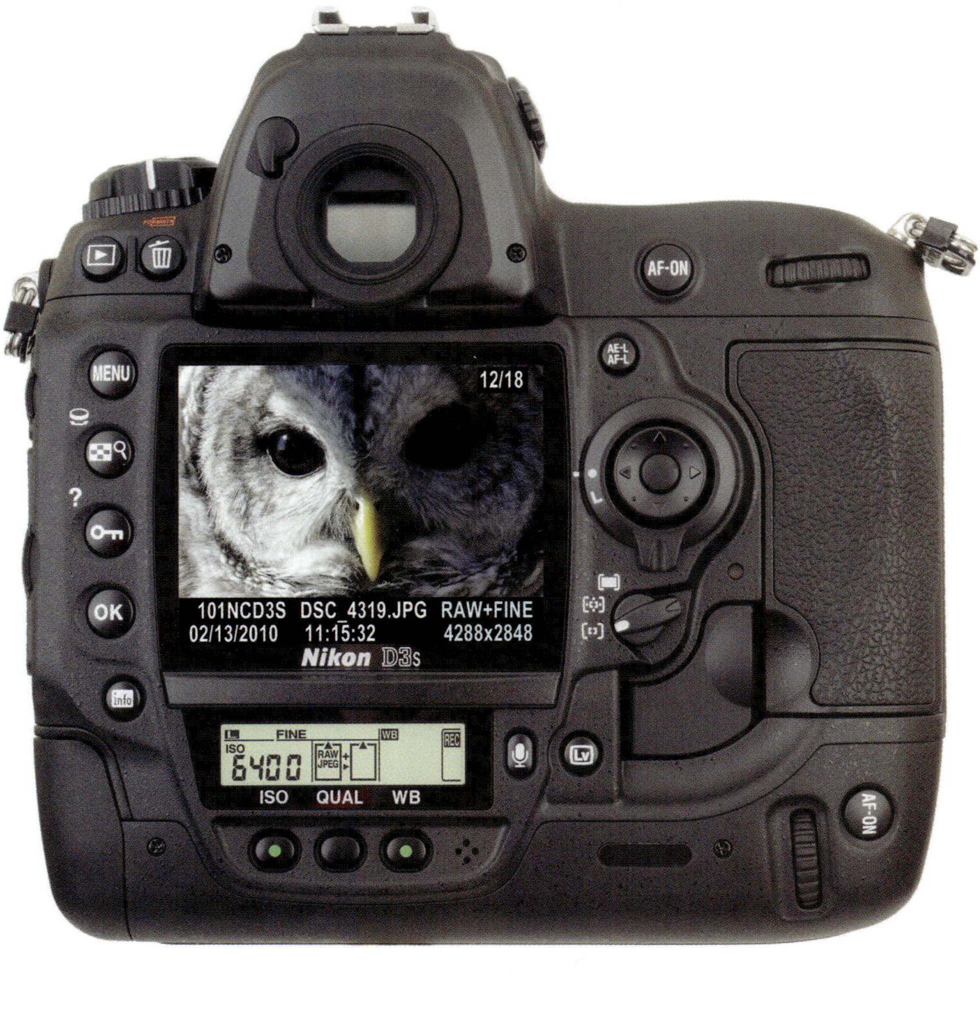


**Figure 2.6**
Back panel of Nikon D3s.

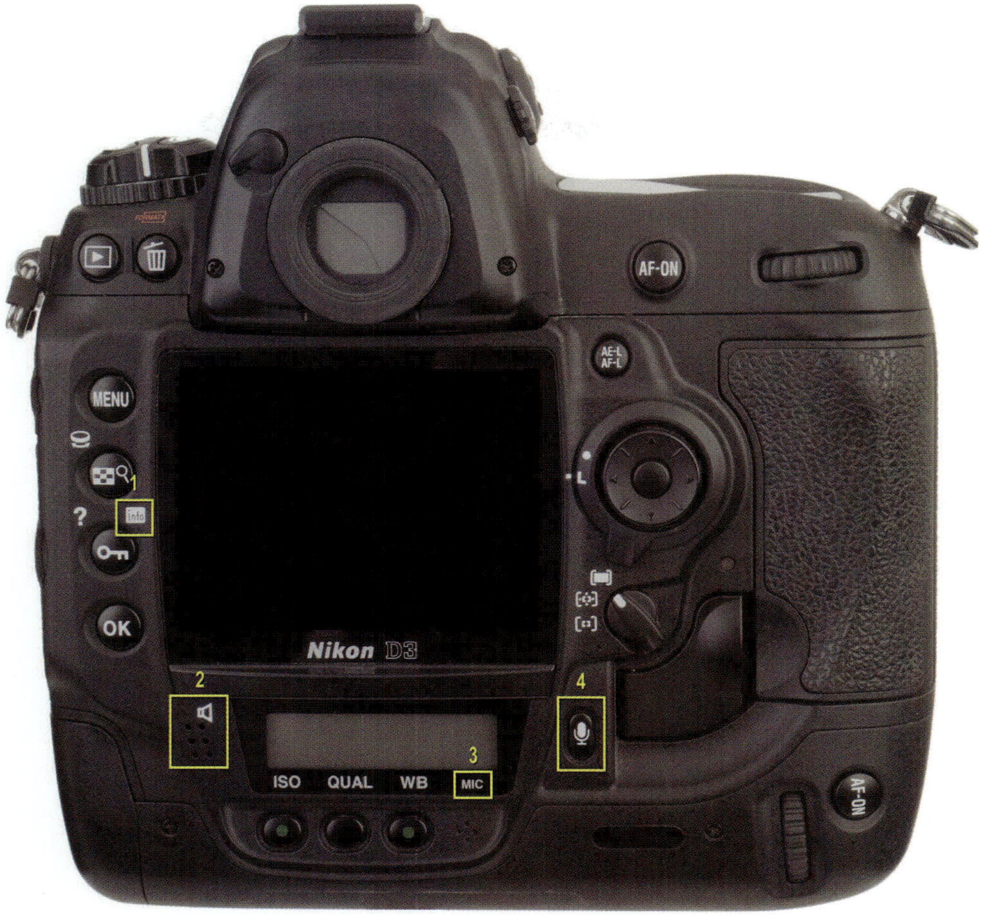


**Figure 2.7**
Back panel of Nikon D3x/D3.

You can see the controls clustered along the top edge of the back panel in Figure 2.8. The key buttons and components and their functions are as follows:

Notations on the tiny differences in control locations are marked with numbered yellow boxes in Figure 2.7. Those differences are as follows:

- **1. Info button.** On the Nikon D3x and original D3, the Info button shares its duties with the Zoom button. For the Nikon D3s, a dedicated button was added just below the OK button on the left side of the back panel. I'll explain how to use this button later in the chapter.
- **2. Speaker.** The external speaker of the Nikon D3x/D3 is located here, to the left of the rear monochrome control panel LCD. On the Nikon D3s, the speaker is tucked away under the small door that is flipped up to reveal the button that releases the larger memory card door.

- **3. Mic label.** On all D3-series cameras, the voice memo microphone is located to the right of the ISO/QUAL/WB button trio, but on the D3s, the label shown here is not present.
- **4. Voice memo microphone button.** On the D3x/D3, this button, which activates recording of voice memos, is located at this position. On the D3s, it is moved a bit to the left to allow adding a dedicated Live View button.

On the upper half of the back panel of the Nikon D3-series cameras, you'll find the following controls, shown in Figure 2.8:

- **Playback button.** Press this button to review images you've taken, using the controls and options I'll explain in the next section. To clear the displayed image, press the Playback button again, or simply tap the shutter release button.
- **Trash/Format #1.** Press to erase the image shown on the LCD. A display will pop up on the LCD asking you to press the Trash button once more to delete the photo, or press the Playback button to cancel. Hold down this button and the Mode button on the top-right surface of the camera (both are marked with red Format labels). "For" will appear in the monochrome status LCD. Choose which memory card you want to erase (rotate the main command dial). Press the buttons again to begin formatting your memory card.
- **Viewfinder eyepiece.** You can frame your composition by peering into the viewfinder. It's surrounded by a soft rubber frame that seals out extraneous light when pressing your eye tightly up to the viewfinder, and it also protects your eyeglass lenses (if worn) from scratching. The lever to the left of the eyepiece can be rotated to close a shutter that ensures that light coming from the back of the camera doesn't venture inside and possibly affect the exposure reading.

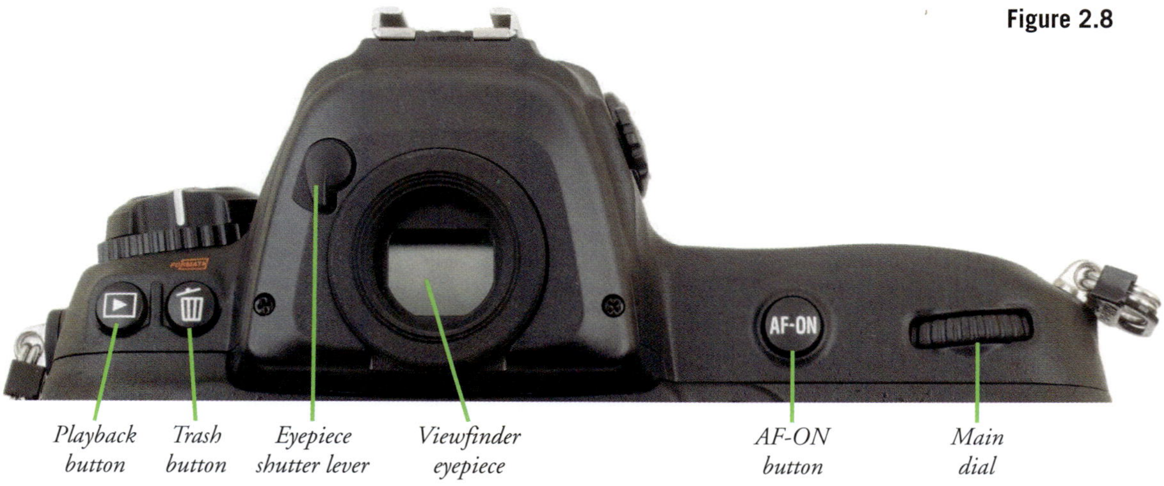


**Figure 2.8**

- **AF-ON.** Press this button to activate the autofocus system without needing to partially depress the shutter release. This control, used with other buttons, allows you to lock exposure and focus separately: Lock exposure by pressing the shutter release halfway, or by pressing the AE lock (AE-L) button; autofocus by pressing the shutter release halfway, or by pressing the AF-ON button. There are lots of cool ways you can use the AF-ON button, and I'll explain them in detail in Chapter 6.
- **Main command dial.** This is the main control dial of the D3s/D3x, used to set or adjust most functions, such as shutter speed, bracketing sequence, white balance, ISO, and so forth, either alone or when another button is depressed simultaneously. It is often used in conjunction with the sub-command dial on the front of the camera when pairs of settings can be made, such as image formats (main command dial: image format; sub-command dial: resolution); exposure (main: shutter speed; sub: aperture); flash (main: flash mode; sub: flash compensation); or white balance (main: WB preset; sub: fine-tune WB). You can swap functions of the main and sub-command dials, reverse the rotation direction, choose whether the aperture ring on the lens or the sub-command dial will be used to set the f/stop, and activate the main command dials to navigate menus and images. You'll learn about these Custom Setting menu options in Chapter 4.

On the right side of the camera, you'll find the controls shown in Figure 2.9.

What they are:

- **AE-L/AF-L (auto exposure/autofocus) lock.** This button can be programmed by you to provide a variety of autoexposure/autofocus locking functions, which I'll explain in Chapter 4. By default, it locks the exposure or focus that the camera sets when you partially depress the shutter button. The exposure lock indication (AE-L icon) appears in the viewfinder. If you want to recalculate exposure or autofocus with the shutter button still partially depressed, press the button again. The exposure/autofocus will be unlocked when you release the shutter button or take the picture. To retain the exposure/autofocus lock for subsequent photos, keep the button pressed while shooting.
- **Multi selector.** This joypad-like button can be shifted up, down, side to side, and diagonally for a total of eight directions, or pressed. It can be used for several functions, including AF point selection, scrolling around a magnified image, trimming a photo, or setting white balance correction. Within menus, pressing the up/down arrows moves the on-screen cursor up or down; pressing towards the right selects the highlighted item and displays its options; pressing left cancels and returns to the previous menu.
- **Center button.** The button in the center of the multi selector can be pressed to choose a highlighted selection in a menu, or to start/stop capturing movie clips (D3s only; the D3x does not have movie functions).

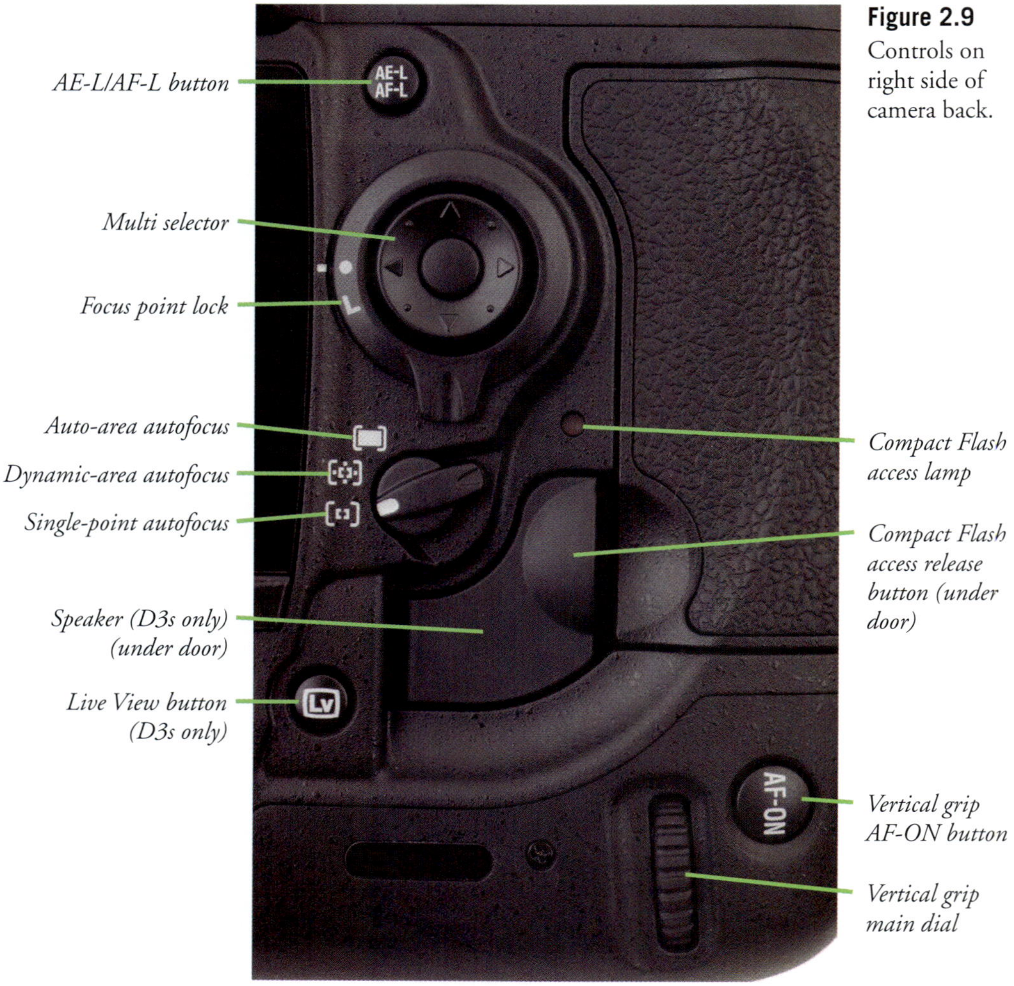


**Figure 2.9** Controls on right side of camera back.

- **AF-Area mode selector.** Use this rotating switch to choose among auto-area autofocus (the camera selects the focus point); dynamic-area AF (you select the focus point from a selectable number of available zones); and single-point AF (you choose a single focus point only). These three modes have several options and may behave differently in single-servo AF and continuous-servo AF, as I'll explain in Chapter 6.
- **Focus selector lock.** Rotate this switch to the L position to disable changing the focus point with the multi selector.
- **Compact flash access lamp.** When lit or blinking, this lamp indicates that a memory card is being accessed.
- **Live View button (D3s only).** Press this button to activate live view when using the D3s. The D3x uses the release mode dial's live view position to prep the camera for displaying a live view of the sensor image.

- **Compact flash access release button door.** Flip up this door to access the button that opens the door to the right that protects the Compact Flash card slots.
- **Speaker.** The D3s speaker is located under the release button door.
- **Vertical grip main dial.** This dial functions as the main command dial when the D3s or D3x are used in vertical orientation.
- **Vertical grip AF-ON button.** This serves the same function as the AF-ON button when the camera is used in vertical orientation.

You'll be using the five buttons to the left of the LCD (shown in Figure 2.10) quite frequently, too, so learn their functions now.

- **Menu button.** Summons/exits the menu displayed on the rear LCD of the D3s/D3x. When you're working with submenus, this button also serves to exit a submenu and return to the main menu.
- **Zoom In button.** Press to zoom in on an image. Hold the button down, while rotating the main command dial to zoom in and out.

Figure 2.10

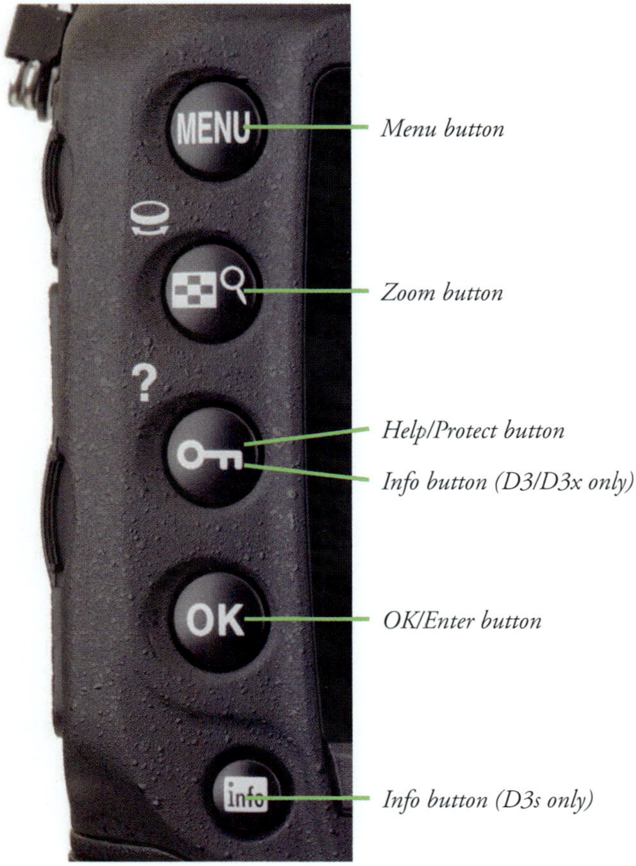

- **Help/Protect button/Info button (D3/D3x only).** When viewing most menu items on the LCD, pressing this button produces a concise Help screen with tips on how to make the relevant setting. This double-duty button also can be used to protect an image from accidental erasure when reviewing a picture on the LCD. Press once to protect the image, a second time to unprotect it. A key symbol appears when the image is displayed to show that it is protected. (This feature safeguards an image from erasure when deleting or transferring pictures only; when you format a card, protected images are removed along with all the others.)
- **OK/Enter button.** Use this button to confirm a selection. When working with menus, press the Menu button instead to back out without making a selection.
- **Info button (D3s only).** Press this button to activate the shooting information display. Press again to change any of the parameters in the bottom rows of the display. Press OK to summon a screen that lets you make the changes. Or, press a third time to remove the information display (or simply tap the shutter release button). The display will also clear after the period you've set for LCD display (the default value is 20 seconds). The information display can be set to alternate between modes that are best viewed under bright daylight, as well as in dimmer illumination. I'll describe the use of the shooting information display in more detail later in this chapter.

## Using the Shooting Information Display

The shooting information display appears when you press the Info button to the left of the color LCD. It shares button space with the Help/Protect button on the D3 and D3x, and is activated by a dedicated Info button on the D3s. This display shows for about 10 seconds by default, but you can change this to a period of up to 10 minutes using the Monitor Off Custom Setting c4, as described in Chapter 5. (The D3/D3x have just one display timing available, from 10 seconds to 10 minutes, for *everything*, while the D3s allows you to set playback, menus, information display, and image review separately.)

Hide this display by pressing the Info button twice, or by tapping the shutter release button. (The D3/D3s/D3x will always clear the LCD screen when you depress the shutter release button, and activate the exposure meter at the same time, so you'll be ready to take a shot if you want.)

The shooting information display provides a lot of basic shooting data. There is a different layout and content between the D3/D3x and D3s, and you can choose light-on-dark or dark-on-light color schemes (either manually, or selected automatically and appropriately based on ambient light conditions where you are shooting). A typical set of displays is shown in Figures 2.11 and 2.12.

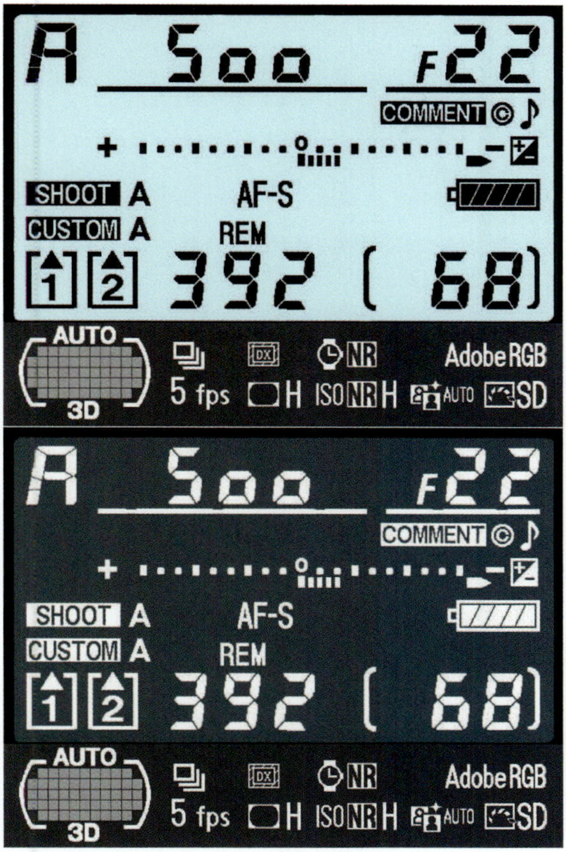


**Figure 2.11** This is a typical shooting information display for the Nikon D3x (and original D3).

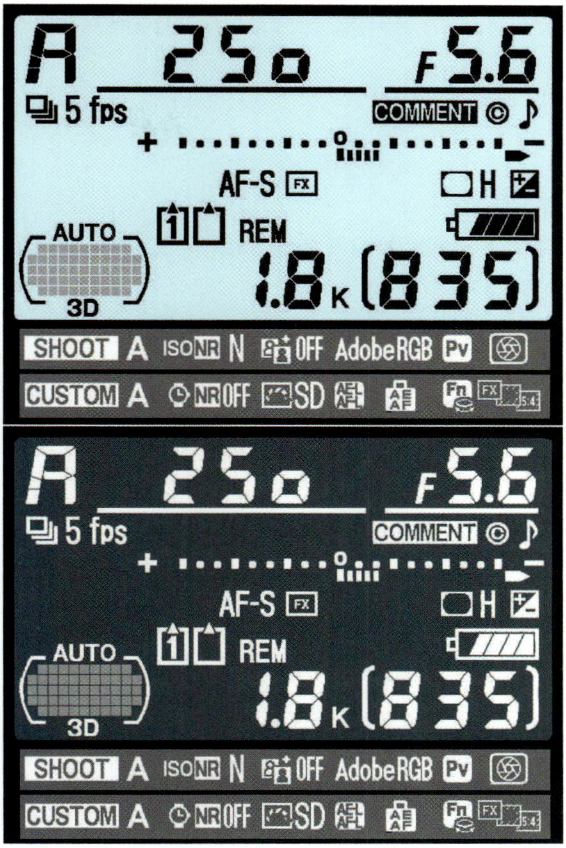


**Figure 2.12** The shooting information display for the Nikon D3s looks like this.

As you can see, the positioning of the information is different with each camera. For the D3x (and the original D3) the display of all possible information is shown in color-coded form in Figures 2.13 and 2.14. The information display for the Nikon D3s is shown in color-coded format in Figure 2.15. The display is *not* color-coded on your LCD; I've added the colors simply to make it easier to label the different bits of information that appear on the screen. I've simplified the labels here; you'll find similar callouts of the individual icons later in this chapter in the section on the top-panel monochrome display, which largely duplicates the information you see here. This rendition just provides an overview of the kind of data you'll find on the color LCD; not every readout will appear on your screen, and certainly not all at once.

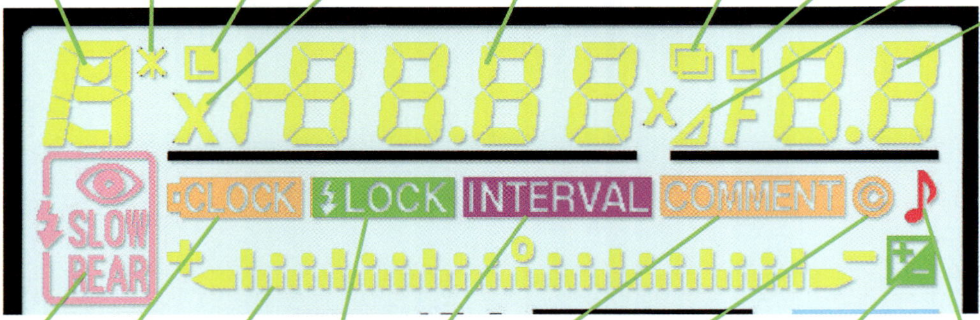


**Figure 2.13** Shooting information display for the Nikon D3 and D3x.

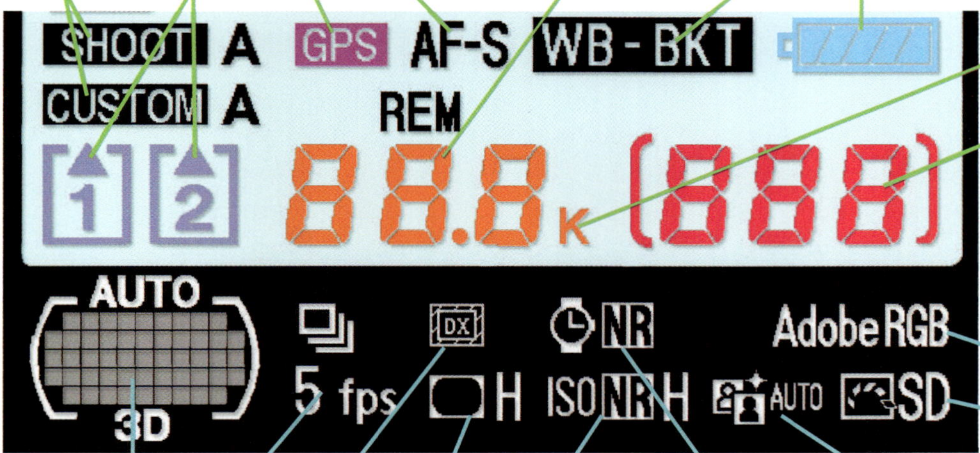


**Figure 2.14** Additional information displayed for the Nikon D3 and D3x.

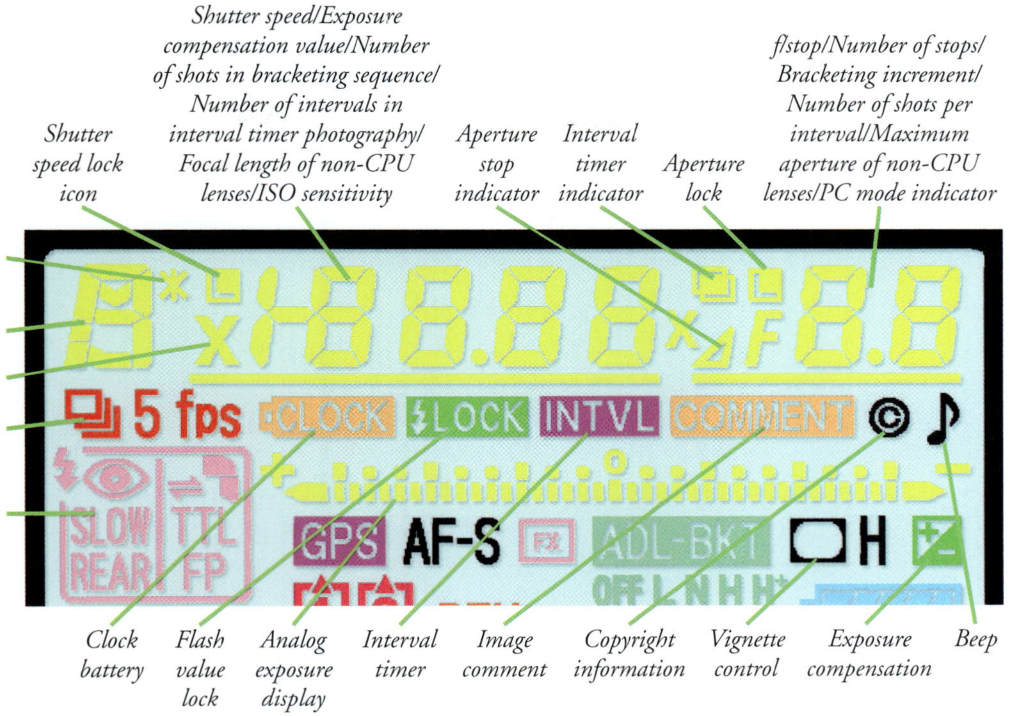


**Figure 2.15** Shooting information display for the Nikon D3s.

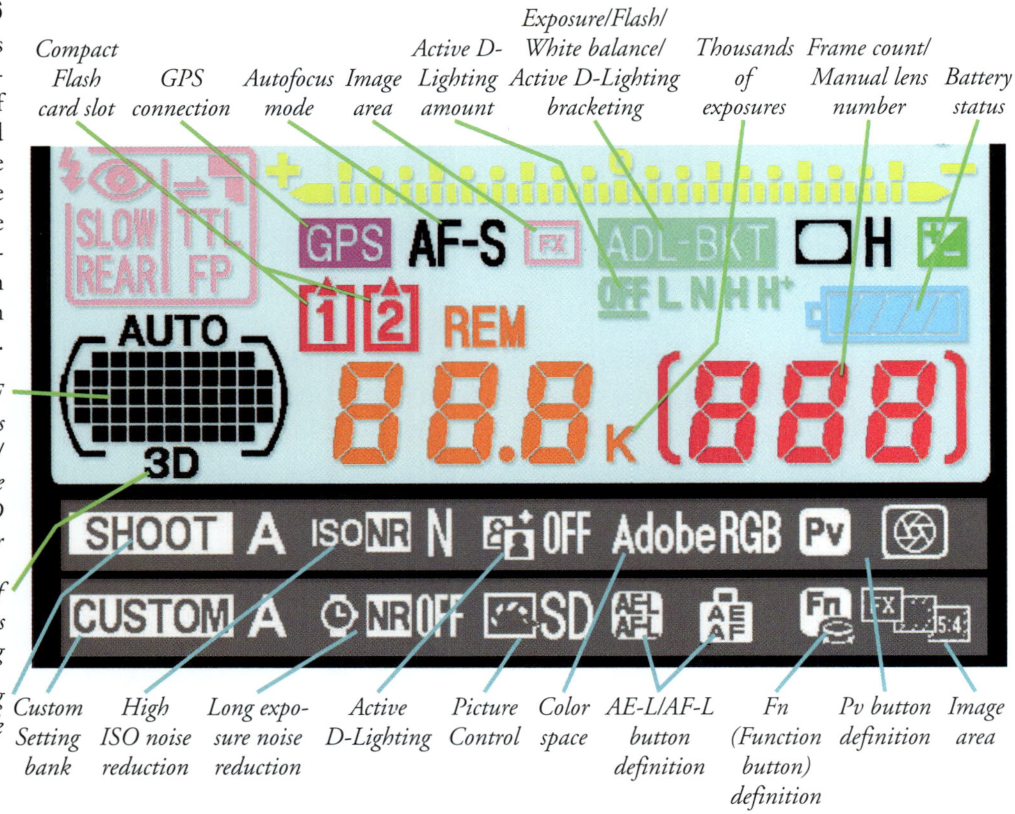


**Figure 2.16** The parameters shown at the bottom two rows of the figure and marked with blue indicators can be changed from the shooting information screen with the Nikon D3s (only).

## MORE FLEXIBILITY WITH THE D3s

On the original Nikon D3 and the D3x, the shooting information display serves an informational purpose *only*. However, with the D3s, when the shooting information display is shown, press the Info button a second time, and you'll be able to *change* the parameters in the bottom two rows, shown in Figure 2.16.

To change the settings using the information display, use the multi selector buttons to navigate to the parameter you want to adjust and press the OK button or the multi selector center button to produce a menu with your options. If you've set Custom Setting d7 (Screen Tips) to On (the default), a handy tool tip appears near a highlighted entry, so you can easily tell what each of the parameters does. Once you've learned the functions, you can turn the screen tips off in the Custom Setting menu. (The original D3 and D3x do not have the Screen Tips feature, because these settings cannot be changed in the information screen.) The specs you can change are described next. (I'll describe the options for each of them in Chapters 4, 5, and 6, too.)

- **Active shooting bank (D3s only).** The D3s/D3x allows you to set up four "banks" of settings, labeled A, B, C, and D, each tailored for a specific type of shooting situation. You can switch among banks quickly. With models other than the D3s, you must use the Setup menu to change these settings.
- **Custom shooting bank (D3s only).** You also get four banks of custom settings that control other D3s/D3x parameters, and can switch between custom shooting banks A, B, C, and D here. With models other than the D3s, you must use the Custom menu system to change these settings.
- **Pv (depth-of-field preview) button/ Fn (Function button)/AE-L/AF-L button (D3s only).** Change the function of each of these three buttons, so that pressing them (either alone or in combination with the main command dial) performs a function of your choice (such as locking the flash off, changing metering mode, or triggering a burst of bracketed shots). You'll find out how to use these (seemingly) infinite combinations of useful shortcuts in Chapter 4. With models other than the D3s, you must use the Custom Setting menu's f (controls) entries to change these settings.
- **ISO Noise Reduction/Long Exposure Noise Reduction (D3s only).** You can turn each of these two types of noise reduction off, or to high, normal, or low settings. These settings can also be adjusted in the Shooting menu.
- **Active D-Lighting (D3s only).** Choose to extend the dynamic range of your image to one of four levels (Low, Normal, High, Extra High), plus Auto or Off. I'll explain the pitfalls/advantages of Active D-Lighting in Chapter 4. These settings can also be adjusted in the Shooting menu.

- **Color space (D3s only).** Use this option to switch between Adobe RGB and sRGB color spaces, described in more detail in Chapter 4. This setting can also be adjusted in the Shooting menu.
- **Picture Control (D3s only).** You can select from various Picture Control styles, described in Chapter 4, using this option. These settings can also be adjusted in the Shooting menu.

## Rear Control Panel

One distinctive feature of the "pro" model Nikon dSLRs is the small monochrome LCD mounted below the color "monitor" LCD, and called the *rear control panel* in Nikon-speak. This panel, shown in Figure 2.17, shows a variety of types of information (see Figure 2.18), and is adjacent to a microphone and microphone button (used to record voice memos that can accompany each image you shoot), a trio of buttons for adjusting ISO, quality, and white balance settings, and, with the Nikon D3s, a Live View button. The three buttons are used to change the following parameters:

- **ISO button.** Press this button while spinning the main command dial to set an ISO sensitivity from ISO 100 to ISO 1600 on the D3x, or ISO 200 to ISO 12800 on the D3s. Higher settings, up to H2 on the D3x (ISO 6400 equivalent) or up to H3 on the D3s (ISO 102400) are also available. Lower settings down to L1.0 (ISO 50 on the D3x and ISO 100 on the D3s) can be dialed in as well. You can also use the ISO Sensitivity entry in the Shooting menu. You'll learn more about ISO, and the option of having the D3s/D3x set it for you automatically based on parameters you enter, in Chapter 6.

**Figure 2.17**

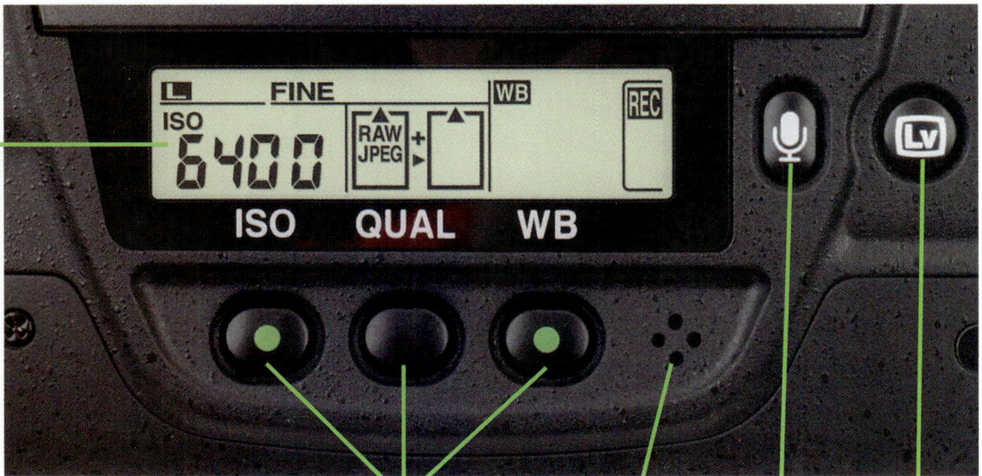

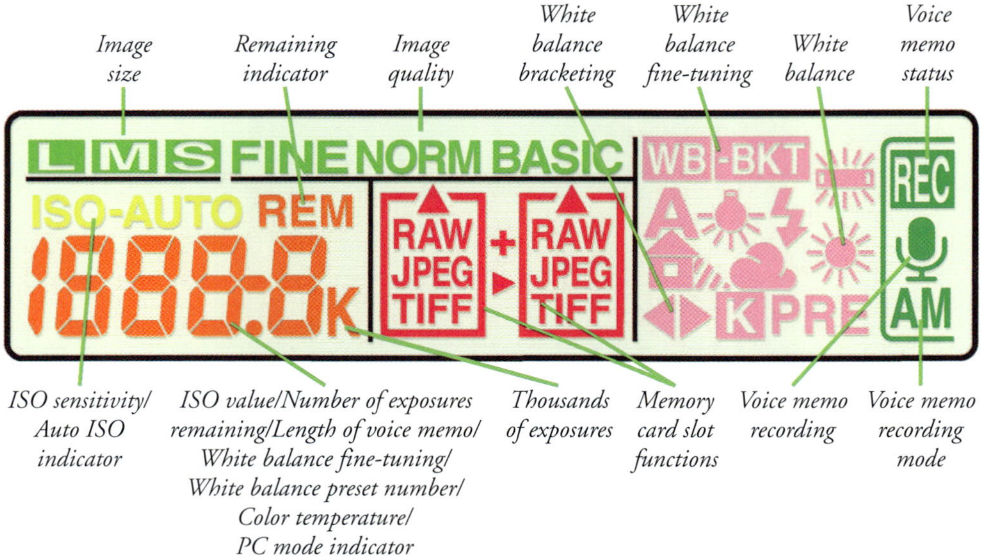


**Figure 2.18**

- **Qual button.** Hold down this button and rotate the main command dial to choose from among three JPEG options (Fine, Norm, and Basic), RAW (only), RAW+ one of the three JPEG quality levels, plus TIFF, which is a loss-free file format that provides high quality files, but, like JPEG, doesn't offer the option of changing the camera settings in your image editor (as RAW does). Hold down the Qual button while rotating the sub-command dial to change resolution among Large (L), Medium (M), or Small (S).

  On the D3s, those resolutions correspond to 4288 × 2848 pixels/12 megapixels (L); 3216 × 2136/6.8 megapixels (M); and 2144 × 1424/3 megapixels (S) sizes. If you're using the D3x, those resolutions correspond to 6048 × 4032 pixels/24.5 megapixels (L); 4544 × 3024/14 megapixels (M); and 3024 × 2016/6 megapixels (S) sizes. These figures are all for the full-frame FX image area, which Nikon calls *(36× 24) 1.0x* in the Image area entry of the Shooting menu. Resolutions and megapixels for both cameras depart from those values when using DX format *(24× 16) 1.5x*, 5:4 format *(30× 24)*, and (on the D3s) 1.2x, which is called *(30× 20) 1.2x*.

- **WB button.** Hold down this button and rotate the main command dial to choose one of the predefined white balance settings available (such as Auto, Daylight, Fluorescent, or Tungsten). When any predefined setting is chosen, other than PRESET or K (choose your own color temperature), you can fine-tune the white balance by holding down the WB button and rotating the sub-command dial to the right to increase the amount of blue, or to the left to increase the amount of amber (indicators will appear to the left on the rear monochrome LCD status panel showing b1…b6 and A1…A6).

When using a preset white balance value that you've captured yourself, rotating the sub-command dial rotates among four stored white balance values, labeled d0, d1, d2, and d3. When K is chosen, the sub-command dial lets you dial in a color temperature from 2,500K to 10,000K. You can also make these same settings using the white balance adjustments in the Shooting menu. If white balance and color temperatures are a mystery to you now, I'll cover them thoroughly in Chapters 3 and 6.

With all D3-series cameras, you can change the information that appears in the lower-left corner of the rear control panel LCD (shown in yellow and orange in Figure 2.18). This is done through Custom Setting d5 (Control panel/viewfinder), described in Chapter 5, which allows you to specify whether the designated area shows ISO sensitivity *or* the number of exposures remaining, as you prefer. (You can also choose to display *either* frame count or exposures remaining at the right side of the viewfinder using this menu option.)

## Recording Voice Memos

Your Nikon D3s/D3x allows you to optionally annotate each image as you shoot, with a voice recording of up to 60 seconds in length, which is stored as a separate .WAV (waveform audio file format) file on your Compact Flash card. The memo will have the same name (other than extension) as the image file, and, if you have a memory card inserted in Slot 1 and Slot 2, will always be recorded to the card in Slot 1 if you've chosen Backup or RAW/Slot 1-JPEG/Slot 2 as the function for the second card slot. If you've selected Overflow as the function for Slot 2, the .WAV file will be recorded on the memory card where the original image is stored.

Although I'd love to explain every single feature of the Nikon D3s/D3x the first time it is mentioned, that's not always possible, especially in a roadmap overview like this chapter. Because the voice memo feature has many options, including a clutch that are specified using Shooting menu options, I'm going to reserve the full discussion of this capability for Chapter 3, which delves into the Shooting menu entries in depth. (The alternative is to let this chapter swell to 100 pages full of diverging topics.)

However, basic voice memo recording is fairly easy. Once you've set up all the options, including enabling the feature and choosing maximum recording length, as explained in Chapter 3, you can record voice memos either automatically (with a recording for each photo) or manually (activated by pressing the button with the microphone on it) as you've set the camera up. The basic steps are these:

- **Start recording.** If you've selected automatic mode, recording will begin after a shot has been taken. If you've selected manual mode, you must either hold down the Record button (it's marked with the microphone icon) to begin recording, or press it once to begin (depending on how you've set this option in the menus).

- **End recording.** If you've selected automatic mode, press the Record button to end the recording (it will end automatically after the maximum time you've specified has elapsed). If you've selected manual mode, end the recording by releasing the button, or by pressing it a second time (again, depending on which option you've selected in the menus).
- **Interrupt a recording.** Don't worry about missing a shot if an opportunity comes up while you're recording a voice memo. Pressing the shutter release halfway ends a recording automatically. So does pressing the menu button, playback button, or turning the camera off.
- **Add memo to an existing image.** If you later decide you want to add a memo to an existing image, view the image using the Playback options (described next). If a musical note icon is overlaid on the review image, a voice memo has already been recorded, and a second one cannot be added, unless you've activated the Overwrite option in the memos. Press and hold the Record button to add a voice memo to that image.
- **Play back a memo.** Review the image in playback mode, either as a full-frame image or a highlighted thumbnail. Images with voice memos available have a musical note icon superimposed in the upper-right corner of the full-frame image. Press the Record button to start playback. Playback will stop when the entire voice memo has been played or the Record button is pressed a second time.
- **Delete a memo.** Press the Trash button. A screen will pop up offering the choice of deleting both the image and sound recording, or of deleting only the sound. Use the up/down buttons to choose, then press the Trash button a second time to delete. Press the Play button to exit without deleting either.

## Playing Back Images

Reviewing images is a joy on the Nikon D3s/D3x's big three-inch LCD. The display is big and bright, and there is abundant detail on that 920,000-dot, VGA-resolution screen. Here are the basics involved in reviewing images on the LCD screen (or on a television/HDTV screen you have connected with a cable). You'll find more details about some of these functions later in this chapter, or, for more complex capabilities, in the chapters that I point you to. This first section just lists the must-know information.

- **Start review.** To begin review, press the Playback button at the upper-left corner of the back of the D3s/D3x. The most recently viewed image will appear on the LCD.
- **Playback folder.** Image review generally shows you the images in the currently selected folder on your Compact Flash card. A given card can contain several folders (a new one is created anytime you exceed 999 images in the current folder).

You can use the Playback folder menu option in the Playback menu (as I'll explain in Chapter 3) to select a specific folder on one of the two memory cards, or direct the D3s/D3x to display images from all the folders on the memory card(s).

- **View thumbnail images.** To change the view from a single image to four or nine thumbnails (or, with the D3s, to 72 thumbnails), follow the instructions in the "Viewing Thumbnails" section that follows.
- **Zoom in and out.** To zoom in or out, press the Zoom/Thumbnail button, following the instructions in the "Zooming the Nikon D3s/D3x Playback Display" in the next section. (It also shows you how to move the zoomed area around using the multi selector keypad.) Rotate the main command dial to change the zoom level.
- **Move back and forth.** To advance to the next image, press the right edge of the multi selector pad; to go back to a previous shot, press the left edge. When you reach the beginning/end of the photos in your folder, the display "wraps around" to the end/beginning of the available shots.
- **See different types of data.** To change the type of information about the displayed image that is shown, press the up and down portions of the multi selector pad. To learn what data is available, read the "Using Shooting Data" section later in this chapter.

**Note**

You can swap the functions of the up/down and right/left keys during playback using Custom Setting f4, as described in Chapter 3.

- **Remove images.** To delete an image that's currently on the screen, press the Trash button once, then press it again to confirm the deletion. To select and delete a group of images, use the Delete option in the Shooting menu to specify particular photos to remove, as described in more detail in Chapter 3.
- **Cancel playback.** To cancel image review, press the Playback button again, or simply tap the shutter release button.

**CENTER FUNCTIONS**

The center button of the multi selector can be programmed to perform one of four different functions during playback, as I'll describe in Chapter 3. Those functions are thumbnails on/off (the default); view histograms; zoom on/off; and choose the memory card folder used for image review.

## Zooming the Nikon D3s/D3x Playback Display

The Nikon D3s/D3x zooms in and out of preview images in a way that's slightly different than used with other cameras, such as the Nikon D700 and D300s. That's annoying (if you're coming from a Nikon camera that used an alternate system, or if you currently use two different models), but it's something we must learn to live with. The procedure is as follows:

1. **View image.** When an image is displayed (use the Playback button to start), press the Zoom in button while rotating the main command dial to fill the screen with a slightly magnified version of the image.
2. **Zoom in.** Continue to rotate the main command dial to the right while holding down the Zoom button to change zoom levels, up to 27X when shooting in Large image size; to 20X when shooting in Medium image size; or 13X when shooting in Small image size. The zoomed area will be highlighted with a yellow box (see top in Figure 2.19); release the Zoom button and the frame will fill with the highlighted portion (bottom in Figure 2.19).

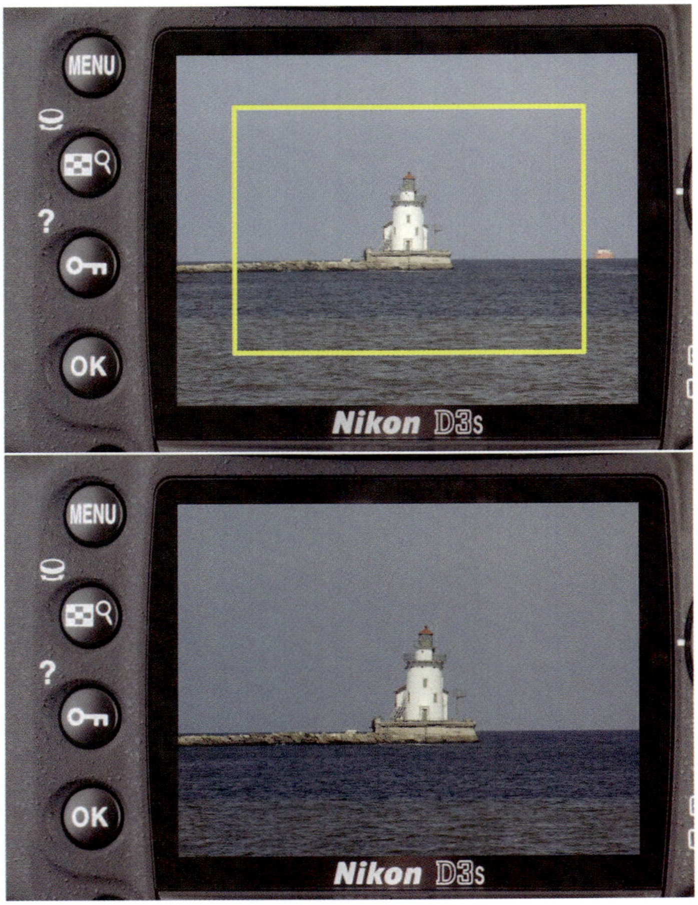


**Figure 2.19**
Hold down the Zoom button and rotate the main command dial to select an area to zoom in to (top); release the button and the frame fills with the area highlighted (bottom).

3. **Move within zoomed area.** When the Zoom button is pressed, the yellow box appears (to allow zooming in or out). When the box is visible, you can press the multi selector up/down/left/right buttons to move the location of the box around the frame; you don't need to confine your zooming to the center area. When the Zoom button is released and the zoomed area fills the frame, the yellow box vanishes, and you can use the directional keys to move the viewed portion of the image around within the frame.
4. **View other images at same zoom level.** When zoomed in, rotate the main command dial left and right to move to the same zoomed area of the next/previous image.
5. **Zoom out.** Hold the Zoom button while rotating the main command dial to the left to zoom back out of a zoomed image. Once you reach full-frame mode, continue to rotate the dial to view 4, 9, or (with the D3s only) 72 thumbnail images. The section that follows this one explains how to work with these thumbnail views.
6. **Protect image.** In zoomed, full-frame, or thumbnail views, press the Protect button to mark an image to prevent it from being deleted until protection is removed, or the card is formatted.
7. **Cancel playback.** As always, you can press the shutter release button halfway to cancel playback and ready the camera to take a picture.

This scheme isn't a bad one. The big problem for those who have more than one advanced Nikon dSLR is that it's different from the system used with the D700, D300s, and D300, as well as the earlier cameras. There is no Zoom out button on the D3/D3s/D3x. Simply press the single Zoom/Thumbnail button and spin the main command dial to the right to zoom in and to the left to zoom out. A yellow box shows the zoomed area, and when you release the Zoom button, the screen fills with the area you've chosen. Of course, if you're not planning to use the D3s/D3x side-by-side with any of the other advanced Nikon dSLRs, all you need to do is learn the new system and forget about the alternate sequences.

## Viewing Thumbnails

The Nikon D3s/D3x provides other options for reviewing images in addition to zooming in and out. You can switch between single image view and either 4, 9, or (with the D3s only), 72 reduced-size thumbnail images on a single LCD screen.

Pages of thumbnail images offer a quick way to scroll through a large number of pictures quickly to find the one you want to examine in more detail. The D3s/D3x lets you switch quickly from single- to 4- to 9-, and 72-image views, with a scroll bar displayed at the right side of the screen to show you the relative position of the displayed thumbnails within the full collection of images in the active folder on your memory card. Figure 2.20 offers a comparison between the three levels of thumbnail views.

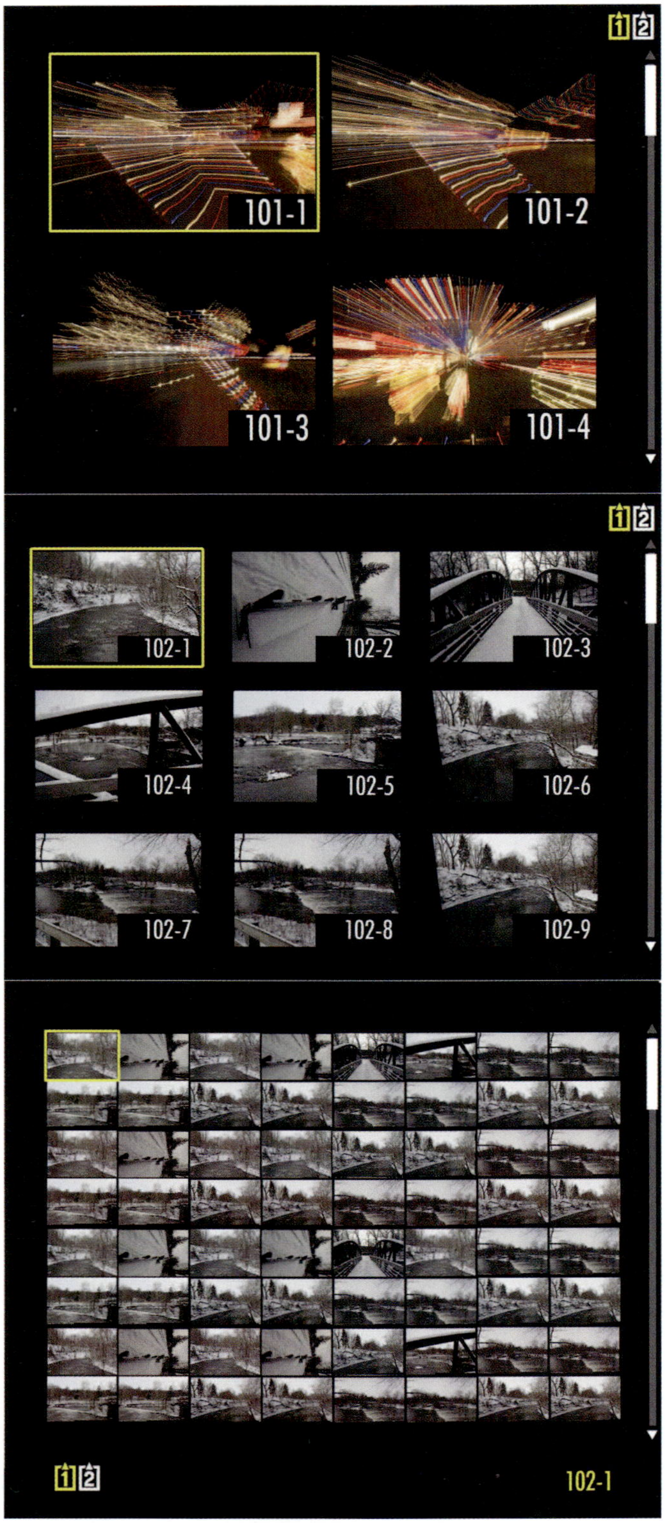


**Figure 2.20**
Switch between four thumbnails (top ) or nine thumbnails (middle) by pressing the Zoom in button and rotating the main command dial to the left. The Nikon D3s has an additional 72-thumbnail mode (bottom).

- **Add thumbnails.** To increase the number of thumbnails on the screen, press the Zoom button and rotate the main command dial to the left. The D3s/D3x will switch from single image to 4 thumbnails to 9 thumbnails to (with the D3s) 72 thumbnails. (The display doesn't cycle back to single image again.)
- **Reduce number of thumbnails.** To decrease the number of thumbnails on the screen, press the Zoom button and rotate the command dial to the right to change from 72 thumbnails (with the D3s) to 9 thumbnails to 4 thumbnails, or from 4 to single-image display. Continuing to press the Zoom button and rotating the command dial once you've returned to single-image display starts the zoom process described in the previous section.
- **Toggle between thumbnails and full image.** When viewing thumbnails, you can quickly toggle between thumbnail view and full image display by pressing the center of the multi selector (unless you've redefined it for some other function or turned it off completely during playback, using Custom Setting f2, as described in Chapter 4). Pressing it again returns to the previously chosen thumbnail view.
- **Change highlighted thumbnail area.** Use the multi selector to move the yellow highlight box around among the thumbnails.
- **Protect and delete images.** When viewing thumbnails or a single page image, press the Protect button to preserve the image against accidental deletion (a key icon is overlaid over the full-page image; press Protect again to remove protection). Press the Protect button again to remove the protection.
- **Exit image review.** Tap the shutter release button or press the Playback button to exit image review. You don't have to worry about missing a shot because you were reviewing images; a half-press of the shutter release automatically brings back the D3s/D3x's exposure meters, the autofocus system (unless you've redefined your controls or are using manual focus), and cancels image review.

## Working with the Photo Data Displays

Your Nikon D3s/D3x can display two types of information on the color LCD as you are reviewing or taking pictures. As a quick review, they are:

- **Shooting information display.** This is the screen of information (illustrated by Figures 2.11 and 2.12 earlier) that provides a readout of various settings for the D3s/D3x's shooting parameters. It appears when you press the Info button on the back of the camera. The shooting information display partially duplicates some of the data shown on the top-panel monochrome LCD, but, with the Nikon D3s only, has an additional feature: you can change any of the parameters listed in the bottom two rows of the display, without the need to press a function button or visit the menus. I explained exactly how to do this earlier in the chapter.

- **Photo Data.** These are a series of up to nine screens (including GPS data, which appears only if you used a GPS device to take the picture) that provide various types of shooting and other information *about a particular image* that you are reviewing. The data shown applies only to that image, and does not reflect your D3s/D3x's current shooting settings (unless you're viewing an image you've just taken). I'll show you each of these screens next, and explain how you can use them.

When reviewing an image on the screen, your D3s/D3x can supplement the image itself with a variety of shooting data, ranging from basic information presented at the bottom of the LCD display, to three text overlays that detail virtually every shooting option you've selected. There is also a display for GPS data if you're using a GPS device, and two views of histograms. There's actually a third histogram view that can be summoned when you reprogram the center button of the multi selector. I'll explain how to do that (Custom Setting f2 for the impatient) and how to work with histograms in the discussion on achieving optimum exposure in Chapter 6. However, this is a good place to provide an overview of the kind of information you can view when playing back your photos.

You can change the *types* of information displayed using the Display mode entry in the Playback menu. There you will find checkboxes you can mark for both basic photo information (overexposed highlights and the focus point used when the image was captured) and detailed photo information (which includes an RGB histogram and various data screens). I'll show you how to activate these info options in Chapter 3, and provide more detailed reasons why you might want to see this data when you review your pictures. This section will simply show you the type of information available. Most of the data is self-explanatory, so the labels in the accompanying figures should tell you most of what you need to know. To change to any of these views while an image is on the screen in Playback mode, press the multi selector up/down buttons (unless you've swapped the up/down functions with the left/right functions in the Custom Setting menu).

- **File information screen.** The basic full image review display is officially called the File Information screen, and looks like Figure 2.21. Press the multi selector down button to advance to the next information screen.
- **Highlights.** When Highlights display is active (after being chosen in the Display mode entry of the Playback menu, as described in Chapter 3), any overexposed areas will be indicated by a flashing black border. As I am unable to make the printed page flash, you'll have to check out this effect for yourself. You can visualize what these "blinkies" look like in Figure 2.22, where they appear as black areas in the girls' clothing and hair.

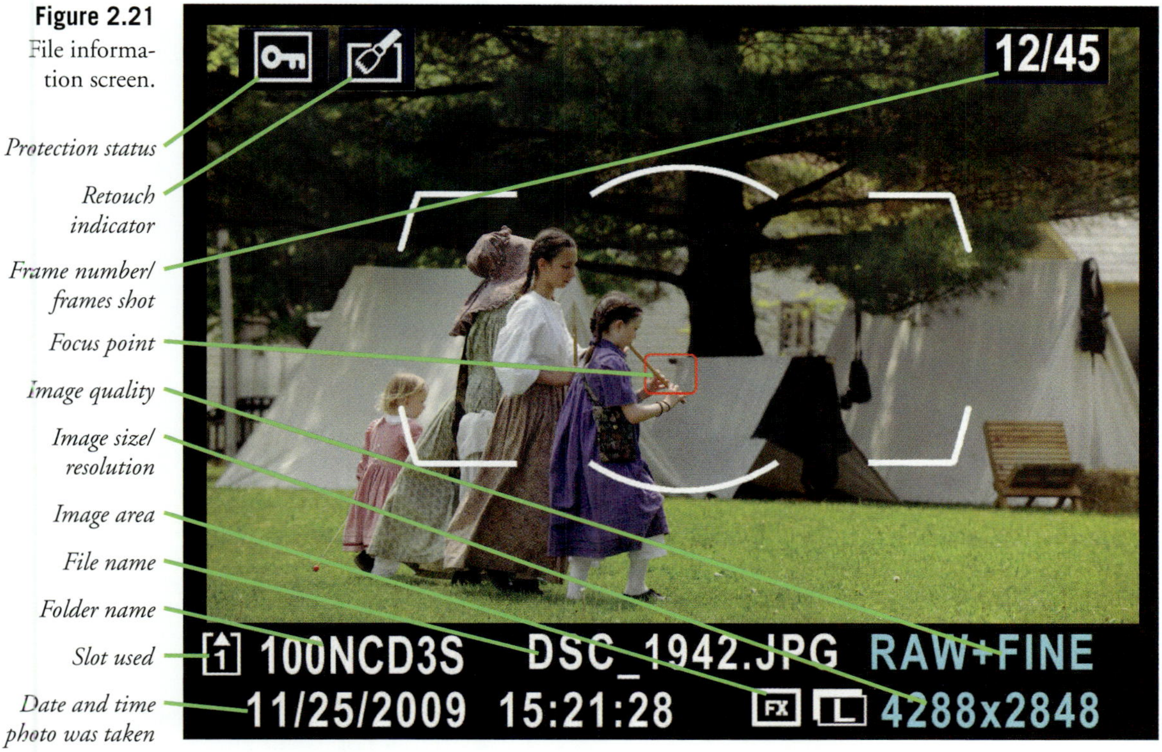


**Figure 2.21**
File information screen.

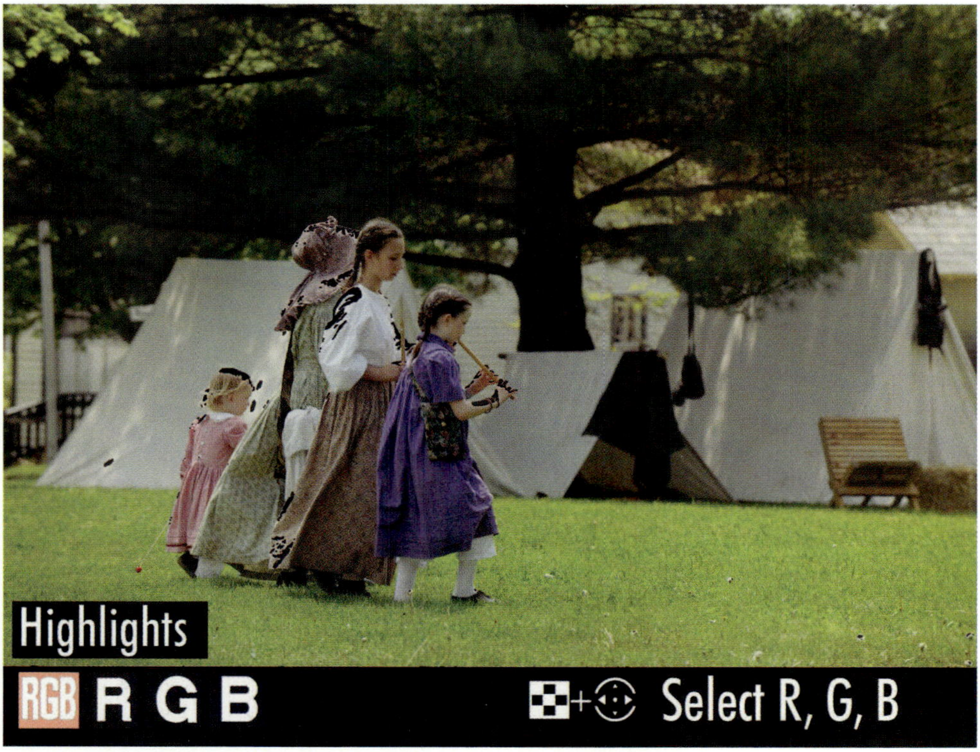


**Figure 2.22**
Highlights screen.

- **RGB histogram.** Another optional screen is the RGB histogram, which you can see in its D3s version in Figure 2.23. (The original D3 and D3x version is only slightly different, moving the brightness "white" histogram over to middle left, under the reduced-size image.) As I mentioned earlier, if you've reprogrammed the center button of the multi selector, pressing it can produce a large luminance (brightness) histogram like the one shown in Figure 2.24. I'm going to leave the discussion of histograms for Chapter 6.
- **Shooting Data 1.** This is the first in a series of three screens that collectively provide everything else you might want to know about a picture you've taken. I'm not providing any labels in Figure 2.25, because the information in the first seven lines in the screen should be obvious.

**Note**

The ISO setting appears in red when the ISO Auto option, which allows the D3s/D3x to adjust the ISO for you, has been selected. (More info in Chapter 6.) The cluster of settings at the bottom of the screen deal with flash settings in commander mode, which comes into play when the D3s/D3x is used to control one or more external flash units. (That's a topic for Chapter 10.)

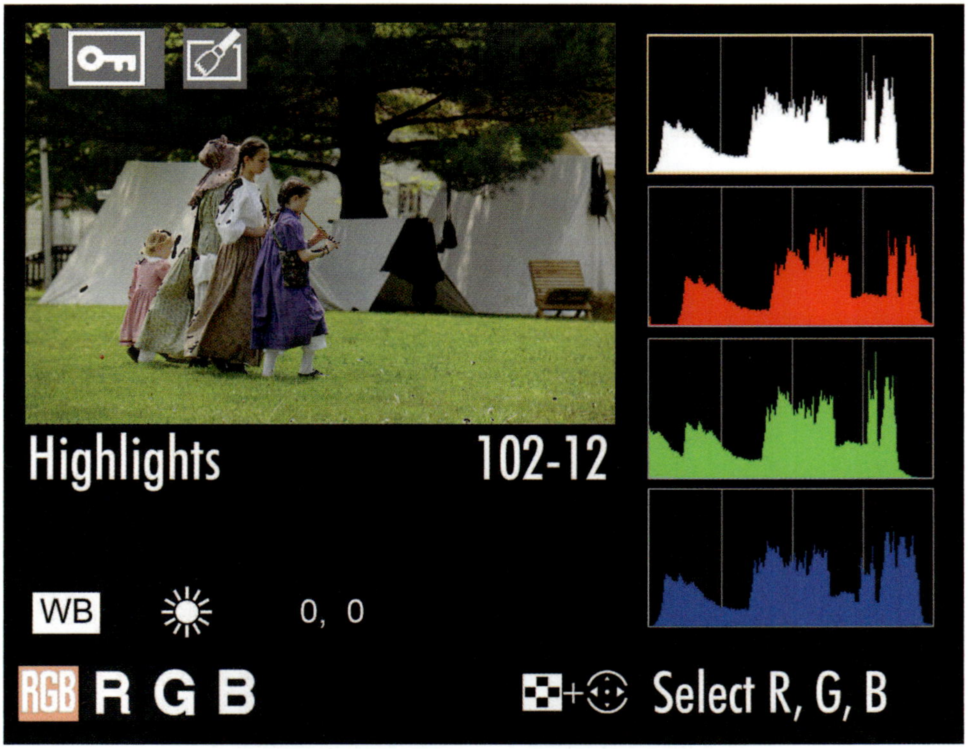


**Figure 2.23**
RGB histogram screen.

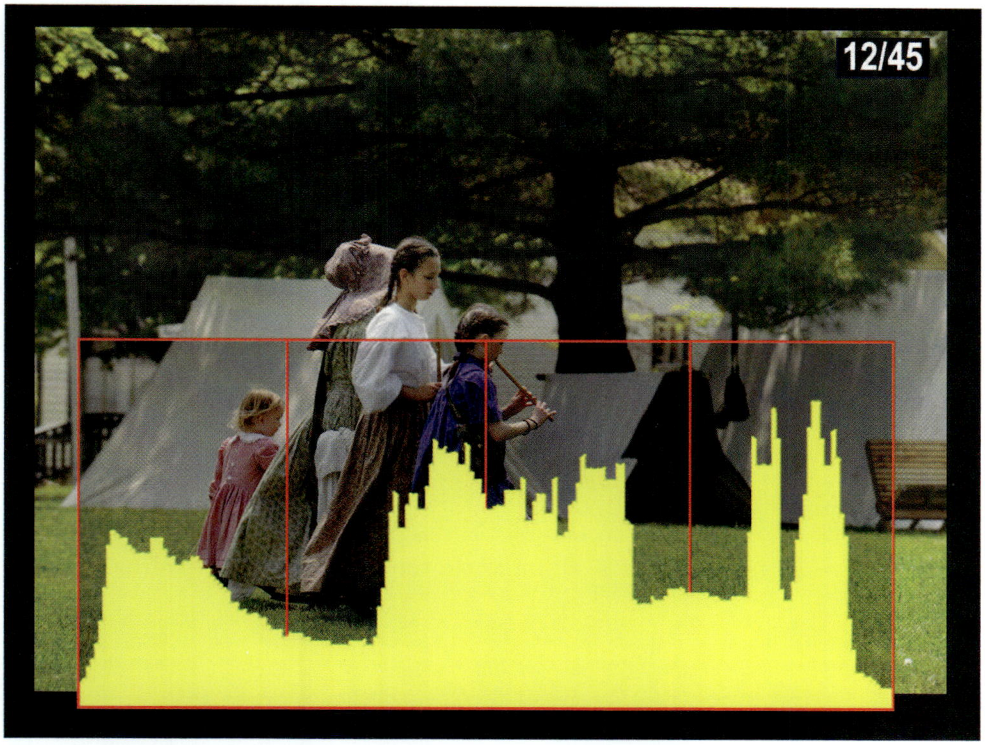


**Figure 2.24** Luminance histogram.

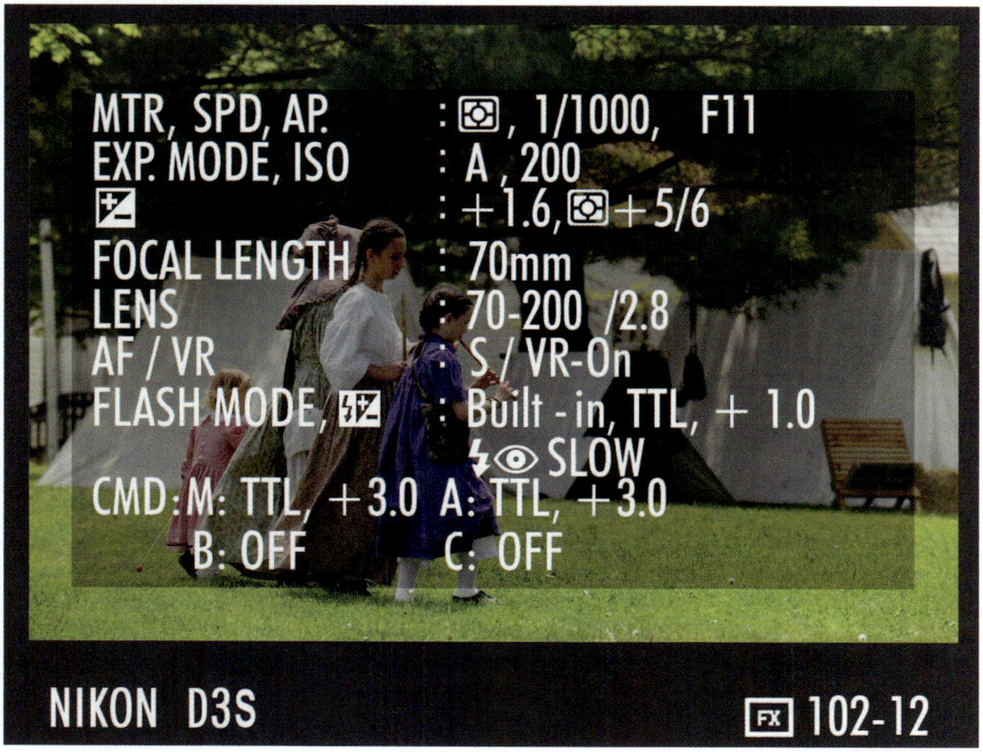


**Figure 2.25** Shooting Data 1 screen.

- **Shooting Data 2.** This screen shows white balance data and adjustments, the color space you've selected, and lists any Picture Control tweaks you've entered. (See Figure 2.26.)
- **Shooting Data 3.** The next screen shows any noise reduction you've specified, Active D-Lighting status, vignette control (if used), and any Retouch menu changes you may have made. Although none of them apply to the background image shown in Figure 2.27, I've added a few entries to show the kind of changes that can be made. You'll learn more about the Retouch menu in Chapter 5, which also will tell you how to create an image comment, like the one shown in the figure.
- **Shooting Data 4.** This screen appears *only* if you've entered Artist and/or Copyright information in the Copyright Information setting of the Setup menu, as described in Chapter 5. I'm not providing an illustration for this screen, because it shows nothing except the name of the photographer (artist) and the copyright.
- **GPS data.** This screen appears *only* if the image was taken using the GPS device. It includes latitude, longitude, altitude, and time information, as shown in Figure 2.28.

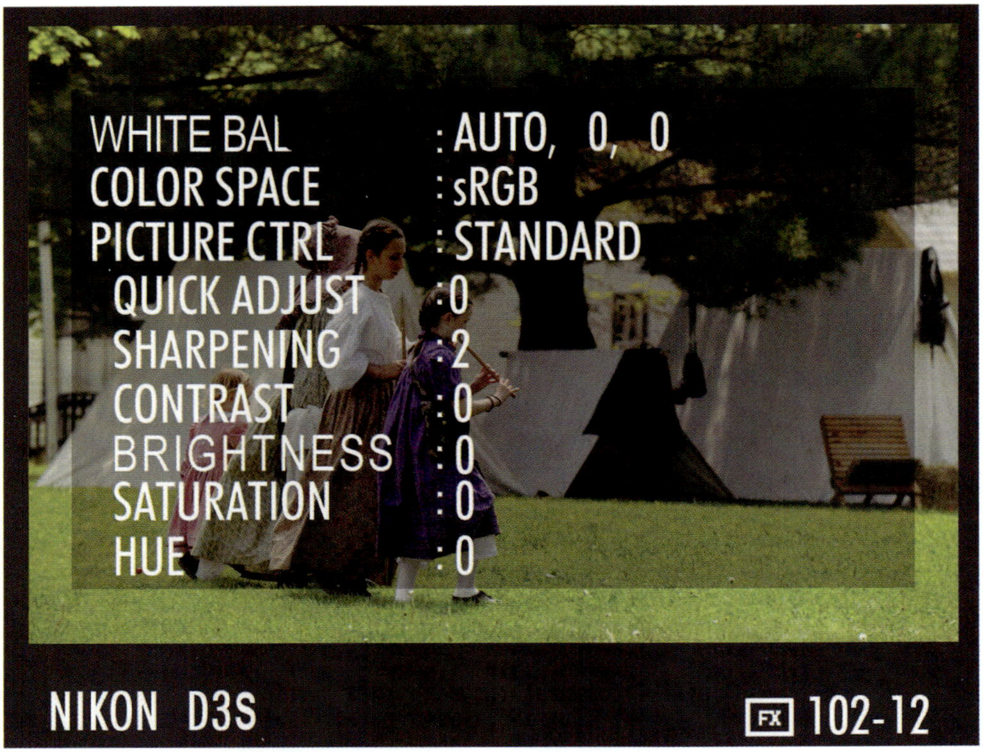


**Figure 2.26**
Shooting Data 2 screen.

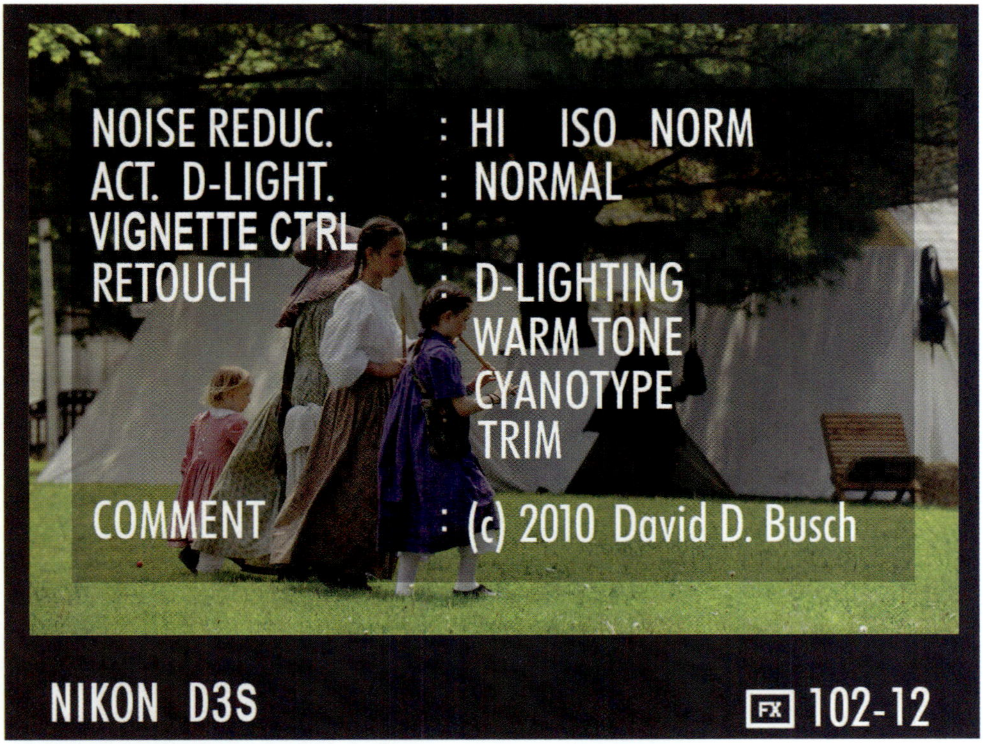


**Figure 2.27** Shooting Data 3 screen.

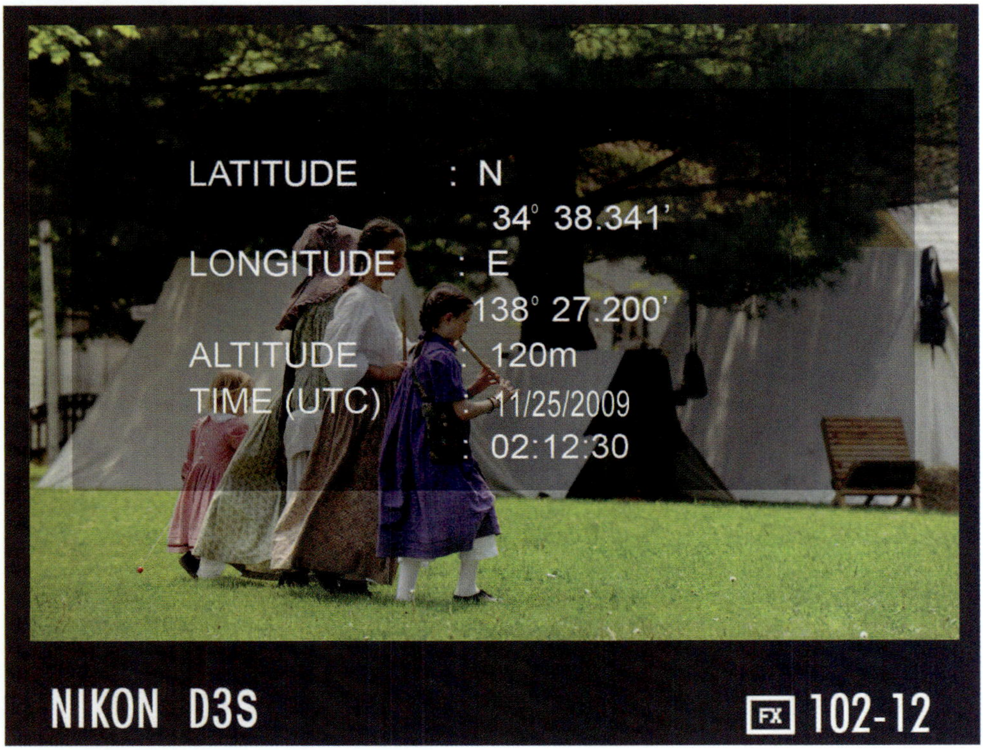


**Figure 2.28** GPS data screen.

- **Overview data.** This screen, shown in Figure 2.29, provides a smaller image of your photo, but more information, including a luminance (brightness) histogram, metering mode used, lens focal length, exposure compensation, flash compensation, and lots of other data that's self-explanatory. The only puzzler in this dense screen is likely to be the image authentication indicator, used with a special authentication kit by law enforcement and judicial agencies to ensure that a digital image presented as evidence has not been modified. It also can show up on the File information screen, but I left it out of the illustration, because 99.9 percent of the readers of this book will not be using that feature.

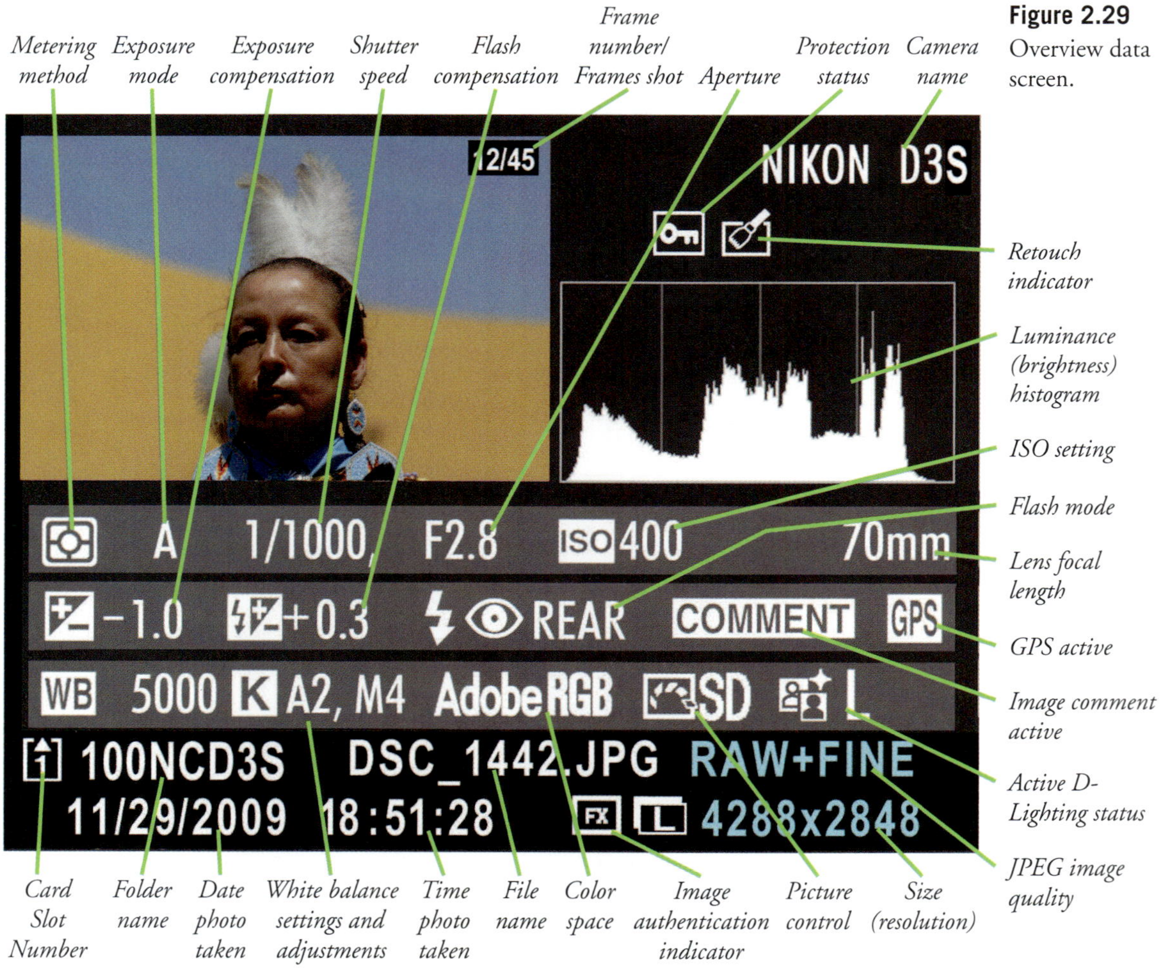


**Figure 2.29**
Overview data screen.

# Going Topside

The top surface of the Nikon D3s/D3x (see Figure 2.30) has its own set of frequently accessed controls. I'm going to divide them into two parts: those to the left side of the camera, and those on the right side. The left side controls offer some settings that you may change frequently, perhaps even during a shooting session, such as flash mode for any attached external flash unit and bracketing parameters. There's also a button to lock the shutter speed or aperture when using shutter-priority, aperture-priority, or manual exposure modes. (I'll explain why you'd want to do this in a moment.) Also on the left side of the camera is the release mode dial, which you'll use to flip among single-frame, continuous shooting, self-timer, and other modes. Figure 2.31 shows this side of the D3s/D3x's top panel up close.

- **Mode dial lock release.** Before you can choose any of the release mode dial's settings, you must hold down this button to free the dial so it can rotate.

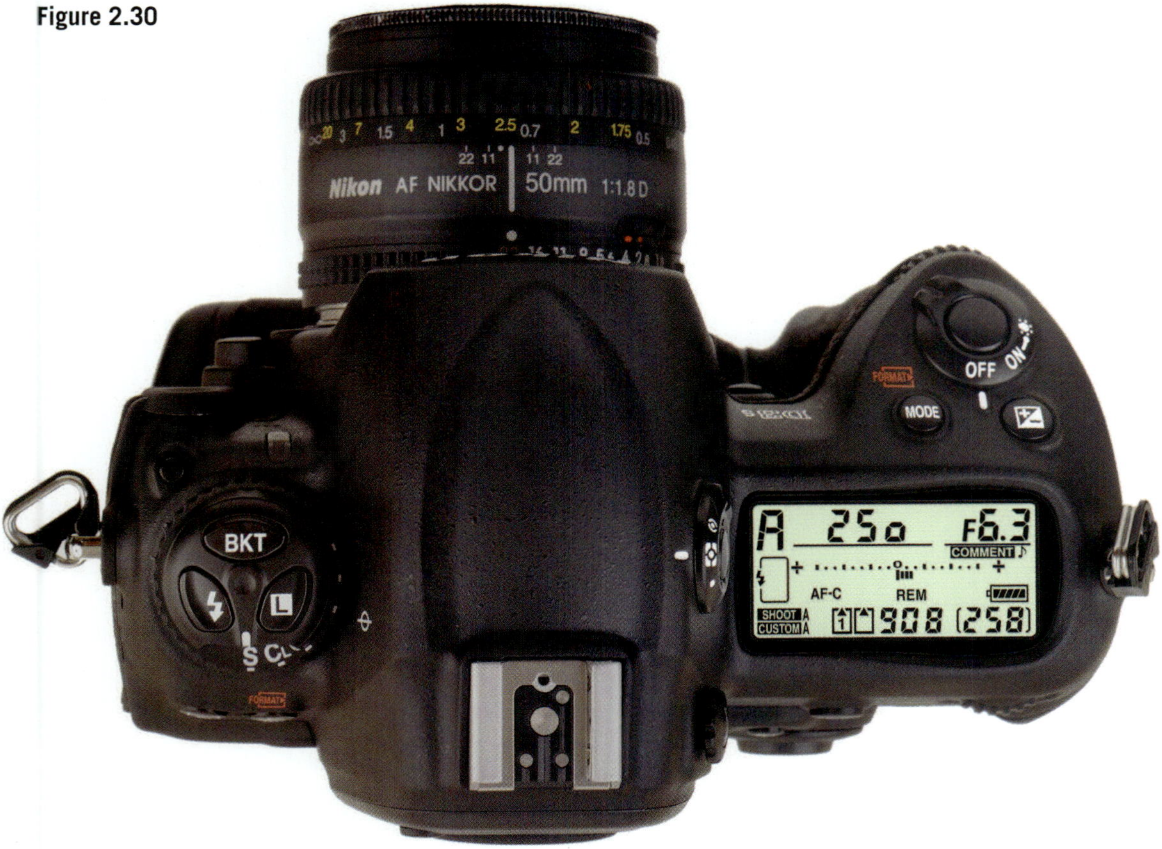


Figure 2.30

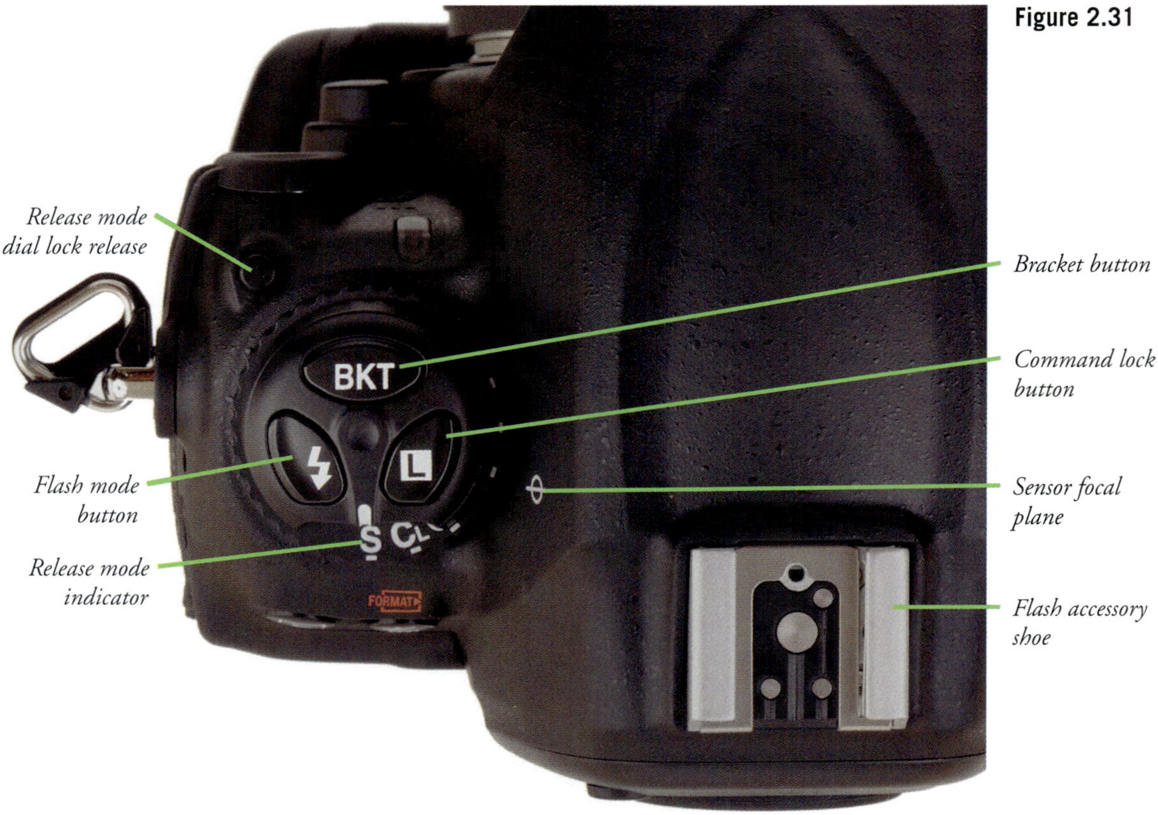


**Figure 2.31**

- **Release mode dial.** Your choices include S (single-frame), CL (continuous low speed), CH (continuous high speed), live view (on the D3x; the D3s has a dedicated button on the right side of the back of the camera), quiet release (on the D3s; the D3x lacks this mode), self-timer, and Mup (Mirror Up). I'll have more information on using these modes in Chapter 7.
- **Bracket button.** Hold down this button and rotate the main command dial to specify number of bracketed shots (from 2 to 9), and whether they should be grouped evenly around the metered exposure or biased towards over- or under-exposure. Rotate the sub-command dial to choose the bracketing increment, in either 1/3, 1/2, or 1-stop steps. I'll show you how to set fractional exposure increments in Chapter 3, and simplify the mysteries of bracketing in Chapter 6.
- **Flash mode button.** Hold this button and rotate the main command dial to select one of the five available flash synchronization modes that can be set for any external flash units attached to the Nikon D3s or D3x. I'll explain each of these modes in detail in Chapter 10.

- **Command lock button.** Hold this button and rotate the main command dial until an L icon appears in the viewfinder and top-panel monochrome LCD. When command lock is active, the shutter speed is locked at the currently selected value when using shutter-priority or manual exposure modes; if using aperture-priority, then the aperture is locked at the current setting. Command lock has no effect when using P (programmed auto) mode. Use this feature when you want to avoid accidentally changing from your preferred value. For example, you *really* want to use 1/500th second, but find that sometimes when adding EV adjustments you forget to press the EV button while rotating the main command dial. So, instead of adding or subtracting exposure from your next shot, you've changed the shutter speed instead. A double whammy: wrong shutter speed, and you've failed to make the exposure correction you intended.
- **Focal plane indicator.** This indicator shows the *plane* of the sensor, for use in applications where exact measurement of the distance from the focal plane to the subject are necessary. (These are mostly scientific/close-up applications.)
- **Accessory shoe.** Slide an electronic flash into this mount when you need a more powerful speedlight. A dedicated flash unit, like the Nikon SB-900, can use the multiple contact points shown to communicate exposure, zoom setting, white balance information, and other data between the flash and the camera. There's more on using electronic flash in Chapter 10. You can also mount other accessories on this shoe, such as the Nikon GP-1 GPS adapter.

On the right side of the camera is another batch of controls and a display panel, as shown in Figure 2.32:

- **Power switch.** Rotate this switch clockwise to turn on the Nikon D3s/D3x (and virtually all other Nikon dSLRs). Continue past the ON position to illuminate the monochrome LCD control panel's backlight for a few seconds. If you'd rather have the backlight remain on for the length of time the exposure meters are active, you can specify this using Custom Setting d7 (D3x) or d8 (D3s) (set to On). For this setting to be useful, you'll need to set the automatic meter-off delay to something other than the default six seconds. If you're carefree about battery usage, you can specify meter-off delays of four seconds to 10 minutes using Custom Setting c2, as described in Chapter 4.
- **Shutter release button.** Partially depress this button to activate the exposure meter (and the main and sub-command dials that adjust metering settings), lock in exposure, and focus (unless you've redefined the focus activation button, as outlined in Chapter 4). Press all the way to take the picture. Tapping the shutter release when the camera has turned off the auto exposure and autofocus mechanisms reactivates both. When a review image is displayed on the back-panel color LCD, tapping this button removes the image from the display and reactivates the autoexposure and autofocus mechanisms.

Figure 2.32

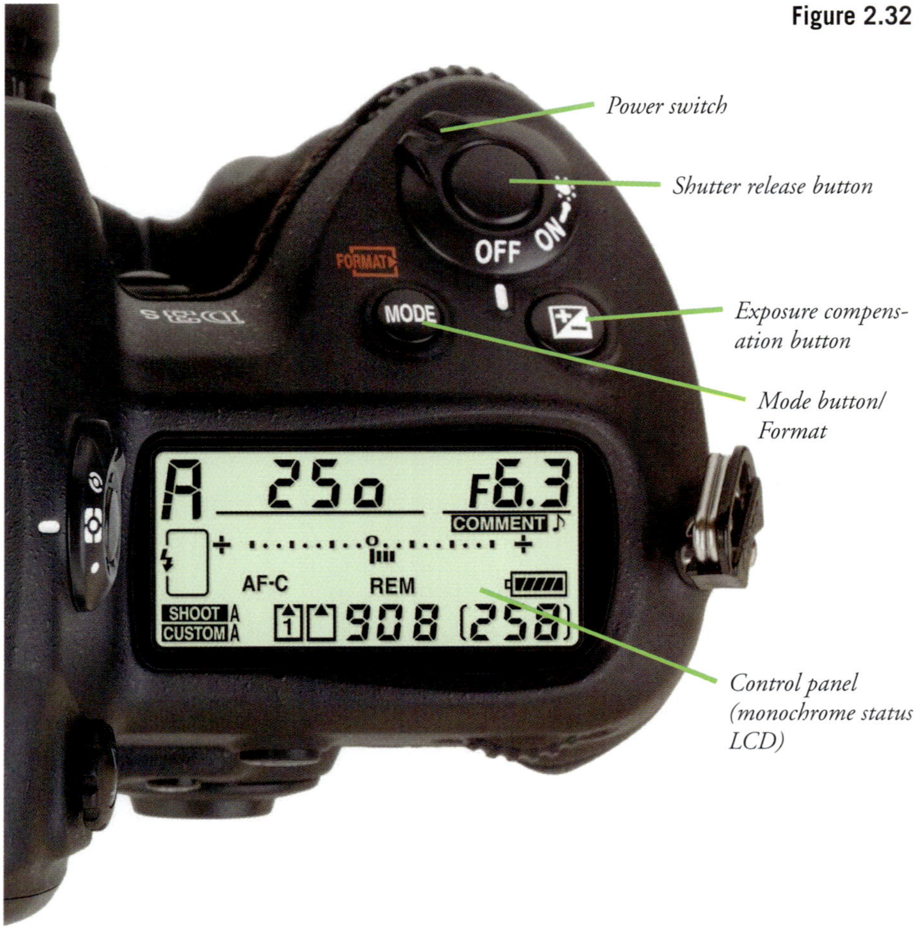


- **Exposure compensation button.** Hold down this button and spin the main command dial to add or subtract exposure when using programmed, aperture-priority, or shutter-priority modes. (In manual mode, the exposure remains the same, but the "ideal" exposure shown in the electronic analog display [more on that in the next section] is modified to reflect the extra/reduced exposure you're calling for.) The exposure compensation amount is shown on the monochrome status panel as plus or minus values.
- **Control panel.** I find Nikon's term for the top monochrome LCD status panel confusing, so top-panel LCD or control panel are the terms I use most of the time. This useful indicator shows the status of many settings. Unfortunately, because it's on top of the camera, you may not be able to *see* those settings when the camera is elevated (especially on a tripod). In that case, use the shooting information display, described earlier in this chapter, which can show much of the same information on the back-panel color LCD when you press the Info button.

- **Mode button.** Hold down this button and rotate the main command dial to choose between programmed, aperture-priority, shutter-priority, and manual exposure modes. Your choice will be displayed on the monochrome status panel and in the viewfinder, both described in the next sections. You can also hold down this button and the Trash button on the back left surface of the camera to initiate a memory card format.

## LCD Control Panel Readouts

The top panel of the Nikon D3s/D3x (see Figure 2.33) contains a monochrome LCD readout (the "control panel") that displays status information about most of the shooting settings. All of the information segments available are shown in Figures 2.34 and 2.35. I've color-coded the display and divided the figure into two parts to avoid drowning you in labels for this intensely dense readout. The information does *not* appear in color on the actual D3s/D3x, and all of these indicators will not appear at once. Many of the information items are mutually exclusive (that is, while all the flash sync options are shown in pink at the right side of Figure 2.34, only the flash sync information relating to the mode you've chosen will actually appear).

Some of the items on the status LCD also appear in the viewfinder, such as the shutter speed and aperture, and the exposure level (in yellow at the middle). This is a thicket of information, but I'll spell out what the categories of data include. First, in Figure 2.34:

- **Exposure mode.** This indicator tells you whether the D3s/D3x is set for programmed, aperture-priority, shutter-priority, or manual exposure modes. An asterisk appears next to the P when you have used flexible program mode, which allows you to depart from the camera's programmed exposure setting to set a different combination of shutter speed/aperture that produces the same exposure. You'll find more about this feature in Chapter 6.

Figure 2.33

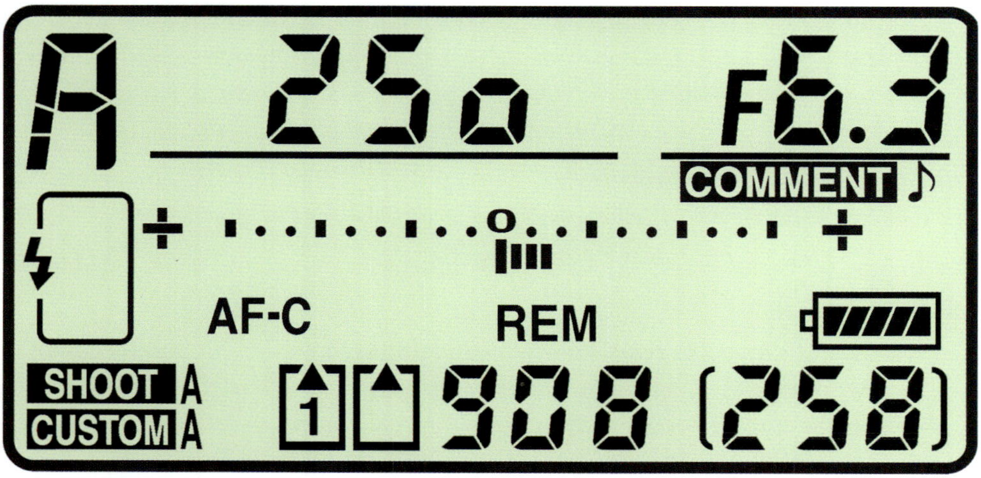

Figure 2.34

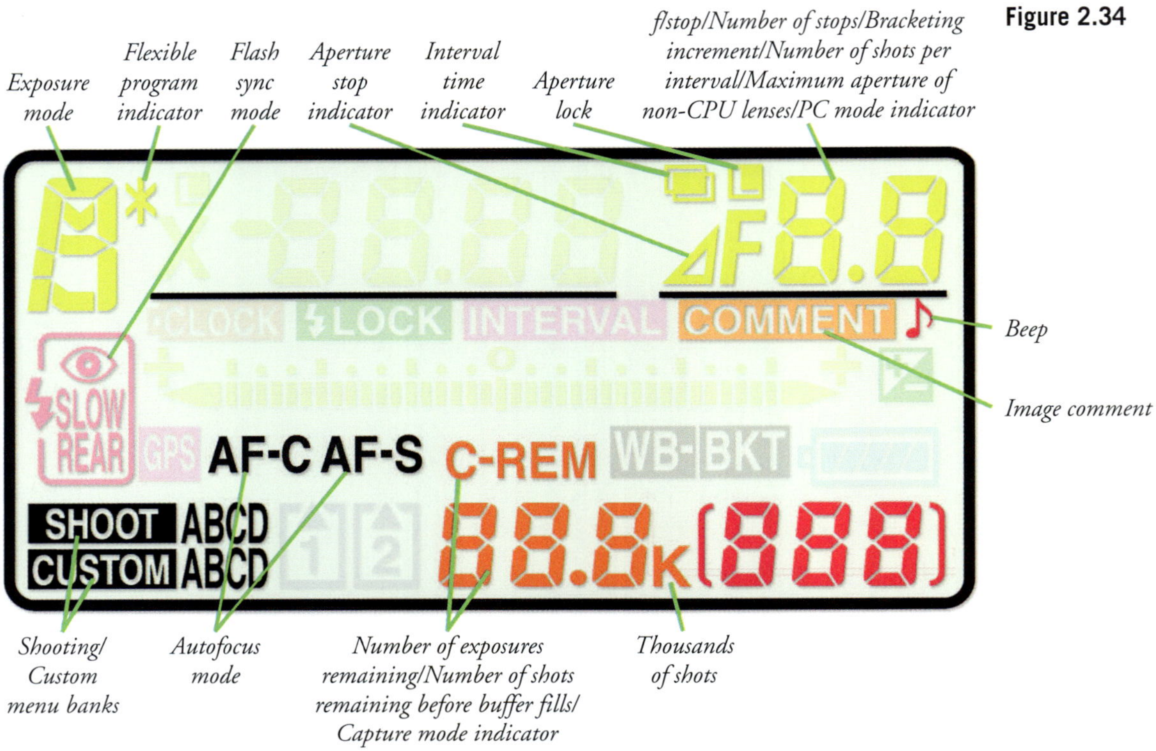


- **Flash sync mode.** The current mode for the D3s/D3x's attached external electronic flash unit is shown here.
- **Interval timer indicator.** Displays when you're shooting delayed exposures using the camera's interval timer.
- **Aperture lock.** Shown when you've used the Command Lock button to lock the aperture at the current setting when using aperture-priority mode.
- **Beep indicator.** Indicates that a helpful beep will sound when using the self-timer or when the D3s/D3x successfully focuses when in single-servo autofocus mode (AF-S) (as long as release priority hasn't been specified in Custom Setting a2). You can specify a loud, soft beep, or none at all in Custom Setting d1.
- **Aperture/additional functions.** The selected f/stop appears here, along with a lot of other alternate information, as shown in the label in the figure.
- **Image comment.** Displayed when you've entered a comment to be included in the image file.
- **Number of exposures remaining/additional functions.** This indicator shows the number of exposures remaining on your memory card, as well as other functions, such as the number of shots remaining until your memory buffer fills. A K (for thousands of shots) appears when the remaining exposures exceeds 999.

- **Autofocus mode.** Shows whether you've selected single-servo AF (AF-S) or continuous-servo AF (AF-C).
- **Shooting/Custom menu banks.** Shows which banks you've selected from among shooting and custom menu banks A, B, C, and D.

In Figure 2.35, you'll find the following readouts highlighted:

- **Exposure/Flash/White balance bracketing indicator.** Shows that exposure, flash, or white balance bracketing is underway.
- **Battery status.** Five segments show the approximate battery power remaining. A better indicator is the Battery info entry in the Setup menu.
- **Clock battery.** This indicator is displayed when your clock needs to be reset. You'll see it when your camera is activated for the first time, any time that the internal clock battery runs down (say, when you've removed the main battery for a few days), and when your internal clock battery wears out and will no longer hold a charge.
- **Flash value lock.** This appears when you've locked in a particular flash value setting.
- **Electronic analog display/additional functions.** This is a continuous scale that shows that correct exposure is achieved when the indicator is in the center, and how

**Figure 2.35**

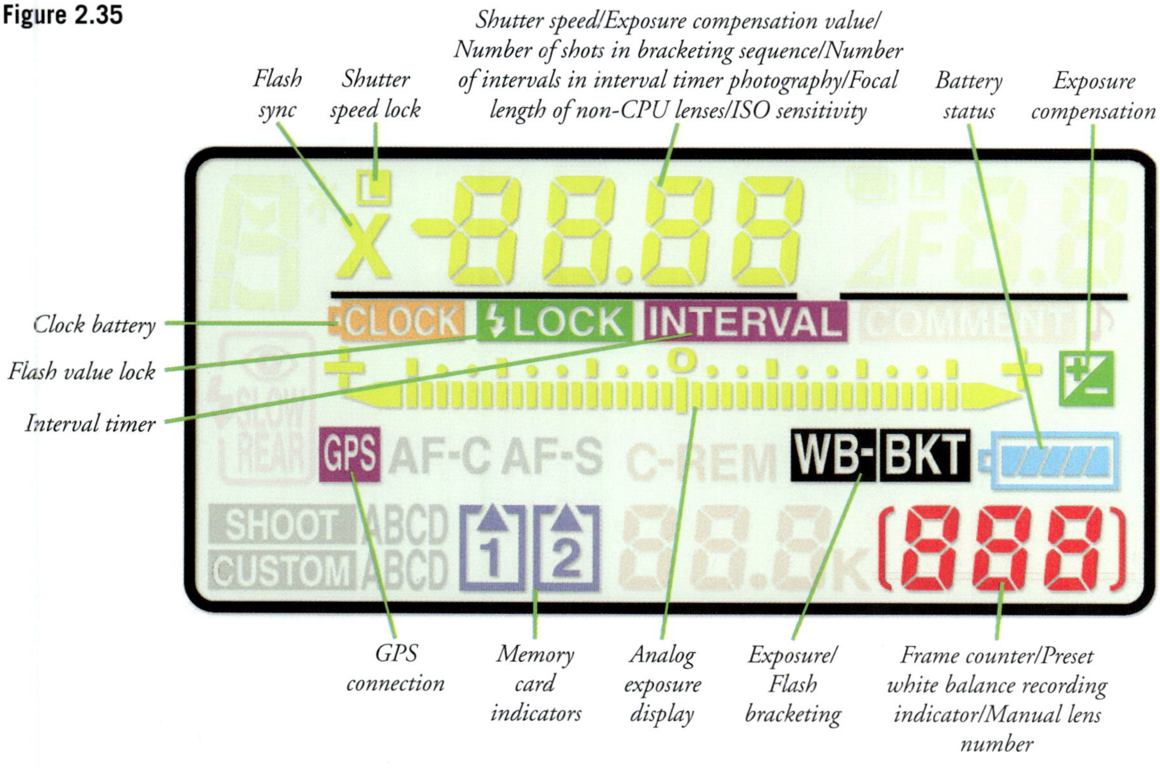

many stops off exposure is when the indicator veers to the right (underexposure) or left (overexposure). This scale is also used to display other information, such as exposure compensation and bracketing progress.

- **Exposure compensation active.** Appears when you've dialed in exposure compensation. Monitor this indicator, as it's easy to forget that you've told the Nikon D3s/D3x to use more or less exposure than what its (reasonably intelligent) metering system would otherwise select.
- **GPS connection.** If you have a GPS device attached and working, you'll know it when this indicator shows up.
- **Interval timer active.** When using the D3s/D3x's interval timer facility (as described in Chapter 5), this indicator appears.
- **Shutter speed/additional functions.** Here you'll find the shutter speed, ISO setting, color temperature, and other useful data.
- **Memory card indicators.** Shows the functions of each of the two memory cards.
- **Frame counter/additional functions.** Shows the number of frames shot, preset white balance recording underway, and manual lens number.

## Lens Components

The typical lens, like the one shown in Figure 2.36, has several common features:

- **Filter thread.** Most lenses have a thread on the front for attaching filters and other add-ons. Some also use this thread for attaching a lens hood (you screw on the filter first, and then attach the hood to the screw thread on the front of the filter). Some lenses, such as the AF-S Nikkor 14-24mm f/2.8G ED lens, have no front filter thread because their front elements are too curved to allow mounting a filter and/or because the front element is so large that huge filters would be prohibitively expensive. Some of these front-filter-hostile lenses allow using smaller filters that drop into a slot at the back of the lens.
- **Lens hood bayonet.** This is used to mount the lens hood for lenses that don't use screw-mount hoods (the majority). Such lenses generally will have a dot on the edge showing how to align the lens hood with the bayonet mount.
- **Focus ring.** This is the ring you turn when you manually focus the lens, or fine-tune autofocus adjustment.
- **Focus scale.** This is a readout that rotates in unison with the lens' focus mechanism to show the distance at which the lens has been focused. It's a useful indicator for double-checking autofocus, roughly evaluating depth-of-field, and for setting manual focus guesstimates. Chapter 8 deals with the mysteries of lenses and their controls in more detail.

Figure 2.36

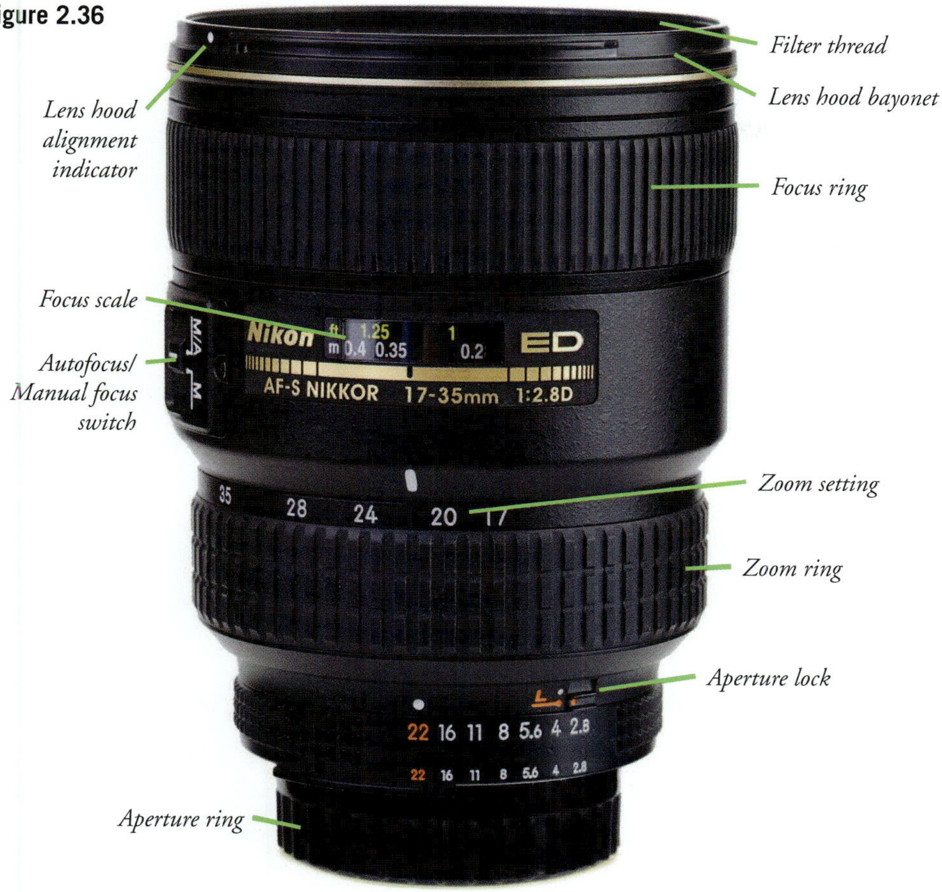


- **Zoom setting.** These markings on the lens show the current focal length selected.
- **Zoom ring.** Turn this ring to change the zoom setting.
- **Autofocus/Manual switch.** Allows you to change from automatic focus to manual focus.
- **Aperture ring.** Some lenses have a ring that allows you to set a specific f/stop manually, rather than use the camera's internal electronic aperture control. An aperture ring is useful when a lens is mounted on a non-automatic extension ring, bellows, or other accessory that doesn't couple electronically with the camera. Aperture rings also allow using a lens on an older camera that lacks electronic control.
- **Aperture lock.** If you want your D3s/D3x (or other Nikon dSLR) to control the aperture electronically, you must set the lens to its smallest aperture (usually f/22 or f/32) and lock it with this control.

- **Focus limit switch.** Some lenses have this switch (shown in Figure 2.37), which limits the focus range of the lens, thus potentially reducing focus seeking when shooting distant subjects. The limiter stops the lens from trying to focus at closer distances (in this case, closer than 2.5 meters).
- **Vibration reduction switch.** Lenses with Nikon's Vibration Reduction (VR) feature include a switch for turning the stabilization feature on and off, and for changing from normal vibration reduction to a more aggressive "active" VR mode useful for, say, shooting from moving vehicles. More on VR and other lens topics in Chapter 8.

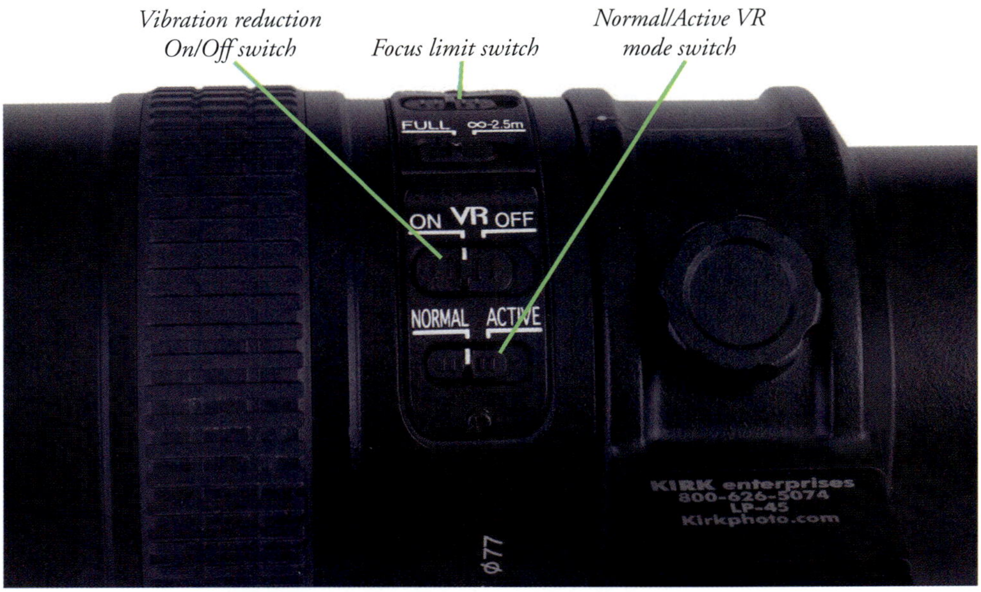


**Figure 2.37**
Some lenses have focus limit switches and controls for vibration reduction (VR) features.

The back end of a lens intended for use on a Nikon camera has other components that you seldom see (except when you swap lenses), shown in Figure 2.38, but still should know about:

- **Lens bayonet mount.** This is the mounting mechanism that attaches to a matching mount on the camera. Although the lens bayonet is usually metal, some lower-priced lenses use a rugged plastic for this key component.
- **Automatic diaphragm lever.** This lever is moved by a matching lever in the camera to adjust the f/stop from wide open (which makes for the brightest view) to the *taking aperture*, which is the f/stop that will be used to take the picture. The actual taking aperture is determined by the camera's metering system (or by you when the D3s/D3x is in manual mode), and is communicated to the lens through the electronic contacts described next. (An exception is when the aperture ring on the lens itself is unlocked and used to specify the f/stop.) However, the spring-loaded

Figure 2.38

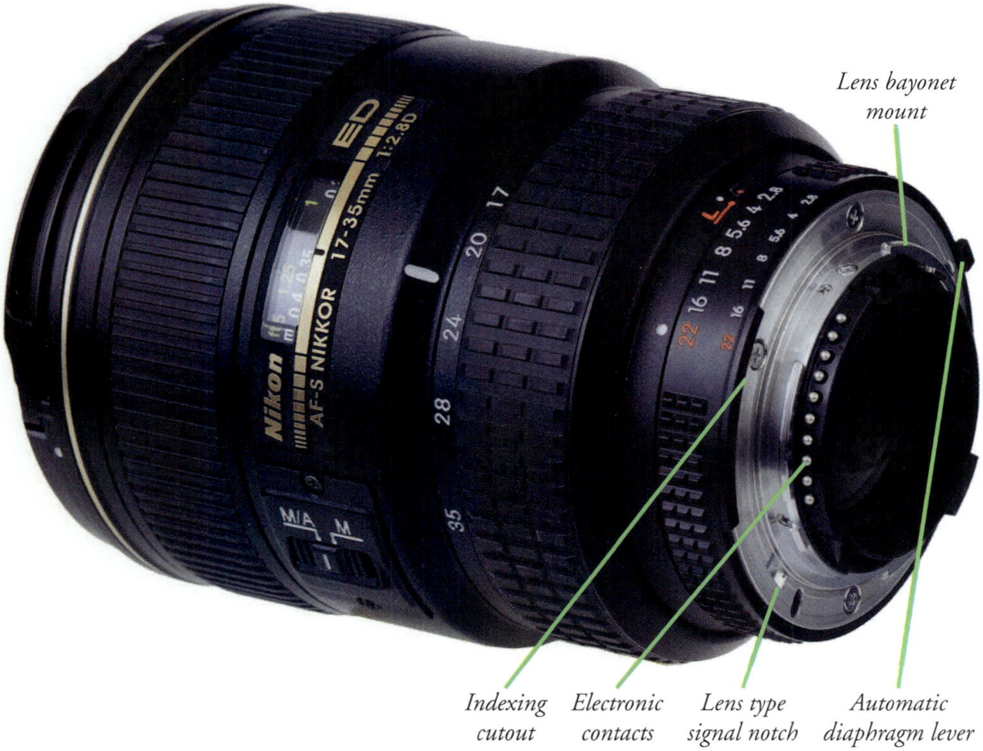


physical levers are what actually push the aperture to the selected f/stop—even with advanced cameras like the D3-series. The aperture lever is also activated when you press the DOF button.

- **Electronic contacts.** These metal contacts pass information to matching contacts located in the camera body allowing a firm electrical connection so that exposure, distance, and other information can be exchanged between the camera and lens.
- **Lens type signal notch.** This is a machined groove in the lens mount, designed to tell older (non-dSLR) cameras that the aperture stops were linear. Today, this information would be conveyed electronically, except that all current lenses already have linear f/stops.
- **Indexing cutout.** The base of any Nikon lens made after 1977 that has an aperture ring includes a cutout notch that mates with a ring around the lens mount of Nikon's advanced cameras (D200, D300/D300s, D2x/D2xs, D3/D3x/D3s, and some older pro models). It tells the camera what the maximum aperture is and what f/stop has been set. For a D3s/D3x owner, this means that older manual focus lenses (including pre-1977 lenses that have been converted to this system) can be used for automatic metering with the aperture-priority exposure mode, and for manual metering in manual exposure mode.

- **Autofocus drive screw slot.** (Not shown in the figure.) As you'll learn in Chapter 8, older autofocus lenses (given the AF designation in Nikon nomenclature) lack an internal autofocus motor. Focus is set using a screw drive built into the camera body of every Nikon autofocus camera (film or digital) except (at the time I write this) the Nikon D40/D40x, D60, D3000, and D5000. Lenses given the AF-S designation lack this connection, because autofocus is achieved internally using a tiny motor.

## Looking Inside the Viewfinder

Much of the important shooting status information is shown inside the viewfinder of the Nikon D3s/D3x. As with the status LCD up on top, not all of this information will be shown at any one time. Figure 2.39 shows what you can expect to see. These readouts include:

- **Focus points.** Can display the 51 areas used by the D3s/D3x to focus. The camera can select the appropriate focus zone for you, or you can manually select one or all of the zones.
- **AF-area bracket.** Shows the area covered by the autofocus sensors.
- **Focus indicator.** Left/right triangles appear on either side of the green dot to indicate focus progress, whether focus was achieved by the AF system, or by you using manual focusing.
- **Metering mode.** Shows whether you've selected matrix, center-weighted, or spot metering.
- **Auto exposure lock.** Shows that exposure has been locked.
- **Flash value lock indicator.** A reminder that flash exposure has been locked.
- **Flash sync.** Shows that the shutter speed has been locked at the x250 (1/250th second) setting (located, not between 1/125th and 1/500th second, but as the speed past bulb or 30 seconds).
- **Shutter speed.** Displays the current shutter speed selected by the camera, or by you in manual exposure mode.
- **Aperture.** Shows the current aperture chosen by the D3s/D3x's autoexposure system, or specified by you when using manual exposure mode.
- **Exposure mode.** Shows whether you've selected programmed, shutter-priority, aperture-priority, or manual exposure modes.

**Figure 2.39**

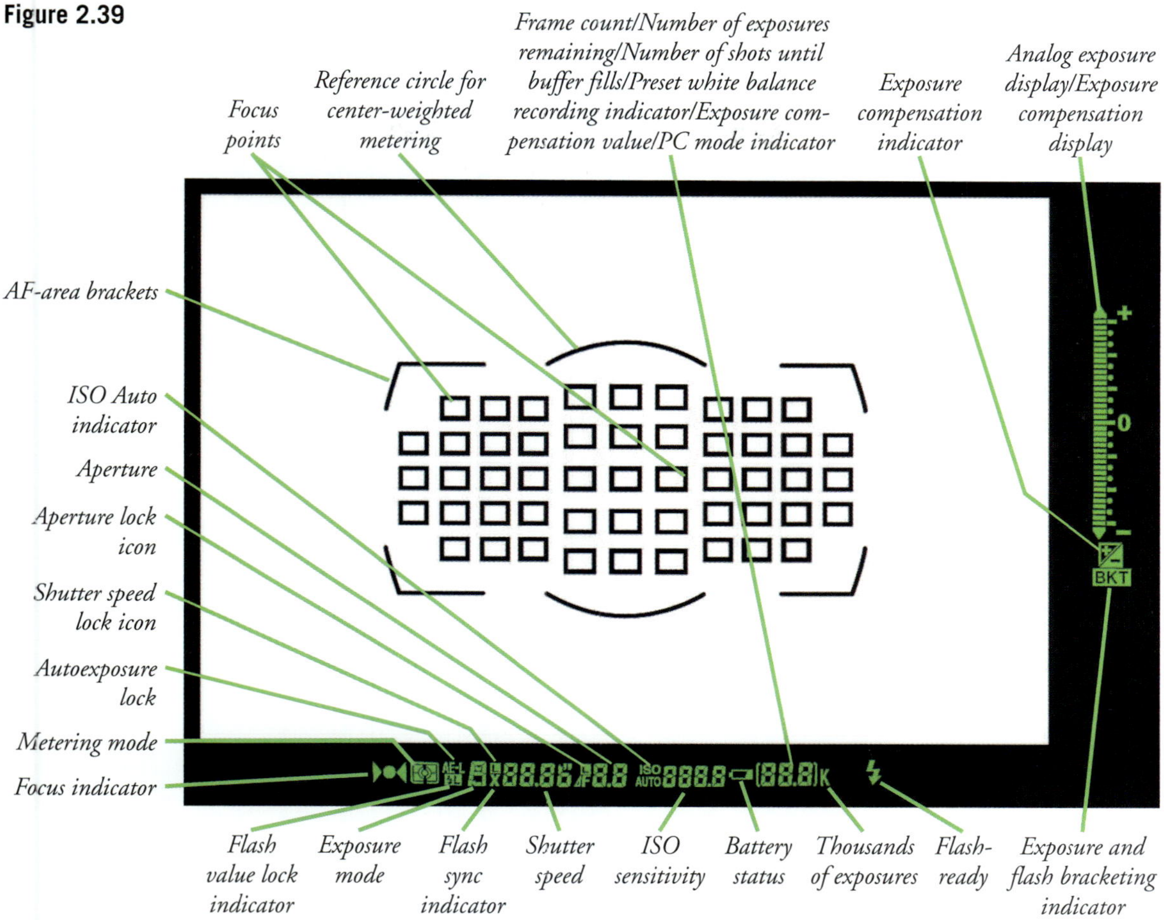


- **Automatic ISO indicator.** Is shown as a reminder that the D3s/D3x has been set to adjust ISO sensitivity automatically.
- **Electronic analog exposure display.** This scale shows the current exposure level, with the bottom indicator centered when the exposure is correct as metered. The indicator may also move to the left or right to indicate over- or underexposure (respectively). The scale is also used to show the amount of exposure compensation dialed in.
- **Flash compensation indicator.** Appears when flash EV changes have been made.
- **Exposure compensation indicator.** This is shown when exposure compensation (EV) changes have been made. It's easy to forget you've dialed in a little more or less exposure, and then shoot a whole series of pictures of a different scene that doesn't require such compensation. Beware!

- **Flash-ready indicator.** This icon appears when the flash is fully charged.
- **ISO sensitivity.** This useful indicator shows the current ISO setting value. Those who have accidentally taken dozens of shots under bright sunlight at ISO 1600 because they forgot to change the setting back after some indoor shooting will treasure this addition.
- **Exposures remaining/maximum burst available.** Normally displays the number of exposures remaining on your memory card, but while shooting it changes to show a number that indicates the number of frames that can be taken in continuous shooting mode using the current settings. This indicator also shows other information, such as exposure/flash compensation values, and whether the D3s/D3x is connected to a PC through a USB cable.

## Underneath Your Nikon D3s/D3x

There's not a lot going on with the bottom panel of your Nikon D3s/D3x. Nestled in the middle of a protective rubber panel, you'll find the tripod socket, which secures the camera to a tripod. The socket accepts other accessories, such as quick release plates that allow rapid attaching and detaching the D3s/D3x from a matching platform affixed to your tripod. Figure 2.40 shows the underside view of the camera.

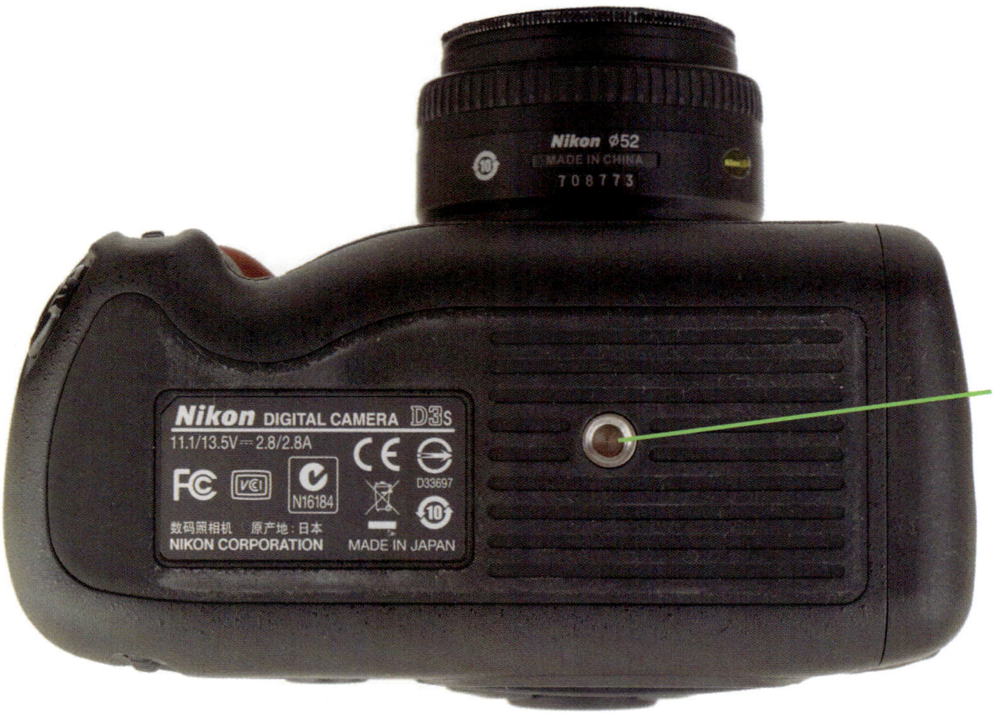


**Figure 2.40**
The underside of the D3x/D3s has a tripod socket and rugged rubber padding.

# 3

# Setup: Playback and Shooting Menus

The Nikon D3s is Nikon's all-time champion in terms of the number of setup and operational options available to its bewildered owners, with a total of 118 different main menu entries scattered among six menu categories. Thanks to its movie-shooting features and a few other new capabilities, the D3s noses out the D3x by a few choices. Of course, those 118 options represent only the *main* menu entries; there are easily an equal number of sub-menu items (I didn't labor to count them all) when you consider that an innocuous entry like Custom Setting f4 has two submenus of its own, with a total of 23 additional options tucked away in ever deeper levels of alternatives.

My job is to be your guide on a wild trip down the rabbit hole, where Menuland rivals Wonderland in its possibility to confuse and confound you. Under that thicket of choices is the kind of versatility that makes the Nikon D3s/D3x the most customizable, tweakable, and fine-tunable camera Nikon has ever offered. If your camera doesn't behave in exactly the way you'd like, chances are you can make a small change in the Playback, Shooting, Custom Settings, and Setup menus that will tailor the D3s/D3x to your needs. In fact, if you don't like the *menus* you can create your own using the clever My Menu system.

However, just telling you what your options are and what they do doesn't really give you the information you need to use your camera to its fullest. What you really want to know is *why* you would want to choose a particular option, and *how* making a particular change will help improve your photographs in a given situation. That's a big job, and I'm going to devote three entire chapters to demystifying the D3s/D3x menu choices for you.

This chapter will help you sort out the settings for the Playback and Shooting menus, which determine how the D3s/D3x displays images on review, and how it uses many of its shooting features to take a photo. The following chapters will focus on the Custom Setting menu (Chapter 4), and Setup, Retouch, and My Menu options (Chapter 5).

As I've mentioned before, this book isn't intended to replace the manual you received with your D3s/D3x, nor have I any interest in rehashing its contents. You'll still find the original manual useful as a standby reference that lists every possible option in exhaustive (if mind-numbing) detail—without really telling you how to use those options to take better pictures. There is, however, some unavoidable duplication between the Nikon manual and the next three chapters, because, like the Nikon book, I'm going to explain all the key menu choices and the options you may have in using them. You should find, though, that I will give you the information you really require in a much more helpful format, with plenty of detail on why you should make some settings that are particularly cryptic.

I'm not going to waste a lot of space on some of the more obvious menu choices in these chapters. For example, you can probably figure out that the Beep option in Custom Setting d1 deals with the solid-state beeper in your camera that sounds off during various activities (such as the self-timer countdown). You can certainly decipher the import of the three options available for the Beep entry (High, Low, and Off). In this chapter, I'll devote no more than a sentence or two to the blatantly obvious settings and concentrate on the more confusing aspects of the D3s/D3x setup, such as automatic exposure bracketing. I'll start with an overview of using the D3s/D3x's menus themselves.

## Anatomy of the Nikon D3s/D3x's Menus

If you used any Nikon digital SLR before you purchased your Nikon D3s/D3x, you're probably already familiar with the basic menu system. Indeed, if you own (or owned) the original Nikon D3, you'll find that its menus are virtually identical to those of the two latest cameras in the D3-series. The menus consist of a series of screens with entries, as shown in the illustration of the Playback menu (discussed next) in Figure 3.1. Navigating among the various menus is easy and follows a consistent set of rules:

- **View menu.** Press the Menu button on the left side of the back of the camera to display the main menu screens.
- **Navigate main menu headings.** Use the multi selector's left/right/up/down buttons to navigate among the menu entries to highlight your choice. Moving the highlighting to the left column lets you scroll up and down among the six top-level menus. From the top in Figure 3.1, they are Playback, Shooting, Custom Setting, Setup, Retouch, and My Menu, with Help access represented by a question mark at the bottom of the column.

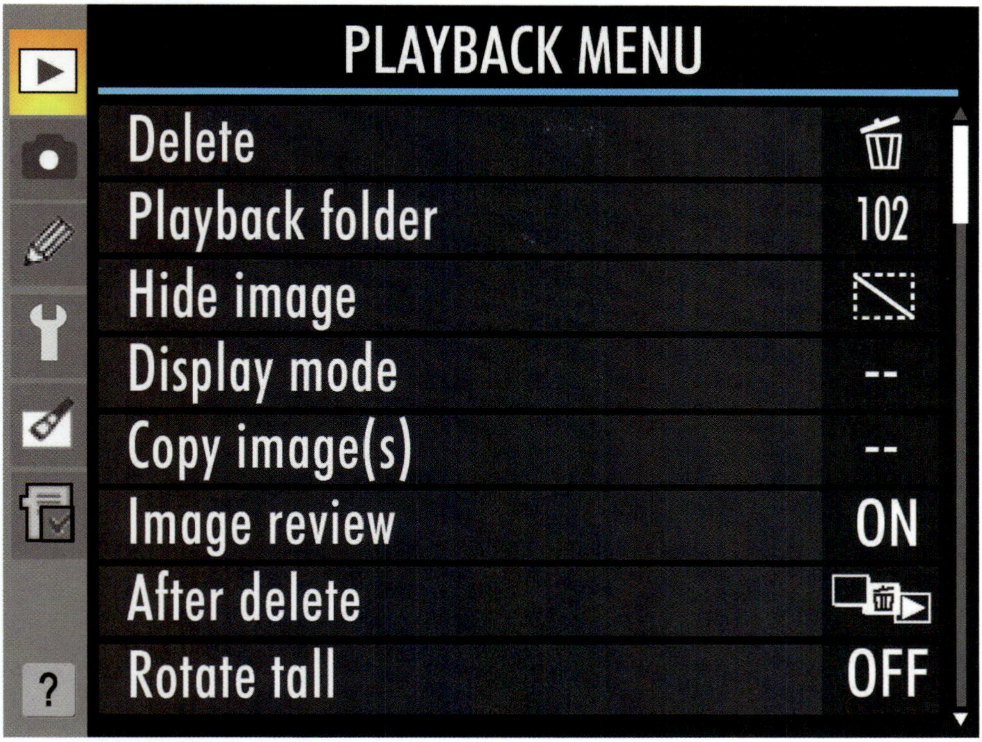


**Figure 3.1**
The multi selector's navigational buttons are used to move among the various menu entries.

**Tip**

Your menus may vary from those shown in this book. Some menu entries are different between the D3s and D3x; for example, World Time in the D3x's Setup menu is labeled Time Zone and Date in the D3s. I'll point out any variations as we go along. The My Menu icon may be replaced by the similar Recent Settings icon if you've chosen to replace My Menu with the Recent Settings feature instead. Rarely, as in Figure 3.1, I may show an element, such as the Question Mark icon, that isn't necessarily active in a given mode, in order to avoid cluttering the book with an additional illustration. (In this case, the question mark doesn't appear until you've actually *selected* one of the menu entries.)

- **Choose a top-level menu entry.** A highlighted top-level menu's icon will change from black-and-white to yellow highlighting. Use the multi selector's right button to move into the column containing that menu's choices, and the up/down buttons to scroll among the entries. If more than one screen full of choices is available, a scroll bar appears at the far right of the screen, with a position slider showing the relative position of the currently highlighted entry.

- **Choose options.** To work with a highlighted menu entry, press the OK button at lower left on the back of the D3s/D3x or, more conveniently, just press the right button on the multi selector. Any additional screens of choices will appear. You can move among them using the same multi selector movements.
- **Confirm your choice.** You can activate a selection by pressing the OK button or, frequently, by pressing the right button on the multi selector once again. Some functions require scrolling to a Done menu choice, or include an instruction to Set a choice using some other button.
- **Exit menus.** Pressing the multi selector left button usually backs you out of the current screen, and pressing the Menu button again usually does the same thing. You can exit the menu system at any time by tapping the shutter release button.
- **Returning to an entry.** The Nikon D3s/D3x "remembers" the top-level menu and specific menu entry you were using (but not any submenus) the last time the menu system was accessed, so pressing the Menu button brings you back to where you left off. So, if you were working with an entry in the Custom Setting menu's Metering/exposure section, then decided to take a photo, the next time you press the Menu button the Custom Setting menu and the Metering/exposure entry will be highlighted, but not the specific submenu (b1 through b6) that you might have selected.
- **Accessing a frequently used entry.** If you use the same menu items over and over, you can create a My Menu listing of those entries. Or, if you'd rather have a rotating listing of the last 20 menu items you accessed, you can convert My Menu to a Recent Settings menu instead. I'll show you exactly how to do that in Chapter 5.

The top-level menus are color-coded, and a bar in that color is displayed underneath the menu title when one of those menus is highlighted. The colors are Playback menu (blue); Shooting menu (green); Custom Setting menu (red); Setup menu (orange); Retouch menu (purple); and My Menu (gray). The Custom Setting menu has six submenus that are themselves color-coded to help you keep track of where you are located in the menu system. You'll learn about the Custom Setting, Setup, Retouch, and My Menu options in Chapters 4 and 5.

## Playback Menu Options

The blue-coded Playback menu, shown previously in Figure 3.1, has ten entries where you select options related to the display, review, transfer, and printing of the photos you've taken. The choices you'll find include the following entries (the last two, Slide show and Print set [DPOF] are not pictured in Figure 3.1, and don't appear until you scroll the listing on the screen to the bottom):

- Delete
- Playback folder
- Hide image
- Display mode
- Copy image(s)
- Image review
- After delete
- Rotate tall
- Slide show
- Print set (DPOF)

## Delete

Choose this menu entry and you'll be given two choices: Selected and All. If you choose All, then all the pictures in the folder currently selected for playback (as described next) will be removed. When two memory cards are in the camera and have photos, you can choose which card to use to select images for removal. To delete only some pictures from a folder, choose Selected; you'll see an image selection screen like the one shown in Figure 3.2. Then, follow these instructions:

1. **Select image.** Use the multi selector cursor keys to scroll among the available images.
2. **Evaluate image.** When you highlight an image you think you might like to delete, press the Zoom/Thumbnail button to temporarily enlarge that image so you can evaluate it further. When you release the button, the selection screen returns.

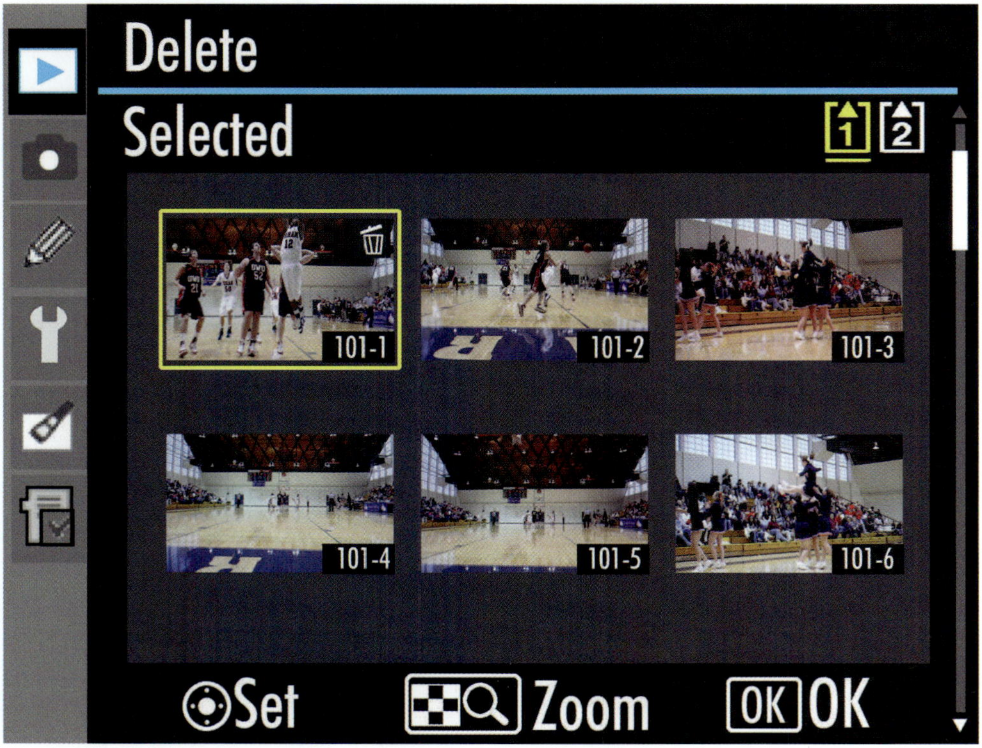


**Figure 3.2** Select images to delete.

3. **Mark images.** To mark an image for deletion, press the multi selector center button (*not* the Trash button). A trash can icon will appear overlaid on that image's thumbnail. To unmark an image, press the multi selector center button again.
4. **Delete images.** When you've finished marking images to delete, press OK. A final screen will appear asking you to confirm the removal of the image(s). Choose Yes to delete the image(s) or No to cancel deletion, and then press OK. If you selected Yes, then you'll return to the Playback menu; if you chose No, you'll be taken back to the selection screen to mark/unmark images.
5. **Exit Delete menu.** To back out of the selection screen, press the Menu button.

Using this menu to delete images will have no effect on images that have been marked as protected with the Protect key. Keep in mind that deleting images in this way is slower than just wiping out the whole card with the Format command, so using Format is generally much faster than choosing Delete: All, and also is a safer way of returning your memory card to a fresh, blank state.

## Playback Folder

Your Nikon D3s/D3x will create folders on your memory card to store the images that it creates. It assigns the first folder a number, like 100D3s/D3x, and when that folder fills with 999 images, the camera automatically creates a new folder numbered one higher, such as 101D3s/D3x. If you use the same memory card in another camera, that camera will also create its own folder. Thus you can end up with several folders on the same memory card, until you eventually reformat the card and folder creation starts anew.

This menu item allows you to choose which folders are accessed when displaying images using the D3s/D3x's Playback facility. Your choices are as follows:

- **NCD3S/NCD3X.** The camera will use only the folders on your memory card created by the D3s or D3x and ignore those created by other cameras. Images in all the D3s/D3x's folders will be displayed. This is the default setting.
- **All.** All folders containing images that the D3s/D3x can read will be accessed, regardless of which camera created them. You might want to use this setting if you swap memory cards among several cameras and want to be able to review all the photos (especially when considering reformatting the memory card). You will be able to view images even if they were created by a non-Nikon camera if those images conform to the Design Rule for Camera File system (DCF) specifications.

- **Current.** The D3s/D3x will display only images in the current folder. For example, if you have been shooting heavily at an event and have already accumulated more than 999 shots in one folder and the D3s/D3x has created a new folder for the overflow, you'd use this setting to view only the most recent photos, which reside in the current folder. You can change the current folder to any other folder on your memory card using the Active Folder option in the Shooting menu, described later in this chapter.

## Hide Image

Use this menu option to protect *and* hide images. When you choose Hide image, you'll be given a choice to select/set images (using a selection screen almost identical to the one used to delete images, as shown earlier in Figure 3.2) or the option of deselecting all hidden images.

Unlike the Protect option, which just *marks* images to keep them from accidental deletion, this selection also hides them from view using the regular Playback functions. Pictures that have been hidden can only be viewed from the selection screen. I use this facility in two different ways:

- **Hide non-relevant images.** Sometimes I have a memory card filled with images and I want to show some of the images, perhaps as a slide show, or sometimes just by handing the camera to someone and asking them to browse through the photos. I can hide the non-relevant images so only the relevant pictures appear.
- **Bury your mistakes.** Hiding images is a good way to make your real stinkers invisible from the eyes of those who otherwise respect your work, if you haven't quite made up your mind to delete them. Tuck them out of view until you move them to your computer, or get up the courage to nuke them forever.

Remember that if you "unhide" an image you are also removing the Protect attribute. If you want the photo to be visible, but still protected, press the Protect button (it has a key icon as a label) while viewing the image on the LCD. The key icon will be superimposed on the image, showing you that it is now protected from accidental erasure. Reformatting the card removes the Hidden and Protected attributes, of course—because it removes those images as well!

## Display Mode

You'll recall from Chapter 2 that a great deal of information, available on multiple screens, can be displayed when reviewing images. This menu item helps you reduce/increase the clutter by specifying which information and screens will be available. To activate or deactivate an info option, scroll to that option and press the right multi selector button to add a check mark to the box next to that item. Press the right button to unmark an item that has previously been checked. Important: when you're finished, you must scroll up to Done and press OK or the right multi selector button to confirm your choices. Exiting the Display mode menu any other way will cause any changes you may have made to be ignored. Your info options include

- **Focus point.** Activate this option to display the active focus point(s) with red highlighting, as shown in Figure 3.3.
- **Highlights.** When enabled, overexposed highlight areas in your image will blink with a black border during picture review. That's your cue to consider using exposure compensation to reduce exposure, unless a minus-EV setting will cause loss of shadow detail that you want to preserve. You can read more about correcting exposure in Chapter 6.
- **RGB histogram.** Displays both luminance (brightness) and RGB histograms on a screen that can be displayed using the up/down multi selector buttons, as shown in Chapter 2. If you're viewing this histogram with the Highlights display enabled, you can change the Highlights focus from the luminance histogram to any of the three RGB channels by holding down the Thumbnail button and pressing the multi selector right button until the channel you want is selected. I'll explain the use of this feature in more detail in Chapter 6.
- **Data.** Activates the four pages of shooting data shown in Chapter 2.

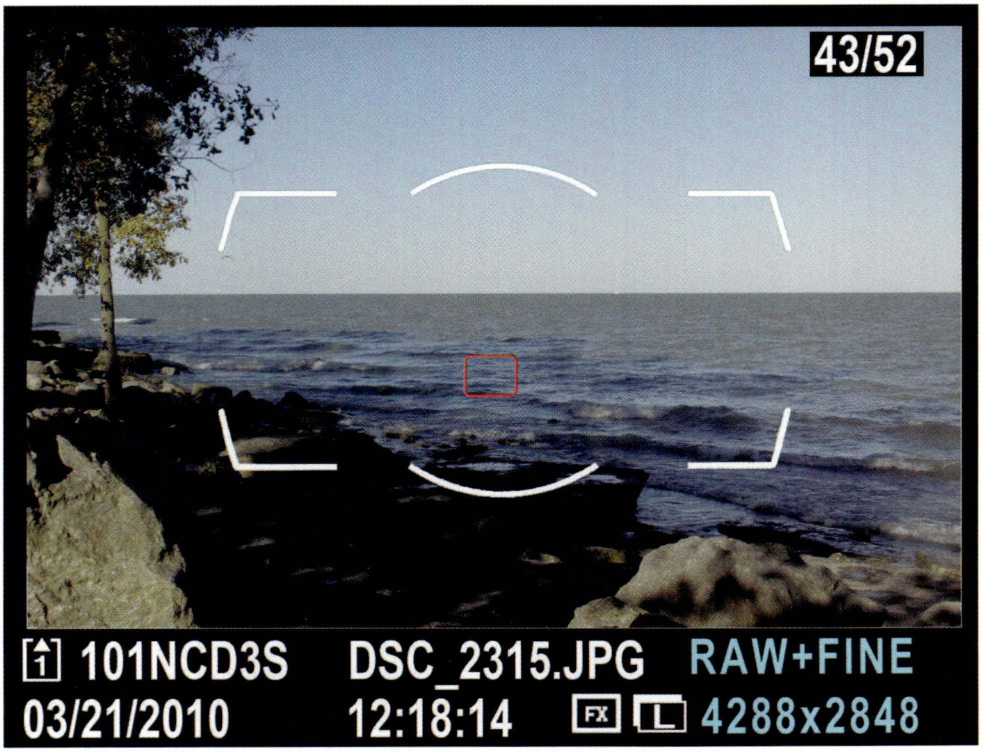


**Figure 3.3**
Use the Display mode menu entry to activate data display, like the focus point shown in this reviewed image.

## Copy Image(s)

The ability to work with two memory cards simultaneously ranked as my absolutely favorite new feature when the original Nikon D3 was introduced in 2007. One of the best uses for two cards is to make backup images while traveling, or at any other time that your computer isn't easily accessible. Here are some examples of what I do:

- **Shoot to two cards simultaneously.** This gives you an instant backup in case pictures on your primary card become corrupt or are erased. Ideally, your two cards should be equal in size.
- **Make a copy.** Use this Copy image(s) facility to make a copy of images you shot on one card to your second card. Instead of shooting on two cards at once (which does slow down the D3s/D3x a bit), use only one card when you take photos, then make a backup onto a second card at the end of the day. You can copy all or only some of the photos you've shot.
- **Make copies to distribute.** I bought a bunch of 2GB memory cards for $4.98 each, and find it's quick and easy to make multiple copies of photos, not for backup, but for distribution either on the spot, say, to provide models I've hired with some raw (not RAW) images, or to send by snail mail to colleagues, friends, or family that I want to share photos with. No computer required!
- **Leave your PSD at home.** Since I've begun using Nikon cameras with dual memory card slots, I leave my hard disk/personal storage device with its built-in reader at home more often. If I am going to be gone for only a day or two, it's easier to just make copies in the camera, and not bother with another external device.

To copy images from the memory card in Slot 1 to the memory card in Slot 2, just follow these steps:

### Tip

Copying from one card to another must always begin with images that reside in the card in Slot 1. If you want to copy photos that are contained in the Slot 2 card, simply swap them before beginning the copying process. You might find this inconvenient, especially if you have used a Nikon D300s, which has an additional option, Select Source, and can initiate the copy process from either slot. However, because the D300s uses one Compact Flash card and one SD card, swapping isn't possible, so the extra choice is necessary. Nikon has kept the process simple with the D3-series cameras.

1. **Access copy menus.** Choose Copy image(s) from the Playback menu. There are three choices that may be available to you: Select image(s); Select destination folder; and Copy image(s)?. Unless you have selected some images on the card in Slot 1, the other choices will be grayed out and Select image(s) will be preselected for you, as shown in Figure 3.4.

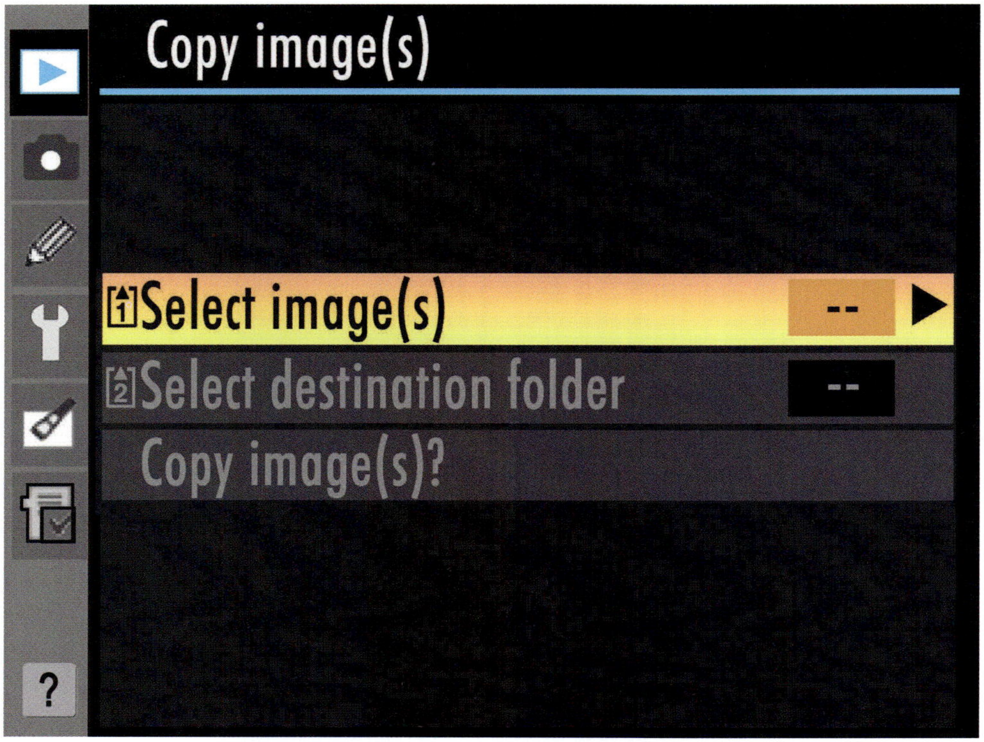


**Figure 3.4**
Selecting images is usually the first step in copying from one card to another.

2. **Select images and/or Destination folder or Copy image(s).** Perform these tasks in order.
   - If you are selecting images, you can either Deselect all images to cancel previous selections; Select all images to view a screen similar to the one shown previously in Figure 3.2, where you can mark and unmark specific thumbnails (Hidden images cannot be copied); or Select protected images to choose from among images you've previously marked with the Protect key (located just under the Zoom button). Press OK when finished to return to the Copy image(s) menu.
   - If you are choosing a destination folder, you can select by folder number (either a current folder number or one you create by specifying a number for the new folder), or choose from a list of existing folders. Press OK when finished to return to the Copy image(s) menu.
3. **Start copying.** When you choose Copy image(s)? you'll see a confirmation screen. Highlight Yes, press OK, and a progress screen with a green progress bar appears while the copying is underway. You'll see a Copy Complete message when the task is finished. Any voice memos associated with an image will be copied along with the image file itself. Press OK, and then the Menu button twice to back out of the menus; or just tap the shutter release button.

**Tip**

The Copy command will ask for confirmation before overwriting images on the destination card that have the same name as the source images. You can choose Replace existing image, Replace all, Skip, or Cancel the rest of the copying operation.

## Image Review

There are certain shooting situations in which it's useful to have the picture you've just shot pop up on the LCD automatically for review. Perhaps you're fine-tuning exposure or autofocus and want to be able to see whether your most recent image is acceptable. Or, maybe you're the nervous type and just want confirmation that you actually took a picture. Instant review has saved my bacon a few times; for example, when I was shooting with studio flash in manual mode and didn't notice that the shutter speed had been set to a (non-syncing) 1/500th second by mistake.

A lot of the time, however, it's a better idea to *not* automatically review your shots in order to conserve battery power (the LCD is one of the major juice drains in the camera) or to speed up or simplify operations. For example, if you've just fired off a burst of eight shots with your D3s at 9 fps during a football game, do you *really* need to have each and every frame display as the camera clears its buffer and stores the photos on your memory card? This menu operation allows you to choose which mode to use:

- **On.** Image review is automatic after every shot is taken.
- **Off.** Images are displayed only when you press the Playback button. Nikon, in its wisdom, has made this the default setting.

## After Delete

When you've deleted an image, you probably will want to do one of three things: have the D3s/D3x display the next picture (in the order shot); show the *previous* picture; or show either the next *or* previous picture, depending on which way you were scrolling during picture review. Your D3s/D3x lets you select which action to take:

- **Show next.** It's likely that you'll want to look at the picture taken after the one you just deleted, so Nikon makes this the default action.
- **Show previous.** I use this setting a lot when shooting sports with a continuous shooting setting. After the sequence is taken, I press the Playback button to see the last picture in the series and sometimes discover that the whole sequence missed the boat. I sometimes go ahead and press the Trash button twice to delete the offending image, then continue moving backwards to delete the five or six or eleven other

pictures in the wasted sequence. You'll often find yourself with time on your hands at football games, and the urge to delete some stinkers to save your time reviewing back at the computer, while freeing up a little space on your card.

- **Continue as before.** This setting actually makes a lot of sense: if you were scrolling backward or forward and deleting photos as you go, you might want to continue in the same direction, weeding out bad shots. Use this setting to set your Nikon D3s/D3s to behave that way.

## Rotate Tall

When you rotate the D3s/D3x to photograph vertical subjects in portrait (tall), rather than landscape (wide) orientation, you probably don't want to view them tilted onto their sides later on, either on the camera LCD or within your image-viewing/editing application on your computer. The D3s/D3x is way ahead of you. It has a directional sensor built in that can detect whether the camera was rotated when the photo was taken and hide this information in the image file itself.

The orientation data is applied in two different ways. It can be used by the D3s/D3x to automatically rotate images when they are displayed on the camera's LCD monitor, or you can ignore the data and let the images display in non-rotated fashion (so you have to rotate the camera to view them in their proper orientation). Your image-editing application, such as Adobe Photoshop Elements, can also use the embedded file data to automatically rotate images on your computer screen.

Rotation works only if you've set Auto image rotation to On in the Setup menu (I'll show you how to do that later in this chapter). Once you've done that, the D3s/D3x will embed information about orientation in the image file, and your image editor (such as Adobe Photoshop or Photoshop Elements) will rotate the images for you as the files are loaded.

This menu choice deals only with whether the image should be rotated when displayed on the *camera's LCD monitor.* (If you de-activate this option, your image-editing software can still read the embedded rotation data and properly display your images.) When Rotate tall is turned off, the Nikon D3s/D3x does not rotate pictures taken in vertical orientation, displaying them as shown in Figure 3.5. The image is large on your LCD screen, but you must rotate the camera to view it upright.

When Rotate tall is turned on, the D3s/D3x rotates pictures taken in vertical orientation on the LCD screen so you don't have to turn the camera to view them comfortably. However, this orientation also means that the longest dimension of the image is shown using the shortest dimension of the LCD, so the picture is reduced in size, as you can see in Figure 3.6.

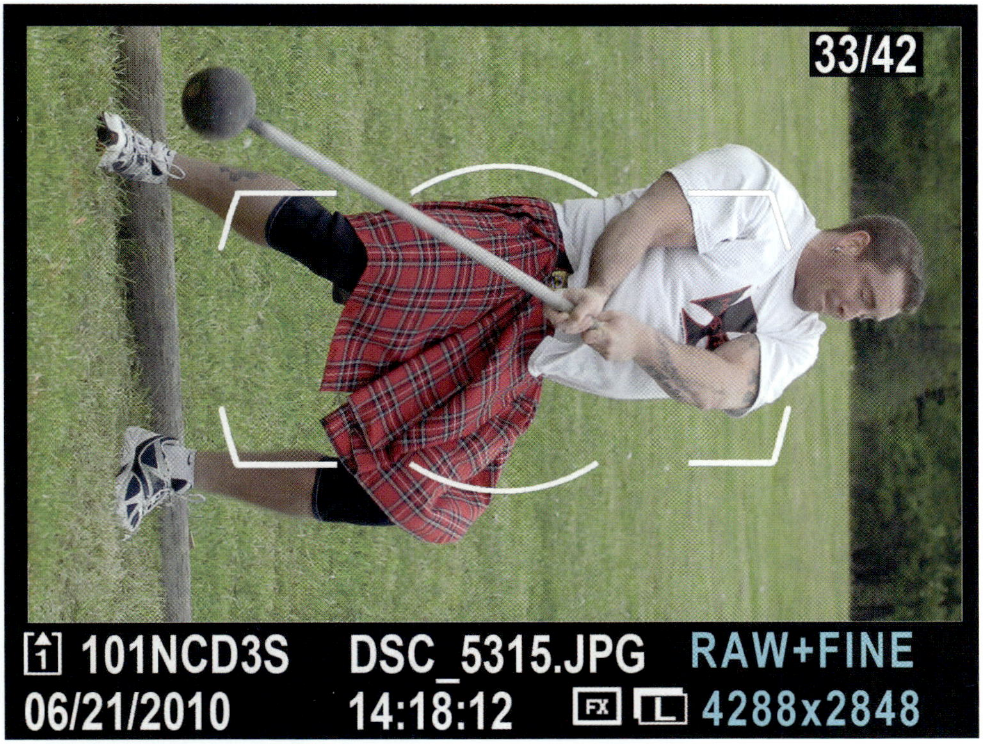


**Figure 3.5**
With Rotate tall turned off, vertical images appear large on the LCD, but you must turn the camera to view them upright.

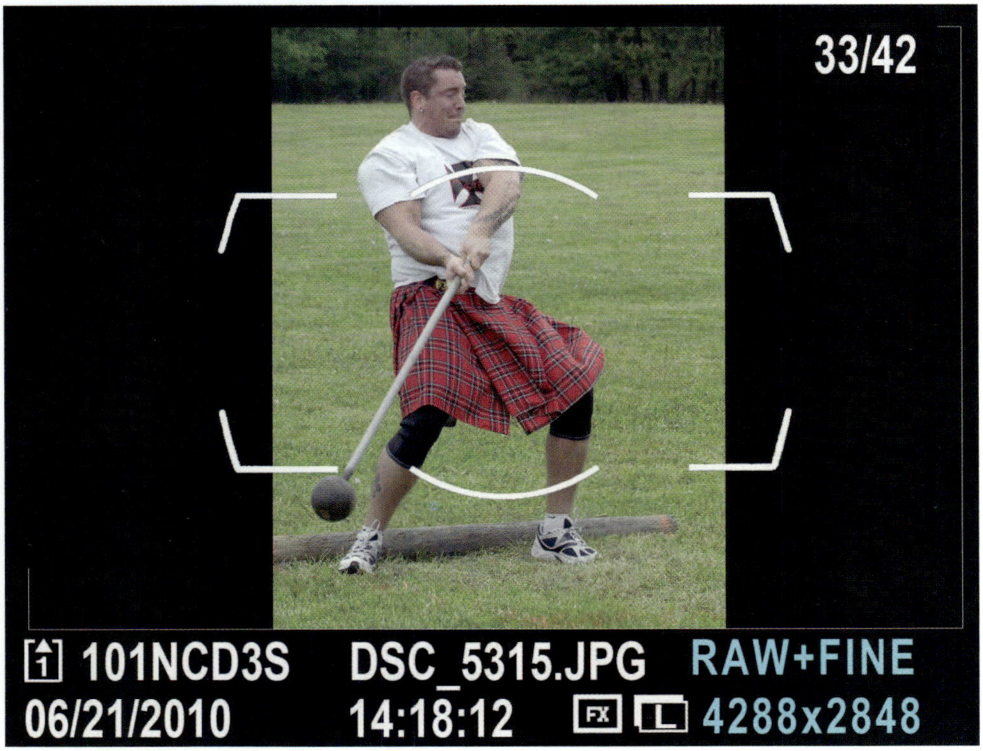


**Figure 3.6**
With Rotate tall turned on, vertical images are shown in a smaller size, but oriented for viewing without turning the camera.

So, turn this feature On (as well as Auto image rotation in the Setup menu), if you'd rather not turn your camera to view vertical shots in their natural orientation, and don't mind the smaller image. Turn the feature Off if, as I do, you'd rather see a larger image and are willing to rotate the camera to do so.

## Slide Show

The D3s/D3x's Slide show feature is a convenient way to review images in the current playback folder one after another, without the need to manually switch between them. If you've recorded voice memos for some or all of the images you display in your slide show, you can opt to have them played back as narration. Re-direct the output of your camera's video to an HDTV television, and you've got an instant camera-based large-screen audiovisual extravaganza. Your options include

- **Start.** To activate a slide show, just choose Start from this entry in the Playback menu. During playback, you can press the OK button to pause the "slide show." When the show is paused, a menu pops up, as shown in Figure 3.7, with choices to restart the show (by pressing the OK button again); change the interval between frames; adjust audio playback options; or to exit the show entirely.
- **Frame interval.** If you like, you can choose Frame interval before commencing the show in order to select an interval of 2, 3, 5, or 10 seconds between "slides."

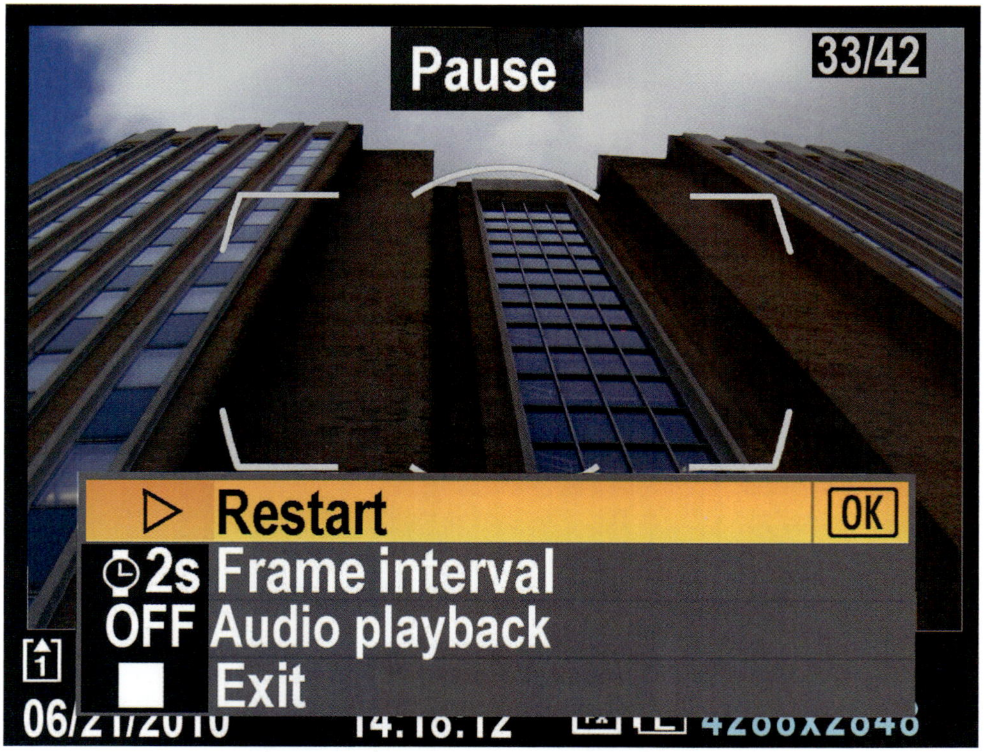


**Figure 3.7**
Press the OK button to pause the slide show, change the interval between slides, or to exit the presentation.

- **Audio playback.** This option allows you to turn the playback of voice memos associated with each image on or off. In effect, this is a very cool feature that allows you to create, in your camera, a slide show complete with narration. If you select On, you can press the right directional key to view a Display image for: submenu that specifies that the voice memo play only as long as the specified frame interval (it will be cut off when the image changes to the next in the series), or that the playback should continue for the full length of the voice memo. In that case, the slide show will not progress to the next image until the entire voice memo has been played back, even if the frame interval has been set for a shorter time.

As the images are displayed, press the up/down multi selector buttons to change the amount of information presented on the screen with each image. For example, you might want to review a set of images and the settings used to shoot them. At any time during the show, press the up/down buttons until the informational screen you want is overlaid on the images.

As the slide show progresses, you can press the left/right multi selector buttons to move back to a previous frame or jump ahead to the next one. The slide show will then proceed as before. Press the Menu button to exit the slide show and return to the menu, or press the Playback button to exit the menu system totally. As always, while reviewing images you can tap the Menu button to exit the show and return to the menus, or tap the shutter release button if you want to remove everything from the screen and return to shooting mode.

At the end of the slide show, as when you've paused it, you'll be offered the choice of restarting the sequence, changing the frame interval, or exiting the Slide show feature completely.

## Print Set (DPOF)

The Nikon D3s/D3x supports the DPOF (Digital Print Order Format) that is now almost universally used by digital cameras to specify which images on your memory card should be printed, and the number of prints desired of each image. This information is recorded on the memory card and can be interpreted by a compatible printer when the camera is linked to the printer using the USB cable (using the Direct Print facility, discussed in the next section), or when the memory card is inserted into a card reader slot on the printer itself. Photo labs are also equipped to read this data and make prints when you supply your memory card to them.

When you choose this menu item, you're presented with a set of screens that look very much like the Delete photos screens described earlier, only you're selecting pictures for printing rather than deleting them. The button sequences are slightly different, however:

1. **Review images.** Use the multi selector cursor keys to scroll among the available images.

2. **Evaluate image.** When you highlight an image you might want to print, press the Zoom button to temporarily enlarge that image so you can evaluate it further. When you release the button, the selection screen returns.
3. **Mark for printing.** To mark an image for printing, press the Protect button and hold it down while pressing the multi selector up and down buttons to choose the number of prints you want, up to 99 per image. A printer icon and the number specified will appear overlaid on that image's thumbnail. (See Figure 3.8.)
4. **Unmark unwanted images.** To unmark an image for printing, highlight and hold down the Protect button while pressing the down button until the number of prints reaches zero. The printer icon will vanish.
5. **Exit image selection.** When you've finished marking images to print, press OK.
6. **Choose imprint options.** A final screen will appear in which you can request a data imprint (shutter speed and aperture) or imprint date (the date the photos were taken). Use the up/down buttons to select one or both of these options, if desired, and press the left/right buttons to mark or unmark the check boxes. When a box is marked, the imprint information for that option will be included on *all* prints in the print order.
7. **Complete print order.** Scroll up to Done when finished, and press OK or the right cursor button.

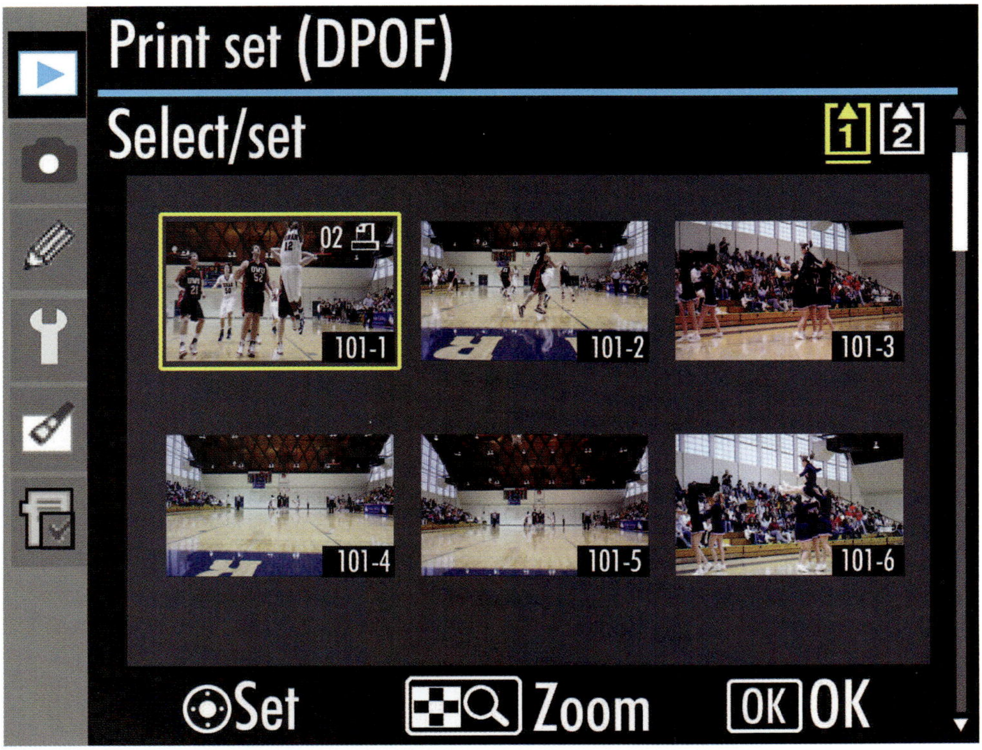


**Figure 3.8**
Select images for printing.

## Direct Printing

Direct printing from your D3-series camera to a PictBridge-compatible printer is not one of the Playback menu options; the PictBridge menu appears when the camera is connected to a PictBridge printer using the USB cable. In that mode, you can print any images you've selected using the Print Set (DPOF) menu entry in the Playback menu, or you can print directly. Just follow these steps to print a single image:

1. Visit the Setup menu and make sure the USB menu entry has been set to MTP/PTP, and not Mass storage. (I'll explain this menu option, which appears only on the D3x menu, in Chapter 5.)
2. Turn off the camera.
3. Connect the camera to the PictBridge printer using the USB cable; do not connect through a USB hub.
4. Turn the camera back on. The PictBridge display will appear.
5. Use the left/right directional buttons on the multi selector to browse among available images. You can press the Zoom button and rotate the main command dial to zoom in and out of a frame being viewed. (Press the Playback button to return to full-frame view.)
6. Press the multi selector center button to view up to six thumbnails at once. Press the button a second time to view a highlighted picture in full-frame mode.
7. When you've highlighted a picture you want to print, press OK to view the PictBridge printing options.
8. Use the up/down directional buttons to highlight an option, and the right directional button to select it. Your choices are
   - **Page size.** Choose from your printer's default page size, 3.5 × 5 in., 5 × 7 in., or A4 sizes.
   - **No. of copies.** Choose from 1 to 99 copies, and press OK.
   - **Border.** Select from Printer default (the border setting already stored in your printer), Print with border, or No border. Press OK to return to the menu.
   - **Time stamp.** Select from Printer default (the time stamp setting already stored in your printer), Print time stamp, or No time stamp. Press OK to return to the menu.
   - **Cropping.** A dialog box will appear, and you can rotate the main command dial to zoom cropping in or out, and use the multi selector directional buttons to position the cropping frame.
9. When ready to print, select Start printing. Once printing has begun, press OK to cancel before all the copies have been output. Press OK to return to the menu.

To print multiple images, follow these steps:

1. Press the Menu button in the PictBridge playback display.
2. Select one of the following:
   - Choose Print select to choose the images now that you want to print.
   - Choose Print (DPOF) to print the images that you have previously marked using the Playback menu's Print set (DPOF) menu.
   - Choose Index print to create an index print of all the JPEG images on the memory card.
3. If you've chosen Print select, choose the images to be printed, using the left/right directional buttons, the Protect button to mark them, and the up/down buttons to select the number of prints from 1 to 99 copies.
4. Press the OK button to display PictBridge printing options, as in Step 8 above, except that only Page size, Border, and Time stamp may be specified.
5. When ready to print, select Start printing. Once printing has begun, press OK to cancel before all the copies have been output. Press OK to return to the menu.

## Shooting Menu Options

The various direct setting buttons and dials on the D3s/D3x, for image quality, autofocus mode, white balance, release mode, ISO sensitivity, metering mode, and flash, along with exposure compensation (EV) adjustments, are likely to be the settings you adjust the most, with changes during a particular session fairly common. You'll find some of these duplicated in the Shooting menu (see Figure 3.9), along with options that you access second-most frequently when you're using your Nikon D3s/D3x, such as specifying noise reduction for long exposures or high ISO settings. You might make such adjustments as you begin a shooting session, or when you move from one type of subject to another. Nikon makes accessing these changes very easy.

This section explains the options of the Shooting menu and how to use them. The options you'll find in these green-coded menus include

- Shooting menu bank
- Reset shooting menu
- Extended menu banks (D3s only)
- Active folder
- File naming
- Slot 2
- Set Picture Control
- Manage Picture Control
- Color space
- Active D-Lighting
- Vignette control
- Long exp. NR

- Image quality
- Image size
- Image area
- JPEG compression
- NEF (RAW) recording
- White balance
- High ISO NR
- ISO sensitivity settings
- Live view (mode D3s)
- Multiple exposure
- Movie settings (D3s)
- Interval timer shooting

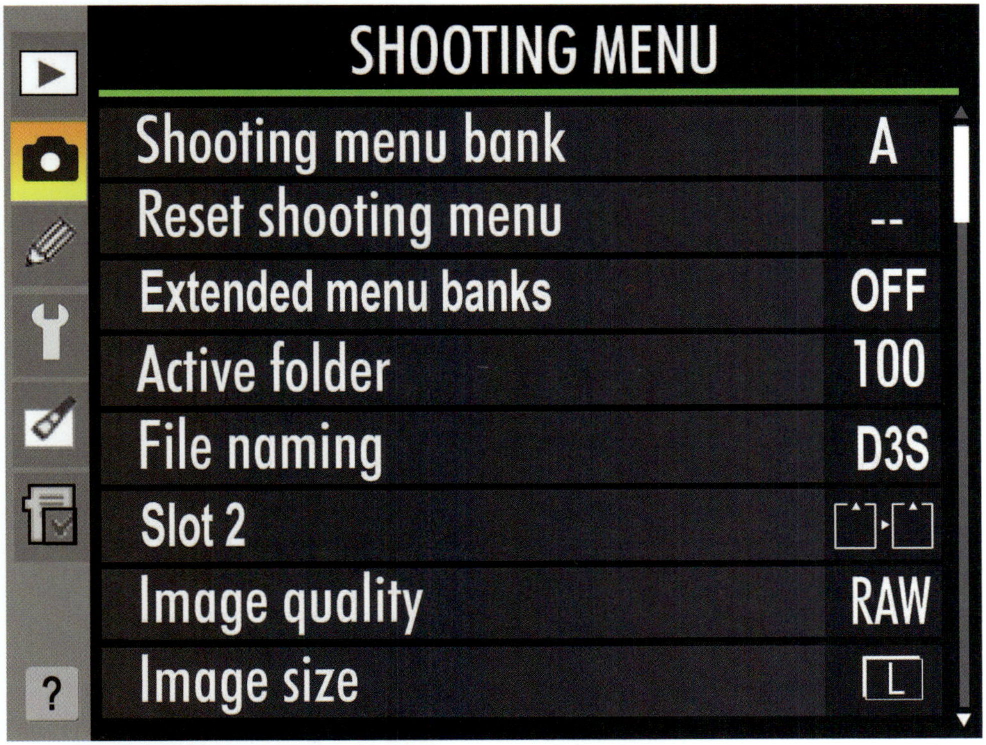


**Figure 3.9** Common shooting settings can be changed in this menu.

## Shooting Menu Banks

The Nikon D3s/D3x's Shooting menu banks are four groups named, initially, A, B, C, and D that store specific collections of Shooting menu settings that you can recall at any time by switching to the bank containing the preferences you want to use. These banks are one of the primary reasons why the D3s/D3x is more versatile than Nikon's entry-level dSLRs, which lack the ability to change shooting specifications *en masse* using a simple menu command. The Shooting menu banks A, B, C, and D should not be confused with the four similarly named Custom Setting menu banks A, B, C, and D, which provide similar, but *separate* storage of your CSM settings. You can use your

Shooting menu banks and Custom Setting menu banks in any combination. That is, you can be using Shooting menu bank A, and Custom Setting menu bank C at the same time.

The D3s/D3x uses bank A by default. To switch to another bank

- **Navigate to the Shooting menu.** Press Menu and select the Shooting menu.
- **Choose the menu bank option.** Scroll to Shooting menu bank and press the multi selector right button.
- **Select the bank to activate.** Scroll to the bank you want to use with the multi selector up/down buttons, and either press OK or press the multi selector right button to confirm your choice.
- **Exit menus.** The Shooting menu appears again. Press the Menu button to back out of the menu, or simply tap the shutter release.

Any changes you make to one menu bank do not affect the other banks, so you can set one up with the settings you like to use in particular situations. For example, you could use bank A for sports, bank B for landscapes, bank C for portraits, and bank D for general shooting. Or, if you're a specialist, one bank could be dedicated to indoor sports (with high ISO settings and tungsten or fluorescent light balance) and another for outdoor sports (normal ISO and daylight white balance), with both specifying JPEG FINE capture only, because RAW or RAW+JPEG can slow down continuous shooting. You could even tailor a D3s/D3x's operation using parameters other than typical shooting sessions. For example, a wedding photography studio that shares a pool of Nikon D3s/D3x cameras among several photographers could have one bank named Peter, another named Paul, and a third dedicated to shooter Mary. The currently selected bank is indicated in the monochrome LCD status panel, and in the shooting information display.

## Entering Text on the Nikon D3s/D3x

Customized names of up to 20 characters each can be used to replace the generic A, B, C, and D designations. You can use the standard Nikon text entry screen to enter the name you want to use. Now is a good time to master text entry, because you can use it to enter comments, rename folders, and perform other functions.

The Nikon D3s/D3x uses a fairly standardized text entry screen to name files, Picture Controls, create new folder names, enter image comments, and other text. You'll be using text entry with other functions that I'll describe later in this book. The screen looks like the one shown in Figure 3.10, with some variations (for example, some functions have a less diverse character set, or offer more or fewer spaces for your entries). To name a menu bank, just use the multi selector navigational buttons to scroll around within the array of alphanumerics.

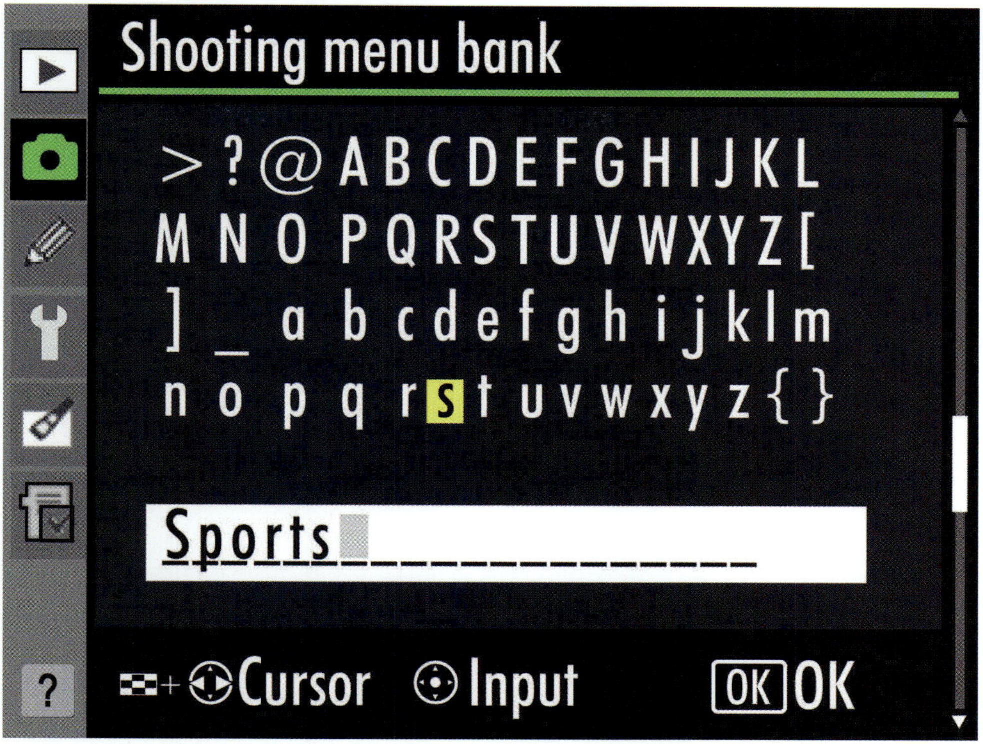


**Figure 3.10** Use this D3s/D3x screen to enter text.

Then, enter your text:

- **Highlight a character.** Use the multi selector keys to scroll around within the array of characters.
- **Insert highlighted character.** Press the multi selector center button to insert the highlighted character. The cursor will move one place to the right to accept the next character.
- **Non-destructively backspace.** Hold down the Thumbnail/Zoom out button and use the left/right buttons to move the cursor within the line of characters you've entered. This allows you to backspace and replace a character without disturbing the others you've entered.
- **Erase a highlighted character.** To remove a character you've already input, move the cursor to highlight that character, and then press the Trash button.
- **Confirm your entry.** When you're finished entering text, press the OK button to confirm your entry, then press the left button twice to return to the Shooting menu, or just tap the shutter release to exit the menu system entirely.

As you work with menu banks, keep in mind that while changes you make to a particular bank don't affect the other banks, they are "sticky" within that bank once you've made them. That is, if you've set up a "sports" menu bank to use a high ISO sensitivity setting, and then during a session change the value to ISO 200, that's what you'll get the next time you access that menu bank (unless you remember to change it back to your preferred value at the end of the session).

In Chapter 8, I'll provide a list of recommended Shooting menu bank settings for typical photo environments, from sports and landscapes to portraits and macros.

## Reset Shooting Menu

Don't feel bad over being confused about what this menu item does. The Nikon D3s/D3x has, in effect, *three* different kinds of resets. This is one of them.

- **Shooting menu reset.** Use this option to reset the values of the currently selected Shooting menu bank *except for image quality, image size, white balance, and ISO sensitivity* to their default values. When you select this menu item, your choices are Yes and No. Note that the defaults are restored *only* for the menu bank that is active, and not any of the other three Shooting menu banks, except for multiple exposure and interval timer shooting settings, which are reset for all four banks. A reset has no effect on the four settings noted above.
- **Custom Setting menu reset.** This option, which I'll describe later in this chapter, is used to reset any of the four Custom Setting menu banks. It has no effect on camera settings or Shooting menu banks.
- **Two-button reset.** The Nikon D3s/D3x's two-button reset (holding down the ISO and White Balance buttons [on the back of the camera below the rear control panel, marked with green dots] simultaneously for more than two seconds) will *not* reset your Shooting menu banks or Custom Setting menu banks. This particular reset is for basic settings, such as focus point, exposure mode, flexible program, exposure/flash compensation, autoexposure hold, bracketing, flash mode, flash value lock, and multiple exposure settings.

Table 3.1 shows the default values that are set using the Reset shooting menu option. If you don't know what some of these settings are, I'll explain them later in this section.

## Extended Menu Banks (D3s Only)

The Nikon D3s added the ability to include several additional parameters—exposure mode, shutter speed, and aperture—to the values stored in a particular Shooting menu bank. So, if you have a sports mode especially for action photography and always begin a sports session using shutter-priority and a shutter speed of 1/1,000th second, you can include that information in each of your Shooting menu banks. Or, perhaps you have a bank set up for portraits, and you like to use aperture-priority with an f/stop of f/5.6 to reduce depth-of-field. The extended menu banks can keep that information on file, too.

**Table 3.1 Default Shooting Menu Values**

| Function | Value | Function | Value |
|---|---|---|---|
| Extended menu banks (D3s) | ***Off*** | Vignette control | ***Normal*** |
| File naming | ***DSC*** | Long exp. NR | ***Off*** |
| Slot 2 | ***Overflow*** | High ISO NR | ***Normal*** |
| Image quality | ***JPEG normal*** | ISO sensitivity settings | |
| Image size | ***Large*** | ISO sensitivity | ***200*** |
| Image area | | ISO sensitivity auto control | ***Off*** |
| Auto DX crop | ***On*** | Live view mode (D3s) | ***Tripod*** |
| Choose image area | ***FX (36× 24)*** | Live view mode (D3x) | ***Hand-held*** |
| JPEG compression | ***Size priority*** | Release mode (D3x) | ***Single frame*** |
| NEF (RAW) recording | | Multiple exposure | |
| Type | ***Lossless compressed*** | Multiple exposure mode | ***Off/Reset*** |
| NEF (RAW) bit depth | ***12-bit*** | Number of shots | ***2*** |
| White balance | | Auto gain | ***On*** |
| Fine tuning | ***Auto*** | Movie settings (D3s) | |
| Choose color temp | ***5000K*** | Quality | ***640× 424 (3:2)*** |
| Set Picture Control | ***Standard*** | Microphone | ***Auto sensitivity (A)*** |
| Color space | ***sRGB*** | Destination | ***Slot 1*** |
| Active D-Lighting | ***Off*** | High sensitivity movie mode | ***Off*** |
| | | Interval timer shooting | ***Reset*** |

When would you *not* want to use extended menu banks? You'd probably want to switch this feature off if you change exposure modes frequently and don't care (or don't want) a particular shutter speed or aperture to be preset for you when you change to a particular menu bank. (Keep in mind that, once a bank has been loaded, you can always change to a different mode or setting, and that your new setting will become the default for that bank when you reload it in the future.)

With this option set to Off (the default), the D3s will not store exposure mode, f/stop, or shutter speed in a menu bank. If you select On, then exposure mode *will* be stored. If the exposure mode that is stored is shutter-priority or manual, then the shutter speed will be remembered as well. If the exposure mode is aperture-priority or manual, the aperture will be remembered.

## Active Folder

If you want to store images in a folder other than the one created and selected by the Nikon D3s/D3x, you can switch among available folders on your Compact Flash card, or create your own folder. Remember that any folders you create will be deleted when you reformat your memory card.

Why create your own folders? Perhaps you're traveling and have a high-capacity memory card and want to store the images for each day (or for each city that you visit) in a separate folder. Maybe you'd like to separate those wedding photos you snapped at the ceremony from those taken at the reception. As I mentioned earlier, the Nikon D3s/D3x automatically creates a folder on a newly formatted memory card with a name like 100NCD3S, and when it fills with 999 images, it will automatically create a new folder with a number incremented by one (such as 101NCD3S). To create your own folder or select an existing folder

1. **Access Active folder entry.** Choose Active folder in the Shooting menu, and press the right multi selector button.
2. **Choose selection method.** Highlight either Select folder by number (D3s) or New folder number (D3x and original D3) (to create a new folder or to choose an existing folder) or Select folder from list (D3s) or Select folder (D3x and original D3) (to choose a folder that you know already exists). Press the right directional button to confirm your choice. One of two screens appears, with the card in the currently active slot highlighted. Perform the tasks in either Step 3 or Step 4.
3. **Select folder by number/New folder number.** If you've chosen this option, a screen appears with three digits representing the possible folder numbers from 100-999, as shown in Figure 3.11. Use the left/right buttons to move between the digits, and the up/down buttons to increase or decrease the value of the digit. If a folder already exists with the number you dial in, an icon appears showing the folder is empty, partially full, or has 999 or a picture numbered 9999 and can contain no more images. Press OK to create the new folder and make it the active folder. You'd want to use this option to create a new folder *or* when you don't know whether a folder by a particular number already exists. If a folder with that number already resides on the memory card, you can use it (if it is not full); if it doesn't exist, you can create it.
4. **Select folder from list/Select folder.** From among the available folders shown, scroll to the one that you want to become active for image storage and playback. This feature is handy when you want to display a slide show located in a particular folder. Use this option if you know that the folder you want to use already resides on the memory card. Press OK to confirm your choice and make the folder active.
5. **Exit menus.** Press the Menu button or tap the shutter release to exit.

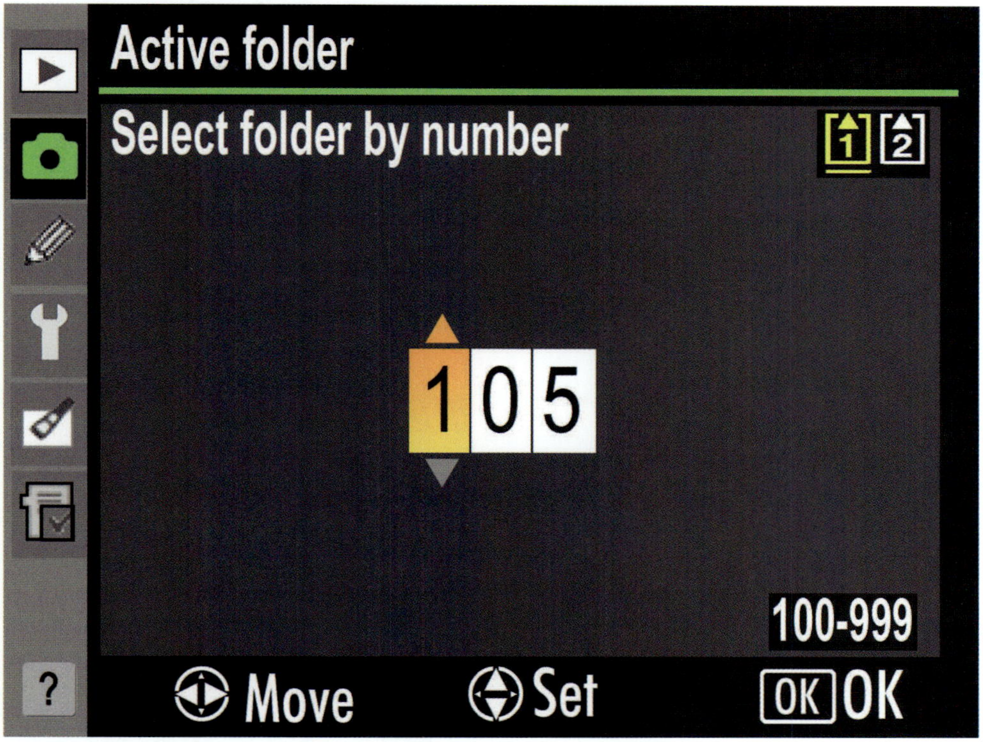


**Figure 3.11** Create a new folder or select an existing folder number.

## File Naming

The D3s/D3x, like other cameras in the Nikon product line, automatically applies a name like _DSC0001.jpg or DSC_0001.nef to your image files as they are created, with matching numbers for the voice memos, using a .wav extension. You can use this menu option to change the names applied to your photos and associated voice memos—but only within certain strict limitations. In practice, you can change only three of the eight characters, the *DSC* portion of the file name. The other five are mandated either by the Design Rule for Camera File System (DCF) specification that all digital camera makers adhere to or to industry conventions.

DCF limits file names created by conforming digital cameras to a maximum of eight characters, plus a three-character extension (such as .jpg, .tif, .nef, or .wav in the case of audio files) that represents the format of the file. The eight-plus-three (usually called 8.3) length limitation dates back to an evil and frustrating computer operating system that we older photographers would like to forget (its initials are D.O.S), but which, unhappily, lives on as the wraith of a file-naming convention.

Of the eight available characters, four are used to represent, in a general sense, the type of camera used to create the image. By convention, one of those characters is an underline, placed in the first position (as in _DSCxxxx.xxx) when the image uses the Adobe

RGB color space (more on color spaces later), and in the fourth position (as in DSC_xxxx.xxx) for sRGB and RAW (NEF) files. That leaves just three characters for the manufacturer (and you) to use. Nikon, Sony, and some other vendors use DSC (which may or may not stand for Digital Still Camera, depending on who you ask), while Canon prefers IMG. The remaining four characters are used for numbers from 0000 to 9999, which is why your D3s/D3x "rolls over" to DSC_0000 again when the 9999 number limitation is reached.

When you select File naming in the Shooting menu, you'll be shown the current settings for both sRGB (and RAW) and Adobe RGB. Press the right multi selector button, and you'll be taken to the (mostly) standard Nikon text entry screen (go back to Figure 3.10 if you've forgotten what it looks like) and allowed to change the DSC value to something else. In this version of the text entry screen, however, only the numbers from 0 to 9 and characters A-Z are available; the file name cannot contain other characters. As always, press the OK button to confirm your new setting.

Because the default DSC characters don't tell you much, don't hesitate to change them to something else. I own, or used to own, a whole collection of Nikon digital cameras, so I've used D40_, D50_, D70_, and D80_ as my templates over the years. My D2X and D200 received D2X_ and D20_ assignments to help me differentiate between pictures taken with each camera. When the D3, D3x, and D700 cameras were introduced, I used 0D3_, D3x_, and 700_. (I used 700 instead of D70 to avoid confusion with the older Nikon D70.) I now use D3S_ for my Nikon D3s files.

If you don't need to differentiate between different camera models, you can change the three characters to anything else that suits your purposes, including your initials (DDB_ or JFK_ for example) or even customize for particular shooting sessions (EUR_, GER_, FRA_, and JAP_ when taking vacation trips). You can also use the file name flexibility to partially overcome the 9999 numbering limitation. You could, for example, use the template 701_ to represent the first 10,000 pictures you take with your D3s/D3x, and then 702_ for the next 10,000, and 703_ for the 10,000 after that.

That's assuming that you don't rename your image files in your computer. In a way, file naming verges on a moot consideration, because, they apply *only* to the images as they exist in your camera. After (or during) transfer to your computer you can change the names to anything you want, completely disregarding the 8.3 limitations (although it's a good idea to retain the default extensions). If you shot an image file named DSC_4832.jpg in your camera, you could change it to Paris_EiffelTower_32.jpg later on. Indeed, virtually all photo transfer programs, including Nikon Transfer and Photoshop Elements Transfer, allow you to specify a template and rename your photos as they are moved or copied to your computer from your camera or memory card.

I usually don't go to that bother (I generally don't use transfer software; I just drag and drop images from my memory card to folders I have set up), but renaming can be useful for those willing to take the time to do it.

## Slot 2

This menu entry allows you to specify the function of the second memory card slot in the Nikon D3s/D3x. You can choose to use the secondary slot to accept overflow images when the slot 1 card fills up; use it to create a backup of all the files stored on the slot 1 card; or elect a third option that splits your RAW+JPEG files between Slot 1 and Slot 2. The function you've selected is displayed in icon form in the center of the rear control panel, as explained in Chapter 2. The D3s's Movie Settings functions (explained later in this chapter) offer a fourth option: you can select which slot is used to store your movie clips (and can therefore choose the largest memory card or fastest memory card for your movies).

As I've mentioned before, the second memory card slot, introduced to the Nikon world with the original D3 (Canon has had this feature on its high-end dSLRs for some time) is one of my favorite features. Nikon has expanded its use to the D3x and D3s, as well as the Nikon D300s (which can use one Compact Flash card and one Secure Digital card simultaneously). My only gripe is that, of currently produced cameras, only the D3x has the ability to use a full-thickness Compact Flash Type II card, which means that my D3x is my only CF-card-using camera that will accept a CF-to-SD adapter that lets me use the EyeFi wireless card. (At least, until EyeFi comes out with a Compact Flash version of their card.)

I'll explain your choices for Slot 2 functions—and the importance of each of them—in the next sections.

### Overflow

In this case, when the memory card in Slot 1 fills up, the D3s/D3x automatically switches over to the card in Slot 2. The changeover happens quickly, and you're not even likely to notice, unless you have your eye on the "slot" indicators on the top LCD monochrome control panel or the shooting information display. There are dozens of ways to use this capability:

- **"Limitless" capacity.** My standard operating procedure is to put one 32GB memory card in each slot. As a practical matter, that means I can shoot all day without changing memory cards, even if I am shooting landscapes and bracketing everything with three- or five-shot sets (either to optimize exposure, or, when the camera is mounted on a tripod, to capture files for later HDR processing). Or, I might be shooting sports/photojournalism, where the practice is to change memory cards when your media is 80 percent full to eliminate the possibility of missing anything important due to a card change at an inopportune time.

- **Small/fast—with backup.** For some sports, if I am shooting at 9 fps, I may want my fastest memory card in Slot 1 to maximize write speed out of the camera's buffer, but the real speed demons in the Compact Flash world can be expensive. So, instead of a 32GB medium-speed card, I may put an 8GB or 16GB UDMA (Ultra Direct Memory Access) card in Slot 1, and back it up with a slightly slower (and cheaper) 16GB or 32GB card. I can capture images with the fastest card I've got, yet not have to worry about missing shots, because I have a backup card installed in Slot 2.
- **Put smaller cards to use.** If you don't think you'll need the overflow capacity, but still want to have it just in case, put a smaller card that you don't use much anymore in Slot 2. If your large card that you didn't think would fill *does* come up short, you won't lose any shots. They'll be directed to that old 4GB card you put in Slot 2 for insurance. I sometimes do this when I am using several cameras and have a limited number of large cards at my disposal. I'll save the big cards for primary use, knowing that any overflow shots will be stored on the small backup cards if necessary.
- **Stretch your budget.** Your D3x produces files that are twice as large as your old 12-megapixel model, but after spending an arm and a leg for a 24.5-megapixel camera, you'd like to avoid replacing your old fast but limited-capacity 8GB memory cards (which have only enough room for 132 RAW+JPEG Fine images) for a little while. (Perhaps you're waiting for those new 64GB cards to come down in price.) With one 8GB card in each slot, you can double your shooting before it's time to swap cards.

## Backup

In this case, each photograph you take is recorded on the memory cards in both Slot 1 and Slot 2. The write process takes slightly longer (so it may not be your best option when shooting sports), but it's otherwise a seamless way to create a backup copy of each and every image you take. If you're shooting RAW+JPEG and voice memos, all three files associated with each image are recorded on both slots. I absolutely love this feature, as I've mentioned before in this book. Here are some of my favorite applications:

- **Critical shots backed up instantly.** When I was a photojournalist, a lot of the images I took, particularly of spot news events, were literally once-in-a-lifetime shots that couldn't be duplicated under any circumstances. I also shot weddings, and while it was sometimes possible to restage a particular setup or pose, that was never a satisfactory option, even if done on the day of the nuptials. So, there was always a degree of trepidation until the film was processed or digital files backed up. With the dual-slot backup capabilities of the D3-series cameras, backup files can be made instantly, as you shoot. What a relief!

- **Great when there's No-Fi.** Many pros (and more than a few amateurs) rely on in-camera Wi-Fi connectivity to beam backups to a nearby laptop computer for safe-keeping, or, at events, so that an assistant can be processing some images while photography continues. But, sometimes that's not possible, or, perhaps, you don't own the necessary equipment. Making a backup in your camera is a great alternative when wireless capabilities are unavailable or impractical. You can even shuttle that Slot 2 card to an assistant at intervals while retaining the "main" copy of your images in the camera.
- **Leave your PSD at home.** When I travel overseas, I like to pack light, with only a carry-on bag that holds my camera gear and some of my clothing, with the rest of my apparel relegated to the second tote that qualifies as a "personal" item. But I've always carried two card reader/personal storage devices so I can make backup copies of my images while I travel. I've found that my dual-card Nikon cameras can easily replace the PSD. I can back up each image as it's shot automatically, or shoot on one card (to allow faster capture) and make a duplicate with a card-to-card copy back in my hotel room in the evening. Or I can use the D3s/D3x's Copy image(s) feature to make an extra copy of only the images I want.
- **Instant copy to share.** Want to give a traveling companion copies of all the images you shoot? Make a backup as you take the photos and hand over the copy on the spot. (Again, if you want to share only *some* of your pictures, you can use the Copy image(s) feature instead.)

## RAW Slot 1—JPEG Slot 2

In this mode, when you're shooting RAW+JPEG, the NEF (RAW) files are saved to the card in Slot 1, and the JPEG files are saved to the card in Slot 2. When you're using any other Quality setting (any JPEG option, or TIFF), the images are stored in Slot 1, until that card fills; then the photos overflow to Slot 2. (This is effectively the same as the Backup option.) You'll find this mode useful under the following conditions:

- **Separate RAW and JPEG.** Perhaps you like to store your RAW and JPEG files in separate locations. This mode makes it easy to do that. Copy the card containing the RAW files to one destination on your computer, and the JPEG files from the other card to a second destination. The only complication is that the memory card in Slot 1 is likely to fill up more quickly than the card with the smaller JPEG files in Slot 2, so if you shoot to the capacity of the card in Slot 1, you'll need to replace it more often than you will the card with the JPEG files. Or, if you want the two cards to be mirror images of each other (but in different formats), you can swap them both out at the same time, with the Slot 2 card only partially full. You can also use a larger card in Slot 1 to allow extra room for the bigger RAW files.

- **Faster backup of RAW+JPEG.** If you shoot RAW+JPEG, using the Backup option (described earlier) means that you're saving *four* files each time you press the shutter release. That can slow you down in some situations if you're rapid-firing a sequence of images. Storing RAW files on one card, and JPEG files on the other is a faster way of capturing a backup, because only two files are saved per click. If you have a problem with one of your JPEG files, you can easily produce a new JPEG from the RAW file. (Nikon Capture NX 2—see Chapter 11—has a batch mode that simplifies creating JPEGs from NEFs *en masse,* in fact.) The reverse is not true, however. If your NEF file gets munged, your RAW information is lost forever, even though you still have the JPEG version. So, use this option carefully if your RAW files are especially important for a particular shooting session.

## Image Quality

As I noted in Chapter 2, you can choose the image quality settings used by the D3s/D3x to store its files. The quickest way to do that is to hold down the Qual button under the rear control panel on the back of the camera and spin the main command dial until the quality setting you want is shown. You can also use this menu option to make the quality settings using the bigger, brighter three-inch color LCD. You might want to do that when you simply prefer the color LCD's display, which can be easier to read. You have three choices to make:

- **JPEG compression.** To reduce the size of your image files and allow more photos to be stored on a given memory card, the D3s/D3x uses JPEG compression to squeeze the images down to a smaller size. This compacting reduces the image quality a little, so you're offered your choice of Fine (a 1:4 reduction), Normal (1:8 reduction), and Basic (1:16) compression. You can see an exaggerated version of the effects of JPEG compression in Figure 3.12. There is a further tweak you can make, specifying whether JPEG compression should be optimized for the smallest possible image size at a given compression level, or whether you'd prefer to sacrifice some compression for optimal quality. You won't find those options in this menu entry; instead, use the JPEG compression menu item, described later in this section.
- **JPEG, RAW, or both.** You can elect to store only JPEG versions of the images you shoot, or you can save your photos as RAW files, which consume more than twice as much space on your memory card. Or, you can store both at once as you shoot (and store them to different memory cards, if you like, using the Slot 2 function described previously). Many photographers elect to save *both* JPEG and a RAW, so they'll have a JPEG version that might be usable as-is, as well as the original "digital negative" RAW file in case they want to do some processing of the image later. You'll end up with two different versions of the same file: one with a .jpg extension, and one with the .nef extension that signifies a Nikon RAW file.

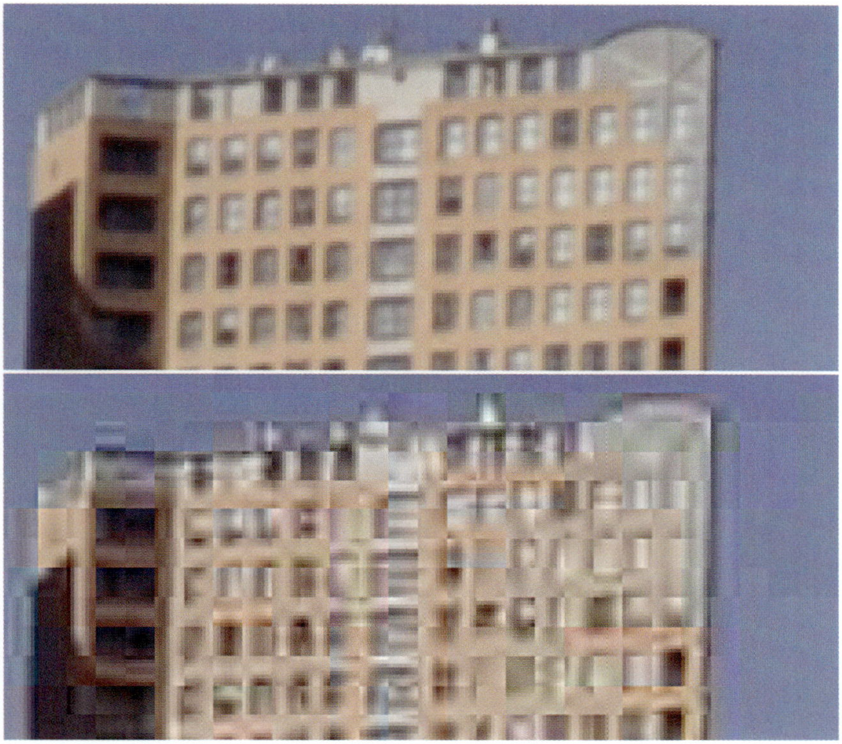

**Figure 3.12**
At low levels of JPEG compression the image looks sharp even when you enlarge it enough to see the actual pixels (top); when using extreme JPEG compression (bottom) an image obviously loses quality.

- **TIFF.** The TIFF format is a lossless uncompressed 8-bit format (at least, in its Nikon incarnation) that is preferred for some applications, such as stock photography. TIFFs are several times larger than RAW files, however, and it takes a long time to store a TIFF file on a memory card (a second or two, at least), so most photographers don't create TIFFs in the camera. It's usually a better idea to produce a TIFF file from a RAW file, which, because it can contain up to 14 bits of information (instead of the Nikon TIFF format's 8 bits), has potentially a wider range of colors captured.

**Tip**

The D3s/D3x always saves a full-resolution 4288 × 2848 pixel (D3s) or 6048 × 4032 pixel (D3x) RAW image even if you choose a smaller image size (resolution) for the JPEG version (such as Medium (M) or Small (S)).

To choose the combination you want, access the Shooting menu, scroll to Image quality, and select it. A screen similar to the one shown in Figure 3.13 will appear. Scroll to highlight the setting you want, and either press OK or push the multi selector right button to confirm your selection.

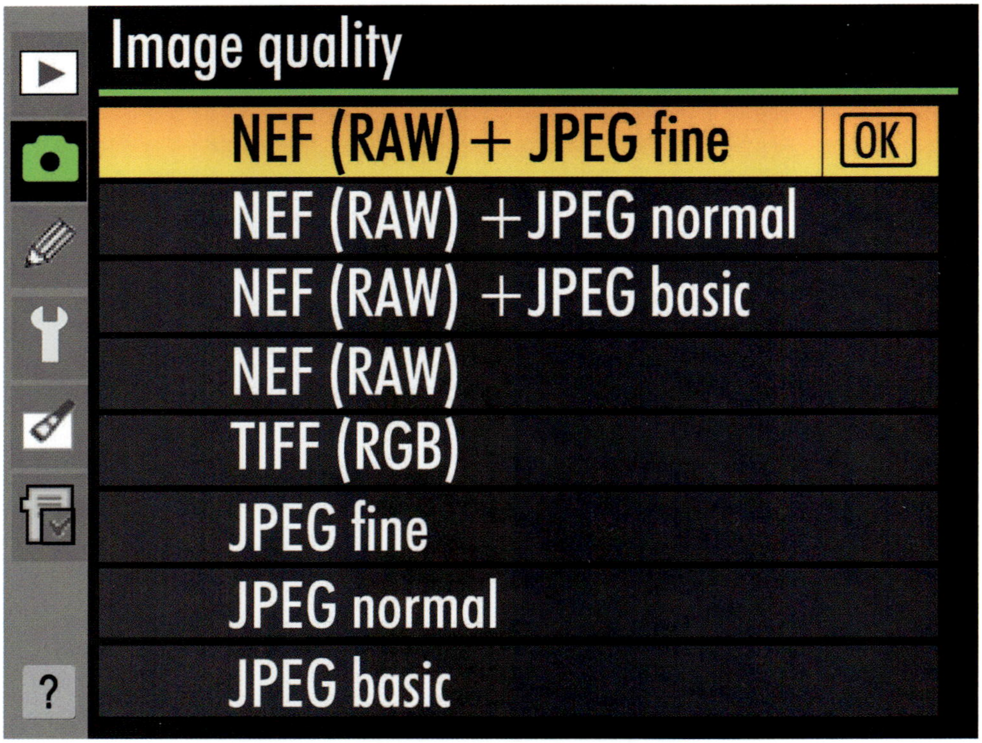


**Figure 3.13** You can choose RAW, JPEG, RAW+JPEG, or TIFF formats here.

In practice, you'll probably use the JPEG Fine, RAW+JPEG Fine selections most often. Why so many choices, then? There are some limited advantages to using the JPEG Normal and JPEG Basic settings, either at full resolution (Large) or when using the Medium and Small resolution settings. Settings that are less than max allow stretching the capacity of your memory card so you can shoehorn quite a few more pictures onto a single memory card. That can come in useful when on vacation and you're running out of storage, or when you're shooting non-critical work that doesn't require 12 megapixels of resolution (such as photos taken for real estate listings, web page display, photo ID cards, or similar applications). Some photographers like to record RAW+JPEG Normal so they'll have a moderate quality JPEG file for review only and no intention of using for editing purposes, while retaining access to the original RAW file for serious editing.

For most work, using lower resolution and extra compression is false economy. You never know when you might actually need that extra bit of picture detail. Your best bet is to have enough memory cards to handle all the shooting you want to do until you have the chance to transfer your photos to your computer or a personal storage device.

However, reduced image quality can sometimes be beneficial if you're shooting sequences of photos rapidly, as the D3s/D3x is able to hold more of them in its internal memory buffer before transferring to the memory card. Still, for most sports and other applications, you'd probably rather have better, sharper pictures than longer periods of continuous shooting. Do you really need 20 or 30 shots of a pass reception in a football game, or a dozen or two slightly different versions of your local basketball star driving in for a lay-up?

## JPEG vs. RAW

You'll sometimes be told that RAW files are the "unprocessed" image information your camera produces, before it's been modified. That's nonsense. RAW files are no more unprocessed than your camera film is after it's been through the chemicals to produce a negative or transparency. A lot can happen in the developer that can affect the quality of a film image—positively and negatively—and, similarly, your digital image undergoes a significant amount of processing before it is saved as a RAW file. Nikon even applies a name (EXPEED) to the digital image processing (DIP) chip used to perform this magic.

A RAW file is more similar to a film camera's processed negative. It contains all the information, captured in 12-bit or 14-bit channels per color (and stored in a 16-bit space), with no sharpening and no application of any special filters or other settings you might have specified when you took the picture. Those settings are *stored* with the RAW file so they can be applied when the image is converted to a form compatible with your favorite image editor. However, using RAW conversion software such as Adobe Camera Raw or Nikon Capture NX, you can override those settings and apply settings of your own. You can select essentially the same changes there that you might have specified in your camera's picture-taking options.

RAW exists because sometimes we want to have access to all the information captured by the camera, before the camera's internal logic has processed it and converted the image to a standard file format. Even Compressed RAW doesn't save as much space as JPEG. What it does do is preserve all the information captured by your camera after it's been converted from analog to digital form.

So, why don't we always use RAW? Some photographers avoid using Nikon's RAW NEF files on the misguided conviction that they don't want to spend time in post-processing, forgetting that, if the camera settings you would have used for JPEG are correct, each RAW image's default attributes will use those settings and the RAW image will not need much manipulation. Post-processing in such cases is *optional*, and overwhelmingly helpful when an image needs to be fine-tuned.

Although some photographers do save *only* in RAW format, it's more common (and frequently more convenient) to use RAW plus one of the JPEG options, or, if you're confident about your settings, just shoot JPEG and eschew RAW altogether. In some situations, working with a RAW file can slow you down a little. RAW images take longer to store on the memory card, and must be converted from RAW to a format your image editor can handle, whether you elect to go with the default settings in force when the picture was taken, or make minor adjustments to the settings you specified in the camera.

As a result, those who depend on speedy access to images or who shoot large numbers of photos at once may prefer JPEG over RAW. Wedding photographers, for example, might expose several thousand photos during a bridal affair and offer hundreds to clients as electronic proofs for inclusion in an album. Wedding shooters take the time to make sure that their in-camera settings are correct, minimizing the need to post-process photos after the event. Given that their JPEGs are so good, there is little need to get bogged down shooting RAW.

Sports photographers also avoid RAW files. I visited a local Division III college one sunny September afternoon. I covered the first half of a football game, trotted down a hill to shoot a women's soccer match later that afternoon, and ended up in the adjacent field house shooting a volleyball invitational tournament an hour later. I managed to shoot 1,920 photos, most of them at a 9 fps clip, in about four hours. I certainly didn't have any plans to do post-processing on very many of those shots, and firing the camera at its maximum frame rate didn't allow RAW shooting, so carefully exposed and precisely focused JPEG images were my file format of choice that day.

JPEG was invented as a more compact file format that can store most of the information in a digital image, but in a much smaller size. JPEG predates most digital SLRs and was initially used to squeeze down files for transmission over slow dial-up connections. Even if you were using an early dSLR with 1.3-megapixel files for news photography, you didn't want to send them back to the office over a modem at 1,200 bps.

But, as I noted, JPEG provides smaller files by compressing the information in a way that loses some image data. JPEG remains a viable alternative because it offers several different quality levels. At the highest quality Fine level, you might not be able to tell the difference between the original RAW file and the JPEG version, even though a lossless compressed, 14-bit RAW file (I'll explain the bit-business later in this chapter) occupies, by Nikon's estimate, 35.7MB (for the D3x) or 14.3 MB (for the D3s) on your memory card, while the Fine JPEG takes up only 14.1/5.9MB (D3x/D3s, respectively) of space. You've squeezed the image by more than 70 percent without losing much visual information at all. If you don't mind losing some quality, you can use more aggressive Normal compression with JPEG to cut the size in half again.

In my case, I shoot virtually everything at RAW+JPEG Fine. Most of the time, I'm not concerned about filling up my memory cards, even when shooting in dual-slot Backup mode, as I usually have a minimum of five 32GB memory cards with me. If I know I may fill up all those cards, I still can resort to my tiny battery-operated personal storage device that can copy 8GB worth of images in about 15 minutes. I also use a netbook with a 160GB internal and an external 320GB hard drive, and (as I mentioned earlier) for short trips, rely on my D3s/D3x's capability of copying directly from one memory card to the other in the camera. When shooting sports I'll shift to JPEG FINE

> **HIDDEN JPEGS**
>
> You may not be aware that your RAW file contains an embedded JPEG file, hidden inside in the JPEG Basic format. It's used to provide thumbnail previews of JPEG files, which is why you may notice an interesting phenomenon when loading a RAW image into a program like Nikon Capture NX2 or Adobe Lightroom. When the software first starts interpreting the RAW image, it may immediately display this hidden JPEG view which has, as you might expect, all the settings applied that you dialed into the camera. Then, as it finishes loading the RAW file, the application (Lightroom in particular) uses its own intelligence to fine-tune the image and display what it thinks is a decent version of the image, replacing the embedded JPEG. That's why you may see complaints that Lightroom or another program is behaving oddly: the initial embedded JPEG may look better than the final version, so it looks as if the application is degrading the image quality as the file loads. Of course, in all cases, once the RAW file is available, you can make your own changes to optimize it to your taste.
>
> There is a second use for these hidden JPEG files. If you shoot RAW without creating JPEG files and later decide you want a JPEG version, there are dozens of utility programs that will extract the embedded JPEG and save it as a separate file. (Google "JPEG extractor" to locate a freeware program that will perform this step for your Mac, PC, or other computer.)

(with no RAW file) to squeeze a little extra speed out of my camera's continuous shooting mode, and to reduce the need to wade through eight-photo bursts taken in RAW format.

You may notice that I am not going into the TIFF option in any detail. To oversimplify things, for most of us, TIFF provides the worst of both worlds: it has heftier storage space requirements than the "worst" case RAW file. For the D3x, the comparative figures are 50.6 megabytes for NEF, uncompressed, 14-bit files, and a whopping 73.5 MB for full-resolution TIFF, and the same relatively limited image editing flexibility as JPEG files. Those who don't mind waiting up to four or five seconds for a single image to be stored to the memory card, and who have prodigious skills at getting their in-camera settings correct the first time, can use TIFF if necessary. The main reason to use TIFF is because of its ability to include an embedded ICC color profile. The format itself doesn't provide much in the way of perceptible quality improvement, and if the image requires extensive editing, it may actually limit the quality of the photo.

## Image Size

The next menu command in the Shooting menu lets you select the resolution, or number of pixels captured as you shoot with your Nikon D3s/D3x. Your choices range from Large (L), Medium (M), and Small (S). On the D3s, those resolutions correspond to

4288 × 2848 pixels/12 megapixels (L); 3216 × 2136/6.8 megapixels (M), and 2144 × 1424/3 megapixels (S) sizes. If you're using the D3x, those resolutions correspond to 6048 × 4032 pixels/24.5 megapixels (L); 4544 × 3024/14 megapixels (M); and 3024 × 2016/6 megapixels (S) sizes. These figures are all for the full-frame FX image area, which Nikon calls *(36 × 24) 1.0x* in the Image area entry of the Shooting menu. Resolutions and megapixels for both cameras depart from those values when using DX format *(24 × 16) 1.5x*, 5:4 format *(30 × 24)* and (on the D3s) 1.2x, which is called *(30 × 20) 1.2x*.

Select image sizes by holding down the Qual button under the rear control panel, while rotating the sub-command dial to change resolution among Large (L), Medium (M), or Small (S). Or, you can use this menu to perform the task (usually because you find the color LCD easier to view under the particular circumstances). There are no additional options available from the Image size menu screen.

## Image Area

This is the first entry on the second page of the Shooting menu (see Figure 3.14) with the Nikon D3s, or the last entry on the first page of the D3x Shooting menu.

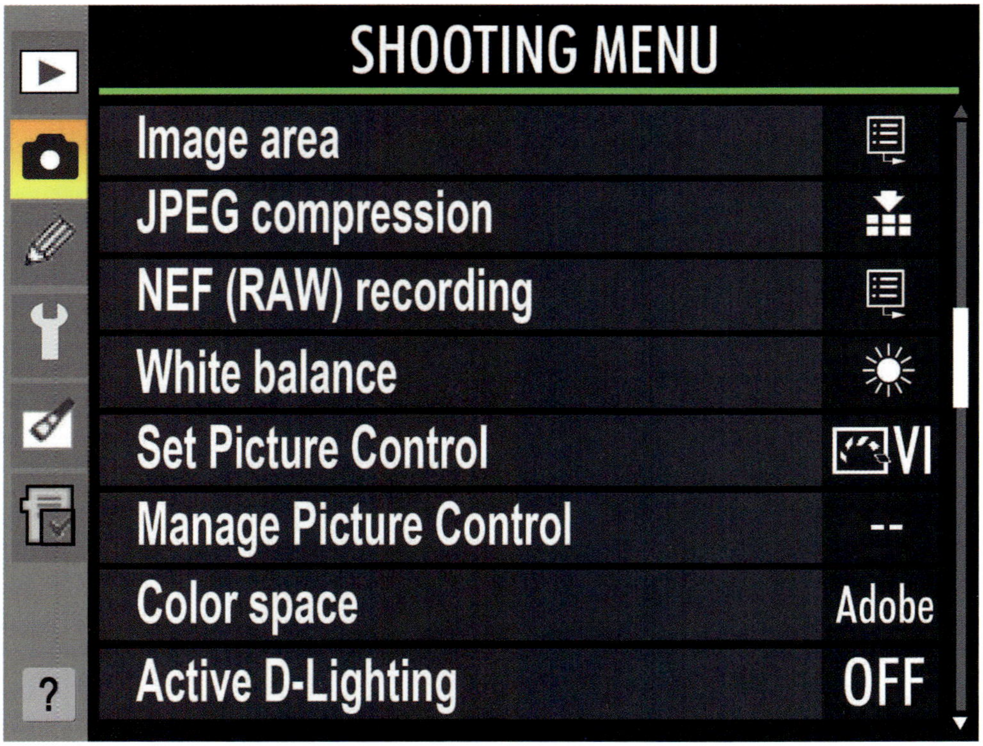


**Figure 3.14**
Image area is the first choice on the second "page" of the Shooting menu of the D3s.

You have two options, Auto DX crop and Choose image area:

- **Auto DX crop.** You can switch this feature On or Off. When activated, the D3s/D3x will detect when a Nikon-brand DX lens is mounted and automatically crop the image to produce a frame filled with the DX coverage area, reducing the resolution of the photo to 5 megapixels (with the D3s) or 10 megapixels (with the D3x). The camera may not detect DX-format lenses from other vendors, in which case you'll need to use the manual image area option described next. Turn Auto DX crop off, and the camera always captures the full frame. You'd want to use that option if you don't mind the vignetting that a DX lens can produce in full-frame mode, or if you're using a lens that you know will cover the full-frame acceptably at the focal length you plan to use.
- **Choose image area.** You can manually specify the image area to be used, which the D3s/D3x will apply regardless of what type of lens is mounted on the camera. Use this option to force the image area issue (as when you're using a DX-format lens that the D3s/D3x can't detect automatically), or to use a particular image area for all your shots in a session. Your choices include:
  - FX format (36 × 24). This is the full FX image format area, roughly 36mm × 24mm.
  - DX format (24 × 16). This fills the image frame with the image in the center 24 × 16mm of the sensor, creating a 1.5x *crop factor*. (See Chapter 9 for more about the crop factor and lenses.)
  - 5:4 (30 × 24). Images are captured using a 5:4 aspect ratio, the same as a 4 × 5 or 8 × 10-inch print.
  - 1.2x (30 × 20) (D3s only). This image area produces an image that fills the frame with a 3:2 aspect ratio (the same proportions as the full-frame image area), but with a 1.2x crop factor. I like to use this setting with some DX-format lenses that don't quite cover the full 36 × 24mm frame, but which do fill up the entire 30 × 20mm image area. For example, I have a 10-17mm fisheye zoom lens that I like to use on my full-frame cameras, but, while I can get an acceptable 10-megapixel image with my D3x in DX mode, I get only a 5-megapixel image in DX mode on the D3s. However, when switching to the 1.2x crop mode, I lose a little bit of the fisheye effect, but get corner-to-corner coverage in a usable 8.4-megapixel image file.

## JPEG Compression

This menu entry is a simple one, offering you the choice of specifying either Size priority (variable compression) or Optimal quality (minimal compression) when the D3s/D3x creates JPEG files. I'll explain image compression in more detail in the next section.

- **Size priority.** When this option is selected, the D3s/D3x will create files that are fairly uniformly sized at roughly 5.8MB for a JPEG Fine image (with the D3s; about twice that for the D3x). Because some photos have content that is more easily compressible (for example, plain areas of sky can be squeezed down more than areas filled with detail), to maintain the standard file size the camera must apply more compression to some images, and less to others. As a result, there may be a barely noticeable loss of detail in the more heavily compressed images. The uniform file size also means that the D3s/D3x's buffer will hold the maximum number of shots during continuous shooting, allowing you to shoot longer sequences without the need to pause and wait for some images to be written to the memory card. I almost never shoot very long sequences, even with sports, so I don't bother with the Size priority option.
- **Optimal quality.** Choose this option if you want to maintain the best image quality possible at a particular JPEG setting (Fine, Normal, or Basic) and don't care if the file size varies. Because the D3s/D3x will use only the minimum amount of compression required at each JPEG setting, file size will vary depending on scene content, and your buffer may hold fewer images during continuous shooting.

## NEF (RAW) Recording

Here you can choose the type (amount) of compression applied to NEF (RAW) files as they are stored on your memory card, and whether the images are stored using 12-bit or 14-bit depth. The default values for type (Lossless compressed) and color depth (12-bit) work best for most situations, but there are times when you might want to use one of the other choices.

Compression is a mathematical technique for reducing the size of a collection of information (such as an image; but other types of data or even programs can be compressed, too) in order to reduce the storage requirements and/or time required to transmit or transfer the information. Some compression algorithms arrange strings of bits that are most frequently used in a table, so that a binary number like, say, 1001011011100111 (16 digits long) doesn't have to be stored as two 8-bit bytes every time it appears in the image file. Instead, a smaller number that points to that position in the table can be used. The more times the pointer is used rather than the full number, the more space is saved in the file. Such a compression scheme can be used to reproduce exactly the original string of numbers, and so is called *lossless* compression.

Other types of compression are more aggressive and actually discard some of the information deemed to be redundant from a visual standpoint, so that, theoretically, you won't *notice* that details are missing, and the file can be made even more compact. The Nikon D3s/D3x's RAW storage routines can use this kind of size reduction, which is called *lossy* compression, to reduce file size by up to about half with very little effect on image quality. JPEG compression can be even more enthusiastic, resulting in images that are 15X smaller (or more) and which display noticeable loss of image quality.

Under Type in the NEF (RAW) recording menu, you can select from

- **Lossless compressed.** This is the default setting, and uses what you might think of as reversible algorithms that discard no image information, so that the image can be compressed from 20-40 percent for a significantly smaller file size. Typically, you'll get up to 400 RAW 12-bit images on a single 8GB memory card with the D3s (or half as many with the D3x) at this setting. The squeezed file can always be restored to its original size precisely, with no effect on image quality.
- **Compressed.** Use this setting if you want to store more images on your memory card and are willing to accept a tiny potential loss in image quality in the highlights, after significant editing (I've never been able to detect any effect at all). The D3s/D3x can achieve from 40-55 percent compression with this option, giving you 550 or more RAW 12-bit exposures on an 8GB Compact Flash card (with the D3s, or about 225 with the D3x). It uses a two-step process, first grouping some very similar tonal values in the mid-tone and lighter areas of the image together, and then storing each group as a single value, followed by a lossless compression scheme that is applied to the dark tones, further reducing the file size. The process does a good job of preserving tones in shadow areas of an image, with only small losses in the midtone and lighter areas. The differences may show up only if you perform certain types of extensive post-processing on an image, such as image sharpening or some tonal corrections.
- **Uncompressed.** At this setting, RAW images are not compressed at all, giving you 350-400 RAW images on an 8GB memory card with the D3s (and up to 200 with the D3x), and also increasing the time needed to transfer these slightly larger files to your memory card. The files are identical to those produced by the lossless compressed option. The only real difference is that some software can handle uncompressed NEF files more readily than lossless compressed files. If you use an up-to-date RAW converter, there's no real reason to use this format.

The Bit Depth setting is another option that looks good on paper but, in the real world, is less useful than you might think. For most applications, the default value that produces 12-bit image files is probably your best choice, unless you're exposing images that will be combined using HDR (high dynamic range) software later on. In that case, you can definitely gain some extra exposure "headroom" using 14-bit processing.

As you may know, bit depth is a way of measuring the amount of color data that an image file can contain. What we call "24-bit color" actually consists of three channels of information—red, green, and blue—with one eight-bit byte assigned to each channel, so a 24-bit image contains three 8-bit channels (each with 256 different shades of red, green, or blue). A 24-bit color image can contain up to 16.8 million different colors (256 × 256 × 256; you do the math). Because each of the red, green, and blue channels always is stored using the same number of bits, it's become the custom to refer only to the channel bit depth to describe the amount of color information that can be collected.

So, when we're talking about 12-bit color, what we really mean are three 12-bit RGB channels, each capable of recording colors from 000000000000 to 111111111111 hues in a particular channel (in binary), or 4096 colors per channel (decimal) and a total of 68,719,476,736 (68.7 billion) different hues. By comparison, 14-bit color offers 16,384 colors per channel and a total of 4,398,046,511,104 (4.4 trillion) colors.

The advantage of having such a humongous number of colors for an image that will, in the end, be boiled down to 16.8 million hues in Photoshop or another image editor is that, to simplify things a little, there is a better chance that the mere millions of colors you end up with have a better chance of being the *right* colors to accurately represent the image. For example, if there are subtle differences in the colors of a certain range of tones that represent only, say, 10 percent of a channel's colors, there would be only 26 colors to choose from in an 8-bit channel, but 410 colors in a 12-bit channel, and a whopping 1638 colors in a 14-bit channel. The larger number of colors improves the odds of ending up with accurate hues.

It's not quite that simple, of course, because bit depth also improves the chances of having the right number of colors to choose from after the inevitable loss of some information due to noise and other factors. But in the real world, the difference between 26 colors and 410 colors is significant (which is why digital cameras always capture at least 12 bits per channel), and the difference between 12 bits and 14 bits (410 and 1638 colors, respectively in our example) is less significant. Because there is a penalty in terms of file size and the amount of time needed to process the image as it is recorded to your memory card, 14-bits-per-channel is usually not your best option. Your two choices look like this:

- **12 bit.** This is the default bit depth for the Nikon D3s/D3x. Images are recorded at 12-bits per channel in the RAW file, and end up with 12 bits of information per channel that is translated during conversion for your image editor either into 12 bits within a 16-bits-per-channel space or interpreted down to 8 bits per channel.
- **14 bit.** At this setting, the D3s/D3x grabs 16,384 colors per channel instead of 4096, ending up as 14 bits in a 16 channel space or reduced to 256 colors by the RAW conversion software that translates the image for your image editor. You'll find that such 14-bit files end up almost one-third larger than 12-bit files, and that your camera's continuous shooting rate falls to 2.5 frames per second (which alone is a good argument for not using the 14-bit setting any time you may need to shoot bursts of images). 14-bit images are great for HDR photography, however.

## White Balance

This menu entry allows you to choose one of the white balance values from among auto, incandescent, seven varieties of fluorescent illumination, direct sunlight, flash, cloudy, shade, a specific color temperature of your choice, a preset value taken from an existing photograph, or a measurement you make. Some of the settings you make here can be duplicated using the WB button on the camera's top-left panel and main and sub-command dials, but the menus offer even more choices, as you'll see. Your white balance settings can have a significant impact on the color rendition of your images, as you can see in Figure 3.15.

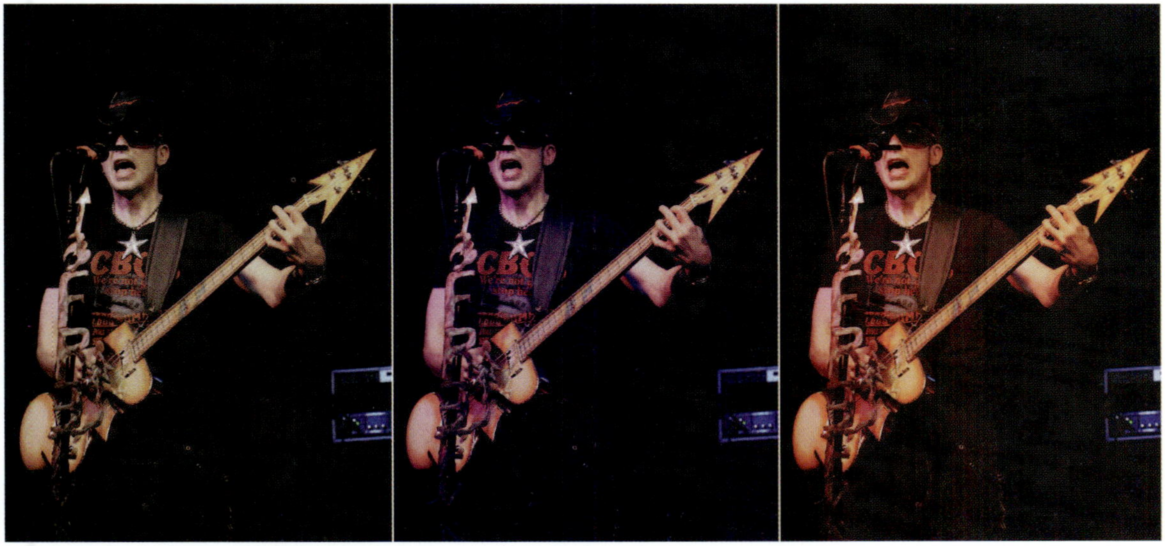

**Figure 3.15** Adjusting color temperature can provide different results of the same subject at settings of 3,400K (left), 5,000K (middle), and 2,800K (right).

In this section, I'm going to describe only the menu commands at your disposal for setting white balance. To learn more about the theory behind why and when you should make white balance adjustments, check out the more complete description in Chapter 6.

When you select the White balance entry on the Shooting menu, you'll see an array of choices like those shown in Figure 3.16. (One additional choice, PRE Preset manual is not visible until you scroll down to it.) If you choose Fluorescent, you'll be taken to another screen that presents seven different types of lamps, from sodium-vapor through warm-white fluorescent down to high temperature mercury-vapor. If you know the exact type of non-incandescent lighting being used, you can select it, or settle on a likely compromise.

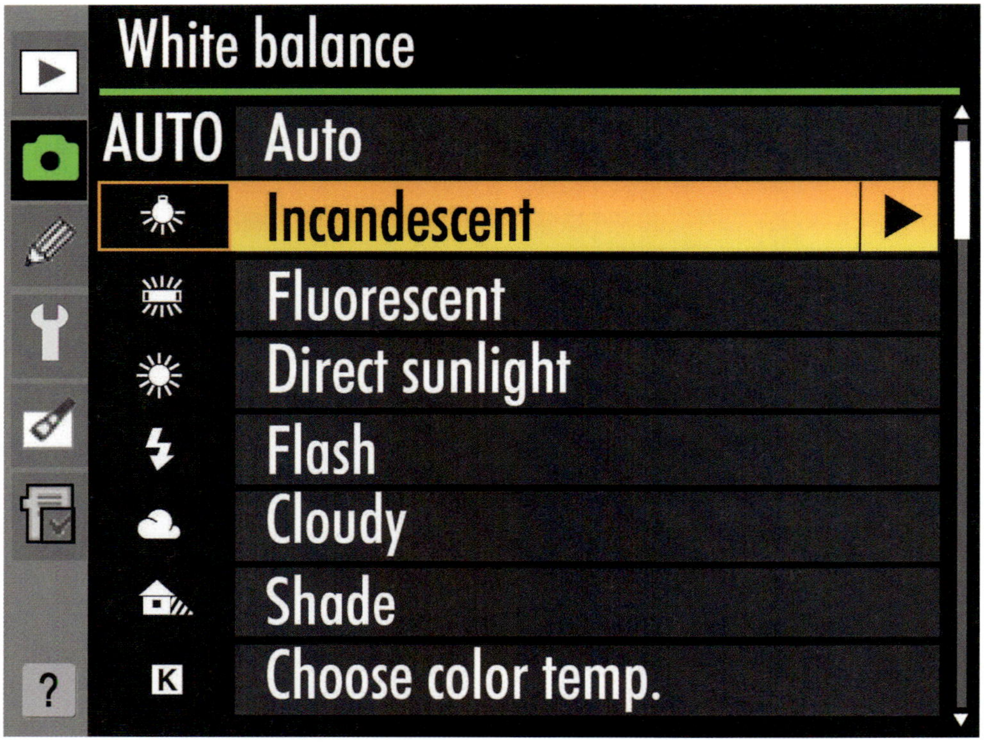


**Figure 3.16** The White Balance menu has predefined values, plus the option of setting color temperature and presets you measure yourself.

### BIG CHANGES

There have been some significant changes in the way white balance is set on the Nikon D3-series cameras, so if you've used earlier cameras (prior to the D300/D300s or D700) you'll want to read this section carefully. Previous mid- and pro-level cameras in the Nikon line offered similar predefined white balance settings, which you could fine-tune by pressing the multi selector right button and then adjusting plus/minus three "levels," which are actually values corresponding to 10 *mireds* (or *micro reciprocal degrees*; more on that measurement in Chapter 6). With earlier cameras, pressing the up button dialed in a slightly cooler color temperature while the down button dialed in a warmer color temperature. No more. The D3s/D3x (as well as the D300s/D3/D700) gives you a *lot* more flexibility than that, as you'll learn from reading on.

The Choose color temp. selection allows you to select from an array of color temperatures in degrees Kelvin (more on this in Chapter 6) from 2,500K to 10,000K, and then further fine-tune the color bias using the fine-tuning feature described next. Select Preset manual to record or recall custom white balance settings suitable for environments with unusual lighting or mixed lighting, as described later in this section.

For all other settings (auto, incandescent, direct sunlight, flash, cloudy, or shade), highlight the white balance option you want, then press the multi selector right button (or press OK) to view the fine-tuning screen shown in Figure 3.17 (and which uses the incandescent setting as an example). The screen shows a grid with two axes, a blue/amber axis extending left/right, and a green/magenta axis extending up and down the grid. By default, the grid's cursor is positioned in the middle, and a readout to the right of the grid shows the cursor's coordinates on the A-B axis (yes, I know the display has the end points reversed) and G-M axis at 0,0.

You can use the multi selector's up/down and right/left buttons to move the cursor to any coordinate in the grid, thereby biasing the white balance in the direction(s) you choose. The amber-blue axis makes the image warmer or colder (but not actually yellow or blue). Similarly, the green-magenta axis preserves all the colors in the original image, but gives them a tinge biased toward green or magenta. Each increment equals about five mired units, but you should know that mired values aren't linear; five mireds at 2,500K produces a much stronger effect than five mireds at 6,000K. If you really want to fine-tune your color balance, you're better off experimenting and evaluating the results of a particular change.

When you've fine-tuned white balance, either using the Shooting menu options or the WB button, left/right triangles appear in the white balance section of the monochrome LCD at lower right to remind you that this tweaking has taken place.

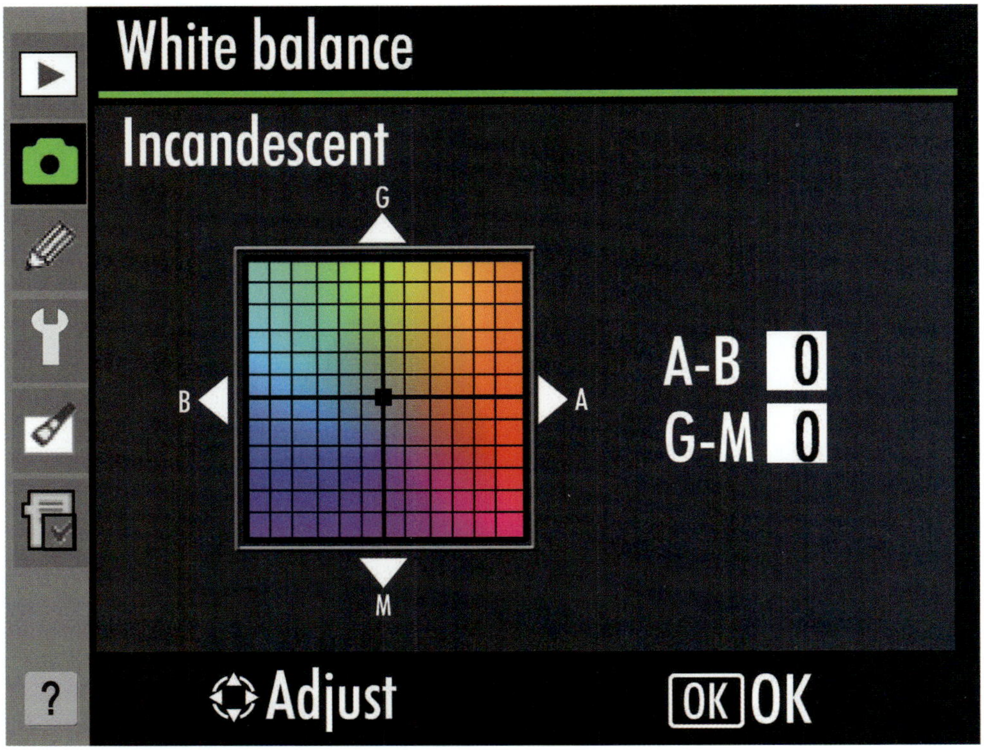


**Figure 3.17** Specific white balance settings can be fine-tuned by changing their bias in the amber/blue, magenta/green directions—or along both axes simultaneously.

## Using Preset Manual White Balance

If automatic white balance or one of the predefined settings available aren't suitable, you can set a custom white balance using the Preset manual menu option. You can apply the white balance from a scene, either by shooting a new picture on the spot and using the resulting white balance (Direct measurement), or using an image you have already shot (Copy from existing photograph). To perform direct measurement from your current scenes, use a reference object. This should preferably be a neutral gray object, such as a commercial gray card available from dealers in Kodak products. In a pinch, a white card can be used, but cards that appear to be white can, in fact, have a slight color cast. Gray cards are more reliably neutral. Then, follow these steps:

1. Place the neutral reference under the lighting you want to measure and fill the frame with it.
2. Hold down the WB button on the rear LCD control panel of the camera and rotate the main command dial until you see PRE displayed in the monochrome LCD.
3. Release the WB button for a moment, then press and hold it again until the PRE icon on the monochrome LCD begins a flashing cycle of about six seconds.
4. While the PRE icon is flashing, take a picture of the reference object. The white balance will be stored in a preset menu slot numbered d-0, as shown in Figure 3.18. No photo is actually taken, so the preset slot appears to be blank.

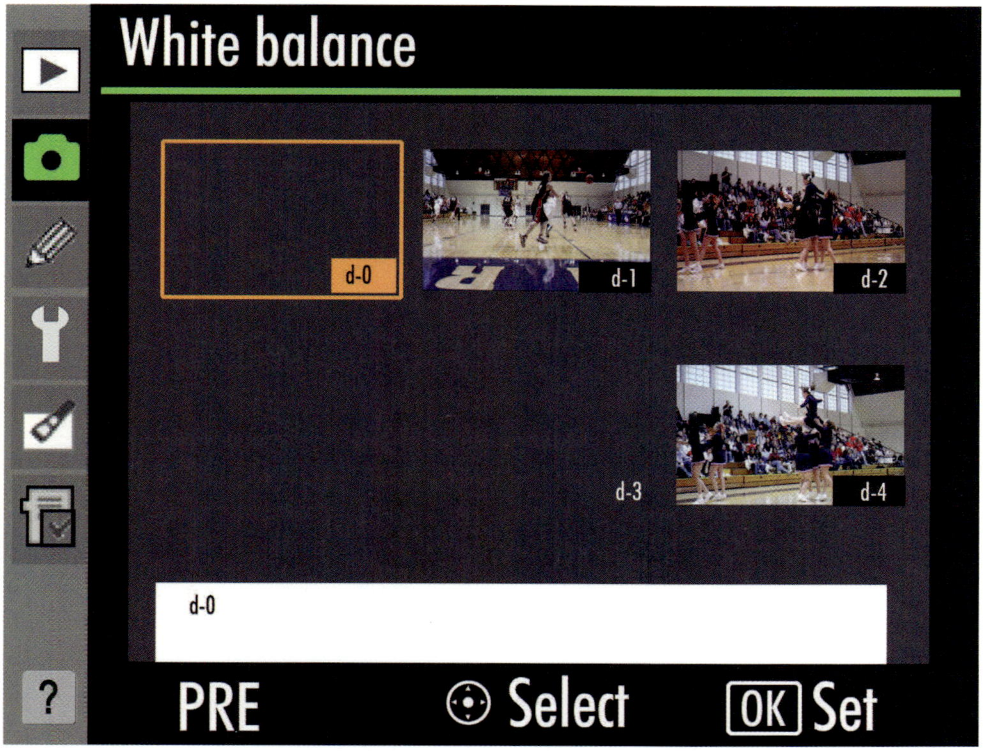


**Figure 3.18**
When you capture a scene's white balance, it will be stored in slot d-0.

5. If the camera successfully measured white balance, Good will flash on the monochrome LCD for about six seconds, and Gd will appear in the bottom line of the viewfinder. Otherwise, you'll see no Gd on the LCD and viewfinder. White balance measurement can fail when the reference object is too brightly or poorly illuminated. In that case, repeat steps 2-5 until the measurement is successful.

The preset value you've captured will remain in slot d-0 until you replace that white balance with a new captured value. It can be summoned at any time (press the WB button on the top left of the camera and dial it in by rotating the sub-command dial until d-0 is displayed on the monochrome LCD). If you want to preserve the captured white balance, it can be copied to one of four additional slots, numbered d-1 to d-4. You can also use those four slots to store white balance information from a picture you've already taken, using the Copy from existing photograph option, as described next:

1. Choose Preset manual from the White balance menu.
2. A screen of thumbnails appears, showing the additional four "slots" numbered d-1 to d-4, which you can use to store information from slot d-0, or from images that contain the white balance information you want to apply. Use the multi selector buttons to highlight one of the four thumbnail slots, and press the multi selector center button.
3. The next screen that appears (see Figure 3.19) has four options: Set, Edit comment, Select image, and Copy d-0.
   - Choose Set to fine-tune the amber/blue/magenta/green white balance of an image already stored in d-0 or one of the four user slots.
   - Choose Edit comment to add or change the comment applied to d-0 to d-4. The comment can be used as a label to better identify the white balance information in the slot, with terms like Gymnasium daytime or Rumpus room. (The standard D3s/D3x Edit comment screen, as in Figure 3.10, appears.)
   - Choose Select image to view the D3s/D3x's standard image selection screen (see Figure 3.8 again) and highlight and choose the existing image slot you want to use. Press the multi selector center button to confirm your choice and copy the white balance of the selected image to the slot you selected in Step 2.
   - Choose Copy d-0 to copy the white balance setting currently stored in slot d-0 to the slot you selected in Step 2. Use this to preserve a captured white balance setting, freeing d-0 for a new capture.
4. Press OK to confirm your white balance setting.

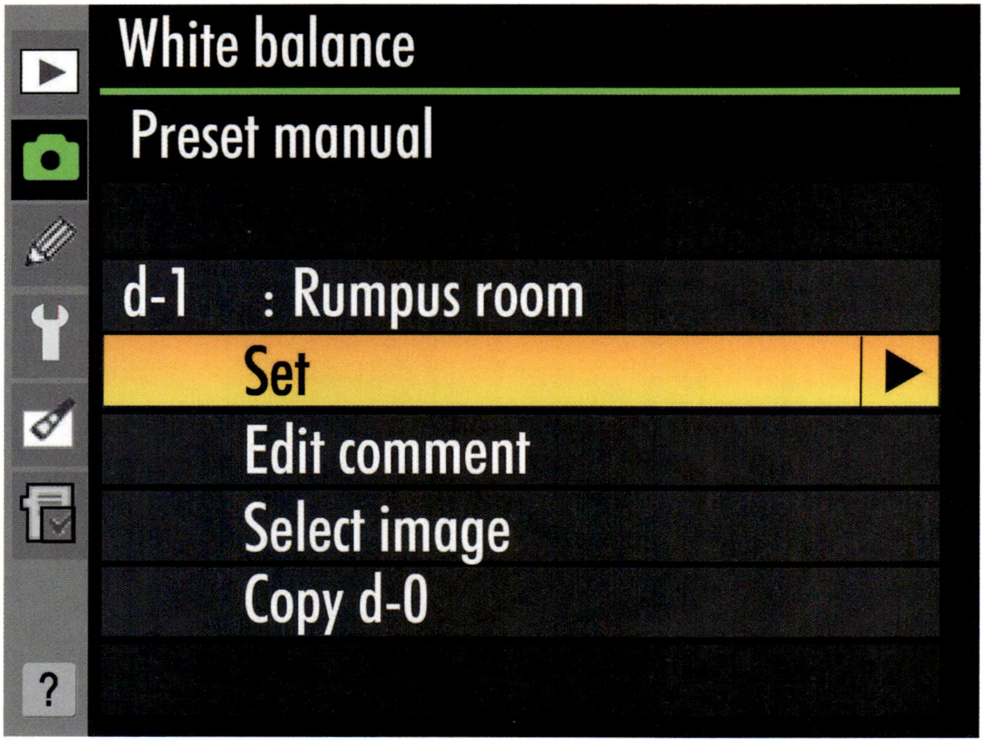


**Figure 3.19**
The Preset manual screen lets you fine-tune preset white balance settings, label them with a comment, select an image to use as a white balance reference, and copy captured settings.

**A WHITE BALANCE LIBRARY**

Consider dedicating a low-capacity memory card to stow a selection of images taken under a variety of lighting conditions. If you want to "recycle" one of the color temperatures you've stored, insert the card and load one of those images into your choice of preset slots d-1 to d-4, as described above.

## Set Picture Control

Nikon's Picture Control styles are a major improvement over the Optimize image feature found in some earlier Nikon cameras when it comes to choosing your own sharpness, contrast, color saturation, and hue settings applied to your images. If you have used a camera with the Optimize image option, you'll recall that it offered five fixed settings to choose from (Normal, Softer, Vivid, More vivid, Portrait), plus Black-and-white, and a single Custom entry that allowed you to specify sharpening, tone compensation (contrast), color mode, saturation, and hue. Yes, that's right—you got *one* Custom Setting slot, and although you could create your own custom settings on your computer and upload them to the camera, the five predefined settings and single set of custom parameters was quite a limitation.

Happily, the Nikon D3s/D3x sweeps those limitations aside with the Picture Control styles. There are only four predefined styles offered, which Nikon calls Original Picture Controls: Standard, Neutral, Vivid, and Monochrome. However, you can *edit* the settings of any of those styles so they better suit your taste. But that's only the beginning; the D3s/D3x also offers *nine* (count 'em) user-definable Picture Control styles, which you can edit to your heart's content, assign descriptive names, and deploy at the press of a few buttons. Even better, you can *copy* these styles to a memory card, edit them on your computer, and reload them into your camera at any time. So, effectively, you can have a lot more than nine custom Picture Control styles available: the nine in your camera, as well as a virtually unlimited library of user-defined styles that you have stored on memory cards.

Moreover, Nikon insists that these styles have been standardized to the extent that if you re-use a style created for one camera (say, your D3s/D3x) and load it into a different compatible camera (such as a Nikon D3), you'll get substantially the same rendition. In a way, Picture Control styles are a bit like using a particular film. Do you want the look of Kodak Ektachrome or Fujifilm Velvia? Load the appropriate style created by you—or anyone else.

Using and managing Picture Control styles is accomplished using two different menu entries, Set Picture Control, which allows you to choose an existing style and to edit the predefined styles that Nikon provides, and Manage Picture Control, discussed in the next section, which gives you the capability of creating and editing user-defined styles.

## Choosing a Picture Control Style

To choose from one of the predefined styles (Standard, Neutral, Vivid, or Monochrome) or select a user-defined style (numbered C-1 to C-9), follow these steps:

1. Choose Set Picture Control from the Shooting menu. The screen shown in Figure 3.20 appears. Note that Picture Controls that have been modified from their standard settings have an asterisk next to their name.
2. Scroll down to the Picture Control you'd like to use.
3. Press OK to activate the highlighted style. (Although you can usually select a menu item by pressing the multi selector right button, in this case, that button activates editing instead.)
4. Press the Menu button or tap the shutter release to exit the menu system.

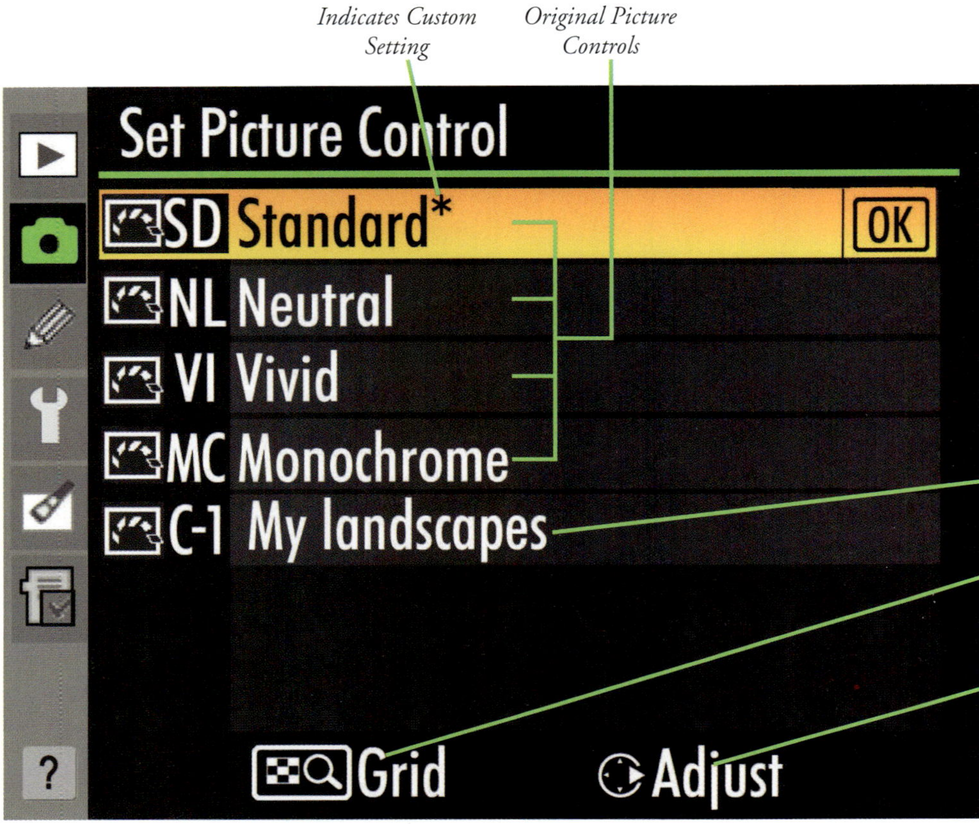


**Figure 3.20**
You can choose from the four predefined Picture Controls, or select a user-defined style, such as *C-1 My landscapes* shown here.

## Editing a Picture Control Style

You can change the parameters of any of Nikon's predefined Picture Controls, or any of the nine user-defined styles you create. You are given the choice of using the quick adjust/fine-tune facility to modify a Picture Control with a few sliders, or to view the relationship of your Picture Controls on a grid. To make quick adjustments to any Picture Control except the Monochrome style, follow these steps:

1. Choose Set Picture Control from the Shooting menu.
2. Scroll down to the Picture Control you'd like to edit.
3. Press the multi selector right button to produce the adjustment screen shown in Figure 3.21.
4. Use the Quick adjust slider to exaggerate the attributes of the Standard or Vivid styles (Quick adjustments are not available with other styles).
5. Scroll down to the Sharpening, Contrast, Brightness, Saturation, and Hue sliders with the multi selector up/down buttons, then use the left/right buttons to decrease or increase the effects. A line will appear under the original setting in the slider whenever you've made a change from the defaults. Note: You can't adjust contrast

and brightness when Active D-Lighting (discussed later in this chapter) is active. Turn it off to make those Picture Control adjustments.

6. Instead of making changes with the slider's scale, you can move the cursor to the far left and choose A (for auto) instead when working with the Sharpening, Contrast, and Saturation sliders. The D3s/D3x will adjust these parameters automatically, depending on the type of scene it detects.
7. Press the Trash button to reset the values to their defaults.
8. Press the Thumbnail/Zoom out button to view an adjustment grid (discussed next).
9. Press OK when you're finished making adjustments.

Editing the Monochrome style is similar, except that the parameters differ slightly. Sharpening, Contrast, and Brightness are available, but, instead of Saturation and Hue, you can choose a filter effect (Yellow, Orange, Red, Green, or none) and a toning effect (black-and-white, plus seven levels of Sepia, Cyanotype, Red, Yellow, Green, Blue Green, Blue, Purple Blue, and Red Purple). (Keep in mind that once you've taken a JPEG photo using a Monochrome style, you can't convert the image back to full color.)

You can create your own Picture Control styles using Nikon ViewNX, and save them using a .ncp extension. You can also try Googling for more styles online, but I haven't found an extensive stash of them in my searches.

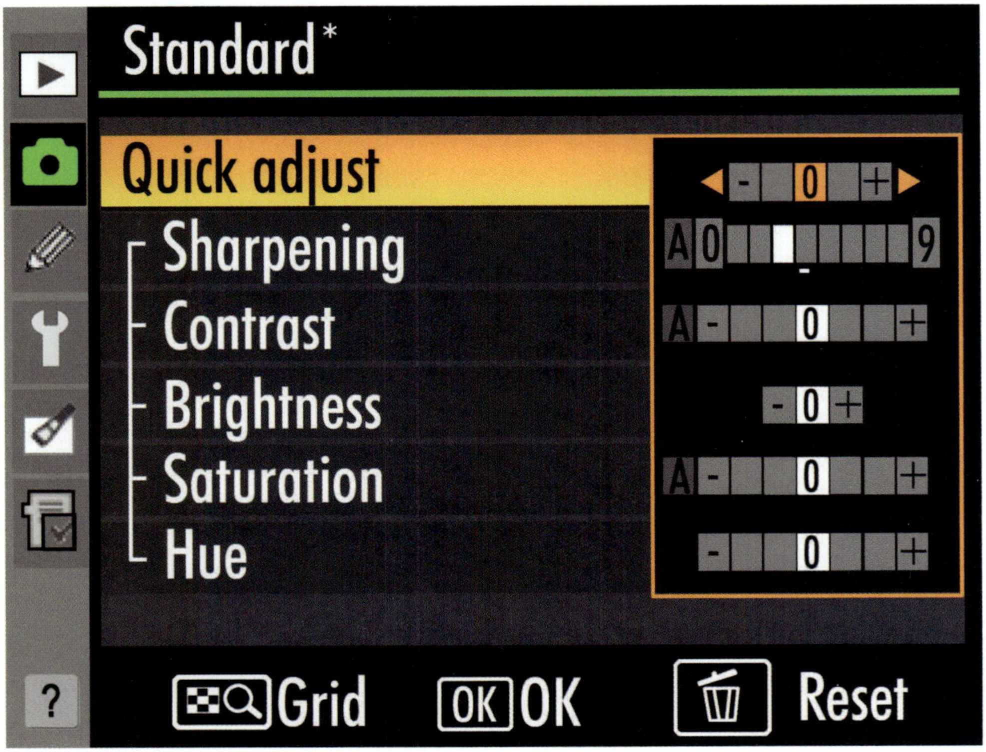


**Figure 3.21** Sliders can be used to make quick adjustments to your Picture Control styles.

## FILTERS VS. TONING

Although some of the color choices seem to overlap, you'll get very different looks when choosing between Filter Effects and Toning. Filter Effects add no color to the monochrome image. Instead, they reproduce the look of black-and-white film that has been shot through a color filter. That is, Yellow will make the sky darker and the clouds will stand out more, while Orange makes the sky even darker and sunsets more full of detail. The Red filter produces the darkest sky of all and darkens green objects, such as leaves. Human skin may appear lighter than normal. The Green filter has the opposite effect on leaves, making them appear lighter in tone. Figure 3.22 shows the same scene shot with no filter, then Yellow, Green, and Red filters.

The Sepia, Blue, Green, and other toning effects, on the other hand, all add a color cast to your monochrome image. Use these when you want an old-time look or a special effect, without bothering to recolor your shots in an image editor.

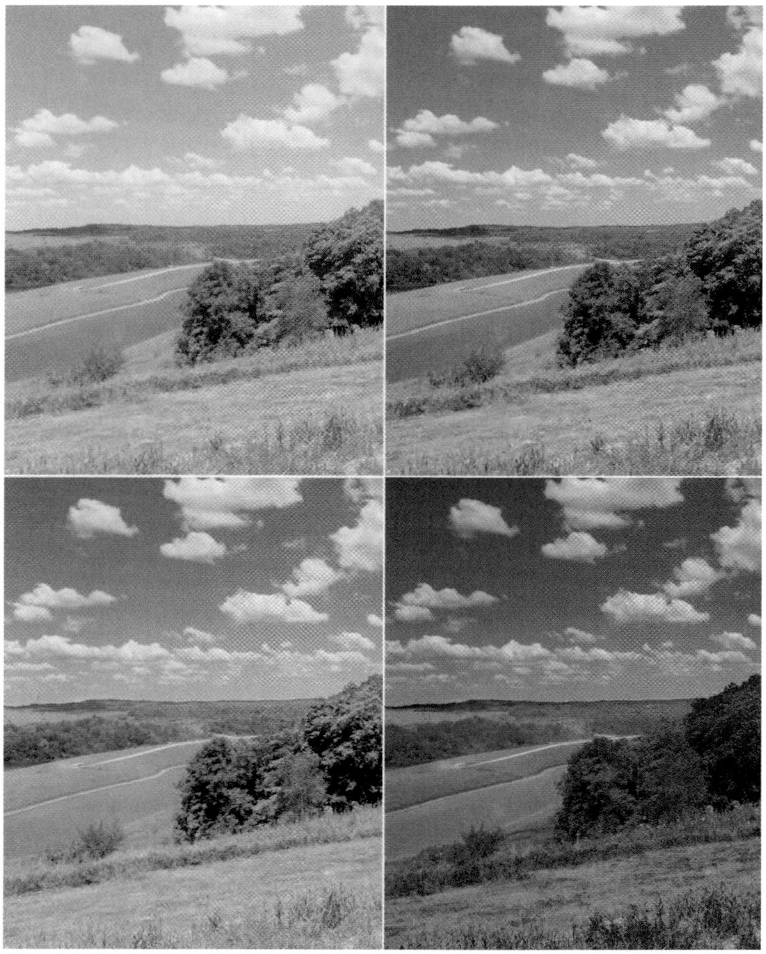

**Figure 3.22**
No filter (upper left); yellow filter (upper right); green filter (lower left); and red filter (lower right).

When you press the Thumbnail/Zoom out button, a grid display, like the one shown in Figure 3.23, appears, showing the relative contrast and saturation of each of the predefined Picture Controls. If you've created your own custom Picture Controls, they will appear on this grid, too, represented by the numbers 1-9. Because the values for autocontrast and autosaturation may vary, the icons for any Picture Control that uses the Auto feature will be shown on the grid in green, with lines extending up and down from the icon to tip you off that the position within the coordinates may vary from the one shown.

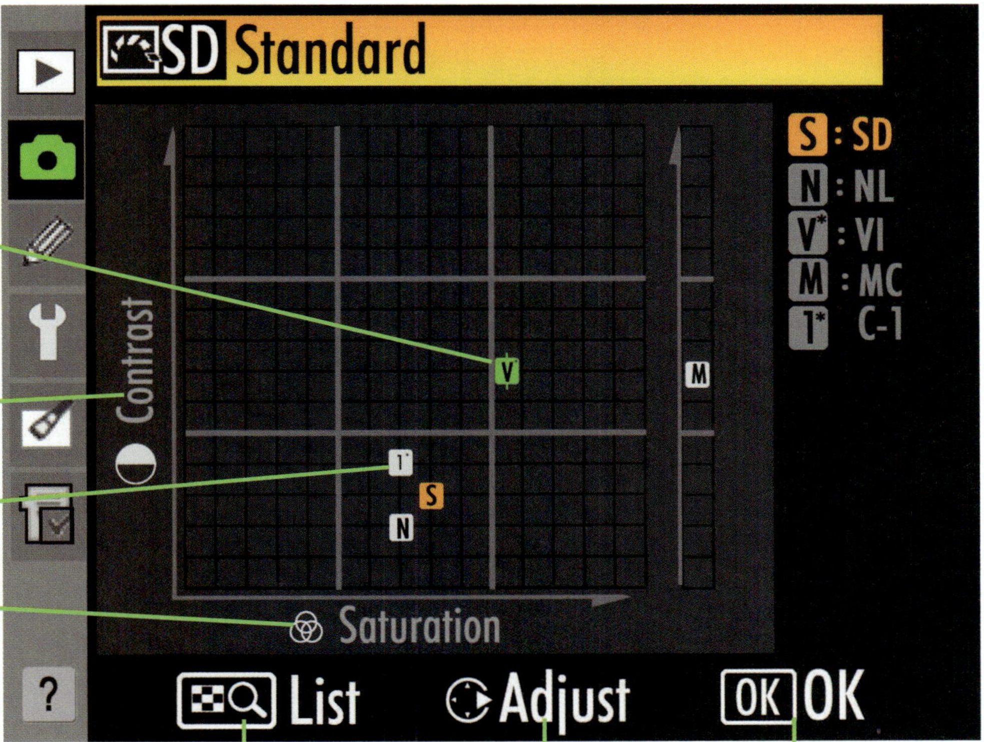


**Figure 3.23** This grid shows the relationship of the Picture Controls being used.

## Manage Picture Control

The Manage Picture Control menu entry can be used to create new styles, edit existing styles, rename or delete them, and store/retrieve them from the memory card. Here are the basic functions of this menu item, which can be found on the Shooting menu directly below the Set Picture Control entry:

- **Make a copy.** Choose Save/edit, select from the list of available Picture Controls, and press OK to store that style in one of the user-defined slots C-1 to C-9 (with slots C1 to C7 shown in Figure 3.24).

- **Save an edited copy.** Choose Save/edit, select from the list of available Picture Controls, and then press the multi selector right button to edit the style, as described in the previous section. Press OK when finished editing, and then save the modified style in one of the user-defined slots C-1 to C-9.
- **Rename a style.** Choose Rename, select from the list of user-defined Picture Controls (you cannot rename the default styles), and then enter the text used as the new label for the style, using the standard D3s/D3x text entry screen shown earlier in Figure 3.10. You may use up to 19 characters for the name.
- **Remove a style.** Select Delete, choose from the list of user-defined Picture Controls (you can't remove one of the default styles), press the multi selector right button, then highlight Yes in the screen that follows, and press OK to remove that Picture Control.
- **Store/retrieve style on card.** Choose Load/save, then select Copy to camera to locate a Picture Control on your Compact Flash card and copy it to the D3s/D3x; Delete from card to select a Picture Control on your memory card and remove it; or Copy to card to duplicate a style currently in your camera onto the Compact Flash card. This last option allows you to create and save Picture Controls in excess of the nine that can be loaded into the camera at one time. Once you've copied a style to your memory card, you can modify the version in the camera, give it a new name, and, in effect, create a whole new Picture Control.

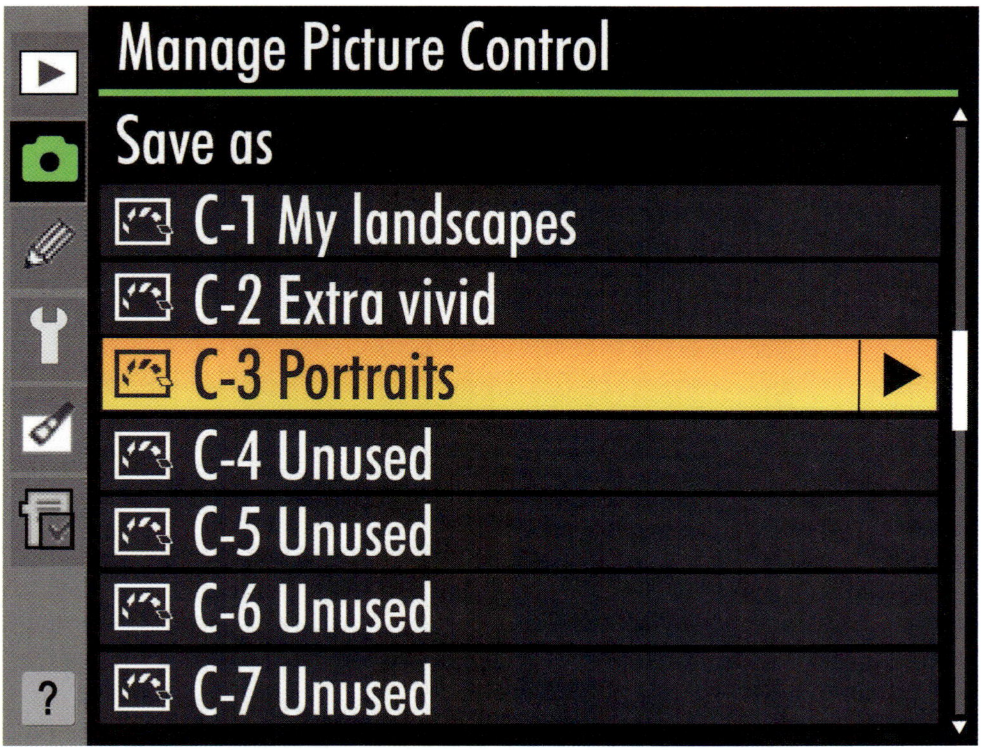


**Figure 3.24** Picture Controls that you define can be stored in your D3s/D3x's settings.

## Color Space

The Nikon D3s/D3x's Color space option gives you two different color spaces (also called *color gamuts*), named Adobe RGB (because it was developed by Adobe Systems in 1998), and sRGB (supposedly because it is the *standard* RGB color space). These two color gamuts define a specific set of colors that can be applied to the images your D3s/D3x captures.

You're probably surprised that the Nikon D3s/D3x doesn't automatically capture *all* the colors we see. Unfortunately, that's impossible because of the limitations of the sensor and the filters used to capture the fundamental red, green, and blue colors, as well as that of the phosphors used to display those colors on your camera and computer monitors. Nor is it possible to *print* every color our eyes detect, because the inks or pigments used don't absorb and reflect colors perfectly.

On the other hand, the D3s/D3x does capture quite a few more colors than we need. The original 12-bit RAW image contains a possible 68 *billion* different hues, which are condensed down to a mere 16.8 million possible colors when converted to a 24-bit (eight bits per channel) image. While 16.8 million colors may seem like a lot, it's a small subset of 68 billion captured, and an even smaller subset of all the possible colors we can see.

The set of colors, or gamut, that can be reproduced or captured by a given device (scanner, digital camera, monitor, printer, or some other piece of equipment) is represented as a color space that exists within the larger full range of colors. That full range is represented by the odd-shaped splotch of color shown in Figure 3.25, as defined by scientists

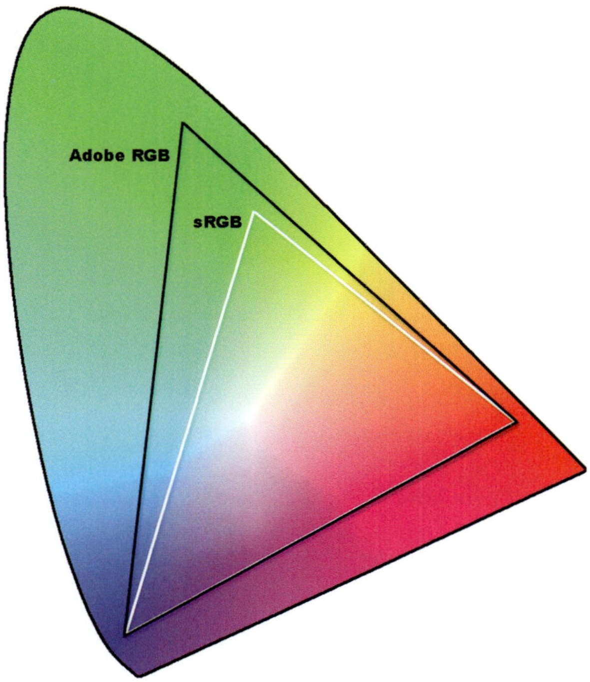


**Figure 3.25** The outer figure shows all the colors we can see; the two inner outlines show the boundaries of Adobe RGB (black triangle) and sRGB (white triangle).

at an international organization back in 1931. The colors possible with Adobe RGB are represented by the larger, black triangle in the figure, while the sRGB gamut is represented by the smaller white triangle.

Regardless of which triangle—or color space—is used by the D3s/D3x, you end up with some combination of 16.8 million different colors that can be used in your photograph. (No one image will contain all 16.8 million! If each and every pixel in a D3s/D3x's 12-megapixel image were a different color—which is extremely unlikely—you'd need only 12 million different colors.) But, as you can see from the figure, the colors available will be *different.*

Adobe RGB is an expanded color space useful for commercial and professional printing, and it can reproduce a wider range of colors. It can also come in useful if an image is going to be extensively retouched, especially within an advanced image editor, like Adobe Photoshop, which has sophisticated color management capabilities that can be tailored to specific color spaces. As an advanced user, you don't need to automatically "upgrade" your D3s/D3x to Adobe RGB, because images tend to look less saturated on your monitor and, it is likely, significantly different from what you will get if you output the photo to your personal inkjet. (You can *profile* your monitor for the Adobe RGB color space to improve your on-screen rendition.)

While both Adobe RGB and sRGB can reproduce the exact same 16.8 million absolute colors, Adobe RGB spreads those colors over a larger portion of the visible spectrum, as you can see in the figure. Think of a box of crayons (the jumbo 16.8 million crayon variety). Some of the basic crayons from the original sRGB set have been removed and replaced with new hues not contained in the original box. Your "new" box contains colors that can't be reproduced by your computer monitor, but which work just fine with a commercial printing press. For example, Adobe RGB has more "crayons" available in the cyan-green portion of the box, compared to sRGB, which is unlikely to be an advantage unless your image's final destination are the cyan, magenta, yellow, and black inks of a printing press.

The other color space, sRGB, is recommended for images that will be output locally on the user's own printer, as this color space matches that of the typical inkjet printer fairly closely. You might prefer sRGB, which is the default for the Nikon D3s/D3x and most other cameras, as it is well suited for the range of colors that can be displayed on a computer screen and viewed over the Internet.

## BEST OF BOTH WORLDS

If you plan to use RAW+JPEG for most of your photos, go ahead and set sRGB as your color space. You'll end up with JPEGs suitable for output on your own printer, but you can still extract an Adobe RGB version from the RAW file at any time. It's like shooting two different color spaces at once—sRGB and Adobe RGB—and getting the best of both worlds.

Of course, choosing the right color space doesn't solve the problems that result from having each device in the image chain manipulating or producing a slightly different set of colors. To that end, you'll need to investigate the wonderful world of *color management*, which uses hardware and software tools to match or *calibrate* all your devices, as closely as possible, so that what you see more closely resembles what you capture, what you see on your computer display, and what ends up on a printed hardcopy. Entire books have been devoted to color management, and most of what you need to know doesn't directly involve your Nikon D3s/D3x, so I won't detail the nuts and bolts here.

To manage your color, you'll need, at the bare minimum, some sort of calibration system for your computer display, so that your monitor can be adjusted to show a standardized set of colors that is repeatable over time. (What you see on the screen can vary as the monitor ages, or even when the room light changes.) I use Pantone's Huey monitor color correction system for my computer's main 26-inch wide-screen LCD display, as well as for the matching 26-inch wide-screen secondary display that flanks it. The Huey checks room light levels every five minutes, and reminds me to recalibrate every week or two, using the small sensor device shown in Figure 3.26, which attaches temporarily to the front of screen with tiny suction cups, and interprets test patches that the Huey software displays during calibration. The rest of the time, the Huey sensor sits in the stand shown, measuring the room illumination and adjusting my monitors for higher or lower ambient light levels.

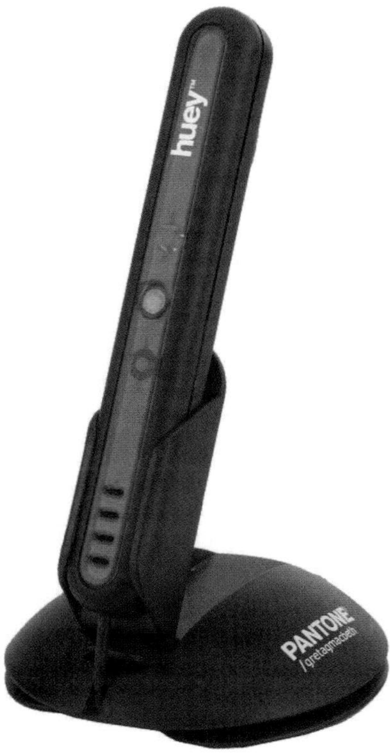


**Figure 3.26**
Pantone's Huey monitor color correction system is an inexpensive device for calibrating your display.

The Huey (www.pantone.com) is an inexpensive (under $100) system that does a good job of calibrating a single monitor. You can upgrade it, as I did, for use with multiple monitors using a $40 software download. If you want more advanced capabilities for adjustments for accurate color and making prints, you might want a more advanced system (up to $500) like the various Spyder products from Datacolor (www.datacolor.com), or Colormunki from X-Rite (www.colormunki.com).

## Active D-Lighting

Active D-Lighting is a feature that improves the rendition of detail in highlights and shadows when you're photographing high contrast scenes. It's been available as an internal retouching option in Nikon's lower-end cameras (by that I mean the CoolPix point-and-shoot line) for some time, and has gradually worked its way up through the company's dSLR products, eventually reaching the D300-series and the "pro" cameras like the D3/D3s/D3x, and D700. You'll find the "non-active" D-Lighting feature in the Retouch menu, which I'll describe in Chapter 5.

A new wrinkle, however, is the Active D-Lighting capability introduced with Nikon's new higher-end models, which, unlike the Retouch menu post-processing feature, applies its tonal improvements *while you are actually taking the photo.* That's good news and bad news. It means that, if you're taking photos in a contrasty environment, Active D-Lighting can automatically improve the apparent dynamic range of your image as you shoot, without additional effort on your part. However, you'll need to disable the feature once you leave the high contrast lighting behind, and the process does take some time. You wouldn't want to use Active D-Lighting for continuous shooting of sports subjects, for example. There are many situations in which the selective application of D-Lighting using the Retouch menu is a better choice.

You have six choices: Auto, Extra High, High, Normal, Low, and Off. You may need to experiment with the feature a little to discover how much D-Lighting you can apply to a high contrast image before the shadows start to darken objectionably. Note that when this feature is activated, brightness and contrast Picture Control settings cannot be changed. Figure 3.27 shows some examples of Active D-Lighting applied. By the time the sample images shown have been half-toned and rendered to the printed page, the differences may be fairly subtle. For that reason, I'm not illustrating the effects of the Auto setting (which varies, of course, depending on the scene) or the Extra High setting. Look at the amount of detail in the shadow cast by overhanging rock in the upper-right area of each version.

For best results, use your D3s/D3x's matrix metering mode, so the Active D-Lighting feature can work with a full range of exposure information from multiple points in the image. Active D-Lighting works its magic by subtly *underexposing* your image so that details in the highlights (which would normally be overexposed and become featureless white pixels) are not lost. At the same time, it adjusts the values of pixels located in

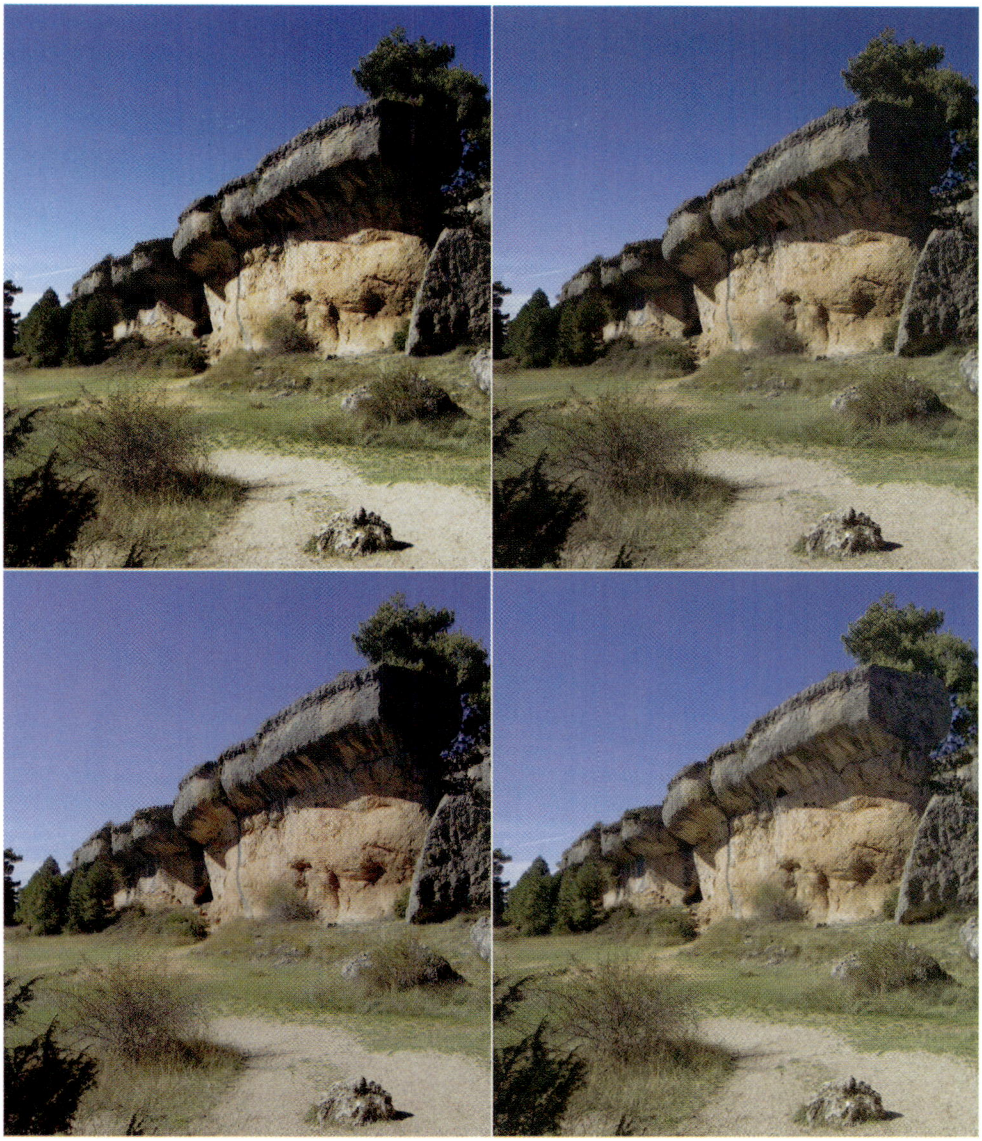

**Figure 3.27**
No D-Lighting (upper left); low (upper right); normal (lower left); and high (lower right).

midtone and shadow areas so they don't become too dark because of the underexposure. Highlight tones will be preserved, while shadows will eventually be allowed to go dark more readily. Bright beach or snow scenes, especially those with few shadows (think high noon, when the shadows are smaller) can benefit from using Active D-Lighting.

It's important to *always* keep in mind that Active D-Lighting not only adjusts the contrast automatically of your image (that's why you can't adjust the brightness/contrast of a Picture Control when Active D-Lighting is turned on), it modifies exposure for both existing light and flash as well, as I've noted. Exposure for both is reduced from about 1/3 stop (at the Low setting) to as much as 1 full stop less at the Extra High setting.

**Tip**

In manual exposure mode, Active D-Lighting does not adjust the exposure of your image; it simply shifts the center (zero) point of the analog exposure indicator in the viewfinder/LCD.

Nikon gives you a lot of flexibility in using Active D-Lighting. You can choose the setting yourself, or let the camera *vary* the amount of tweaking by using Active D-Lighting bracketing, which I'll explain in the general bracketing discussion in Chapter 6. You'll find this is a useful feature, if used with caution.

## Vignette Control

This is the first entry in the third page of the Shooting menu with the D3s (see Figure 3.28) or the last entry on the second page of the D3x Setup menu. Some lenses may not be up to the challenge of covering the full FX frame evenly, producing darkening in the corners of your images at certain focal lengths. That was the chief beef many D3-series and D700 users had with the otherwise superb original version of the Nikon 70-200 f/2.8 VR zoom. (It's since been replaced with a new VR II version that does a better job of avoiding vignetting effects.)

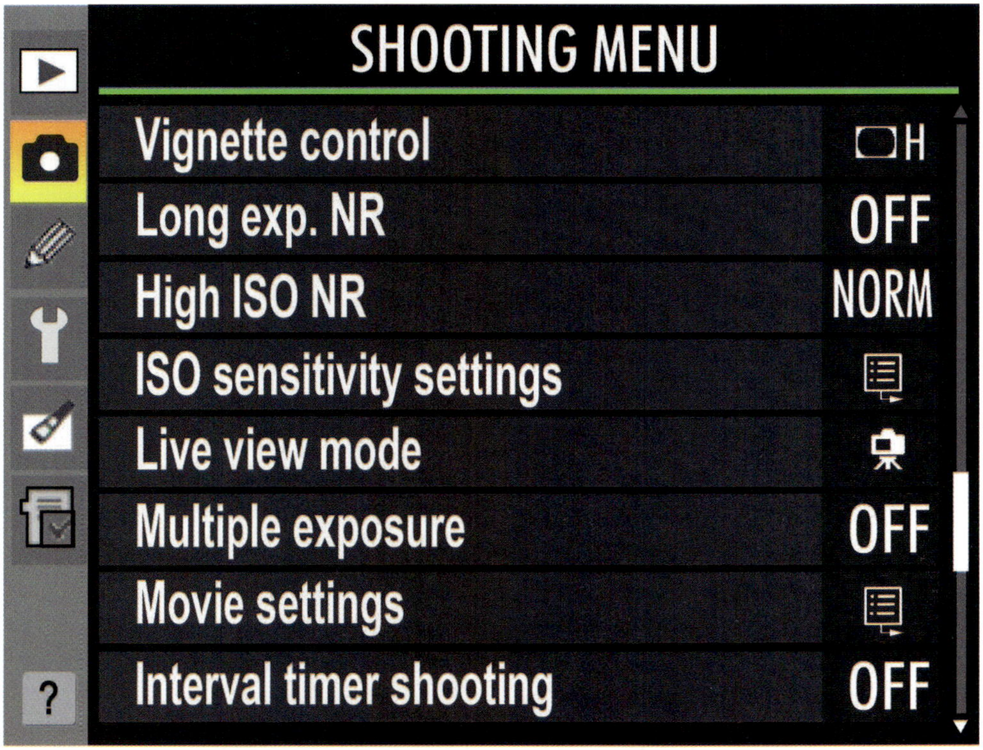


**Figure 3.28** Vignette control is the first entry on the third page of the D3s Shooting menu.

If you consistently encounter vignetting, this option may help. It reduces darkening at the periphery of images when using non-DX/non-perspective control lenses of the G and D type. (I explain the nomenclature of Nikon's lens alphabet soup in Chapter 9.) You can choose from High, Normal, Low, and Off. It's difficult to quantify exactly how much corner-brightening each setting provides. Your best bet is to shoot some blank walls of a single color with lenses that seem to have this problem, and try a few at each of the settings. Then select the value that best seems to counter vignetting with your particular lenses. You may want to use this feature selectively. While most lenses have some vignetting, especially wide open, different lenses exhibit different amounts of vignetting. A single lens may have more or less vignetting at various focal lengths in its zoom range, from half a stop in the corners to as much as a full f/stop's worth at the periphery of your image. I tend to leave this control set at Normal, and change to High when I mount my (original version) 70-200 f/2.8 VR Zoom lens.

## Long Exp. NR

Visual noise is that awful graininess caused by long exposures and high ISO settings, and which shows up as multicolored specks in images. This setting helps you manage the kind of noise caused by lengthy exposure times. In some ways, noise is like the excessive grain found in some high-speed photographic films. However, while photographic grain is sometimes used as a special effect, it's rarely desirable in a digital photograph. There are easier ways to add texture to your photos.

Some noise is created when you're using shutter speeds longer than eight seconds to create a longer exposure. Extended exposure times allow more photons to reach the sensor, but increase the likelihood that some photosites will react randomly even though not struck by a particle of light. Moreover, as the sensor remains switched on for the longer exposure, it heats, and this heat can be mistakenly recorded as if it were a barrage of photons. This menu setting can be used to activate the D3s/D3x's long exposure noise-canceling operation performed by the EXPEED digital signal processor.

- **Off.** This default setting disables long exposure noise reduction. Use it when you want the maximum amount of detail present in your photograph, even though higher noise levels will result. This setting also eliminates the extra time needed to take a picture caused by the noise reduction process. If you plan to use only lower ISO settings (thereby reducing the noise caused by ISO amplification), the noise levels produced by longer exposures may be acceptable. For example, you might be shooting a waterfall at ISO 50 (L1.0 on the D3x) or ISO 100 (L 1.0 on the D3s) with the camera mounted on a tripod, using a neutral-density filter and a long exposure to cause the water to blur. (Try exposures of 2 to 16 seconds, depending on the intensity of the light and how much blur you want.) (See Figure 3.29.) To maximize detail in the non-moving portions of your photos for the exposures that are eight seconds or longer, you can switch off long exposure noise reduction.

- **On.** When exposures are eight seconds or longer, the Nikon D3s/D3x takes a second, blank exposure to compare that to the first image. (While the second image is taken, the warning Job nr appears on the monochrome LCD panel and in the viewfinder.) Noise (pixels that are bright in a frame that *should* be completely black) in the "dark frame" image is subtracted from your original picture, and only the noise-corrected image is saved to your memory card. Because the noise-reduction process effectively doubles the time required to take a picture, you won't want to use this setting when you're rushed. Some noise can be removed later on, using tools like the noise reduction features built into Photoshop, Bibble Pro, or Nikon Capture NX.

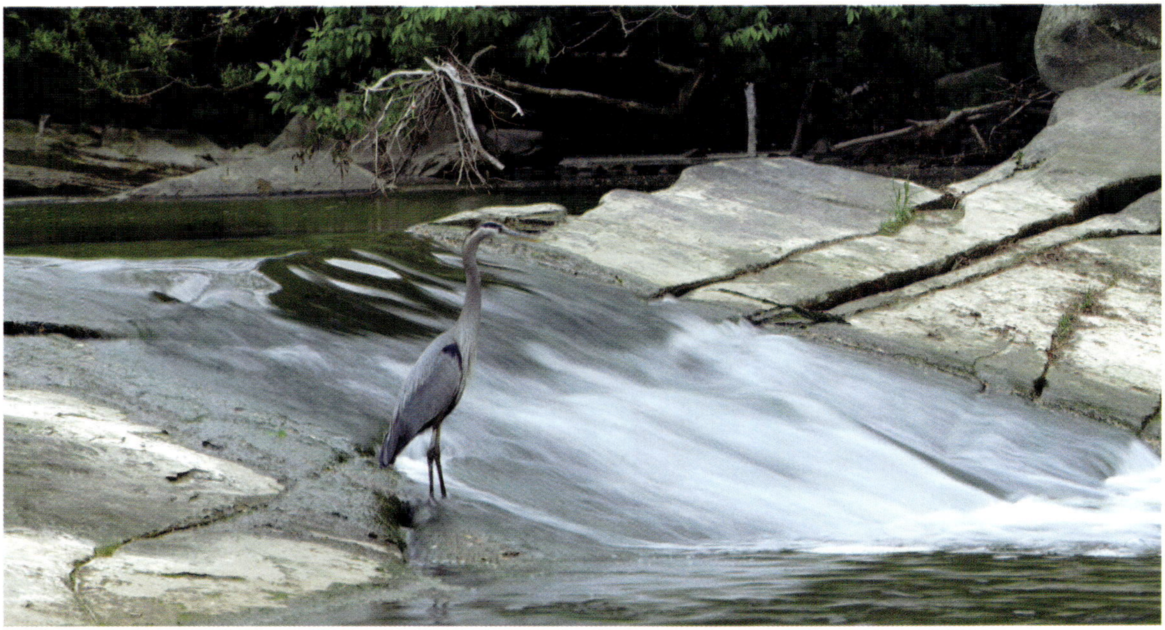

**Figure 3.29** A long exposure with the camera mounted on a tripod produces this traditional moving water photo.

## High ISO NR

Noise can also be caused by higher ISO sensitivity settings, and the Nikon D3s/D3x offers direct settings up to ISO 1600/12800 (on the D3x and D3s, respectively) and extended settings that go even higher. The D3x has intermediate settings between its Hi 1.0 (ISO 3200 equivalent) and Hi 2.0 (ISO 6400 equivalent), while the D3s has a loftier ceiling that goes in fractional increments through Hi 1.0 (ISO 25600) to Hi 2.0 (ISO 51200) to the incredible Hi 3.0 (ISO 102400). Indeed, both the D3s and D3x use reduced-noise CMOS sensors, and the D3s, in particular, gives you results that are at least three to four stops better than its DX-format stablemates. Even so, high ISO noise reduction, which can be set with this menu option, may be a good option in many cases. You can choose Off when you want to preserve detail at the cost of some noise graininess, and the D3s/D3x will apply high ISO NR only at the "boosted" settings of Hi 0.3, Hi 0.6, Hi 1.0, Hi 1.3, Hi 1.6, and Hi 2.0 (and additional settings up to Hi 3.0 with the D3s). Or, you can select Low, Normal, and High noise reduction, which is applied when ISO sensitivity has been set to ISO 800 or higher.

The effects of high ISO noise are something like listening to a CD in your car, and then rolling down all the windows. You're adding sonic noise to the audio signal, and while increasing the CD player's volume may help a bit, you're still contending with an unfavorable signal to noise ratio that probably mutes tones (especially higher treble notes) that you really want to hear.

The same thing happens when the analog image signal is amplified: You're increasing the image information in the signal, but boosting the background fuzziness at the same time. Tune in a very faint or distant AM radio station on your car stereo. Then turn up the volume. After a certain point, turning up the volume further no longer helps you hear better. There's a similar point of diminishing returns for digital sensor ISO increases and signal amplification as well.

As the captured information is amplified to produce higher ISO sensitivities, some random noise in the signal is amplified along with the photon information. Increasing the ISO setting of your camera raises the threshold of sensitivity so that fewer and fewer photons are needed to register as an exposed pixel. Yet, that also increases the chances of one of those phantom photons being counted among the real-life light particles, too.

Fortunately, the Nikon D3s/D3x's CMOS sensor and its EXPEED digital processing chip are optimized to produce the low noise levels, so ratings as high as ISO 1600 (with the D3x), and up to ISO 12800 (with the D3s) can be used routinely (although there will be some noise, of course), and even ISO 6400 can generate good results. I regularly shoot concerts at ISO 3200, and indoor sports at ISO 6400 with my D3s. Some kinds of subjects may not require this kind of noise cancellation, particularly with images that have a texture of their own that tends to hide or mask the noise.

## ISO Sensitivity Settings

This menu entry has two parts, ISO sensitivity and ISO sensitivity auto control. The former is simply a screen that allows you to specify the ISO setting, just as you would by spinning the main command dial while holding down the ISO button on back of the D3s/D3x under the rear control panel. The available settings range from LO 1 (ISO 50/100 equivalent with the D3x and D3s, respectively) through ISO 1600/12800 (D3s/D3s) to Hi 1.0 (ISO 3200/25600 equivalent with the D3x/D3s), Hi 2.0 (ISO 6400/51200 equivalent with the D3x/D3x). The D3s (only) also has settings up to Hi 3.0 at ISO 102400. The available settings are determined by the size of the increment you've specified in Custom Setting b1: 1/3, 1/2, or 1 step values. For example, if you had chosen 1-step increments for the D3x, then LO 1.0, 100, 200, 400, 800, 1600, Hi 1.0, and Hi 2.0 would be available. (I'll explain the use of increments in Chapter 4.) Use the ISO sensitivity menu when you find it more convenient to set ISO using the three-inch color LCD.

The ISO sensitivity auto control menu entry lets you specify how and when the D3s/D3x will adjust the ISO value for you automatically under certain conditions. This capability can be potentially useful, although experienced photographers tend to shy away from any feature that allows the camera to change basic settings like ISO that have been carefully selected. Fortunately, you can set some boundaries so the D3s/D3x will use this adjustment in a fairly intelligent way.

When Auto ISO is activated, the camera can bump up the ISO sensitivity, if necessary, whenever an optimal exposure cannot be achieved at the current ISO setting. Of course, it can be disconcerting to think you're shooting at ISO 400 and then see a grainier ISO 1600 shot during LCD review. While the D3s/D3x provides a flashing ISO-Auto alert in the viewfinder and top-panel status LCD, the warning is easy to miss. Here are the important considerations to keep in mind when using the options available for this feature:

- **Off.** Set ISO sensitivity auto control to off, and the ISO setting will not budge from whatever value you have specified. Use this setting when you don't want any ISO surprises, or when ISO increases are not needed to counter slow shutter speeds. For example, if the D3s/D3x is mounted on a tripod, you can safely use slower shutter speeds at a relatively low ISO setting, so there is no need for a speed bump. On the other hand, if you're hand-holding the camera and the D3s/D3x set for programmed (P) or aperture-priority (A) mode wants to use a shutter speed slower than, say, 1/30th second, it's probably a good idea to increase the ISO to avoid the effects of camera shake. If you're using a longer lens, a shutter speed of 1/125th second or higher might be the point where an ISO bump would be a good idea. In that case, you can turn the ISO sensitivity auto control on, or remember to boost the ISO setting yourself.
- **Maximum sensitivity.** Use this parameter to indicate the highest ISO setting you're comfortable having the D3s/D3x set on its own. You can choose the max ISO setting the camera will use from ISO 200, 400, 800, 1600, and Hi 1.0 and Hi 2.0 (ISO 3200 and ISO 6400 equivalent) with the D3x. With the D3s, you can choose from ISO 400 through 12800 in one-third stop increments, then Hi 0.3, Hi 0.7, Hi 1.0, Hi 2.0, and Hi 3.0. (Note that the increments are fixed at those listed, regardless of how the exposure increments in Custom Setting b1 is set.) Use a low number if you'd rather not take any photos at a high ISO without manually setting that value yourself. Dial in a higher ISO number if getting the photo at any sensitivity setting is more important than worrying about noise.

- **Minimum shutter speed.** This setting allows you to tell the D3s/D3x how slow the shutter speed must be before the ISO boost kicks in, within the range 1 second to 1/250th second. The default value is 1/30th second, because for most shooters in most situations, any shutter speed longer than 1/30th is to be avoided, unless you're using a tripod, monopod, or looking for a special effect. If you have steady hands, or the camera is partially braced against movement (say, you're using that monopod), a slower shutter speed, down to 1 full second, can be specified. Similarly, if you're working with a telephoto lens and find even a relatively brief shutter speed "dangerous," you can set a minimum shutter speed threshold of 1/250th second. When the shutter speed is faster than the minimum you enter, auto ISO will not take effect.

## Live View

Live view, which allows you to preview your image on the LCD before the picture is taken, is the feature that new users of the D3s/D3x often rave about, but may not understand fully. So, I'll cover live view more completely in Chapter 8. This brief section simply outlines the two options you can set for Live view in the Shooting menu. Live view is activated by rotating the release Mode dial to the Lv position with the D3x, or by pressing the dedicated Lv (live view) button on the back of the D3s. This menu entry allows you to specify which of two live view modes is used, and, with the D3x, whether you want to take pictures using single frame, continuous low speed, or continuous high speed release modes.

- **Hand-held** (the default value) **mode**. Hand-held mode is useful for shooting moving subjects and for framing images at angles that might not be convenient to compose with the camera mounted on a tripod. Hand-held mode uses phase-detection autofocus, using focus information provided from the same sensor used to focus the D3s/D3x when live view is not active. As you'll learn in Chapter 8, the mirror temporarily flips down when the shutter release or AF-ON button is pressed and the camera focuses (automatically in AF-S or AF-C modes, or manually in M mode), returning to live view when either button is released.
- **Tripod mode.** This is better for non-moving subjects and allows zooming your view in for easier and more precise manual or automatic focus. Tripod mode focuses with contrast-detect autofocus, a slower method that evaluates the contrast of the image reaching the sensor and adjusts autofocus until the highest contrast image is achieved. You can select the focus point yourself using the multi selector, and then autofocus by pressing the AF-ON button (but *not* by pressing the shutter release halfway) or manually focus. Chapter 8 has all the details.

- **Release mode (D3x and original D3 only).** Because the D3x and original D3 activate live view using a release mode dial setting, that prevents you from using another release mode at the same time—unless you select single frame, continuous low speed, or continuous high speed from this menu entry. This option is not needed with the D3s, because live view works with any release mode you care to use.

## Multiple Exposure

This option lets you combine two exposures into one image without the need for an image editor like Photoshop, and can be an entertaining way to return to those thrilling days of yesteryear, when complex photos were created in the camera itself. In truth, prior to the digital age, multiple exposures were a cool, groovy, far-out, hep/hip, phat, sick, fabulous way of producing composite images. Today, it's more common to take the lazy way out, snap two or more pictures, and then assemble them in an image editor like Photoshop.

However, if you're willing to spend the time planning a multiple exposure (or are open to some happy accidents), there is a lot to recommend the multiple exposure capability that Nikon has bestowed on the D3s/D3x. For one thing, the camera is able to combine two or more images using the RAW data from the sensor, producing photos that are blended together more smoothly than is likely for anyone who's not a Photoshop guru. In addition, with the D3s, Nikon has eliminated one annoying aspect of the feature in previous incarnations—including that on the D3x: it's no longer necessary to return to the menu to activate multiple exposures for each and every set. If you want to take a series of pictures, you can set it once, and forget it. (But don't forget to turn it off when you're done!)

To take your own multiple exposures, just follow these steps (although it's probably a good idea to do a little planning and maybe even some sketching on paper first):

1. **Activate the feature.** Choose Multiple exposure from the Shooting menu.
2. **Choose exposures per frame.** Select Number of shots, choose a value from 2 to 10 with the multi selector up/down buttons, and press OK.
3. **Specify ratio of exposure between frames.** Choose Auto gain and specify either On (the default) or Off. When On is selected, the D3s/D3x will divide the total exposure of the image by the number of shots specified; for example, applying 1/4 of the exposure time to each shot in a four-image series. Choose Off, and the full exposure is applied to each picture. You'd want to use Off when using a dark background that would allow successive exposures to add details, and On to avoid the risk of overlapping images washing each other out.
4. **Confirm gain setting.** Press OK to set the gain.

5. **Exit settings (D3x only).** If you're using the D3x, move the cursor up to Done and press OK. The multiple exposure icon appears in the monochrome LCD status panel. Multiple exposure is active only for the next series of images you take (for the number of shots you specified). If you want to take additional multiple exposures, you'll need to repeat steps 1-5.
6. **Choose multiple exposure mode (D3s only).** If you're using the D3s, select Multiple exposure mode. A submenu appears with three choices:
   - On (series). The multiple exposure feature remains active even after you've taken a complete set of exposures for the number of shots you specified. Use this if you want to shoot several multiple exposures in a row. Remember to turn it off when you're done.
   - On (single photo). Once you've taken a single set of multiple exposures, the feature turns itself off (exactly like the D3x and original D3).
   - Off. Use this option to cancel multiple exposures.
7. **Shoot your multiple exposure set.** Take the photo by pressing the shutter release button multiple times until all the exposures in the series have been taken. (In continuous shooting mode, the entire series will be shot in a single burst.) The blinking multiple exposure icon vanishes when the series is finished. Reminder: you'll need to reactivate the Multiple exposure feature once you've finished taking a set with the D3x or the D3s when set to On (single photo); it shuts off automatically.

Keep in mind if you wait longer than 30 seconds between any two photos in the series, the sequence will terminate and combine the images taken so far. If you want a longer elapsed time between exposures, go to the Playback menu and make sure On has been specified for Image review, and then extend the monitor display time using Custom Setting c2 (Auto meter-off delay) to an appropriate maximum interval. The camera will grant you an additional 30 seconds beyond that. The Multiple exposure feature will then use the monitor-off delay as its maximum interval between shots. Figure 3.30 shows an odd multiple exposure created at a bluegrass concert.

## Movie Settings (D3s Only)

This menu entry allows you to choose three movie making parameters for the D3s (the D3x and original D3 lack the movie feature), which I'll discuss in much more detail in Chapter 8. The three are

- **Quality.** Choose from 1280 × 720 pixels (HDTV at 16:9 aspect ratio); 640 × 424 (3:2/VGA resolution); 320 × 216 (3:2 ratio for presentation on web pages and similar applications).
- **Microphone.** Select from low, medium, high sensitivity microphones, auto sensitivity, or off.

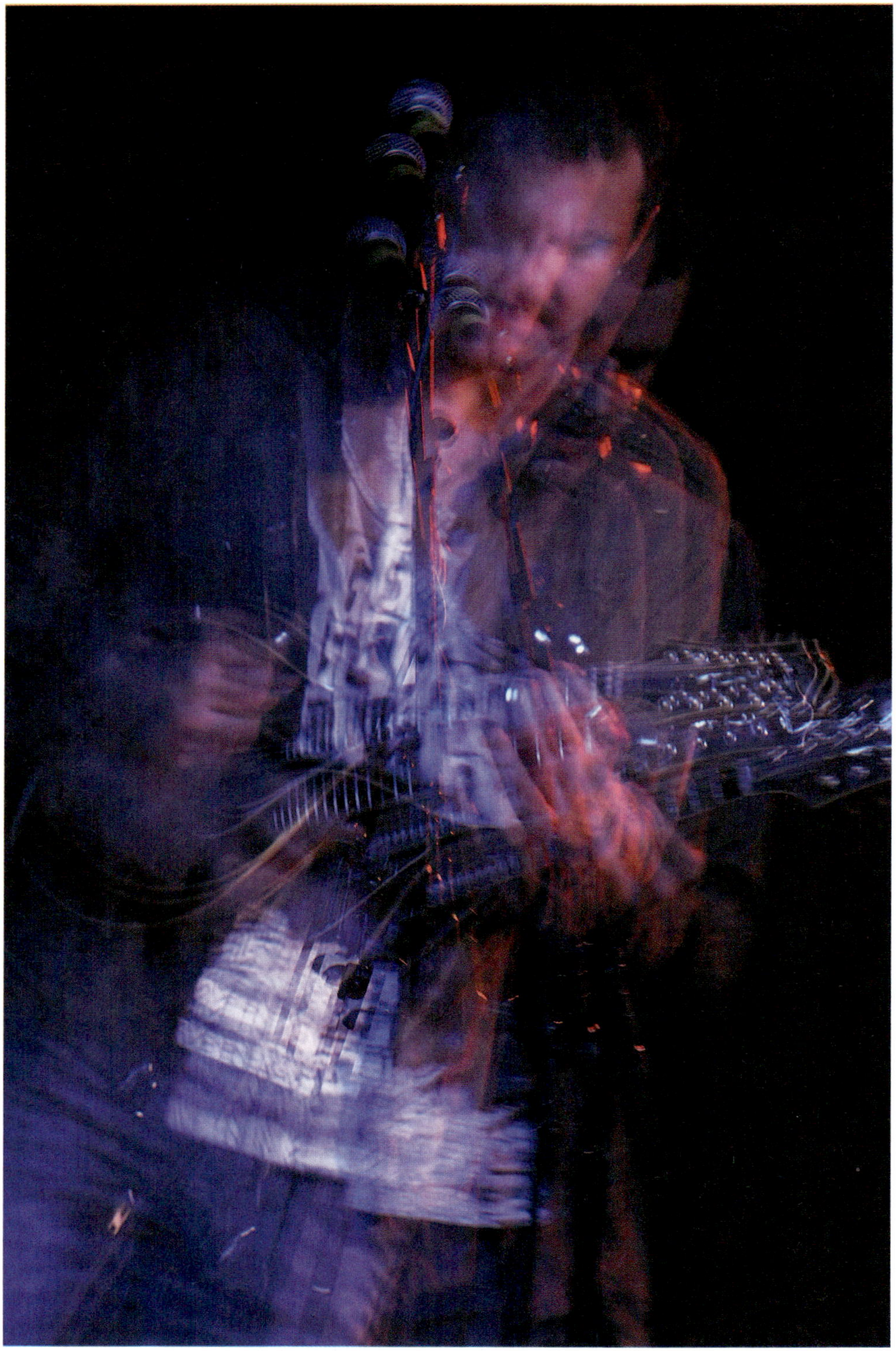

**Figure 3.30**
The D3s/D3x's Multiple exposure capability allows combining images without an image editor.

- **Destination.** Choose the slot containing the Compact Flash card you want to store your movies on; generally, use the slot containing the fastest memory card.
- **High-sensitivity movie mode.** You can elect to shoot movies under the highest ISO settings (ISO 6400 to Hi 3) if you're willing to accept grain and some washed out highlights. Set to On to allow shooting movies at ISO 6400 to Hi 3. Switch to Off to limit movie-making to ISO 200 to ISO 12800 (which is still fairly high, in my book).

## Interval Timer Shooting

Nikon D3s/D3x's built-in time-lapse photography feature allows you to take pictures for up to 999 intervals in bursts of as many as nine shots, with a delay of up to 23 hours and 59 minutes between shots/bursts, and an initial start-up time of as long as 23 hours and 59 minutes from the time you activate the feature. That means that if you want to photograph a rosebud opening and would like to photograph the flower once every two minutes over the next 16 hours, you can do that easily. If you like, you can delay the first photo taken by a couple hours so you don't have to stand there by the D3s/D3x waiting for the right moment.

Or, you might want to photograph a particular scene every hour for 24 hours to capture, say, a landscape from sunrise to sunset to the following day's sunrise again. The D3s/D3x can do that, too, and, in fact, offers most of the features of the expensive ($130) Nikon MC-36 Multi-Function Remote control. Nikon has done us all a huge favor by including this functionality essentially for free! I will offer two practical tips right now, in case you want to run out and try interval timer shooting immediately: *use a tripod, and for best results over longer time periods, plan on connecting your D3s/D3x to an external power source!*

The Interval timer shooting screen (see Figure 3.31) is confusingly designed, in my opinion. It's needlessly complex; the display changes in a quirky way depending on what information you're entering, and some portions of the screen aren't accessible until you've performed a prerequisite function. I would have set up this menu with nothing more than five entries, each with their own screen of options: On/Off, start time, interval delay, total number of shots to expose, and the number of shots in the burst per interval (if more than one image per interval is desired).

To set up interval timer shooting, just follow these steps.

Before you start:

1. **Check your time.** The D3s/D3x uses its internal clock to activate, so make sure the time has been set accurately in the Setup menu before you begin.
2. **Choose release mode.** If you want to shoot bursts of images each time an interval elapses, set the release mode dial to $C_L$ (continuous low speed; pictures will be taken

at the rate specified in Custom Setting d2) or $C_H$ (continuous high speed). If you prefer to take one picture per interval, set the release mode dial to S. However, you can still specify multiple shots per interval when using S; the D3s/D3x will use the frame rate specified in Custom Setting d5 just as if you had set the release mode to $C_L$. You can't use the self-timer or Mup release mode with interval timing.

3. **Set up optional bracketing.** If you'd like to bracket exposures during interval shooting, set up bracketing prior to beginning. (You'll learn how to bracket in Chapter 6.)
4. **Position camera.** Mount the camera on a tripod or other secure support.
5. **Fully charge the battery.** You might want to connect the D3s/D3x to the Nikon AC Adapter EH-6 if you plan to shoot long sequences. Although the camera more or less goes to sleep between intervals, some power is drawn, and long sequences with bursts of shots can drain power even when you're not using the interval timer feature.
6. Make sure the camera is protected from the elements, accidents, and theft, and that the viewfinder is covered (use the eyepiece shutter if necessary) if you need to keep strong ambient light from entering the viewfinder and affecting exposure.

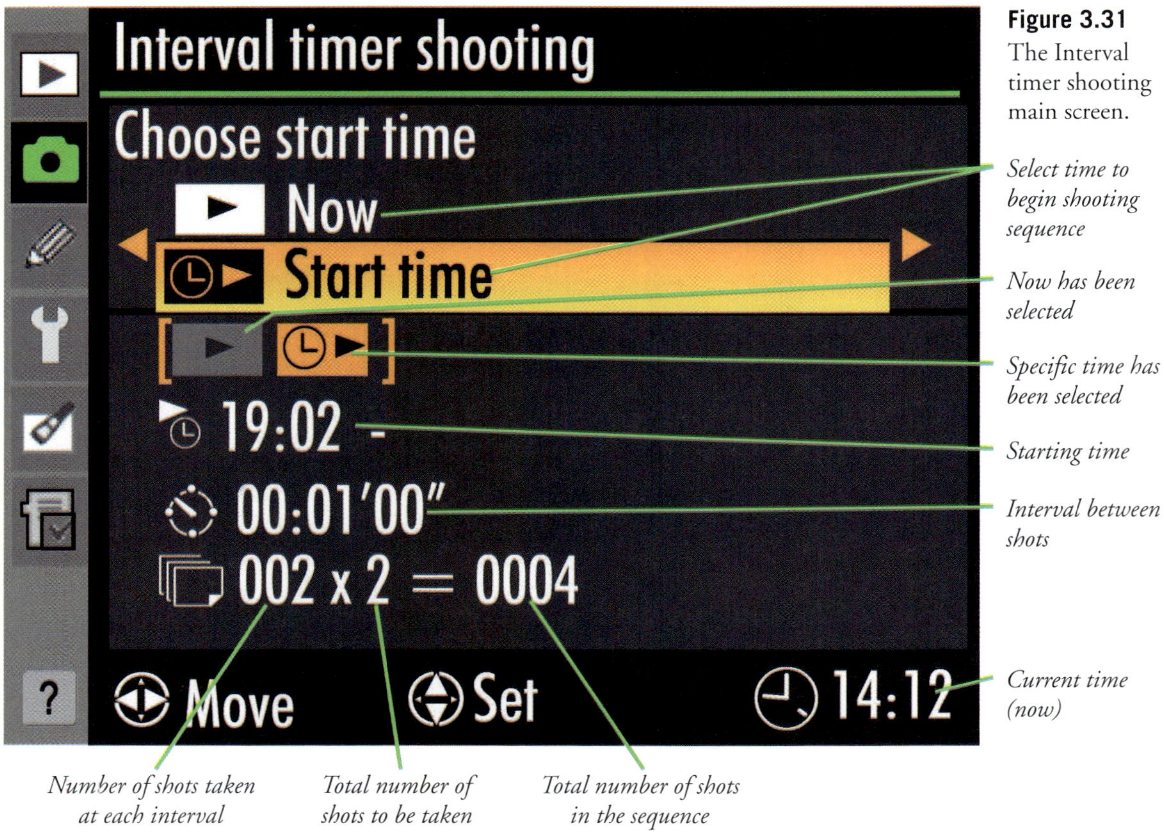


**Figure 3.31**
The Interval timer shooting main screen.

When you're ready to go, set up the D3s/D3x for interval shooting:

1. **Access feature.** Choose Interval timer shooting from the Shooting menu.
2. **Specify a starting time.** You must choose a start time before the D3s/D3x will let you set other parameters. Highlight either Now or Start time and press the multi selector right button. If you choose Now, the interval shooting will begin approximately three seconds after you've finished setting the parameters beginning with Step 5. If you select Start time, you'll be able to enter a specific time, as described in Steps 3 and 4.
3. **Select initial delay.** When the Start time sub-screen appears, use the multi selector left/right buttons to highlight the hours or minutes, and the up/down buttons to increase or decrease the hours/minutes entry. The 24-hour clock is used, so you can specify a time from 00:00 (midnight) to 23:59 (one minute to midnight). When both hours and minutes have been set, press the multi selector right button to move the highlighting to the Interval section of the sub-screen.
4. **Set the interval between exposures.** You can use the left/right buttons to move among hours, minutes, and seconds, and use the up/down buttons to choose an interval from one second to 24 hours. Press the right button when finished to move down to the number of intervals/shots per interval sub-screen.

**Tip**

The interval cannot be shorter than the shutter speed; for example, you cannot set one second as the interval if the images will be taken at two seconds or longer.

5. **Set number of intervals and shots per interval.** Use the left/right buttons to highlight the number of intervals, the number of shots taken after each interval has elapsed, and the total number of shots to be exposed overall. You can highlight each number column separately, so that to enter, say, 250 intervals you can set the 100s, 10s, and 1s columns individually (rather than press the up button 250 times!). You can select up to 999 intervals, and 9 shots per interval for a maximum of 8991 exposures with one interval shooting cycle.
6. **Activate shooting.** When all the parameters have been entered, press the multi selector right button once more, and the Start subscreen appears, with the choices On or Off. Choose either one and press OK. If you activate interval shooting, a message is displayed on the monitor one minute before each series of shots begins.

## PAUSE OR CANCEL INTERVAL SHOOTING

Press the Menu button between intervals (but not when images are still being recorded to the memory card), choose the Interval timer shooting menu entry, and select Pause. Interval shooting can also be paused by turning the camera on or off, or by rotating the release mode dial to live view, self-timer, or Mup positions. With the D3s, just press the Live view (Lv) button to pause. To resume the Interval timer shooting menu again, press the multi selector left button, and choose Restart. You may also select Off to stop the shooting.

# 4

# Setup: The Custom Setting Menu

Unlike the Shooting menu options, which you are likely to modify frequently as your picture-taking environment changes, Custom Settings are slightly more stable sets of preferences that let you tailor the behavior of your camera in a variety of different ways for longer-term use.

Some options are minor tweaks useful for specific shooting situations. You can turn off the autofocus assist lamp, the back-panel LCD's shooting information display, and the D3s/D3x's built-in beeper when you are shooting an acoustic music concert, when you'd rather not disrupt the environment. Others make the camera more convenient to use. Perhaps you'd like to assign a frequently used feature to the Fn button, or turn on the viewfinder grid display to make it easier to align vertical or horizontal shapes.

Best of all are the settings that actually *improve* the way the D3s/D3x operates. Custom Setting b6, for example, provides a way to fine-tune the exposures your camera calculates for each of the metering modes: matrix, center-weighted, and spot. If you find that one or the other consistently over- or underexposes more than you like, it's easy to dial in a permanent correction. Should you feel that the D3s/D3x is taking a few pictures that are out of focus, Custom Settings a1 and a2 can be used to tell it not to fire until optimum focus is achieved.

This chapter concentrates on explaining all the options of the Custom Setting menu and, most importantly, when and why you might want to use each setting.

## Custom Setting Menu Layout

There are 50-plus different Custom Settings, arranged in six different categories, as shown in Figure 4.1: Autofocus, Metering/exposure, Timers/AE lock, Shooting/display, Bracketing/flash, and Controls. Some of those may seem to be an odd match. What does bracketing have to do with flash? Oh, wait! You can *bracket* flash (as well as non-flash) exposures. The category system does have an advantage. Once you've learned what settings are available within each category, you can select the Custom Setting menu, scroll down to the specific category you want, and enter the Custom Setting system at that point, skipping the other entries.

However, once you get past the main Custom Setting screen, the entries are one long scrolling list, so if you've guessed wrong about where you want to start, you can enter the list at any point and then scroll up or down until you find the entry you want. Or, press the left directional key to get back to the main screen, then move down to another entry point and re-enter. The Custom Setting menu items are all color- and letter-coded: **a** (red) for autofocus functions; **b** (orange) for metering/exposure; **c** (green) for timers and AE lock features; **d** (light blue) for shooting/display functions; **e** (dark blue) for bracketing/flash; and **f** (purple) for adjustments to the D3s/D3x's controls.

For simplicity, in this book I have been consistently referring to the Custom Setting menu entries by their letter/names, so that you always know that when I mention

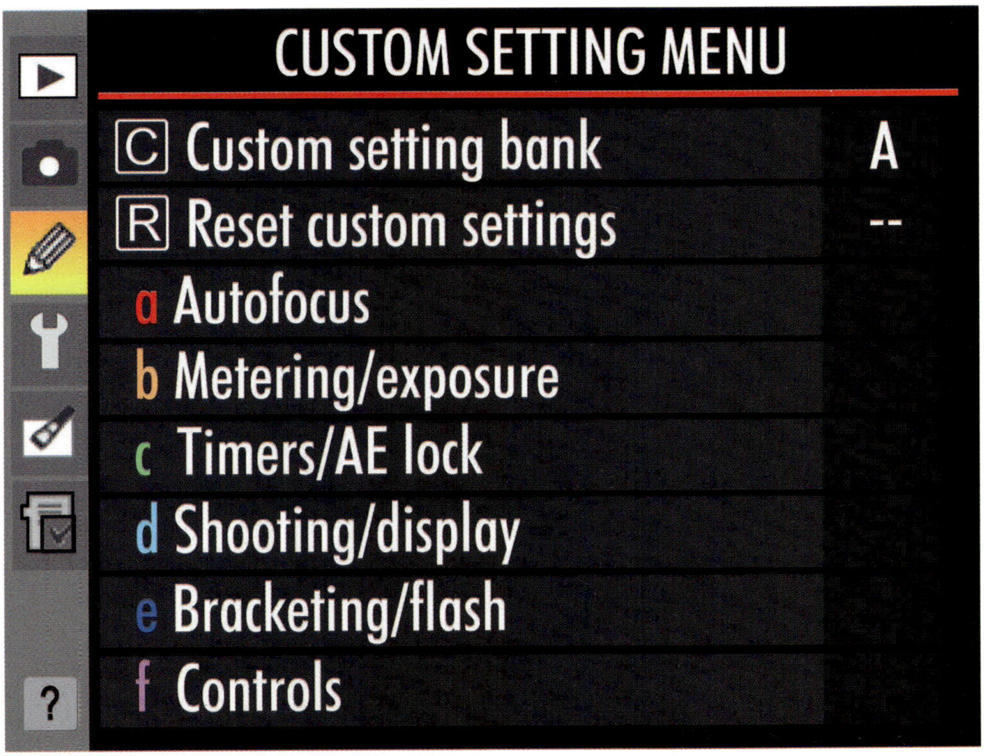


**Figure 4.1**
These six categories include more than four dozen different entries in the Custom Setting menu.

Custom Setting a8, I am describing the eighth entry in the Autofocus menu, AF point selection. That terminology makes it easy to jump quickly to the specific entry. There are some minor differences in the Custom Setting menus of the D3s and D3x, and I'll point them out as we go along.

You can select a Custom Setting function as you do any menu entry, by pressing the multi selector right button, and navigating through the screen that appears with the up/down (and sometimes left/right) buttons. Confirming an option is usually done by pressing the OK button, pushing the multi selector right button, or sometimes by choosing Done when a series of related options have been chosen.

At the top level, you'll see these entries:

- Custom Setting bank
- Reset custom settings
- a. Autofocus
- b. Metering/exposure
- c. Timers/AE lock
- d. Shooting/display
- e. Bracketing/flash
- f. Controls

## Custom Setting Bank

The Custom Setting menu has four banks, counterparts to the A, B, C, and D banks in the Shooting menu, that store specific collections of Custom Setting settings. As with the Shooting menu banks, you can recall any of the four at any time. As I mentioned in Chapter 3, the Custom Setting banks A, B, C, and D should not be confused with the four similarly named Shooting menu banks A, B, C, and D, which provide storage of separate sets of options. You can use your Shooting menu banks and Custom Setting menu banks in any combination.

The D3s/D3x uses bank A by default. To switch to another bank:

- Press Menu and select the Custom Setting menu.
- Scroll to Custom Setting bank and press the multi selector right button.
- Scroll to the bank you want to use with the multi selector up/down buttons, and either press OK or press the multi selector right button to confirm your choice.
- The Custom Setting menu appears again. Press the Menu button to back out of the menu, or simply tap the shutter release.

If you've changed a bank from its default values, the active bank's letter will be shown in the monochrome LCD status panel and the shooting information display. As with Shooting menu banks, any changes you make to one menu bank do not affect the other banks, so you can set one up with the settings you like to use in particular situations, and assign each of them customized names of up to 20 characters to replace the generic

A, B, C, and D designations. As with the Shooting menu banks, use the standard Nikon text-entry screen to enter the name you want to use.

- Press Menu and select the Custom Setting menu.
- Scroll to the Custom Setting menu bank entry and press the multi selector right button.
- Scroll down to Rename and press the multi selector right button to confirm your choice.
- Scroll down to the bank you want to rename, and press the multi selector right button to activate the text entry screen.
- Use the multi selector navigational buttons to scroll around within the array of alphanumerics, as described in Chapter 3. Press the multi selector's center button to insert the highlighted character; hold down the Thumbnail/Zoom out button and use the left/right buttons to move the cursor within the line of characters; remove a character by highlighting the character and pressing the Trash button. Press OK when finished, then press the left button twice to return to the Custom Setting menu, or just tap the shutter release to exit the menu system entirely.

## Reset Custom Settings

You can restore the settings of the Custom Setting banks to their default values by choosing this menu entry and selecting Yes or No. Only the currently active bank is reset; the other three are untouched. In Chapter 8, I'll provide a list of recommended Custom Setting menu bank settings for typical photo environments. Tables 4.1–4.6 show the default values as the Nikon D3s/D3x comes from the factory, and after a reset. If you don't know what some of these settings are, I'll explain them later in this chapter. Be careful when changing any of your carefully tailored customized settings back to the defaults.

**Table 4.1 Default Custom Setting Bank Values: Autofocus**

| Function | Option | Default |
|---|---|---|
| a1 | AF-C priority selection | Release |
| a2 | AF-S priority selection | Focus |
| a3 | Dynamic AF area | 9 points |
| a4 | Focus tracking with lock-on | Normal |
| a5 | AF activation | Shutter/AF-ON |

**Table 4.1 Continued**

| Function | Option | Default |
|---|---|---|
| a6 | Focus point illumination | |
| | Manual focus mode | On |
| | Continuous focus mode | On |
| | Focus point brightness | Normal |
| a7 | Focus point wrap-around | No wrap |
| a8 | AF point selection | 51 points |
| a9 | AF-ON button | On |
| a10 | Vertical AF-ON button | AF-ON |

**Table 4.2 Default Custom Setting Bank Values: Metering/Exposure**

| Function | Option | Default |
|---|---|---|
| b1 | ISO sensitivity step value | 1/3 step |
| b2 | EV steps for exposure cntrl. | 1/3 step |
| b3 | EV steps for exposure comp. | 1/3 step |
| b4 | Easy exposure compensation | Off |
| b5 | Center-weighted area | 12mm |
| b6 | Fine-tune optimal exposure | |
| | Matrix metering | 0 |
| | Center-weighted metering | 0 |
| | Spot metering | 0 |

**Table 4.3 Default Custom Setting Bank Values: Timers/AE Lock**

| Function | Option | Default |
|---|---|---|
| c1 | Shutter release button AE-L | Off |
| c2 | Auto meter-off delay | 6 seconds |
| c3 | Self-timer delay | 10 seconds |
| c4 | Monitor off delay | |
| | Playback | 20 seconds |
| | Menus | 10 seconds (D3s only) |
| | Information display | 10 seconds |
| | Image review | 4 seconds |

**Table 4.4 Default Custom Setting Bank Values: Shooting/Display**

| Function | Option | Default |
|---|---|---|
| d1 | Beep | Off |
| d2 | Shooting speed | |
| | Continuous high-speed | 5 fps (D3x); 9 fps (D3s) |
| | Continuous low-speed | 5 fps |
| d3 | Max. Continuous release | 130 |
| d4 | File number sequence | On |
| d5 | Control panel/viewfinder | Rear control panel: ISO sensitivity/Viewfinder: Frame count |
| d6 | Shooting info display (Information Display) | Auto |
| d7 (D3x) | LCD illumination | Off |
| d8 | Exposure delay mode | Off |

**Table 4.5 Default Custom Setting Bank Values: Bracketing/Flash**

| Function | Option | Default |
|---|---|---|
| e1 | Flash sync speed | 1/250th second |
| e2 | Flash shutter speed | 1/60th second |
| e3 | Modeling flash | On |
| e4 | Auto bracketing set | AE & Flash |
| e5 | Auto bracketing (Mode M) | Flash/speed |
| e6 | Bracketing order | MTR>under>over |

**Table 4.6 Default Custom Setting Bank Values: Controls**

| Function | Option | Default |
|---|---|---|
| f1 | Multi selector center button | |
| | Shooting mode | Select center focus point |
| | Playback mode | Thumbnail on/off |

**Table 4.6 Continued**

| Function | Option | Default |
|---|---|---|
| f2 | Multi selector | Do nothing |
| f3 | Photo info/playback | Info (up/down)<br>Playback (left/right) |
| f4 | Assign Fn Button | |
| | Fn button press | None |
| | Fn button + command dials | Autobracketing<br>Choose image area |
| f5 | Assign preview button | |
| | Preview button press | Preview |
| | Preview + command dials | None |
| f6 | Assign AE-L/AF-L button | |
| | AE-L/AF-L button press | AE/AF lock |
| | AE-L/AF-L + command dials | None |
| f7 | (D3s) Assign BKT button | |
| f7/8 | Customize command dials | |
| | Reverse rotation | No |
| | Change main/sub | Off |
| | Aperture setting | Sub-command dial |
| | Menus and playback | Off |
| f8/9 | Release button to use dial | No |
| f9/10 | No memory card? | Enable release |
| f10/11 | Reverse indicators | + / - |

# a. Autofocus

The red-coded Autofocus options (see Figure 4.2, which shows all but the last two entries) deal with some of the potentially most vexing settings available with the Nikon D3s/D3x. After all, incorrect focus is one of the most damaging picture killers of all the attributes in an image. You may be able to compensate for bad exposure, partially fix errant color balance, and perhaps even incorporate motion blur into an image as a creative element. But if focus is wrong, the photograph doesn't look right, and no amount of "I meant to do that!" pleas are likely to work. The D3s/D3x's autofocus options enable you to choose how and when focus is applied (using the AF-S or AF-C focus mode you selected on the camera body), the controls used to activate the feature, and the way focus points are selected from the available 51 zones.

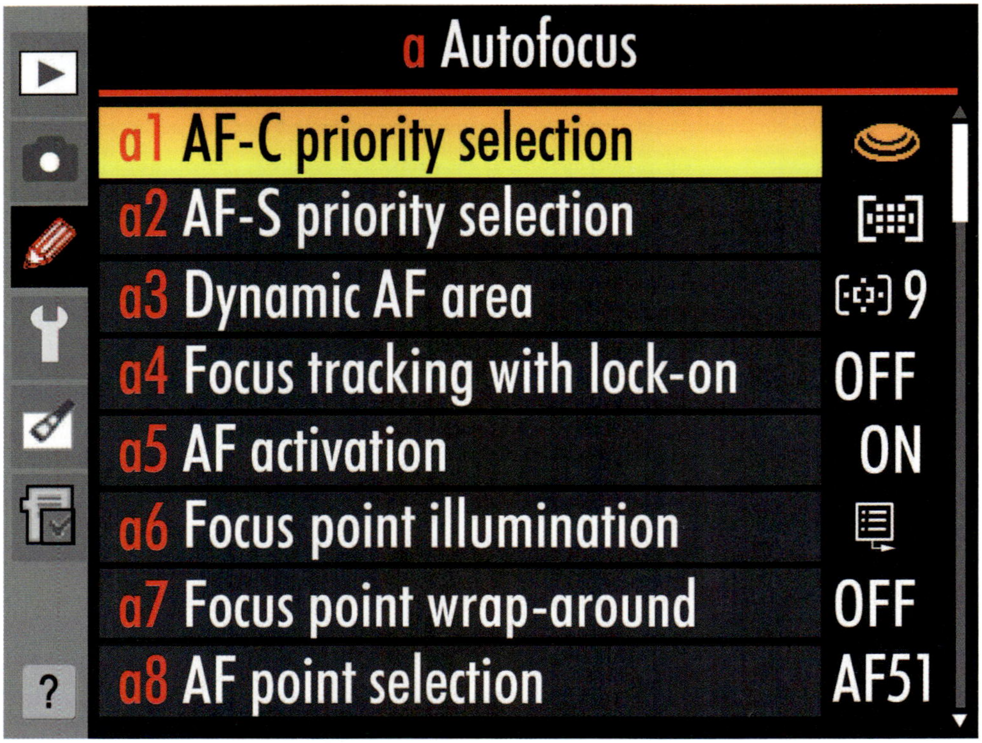


**Figure 4.2**
The first eight entries in the autofocus options menu.

## a1 AF-C Priority Selection

As you'll learn in Chapter 7, the Nikon D3s/D3x has two primary autofocus modes, continuous-servo autofocus (AF-C) and single-servo autofocus (AF-S). This menu entry allows you to specify what takes precedence when you press the shutter release all the way down to take a picture: focus (called *focus priority*) or the release button (called *release priority*). You can choose from:

- **Release.** When this option is selected (the default), the shutter is activated when the release button is pushed down all the way, even if sharp focus has not yet been achieved. Because AF-C focuses and refocuses constantly when autofocus is active, you may find that an image is not quite in sharpest focus. Use this option when taking a picture is more important than absolute best focus, such as fast action or photojournalism applications. (You don't want to miss that record-setting home run, or the protestor's pie smashing into the Governor's face.) Using this setting doesn't mean that your image won't be sharply focused; it just means that you'll get a picture even if autofocusing isn't quite complete. If you've been poised with the shutter release pressed halfway, the D3s/D3x probably has been tracking the focus of your image.

- **Release + focus.** The shutter is released when the button is pressed, but the frame rate is reduced slightly to give the D3s/D3x more time to autofocus when AF-C mode is used. (In non-live view modes, the D3s/D3x is able to autofocus *only* between shots when the mirror is down and the autofocus sensors can read the incoming light.) You would not want to use this setting if the highest possible continuous shooting rates are important to you.
- **Focus.** The shutter is not activated until sharp focus is achieved. This is best for subjects that are not moving rapidly. AF-C will continue to track your subjects' movement, but the D3s/D3x won't take a picture until focus is locked in. You might miss a few shots, but you will have fewer out-of-focus images.

## a2 AF-S Priority Selection

This is the counterpart setting for single-servo autofocus mode. Note that the order of your two choices is reversed, compared to the Nikon D200; the Release choice is now on top, and Focus (the default) is on the bottom:

- **Release.** The shutter is activated when the button is depressed all the way, even if sharp focus is not quite achieved. Keep in mind that, unlike AF-C, the D3s/D3x focuses only *once* when AF-S mode is used. So, if you've partially depressed the shutter release, paused, and then pressed the button down all the way, it's possible that the subject has moved and release priority will yield more out-of-focus shots than release priority with AF-C. This setting is most viable if you're using a fast lens with a speedy internal focus motor (designated AF-S, which is *not* the same as the AF-S focus mode).
- **Focus.** This default prevents the D3s/D3x from taking a picture until focus is achieved and the in-focus indicator in the viewfinder glows a steady green. If you're using single-servo autofocus mode, this is probably the best setting. Moving subjects really call for AF-C mode in most cases.

## a3 Dynamic AF Area

The D3s/D3x has three focus area selection modes: auto-area, dynamic-area, and single point. These three have some significant differences from the dynamic-area/closest subject, group dynamic, dynamic-area, and single point modes found in the D200 (which is why I'll devote some space to describing AF area selection in Chapter 7).

In the D3s/D3x's dynamic-area mode, you choose the initial autofocus point using the multi selector's up/down and left/right buttons. The camera will initially focus on the specified focus point, but in continuous-servo autofocus (AF-C) mode, the camera will refocus if the subject moves outside that point. This setting lets you determine how the camera diverts its attention from your specified active focus point to choose a new point when the subject leaves the primary focus zone. Your choices (shown in Figure 4.3) include

- **9 points.** Should the subject leave the selected focus point, the camera will refocus using information from eight surrounding focus points. This mode is best when your subjects are moving in a predictable way, or you have time to re-compose the image. The D3s/D3x responds by using only a limited number of points outside the initial zone, but acting very quickly within that range of points.
- **21 points.** Should the subject leave the selected focus point, the D3s/D3x will refocus based on information from 20 surrounding focus points. This mode is best for subjects that are moving erratically. Autofocus may take slightly longer because more points are considered.
- **51 points.** Should the subject leave your selected focus point's coverage area, the camera will refocus based on information from all 50 surrounding focus points. This setting is best with subjects that are moving very quickly and/or not cooperative enough to be captured by your selected focus point. Nikon uses the example of birds and other hard-to-track subjects as suitable fodder for this mode.

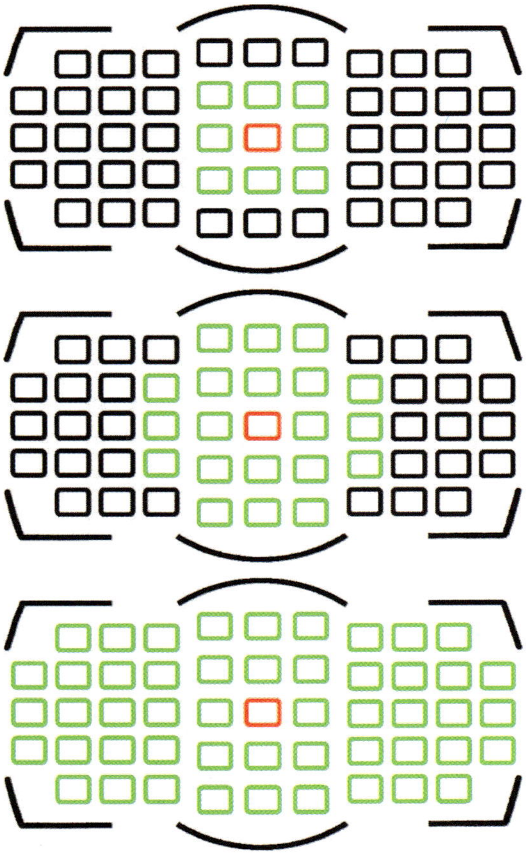

**Figure 4.3**
You can select from 9 (top), 21 (middle), or 51 (bottom) active focus points.

- **51 points (3D-tracking).** Should the subject leave your selected focus zone, the D3s/D3x uses distance information to calculate the path of the subject and select a new focus point. Nikon recommends using this setting to focus subjects that move erratically from side to side (a halfback running towards you with the ball tucked under one arm comes to mind), because the camera can use the distance information to differentiate the original subject from objects that are closer or farther away.

## a4 Focus Tracking with Lock-on

Sometimes new subjects interject themselves in the frame temporarily. Perhaps you're shooting an architectural photo from across the street and a car passes in front of the camera. Or, at a football game, a referee dashes past just as a receiver is about to make a catch. This setting lets you specify how quickly the D3s/D3x reacts to these transient interruptions that would cause relatively large changes in focus before refocusing on the "new" subject matter. You can specify a long delay, so that the interloper is ignored, a shorter delay, or turn off lock-on completely so that the D3s/D3x immediately refocuses when a new subject moves into the frame. Your options differ slightly between the D3s and D3x. The D3s provides intermediate settings between long/normal and normal/short, and numbers each of the settings. In the labels below, the D3s's number system is shown first. The options are as follows:

- **AF 5/Long.** The longest delay causes the D3s/D3x to ignore the intervening subject matter for a significant period of time. Use this setting when shooting subjects, such as sports, in which focus interruptions are likely to be frequent and significant.
- **AF 4 (D3s only).** A slightly shorter delay (Nikon does not provide the exact timings).
- **AF 3/Normal.** This default setting provides an intermediate delay before the camera refocuses on the new subject. It's usually the best choice when shooting sports in either of the continuous shooting modes, as the long delay can throw off autofocus accuracy at higher fps settings.
- **AF 2 (D3s only).** A slightly shorter delay than Normal.
- **AF 1/Short.** Choose this setting to tell the D3s/D3x to wait only a moment before refocusing. Very high frame rates may work better when you allow refocusing to take place rapidly, without a lock-on delay.
- **Off.** Turn off focus lock-on if you want the D3s/D3x to refocus immediately. This may be the best choice for general subjects, because it allows the camera to smoothly follow focus on a moving subject with no delay.

## a5 AF Activation

This setting lets you change which controls are used to activate autofocus, either the shutter release button *and* the AF-ON button or the AF-ON button only. Most of us learned to use a half-press of the shutter release button to activate autofocus at the same time the exposure is calculated, but if you're willing to retrain yourself to use the AF-ON button, there are some nifty things you can do. For example, the AF-ON button can be used to lock in focus separately from exposure and taking the picture, and to produce the effect called *trap focus* in which you pre-focus at a certain point, press the shutter release, and the D3s/D3x doesn't take a picture until your subject (say, a horse crossing the finish line) moves into the pre-focused position. I'll describe trap focus in more detail in Chapter 7, but you can learn the basic use of this Custom Setting now.

- **Shutter/AF-ON.** With this default setting, you can use either the shutter release button or the AF-ON button to initiate focus. For example, you could press the AF-ON button to start the autofocus operation as you initially frame the image, then press the shutter release when you're ready to take the picture to meter the scene. Or, without changing anything, you could press the shutter release button to perform autofocus and metering at the same time.
- **AF-ON only.** This setting decouples metering from autofocus activation. You must press AF-ON to start autofocus, and you must press the shutter release to start metering. So, you can activate and re-activate autofocus at any time. For example, suppose you're photographing a field goal attempt in a football game. Press AF-ON to lock in focus on the player who will be holding the ball for the kicker. When the play begins, focus will remain locked on the holder, even if defenders suddenly burst into the frame. As the kicker goes into motion, press the shutter release button to meter the scene and take the picture, confident that the focus you've set will not change. (In fast-moving situations, this is obviously more precise than manually focusing.) As a bonus, you don't have to worry about autofocus lag; the D3s/D3x will snap the picture virtually instantly. AF-ON can also be used in sneaky ways with the AE-L/AF-L button, and I'll cover those in Chapter 7.

**Tip**

The D3s/D3x's built-in vertical grip has an AF-ON button for use in a vertical orientation, but does *not* have an AE-L/AF-L button (unless you reprogram the AF-ON button using Custom Setting a10 described later in this section).

## a6 Focus Point Illumination

It's usually helpful to have the active focus point highlighted in red in the viewfinder, although the flashing indicator does use a minuscule amount of power. This setting lets you specify when/if this highlighting happens. Your choices include

- **Manual focus mode.** Choose On if you want the active focus point to be highlighted in red when using manual focus. Choose Off to disable this display.
- **Continuous mode.** Select On to display the active focus point when using continuous high speed or continuous low speed release modes. As these modes are frequently used for sports photography, you might find it useful to have the focus point displayed as you shoot. If you find the display distracting, set this option to Off.
- **Focus point brightness.** When the selected focus point is highlighted in red it will be shown at the brightness level you choose here, from –1 (Low) to +2 (Extra high). Use the brighter levels if you have trouble distinguishing the focus point against a background; a dimmer level if you want to minimize the distraction, especially when shooting in a dark environment, such as at a concert.

## a7 Focus Point Wrap-Around

This setting is purely a personal preference parameter. When you press the multi selector left/right and up/down buttons to choose a focus point, the D3s/D3x can be told to stop when the selection reaches the edge of the 51-point array—or, it can continue, wrapping around to the opposite edge, like Pac-Man leaving the playing area on one side or top/bottom to re-emerge on the other. (I hope I'm not revealing my age, here.) Your choices are simple; decide which behavior you prefer:

- **Wrap.** Pressing the left/right or up/down buttons when you've reached the edge of the focus point display wraps the selection to the opposite side, still moving in the same direction.
- **No Wrap.** The focus point selection stops at the edge of the focus zone array.

## a8 AF Point Selection

You can choose the number of focus points available when you manually select a zone using the multi selector up/down and left/right buttons. Your choices, shown in Figure 4.4, are as follows:

- **51 points.** This is the default. All 51 focus points can be selected.
- **11 points.** A more widely spaced array of points is available. This can be the best choice for faster focus point selection when taking pictures of relatively large, evenly illuminated subject matter such that choosing precise focus zones is not particularly beneficial. I often use the 11-point option when photographing basketball games.

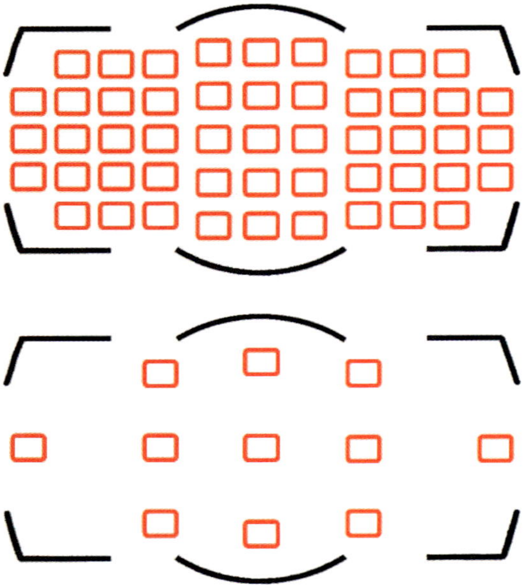

**Figure 4.4**
Select from all 51 focus points (top), or 11 more widely spaced points (bottom).

## a9 AF-ON Button

Use this setting (it's not shown in Figure 4.2; you must scroll to see it in the camera) to choose the function performed when you press the AF-ON button. This option lets you define the AF-ON button for three different functions: normal AF-ON behavior; AE-L/AF-L exposure lock/focus lock functions; and whatever action you've defined for the Fn button. Your choices are as follows:

- **AF-ON.** This default setting defines the AF-ON button as an AF-ON button. Autofocus is initiated when the button is pressed.
- **AE/AF lock.** With this setting, both focus and exposure are locked when the AF-ON button is held down.
- **AE lock only.** Exposure is locked while this button is held down.
- **AE lock (Reset on release).** Exposure locks when the button is held down, and remains locked even when the button is released. You can cancel the AE lock by pressing the button a second time, by taking a picture, or allowing the exposure meters to turn off at the end of their normal meter-off delay.
- **AE lock (Hold).** This Exposure locks when the AF-ON button is pressed, and remains locked at that exposure until the button is pressed again, or the meters turn off.
- **AF lock only.** This setting locks autofocus as long as the button is pressed.

## a10 Vertical AF-ON Button

You can use the AF-ON button included in the built-in grip for its intended purpose when firing the camera in vertical orientation, or you can redefine the button to a related function, depending on your working preferences. While the options for this button are similar to those for the main AF-ON button, this setting changes *only* the behavior of the AF-ON button on the vertical grip; the AF-ON button on the D3s/D3x camera body next to the viewfinder may be set up to do something different (which can be *very* confusing).

Your choices let you define the AF-ON button for three different functions: normal AF-ON behavior; AE-L/AF-L exposure lock/focus lock functions; and whatever action you've defined for the Fn button. Your choices are as follows:

- **Same as AF-ON.** The vertical grip's AF-ON button performs the same function you've specified in Custom Setting a9 for the main AF-ON button. Use this for consistency; you can change the action of the vertical grip's AF-ON button by changing the main button's function.
- **AF-ON.** This default setting defines the AF-ON button as an AF-ON button, natch. Autofocus is initiated when the button is pressed.
- **AE/AF lock.** With this setting, both focus and exposure are locked when the AF-ON button is held down.
- **AE lock only.** Exposure is locked while this button is held down.
- **AE lock (Reset on release).** Exposure locks when the button is held down, and remains locked even when the button is released. You can cancel the AE lock by pressing the button a second time, by taking a picture, or allowing the exposure meters to turn off at the end of their normal meter-off delay.
- **AE lock (Hold).** This exposure locks when the AF-ON button is pressed, and remains locked at that exposure until the button is pressed again, or the meters turn off.
- **AF lock only.** This setting locks autofocus as long as the button is pressed.

# b. Metering/Exposure

The orange-coded Metering/exposure Custom Settings (see Figure 4.5) let you define six different parameters that affect exposure metering in the Nikon D3s/D3x.

## b1 ISO Sensitivity Step Value

This setting determines the size of the "jumps" it should use when making ISO adjustments—either one-third or one full stop. At the 1/3 stop setting, typical ISO values

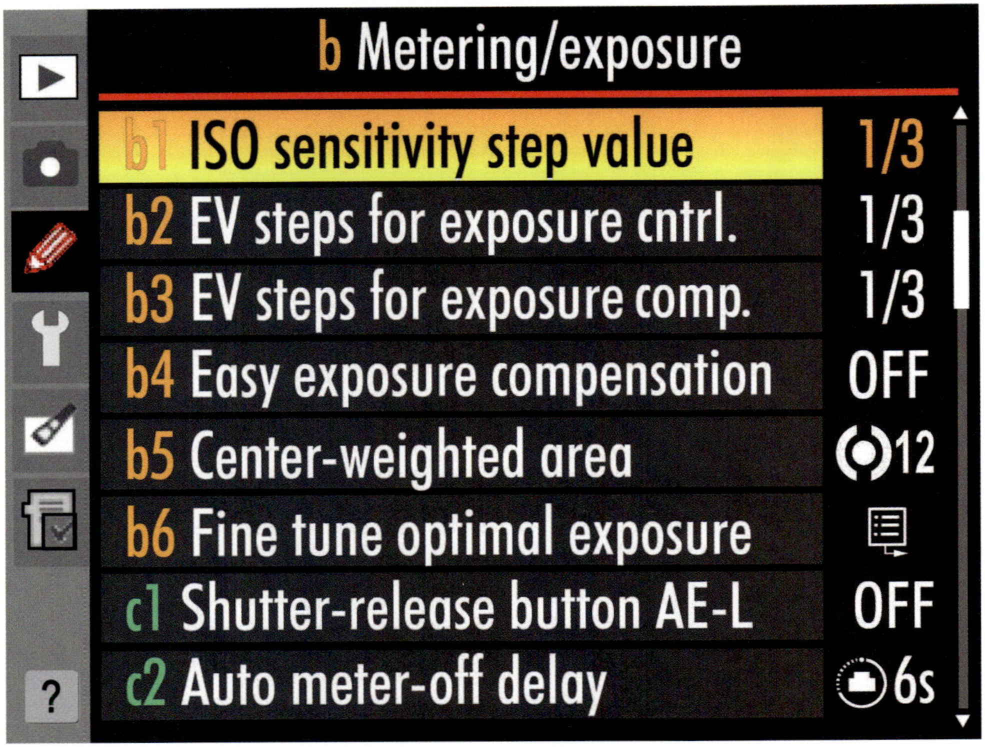


**Figure 4.5**
There are six metering/exposure options.

would be 200, 250, 320, 400, 500, 640, 800, 1000, 1250, 1600, and so forth. Choose 1/2 stop settings, and your choices would be 200, 280, 400, 560, 800, 1100, and 1600 over the same range. For really large increments, set the full-stop option, and choose 200, 400, 800, and 1600, and so forth. The larger increment can help you leap from one ISO setting to one that's much larger with one click in environments where you don't care to fine-tune sensitivity. As you've surmised, your choices include 1/3 step (the default); 1/2 step; and 1 step.

## b2 EV Steps for Exposure Cntrl.

This setting tells the Nikon D3s/D3x the size of the "jumps" it should use when making exposure adjustments—either one-third, one-half, or one full stop. The increment you specify here applies to f/stops, shutter speeds, EV changes, and autoexposure bracketing. As with ISO sensitivity step value, you can select from 1/3 step (the default); 1/2 step; and 1 step increments.

Choose the 1/3 stop setting when you want the finest increments between shutter speeds and/or f/stops. For example, the D3s/D3x will use shutter speeds such as 1/60th, 1/80th, 1/100th, 1/125th, and 1/160th second, and f/stops such as f/5.6, f/6.3, f/7.1, and f/8, giving you (and the autoexposure system) maximum flexibility.

With 1/2 stop increments, you will have larger and more noticeable changes between settings. The D3s/D3x will apply shutter speeds such as 1/60th, 1/125th, 1/250th, and 1/500th second, and f/stops including f/5.6, f/6.7, f/8, f/9.5, and f/11. These coarser adjustments are useful when you want more dramatic changes between different exposures.

## b3 EV Steps for Exposure Comp.

This third "increment" setting functions identically to the other two but applies to exposure compensation and flash exposure compensation adjustments you make by holding down the relevant EV adjustment buttons on the camera. (The Exposure Compensation button is on the top panel, just southeast of the shutter release button, as introduced in Chapter 2.) The flash compensation button can be found on the left side of the pentaprism, just below the flash pop-up button. Both add or subtract from the exposure when held down while the main command dial is rotated. This setting tells the Nikon D3s/D3x the size of the "jumps" it should use when making these exposure adjustments. As with ISO sensitivity and exposure control step values, you can select from 1/3 step (the default); 1/2 step; and 1 step increments.

## b4 Easy Exposure Compensation

This setting potentially simplifies dialing in EV (exposure value compensation) adjustments by specifying whether the Exposure Compensation button must be pressed while adding or extracting EV compensation. Because of the possibility of confusion or error, I tend to leave this setting turned off. Your choices are as follows:

- **On (Auto reset).** This setting allows you to add or subtract exposure by rotating the sub-command dial when in programmed (P) or shutter-priority (S) exposure modes, or by rotating the main command dial when using aperture-priority (A) mode. Rotating either dial has no effect in manual (M) exposure mode. (If you've reversed the behavior of the command dials using Custom Setting f7, the "opposite" command dial must be used to make the changes.) Any adjustments you've made are canceled when the camera is shut off, or the meter-off time expires and the D3s/D3x's exposure meters go back to sleep. That's a useful mode, because most of us have made an EV adjustment and then forgotten about it, only to expose a whole series of improperly exposed photos. You can still have "sticky" EV settings when Easy Exposure Compensation is turned on: just hold down the Exposure Compensation button when you make your changes.
- **On.** This setting brings the Easy compensation mode into conformance with the D3s/D3x's behavior when the Exposure compensation button is pressed: in either case, any EV modifications you make will remain until you countermand them. As I have mentioned several times, forgetting to "turn off" EV changes after you've

moved on to a different shooting environment is a primary cause of over and underexposure among those of us who are forgetful or who ignore the D3s/D3x's flashing EV warnings.

- **Off.** With this default setting, you must always press the Exposure Compensation button while rotating the main command dial to add or subtract exposure. Use this choice when you don't want any EV changes unless you deliberately make them by pressing the button.

## b5 Center-Weighted Area

This setting changes the size of the center-weighted exposure spot when the D3s/D3x is used with a non-CPU (generally older AI and AI-S and earlier lenses that haven't been updated with a "computer" chip). Your choices include 8mm, 12mm, 15mm, 20mm, or full-frame average (which turns the metering mode from a center-weighted system to an old-fashioned averaging system). If you're using a non-CPU lens, the center-weighted area is fixed at 12mm, and the camera ignores whatever choice you may have entered here. Because the D3s/D3x shows the default 12mm area in the viewfinder, you have a visual indication of what area is being emphasized by the metering system.

## b6 Fine Tune Optimal Exposure

This setting is a powerful adjustment that allows you to dial in a specific amount of exposure compensation that will be applied, invisibly, to every photo you take using each of the three metering modes. No more can you complain, "My D3s/D3x always underexposes by 1/3 stop!" If that is actually the case, and the phenomenon is consistent, you can use this custom menu adjustment to compensate.

Exposure compensation is usually a better idea (does your camera *really* underexpose that consistently?), but this setting does allow you to "recalibrate" your D3s/D3x yourself. You can fine-tune exposure separately in each of the four A, B, C, D Custom Setting banks, and your dialed in modifications will survive a two-button reset. However, you have no indication that fine-tuning has been made, so you'll need to remember what you've done. After all, you someday might discover that your camera is consistently *over*-exposing images by 1/3 stop, not realizing that your Custom Setting b6 adjustment is the culprit.

In practice, it's rare that the Nikon D3s/D3x will *consistently* provide the wrong exposure in any of the three metering modes, especially matrix metering, which can alter exposure dramatically based on the D3s/D3x's internal database of typical scenes. This feature may be most useful for spot metering, if you always take a reading off the same type of subject, such as a human face or 18-percent gray card. Should you find that the gray card readings, for example, always differ from what you would prefer, go ahead and fine-tune optimal exposure for spot metering, and use that to read your gray cards. To use this feature:

1. **Select fine-tuning.** Choose b6 Fine Tune Optimal Exposure from the Custom Setting menu.
2. **Consider yourself warned.** In the screen that appears, choose Yes after carefully reading the warning that Nikon insists on showing you each and every time this option is activated.
3. **Select metering mode to correct.** Choose matrix metering, center-weighted, or spot metering in the screen that follows by highlighting your choice and pressing the multi selector right button.
4. **Specify amount of correction.** Press the up/down buttons to dial in the exposure compensation you want to apply. You can specify compensation in increments of 1/6 stop, half as large a change as conventional exposure compensation. This is truly *fine-tuning.*
5. **Confirm your change.** Press OK when finished. You can repeat the action to fine-tune the other two exposure modes if you wish.

# c. Timers/AE Lock

This category (see Figure 4.6) is a mixed bag of settings, covering both entries that adjust delay times (c2 through c4) and how the shutter release and AE-L buttons interact (c1). I think the latter setting, changed slightly for the D3s/D3x, should have been placed in the purple f-coded Controls section, especially since with the original D300, Nikon moved the assignment of the AE-L/AF-L button setting (which used to reside here with some earlier cameras) to that location. They moved one of the settings, but not the other. Go figure.

## c1 Shutter Release Button AE-L

This is another of Nikon's easily confusing options for controlling how and when autofocus and exposure are activated and locked. The intent is to allow you to separate autofocus and autoexposure activation and locking. Because the options are scattered in various places in the Custom Setting menu, I'll sort out the interaction for you in Chapter 6. Meanwhile, all you need to know is

- **Off.** Exposure is locked *only* when the AE-L/AF-L button is pressed. This is the default.
- **On.** Exposure locks when either the shutter release button is depressed halfway or the AE-L/AF-L button is held down.

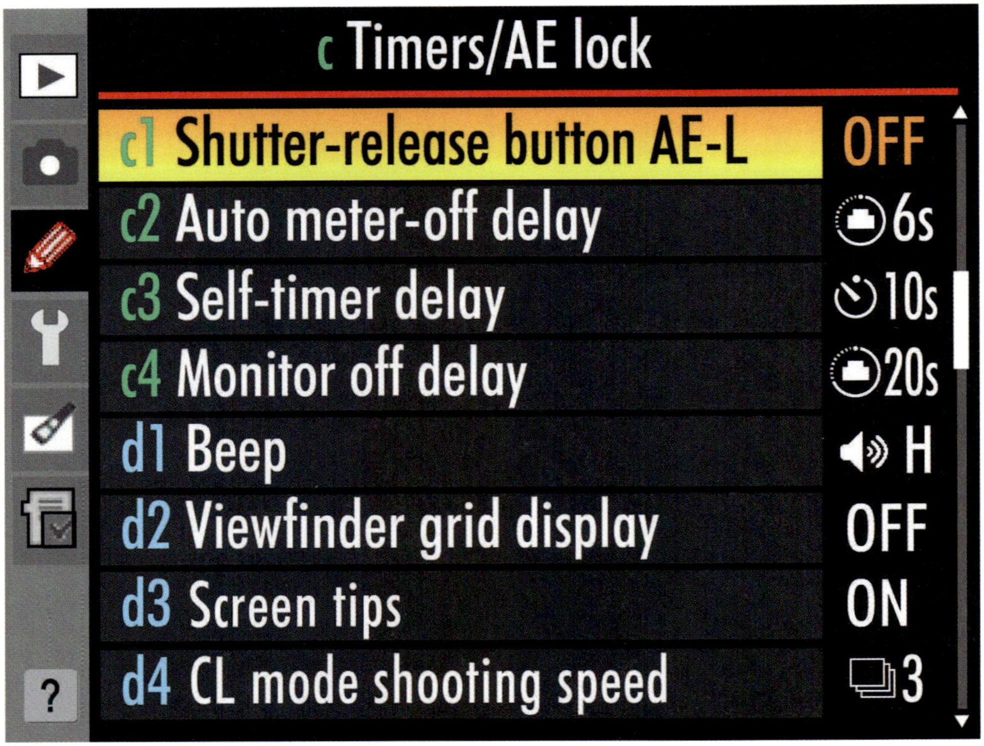


**Figure 4.6**
The Timers/AE lock settings.

## c2 Auto Meter-Off Delay

Use this setting to determine how long the D3s/D3x's exposure meter continues to operate after the last operation, such as autofocusing, focus point selection, and so forth, was performed. The default value is 6 seconds, but you can also select 4, 8, 16, and 30 seconds, as well as 1, 5, 10, and 30 minutes, or No limit, which keeps the meter active until the camera is switched off.

To save power, you should select an intermediate value, such as 8, 16, or 30 seconds if the default 6 seconds is not long enough. When the Nikon EH-6 AC adapter is connected to the D3s/D3x, the exposure meter will remain on indefinitely, just as if you'd specified No limit. Absent an external power source, any setting longer than 8 seconds will definitely eat up power.

Even so, sports shooters and some others prefer a longer delay, because they are able to keep their camera always "at the ready" with no delay to interfere with taking an action shot that unexpectedly presents itself. Extra battery consumption is just part of the price paid. For example, when I am shooting football, a meter-off delay of 16 seconds is plenty, because the players lining up for the snap is my signal to get ready to shoot. But for basketball or soccer, I typically set the meter-off delay for No limit, because action is virtually continuous. My D3s/D3x has plenty of power, and I carry two sets of spares.

I rarely shoot much more than 1000-1200 shots at any sports event, so with the big EN-EL4a battery, that's sufficient juice even with meter-off delay set for No limit.

Of course, if the meters have shut off, and the power switch remains in the On position, you can bring the camera back to life by tapping the shutter button.

## c3 Self-Timer Delay

This setting lets you choose the length of the self-timer shutter release delay. The default value is 10 seconds. You can also choose 2, 5, or 20 seconds. If I have the camera mounted on a tripod or other support and am too lazy to attach the MC-30 cable release (I have three, one for each camera bag, so I *always* have one available), I can set a 2-second delay that is sufficient to let the camera stop vibrating after I've pressed the shutter release. I use a longer delay time if I am racing to get into the picture myself and am not sure I can make it in 10 seconds.

**Tip**

If you want a longer delay and are *really* lazy, just turn the D3s/D3x's release mode dial to the Mup position. No menu changes required! When you press the shutter release all the way down, the mirror will raise (reducing vibration so you can take a picture immediately), but if you do nothing else, the picture will be taken anyway 30 seconds later. (To take a picture immediately after the mirror is raised, press the shutter release a second time.) Return the release mode dial to the single frame or continuous shooting modes to cancel this temporary self-timer option.

## c4 Monitor Off Delay

You can adjust the amount of time the monitor remains on when no other operations are being performed. As with the meter-off delay, if the EH-6 AC adapter is attached, the monitor will remain on for the maximum amount, about 10 minutes. The D3s and D3x differ in how much control you have. The D3x (and original D3) lets you set only one value that is used for *everything* monitor related, with a default value of 20 seconds; but you can also select 10 seconds, plus 1, 5, or the full 10 minutes. With the D3s, you can specify separate values for Playback (the default is 10 seconds); Menus (the default is 20 seconds); Information display (default is 10 seconds); and Image review (4 seconds). Choosing a brief duration for all or each of these can help preserve battery power. However, the D3s/D3x will always override the review display when the shutter button is partially or fully depressed, so you'll never miss a shot because a previous image was on the screen.

## SAVING POWER WITH THE Nikon D3s/D3x

There are several settings and techniques you can use to help stretch the longevity of your D3s/D3x's battery. To get the most from each charge, consider these steps:

- **Playback menu.** Image review: Turn off image review after each shot. You can still review your images by pressing the Playback button.
- **Auto meter-off delay.** Set to 4 seconds if you can tolerate such a brief active time.
- **Monitor off delay.** Set values for the minimum length, 10 seconds. That big three-inch LCD uses a lot of juice, so reducing the amount of time it is used when you don't turn it off manually (either for automatic review or for playing back your images) can boost the effectiveness of your battery.
- **Reduce LCD illumination.** Set Custom Setting d7 (on the D3x) or d8 (on the D3s) to Off, so the monochrome LCD status panel will be backlit only when you manually use the switch around the shutter release.
- **Reduce LCD brightness.** In the Setup menu, select the lowest of the seven brightness settings that work for you under most conditions. If you're willing to shade the LCD with your hand, you can often get away with lower brightness settings outdoors, which will further increase the useful life of your battery.
- **Cancel VR.** Turn off vibration reduction if your lens has that feature and you feel you don't need it.
- **Use a card reader.** When transferring pictures from your D3s/D3x to your computer, use a card reader instead of the USB cable. Linking your camera to your computer and transferring images using the cable takes longer and uses a lot more power.

# d. Shooting/Display

This menu section (see Figure 4.7) offers a variety of mostly unrelated shooting and display options not found elsewhere, but which are not frequently changed, making them suitable for a Custom Setting entry. The figure shows only the first eight entries; you must scroll down to see the last three.

## d1 Beep

The Nikon D3s/D3x's internal beeper provides a (usually) superfluous chirp to signify various functions, such as the countdown of your camera's self-timer or autofocus confirmation in AF-S mode (unless you've selected release priority in Custom Setting a2). You can (and probably should) switch it off if you want to avoid the beep because it's annoying, impolite, distracting (at a concert or museum), or undesired for any other reason. It's one of the few ways to make the D3s/D3x a bit quieter. (I've actually had

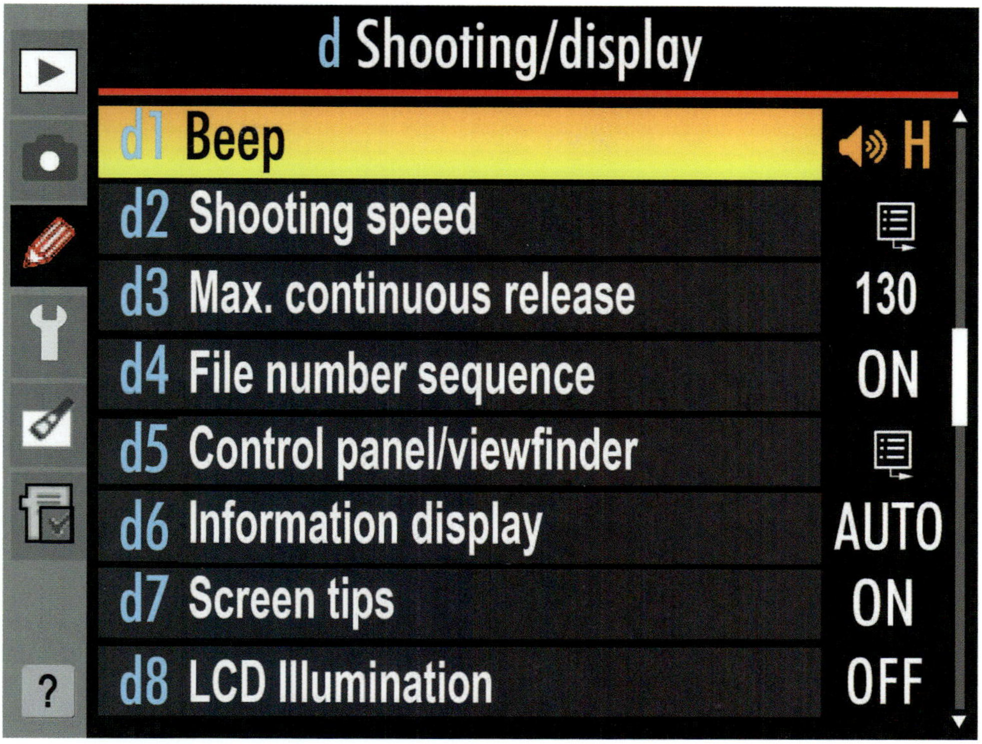


**Figure 4.7**
A mixed bag of entries is found in the Shooting/display submenu.

new dSLR owners ask me how to turn off the "shutter sound" the camera makes; such an option was available in the point-and-shoot camera they'd used previously.) Select d1 Beep from the menu, and select one of the following:

- **High.** This default value produces a high-pitched beep, and a quarter-note icon appears in the monochrome LCD status panel and the shooting information display.
- **Low.** A low-pitched beep is emitted, and the quarter-note icon appears in the status panel and shooting information display.
- **Off.** Turns the beeper off completely.

## d2 Shooting Speed

You can specify the frames per second shooting rate for both continuous high speed mode ($C_H$) and continuous low speed mode ($C_L$.) The rates available depend on whether you're using a Nikon D3x or D3s.

- **D3x: Continuous high speed.** Choose 5, 6, or 7 frames per second when using DX Image area. For FX and other image areas, the frame rate is fixed at 5 frames per second.

- **D3x: Continuous low speed.** All values from 1 to 5 fps are available for any Image area mode. The default value is 3 fps.
- **D3s: Continuous high speed.** Choose 9, 10, or 11 frames per second when using DX Image area. For FX and other image areas, the frame rate is fixed at 9 frames per second, and useful for capturing critical moments, like the one shown in Figure 4.8.
- **D3x: Continuous low speed.** All values from 1 to 9 fps are available for any Image area mode.

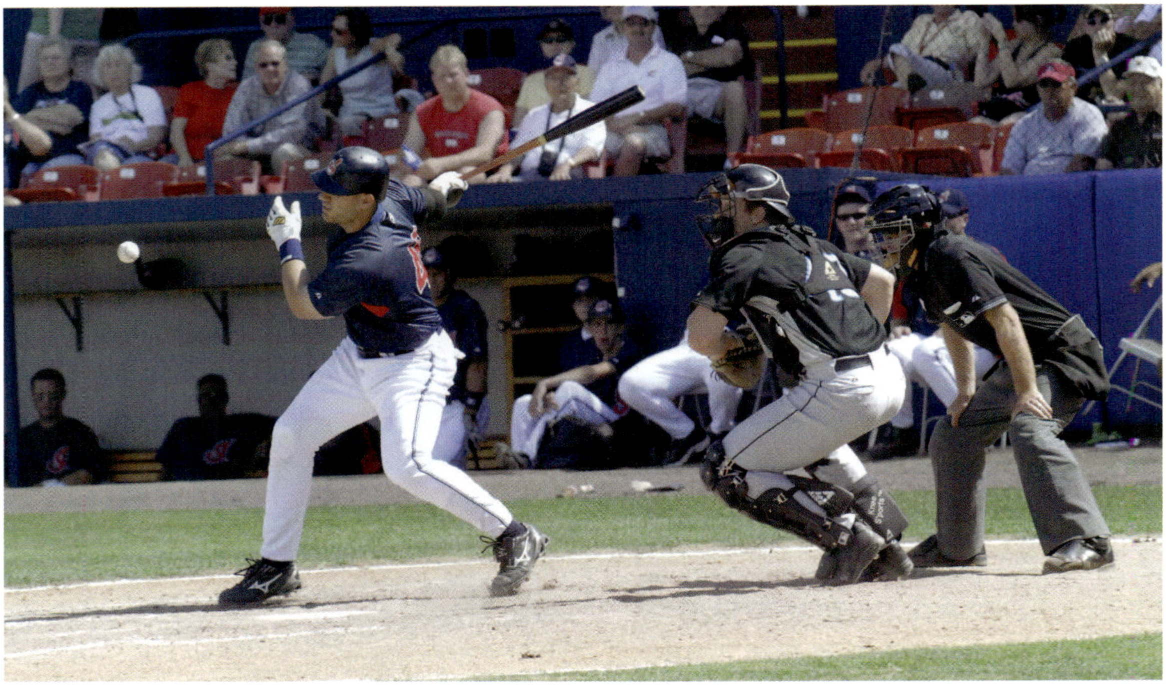

**Figure 4.8** High frame rates can capture a critical moment when shooting sports action.

Choose one of these firing speed ranges for $C_L$ and $C_H$ from among those available that is suitable for the kind of shooting environment you're in:

- **Normal continuous shooting.** I set my D3s/D3x to the 1 fps rate most of the time, so that I can take multiple shots quickly without needing to press the shutter release repeatedly. A one-second rate isn't so fast that I end up taking a bunch of shots that I don't want, but it is fast enough that I can shoot a series.
- **Bracketing.** When I'm using bracketing, I generally have the D3s/D3x set to shoot a bracketed set of three pictures: normal, over-, and underexposure. With the camera set to 3 fps, I can press the shutter once and take all three bracketed shots, with basically the same framing, within about one second.

- **Slower action sequences.** The 5 fps and faster rates available for sports photography often produce an embarrassing plethora of pictures that are a pain to wade through after the event is over. For some types of action, such as long distance running, golf, swimming, or routine baseball plays, a rate of 3 to 5 fps might be sufficient. You can make this more reasonable speed available by defining it here as the continuous low speed frame rate.

## d3 Max. Continuous Release

Use this setting to limit the number of consecutive shots that can be taken in one burst when using continuous shooting modes. Your choices are any value between 1 and 130. Choosing a particular setting does not mean that the D3s/D3x will actually *take* that many shots if you hold down the shutter button long enough. As your buffer fills, continuous shooting will slow down and eventually pause while the D3s/D3x dumps pictures to the memory card. Nikon beefed up the size of the buffer for the D3s (and offered a buffer upgrade for the original D3), so it's likely that you probably will never outrun your D3s's buffer. However, the D3x's file sizes are twice as large, so you can easily find yourself waiting for the memory card to store images, especially if you're shooting RAW+JPEG at a 5 fps rate.

However, there are many image quality and size settings that will allow the D3s/D3x to shoot more or less forever when equipped with a very fast memory card. For example, at the JPEG Normal setting, you can theoretically shoot 122 full-resolution images consecutively, and even using JPEG Fine you may be able to fire off more than 82 pictures in one burst with the D3s. The D3x isn't far behind with a buffer capacity of 80 full-resolution images at the JPEG Normal and 44 when using JPEG Fine. If you'd rather not accumulate that many images of one action and don't trust yourself to let up on the shutter release (it would take about 12 seconds to shoot 100 pictures at 9 fps), you can limit the maximum burst here.

## d4 File Number Sequence

The Nikon D3s/D3x will automatically apply a file number to each picture you take, using consecutive numbering for all your photos over a long period of time, spanning many different memory cards, starting over from scratch when you insert a new card, or when you manually reset the numbers. Numbers are applied from 0001 to 9999, at which time the D3s/D3x "rolls over" to 0001 again.

The camera keeps track of the last number used in its internal memory and, if File number sequence is turned On, will apply a number that's one higher, or a number that's one higher than the largest number in the current folder on the memory card inserted in the camera. You can also start over each time a new folder has been created on the memory card, or reset the current counter back to 0001 at any time.

Here's how it works:

- **On.** At this default setting, the D3s/D3x will use the number stored in its internal memory any time a new folder is created, a new memory card inserted, or an existing memory card formatted. If the card is not blank and contains images, then the next number will be one greater than the highest number on the card *or* in internal memory (whichever is higher). Here are some examples.
  - You've taken 1,235 shots with the camera, and you insert a blank/reformatted memory card. The next number assigned will be 1,236, based on the value stored in internal memory.
  - You've taken 1,235 shots with the camera, and you insert an old memory card you previously used with the D3s/D3x, but which has a picture numbered 0728. The next picture will be numbered 1,236.
  - You've taken more than 9,999 shots with the camera and the counter has rolled over to 0001 again, and your new total is 1,235 shots. You insert an old memory card with a picture from before the rollover that's numbered 8,281. The next picture will be numbered 8,282, and that value will be stored in the camera's menu as the "high" shot number (and will be applied when you next insert a blank card). This misnumbering makes it a good idea to always reformat your memory cards before taking a photo, if at all possible.
- **Off.** If you're using a blank/reformatted memory card, or a new folder is created, the next photo taken will be numbered 0001. File number sequences will be reset every time you use or format a card, or a new folder is created (which happens when an existing folder on the card contains 999 shots).
- **Reset.** The D3s/D3x assigns a file number that's one larger than the largest file number in the current folder, unless the folder is empty, in which case numbering is reset to 0001. At this setting, new or reformatted memory cards will always have 0001 as the first file number.

## HOW MANY SHOTS, REALLY?

The file numbers produced by the D3s/D3x don't provide information about the actual number of times the camera's shutter has been tripped—called actuations. For that data, you'll need a third-party software solution, such as the free Opanda iExif (www.opanda.com) for Windows (see Figure 4.9) or the non-free ($34.95) GraphicConverter for Macintosh (www.lemkesoft.com). These utilities can be used to extract the true number of actuations from the Exif information embedded in a JPEG file.

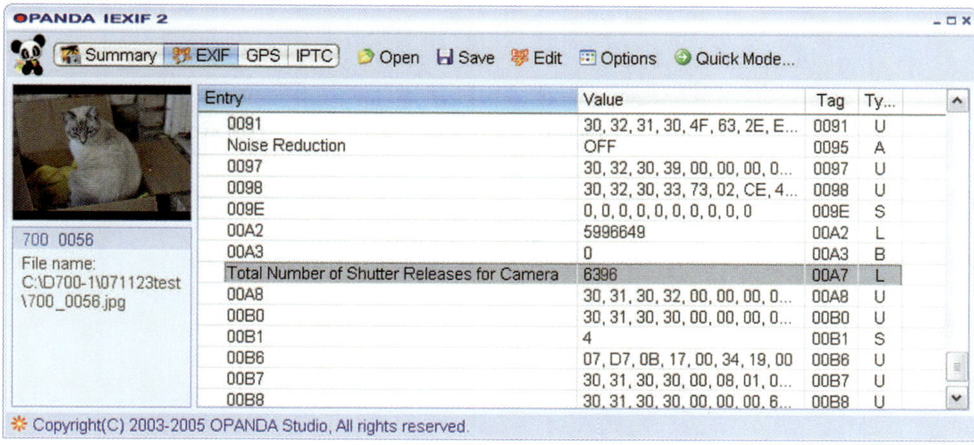


**Figure 4.9**
Opanda iExif shows the exact number of pictures that have been taken with your camera.

## d5 Control Panel/Viewfinder

You can change the information displayed in the rear control panel and in the viewfinder, using this option.

- **Rear control panel.** By default, the current ISO sensitivity setting is displayed at the left side of the rear control panel. Most of us like to keep track of the ISO we're using, if only to keep us reminded of the amount of grain that can be produced at higher settings. However, you can opt to have the number of exposures remaining on your memory card shown instead. The ISO setting can still be viewed at any time by pressing the ISO button just beneath the rear control panel. You might want to have the remaining exposures visible on the back of the camera when the D3s/D3x is mounted on a tripod at roughly eye-level (and the exposure counters on the top-panel LCD aren't readily available). This might be especially true if you're shooting a lot of photos and don't want to run out unexpectedly.
- **Viewfinder display.** By default, the number of frames you've taken with the current memory card is shown at the right edge of the viewfinder display. If you'd rather keep track of the number of exposures remaining instead, you can choose that option here. In either case, the memory buffer capacity will be displayed when the shutter release is pressed.

## d6 Information Display/Shooting Info Display

This menu entry is labeled Information display on the D3s, and Shooting info display in the D3x menu. In either case, the nomenclature refers to the shooting information display that appears when you press the Info button. You can set this display to change automatically from dark lettering on a light background to light lettering on a dark background (as seen previously in Chapter 2), or you can select one or the other to be used all the time. The color LCD monitor will automatically change its brightness to provide the best contrast for the selected text display. Your choices are as follows:

- **Auto.** If the scene as viewed through the lens indicates a bright environment, the shooting info display will appear as black letters on a white background, producing an improved view in full daylight. If the scene appears dark, the display will have lighter letters on a dark background. Note that it's easy to "fool" the camera. Until you take the lens cap off, you'll see the dark background display regardless of your shooting environment. If you're standing in a darkened location, but point the camera at a bright scene, the D3s/D3x will show you the "daylight" display.
- **Manual.** Select this option and you can choose B (Dark on light) or W (Light on dark) to be used as the display at all times.

## d7 Screen Tips (D3s Only)

Screen tips are the Tool Tip type labels that pop up when you've selected an item on the information display that you want to change (available with the Nikon D3s only). Choose On to enable screen tips; Off to disable them (after you've memorized each option's function).

## d7 (D3x)/d8 (D3s) LCD Illumination

When set to Off (the default), the monochrome LCD status panel (and the status LCDs on any attached compatible Nikon Speedlight, such as the Nikon SB-900) will illuminate for as long as the exposure meters are active, but only when the switch around the shutter release is pressed towards the maximum clockwise direction, just past the On indicator. Choose On, and the panel will be illuminated any time the exposure meters are active (and thus using more power), without the need to press the switch.

## d8 (D3x)/d9 (D3s) Exposure Delay Mode

This is a marginally useful feature you can use to force the Nikon D3s/D3x to snap a picture about one second after you've pressed the shutter release button all the way. It's useful when you are using shutter speeds of about 1/8th to 1/60th second hand-held and want to minimize the effects of the vibration that results when you depress the shutter button. It can also be used when the camera is mounted on a tripod, although the self-timer function, set to a two-second delay, is more useful in that scenario. When switched On, the camera will pause while you steady your steely grip on the camera, taking the picture about one second later. When turned Off, the picture is taken when the shutter release is pressed, as normal. One interesting side effect of this mode is that it separates the normally invisible pre-flash produced by any D3s/D3x's external flash that's connected with the delay, so, if you're shooting living subjects (human or animal) they may be startled by the initial flash and close their eyes just before the main flash fires 1,000 milliseconds later.

# e. Bracketing/Flash

There are lots of useful settings in this submenu (see Figure 4.10) that deal with bracketing and electronic flash (hence the cleverly concocted name). I'll provide a thorough description of using bracketing in Chapter 6, and a complete rundown of flash options in Chapter 10. Here, I'll offer an introduction to the settings at your disposal.

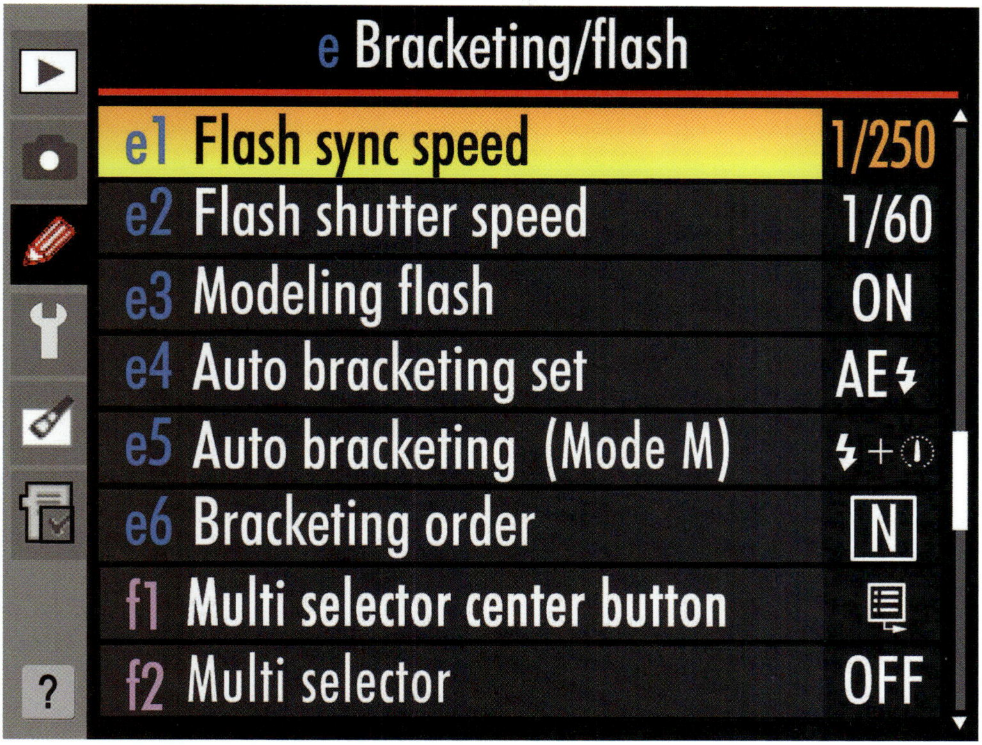


**Figure 4.10** Bracketing and flash options are available in this menu.

## e1 Flash Sync Speed

As you may already know (or will learn in Chapter 8), the focal plane shutter in the Nikon D3s/D3x must be fully open when the flash fires; otherwise, you'll image one edge or the other of the vertically traveling shutter curtain in your photo. Ordinarily, the fastest shutter speed during which the shutter is completely open for an instant is 1/250th second. However, there are exceptions when you can use faster shutter speeds with certain flash units (such as the Nikon SB-900, SB-600, and SB-R200) for automatic FP (focal plane) synchronization. There are also situations in which you might want to set flash sync speed to *less* than 1/250th second, say, because you *want* ambient light to produce secondary ghost images in your frame. (I'll address all these sync issues in Chapter 8.)

You can choose the following settings:

- **1/250 s (Auto FP).** This setting allows using the named external flash units with high-speed synchronization at 1/250th second or faster, and activates auto FP sync when the camera selects a shutter speed of 1/250th second or faster in programmed and aperture-priority modes. Other flash units will be used at speeds no faster than 1/250th second.
- **1/250 s.** At this default setting, only shutter speeds up to 1/250th second can be used with flash, both internal and external. Note: To lock in shutter speed at 1/250th second, choose the x 250 setting located after the 30 s and bulb speeds.
- **1/200 s-1/60 s.** You can specify a shutter speed from 1/200th second to 1/60th second to be used as the synchronization speed for external flash units.

## e2 Flash Shutter Speed

This setting determines the *slowest* shutter speed that is available for electronic flash synchronization when you're not using a "slow sync" mode (described in Chapter 10). As you may know, when you're using flash, the flash itself provides virtually all of the illumination that makes the main exposure, and the shutter speed determines how much, if any, of the ambient light contributes to that second, non-flash exposure. Indeed, if the camera or subject is moving, you can end up with two distinct exposures in the same frame: the sharply defined flash exposure, and a second, blurry "ghost" picture created by the ambient light.

If you *don't* want that second exposure, you should use the highest shutter speed that will synchronize with your flash. This setting prevents programmed or aperture-priority modes (which both select the shutter speed for you) from inadvertently selecting a "too slow" shutter speed. You can select a value from 30 s to 1/60 s, and the D3s/D3x will avoid using speeds slower than the one you specify with electronic flash (unless you've selected slow sync, slow rear-curtain sync, or red-eye reduction with slow sync, as described in Chapter 10). The "slow sync" modes do permit the ambient light to contribute to the exposure (say, to allow the background to register in night shots, or to use the ghost image as a special effect). For brighter backgrounds, you'll need to put the camera on a tripod or other support to avoid the blurry ghosts that can occur from camera shake, even if the subject is stationary.

If you are able to hold the D3s/D3x steady, a value of 1/30 s is a good compromise; if you have shaky hands, use 1/60 s or higher. Those with extraordinarily solid grips or a lens with vibration reduction can try the 1/15 s setting. Remember that this setting only determines the slowest shutter speed that will be used, not the default shutter speed.

## e3 Modeling Flash

The Nikon D3s/D3x, and certain compatible external flash units (like the SB-600 and SB-900) have the capability of simulating a modeling lamp, which gives you the limited capability of previewing how your flash illumination is going to look in the finished photo. The modeling flash is not a perfect substitute for a real incandescent or fluorescent modeling lamp, but it does help you see how your subject is illuminated, and spot any potential problems with shadows.

When this feature is activated, pressing the Depth-of-field button on the D3s/D3x briefly triggers the modeling flash for your preview. Selecting Off disables the feature. You'll generally want to leave it On, except when you anticipate using the Depth-of-field preview button for depth-of-field purposes (imagine that) and do *not* want the modeling flash to fire when the flash unit is charged and ready. Some external flash units, such as the SB-900, have their own modeling flash buttons. Although the SB-600 does not have this button, it works fine with the D3s/D3x's modeling flash feature.

## e4 Auto Bracketing Set

The Nikon D3s/D3x can automatically take several pictures using slightly different settings within a range that you specify, and apply the changes to automatic exposure, electronic flash, white balance, or (with the D3s) Active D-Lighting. This setting allows you to specify whether bracketing is used for both automatic exposure *and* flash (AE & flash), automatic exposure only (AE), flash bracketing only (Flash only), white balance color bracketing alone (WB bracketing) or (with the D3s) Active D-Lighting bracketing alone. No autoexposure or flash bracketing will be performed when white balance bracketing or ADL bracketing is activated. Because you can specify white balance manually when importing a RAW file, WB bracketing is not available when Quality has been set to NEF (RAW) or NEF (RAW)+JPEG. The results you get with flash bracketing can vary quite a bit, depending on the amount of ambient illumination and flash mode you've chosen, but exposure bracketing is fairly consistent. I tend to leave this option set to AE most of the time. White balance bracketing is useful when you're not quite sure of the color balance of your illumination. ADL bracketing with the D3s can come in handy when you're not sure which Active D-Lighting setting will work for a particular situation. You'll find more about bracketing in Chapter 6.

## e5 Auto Bracketing Mode (Mode M)

If you're using manual exposure mode to set the shutter speed and f/stop yourself, you can still take advantage of exposure bracketing. The Nikon D3s/D3x will take the basic settings you specified and adjust the exposure to provide over, under, and as-set variations. This setting determines whether shutter speed, aperture, or both are used to create the bracketing exposures. Remember, *you* set the basic exposure using shutter speed and aperture, and the D3s/D3x brackets around those values. If your flash is used and has been activated for bracketing using Custom Setting e5, the flash will be factored in, as well. The menu entries can be tricky to understand, so I'm going to spell them out:

- **Flash/Speed.** With this default value, the D3s/D3x will vary the shutter speed to produce bracketed exposures and, if flash bracketing is available, will vary flash output as well. Use this option to keep your aperture set at the f/stop you select, say, to provide a certain desired amount (or lack) of depth-of-field. This setting works best when bracketing a moderate number of shots—say, 2 to 5 exposures—because the shutter speed changes among the bracketed set won't be dramatic.
- **Flash/Speed/Aperture.** This option tells the D3s/D3x to vary both shutter speed and aperture from your manual settings, and to vary flash output if flash bracketing is available. This setting is useful when creating a large bracket set, up to nine different exposures, because you'll rarely want to vary shutter speed or aperture alone over such a large range of shots. The Flash/Speed/Aperture option spreads the variation over a combination of shutter speeds and apertures.
- **Flash/Aperture.** The D3s/D3x will use the aperture to bracket your photos taken by ambient light, and if flash bracketing is available, will use flash output as well. This option is best if you're shooting sports with manual exposure and want to lock in a specific shutter speed. As with Flash/Speed, this setting works best when the number of exposures in your bracket set is limited to 2 to 5 exposures; otherwise, the f/stop selected can vary wildly.
- **Flash Only.** The D3s/D3x will bracket only flash exposure.

## e6 Bracketing Order

Use this setting to define the sequence in which bracketing is carried out. Your choices are the default: MTR > Under > Over (metered exposure, followed by the version receiving less exposure, and finishing with the picture receiving the most exposure) and Under > MTR > Over, which orders the exposures from least exposed to most exposed (for both ambient and flash exposures). The same order is applied to white balance bracketing, too, but the values are Normal > More Yellow > More Blue and More Yellow > Normal > More Blue. (Nikon actually calls "yellow" by the term "amber," but I've found "yellow" easier to understand.) You'll find lots more about bracketing in Chapter 6. When doing ADL bracketing with the D3s, this setting has no effect.

# f. Controls

You can modify the way various control buttons and dials perform by using the options in this submenu, shown in Figure 4.11.

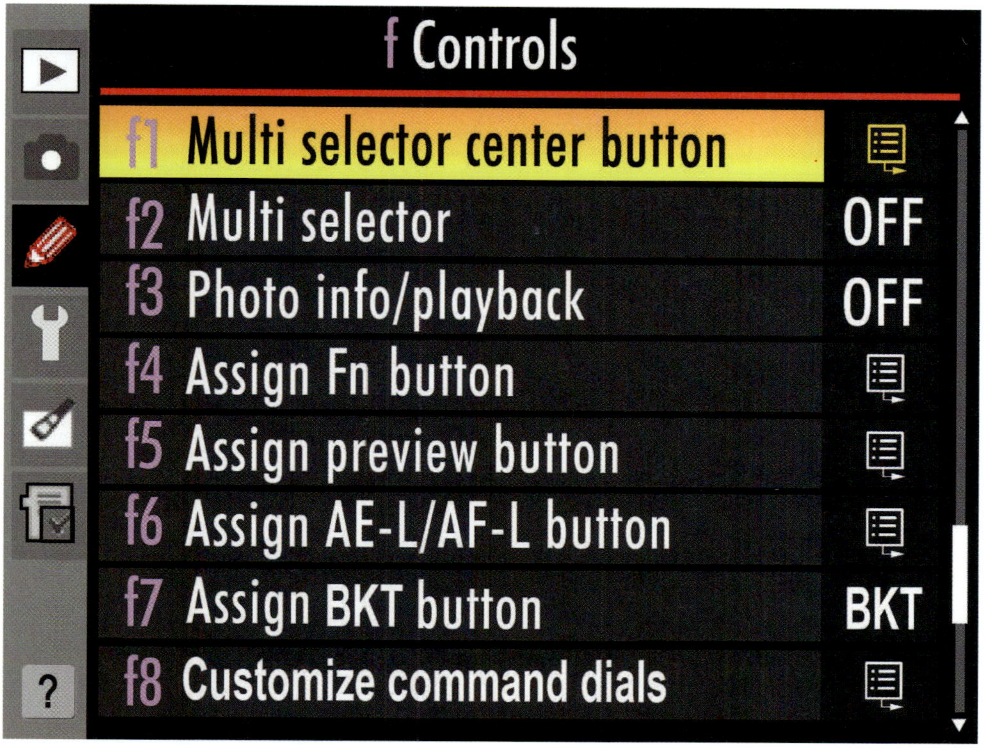


**Figure 4.11** Modify the behavior of the D3s/D3x's controls with these menu options.

## f1 Multi Selector Center Button

There are three groups of options available here, one for use when the camera is in shooting mode, and another when you're reviewing images in playback mode. The third is applied during live view mode. So the multi selector center button can have three different functions. In shooting mode:

- **RESET/Select center focus point.** This default setting lets you quickly select the center focus point in the viewfinder simply by pressing the multi selector center button.
- **Not used.** Nothing happens when the multi selector center button is pressed. If you find yourself sloppily pressing the center button in the heat of the moment while shooting, use this setting to deactivate it and avoid unwanted actions.

In playback mode:

- **Thumbnail on/off.** This default setting alternates between full-frame and thumbnail playback.
- **View histograms.** When selected, a larger histogram is displayed while the multi selector center button is pressed.

- **Zoom on/off.** Use the multi selector center button to toggle between full-frame or thumbnail playback (whichever is active) and playback zoom. You can choose Low magnification, Medium magnification, and High magnification.

In live view mode:

- **RESET/Select center focus point.** This setting selects the center focus point in the viewfinder by pressing the center button.
- **Zoom on/off.** Use the multi selector center button to toggle between full-frame or thumbnail playback (whichever is active) and playback zoom. You can choose Low magnification, Medium magnification, and High magnification.
- **Start movie recording.** Use this setting to begin movie recording when the center button is pressed.
- **Not used.** Nothing happens when you press the multi selector center button.

## f2 Multi Selector

By default, pressing the left/right or up/down buttons on the multi selector when the exposure meters are off does nothing. If you would rather have the meters activated instead, switch from the Do nothing default to Reset meter-off delay. The meters will spring to life when one of the directional buttons is pressed, and remain active until the delay you've set previously in Custom Setting c2 has elapsed.

## f3 Photo Info/Playback

During playback, pressing the multi selector up/down buttons on the Nikon D3s/D3x changes the type of photo information displayed, while pressing the left/right buttons moves forward and back among the available images. This action was reversed in some earlier Nikon dSLRs, and some prefer that the up/down buttons scroll among images and the left/right buttons change the information display. You can use this setting to specify either mode of operation.

## f4 Assign Fn (Function) Button

You can define the action that the Fn button performs when pressed alone, or when pressed while the command dials are rotated. There are no less than 16 different actions you can define for the button alone (including None), and five for the Fn button + a command dial. For the Fn button alone you can choose from:

- **Preview.** Depth-of-field preview. Perhaps you'd like to use the DOF preview button for something else, and substitute the lower of the two buttons for DOF preview. Unfortunately, you cannot use this function if you've also selected a function for the Fn button + command dials. If you do use this function, then any Fn button + command dials function will be canceled and set to None. Conversely, if you go ahead and set a function for Fn button + command dials, this setting will be deactivated and set to None. They are what we like to call "mutually exclusive."

- **FV lock.** Press the Fn button to lock the value of the built-in or external flash, and press again to unlock it. As with Preview, you cannot use this function if you've also selected a function for the Fn button + command dials. If you do set this function, then any Fn button + command dials function will be canceled and set to None. Should you go ahead and set a function for Fn button + command dials, this setting will be deactivated and the Fn button function set to None.
- **AE/AF lock.** Lock both focus and exposure while the Fn button is pressed. Use this setting or one of the next four when you want to have a specific mode of operation normally available from the AE-L/AF-L button, but would prefer to trigger the behavior with the Fn button pressed instead.
- **AE lock only.** Lock only the exposure while the Fn button is pressed.
- **AE lock (Reset on release).** Lock exposure while the Fn button is pressed, and it remains locked until the Fn button is pressed a second time, or a picture is taken, or the exposure meter-off delay expires. This is another of the four settings mutually exclusive with using a Fn button + command dial setting.
- **AE lock (Hold).** Exposure is locked when the Fn button is pressed, and remains locked until the button is pressed again, or the exposure meter-off delay expires. This is the fourth of the settings mutually exclusive with using a Fn button + command dial setting.
- **AF lock only.** Focus is locked in while the Fn button is held down.
- **Flash off.** The attached external flash, if powered up, will not fire while the Fn button is held down. Handy if you want to temporarily disable the flash, say, to take a picture or two by available light, and then return to normal flash operation.
- **Bracketing burst.** If the Fn button is pressed while exposure, flash, or ADL bracketing have been activated in single frame mode, all the shots (from 2 to 9 exposures) will be taken, one after another, each time the shutter release is pressed. If continuous high speed or continuous low speed shooting modes ($C_H$ or $C_L$) are active (or if white balance bracketing is active), the D3s/D3x will repeat the bracketing bursts for as long as the shutter release button is pressed down.
- **Matrix metering.** Switch from the current metering mode to matrix metering while the Fn button is held down.
- **Center-weighted metering.** Switch from the current metering mode to center-weighted metering while the Fn button is held down.

- **Spot metering.** Switch from the current metering mode to spot metering while the Fn button is held down. This is my favorite setting, because I like to switch from matrix to spot metering from time to time.
- **Virtual horizon.** In this clever implementation of the virtual horizon feature, the analog exposure meter scales on the D3s and D3x act as a level, measuring both side-to-side tilt (along the axis of the lens) and forward/back tilt (raising the lens up or down). The top control panel's exposure scale shifts towards the left and right side of the scale to show rotating around the lens axis, and the viewfinder exposure scale at the side of the frame shifts up or down to indicate forward/back tilting. You'll find more information on using this feature in Chapter 5.
- **Playback.** This option redefines the Fn button to provide the same function as the Playback button. You'll find this useful when a long, heavy lens is mounted on your camera and it's difficult to press the Playback button with the left hand.
- **Access top item in My Menu.** Another new option, this one summons the first entry in your My Menu roster. Effectively, you can select *any* menu item that you access frequently, place it at the top of My Menu (as described in Chapter 5), and jump to that item by pressing the Fn button.
- **None.** Deactivates the Fn button.

To define the Fn button + command dials options, choose one of the following. Note that setting any of these while Preview, FV lock, AE lock (Reset on release), or AE lock (Hold) are active will reset the Fn button (alone) to None:

- **Choose image area.** Select from DX, FX formats, 5:4, 1.2x (on the D3s only), or Auto (the D3s/D3x will detect Nikon DX lenses), and some from third-party manufacturers.
- **1 step spd/aperture.** If you sometimes prefer coarser exposure settings of 1 whole step (instead of the 1/3 or 1/2 step increments that are normally set), use this option. When holding down the Fn button and rotating a command dial, shutter speed and aperture changes are made in whole step increments instead.
- **Choose non-CPU lens number.** If you swap out older non-CPU manual lenses frequently, this option provides a quicker way of telling the D3s/D3x which lens number (1 to 9) to use. I often mount an old manual focus 85mm f/1.8 lens or 55mm f/3.5 Micro Nikkor on my D3s/D3x, and can use this facility to switch back and forth between the lens settings I've manually entered for these lenses. (Chapter 5 will show you how to do that in the Setup menu.)
- **Focus point selection.** Press the Fn button and rotate the vertical grip command dials to choose a focus point. You may find this easier than trying to reach the multi selector when holding the camera in a vertical orientation.

- **Shooting menu bank.** Choose a Shooting menu bank by rotating a command dial while the Fn button is pressed. Helpful if you frequently switch among banks.
- **Dynamic AF area.** Switch among the number of focus points active in dynamic-area AF mode when using continuous-servo autofocus, from 9, 21, and 51 points.
- **None.** No action is performed when the Fn button is held down while the command dials are rotated.

### USING BOTH FN PLUS FN + COMMAND DIALS

The settings that preclude the use of the Fn button + command dials combinations can be confusing. To make things simpler, you can define the Fn button to use AE/AF lock, AE lock only, AF lock only, flash off, bracketing burst, matrix, center-weighted, or spot metering options with any of the Fn button + command dial options. If you define the Fn button to provide Preview, FV lock, AE lock (Reset on release), AE lock (Hold), Playback, or +NEF (RAW) functions, you cannot use *any* of the Fn button + command dial options at all. If you elect to use any Fn button + command dial settings, then the antagonistic Fn button functions are disabled. It's as simple (or complicated) as that.

## f5 Assign Preview Button

The Depth-of-field button can also be defined as you wish, with the same options and limitations as for the Fn button, but the default action for the DOF button is Preview, and the focus point-selection option is not available for the Preview button + command dials. The default setting is None.

## f6 Assign AE-L/AF-L Button

As if the Nikon D3s/D3x didn't have enough buttons that are user-definable, you can change the behavior of the AE-L/AF-L button, too, both when it is used alone and when held down while command dials are rotated. The options and limitations are basically the same as for the Fn button described earlier, except that the default value for the AE-L/AF-L button is AE/AF lock, and there is no default action for AE-L/AF-L button + command dials. There are a couple other exceptions, which are spelled out in the revised recap of the options listed next.

- **Preview.** Depth-of-field preview. Perhaps you'd like to use the DOF preview button for something else, and substitute the lower of the two buttons for DOF preview. Unfortunately, you cannot use this function if you've also selected a function for the AE-L/AF-L button + command dials. If you do use this function, then any AE-L/AF-L button + command dials function will be canceled and set to None. Conversely, if you go ahead and set a function for AE-L/AF-L button + command dials, this setting will be deactivated and set to None. They are what we like to call "mutually exclusive."

- **FV lock.** Press the AE-L/AF-L button to lock the value of the built-in or external flash, and press again to unlock it. As with Preview, you cannot use this function if you've also selected a function for the AE-L/AF-L button + command dials. If you do set this function, then any AE-L/AF-L button + command dials function will be canceled and set to None. Should you go ahead and set a function for AE-L/AF-L button + command dials, this setting will be deactivated and the AE-L/AF-L button function set to None.
- **AE/AF lock.** This is the default definition for the AE-L/AF-L button. When active, it locks both focus and exposure while the AE-L/AF-L button is pressed. Use this setting or one of the next four when you want to have a specific mode of operation normally available from the AE-L/AF-L button, but would prefer to trigger the behavior with the AE-L/AF-L button pressed instead.
- **AE lock only.** Lock only the exposure while the AE-L/AF-L button is pressed.
- **AE lock (Reset on release).** Lock exposure while the AE-L/AF-L button is pressed, and it remains locked until the AE-L/AF-L button is pressed a second time, or a picture is taken, or the exposure meter-off delay expires. This is another of the four settings mutually exclusive with using an AE-L/AF-L button + command dial setting.
- **AE lock (Hold).** Exposure is locked when the AE-L/AF-L button is pressed, and remains locked until the button is pressed again, or the exposure meter-off delay expires. This is the fourth of the settings mutually exclusive with using an AE-L/AF-L button + command dial setting.
- **AF lock only.** Focus is locked in while the AE-L/AF-L button is held down.
- **AF-ON.** This option is not available for the Fn key. When active, pressing the AE-L/AF-L button has the same effect as pressing the AF-ON button to initiate autofocus. You can't use this option in combination with the AE-L/AF-L + command dials options.
- **Flash off.** The attached external flash, if powered up, will not fire while the AE-L/AF-L button is held down. Handy if you want to temporarily disable the flash, say, to take a picture or two by available light, and then return to normal flash operation.
- **Bracketing burst.** If the AE-L/AF-L button is pressed while exposure, flash, or ADL bracketing have been activated in single frame mode, all the shots (from 2 to 9 exposures) will be taken, one after another, each time the shutter release is pressed. If continuous high speed or continuous low speed shooting modes ($C_H$ or $C_L$) are active (or if white balance bracketing is active), the D3s/D3x will repeat the bracketing bursts for as long as the shutter release button is pressed down.

- **Matrix metering.** Switch from the current metering mode to matrix metering while the AE-L/AF-L button is held down.
- **Center-weighted metering.** Switch from the current metering mode to center-weighted metering while the AE-L/AF-L button is held down.
- **Spot metering.** Switch from the current metering mode to spot metering while the AE-L/AF-L button is held down. This is my favorite setting, because I like to switch from matrix to spot metering from time to time.
- **Virtual horizon.** In this clever implementation of the virtual horizon feature, the analog exposure meter scales on the D3s and D3x act as a level, measuring both side-to-side tilt (along the axis of the lens) and forward/back tilt (raising the lens up or down). The top control panel's exposure scale shifts towards the left and right side of the scale to show rotating around the lens axis, and the viewfinder exposure scale at the side of the frame shifts up or down to indicate forward/back tilting. You'll find more information on using this feature in Chapter 5.
- **Playback.** This option redefines the AE-L/AF-L button to provide the same function as the Playback button. You'll find this useful when a long, heavy lens is mounted on your camera and it's difficult to press the Playback button with the left hand.
- **Access top item in My Menu.** Another new option, this one summons the first entry in your My Menu roster. Effectively, you can select *any* menu item that you access frequently, place it at the top of My Menu (as described in Chapter 5), and jump to that item by pressing the AE-L/AF-L button.
- **None.** Deactivates the AE-L/AF-L button.

To define the AE-L/AF-L button + command dials options, choose one of the following. Note that setting any of these while Preview, FV lock, AE lock (Reset on release), or AE lock (Hold) are active will reset the AE-L/AF-L button (alone) to None. The 1 step spd/aperture and Focus-point selection options available for the Fn button are not offered for the AE-L/AF-L button + command dials.

- **Choose image area.** Select from DX, FX formats, 5:4, 1.2x (on the D3s only), or Auto (the D3s/D3x will detect Nikon DX lenses), and some from third-party manufacturers.
- **Choose non-CPU lens number.** If you swap out older non-CPU manual lenses frequently, this option provides a quicker way of telling the D3s/D3x which lens number (1 to 9) to use. I often mount an old manual focus 85mm f/1.8 lens or 55mm f/3.5 Micro Nikkor on my D3s/D3x, and can use this facility to switch back and forth between the lens settings I've manually entered for these lenses. (Chapter 5 will show you how to do that in the Setup menu.)

- **Shooting menu bank.** Choose a Shooting menu bank by rotating a command dial while the AE-L/AF-L button is pressed. This is helpful if you frequently switch among banks.
- **Dynamic AF area.** Switch among the number of focus points active in dynamic-area AF mode when using continuous-servo autofocus, from 9, 21, and 51 points.
- **None.** No action is performed when the AE-L/AF-L button is held down while the command dials are rotated. This is the default setting.

## f7 (D3s) Assign BKT Button

Redefining the BKT button, located at the front of the mode dial, is available only with the Nikon D3s. The default action is to perform the actions described in Chapter 2: Holding the button and rotating the main command dial changes the number of shots in the bracketing sequence, while rotating the sub-command dial changes the bracketing increment. You'll find more on bracketing in Chapter 6.

With the D3s, you can change this default action so that holding the BKT button and rotating the command dial changes the bracketing mode, and the sub-command dial changes the number of shots in the multiple exposure set. If you shoot a lot of multiple exposures, or shoot multiple exposures more than you bracket, this behavior can come in quite handy, as it's faster than accessing the Multiple exposure menu entry in the Shooting menu.

## f7/f8 (D3s) Customize Command Dials

This menu entry is labeled f7 with the original D3 and D3x, and f8 with the D3s. You can use the options in this choice to change the behavior of the command dials. Use the available tweaks to change the behavior of the dials to better suit your preferences, or if you're coming to the Nikon world from another vendor's product that uses a different operational scheme. Keep in mind that redefining basic controls in this way can prove confusing if someone other than yourself uses your camera, or if you find yourself working with other Nikon cameras that have retained the normal command dial behavior. The reason that the dials are set for their default directions is to match the direction of rotation of the aperture ring/sub-command dial (when changing the aperture). Turning any of the three to the left decreases exposure, while rotating to the right increases exposure. Your options include

- **Reverse rotation.** Rotating the main command dial (both the regular camera dial and the one on the vertical grip) counterclockwise causes shutter speeds to become shorter in manual and shutter-priority modes; rotating the sub-command dial counterclockwise selects larger f/stops. If you want to reverse the directional orientation of the dials (so you'll need to rotate the main command dial clockwise to specify shorter shutter speeds, etc.), set this option to Yes. Set to No to return to the original D3s/D3x scheme of things.

- **Change main/sub.** Select On to exchange the functions of the main and sub-command dials. When activated, the main dial will set the aperture in manual and aperture-priority modes, and the sub-command dial will adjust the shutter speed in manual and shutter-priority modes. All other normal functions are swapped, as well. Select Off to return to the Nikon D3s/D3x's default arrangement.
- **Aperture setting.** Ordinarily, autofocus lenses having an aperture ring are locked at their smallest aperture when mounted on the Nikon D3s/D3x (and other Nikon models) and f/stops are set using the sub-command dial (unless you've used the Change main/sub option above). The default setting of sub-command dial retains this behavior. If you'd rather unlock the aperture ring on the lens and use that instead, choose Aperture ring. Type G lenses, which lack an aperture ring, will still be adjusted using the sub-command dial, regardless of how this setting is made. Non-CPU lenses, which lack an electronic connection to the camera, are always set using the aperture ring.
- **Menus and playback.** You can change the orientation of the command dials when navigating menus and playback options, too. By default, the main command dial is used to select an image during full-frame playback; move the cursor left or right during thumbnail viewing, and move the menu highlighting up or down. The sub-command dial is used to display additional photo information in full-frame playback, to move the cursor up and down, and to move back and forth between menus and submenus. (Note that you can also use the multi selector directional buttons for these functions.) When set to On, the functions assigned to the dials are reversed. This choice is new to the Nikon D3s/D3x.

## f8/f9 (D3s) Release Button to Use Dial

This menu entry is labeled f8 with the original D3 and D3x, and f9 with the D3s. Normally, any button used in conjunction with a command dial must be held down while the command dial or sub-command dial is rotated. Choose Yes for this option if you want to be able to press the button and release it, and then rotate the command dial. You can continue to make adjustments until the button is pressed again, or you press the Mode, Exposure Compensation, Flash, ISO, Qual, or WB buttons, or the shutter release button is pressed halfway. Exposure meter time-out also turns off setting mode, unless the D3s/D3x is connected to an AC adapter. Chose No to return to the D3s/D3x's default behavior, which requires that the button be held down while the adjustment is made.

## f9/f10 (D3s) No Memory Card?

This menu entry is labeled f9 with the original D3 and D3x, and f10 with the D3s. This option gives you the ability to snap off "pictures" without a memory card installed—or to lock the camera shutter release if that is the case. It is sometimes called play mode, because you can experiment with your camera's features or even hand your D3s/D3x to a friend to let them fool around, without any danger of pictures actually being taken.

Back in our film days, we'd sometimes finish a roll, rewind the film back into its cassette surreptitiously, and then hand the camera to a child to take a few pictures—without actually wasting any film. It's hard to waste digital film, but "shoot without card" mode is still appreciated by some, especially camera vendors who want to be able to demo a camera at a store or trade show, but don't want to have to equip each and every demonstrator model with a memory card. Choose Enable release to activate "play" mode or Release locked to disable it.

The pictures you actually "take" are displayed on the LCD with the legend "Demo" superimposed on the screen, and they are, of course, not saved. Note that if you are using the optional Camera Control Pro 2 software to record photos from a USB-tethered D3s/D3x directly to a computer, no memory card is required to unlock the shutter even if Release locked has been selected.

## f10/f11 (D3s) Reverse Indicators

This menu entry is labeled f10 with the original D3 and D3x, and f11 with the D3s. Refugees from the Canon world or other dSLR product lines are sometimes put off that Nikon cameras place the plus exposure values on the left side of the analog exposure display in the control panel, viewfinder, and shooting information display, with the negative values on the right, to match the rotation of the aperture ring (if used). This default setting (+0–) can be swapped for the opposite orientation (–0+) to change the display. My take is that if you've fled to Nikonland, you might as well get used to it. I suppose this setting is useful for a dedicated Canon shooter who sometimes uses a Nikon dSLR, and who never needs to change exposure using an aperture ring.

# 5

# Setup: The Setup Menu, Retouch Menu, and My Menu

We're not done covering the Nikon D3s/D3x's Setup options yet. There are three more menus to deal with. These include the Setup menu (which deals with adjustments that are outside the actual shooting experience, such as formatting a memory card, adjusting the time, or checking your battery); the Retouch menu (which enables you to fine-tune the appearance of images by trimming, adding filter effects, or removing red-eye); and the My Menu system, which can help you set up a customized menu that contains only the entries you want.

## Setup Menu Options

There is a long list of nearly two-dozen entries in the orange-coded Setup menu, depending on whether you're looking at a Nikon D3s or D3x. The order and arrangement of these items differs between the two cameras, most notably, with the D3s's combining three voice memo options found in the D3x into a single entry. I'm going to show the D3s menu listings in the figures, as in the first page shown in Figure 5.1, and trust you D3x owners to note the slight differences that I will describe as they come up.

All the Setup menu options let you make additional adjustments on how your camera *behaves* before or during your shooting session, as differentiated from the Shooting menu, which adjusts how the pictures are actually taken.

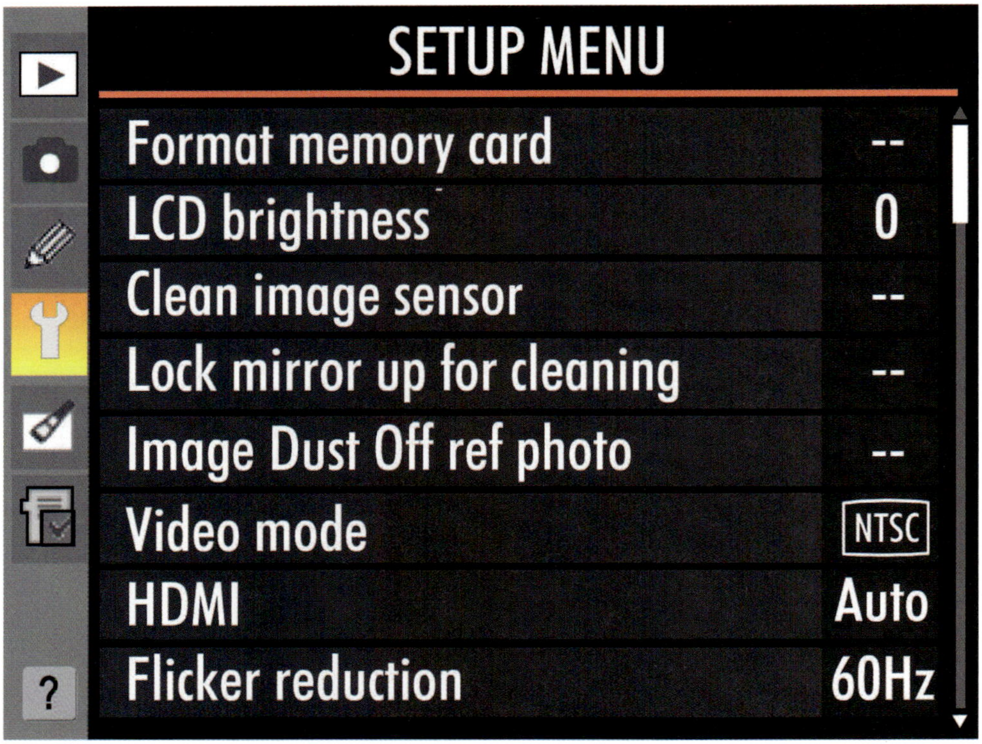


**Figure 5.1**
The Setup menu allows you to adjust how the D3s/D3x behaves.

Your choices include:

- Format memory card
- LCD brightness
- Clean image sensor
- Lock mirror up for cleaning
- Image Dust Off ref photo (D3s)
- Video mode
- HDMI
- Flicker reduction (D3s)
- World Time (Time Zone and date [D3s])
- Language
- Image comment
- Auto image rotation
- Voice memo/Voice memo options (D3s)
- Voice memo overwrite (D3x)
- Voice memo button (D3x)
- Audio output (D3x)
- USB (D3x)
- Image Dust Off ref photo (D3x)
- Battery info
- Wireless transmitter
- Image authentication
- Copyright information
- Save/load settings
- GPS
- Virtual horizon
- Non-CPU lens data
- AF fine tune
- Firmware version

## Format Memory Card

I recommend using this menu entry to reformat your memory card after each shoot. While you can move files from the memory card to your computer, creating a blank card, or delete files using the Playback menu's Delete feature, both of those options can leave behind stray files (such as those that have been marked as Hidden or Protected). Format removes those files completely and beyond retrieval (unless you use a special utility program as described in Chapter 11) and establishes a spanking new fresh file system on the card. All the file allocation table (FAT) pointers (which tell the camera and your computer's operating system where all the images reside) are reset, efficiently pointing where they are supposed to on a blank card.

If you're an efficiency nut, you can reformat a memory card without a visit to the Setup menu by holding down the Mode and Trash buttons (both marked with red Format labels) for about two seconds, until For flashes on the LCD status panel and a slot number appears below. Press the buttons a second time to format the card in the slot indicated. Or, select the Format memory card menu entry, and select Yes from the screen that appears. Press OK to begin the format process. Wait until the For indicator has finished flashing on the monochrome LCD status panel.

## LCD Brightness

Choose this menu option and a grayscale strip appears on the LCD, as shown in Figure 5.2. Use the multi selector up/down keys to adjust the brightness to a comfortable viewing level. Under the lighting conditions that exist when you make this adjustment, you should be able to see all 10 swatches from black to white. If the two left end swatches blend together, the brightness has been set too low. If the two whitest swatches on the right end of the strip blend together, the brightness is too high. Brighter settings use more battery power, but can allow you to view an image on the LCD outdoors in bright sunlight. When you have the brightness you want, press OK to lock it in and return to the menu.

## Clean Image Sensor (D3s)

This entry gives you some control over the Nikon D3s's automatic sensor cleaning feature, which removes dust through a vibration cycle that shakes the sensor until dust, presumably, falls off and is captured by a sticky surface at the bottom of the sensor area. If you happen to take a picture and notice an artifact in an area that contains little detail (such as the sky or a blank wall), you can access this menu choice, place the camera with its base downward, and choose Clean now. A message Cleaning sensor now appears, and the dust you noticed has probably been shaken off.

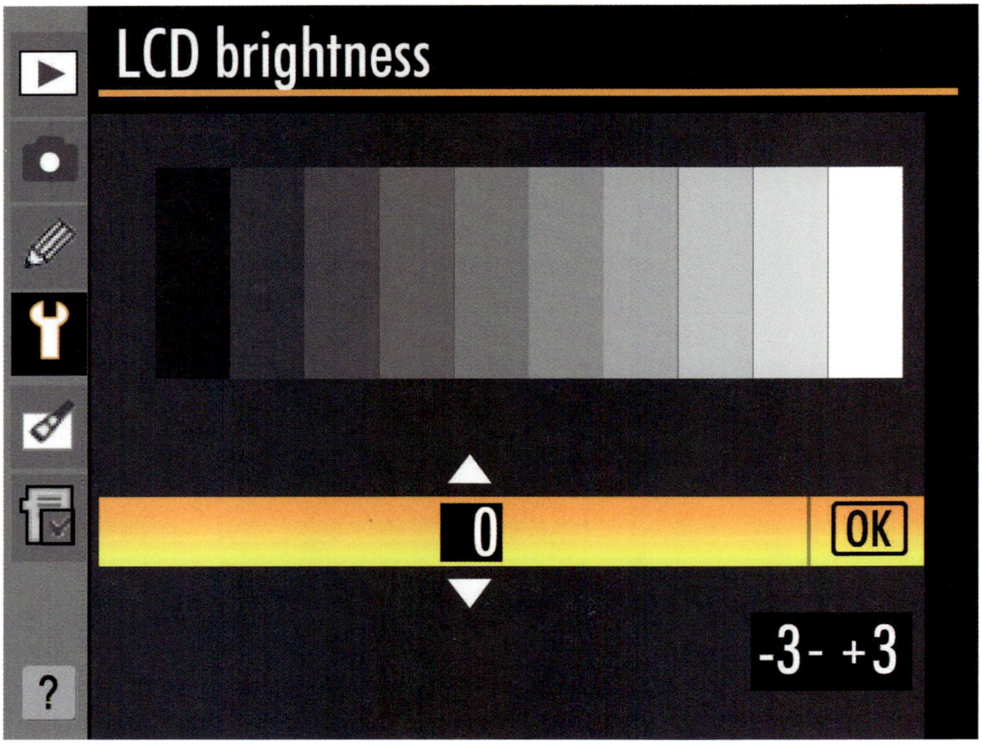


**Figure 5.2**
Adjust the LCD brightness so that all the grayscale strips are visible.

You can also tell the D3s when you'd like it to perform automatic cleaning without specific instructions from you. Select from:

- **ON.** Clean at startup. This allows you to start off a particular shooting session with a clean sensor.
- **OFF.** Clean at shutdown. This removes any dust that may have accumulated since the camera has been turned on, say, from dust infiltration while changing lenses. Note that this choice does not turn off automatic cleaning; it simply moves the operation to the camera power-down sequence.
- **ON/OFF.** Clean at both startup and shutdown. Use this setting if you're paranoid about dust and don't mind the extra battery power consumed each time the camera is turned on or off. If you only turn off the D3s when you're finished shooting, the power penalty is not large, but if you're the sort who turns off the camera every time you pause in shooting, the extra power consumed by the dust removal may exceed any savings you get from leaving the camera off.
- **Cleaning Off.** No automatic dust removal will be performed. Use this to preserve battery power, or if you prefer to use automatic dust removal only when you explicitly want to apply it.

## Lock Mirror Up for Cleaning

You can also clean the sensor manually. Use this menu entry to raise the mirror and open the shutter so you'll have access to the sensor for cleaning with a blower, brush, or swab, as described in Chapter 12. You don't want power to fail while you're poking around inside the camera, so this option is available only when sufficient battery power (at least 60 percent) is available. Using a fully charged battery or connecting the D3s/D3x to an EH-6 AC adapter is an even better idea.

## Image Dust Off Ref Photo

This menu choice (located farther down on the D3x Setup menu, but positioned at this point with the D3s) lets you "take a picture" of any dust or other particles that may be adhering to your sensor. The D3s/D3x will then append information about the location of this dust to your photos, so that the Image Dust Off option in Capture NX can be used to mask the dust in the NEF image.

To use this feature, select Image Dust Off ref photo, choose either Start or Clean sensor, and then press OK. If directed to do so, the camera will first perform a self-cleaning operation by applying ultrasonic vibration to the low-pass filter that resides on top of the sensor. Then, a screen will appear asking you to take a photo of a bright featureless white object 10 cm from the lens. Nikon recommends using a lens with a focal length of at least 50mm. Point the D3s/D3x at a solid white card and press the shutter release. An image with the extension .ndf will be created, and can be used by Nikon Capture NX as a reference photo if the "dust off" picture is placed in the same folder as an image to be processed for dust removal.

## Video Mode

This setting controls the output of the Nikon D3s/D3x to a conventional video system through the video cable when you're displaying images on a monitor or connected to a VCR through the external device's yellow video input jack. You can select either NTSC, used in the United States, Canada, Mexico, many Central, South American, and Caribbean countries, much of Asia, and other countries; or PAL, which is used in the UK, much of Europe, Africa, India, China, and parts of the Middle East.

## HDMI

The Nikon D3s/D3x has a High-Definition Multimedia Interface (HDMI) video connection, so you can play back your camera's images on HDTV or HD monitors using a type A cable, which Nikon does not provide to you, but which is readily available from third parties. Before you link up you'll want to choose the HDMI format to be used, from 480p (640 × 480 progressive scan); 576p (720 × 576 progressive scan); 720p (1280 × 720 progressive scan); or 1080i (1920 × 1080 interlaced scan).

## Flicker Reduction (D3s)

This menu entry, available only with the D3s, helps eliminate the banding and flickering effects that can result from unsynchronized video display when using live view or movie recording modes. All you need to do is match the AC power frequency in your area by selecting 50Hz (used in Europe and many other countries) or 60Hz (used in North America and other places). Some locations, such as Japan, use a mixture of 50Hz and 60Hz current.

## Time Zone and Date/World Time

Use this menu entry, called Time Zone and Date in the D3s menus and World Time in the D3x, to adjust the D3s/D3x's internal clock. It is the first entry on the second "page" of Setup menu entries (see Figure 5.3). Your options include

- **Time zone.** A small map will pop up on the setting screen and you can choose your local time zone. I sometimes forget to change the time zone when I travel (especially when going to Europe), so my pictures are all time-stamped incorrectly. I like to use the time stamp to recall exactly when a photo was taken, so keeping this setting correct is important.
- **Date and time.** Use this setting to enter the exact year, month, day, hour, minute, and second.

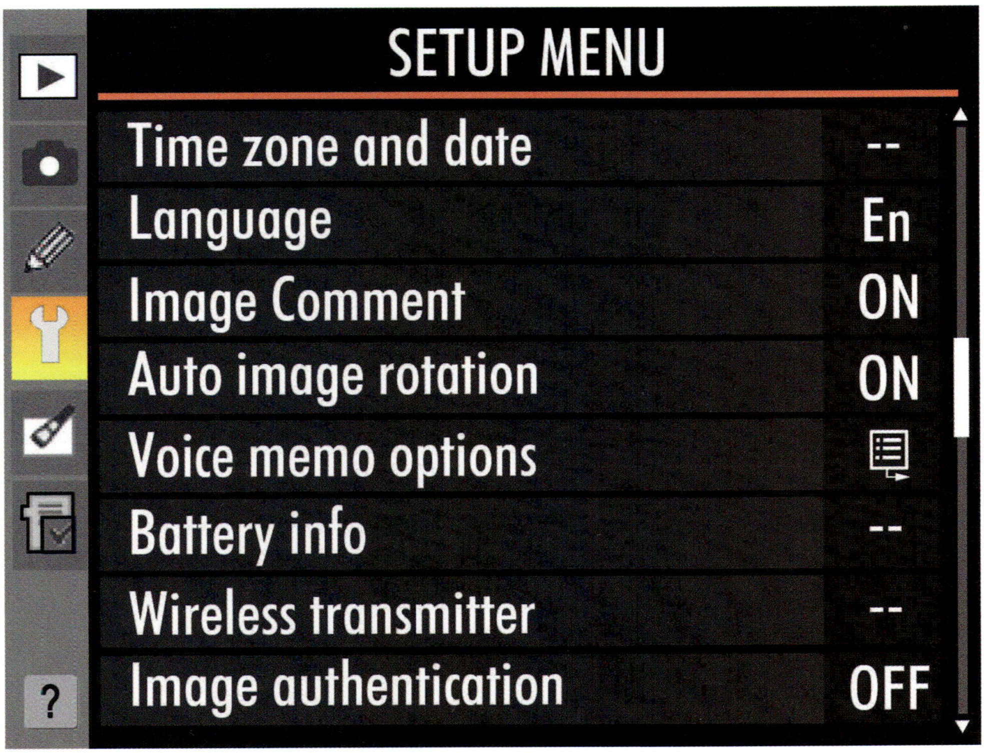


**Figure 5.3**
The second page of Setup menu options starts with the Time zone and date option

- **Date format.** Choose from Y/M/D (year/month/day), M/D/Y (month/day/year), or D/M/Y (day/month/year) formats.
- **Daylight saving time.** Use this to turn daylight saving time On or Off. Because the date on which DST goes into effect each year has been changed from time to time, if you turn this feature on you may need to monitor your camera to make sure DST has been implemented correctly.

## Language

Choose from 15 (D3x) or 20 (D3s) languages for menu display, choosing from Czech, Danish, German, English, Spanish, French, Indonesian, Italian, Finnish, Dutch, Norwegian, Polish, Portuguese, Russian, Swedish, Turkish, Traditional Chinese, Simplified Chinese, Japanese, or Korean. (The D3x lacks Czech, Danish, Norwegian, Indonesian, and Turkish.)

## Image Comment

The Image comment is your opportunity to add a copyright notice, personal information about yourself (including contact info), or even a description of where the image was taken (e.g., Browns Super Bowl 2012), although text entry with the Nikon D3s/D3x is a bit too clumsy for doing a lot of individual annotation of your photos. (But you still might want to change the comment each time, say, you change cities during your travels.) The embedded comments can be read by many software programs, including Nikon ViewNX or Capture NX.

The standard text entry screen described in Chapter 2 can be used to enter your comment, with up to 36 characters available. For the copyright symbol, embed a lowercase "c" within opening and closing parentheses: (c). You can input the comment, turn attachment of the comment On or Off using the Attach Comment entry, and select Done when you're finished working with comments. If you find typing with a cursor too tedious, you can enter your comment in Nikon Capture NX and upload it to the camera through a USB cable.

## Auto Image Rotation

Turning this setting On tells the Nikon D3s/D3x to include camera orientation information in the image file. The orientation can be read by many software applications, including Adobe Photoshop, Nikon ViewNX, and Capture NX, as well as the Rotate tall setting in the Playback menu. Turn this feature Off, and none of the software applications or Playback's Rotate tall will be able to determine the correct orientation for the image. Nikon notes that only the first image's orientation is used when shooting continuous bursts; subsequent photos will be assigned the same orientation, even if you rotate the camera during the sequence (which is something I have been known to do myself when shooting sports like basketball).

## Voice Memo Options

The D3s has a single Voice memo options entry in the Setup menu. The D3x includes the exact same four options, for recording optional notes associated with each image, but assigns each of them to an individual menu entry. The four options are Voice memo, Voice memo overwrite, Voice memo button, and Audio output. I'll explain each of these in turn.

Voice memos are an annotation feature Nikon makes available only to the "pro" cameras in its lineup, currently the D3-series cameras. You can use it to optionally accompany each image you shoot with a voice recording of up to 60 seconds in length, which is stored as a separate WAV (waveform audio file format) file on your Compact Flash card. The memo will have the same name (other than extension) as the image file, and, if you have a memory card inserted in Slot 1 and Slot 2, will always be recorded to the card in Slot 1 if you've chosen Backup or RAW/Slot 1-JPEG/Slot 2 as the function for the second card slot. If you've selected Overflow as the function for Slot 2, the WAV file will be recorded on the memory card where the original image is stored.

Before you start recording voice memos, you'll want to set up the available options.

### Voice Memo

This setting determines whether your D3s/D3x records voice memos automatically after you shoot each photo, or whether you must manually start/stop recording yourself. Your choices are as follows:

- **Off.** Voice memo recording is disabled, and pressing the Record button on the back of the camera (left of the rear control panel and marked with a microphone symbol) has no effect.
- **On (Time).** This choice activates voice memo recording and enables both automatic and manual recording, with a maximum recording time that you select (press the right directional key to see a list of choices). You can select from 5, 10, 20, 30, 45, or 60 seconds as the maximum recording time, and memo recording will begin as soon as the shutter button is released after shooting. Recording will end when the maximum time has elapsed, or when you press the Record button. If you've also activated Image review in the Playback menu, recording does not happen; you'll have to add the memo manually by pressing the Record button during image review.
- **Manual only.** If you select this option, voice memo recording will not begin automatically, and will take place only while you press and hold down the Record button for at least one second.

### Voice Memo Overwrite

This option protects/unprotects the voice memo recorded for the most recent image from being replaced.

- **Disable.** Select this option, and if a voice memo has been recorded for the most recent image, a new one cannot be recorded over it in shooting mode. If you're using voice annotations to provide an important record of your shots, you'll want to use this capability to protect them from being accidentally overwritten.
- **Enable.** Makes it possible to record a new voice memo to replace an existing one. Use this if you want to be able to update your voice memos, say, to add narration for a slide show, as described in Chapter 3.

### Voice Memo Button

This option determines how the Record button is used to control manual recording. There are two possibilities:

- **Press and hold.** Activate this choice, and voice memos will be recorded as long as the Record button is held down, up to a maximum of 60 seconds.
- **Press to start/stop.** Use this option when you want to start recording by pressing the Record button. Recording will continue until the Record button is pressed again, or 60 seconds have elapsed.

### Audio Output

This choice routes the audio output, enabling you to play back your voice memos using the speaker on the camera (located to the left of the rear control panel on the D3x, or under the Compact Flash button access door on the D3s), or to the HDMI or audio-video output ports:

- **Via speaker.** If you choose this option, you can use the up/down directional buttons to increase or decrease the playback volume.
- **HDMI/audio-video output.** Select this choice if you've hooked your D3s/D3x to an HDTV through the HDMI port, or to a monitor using the video part. The sound will be played back through the external device's speakers.
- **Off.** Voice memos are not played back at all.

Basic voice memo recording is fairly easy. Once you've set up all the options, including enabling the feature and choosing maximum recording length, you can record voice memos either automatically (with a recording for each photo) or manually (activated by pressing the button with the microphone on it) as you've set the camera up using the options just named. The basic steps are these:

- **Start recording.** If you've selected automatic mode, recording will begin after a shot has been taken, unless Image review is turned on. If you've selected manual mode, you must either hold down the Record button (it's marked with the microphone icon) to begin recording, or press it once to begin (depending on how you've set this option in the menus).

- **End recording.** If you've selected automatic mode, press the Record button to end the recording (it will end automatically after the maximum time you've specified has elapsed). If you've selected manual mode, end the recording by releasing the button, or by pressing it a second time (again, depending on which option you've selected in the menus).
- **Interrupt a recording.** Don't worry about missing a shot if an opportunity comes up while you're recording a voice memo. Pressing the shutter release halfway ends a recording automatically. So does pressing the Menu button, Playback button, or turning the camera off.
- **Add memo to an existing image.** If you later decide you want to add a memo to an existing image, view the image using the Playback options. If a musical note icon is overlaid on the review image, a voice memo has already been recorded, and a second one cannot be added, unless you've activated the Overwrite option in the memos. Press and hold the Record button to add a voice memo to that image.
- **Play back a memo.** Review the image in Playback mode, either as a full-frame image or a highlighted thumbnail. Images with voice memos available have a musical note icon superimposed in the upper-right corner of the full-frame image. Press the Record button to start playback. Playback will stop when the entire voice memo has been played or the Record button is pressed a second time.
- **Delete a memo.** Press the Trash button. A screen will pop up offering the choice of deleting both the image and sound recording, or of deleting only the sound. Use the up/down buttons to choose, then press the Trash button a second time to delete. Press the Play button to exit without deleting either.

## USB (D3x Only)

This menu entry exists only on the D3x (and original D3), and allows specifying one of two USB modes for the camera, Mass storage and MTP/PTP (Media Transfer Protocol/Picture Transfer Protocol). The D3s uses an appropriate USB mode automatically.

- **MTP/PTP.** This should be used when you connect the camera to a PictBridge-compatible printer, the optional WT-4a wireless transmitter, or when you're controlling the camera remotely from a computer using Nikon Camera Control Pro software. This mode allows two-way communication so that software in the computer can control functions of the camera.
- **Mass storage.** This option connects the camera to your computer and mimics a dumb removable disk drive, so that you can drag and drop files from either of the two memory cards to a folder on your computer. I prefer not to do this (moving files in this way uses a lot of power), so my D3x is always set to MTP/PTP.

## Battery Info

This screen (not shown) is purely informational; there are no settings to be made. When invoked, you can see the following information:

- **Bat. meter.** The current battery level, shown as a percentage from 100 to 0 percent.
- **Pic. meter.** This shows the number of actuations with the current battery since it was last recharged. This number can be larger than the number of photos taken, because other functions, such as white balance presetting, can cause the shutter to be tripped.
- **Calibration.** This shows when the battery should be recalibrated over its useful life, so the camera is able to detect battery power level more accurately. I explained how to calibrate the EN-EL4a battery in Chapter 1.
- **Charging life.** Eventually, a battery will no longer accept a charge as well as it did when it was new, and must be replaced. This indicator shows when a battery is considered new (0); has begun to degrade slightly (1,2,3); or has reached the end of its charging life and is ready for replacement (4). Batteries charged at temperatures lower than 41 degrees F may display an impaired charging life temporarily, but return to their true "health" when recharged above 68 degrees F.

## Wireless Transmitter

This menu entry is used to modify settings for connecting to a wireless network using the optional WT-4a wireless transmitter. Consult the manual furnished with your transmitter for instructions on configuring the device and your computer's WiFi network. This menu entry is available only when the WT-4a is connected.

## Image Authentication

The Nikon D3s/D3x has a special feature that allows determining whether a specific JPEG, TIFF, or NEF (RAW) image has been modified using Nikon's optional Image Authentication software. To embed the encrypted information in an image, turn this feature On. If you don't want image authentication information embedded, set this feature to the default value, Off.

Image authentication is used by law enforcement and government agencies, the media, insurance companies, and for other business applications where it is important to determine whether an image has been edited or modified since it was taken. Even the software is protected from modification, using both a product key and USB device that must be plugged into the computer before the software will run.

## Copyright Information

This is an expansion of the Image Comment capability, allowing you to specify the name of the "artist" (photographer), and enter copyright information. Use the standard Nikon text entry screen described earlier. Highlight the Attach copyright information option and press the right multi selector button to mark/unmark it to control whether your copyright data is embedded in each photo as taken.

## Save/Load Settings

You can store many camera settings to your memory card in a file named NCSETUP5, and then reload them later using this menu item. This is a good way to archive your favorite camera settings for the Playback menu, all four Shooting menu and Custom Setting menu banks, the Setup menu settings, and all My Menu items. You can restore your settings if you've messed them up, or save multiple sets of settings to multiple memory cards. You can save only one group of settings at a time to a particular card (always in Slot 1); the default name NCSETUP3 (D3x) or NCSETUP6 (D3s) cannot be changed. Well, it *can* be changed in your computer, but if you do, the D3s/D3x will not be able to find it on the memory card. If you want to save multiple settings, simply use multiple memory cards. This might be a good use for all those 256MB SD cards you have left over from your point-and-shoot snapshooting days.

Note that storing/restoration is an all-or-nothing proposition. When you select Save settings, all your current settings are stored on the memory card; choose Load settings, and the camera's current settings are replaced with the values stored on the memory card. The following settings are saved:

- **Playback.** Display mode, Image review, After delete, Rotate tall.
- **Shooting menu.** Active shooting menu bank, File naming, Slot 2 function, Image quality, Image size, Image area, JPEG compression, NEF (RAW) recording, White balance, Set Picture Control, Color space, Active D-Lighting, Vignette control, Long exp. NR, High ISO NR, ISO sensitivity settings, Live view mode, Movie settings (D3s only). The settings for all four banks (A, B, C, D) are stored.
- **Custom Setting menu.** All settings for all four banks (A, B, C, D) are stored.
- **Setup menu.** Clean image sensor (D3s only), Video mode, HDMI, Flicker reduction (D3s only), Time zone and date (World time), Language, Image comment, Auto image rotation, Image authentication, Voice memo settings, USB (D3x only), Copyright information, GPS, Non-CPU lens data.
- **My Menu/Recent Settings.** All My Menu entries, All recent settings, active tab.

## GPS

This menu entry has options for using the Nikon GP-1 Global Positioning System (GPS) device, shown mounted on my D3s in Figure 5.4. It has three options, none of which turn GPS features on or off, despite the misleading "Enable" and "Disable" nomenclature (what you're enabling and disabling is the automatic exposure meter turn-off):

- **Enable.** Reduces battery drain by enabling turning off exposure meters while using the GP-1 after the time specified in Custom Setting c2 (Auto meter-off delay, discussed earlier in this chapter) has elapsed. When the meters turn off, the GP-1 becomes inactive and must reacquire at least three satellite signals before it can begin recording GPS data once more.
- **Disable.** Causes exposure meters to remain on while using the GP-1, so that GPS data can be recorded at any time, despite increased battery drain.
- **Position.** This is an information display, rather than a selectable option. It appears when the GP-1 is connected and receiving satellite positioning data. It shows the latitude, longitude, altitude, and Coordinated Universal Time (UTC) values.

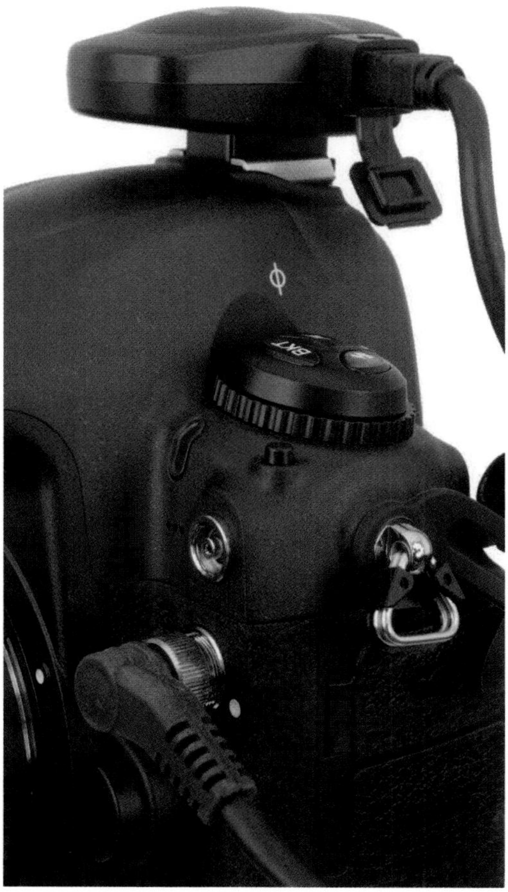

**Figure 5.4**
The Nikon GP-1 GPS device can be clipped to your camera strap or mounted on the accessory shoe on top of the camera.

## Virtual Horizon

Some people like this feature, which provides a virtual bubble level display on the LCD that acts like the horizon indicator in an airplane, ostensibly to help you keep your image level as you shoot. I'm less than enamored, finding it to be an interesting toy that really doesn't do the job sufficiently.

When activated, a circular indicator like the one shown in Figure 5.5 appears on the LCD. When the camera is level, the reference line will be displayed in green. As I noted in Chapter 4 when explaining Custom Setting f4, the Fn (Function) button can be assigned to display this virtual horizon. The analog exposure meter scales on the D3s and D3x act as a level, measuring both side-to-side tilt (along the axis of the lens) and forward/back tilt (raising the lens up or down). The top control panel's exposure scale shifts towards the left and right side of the scale to show rotating around the lens axis, and the viewfinder exposure scale at the side of the frame shifts up or down to indicate forward/back tilting. Tilting may not be shown accurately, however, as the D3-series cameras can't measure it precisely.

In addition, you can't frame a picture through the viewfinder very easily while monitoring this display, and it's difficult to keep the camera on a level plane, so you'll find that the virtual horizon works best when the D3s/D3x is mounted on a tripod and/or

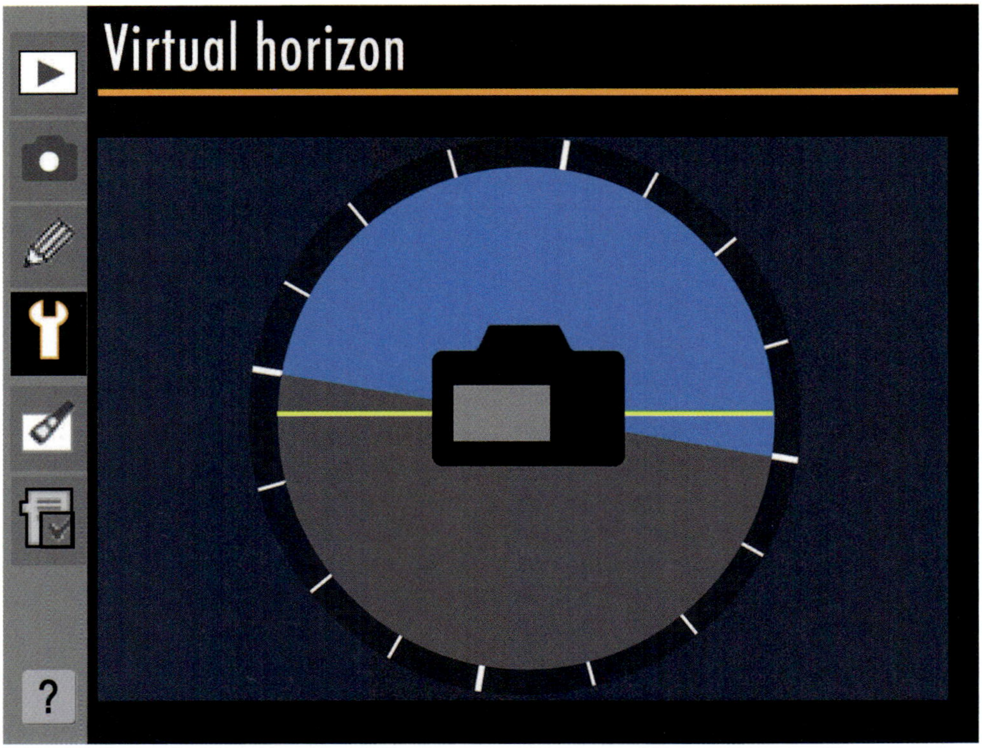


**Figure 5.5** The Virtual horizon serves as a kind of bubble level for your camera

when you're using live view, which has its own Virtual horizon feature (discussed in Chapter 8).

I'm not crazy about the feature because, in my case, all my tripods and tripod heads already *have* bubble levels built in. So, when I'm using the D3s/D3x on a tripod, I really don't need the virtual horizon. In addition, the feature only works best when you've rotated the camera along the axis of the lens. If you tilt it forward or back (pointing the lens a bit towards the sky or ground), that angling won't be detected accurately. The bubble levels on my tripods and tripod heads can do that, with no problems. I know folks who like and use the virtual horizon, but I find it just a cute way to use the sensor built into your camera that sends vertical/horizontal orientation information to the various rotation features. (Incidentally, if you listen carefully when you rotate the camera from horizontal to vertical, you can hear the pendulum-like sensor clanking around inside the D3s/D3x.)

## Non-CPU Lens Data

You can specify lens focal length data and maximum aperture for up to nine older manual focus, non-CPU chipped lenses, using this entry, the first new entry on the last page of the Setup menu, as shown in Figure 5.6. When both values are entered, the D3s/D3x can use older lenses (including AI manual focus lenses) that are not equipped with a CPU

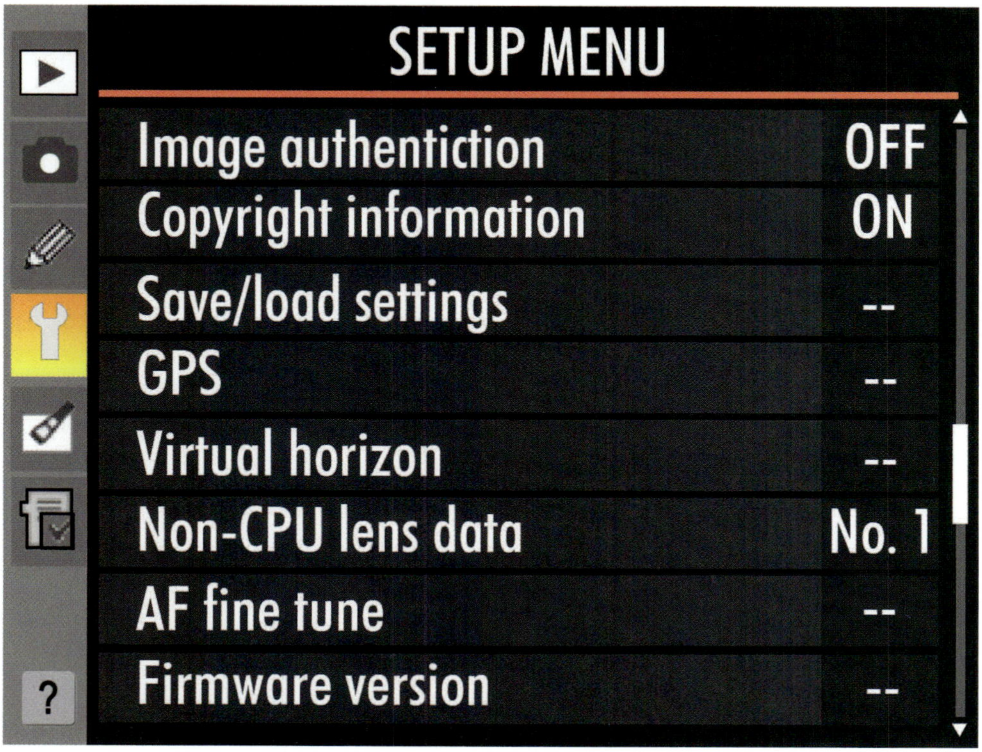


**Figure 5.6**
The Non-CPU lens data entry is located on the third page of the Setup menu.

chip for color matrix metering to calculate exposure in aperture-priority and manual exposure modes. The data also enables automatic power zoom when using the Nikon SB-900, SB-800, and SB-600 Speedlights; as well as improved flash exposures and balanced iTTL fill-flash. In addition, the current aperture can be listed in the monochrome LCD status panel and camera viewfinder, as well as embedded in the photo playback display.

If you're a veteran of some older Nikon cameras, this feature is a dramatic improvement of its implementation in that camera. Previously, the Non-CPU lens data entry screen was in the Shooting menu, and it was possible to enter information about *only one* lens. That's a fatal error for those of us who have a large collection of manual focus lenses that work just fine on modern Nikon digital cameras. Of course, you could enter a different lens's information in each of the Shooting menu banks A, B, C, and D, but you had to switch banks when you mounted a lens. I happen to use a manual focus 16mm f/3.5 Nikkor fisheye, a 55mm f/3.5 Micro-Nikkor, and an 85mm f/1.8 Nikkor several times a week, with other older lenses seeing occasional use. What was I supposed to do?

Switching to the Nikon D3s/D3x proved to be a smart move for me, because it allows defining up to nine different lenses, and I can choose any of them with a quick trip to this menu entry (or to the equivalent menu item in My Menu, described later in this chapter). Nikon wisely moved the feature from the Shooting menu to the Setup menu, so your lens definitions aren't locked into a single menu bank. You can use any defined lens in any Shooting menu or Custom Setting bank.

To enter this information, follow these steps using the screen shown in Figure 5.7:

1. Choose Non-CPU lens data from the Setup menu.
2. Highlight lens number and press the multi selector left/right buttons to choose a number between 1 and 9.
3. Scroll down to Focal length (mm) and use the multi selector left/right buttons to choose a focal length between 6mm and 4000mm.
4. Scroll down to Maximum aperture and use the multi selector left/right buttons to choose a maximum f/stop between f/1.2 and f/22.
5. Choose Done. You can now select the lens number using any of several controls you can define for the Fn button, Depth-of-field preview button, AE-L/AF-L, or BKT buttons as described in Chapter 4 under Custom Setting f4, Custom Setting f5, or Custom Setting f6 and Custom Setting f7.

## AF Fine Tune

Troubled by lenses that don't focus exactly where they should, producing back focus or front focus problems? No need to send your lens and/or camera into Nikon for servicing. The Nikon D3s/D3x allows you to fine-tune focus for up to 12 different lenses.

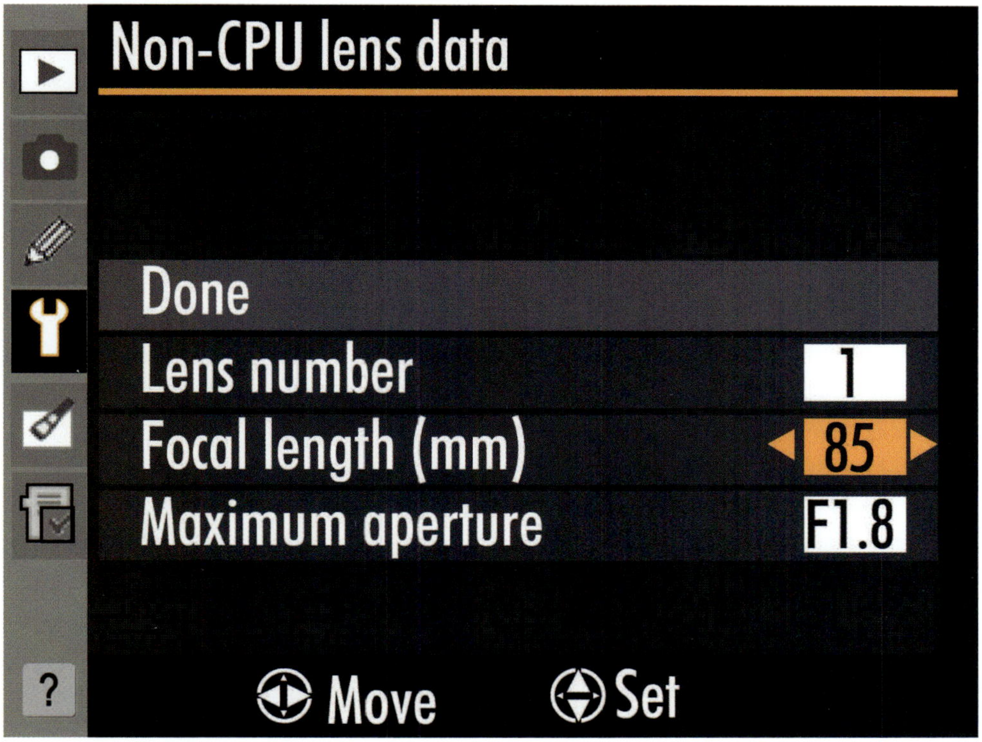


**Figure 5.7**
You can enter focal length and maximum aperture of up to nine manual focus lenses.

You'll probably never need to use this feature, but if you do, it's priceless. To fine-tune your lenses, first perform some tests to see just how much fine-tuning is required. The only problem I've run into is that with some lenses, particularly short focal length lenses, using large negative values (–10 to –20) to move the focal point closer to the camera sometimes results in being unable to focus to infinity. If you run into that, you may be better off sending the lens to Nikon so they can recalibrate the focus for you.

This menu option has four choices, shown in Figure 5.8:

- **AF fine tune (On/Off).** Enable/disable application of your AF fine-tuning changes.
- **Saved value.** View or enter an adjustment for the lens currently mounted on your camera.
- **Default.** Set the default value to be applied to lenses that haven't been recalibrated. You'd use this if your D3s/D3x has a certain amount of front or back focus problems with all lenses. Use with caution, as it affects every CPU lens that you use.
- **List saved values.** View and delete tuning values you've saved for up to 12 different lenses.

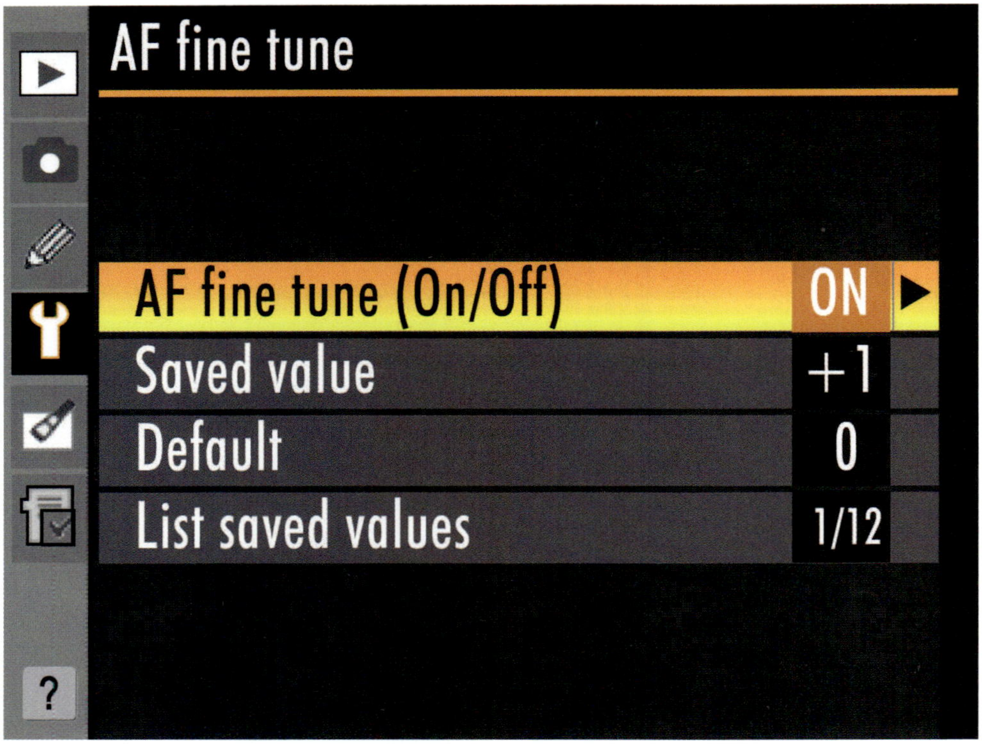


**Figure 5.8**
The autofocus of lenses can be adjusted here.

Because the adjustments made with the AF Fine tune setting are potentially so dangerous to your focusing health, I'm not even going to provide an overview in this chapter. (Knowing just enough to hurt yourself can be a real possibility.) Instead, you'll find a complete discussion of using this feature at the end of Chapter 9, which deals with lens issues.

## Firmware Version

You can see the current firmware release in use in the menu listing. You can learn how to update firmware in Chapter 12.

# Retouch Menu

- D-Lighting
- Red-eye correction
- Trim
- Monochrome
- Filter effects
- Color balance
- Small picture
- Image overlay
- NEF/RAW processing (D3s)
- Resize (D3s)
- Side-by-side comparison
- Edit movie (D3s)

The Retouch menu (see Figure 5.9) is most useful when you want to create a modified copy of an image on the spot, for immediate printing or e-mailing without first importing into your computer for more extensive editing. You can also use it to create a JPEG version of an image in the camera when you are shooting RAW-only photos. You can retouch images that have already been processed by the Retouch menu, except for copies created with the Trim, Resize, or Save Selected Frame (in movie mode) options. Nor can you apply D-Lighting, red-eye correction, filter effects, and color balance to monochrome image copies. You may notice some quality loss when applying more than one retouch option. To create a retouched copy of an image

1. **Choose image retouching option.** From the Retouch menu, select the option you want and press the multi selector right button. The Nikon D3s/D3x's standard image selection screen appears. Scroll among the images as usual with the left/right multi selector buttons, press the Zoom button to examine a highlighted image more closely, and press OK to choose that image.
2. **Manipulate image.** Work with the options available from that particular Retouch menu feature and press OK to create the modified copy, or Playback to cancel your changes.
3. **View copy.** A retouched JPEG image will be the same size and quality as the original, except for copies created from NEF and TIFF images (which are always saved as JPEG Fine images).

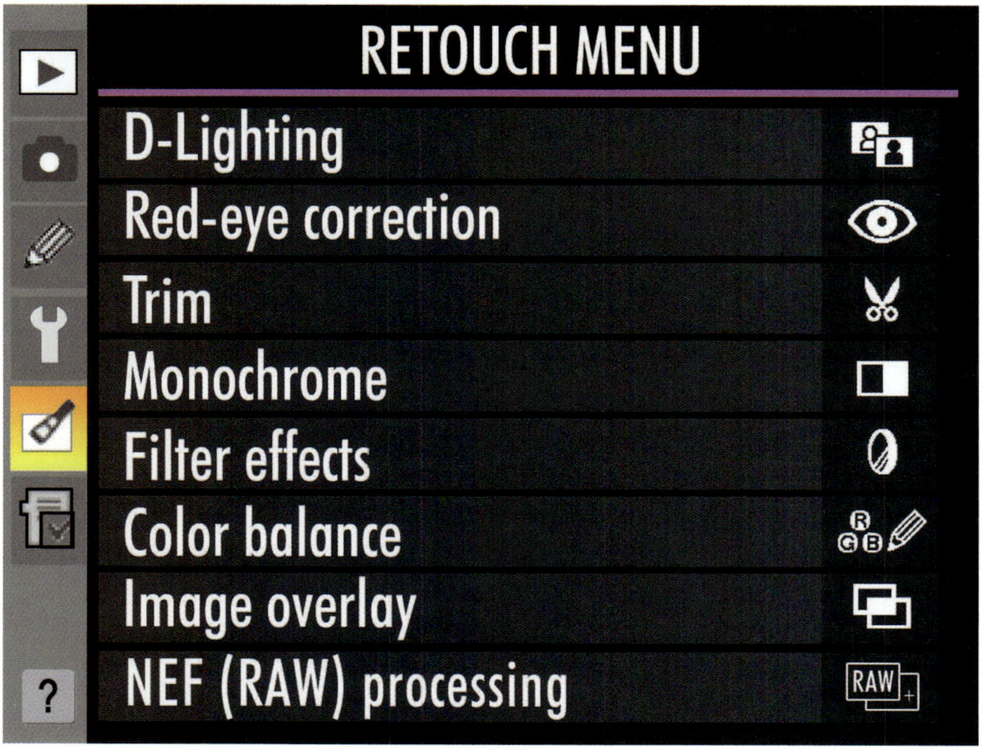


**Figure 5.9** The Retouch menu allows simple in-camera editing.

## D-Lighting

This option brightens the shadows of pictures that have already been taken. Once you've selected your photo for modification, you'll be shown side-by-side images with the unaltered version on the left, and your adjusted version on the right. Press the multi selector's up/down buttons to choose from High, Normal, or Low corrections. Press the Zoom button to magnify the image. When you're happy with the corrected image on the right, compared to the original on the left, press OK to save the copy to your memory card. Typical results are shown in Figure 5.10.

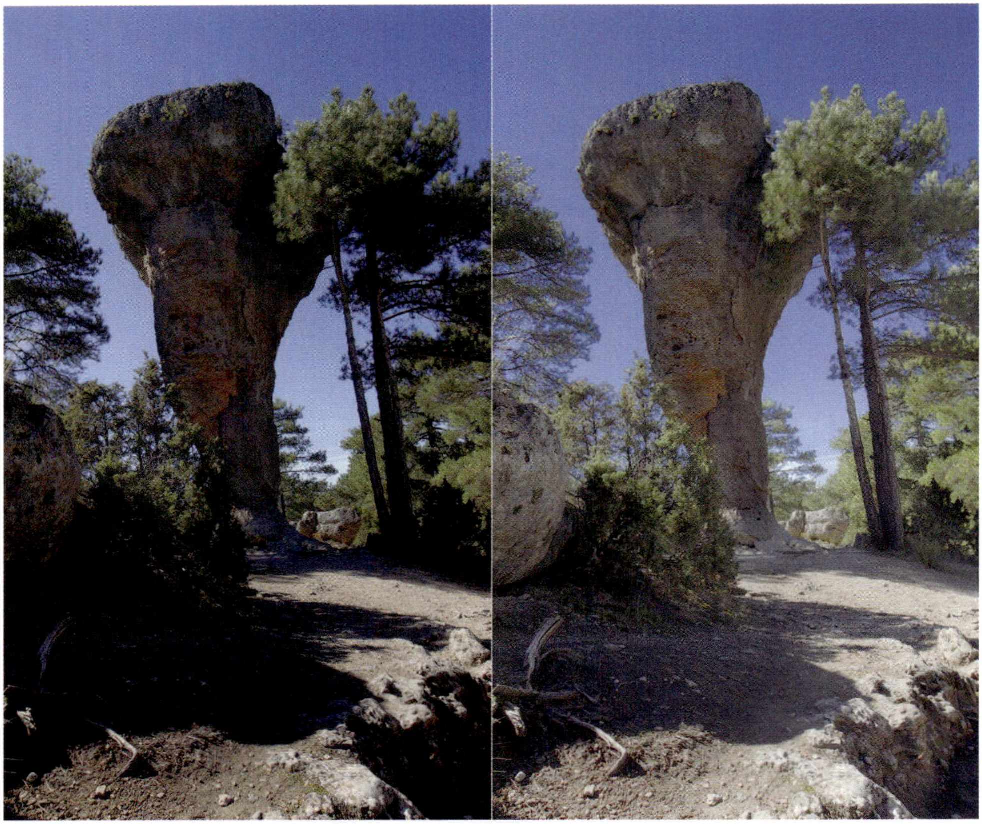

**Figure 5.10**
An image with dark shadows can be improved with post-shot D-Lighting.

## Red-Eye Correction

This Retouch menu tool can be used to remove the residual red-eye look that remains after applying the Nikon D3s/D3x's other remedies, such as the red-eye reduction lamp. (You can use the red-eye tools found in most image editors, as well.)

Your Nikon D3s/D3x has a fairly effective red-eye reduction flash mode. Unfortunately, your camera is unable, on its own, to totally *eliminate* the red-eye effects that occur when an electronic flash (or, rarely, illumination from other sources) bounces off the retinas of the eye and into the camera lens. Animals seem to suffer from yellow or green glowing pupils, instead; the effect is equally undesirable. The effect is worst under low-light conditions (exactly when you might be using a flash) as the pupils expand to allow more light to reach the retinas. The best you can hope for is to *reduce* or minimize the red-eye effect.

The best way to truly eliminate red-eye is to raise the flash up off the camera so its illumination approaches the eye from an angle that won't reflect directly back to the retina and into the lens. That alone is a good reason for using an external flash. If your image still displays red-eye effects, you can use the Retouch menu to make a copy with red-eye reduced further. First, select a picture that was taken with flash (non-flash pictures won't be available for selection). After you've selected the picture to process, press OK. The image will be displayed on the LCD. You can magnify the image with the Zoom button, scroll around the zoomed image with the multi selector buttons, and zoom out with the Zoom out button. While zoomed, you can cancel the zoom by pressing the OK button.

When you are finished examining the image, press OK again. The D3s/D3x will look for red-eye, and, if detected, create a copy that has been processed to reduce the effect. If no red-eye is found, a copy is not created. Figure 5.11 shows an original image (left) and its processed copy (right).

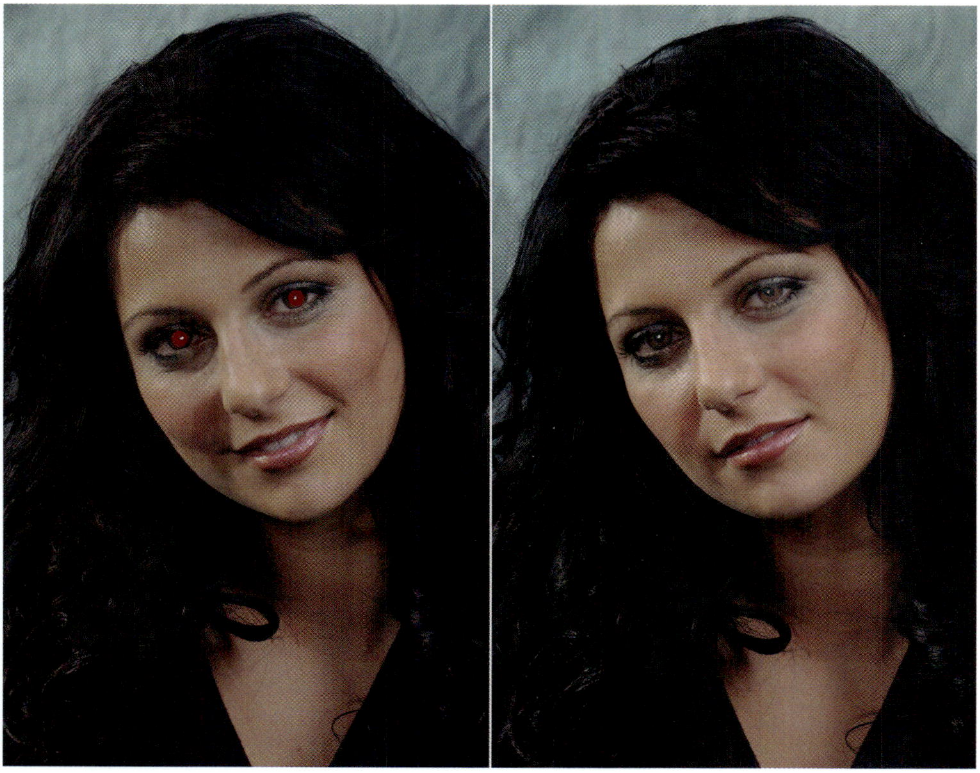

**Figure 5.11**
Wider pupils can lead to red-eye effects.

# Trim

This option creates copies in specific sizes based on the final size you select, chosen from among 3:2, 4:3, and 5:4 aspect ratios (proportions). You can use this feature to create smaller versions of a picture for e-mailing without the need to first transfer the image to your own computer. If you're traveling, create your smaller copy here, insert the memory card in a card reader at an Internet café, your library's public computers, or some other computer, and e-mail the reduced-size version. Just follow these steps:

1. **Select your photo.** Choose Trim from the Retouch menu. You'll be shown the standard Nikon D3s/D3x image selection screen. Scroll among the photos using the multi selector left/right buttons, and press OK when the image you want to trim is highlighted. While selecting, you can temporarily enlarge the highlighted image by pressing the Zoom button.
2. **Choose your aspect ratio.** Rotate the main command dial to change from 3:2, 4:3, 5:4, 1:1, and 16:9 aspect ratios. (See Table 5.1 for sizes.) These proportions happen to correspond to the proportions of common print sizes, including the two most popular sizes: 4 × 6 inches (3:2) and 8 × 10 inches (5:4).
3. **Crop in on your photo.** Press the Zoom button and rotate the main command dial to crop in on your picture. The pixel dimensions of the cropped image at the selected proportions will be displayed in the upper-left corner (see Figure 5.12) as you zoom. The current framed size is outlined in yellow within an inset image in the lower-right corner.
4. **Move cropped area within the image.** Use the multi selector left/right and up/down buttons to relocate the yellow cropping border within the frame.

**Table 5.1 Trim Sizes**

| Aspect Ratio | Sizes Available |
|---|---|
| 3:2 | 3424 × 2280, 2560 × 1704, 1920 × 1280, 1280 × 856, 960 × 640, 640 × 424 |
| 4:3 | 3424 × 2568, 2560 × 1920, 1920 × 1440, 1280 × 960, 960 × 720, 640 × 480 |
| 5:4 | 3216 × 2568, 2400 × 1920, 1808 × 1440, 1200 × 960, 986 × 720, 608 × 480 |
| 1:1 | 2560 × 2560, 1920 × 1920, 1440 × 1440, 960 × 960, 720 × 720, 480 × 480 |
| 16:9 | 3424 × 1920, 2560 × 1440, 1920 × 1080, 1280 × 720, 960 × 536, 640 × 480 |

5. **Save the cropped image.** Press OK to save a copy of the image using the current crop and size, or press the Playback button to exit without creating a copy. Copies created from JPEG Fine, Normal, or Standard have the same Image quality setting as the original; copies made from RAW files or any RAW+JPEG setting will use JPEG Fine compression.

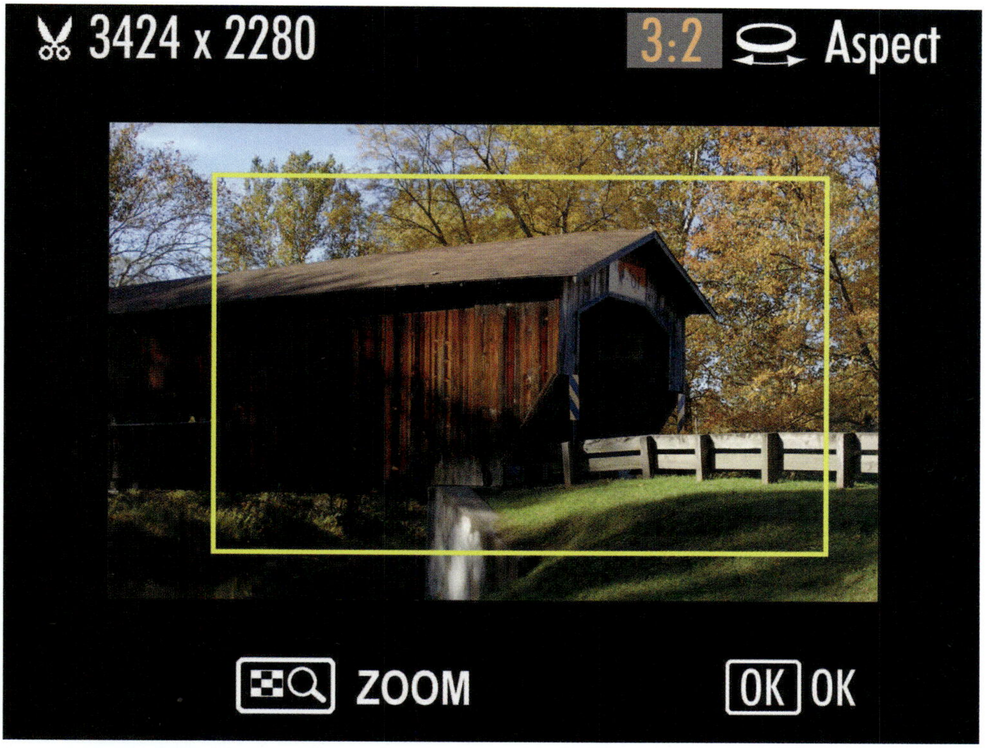


**Figure 5.12** The Trim feature of the Retouch menu allows in-camera cropping.

## Monochrome

This Retouch choice allows you to produce a copy of the selected photo as a black-and-white image, sepia-toned image, or cyanotype (blue-and-white). You can fine-tune the color saturation of the previewed Sepia or Cyanotype version by pressing the multi selector up button to increase color richness, and the down button to decrease saturation. When satisfied, press OK to create the monochrome duplicate.

## Filter Effects

Add a warmer tone to your images using this Retouch option. You have two choices: Skylight, which makes the picture slightly less blue, and Warm filter, which adds a rich warm cast to the duplicate. Preview either effect in the color LCD before pressing OK to create the modified copy.

## Color Balance

This Retouch effect allows you to create a copy with modified color balance. When you press the OK button while viewing a selected image, a screen like the one shown in Figure 5.13 appears with the photo shown in thumbnail size at the upper-left corner, and red/green/blue histograms at the right. You can bias the image along the magenta/green axis or blue/yellow (amber) axis based on your perception of the thumbnail or, as you gain experience, from your estimation of the distribution of tones as shown by the histograms.

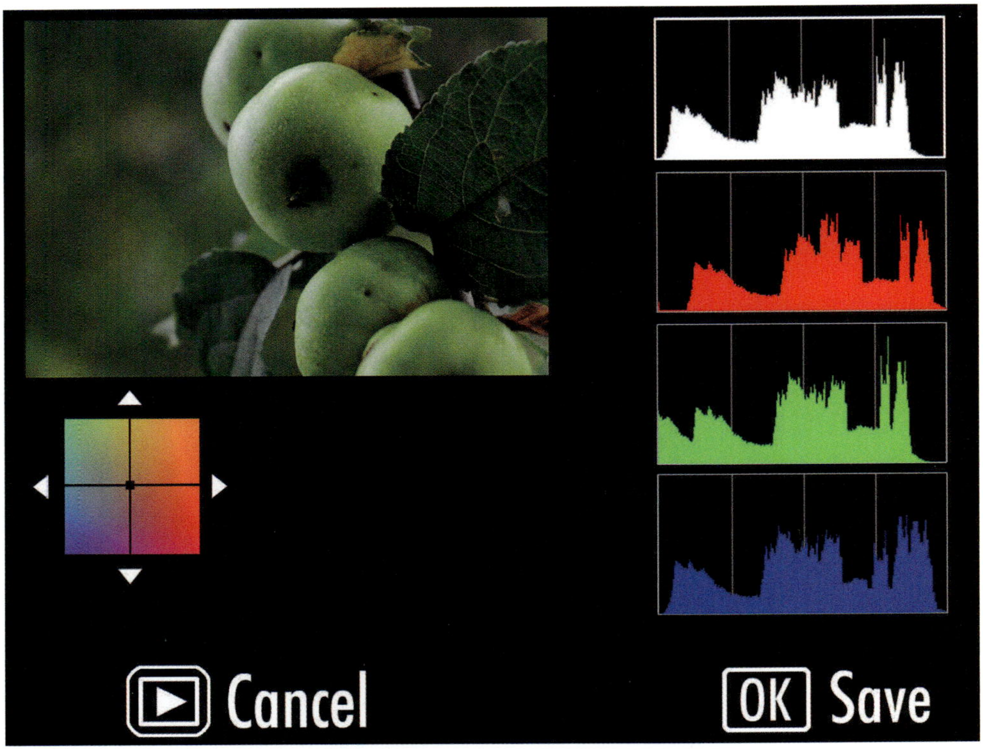


**Figure 5.13** Fine-tune color balance in the camera using this Retouch menu screen.

Press the multi selector up button to increase the amount of green, the down button to increase the amount of magenta, the right button to increase the bias towards yellow/amber, and the left button to increase the amount of blue. As you make these modifications, the changes will be reflected in the histograms. Press OK to save the image, and Menu to back out of the feature.

## Image Overlay

This feature allows you to combine two RAW photos (only NEF files can be used) in a composite image that Nikon claims is better than a "double exposure" created in an image-editing application, because the overlays are made using RAW data. To produce this composite image, follow these steps:

1. Choose Image overlay. The screen shown in Figure 5.14 will be displayed, with the Image 1 box highlighted.
2. Press OK and the Nikon D3s/D3x's image selection screen appears. Choose the first image for the overlay and press OK.
3. Press the multi selector right button to highlight the Image 2 box, and press OK to produce the image selection screen. Choose the second image for the overlay.
4. By highlighting either the Image 1 or Image 2 boxes and pressing the multi selector up/down buttons, you can adjust the "gain," or how much of the final image will be "exposed" from the selected picture. You can choose from X0.5 (half-exposure) to X2.0 (twice the exposure) for each image. The default value is 1.0 for each, so that each image will contribute equally to the final exposure.
5. Use the multi selector right button to highlight the Preview box and view the combined picture. Press the Zoom button to enlarge the view.
6. When you're ready to store your composite copy, press the multi selector down button when the Preview box is highlighted to select Save, and press OK. The combined image is stored on the memory card.

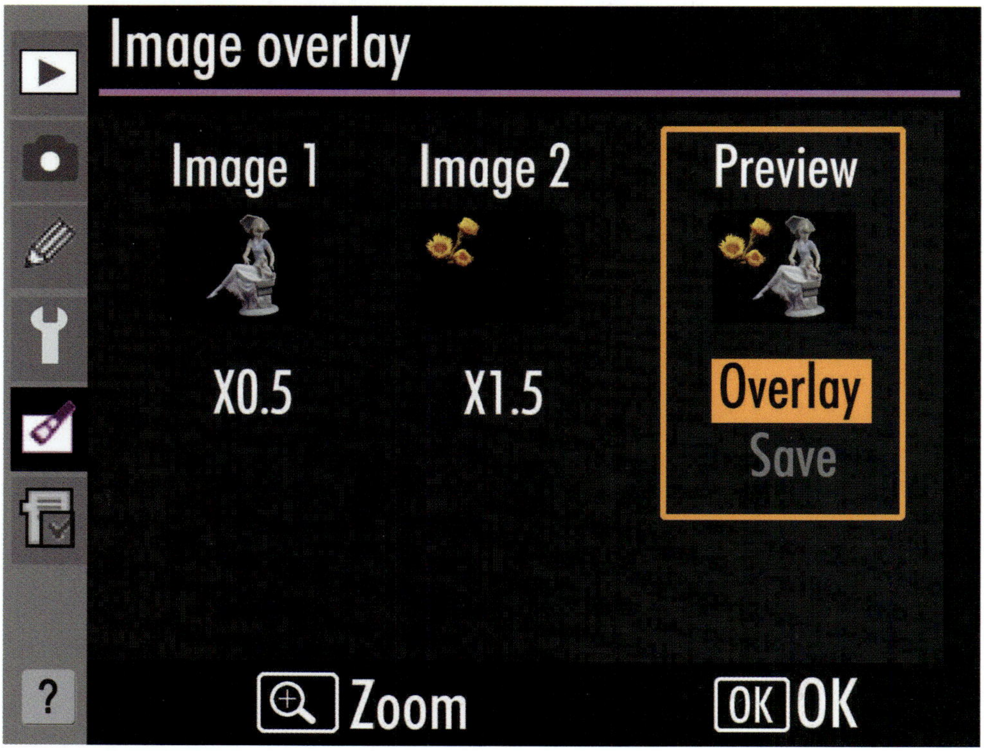


**Figure 5.14** Overlay two RAW images to produce a "double exposure."

## NEF/RAW Processing (D3s Only)

Use this tool to create a JPEG version of any image saved in either straight RAW (with no JPEG version) or RAW+Basic (with a Basic JPEG version). You can select from among several parameters to "process" your new JPEG copy right in the camera.

1. Choose a RAW image. Select NEF (RAW) processing from the Retouch menu. You'll be shown the standard Nikon D3s image selection screen. Use the left/right buttons to navigate among the RAW images displayed. Press OK to select the highlighted image.
2. In the NEF (RAW) processing screen, shown in Figure 5.15, you can use the multi selector up/down keys to select from five different attributes of the RAW image information to apply to your JPEG copy. Choose Image quality (Fine, Normal, or Basic), Image size (Large, Medium, or Small), White balance, Exposure compensation, Set Picture Control, High ISO noise reduction, Color Space, and Vignette control parameters.
3. Press the Zoom button to magnify the image temporarily while the button is held down.

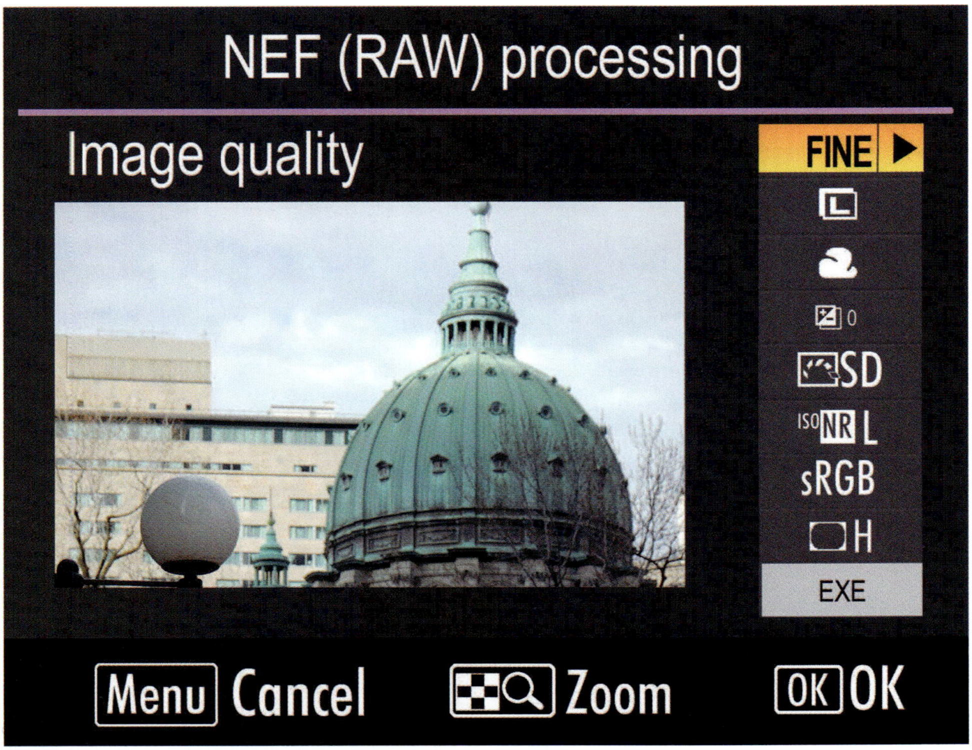


**Figure 5.15** Adjust eight parameters and then save your JPEG copy from a RAW original file.

4. Press the Playback button if you change your mind, to exit from the processing screen.
5. When all parameters are set, highlight EXE (for Execute) and press OK. The D3s will create a JPEG file with the settings you've specified, and show an Image saved message on the LCD when finished.

## Resize (D3s Only)

This option creates smaller copies of the selected images. It can be applied while viewing a single image in full-frame mode (just press the OK button while viewing a photo), or accessed from the Retouch menu (especially useful if you'd like to select and resize multiple images).

1. **Select images.** If accessing from the Retouch menu, you can choose to select multiple images, or jump directly to the following two steps.
2. **Choose destination.** If two memory cards are inserted, you can choose either CF slot as the destination.
3. **Choose size.** Next, select the size for the finished copy, from 2.5, 1.1, 0.6, or 0.3 megabytes.
4. **Confirm.** Press OK to create your copy.

## Side-by-Side Comparison

Use this option to compare a retouched photo side-by-side with the original from which it was derived.

To use Side-by-side comparison

1. Select Side-by-side comparison in the Retouch menu, and choose your image.
2. The original and retouched image will appear next to each other, with the retouching options you've used shown as a label above the images, as you can see in Figure 5.16.
3. Highlight the original or the copy with the multi selector left/right buttons, and press the Zoom button to magnify the image to examine it more closely.
4. If you have created more than one copy of an original image, select the retouched version shown, and press the multi selector up/down buttons to view the other retouched copies. The up/down buttons will also let you view the other image used to create an Image overlay copy.
5. When done comparing, press the Playback button to exit.

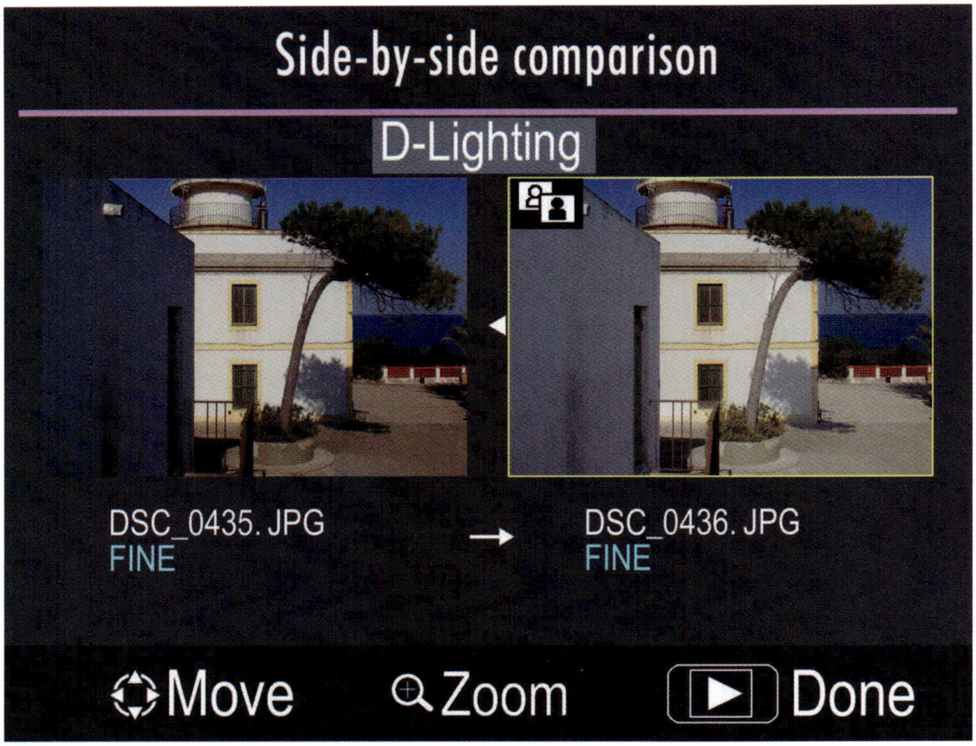


**Figure 5.16**
You can easily compare an original image and the retouched version side-by-side.

## Edit Movie (D3s Only)

You can do limited editing of movies in the camera (actually, just modest trimming), choosing a start point, end point, and also storing a selected frame as a still image.

In-camera editing is limited to trimming the beginning or end from a clip, and the clip must be at least two seconds long. For more advanced editing, you'll need an application capable of editing AVI movie clips, if you want to combine several clips into one movie, add titles, special effects, and transitions between scenes. I'll explain more about movie making in Chapter 8.

To do in-camera editing/trimming, follow these steps:

1. While viewing a movie clip, press the OK button. The Edit movie prompt will appear.
2. Press the right multi selector button and highlight either Choose start point or Choose end point, and press OK.
3. Press the center button of the multi selector to start or resume playback. You can use the Pause, Rewind, Advance, and Single frame controls (described in more detail in Chapter 8) to move around within your clip.

4. When you reach the point where you want to trim, press the Pause button (if the movie is not already paused), and then press the multi selector up button. All frames prior to the pause will be deleted if you're in Choose start point mode; all frames *after* the pause will be deleted if you're in Choose end point mode.
5. A Proceed? prompt appears. Choose Yes or No, and press OK.
6. You'll see a message Saving movie and a green progress bar as the D3s stores the trimmed clip to your memory card. Storage takes some time, and you don't want to interrupt it to avoid losing your saved clip. So, make sure your D3s has a fully charged battery before you start to edit a clip.

## Using My Menu

The last menu in the D3s/D3x's main menu screen has two versions: Recent settings and My Menu. The default mode is Recent settings, which simply shows an ever-changing roster of the 20 menu items you used most recently. You'll probably find it more useful to activate the My Menu option instead, which contains only those menu items that you deposit there extracted from the Playback, Shooting, Custom Setting, Setup, and Retouch menus, based on your own decisions on which you use most. Remember that the D3s/D3x always returns to the last menu and menu entry accessed when you press the Menu button. So you can set up My Menu (see Figure 5.17) to include just

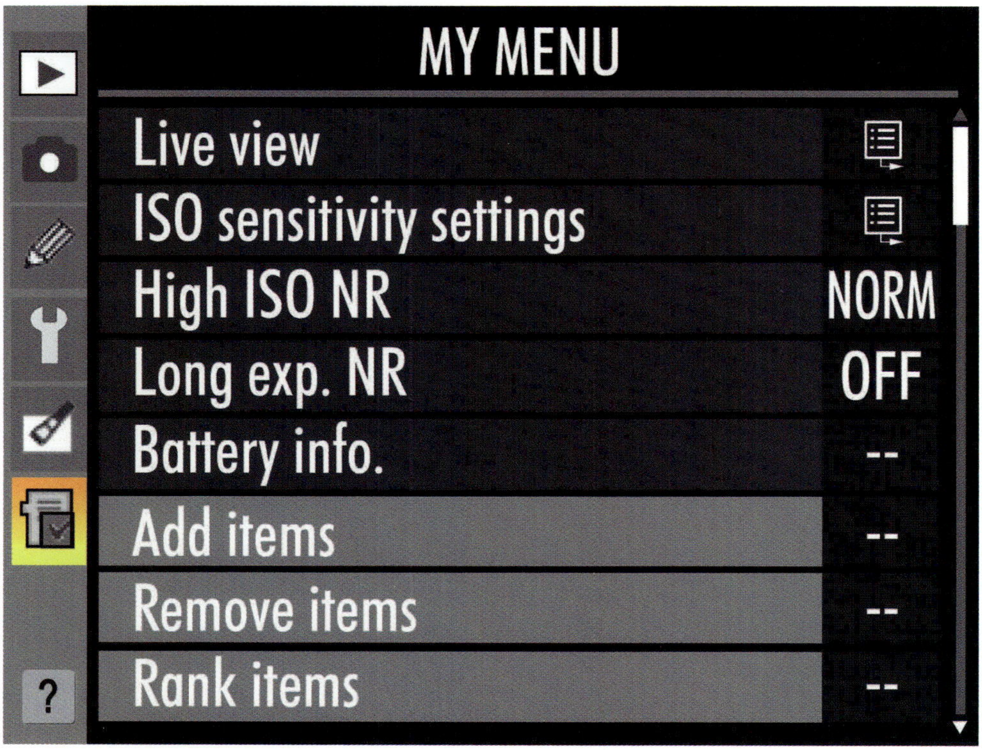


**Figure 5.17** You can include your favorite menu items in the fast-access My Menu.

the items accessed most frequently, and (as long as you haven't used another menu) jump to those items instantly by pressing the Menu button.

Switching back and forth is easy. The My Menu and Recent settings menus each has a menu choice called Choose tab. Highlight that entry and press the right multi selector button to view a screen that allows you to activate either the My Menu or Recent settings menu. Press OK to confirm.

I tend to include frequently used functions that aren't available using direct access buttons in My Menu. For example, I include High ISO NR and Long Exp. NR, and Battery info there, because I may want to turn noise reduction on or off, or check the status of my battery during shooting. I *don't* include ISO, Qual, or WB changes in My Menu, even though they are available in the menu system, because I can quickly change those values by pressing their dedicated buttons and rotating the main and sub-command dials.

You can add or subtract entries on My Menu at any time, and re-order (or rank) the entries so the ones you access most often are shown at the top of the list. Here's all you need to know to work with My Menu. To add entries to My Menu

1. Select My Menu and choose Add items.
2. A list of the available menus will appear (Playback, Shooting, Custom Setting, Setup, and Retouch menus). Highlight one and press the multi selector's right button.
3. Within the selected menu, choose the menu item you want to add and press OK.
4. The label Choose position appears at the top of the My Menu screen. Use the up/down buttons to select a rank among the entries, and press OK to confirm and add the new item.
5. Repeat steps 1-4 if you want to add more entries to My Menu.

To reorder the menu listings:

1. Within the My Menu screen, choose Rank items.
2. Use the up/down buttons to select the item to be moved, and press OK.
3. Use the up/down buttons to relocate the selected item and press OK.
4. Repeat steps 2-3 to move additional entries.

To remove entries from the list, you can simply press the Trash button while an item is highlighted in the My Menu screen. To remove multiple items, follow these steps:

1. Within the My Menu screen, choose Remove items.
2. A list with check boxes next to the menu items appears. Scroll down to an item you want to remove and press the multi selector right button to mark its box. If you change your mind, highlight the item and press the right button again to unmark the box.
3. When finished, highlight Done and press the OK button.
4. Press OK to confirm the deletion.

# 6

# Understanding Exposure

Everyone had their own formula for getting the right exposure in the days before cameras had more processing power inside than the craft that took humans to the Moon. For landscape photographers, it's been the Sunny 16 rule—f/16 with a shutter speed that's the reciprocal of the ISO sensitivity (e.g., 1/400 for ISO 400), with appropriate adjustments for cloudy days, snow, or beach scenes. For photojournalists, the formula is "f/8—and be there," meaning that *any* exposure is less important than being on the spot at a decisive moment. For beginning photographers, the conventional wisdom for getting a decent average of acceptable exposures is to set the camera on P (programmed) and not point the lens at the sun.

For the owner of a Nikon D3s or D3x, these rules of thumb are more conventional than they are wise. You don't want the adjectives "decent," "average," or "acceptable" applied to your photography in any way, shape, or form. For the critical photographer, correct exposure can make or break an image, and it's not something you want to shoot for—you want to *nail* it.

That's why you won't be happy setting and forgetting your camera's controls. While the D3s/D3x is one of the smartest cameras available when it comes to calculating the right exposure for most situations, the brains inside the box can benefit from the experience and vision that you bring to the table. Certainly, you can generally press the mode button and spin the main command dial to switch to programmed (P), aperture-priority (A), or shutter-priority (S) and shoot away. But as you learn to use your D3s/D3x creatively, you're going to find that the right settings—as determined by the camera's exposure meter and intelligence—need to be *adjusted* to account for your creative decisions or special situations.

For example, when you shoot with the main light source behind the subject, you end up with *backlighting*, which can result in an overexposed background and/or an underexposed subject. The Nikon D3s/D3x recognizes backlit situations nicely, and can properly base exposure on the main subject, producing a decent photo. Features like D-Lighting (first discussed in Chapter 3) can fine-tune exposure to preserve detail in the highlights and shadows.

But what if you *want* to underexpose the subject, to produce a silhouette effect? Or, perhaps, you might want to use an external flash unit to fill in the shadows on your subject. The more you know about how to use your D3s/D3x, the more you'll run into situations where you want to creatively tweak the exposure to provide a different look than you'd get with a straight shot.

This chapter shows you the fundamentals of exposure, so you'll be better equipped to override the Nikon D3s/D3x's default settings when you want to, or need to. After all, correct exposure is one of the foundations of good photography, along with accurate focus and sharpness, appropriate color balance, freedom from unwanted noise and excessive contrast, as well as pleasing composition.

The Nikon D3s/D3x gives you a great deal of control over all of these, although composition is entirely up to you. You must still frame the photograph to create an interesting arrangement of subject matter, but all the other parameters are basic functions of the camera. You can let your D3s/D3x set them for you automatically, you can fine-tune how the camera applies its automatic settings, or you can make them yourself, manually. The amount of control you have over exposure, sensitivity (ISO settings), color balance, focus, and image parameters like sharpness and contrast make the D3s/D3x a versatile tool for creating images.

In the next few pages I'm going to give you a solid grounding in one of those foundations, and explain the basics of exposure, either as an introduction or as a refresher course, depending on your current level of expertise. When you finish this chapter, you'll understand most of what you need to know to take well-exposed photographs creatively in a broad range of situations.

## Getting a Handle on Exposure

In the most basic sense, exposure is all about light. Exposure can make or break your photo. Correct exposure brings out the detail in the areas you want to picture, providing the range of tones and colors you need to create the desired image. Poor exposure can cloak important details in shadow, or wash them out in glare-filled featureless expanses of white. However, getting the perfect exposure requires some intelligence—either that built into the camera, or the smarts in your head—because digital sensors can't capture all the tones we are able to see. If the range of tones in an image is extensive, embracing both inky black shadows and bright highlights, we often must settle for an exposure that renders most of those tones—but not all—in a way that best suits the photo we want to produce.

Figure 6.1 presents a pair of tourist snapshots that I've been using in my books to illustrate a typical exposure problem that most of us encounter all the time—a scene with a dynamic range that's so broad that it can't be captured in a single photo. For the image on the left, the camera, set for spot metering, calculated exposure based on the scene in the background that is visible through the archway. While the background is reasonably well-exposed, the interior, the statues, and the ceiling overhead are quite underexposed. For the version at right, spot metering was used to read the ceiling of the scene, producing a more detailed interior shot, but badly overexposing the exterior details. The camera's sensor simply can't capture detail in both dark areas and bright areas in a single shot.

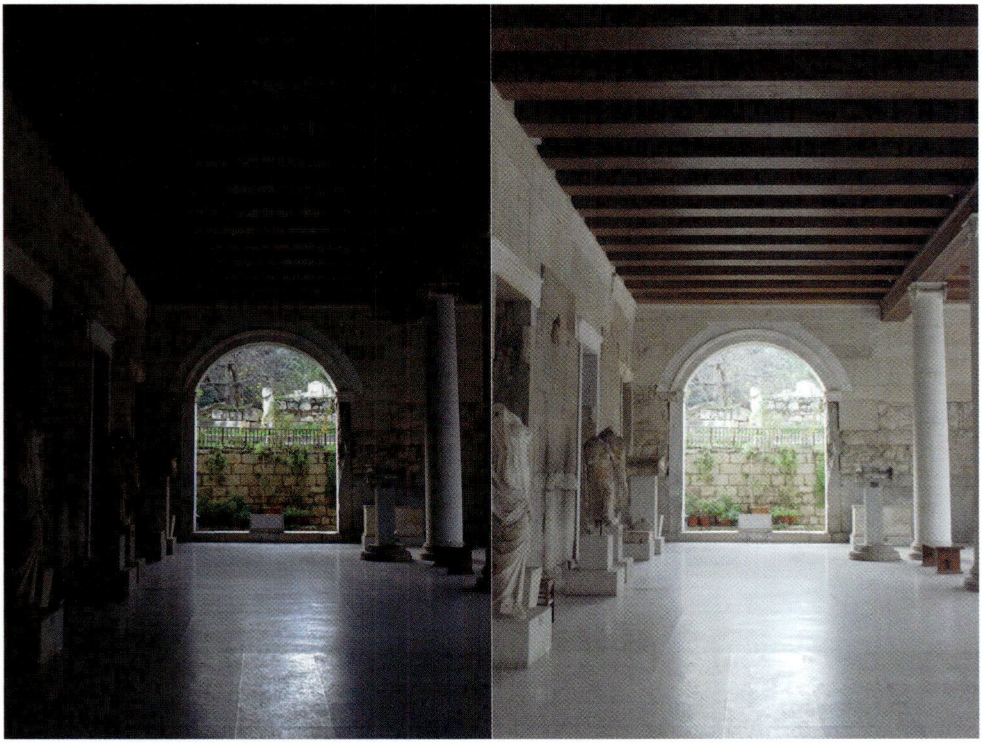

**Figure 6.1** At left, the image is exposed for the background highlights, losing shadow detail. At right, the exposure captures detail in the shadows, but the background highlights are washed out.

The solution, in this particular case, was to resort to a technique called High Dynamic Range (HDR) photography, in which the two exposures from Figure 6.1 were combined in an image editor such as Photoshop, or a specialized HDR tool like Photomatix (about $100 from www.hdrsoft.com). The resulting shot is shown in Figure 6.2. I'll explain more about HDR photography later in this chapter. For now, though, I'm going to concentrate on showing you how to get the best exposures possible without resorting to such tools, using only the features of your Nikon D3s/D3x.

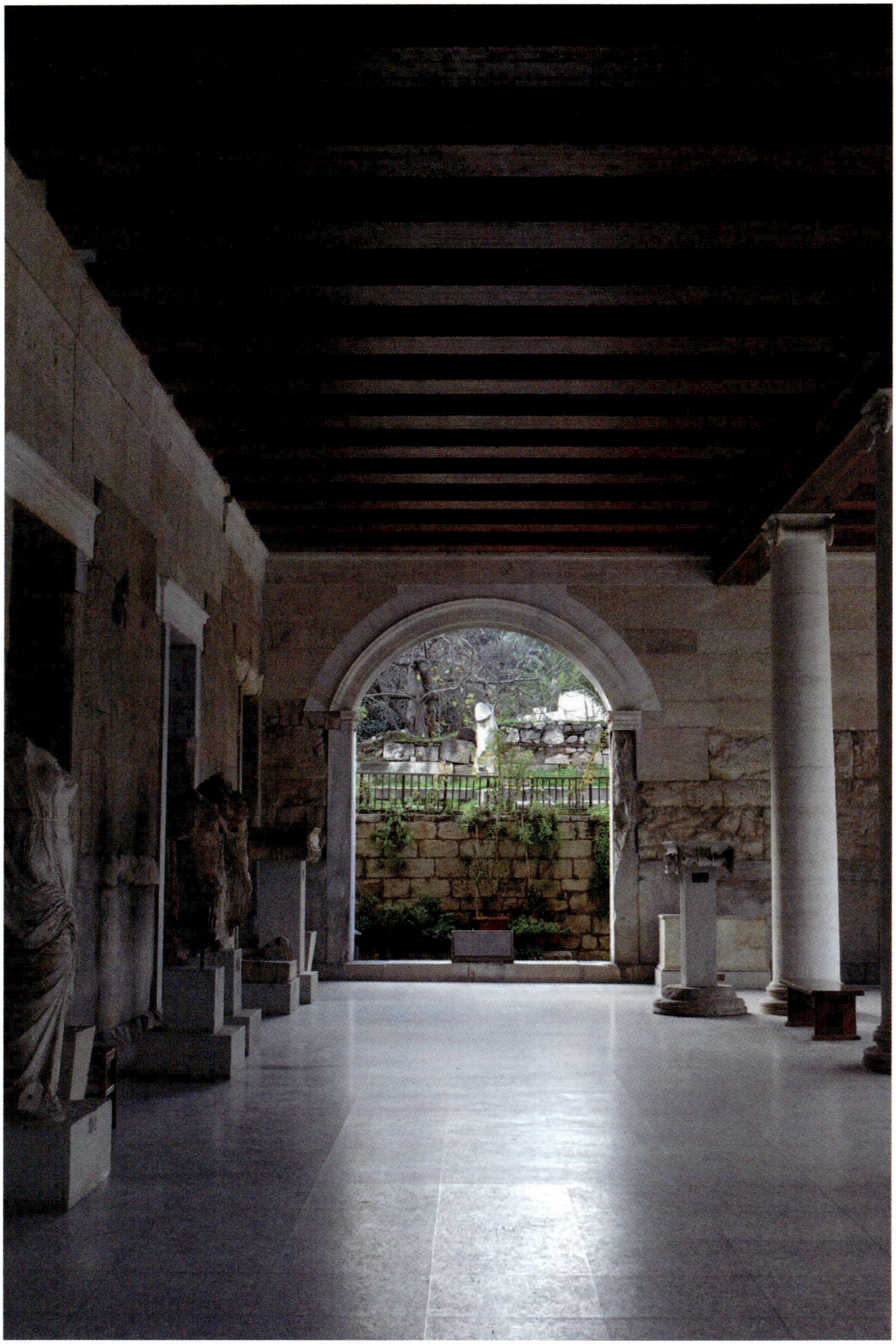

**Figure 6.2**
Combining the two exposures produces the best compromise image.

To understand exposure, you need to understand the six aspects of light that combine to produce an image. Start with a light source—the sun, an interior lamp, or the glow from a campfire—and trace its path to your camera, through the lens, and finally to the sensor that captures the illumination. Here's a brief review of the things within our control that affect exposure, listed in "chronological" order (that is, as the light moves from the subject to the sensor):

- **Light at its source.** Our eyes and our cameras—film or digital—are most sensitive to that portion of the electromagnetic spectrum we call *visible light.* That light has several important aspects that are relevant to photography, such as color, and harshness (which is determined primarily by the apparent size of the light source as it illuminates a subject). But, in terms of exposure, the important attribute of a light source is its *intensity.* We may have direct control over intensity, which might be the case with an interior light that can be brightened or dimmed. Or, we might have only indirect control over intensity, as with sunlight, which can be made to appear dimmer by introducing translucent light-absorbing or reflective materials in its path.
- **Light's duration.** We tend to think of most light sources as continuous. But, as you'll learn in Chapter 10, the duration of light can change quickly enough to modify the exposure, as when the main illumination in a photograph comes from an intermittent source, such as an electronic flash.
- **Light reflected, transmitted, or emitted.** Once light is produced by its source, either continuously or in a brief burst, we are able to see and photograph objects by the light that is reflected from our subjects towards the camera lens; transmitted (say, from translucent objects that are lit from behind); or emitted (by a candle or television screen). When more or less light reaches the lens from the subject, we need to adjust the exposure. This part of the equation is under our control to the extent we can increase the amount of light falling on or passing through the subject (by adding extra light sources or using reflectors), or by pumping up the light that's emitted (by increasing the brightness of the glowing object).
- **Light passed by the lens.** Not all the illumination that reaches the front of the lens makes it all the way through. Filters can remove some of the light before it enters the lens. Inside the lens barrel is a variable-sized diaphragm called an *aperture* that dilates and contracts to control the amount of light that enters the lens. You, or the D3s/D3x's autoexposure system, can control exposure by varying the size of the aperture. The relative size of the aperture is called the *f/stop.* (See Figure 6.3.)
- **Light passing through the shutter.** Once light passes through the lens, the amount of time the sensor receives it is determined by the D3s/D3x's shutter, which can remain open for as long as 30 seconds (or even longer if you use the Bulb setting) or as briefly as 1/8,000th second.

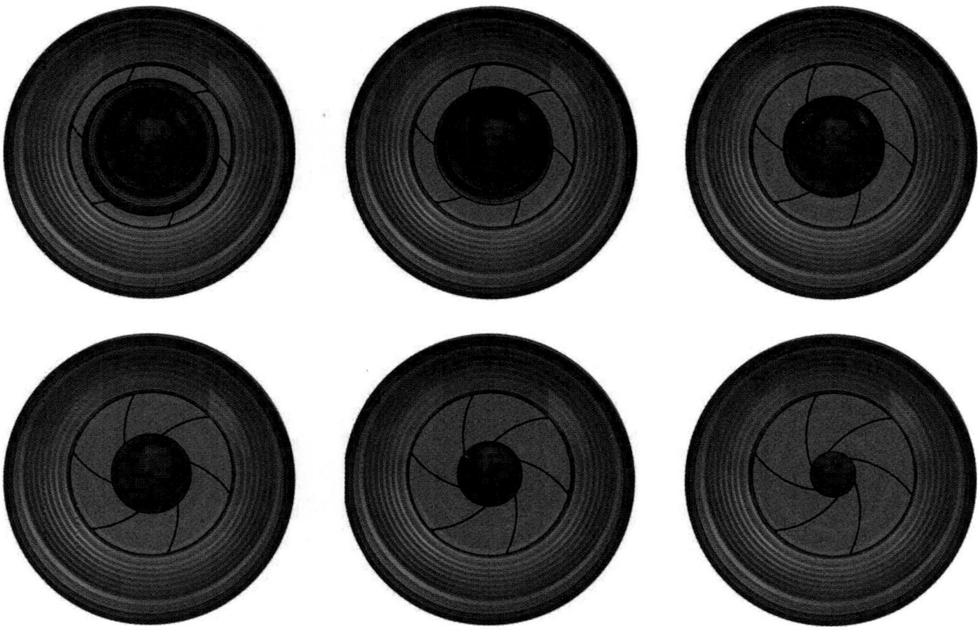

**Figure 6.3**
Top row (left to right): f/2, f/2.8, f/4; bottom row, f/5.6, f/8, f11.

- **Light captured by the sensor.** Not all the light falling onto the sensor is captured. If the number of photons reaching a particular photosite doesn't pass a set threshold, no information is recorded. Similarly, if too much light illuminates a pixel in the sensor, then the excess isn't recorded or, worse, spills over to contaminate adjacent pixels. We can modify the minimum and maximum number of pixels that contribute to image detail by adjusting the ISO setting. At higher ISOs, the incoming light is amplified to boost the effective sensitivity of the sensor.

These four factors—quantity of light, light passed by the lens, the amount of time the shutter is open, and the sensitivity of the sensor—all work proportionately and reciprocally to produce an exposure. That is, if you double the amount of light, increase the aperture by one stop, make the shutter speed twice as long, or boost the ISO setting 2X, you'll get twice as much exposure. Similarly, you can increase any of these factors while decreasing one of the others by a similar amount to keep the same exposure.

Most commonly, exposure settings are made using the aperture and shutter speed, followed by adjusting the ISO sensitivity, if it's not possible to get the preferred exposure (that is, the one that uses the "best" f/stop or shutter speed for the depth-of-field or action stopping we want). Table 6.1 shows equivalent exposure settings using various shutter speeds and f/stops.

When the D3s/D3x is set for P mode, the metering system selects the correct exposure for you automatically, but you can change quickly to an equivalent exposure by holding down the shutter release button halfway ("locking" the current exposure), and then spinning the main command dial until the desired equivalent exposure combination is

### Table 6.1 Equivalent Exposures

| Shutter speed | f/stop | Shutter speed | f/stop |
|---|---|---|---|
| 1/30th second | f/22 | 1/1,000th second | f/4 |
| 1/60th second | f/16 | 1/2,000th second | f/2.8 |
| 1/125th second | f/11 | 1/4,000th second | f/2 |
| 1/250th second | f/8 | 1/8,000th second | f/1.4 |
| 1/500th second | f/5.6 | | |

### F/STOPS AND SHUTTER SPEEDS

If you're *really* new to more advanced cameras (and I realize that some ambitious amateurs do purchase the D3s/D3x as their first digital SLR), you might need to know that the lens aperture, or f/stop, is a ratio, much like a fraction, which is why f/2 is larger than f/4, just as 1/2 is larger than 1/4. However, f/2 is actually *four times* as large as f/4. (If you remember your high school geometry, you'll know that to double the area of a circle, you multiply its diameter by the square root of two: 1.4.)

Lenses are usually marked with intermediate f/stops that represent a size that's twice as much/half as much as the previous aperture. So, a lens might be marked

f/2, f/2.8, f/4, f/5.6, f/8, f/11, f/16, f/22, with each larger number representing an aperture that admits half as much light as the one before, as shown in Figure 6.3.

Shutter speeds are actual fractions (of a second), but the numerator is omitted, so that 60, 125, 250, 500, 1,000, and so forth represent 1/60th, 1/125th, 1/250th, 1/500th, and 1/1,000th second. To avoid confusion, Nikon uses quotation marks to signify longer exposures: 2", 2"5, 4", and so forth representing 2.0, 2.5, and 4.0-second exposures, respectively.

displayed. You can use this Flexible Program feature more easily if you remember that you need to rotate the command dial towards the left when you want to increase the amount of depth-of-field or use a slower shutter speed; rotate to the right when you want to reduce the depth-of-field or use a faster shutter speed. The need for more/less DOF and slower/faster shutter speed are the primary reasons you'd want to use Flexible Program. This program shift mode does not work when you're using flash.

In aperture-priority (A) and shutter-priority (S) modes, you can change to an equivalent exposure, but only by either adjusting the aperture (the camera chooses the shutter speed) or shutter speed (the camera selects the aperture). I'll cover all these exposure modes later in the chapter.

## How the D3s/D3x Calculates Exposure

Your Nikon D3s/D3x calculates exposure by measuring the light that passes through the lens and is bounced up by the mirror to a 1,005-segment RGB sensor located near the focusing surface, using a pattern you can select (more on that later), and based on the assumption that each area being measured reflects about the same amount of light as a neutral gray card with roughly 18-percent reflectance. That assumption is necessary, because different subjects reflect different amounts of light. In a photo containing a white cat and a dark gray cat, the white cat might reflect five times as much light as the gray cat. An exposure based on the white cat will cause the gray cat to appear to be black, while an exposure based only on the gray cat will make the white cat washed out. Light-measuring devices handle this by assuming that the areas measured average a standard value of 18-percent gray, a figure that's been used as a rough standard for many years (most vendors don't calibrate their metering for exactly 18-percent gray; the actual figure may be closer to 13 or 14 percent).

In most cases, your camera's light meter will do a good job of calculating the right exposure, especially if you use the exposure tips in the next section. But if you want to double-check, or feel that exposure is especially critical, take the light reading off an object of known reflectance. Photographers sometimes carry around an 18-percent gray card (available from any camera store) and, for critical exposures, actually use that card, placed in the subject area, to measure exposure (or to set a custom white balance if needed).

You could, in many cases, arrive at a reasonable exposure by pointing your D3s/D3x at an evenly lit object, such as an actual gray card or the palm of your hand (the backside of the hand is too variable). You'll need to increase the exposure by one stop in the latter case, because the human palm—of any ethnic group—reflects about twice as much light as a gray card. It's more practical though, to use your D3s/D3x's system to meter the actual scene.

### F/STOPS VERSUS STOPS

In photography parlance, *f/stop* always means the aperture or lens opening. However, for lack of a current commonly used word for one exposure increment, the term *stop* is often used. (In the past, EV served this purpose, but Exposure Value and its abbreviation has been inextricably intertwined with its use in describing Exposure Compensation.) In this book, when I say "stop" by itself (no *f/*), I mean one whole unit of exposure, and am not necessarily referring to an actual f/stop or lens aperture. So, adjusting the exposure by "one stop" can mean both changing to the next shutter speed increment (say, from 1/125th second to 1/250th second) or the next aperture (such as f/4 to f/5.6). Similarly, 1/3 stop or 1/2 stop increments can mean either shutter speed or aperture changes, depending on the context. Be forewarned.

## Tip

Of course, if you use such a gray card, strictly speaking, you need to use about one-half stop *more* exposure than metered, because the D3s/D3x is calibrated for a lighter tone, rather than the 18-percent gray you just measured. If you're using a human palm instead, add one full stop more exposure.

To meter properly you'll want to choose both the *metering method* (how light is evaluated) and *exposure method* (how the appropriate shutter speeds and apertures are chosen). I'll describe both in the following sections. But first, let's clear up that black cat/gray cat/white cat conundrum, without using any actual cats. Black, white, and gray cats have been a standard metaphor for many years, so I'm going to explain this concept using a different, and more cooperative, life form: peppers.

Figure 6.4 shows three colors of peppers. The yellow peppers at top represent an off-white cat, or any object that is very light but which contains detail that we want to see in the light areas. The red peppers in the center are a stand-in for a gray cat, because they have most of their details in the middle tones. The green peppers serve as our black cat, because it is a dark object with detail in its shadows.

The colors confuse the issue, so I'm going to convert our color peppers to black-and-white. For the version shown in Figure 6.5, the exposure was optimized for the white (yellow) peppers, changing their tonal value to a medium, 18-percent gray. The dark (green) and medium-toned (red) peppers are now *too* dark. For Figure 6.6, the

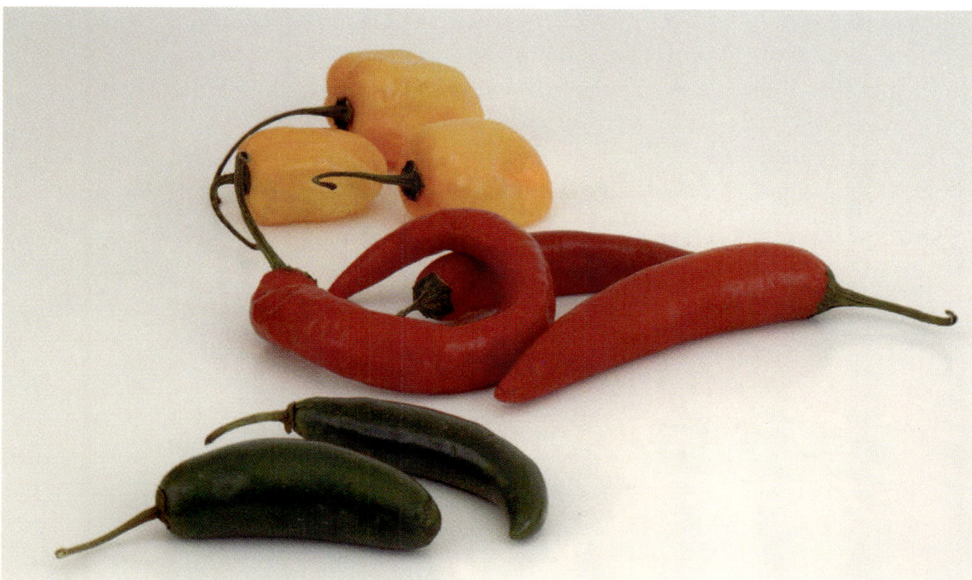

**Figure 6.4**
The yellow peppers, red peppers, and green peppers represent light, middle, and dark tones.

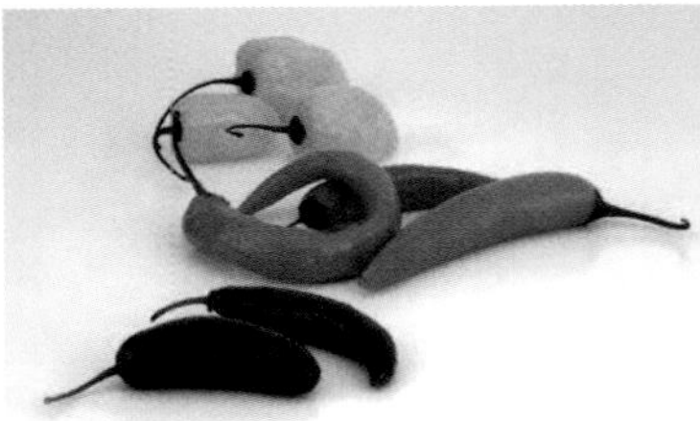

**Figure 6.5** Exposing for the light-colored peppers at top renders the other two types excessively dark.

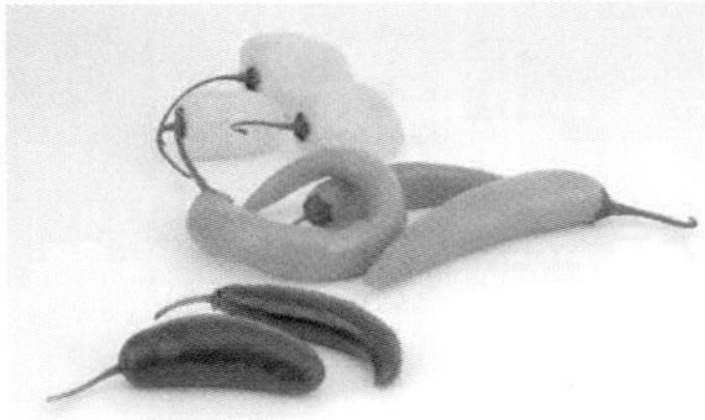

**Figure 6.6** Exposing for the dark peppers (bottom) causes the vegetables in the upper two-thirds of the picture to become too light.

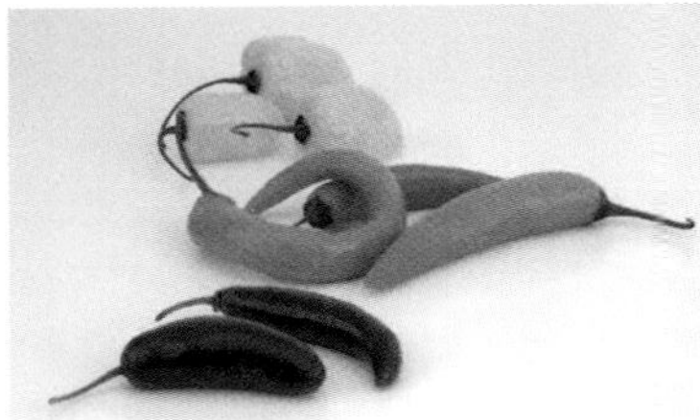

**Figure 6.7** Exposing for the middle-toned red peppers in the center produces an image in which the tones of all three types appear accurately.

exposure was optimized for the dark (green) peppers, making most of their surface, now, fall into the middle-tone, 18-percent gray range. The yellow (light) and midtone (red) peppers are now too light.

The solution, of course, is to measure exposure from the object with the middle tones which most closely correspond to the gray "standard." Do that, and you wind up with a picture that more closely resembles the original tonality of the red, yellow, and green peppers, and which looks, in black-and-white, like Figure 6.7.

### MODES, MODES, AND MORE MODES

Call them modes or methods, the Nikon D3s/D3x seems to have a lot of different sets of options that are described using similar terms. Here's how to sort them out:

- **Metering method.** These modes determine the *parts of the image* within the 1,005-segment sensor array that are examined in order to calculate exposure. The D3s/D3x may look at many different points within the image, segregating them by zone (matrix metering); examine the same number of points, but give greater weight to those located in the middle of the frame (center-weighted metering); or evaluate only a limited number of points in a limited area (spot metering).
- **Exposure method.** These modes determine *which* settings are used to expose the image. The D3s/D3x may adjust the shutter speed, the aperture, or both, depending on the method you choose.

## Choosing a Metering Method

The D3s/D3x has three different schemes for evaluating the light received by its exposure sensors: Matrix (with several variations, depending on what lens you have attached), center-weighted, and spot metering. Select the mode you want to use by rotating the metering method dial immediately forward of the viewfinder window on the pentaprism. Push the central button to unlock the lever used to choose the metering method. Here is what you need to know about each metering method:

## Matrix Metering

For its various matrix metering modes, the D3s/D3x slices up the frame into 1,005 different zones, arrayed in 67 rows of 15 columns that cover most of the sensor area, shown in Figure 6.8. When matrix metering is active, an icon appears in the viewfinder (lower left) and in the monochrome status LCD (enlarged in the upper-right corner). In all cases, the D3s/D3x evaluates the differences between the zones, and compares them with a built-in database of several hundred thousand images to make an educated guess about what kind of picture you're taking. For example, if the top sections of a picture are much lighter than the bottom portions, the algorithm can assume that the scene is a landscape photo with lots of sky. An image that includes most of the lighter portions in the center area may be a portrait.

Color information is available to the metering system because the 1,005-segment exposure array is actually composed of blue, green, and red-sensitive sensors, which alternate across the frame to fill the 67 columns and 15 rows, as you can see in the figures. Note that there are 335 of each color sensor, and that all the rows are identical. That's different from the Bayer filter array that blankets the sensor, which alternates rows of red/green pixels with rows of blue/green pixels. While the Bayer arrangement is needed

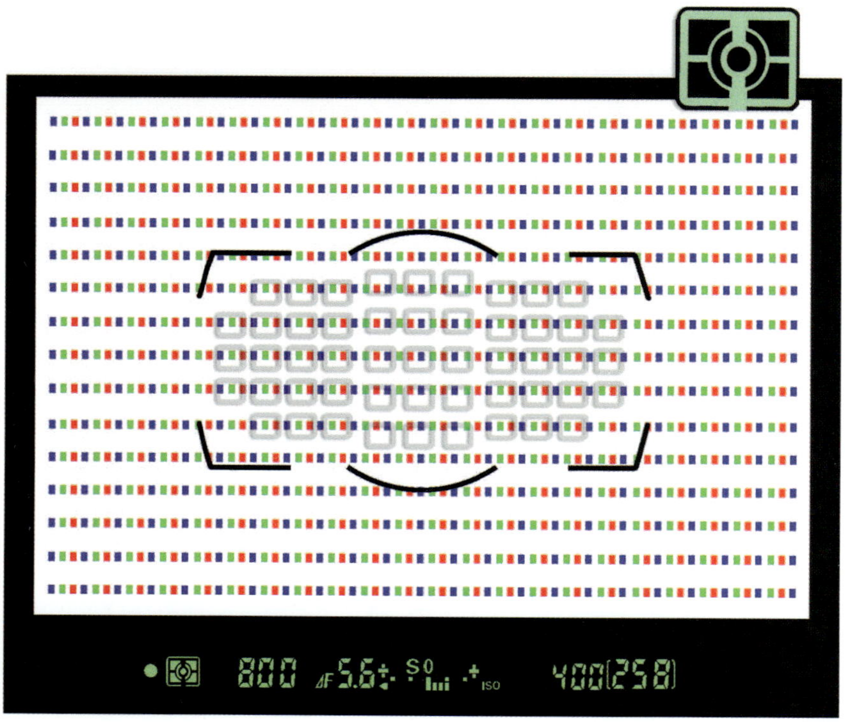

**Figure 6.8** Matrix metering calculates exposure based on 1,005 points in the frame, arranged in an array of alternating red, green, and blue-sensitive pixels.

for the sensor in order to accurately reproduce the colors of the scene, the 1,005-pixel metering array has a much simpler task: just to capture color information that can be used to interpret the scene for exposure and autofocus calculations.

Here are the ways in which the Nikon D3s/D3x uses information other than brightness to make its evaluation:

- **3D color matrix metering II.** This metering mode is used by default when the D3s/D3x is equipped with a lens that has a type G or type D designator in its name, such as the AF-S Nikkor 14-245mm f/2.8G ED lens. The G after the f/2.8 is the giveaway. (More on lens nomenclature in Chapter 9.) The camera calculates exposure based on brightness, colors of the subject matter (that is, blue pixels in the upper part of the image are probably sky; green pixels in the lower half probably foliage), focus point, and distance information. The D3s/D3x is able to use that additional distance data to better calculate what kind of scene you have framed. For example, if you're shooting a portrait with a longer focal-length lens focused to about 5 to 12 feet from the camera, and the upper half of the scene is very bright, the camera assumes you would prefer to meter for the rest of the image, and discount the bright area. However, if the camera has a wide-angle lens attached and is focused at infinity, the D3s/D3x can assume you're taking a landscape photo and take the bright upper area into account to produce better looking sky and clouds.
- **Color matrix metering II.** If you have a non-G or non-D lens equipped with a CPU chip (these are generally older lenses, although chips can be added to optics that lack them), the distance range is not used. Instead, only focus, brightness, and the RGB color information is taken into account to calculate an appropriate exposure.
- **Color matrix metering.** If you're using a non-CPU lens (such as an older manual focus lens) and have specified the focal length and maximum aperture in the Shooting menu (as described in Chapter 5), then the D3s/D3x uses plain old color matrix metering, which evaluates exposure based only on brightness and RGB color information detected in the scene.
- **With other lenses.** If you don't specify focal length or maximum aperture for a non-CPU lens, the D3s/D3x defaults to center-weighted metering.

Matrix metering is best for most general subjects, because it is able to intelligently analyze a scene and make an excellent guess of what kind of subject you're shooting a great deal of the time. The camera can tell the difference between low-contrast and high-contrast subjects by looking at the range of differences in brightness across the scene. Because the D3s/D3x has a fairly good idea about what kind of subject matter you are shooting, it can underexpose slightly when appropriate to preserve highlight detail when image contrast is high. (It's often possible to pull detail out of shadows that are too dark using an image editor, but once highlights are converted to white pixels, they are gone forever.)

**CAUTION**

If you're using a strong filter, including a polarizing filter, split-color filter, or neutral-density filter (particularly a graduated neutral-density filter), you should switch from matrix metering to center-weighted, because the filter can affect the relationships between the different areas of the frame used to calculate a matrix exposure. For example, a polarizing filter produces a sky that is darker than usual, hindering the matrix algorithm's recognition of a landscape photo. Extra dark or colored filters disturb the color relationships used for color matrix metering, too.

## Center-Weighted Metering

In this mode, the exposure meter emphasizes a zone in the center of the frame to calculate exposure, as shown in Figure 6.9. About 75 percent of the exposure is based on that central area, and the remaining exposure is based on the rest of the frame. The theory here is that, for most pictures, the main subject will be located in the center. So, if the D3s/D3x reads the center portion and determines that the exposure for that region should be f/8 at 1/250th second, while the outer area, which is a bit darker, calls for f/4 at 1/125th second, the camera will give the center portion the most weight and arrive at a final exposure of f/5.6 at 1/250th second.

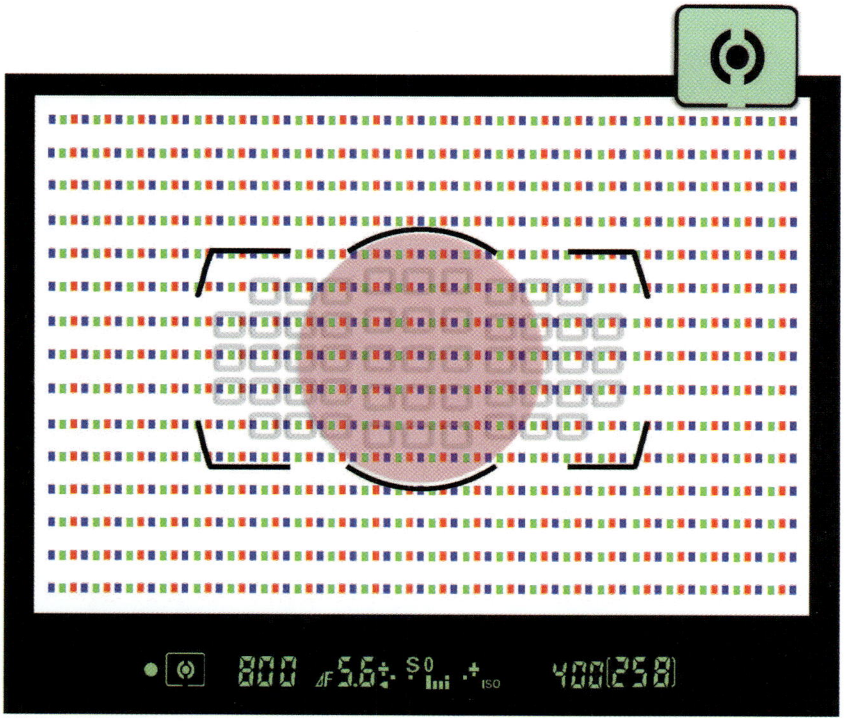

**Figure 6.9** Center-weighted metering calculates exposure based on the full frame, but gives 75 percent of the weight to the center area shown; the remaining 25 percent of the exposure is determined by the rest of the image area.

Center-weighting works best for portraits, architectural photos, backlit subjects with extra-bright backgrounds (such as snow or sand), and other pictures in which the most important subject is located in the middle of the frame. As the name suggests, the light reading is *weighted* towards the central portion, but information is also used from the rest of the frame. If your main subject is surrounded by very bright or very dark areas, the exposure might not be exactly right. However, this scheme works well in many situations if you don't want to use one of the other modes. This mode can be useful for close-ups of subjects like flowers, or for portraits. You can adjust the size of the center area assigned the greatest weight using Custom Setting b5, as described in Chapter 4.

## Spot Metering

Spot metering is favored by those of us who used to utilize a hand-held light meter to measure exposure at various points (such as metering highlights and shadows separately). However, you can use spot metering in any situation where you want to individually measure the light reflecting from light, midtone, or dark areas of your subject—or any combination of areas.

This mode confines the reading to a limited 3mm area in the center of the viewfinder, making up only two percent of the image, as shown in Figure 6.10. The circle is centered on the current focus point, *but is larger than the focus point*, so don't fall into the

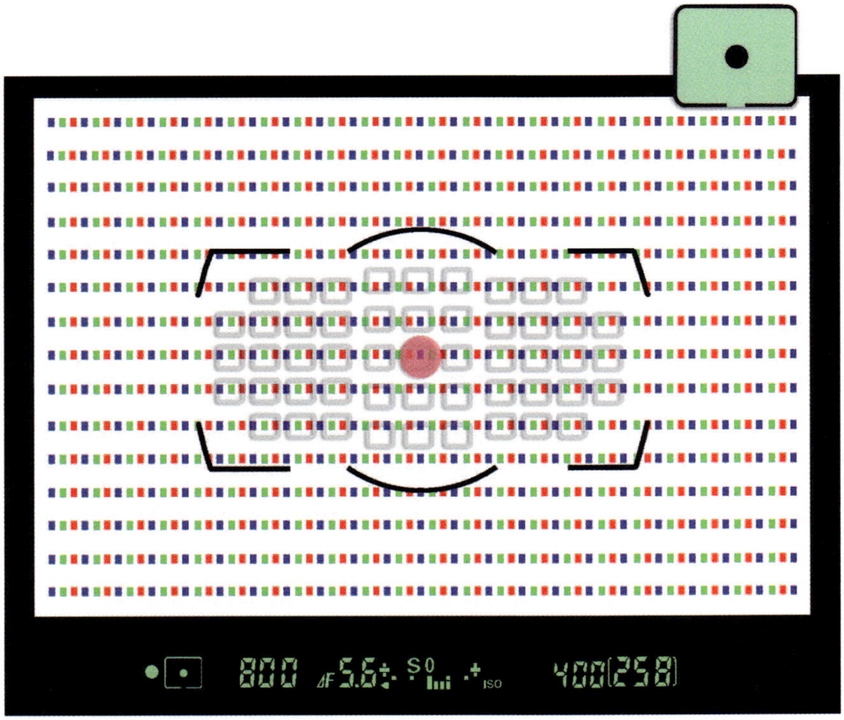


**Figure 6.10** Spot metering calculates exposure based on a spot that's only two percent of the image area, and which is slightly larger than the currently selected focus point. In this figure, the center focus point is the selected focus zone.

trap of believing that exposure is being measured only within the brackets that represent the active focus point. The figure shows the spot metering area based on the center focus area being the current focus point, but, in practice, the metering spot can be any of the 51 points selected by you *or the camera.* That's an important distinction. You might select a particular focus point manually, but in a certain autofocus mode (dynamic-area AF when using continuous-servo autofocus), the D3s/D3x may switch to another focus point if the subject moves outside the autofocus area you've chosen. The spot metering area will follow.

Table 6.2 is a summary of the possibilities to help you keep them straight (if you don't understand the autofocus modes, you may need to skip ahead to Chapter 7 to review them).

Spot metering is the only metering method you can use to tell the D3s/D3x exactly where to measure exposure. However, if a non-CPU lens is mounted, or you have selected auto-area AF, only the center focus point is used to spot meter.

**Table 6.2 Spot Metering Modes**

| Autofocus mode | Autofocus point selection | Action |
|---|---|---|
| Single-servo (AF-S) or manual focus (M) | Single-point AF or Dynamic-area AF | Spot metering at the focus point you select manually. |
| Continuous-servo (AF-C) | Dynamic-area AF | Spot metering initially at the focus point you select, but follows focus point that the camera selects if the subject moves. |
| Single-servo (AF-S) or continuous-servo (AF-C) | Auto-area AF | Spot metering at the focus point selected by the camera. |

**MORE TO COME**

Although some metering modes and autofocus functions are closely intertwined, it's not possible to explain them both in a single chapter without confusing the issues. This chapter concentrates on metering options; if you want to fully understand how they relate to autofocus, you'll need to read Chapter 7, too.

You'll find spot metering useful when you want to base exposure on a small area in the frame. If that area is in the center of the frame, so much the better. If not, you'll have to move the autofocus point to one of the other zones, or else make your meter reading for an off-center subject and then lock exposure by pressing the shutter release halfway, or by pressing the AE lock button. This mode is best for subjects where the background is significantly brighter or darker.

# Choosing an Exposure Method

You'll find four methods for choosing the appropriate shutter speed and aperture. You can choose among them by pressing the Mode button on the top panel, and using the main command dial until the icon for the mode you want appears in the monochrome status LCD. Your choice of which is best for a given shooting situation will depend on things like your need for lots of (or less) depth-of-field, a desire to freeze action or allow motion blur, or how much noise you find acceptable in an image. Each of the D3s/D3x's exposure methods emphasizes one aspect of image capture or another. This section introduces you to all four.

## Aperture-Priority

In A mode, you specify the lens opening used, and the D3s/D3x selects the shutter speed. Aperture-priority is especially good when you want to use a particular lens opening to achieve a desired effect. Perhaps you'd like to use the smallest f/stop possible to maximize depth-of-field in a close-up picture. Or, you might want to use a large f/stop to throw everything except your main subject out of focus, as in Figure 6.11. Maybe you'd just like to "lock in" a particular f/stop because it's the sharpest available aperture with that lens. Or, you might prefer to use, say, f/2.8 on a lens with a maximum aperture of f/1.4, because you want the best compromise between speed and sharpness.

Aperture-priority can even be used to specify a *range* of shutter speeds you want to use under varying lighting conditions, which seems almost contradictory. But think about it. You're shooting a soccer game outdoors with a telephoto lens and want a relatively high shutter speed, but you don't care if the speed changes a little should the sun duck behind a cloud. Set your D3s/D3x to A, and adjust the aperture until a shutter speed of, say, 1/1,000th second is selected at your current ISO setting. (In bright sunlight at ISO 400, that aperture is likely to be around f/11.) Then, go ahead and shoot, knowing that your D3s/D3x will maintain that f/11 aperture (for sufficient DOF as the soccer players move about the field), but will drop down to 1/750th or 1/500th second if necessary should the lighting change a little.

A Lo or Hi indicator in the viewfinder and the top-panel monochrome LCD indicates that the D3s/D3x is unable to select an appropriate shutter speed at the selected aperture and that over- and underexposure will occur at the current ISO setting. That's the major pitfall of using A: you might select an f/stop that is too small or too large to allow an optimal exposure with the available shutter speeds. For example, if you choose f/2.8 as your aperture and the illumination is quite bright (say, at the beach or in snow), even your camera's fastest shutter speed might not be able to cut down the amount of light reaching the sensor to provide the right exposure. Or, if you select f/8 in a dimly lit room, you might find yourself shooting with a very slow shutter speed that can cause blurring from subject movement or camera shake. Aperture-priority is best used by those with a bit of experience in choosing settings. Many seasoned photographers leave their D3s/D3x set on A all the time. The exposure indicator scale in the status panel and viewfinder indicate the amount of under- or overexposure.

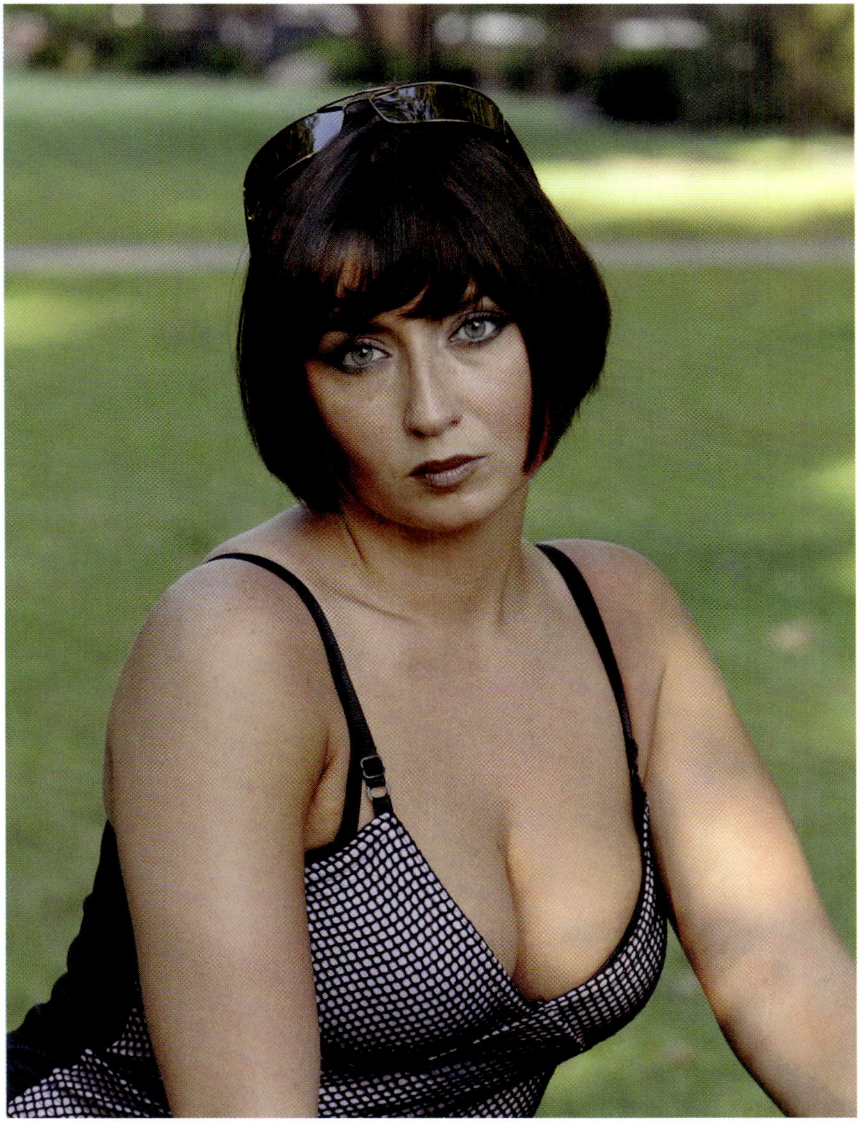

**Figure 6.11**
Use aperture-priority to "lock in" a large f/stop when you want to blur the background.

## Shutter-Priority

Shutter-priority (S) is the inverse of aperture-priority: you choose the shutter speed you'd like to use, and the camera's metering system selects the appropriate f/stop. Perhaps you're shooting action photos and you want to use the absolute fastest shutter speed available with your camera; in other cases, you might want to use a slow shutter speed to add some blur to a sports photo that would be mundane if the action were completely frozen. (See Figure 6.12.) Shutter-priority mode gives you some control over how much action-freezing capability your digital camera brings to bear in a particular situation.

You'll also encounter the same problem as with aperture-priority when you select a shutter speed that's too long or too short for correct exposure under some conditions. I've shot outdoor soccer games on sunny Fall evenings and used shutter-priority mode to lock in a 1/1,000th second shutter speed, only to find my D3s/D3x refused to shoot when the sun dipped behind some trees and there was no longer enough light to shoot at that speed, even with the lens wide open.

Like A mode, it's possible to choose an inappropriate shutter speed. If that's the case, the same Hi and Lo displays will flash.

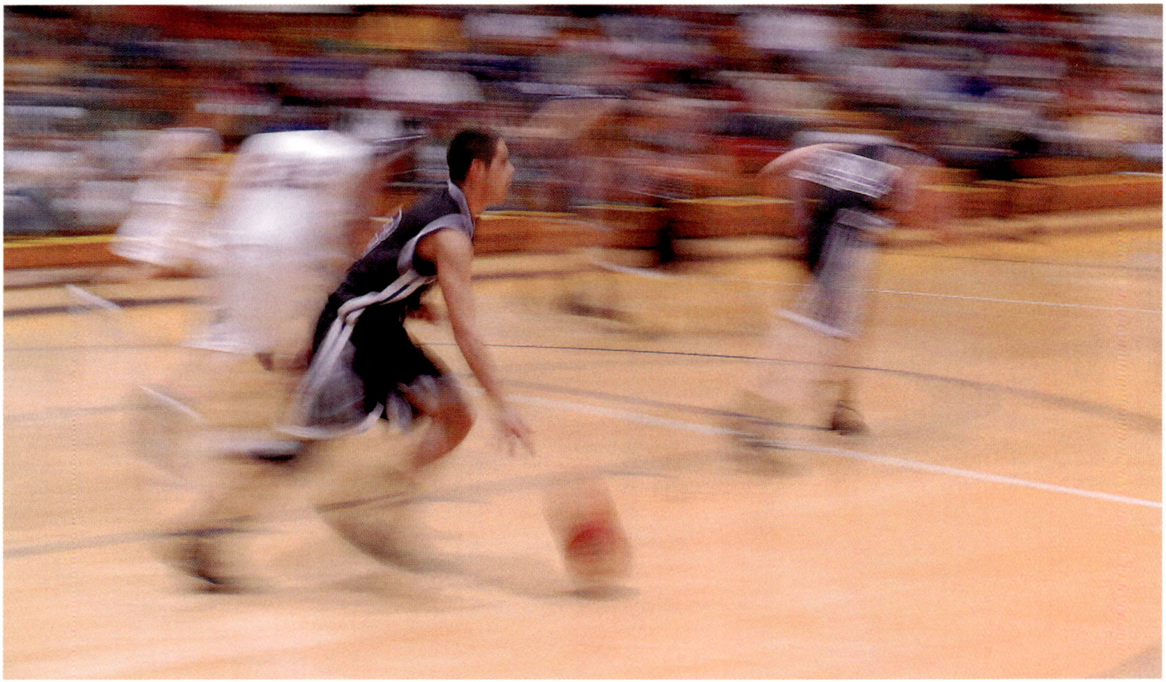

**Figure 6.12** Lock the shutter at a slow speed to introduce blur into an action shot, as with this panned image of a basketball player.

## Programmed Mode

Programmed mode (P) uses the D3s/D3x's built-in smarts to select the correct f/stop and shutter speed using a database of picture information that tells it which combination of shutter speed and aperture will work best for a particular photo. If the correct exposure cannot be achieved at the current ISO setting, the Lo or Hi indicator in the viewfinder and monochrome LCD will appear. You can then boost or reduce the ISO to increase or decrease sensitivity.

The D3s/D3x's recommended exposure can be overridden if you want. Use the EV setting feature (described later, because it also applies to S and A modes) to add or subtract exposure from the metered value. And, as I mentioned earlier in this chapter, in programmed mode you can rotate the main command dial to change from the recommended setting to an equivalent setting (as shown in Table 6.1) that produces the same exposure, but using a different combination of f/stop and shutter speed.

This is called "Flexible Program" by Nikon. Rotate the main command dial counterclockwise to reduce the size of the aperture (going from, say, f/4 to f/5.6), so that the D3s/D3x will automatically use a slower shutter speed (going from, say, 1/250th second to 1/125th second). Rotate the main command dial clockwise to use a larger f/stop, while automatically producing a shorter shutter speed that provides the same equivalent exposure as metered in P mode. An asterisk appears next to the P in the monochrome LCD and viewfinder so you'll know you've overridden the D3s/D3x's default program setting. Your adjustment remains in force until you rotate the main command dial until the asterisk disappears, or you switch to a different exposure mode, or turn off the D3s/D3x.

### MAKING EV CHANGES

Sometimes you'll want more or less exposure than indicated by the D3s/D3x's metering system. Perhaps you want to underexpose to create a silhouette effect, or overexpose to produce a high key look. It's easy to use the D3s/D3x's exposure compensation system to override the exposure recommendations. Press the EV button on the top of the camera (just southeast of the shutter release). Then rotate the main command dial counterclockwise to add exposure, and clockwise to subtract exposure. The EV change you've made remains for the exposures that follow, until you manually zero out the EV setting. The EV plus/minus icon appears in the viewfinder and monochrome status panel to warn you that an exposure compensation change has been entered. You can increase or decrease exposure over a range of plus or minus five stops. (If you've activated easy exposure compensation using Custom Setting b4, as described in Chapter 4, you don't have to hold down the EV button; rotating the main or sub-command dials alone changes the EV value when using programmed, aperture-priority, shutter-priority, or manual exposure modes.)

## Manual Exposure

Part of being an experienced photographer comes from knowing when to rely on your D3s/D3x's automation (with P mode), when to go semiautomatic (with S or A), and when to set exposure manually (using M). Some photographers actually prefer to set their exposure manually, as the D3s/D3x will be happy to indicate when its metering system judges your manual settings provide the proper exposure, using the analog exposure scale at the bottom of the viewfinder and on the status LCD.

Manual exposure can come in handy in some situations. You might be taking a silhouette photo and find that none of the exposure modes or EV correction features give you exactly the effect you want. Set the exposure manually to use the exact shutter speed and f/stop you need. Or, you might be working in a studio environment using multiple flash units. The additional flash are triggered by slave devices (gadgets that set off the flash when they sense the light from another flash unit, or, perhaps from a radio or infrared remote control). Your camera's exposure meter doesn't compensate for the extra illumination, so you need to set the aperture manually.

Because, depending on your proclivities, you might not need to set exposure manually very often, you should still make sure you understand how it works. Fortunately, the D3s/D3x makes setting exposure manually very easy. Just press the Mode button and rotate the main command dial to change to manual mode, and then turn the main command dial to set the shutter speed, and the sub-command dial to adjust the aperture. Press the shutter release halfway or press the AE lock button, and the exposure scale in the viewfinder shows you how far your chosen setting diverges from the metered exposure.

### METERING WITH OLDER LENSES

Older lenses that lack the CPU chip that tells the Nikon D3s/D3x what kind of lens is mounted can be used with aperture-priority and manual exposure modes only, assuming you've entered the Non-CPU lens information in the Setup menu, as described in Chapter 5. If the D3s/D3x knows the maximum aperture of the lens, you can set the aperture using the lens's aperture ring, and, in A mode, the camera will automatically select an appropriate shutter speed. In manual mode, you can set the aperture, and the analog exposure scale in the viewfinder and monochrome LCD status panel will indicate when you've set the correct shutter speed manually. If a non-CPU lens is mounted and you try to set programmed or shutter-priority modes, the D3s/D3x switches to aperture-priority automatically. The process works because the D3s/D3x camera body and other advanced Nikon models (from the old D200 on up through the D3x) have a mechanical linkage built into the lens mount that tells the camera when the f/stop has been changed. Amateur cameras like the Nikon D3000, D5000, D40/D40x, D50, D60, D70/D70s, D80, and D90 lack this linkage and cannot meter with non-CPU lenses.

## Adjusting Exposure with ISO Settings

Another way of adjusting exposures is by changing the ISO sensitivity setting. Sometimes photographers forget about this option, because the common practice is to set the ISO once for a particular shooting session (say, at ISO 200 for bright sunlight outdoors, or ISO 800 when shooting indoors) and then forget about ISO. The reason for that is that ISOs higher than ISO 200 or 400 are seen as "bad" or "necessary evils." However, changing the ISO is a valid way of adjusting exposure settings, particularly with the Nikon D3s/D3x, which produces good results at ISO settings that create grainy, unusable pictures with some other camera models.

Indeed, I find myself using ISO adjustment as a convenient alternate way of adding or subtracting EV when shooting in manual mode, and as a quick way of choosing equivalent exposures when in programmed or shutter-priority or aperture-priority modes. For example, I've selected a manual exposure with both f/stop and shutter speed suitable for my image using, say, ISO 200. I can change the exposure in 1/3 stop increments by pressing the ISO button on back of the camera, and spinning the main command dial one click at a time. The difference in image quality/noise at the base setting of ISO 200 is negligible if I dial in L 0.3 or L 0.7 (ISO 160 or 125 equivalents) to reduce exposure a little, or change to ISO 250 or 320 to increase exposure. I keep my preferred f/stop and shutter speed, but still adjust the exposure.

Or, perhaps, I am using S mode and the metered exposure at ISO 200 is 1/500th second at f/11. If I decide on the spur of the moment I'd rather use 1/500th second at f/8, I can press the ISO button and spin the main command dial three clicks counterclockwise to switch to LO 1.0 (ISO 100 equivalent). Of course, it's a good idea to monitor your ISO changes, so you don't end up at ISO 6400 accidentally. An ISO indicator appears in the monochrome control panel and in the viewfinder to remind you what sensitivity setting has been dialed in.

ISO settings can, of course, also be used to boost or reduce sensitivity in particular shooting situations. The D3x/D3s can use ISO settings from L 1.0 (ISO 50/100, respectively) up to Hi 1.0 (ISO 3200/25600 equivalent, respectively), then Hi 2.0 (6400/51200 equivalent, respectively). Only the D3s has settings up to Hi 3.0, which is the equivalent of ISO 102400.

The camera can also adjust the ISO automatically as appropriate for various lighting conditions. When you choose the Auto ISO setting in the Shooting menu, as described in Chapter 3, the D3s/D3x adjusts the sensitivity dynamically to suit the subject matter, based on minimum shutter speed and ISO limits you have prescribed.

## Dealing with Noise

Visual image noise is that random grainy effect that some like to use as a special effect, but which, most of the time, is objectionable because it robs your image of detail even as it adds that "interesting" texture. Noise is caused by two different phenomena: high ISO settings and long exposures.

High ISO noise commonly appears when you raise your camera's sensitivity setting above ISO 400. With the Nikon D3x, noise may become visible at ISO 1600, and is often fairly noticeable at ISO 3200. For the D3s, the equivalent figures are around ISO 6400 and ISO 12800. With either camera, sensitivity settings higher than that are usually quite bothersome. Nikon tips you off that higher settings may be problematic by labeling them with the Hi 1.0, Hi 2.0, and (with the D3s) Hi 3.0 labels. In all these cases, you can expect noise and increase in contrast in any pictures taken at these lofty ratings. High ISO noise appears as a result of the amplification needed to increase the sensitivity of the sensor. While higher ISOs do pull details out of dark areas, they also amplify non-signal information randomly, creating noise. You'll find a High ISO NR choice in the Shooting menu, where you can specify High, Norm, or Low noise reduction, or turn the feature off entirely. Because noise reduction tends to soften the grainy look while robbing an image of detail, you may want to disable the feature if you're willing to accept a little noise in exchange for more details.

A similar noisy phenomenon occurs during long time exposures, which allow more photons to reach the sensor, increasing your ability to capture a picture under low-light conditions. However, the longer exposures also increase the likelihood that some pixels will register random phantom photons, often because the longer an imager is "hot," the warmer it gets, and that heat can be mistaken for photons. There's also a special kind of noise that CMOS sensors like the one used in the D3s/D3x are potentially susceptible to. With a CCD, the entire signal is conveyed off the chip and funneled through a single amplifier and analog-to-digital conversion circuit. Any noise introduced there is, at least, consistent. CMOS imagers, on the other hand, contain millions of individual amplifiers and A/D converters, all working in unison. Because these circuits don't necessarily all process in precisely the same way all the time, they can introduce something called fixed-pattern noise into the image data.

Fortunately, Nikon's electronics geniuses have done an exceptional job minimizing noise from all causes in the D3-series cameras, particularly so with the amazing D3s. Even so, you might still want to apply the optional long exposure noise reduction that can be activated using Long exp. NR in the Shooting menu, where the feature can be turned On or Off. This type of noise reduction involves the D3s/D3x taking a second, blank exposure, and comparing the random pixels in that image with the photograph you just took. Pixels that coincide in the two represent noise and can safely be suppressed. This noise reduction system, called *dark frame subtraction,* effectively doubles the amount of time required to take a picture, and is used only for exposures longer than one second. Noise reduction can reduce the amount of detail in your picture, as some image information may be removed along with the noise. So, you might want to use this feature with moderation.

You can also apply noise reduction to a lesser extent using Photoshop, and when converting RAW and sRAW files to some other format, using your favorite RAW converter, or an industrial-strength product like Noise Ninja (www.picturecode.com) to wipe out noise after you've already taken the picture.

Both Canon and Nikon have introduced cameras with a top sensitivity setting of ISO 102400. Those of us who thought that processing 400 ASA Tri-X at EI 1600 in Acufine was a miracle may have been watching these outrageous speed increases with some skepticism. Of course, I couldn't believe the results I got with the original Canon EOS 5D at ISO 3200 back in 2005, and have routinely shot indoor sports with my D3 at ISO 6400 since 2007. So, going beyond 2010 with cameras like the Canon EOS 1D Mark IV and Nikon D3s, what do these lofty sensitivity ratings mean to you? In general, the improvement in the latest cameras means you can do all the things I outline below, but with even better quality and less noise.

- **Your lenses are all two or three stops "faster."** I lug all my large, fast, f/2.8 zooms around when traveling within the USA. Slower lenses just don't have the versatility of my 14-24mm, 24-70mm, and 70-200mm optics. But when I venture overseas, I like to travel (much) lighter. I've found that with a Nikon D3s, I can shoot at ISO 1600 with the same image quality I got from my older cameras at ISO 400, and my tiny 28-200mm f/3.5-5.6 zoom can easily replace two hefty lenses with enough speed even for indoor photography in cathedrals and other dimly lit locations. The shot in Figure 6.13 was taken with the 28-200mm zoom at 1/500th second at f/11 under indoor fluorescent illumination, at ISO 25600, and it's good enough for publication. Of course, if you're using fast lenses, higher ISOs let you stop down. My 70-200mm VR lens is great wide open, but it's even better at f/4 and f/5.6.
- **Stop action better.** This is the flip side of the equation. I've always shot concerts and indoor sports at f/4, and continue to favor that aperture range with my favorite lenses because a larger f/stop isolates my subjects. But 1/500th second is not ideal for basketball or volleyball, and the 1/80th second I used for performers often led to *too much* blur in those flying fingers. With ISO 3200 and higher available, I'm shooting indoor sports at 1/1,000th or 1/1,250th second, and concerts at 1/200th second. If the latest cameras give me improved image quality at those ISO settings, so much the better.

- **Sensor R&D is being redeployed in more useful directions.** The Canon 1D Mark IV has "only" 16MP, and Nikon probably surprised some when it unveiled the upgraded D3s with the same 12MP resolution of its predecessor. I, for one, have been delighted that vendors are emphasizing image quality, dynamic range, and noise reduction over more and more megapixels. I've been sorely disappointed in the image quality of several 14- and 15-megapixel cameras I purchased and used extensively while writing guidebooks for them. Cramming more pixels into the same space produced sensors with way too much noise. (Outside the dSLR world, you need only look as far as the Canon PowerShot G11, which takes a step *backward* to 10MP because the earlier 14.7MP G10 was almost unusable at ISO 800 and above.)

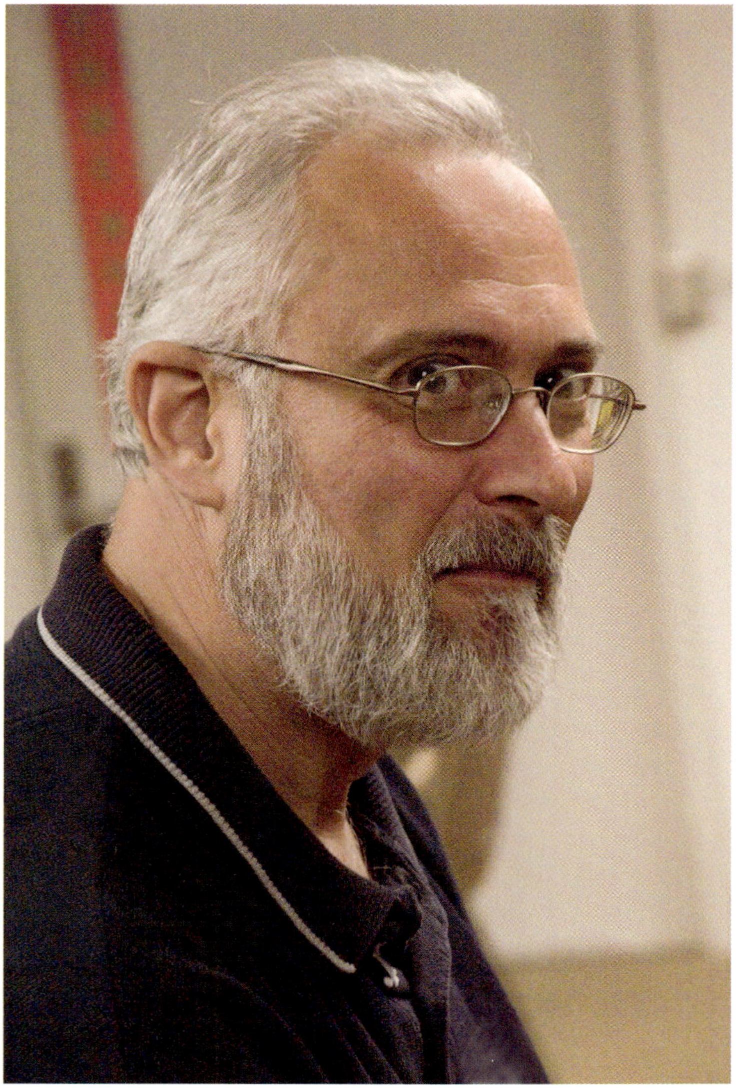

**Figure 6.13**
With the original D3 and the D3s, high ISO pictures like this one, shot at ISO 25600, are good enough for many purposes.

For many photographers, myself included, 12 megapixels is plenty for 90 percent of our work. There are too many things that the D3 and the D3s do better than the D3x (or, at least, sufficiently well) to make them obsolete with 12 megapixels. However, when I'm shooting fashion with plenty of strobe light, landscapes with the D3x mounted on a tripod, or certain types of product photography, those 24.5 megapixels come in very handy. (For example, when doing illustrations for my camera guides, I can take one image of the front and back of a camera, then crop in on details such as specific buttons and dials. Previously, I had to take individual shots of each component I planned to picture.)

But, overall, I welcome the improvements in image quality over more megapixels, and am thankful that sensor design is headed in that direction. I won't say that more 24-30MP cameras won't be introduced in the future. But, I'll say that few photographers actually will need them, until they match the 1D Mark IV and D3s in noise and dynamic range.

- **How much is too much?** I doubt I'll use ISO 102400 very often, but, then, I almost never use ISO 25600 or 12800, either. But, when vendors feel that those ridiculously high settings are viable enough to assign them Hi 2 and Hi 3 labels, that means the more reasonable speeds are likely to be even better and more usable. Certainly, I wouldn't mind owning a dSLR with a 208800 or higher ISO top end someday—if it meant I could use ISO 6400 like I work with ISO 400 now. There's no such thing as too much if the middle territory improves along with it. And, while we're at it, how about an ISO 10 setting with killer image quality so I don't have to remember to carry my neutral-density filters every time I want to shoot long exposures in full daylight?

## Bracketing

Bracketing is a method for shooting several consecutive exposures using different settings, as a way of improving the odds that one will be exactly right. Alternatively, bracketing can be used to create a series of photos with slightly different exposures (or white balances) in anticipation that one of the exposures will be "better" from a creative standpoint. For example, bracketing can supply you with a normal exposure of a backlit subject, one that's "underexposed," producing a silhouette effect, and a third that's "overexposed" to create still another look.

Before digital cameras took over the universe, it was common to bracket exposures, shooting, say, a series of three photos at 1/125th second, but varying the f/stop from f/8 to f/11 to f/16. In practice, smaller than whole-stop increments were used for greater precision, and lenses with apertures that were set manually commonly had half-stop detents on their aperture rings, or could easily be set to a mid-way position between whole f/stops. It was just as common to keep the same aperture and vary the shutter speed, although in the days before electronic shutters, film cameras often had only whole increment shutter speeds available.

I have to confess that I use bracketing a lot more than most people for certain types of shooting, especially street photography. On each of my 15 visits to Spain I've always spent a lot of time roaming the streets and squares during the evening *paseo*, which, during certain times of the year can occur very close to sunset. That means the lighting is constantly changing, and the typical scene can have a mixture of bright sunny areas and dusky shadows. Things happen quickly, too. An interesting person can stride into view unexpectedly and be gone in moments. For street photography, I don't want to be limited by changing light conditions, an exposure system that doesn't know exactly what subject I'm interested in, or the lack of time available to make exposure adjustments on my own.

So, I bracket. A lot. I'll set my D3s or D3x appropriately, probably matrix metering and aperture-priority, with the lens (most often my 70-200mm f/2.8 VR zoom) set for f/5.6 to limit depth-of-field, because most of my street photos concentrate on a single individual or a small group. Then, I'll set the camera to shoot in three-shot brackets, either with a 1/3 stop or 2/3 stop increment, depending on how widely the lighting conditions vary. (With a broader range of lighting, I'll use a larger increment to increase the chances that *one* of my shots will be spot-on.) Then, I'll rotate the release mode dial to continuous high speed ($C_H$) so that each press of the shutter release fires off an entire bracketed set in either 0.6 or .33 second (D3x/D3s, respectively). I can bang away with abandon, without thinking about anything other than my subject, so I'm ready when a weird guy walks out of the shadows, like the one I spotted strolling past a flower vendor at the Plaza Mayor in Madrid one October evening (see Figure 6.14). I caught him—human butterfly next to an array of flowers—at just the right moment. Because I'd bracketed, I was able to choose the shot that showed off the dude's wings, contrasted with the portico behind him.

Today, cameras like the D3s/D3x can bracket exposures much more precisely, and bracket white balance and Active D-Lighting as well. While WB bracketing is sometimes used when getting color absolutely correct in the camera is important, auto exposure bracketing is used much more often, and Active D-Lighting bracketing is seeing increased use as photographers discover how this feature can often "expand" the dynamic range of tones the sensor can capture.

Exposure bracketing is probably easiest to understand. When activated, the D3s/D3x takes three to nine consecutive photos. For example, you might choose three, one at the metered "correct" exposure, one with less exposure, and one with more exposure, using an increment of your choice. (Choose between increments by setting Custom Setting b2.) In S mode, the aperture will change, while in A mode, the shutter speed will change.

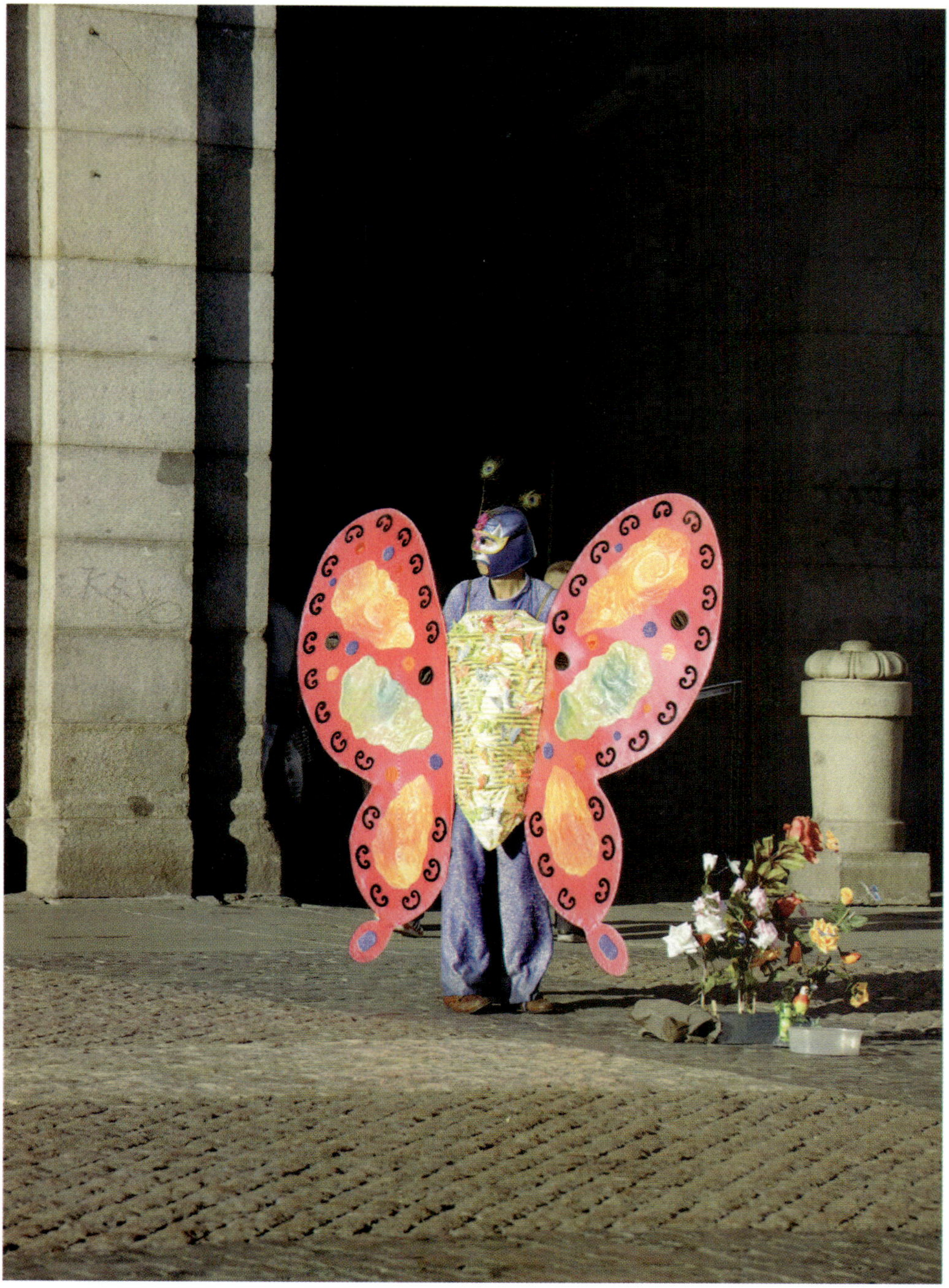

**Figure 6.14**
This grab shot was selected from a set of three bracketed exposures captured on the spur of a moment.

Using auto bracketing is trickier than it needs to be, but you can follow these steps to get results like those shown in Figure 6.15:

1. **Choose type of bracketing.** First, select the type of bracketing you want to do, using Custom Setting e4, as explained in Chapter 4. You can select autoexposure and flash, autoexposure only, flash only, white balance only, or ADL (Active D-Lighting) only. (ADL bracketing is possible with the D3s, but not the D3x). If you plan on shooting in manual exposure mode, you can specify how bracketing is performed using Custom Setting e5. With white balance bracketing, only a single exposure is taken, but the camera saves versions using each of the different white balance bracket settings.
2. **Press bracketing setting button.** Press the button you prefer or defined as the bracketing setting button in Custom Setting f4 (Fn button + command dial), Custom Setting f5 (Preview button + command dial), or Custom Setting f6 (AE-L/AF-L button + command dial), or the BKT button, Custom Setting f7, as described in Chapter 4. The BKT button is the most convenient for the majority and is the default value when the D3s/D3x comes from the factory, but you can choose one of the others if you prefer.

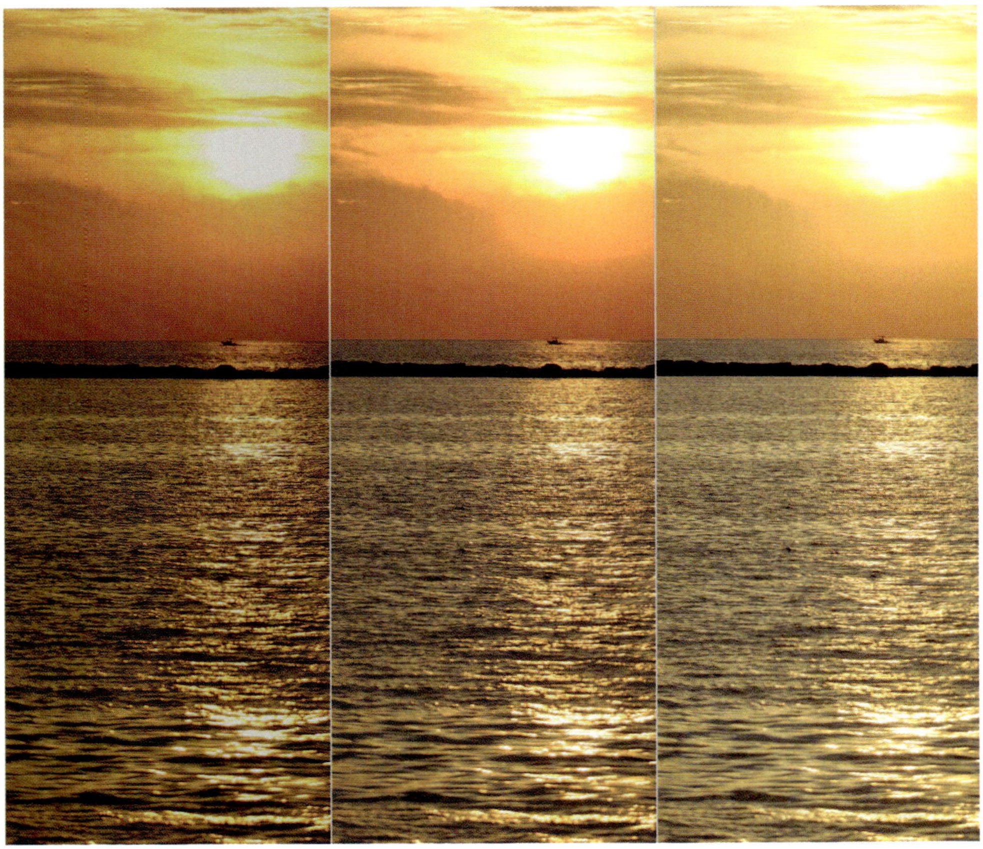

**Figure 6.15**
Bracketing can give you three different exposures of the same subject.

3. **Select number of bracketed exposures.** With the setting button held down, rotate the main command dial to choose the number of shots in the sequence, 0 (which turns bracketing off), 2, 3, 5, 7, or 9 bracketed shots. Rotate the main command dial counterclockwise to center the bracketed shots around the metered exposure (the 2 value is not available if you do this), and rotate it clockwise to choose 2 or 3 bracketed exposures concentrated either over or under the metered exposure. This is the most confusing aspect of bracketing, so I'll explain how this works in more detail next.
4. **Choose bracket increment.** With the setting button still held down, rotate the sub-command dial to choose the exposure increment, either 1/3, 2/3, or 1 EV (unless you've redefined the exposure compensation increment in Custom Setting b2).
5. **Frame and shoot.** As you take your photos the camera will vary exposure, flash level, white balance, or ADL setting for each image, based on the bracketing "program" you selected, and in the order you specified in Custom Setting e6. In single frame mode for exposure bracketing, you'll need to press the shutter release button the number of times you specified for the exposures in your bracketed burst (2, 3, 5, 7, or 9 shots). I've found it easy to forget that I am shooting bracketed pictures, stop taking my sequence, and then wonder why the remaining pictures in my defined burst are "incorrectly" exposed. To avoid that, I often set the D3s/D3x to one of the two continuous shooting modes, so that all my bracketed pictures are taken at once. The D3s/D3x does provide indicators on the monochrome LCD (a BKT indicator as well as a bracketing progress indicator), but they may be overlooked.
6. **Turn bracketing off.** When you're finished bracketing shots, remember to press the bracket setting button and rotate the main command dial until the number of shots in the sequence is 0F, and the BKT indicator is no longer displayed.

## White Balance and ADL Bracketing Exceptions

I concentrated on exposure bracketing in the previous list. Although most of the information applies, there are some differences you should know about when doing white balance bracketing with the D3x or D3s, or Active D-Lighting bracketing (available with the D3s only).

Here are the considerations you must keep in mind:

- **WB for JPEG only.** White balance bracketing can be performed only if you've set the Quality level of the D3s/D3x to JPEG Fine, Normal, or Basic. If you have selected RAW or RAW+JPEG, white balance bracketing is deactivated. That makes sense, because, if you have a RAW file, you can process your image using any white balance you like.

- **WB a single step.** With white balance bracketing, the camera takes only a single exposure, then saves copies at each of the white balance settings. There is no need to press the shutter release several times, or use continuous shooting to fire off a burst. One click is all it takes.
- **Specifying ADL settings.** You can only directly specify which of the five ADL settings (Off, Low, Normal, High, or Extra High) are applied during ADL bracketing if you choose to bracket just two images. If you want to shoot more than two, the camera selects the ADL settings for you, based on the number of shots in the bracket set that you choose. I'll explain the sequence shortly.

## More on Exposure Bracketing Programs

Unless you have previous experience with Nikon's bracketing procedures, the process can seem a little confusing, particularly when it comes time to select the number of bracketed exposures. That's because Nikon combines two functions in one setting: *how many actual shots in the burst* and *where those shots are placed within the overall scheme of exposure.* Both those parameters are set when you hold down your bracket setting button BKT button and spin the main command dial. That's an entirely different operation than setting the exposure increment, which is accomplished by holding down the setting button and spinning the sub-command dial.

Here's what happens. When you set the number of bracketed exposures, there are two "modes" based on which direction you rotate the command dial. Rotate the dial counterclockwise, and the number of exposures increases from 0 to 3, 5, 7, or 9 images. In *all* cases, the bracketed exposure values will be evenly spaced on either side of the metered exposure, using the increment you have selected separately (with the sub-command dial). Suppose you have already chosen 1/3 EV as your increment, and then rotate the main command dial counterclockwise. At the 3F 0.3 position, the exposures will be taken at the metered exposure, plus 1/3 stop less and 1/3 stop more (three shots in all). At the 5F 0.3 position, the exposures will be taken at the metered exposure, plus 1/3 stop and 2/3 stop less, as well as 1/3 stop and 2/3 stop more (five shots in all). The bracketed exposures are evenly spread on either side of the metered exposure.

Now rotate the main dial in the clockwise direction instead. In that case, the first setting that appears on the LCD is –2F 0.3, which will tell the D3s/D3x to shoot one picture at the measured exposure, and one at 1/3 stop less (two shots). The next click produces a readout of +2F 0.3, which produces one shot at the metered exposure, and one at 1/3 stop *more.* You can also select –3F 0.3 or +3F 0.3. In all cases, the additional bracketed shots are biased either towards under- or overexposure. That's as far as the clockwise spin will take you. There are no –5F or +5F or larger numeric settings available.

A lot of people find this concept confusing, because the Nikon manual discusses these variations (which it calls "bracketing programs") in the section that follows the description of exposure increments, set with the *sub*-command dial. Yes, the exposure increment you select does affect the "program," but the number of shots and distribution of the bracketed exposures is an entirely different concept, and is controlled by spinning the *main* command dial.

## More on Active D-Lighting Programs

As I mentioned earlier, you can't specifically choose from among the various Active D-Lighting settings when using ADL bracketing, *unless* you choose to shoot only two images in your bracket set. If you've selected ADL bracketing in Custom Setting e4, here's what happens:

- **Choose number of shots in the set.** When ADL bracketing has been selected in the Custom Setting menu, choose the number of shots in the set by holding down the BKT button and rotating the main command dial. You can select two to five shots. Each number sets the camera to use a different combination of ADL settings.
- **Select two shots.** If you want to specify a particular ADL setting, hold down the BKT button and rotate the main command dial to choose two shots. The D3s/D3x will take one image with ADL switched off, and one at a setting you can choose. To choose, while holding the BKT button, rotate the *sub-command* dial. The display on top of the camera will cycle through the five indicators shown in Figures 6.16 and 6.17 (which is a cropped view, highlighted to show the indicators to watch for). The options represent Auto, Low, Normal, High, and Extra High.

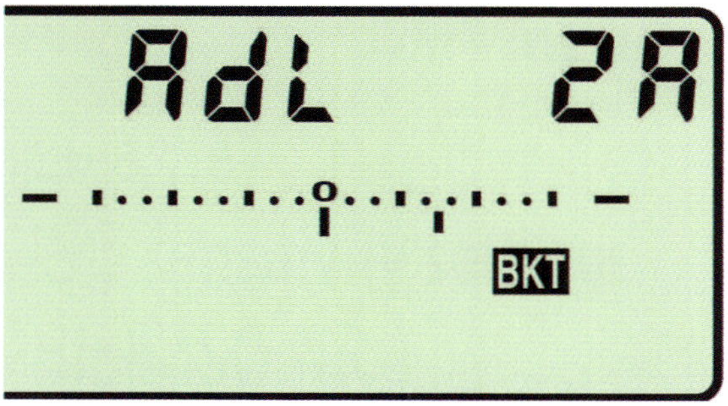


**Figure 6.16**
Hold down the BKT button and select two shots with the main command dial, then set ADL bracketing for Auto by rotating the sub-command dial until this display is shown.

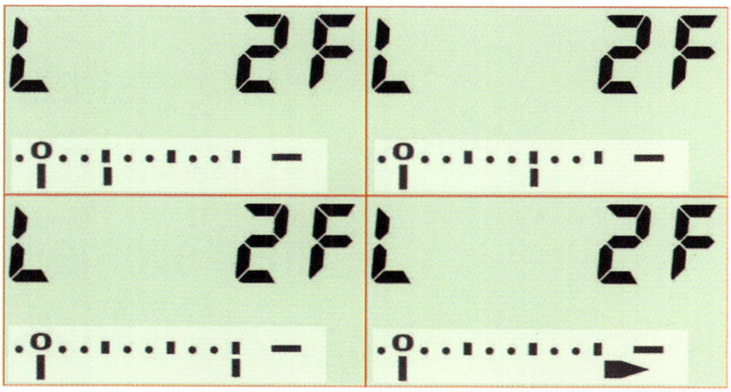

**Figure 6.17**
Hold down the BKT button and select two shots with the main command dial, then set ADL bracket setting by rotating the sub-command dial to specify Low (upper left), Normal (upper right), High (lower left), and Extra High (lower right).

- **Select three shots.** Hold down the BKT button and rotate the main command dial to choose three shots. The camera will take a set with ADL set to Off, Low, and Normal.
- **Select four shots.** Hold down the BKT button and rotate the main command dial to choose three shots. The camera will take a set with ADL set to Off, Low, Normal, and High.
- **Select five shots.** Hold down the BKT button and rotate the main command dial to choose three shots. The camera will take a set with ADL set to Off, Low, Normal, High, and Extra High.
- **Take your pictures.** Shoot your bracketed set. A bracketing indicator will appear on the top LCD control panel as each image is taken.

## More on White Balance Programs

If you've selected White balance bracketing in Custom Setting e4, here's the routine:

- **Choose number of shots.** Hold down the BKT button and rotate the main command dial to the right (counterclockwise) to select 3, 5, 7, or 9 bracketed shots, which will be evenly spaced around the current default white balance setting in the blue and amber directions. For example, if you select 3 shots, one will be saved that's bluer than the base white balance, one that's more amber (yellow), and one in the middle at the base white balance.

  or

- **Choose blue or amber bias instead.** Hold down the BKT button and rotate the main command dial to the left (clockwise), instead, to select a program that saves either two or three shots that are more blue (2bF or 3bF will appear on the display), or two or three shots that are more amber/yellow (2AF or 3AF will appear on the display).
- **Select increment.** Choose how much each bracketed shot will vary by holding down the BKT button and rotating the sub-command dial. You can choose increasing values of 1, 2, or 3, the equivalent of 5, 10, and 15 microreciprocal degrees (mireds). Don't worry about what a mired is; unless you have a color temperature meter, the exact values don't matter. Just keep in mind that the larger the number, the more white balance is changed.
- **Take your picture.** The camera will snap off a single exposure, and save the number of copies you specified with the white balance variations you've requested.

## Bracketing and Merge to HDR

One of the best uses for bracketing is to take a set of pictures that can be merged to create one high dynamic range (HDR) image. While my goal in this book is to show you how to take great photos *in the camera* rather than how to fix your errors in Photoshop, the Merge to HDR (high dynamic range) feature in Adobe's flagship image editor is too cool to ignore. The ability to have a bracketed set of exposures that are identical except for exposure is key to getting good results with this Photoshop feature, which allows you to produce images with a full, rich dynamic range that includes a level of detail in the highlights and shadows that is almost impossible to achieve with digital cameras. In contrasty lighting situations, even the Nikon D3s/D3x has a tendency to blow out highlights when you expose solely for the shadows or midtones.

Suppose you wanted to photograph a dimly lit room that had a bright window showing an outdoors scene. Proper exposure for the room might be on the order of 1/60th second at f/2.8 at ISO 200, while the outdoors scene probably would require f/11 at 1/400th second. That's almost a 7 EV step difference (approximately 7 f/stops) and well beyond the dynamic range of any digital camera, including the Nikon D3s/D3x.

When you're using Merge to HDR, you'd take two to three pictures, one for the shadows, one for the highlights, and perhaps one for the midtones. Then, you'd use the Merge to HDR command to combine all of the images into one HDR image that integrates the well-exposed sections of each version. You can use the Nikon D3s/D3x's bracketing feature to produce those images.

The images should be as identical as possible, except for exposure. So, it's a good idea to mount the D3s/D3x on a tripod, use a remote release like the Nikon MC-30, and take all the exposures in one burst. Just follow these steps:

1. Mount the D3s/D3x on a tripod and connect the remote release cable.
2. Press the bracketing setting button (usually the BKT button) and rotate the sub-command dial to set the increment to 1EV. Merge to HDR works best with a significant difference in exposure between the bracketed shots; subtle changes are not better here.
3. Still holding down the bracketing setting button, rotate the main dial until the 3F 1.0 setting is made. This will take a total of three exposures, one at the metered exposure, one 1 stop under, and one 1 stop over.
4. Rotate the release mode dial to one of the continuous shooting modes. This will ensure that all three bracketed shots are taken consecutively once you've triggered the shutter with the remote release.
5. Set the D3s/D3x to A (aperture-priority). This forces the D3s/D3x to bracket the exposures by changing the shutter speed. You don't want the bracketed exposures to have different aperture settings, because the depth-of-field will change, perhaps enough to disturb a smooth merger of the final shots.

6. Hold down the Qual button and choose RAW exposures. You'll need RAW files to give you the 16-bit high dynamic range images that the Merge to HDR feature processes best.
7. Manually focus or autofocus the D3s/D3x.
8. Trigger the remote release to take all the exposures in the bracketed set. Repeat if you like.
9. Copy your images to your computer and continue with the Merge to HDR steps listed next.

The next steps show you how to combine the separate exposures into one merged high dynamic range image. The sample images shown in Figures 6.18, 6.19, and 6.21 show the results you can get from a two-shot bracketed sequence. I merged only two pictures for simplicity, because the differences between three or more bracketed exposures, even when taken at exposures that are 1 stop apart, can be too subtle to show up well on the printed page. My two examples were taken from a longer sequence, and actually have a two-stop difference.

1. If you use an application to transfer the files to your computer, make sure it does not make any adjustments to brightness, contrast, or exposure. You want the real raw information for Merge to HDR to work with. If you do everything correctly, you'll end up with at least two photos like the ones shown in Figures 6.18 and 6.19.
2. Load the images into Photoshop using your preferred RAW converter. Make sure the 16-bits-per-channel depth is retained (don't reduce them to 8-bit files). You can load them ahead of time and save as 16-bit Photoshop PSD files, as I did for my example photos.
3. Activate Merge to HDR by choosing File > Automate > Merge to HDR.
4. Select the photos to be merged, as shown in Figure 6.20, where I have specified the two 16-bit PSD files. You'll note a check box that can be used to automatically align the images if they were not taken with the D3s/D3x mounted on a rock-steady support.
5. Once HDR merge has done its thing, you must save in PSD, PFM, TIFF, or EXR formats to retain the 16-bit file's floating-point data, in case you want to work with the HDR image later. Otherwise, you can convert to a normal 24-bit file and save in any compatible format.

If you do everything correctly, you'll end up with a photo like the one shown in Figure 6.21, which has the properly exposed foreground of the first shot, and the well-exposed sky of the second image. Note that, ideally, nothing should move between shots. In the example pictures, the river is moving, but the exposures were made so close together that, after the merger, you can't really tell.

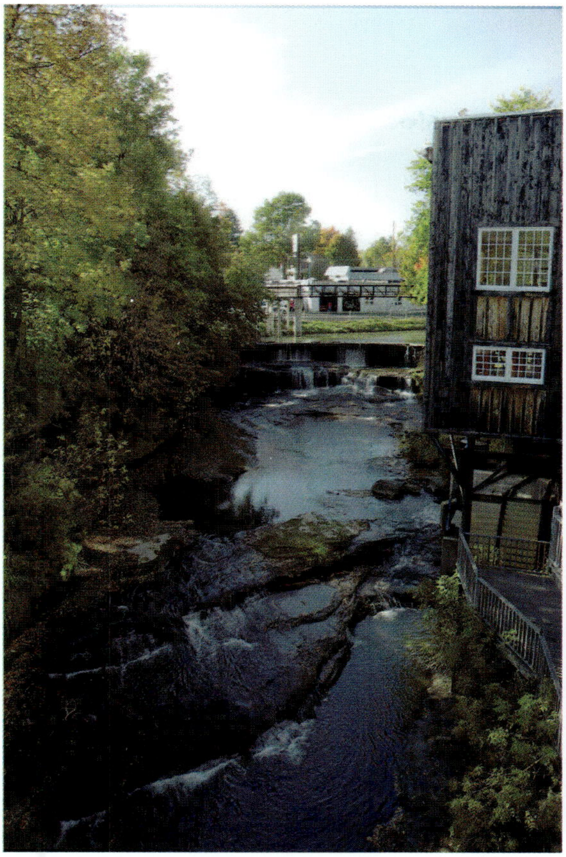

**Figure 6.18** Make one exposure for the shadow areas.

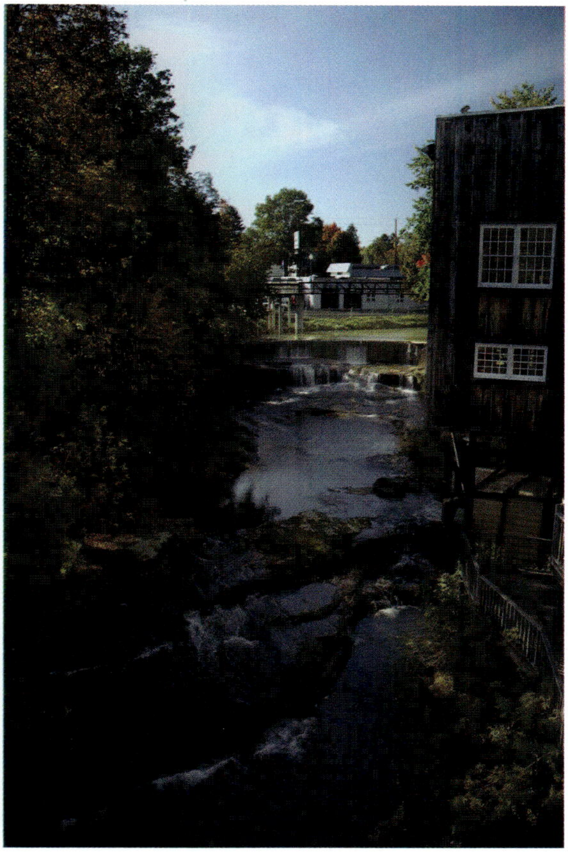

**Figure 6.19** Make a second exposure for the highlights, such as the sky.

**Figure 6.20** Use the Merge to HDR command in Photoshop to combine the two images.

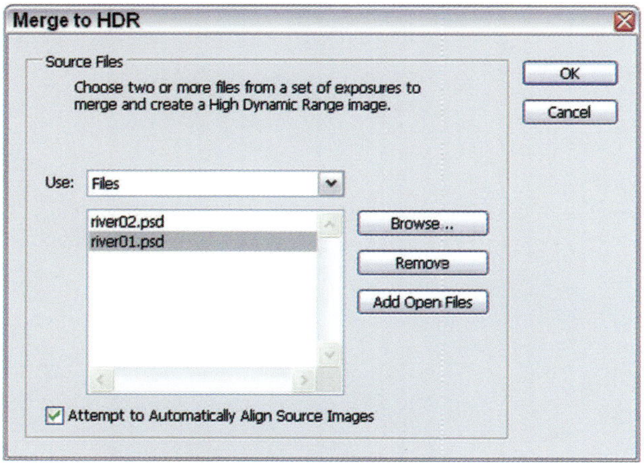

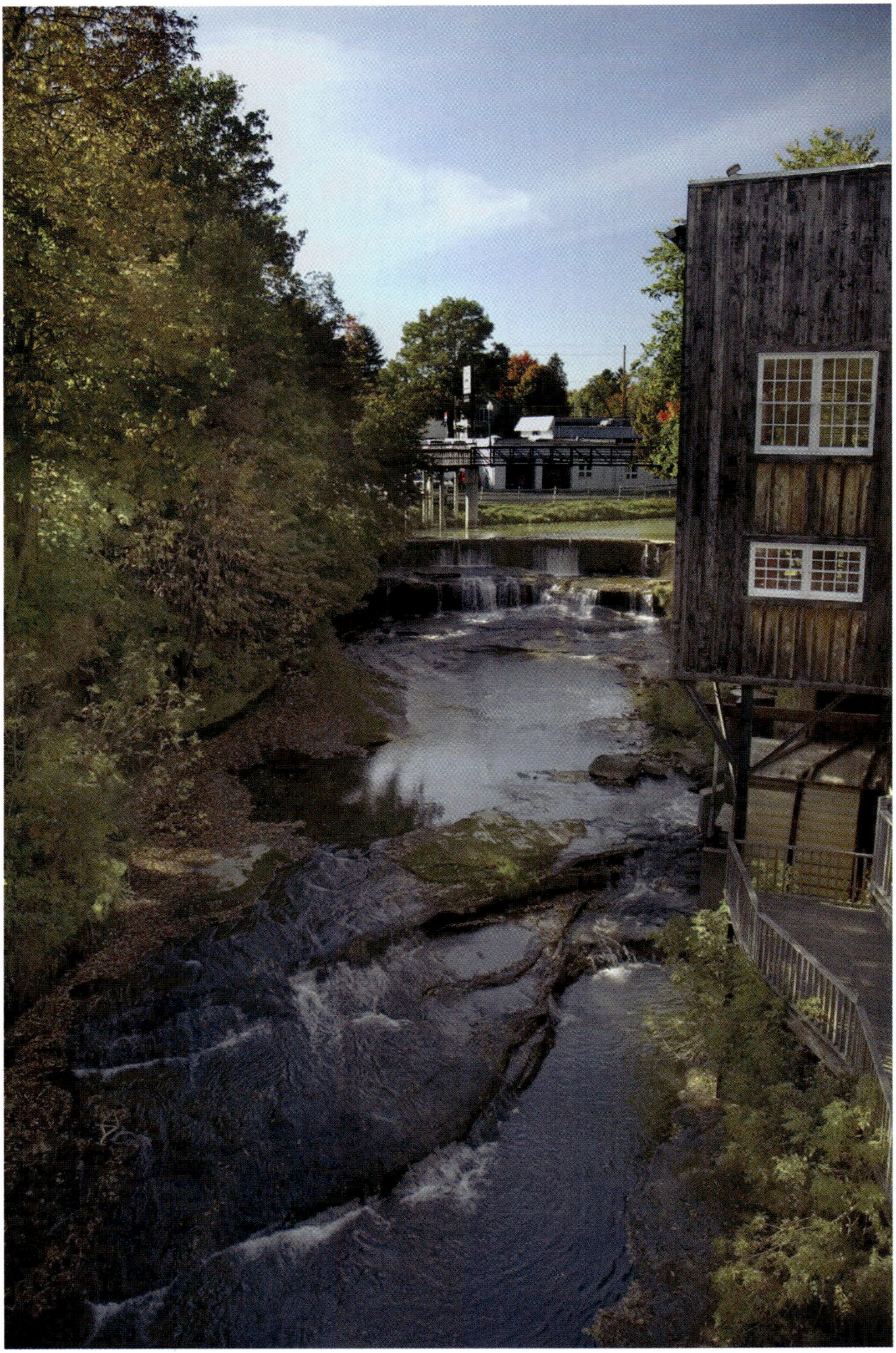

**Figure 6.21**
You'll end up with an extended dynamic range photo like this one.

What if you don't have the opportunity, inclination, or skills to create several images at different exposures, as described? If you shoot in RAW format, you can still use Merge to HDR, working with a *single* original image file. What you do is import the image into Photoshop several times, using Adobe Camera Raw to create multiple copies of the file at different exposure levels.

For example, you'd create one copy that's too dark, so the shadows lose detail, but the highlights are preserved. Create another copy with the shadows intact and allow the highlights to wash out. Then, you can use Merge to HDR to combine the two and end up with a finished image that has the extended dynamic range you're looking for. (This concludes the image-editing portion of the chapter. We now return you to our alternate sponsor: photography.)

# Fixing Exposures with Histograms

While you can often recover poorly exposed photos in your image editor, your best bet is to arrive at the correct exposure in the camera, minimizing the tweaks that you have to make in post-processing. However, you can't always judge exposure just by viewing the image on your D3s/D3x's LCD after the shot is made. Nor can you get a 100 percent accurately exposed picture by using the D3s/D3x's live view feature. Ambient light may make the LCD difficult to see, and the brightness level you've set can affect the appearance of the playback image.

Instead, you can use a histogram, which is a chart displayed on the D3s/D3x's LCD that shows the number of tones being captured at each brightness level. You can use the information to provide correction for the next shot you take. The D3s/D3x offers four histogram variations in three screens: three histograms that show overall brightness levels for an image and an alternate version that separates the red, green, and blue channels of your image into separate histograms.

## DISPLAYING HISTOGRAMS

To view all the available histograms on your screen, you must have the D3s/D3x set up properly. First, you'll need to mark histograms using the Display mode entry in the Playback menu, as described in Chapter 3. That will make the Histograms screen visible when you cycle among the informational screens while pressing the multi selector up/down buttons while an image is displayed.

If you also want to view a larger brightness/luminance histogram overlaid on your image at the press of the multi selector center button, you'll need to specify that behavior using Custom Setting f1, as described in Chapter 4.

The most basic histogram is displayed during playback when you press the multi selector up/down buttons to produce the Overview data screen, as described in Chapter 2, and shown in Figure 6.22. This screen provides a small histogram at the right side that displays the distribution of luminance or brightness. You can also view a larger luminance histogram, like the one shown in Figure 6.23, by pressing the multi selector center button when Custom Setting f1 is properly set up, as mentioned above. The final histogram screen is the one shown in Figure 6.24, which displays both a luminance chart and separate red, green, and blue charts.

Both luminance and RGB histograms are charts that include a representation of up to 256 vertical lines on a horizontal axis that show the number of pixels in the image at each brightness level, from 0 (black) on the left side to 255 (white) on the right. (The three-inch LCD doesn't have enough pixels to show each and every one of the 256 lines, but, instead provides a representation of the shape of the curve formed.) The more pixels at a given level, the taller the bar at that position. If no bar appears at a particular position on the scale from left to right, there are no pixels at that particular brightness level.

As you can see, a typical histogram produces a mountain-like shape, with most of the pixels bunched in the middle tones, with fewer pixels at the dark and light ends of the scale. Ideally, though, there will be at least some pixels at either extreme, so that your

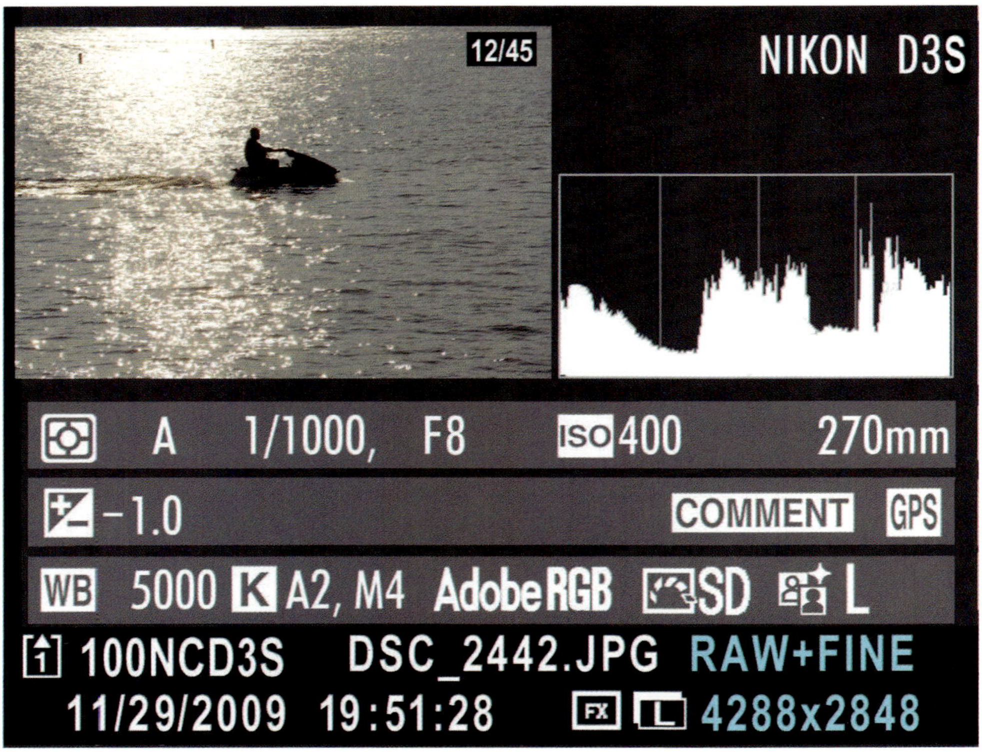


**Figure 6.22**
A histogram shows the relationship of tones in an image.

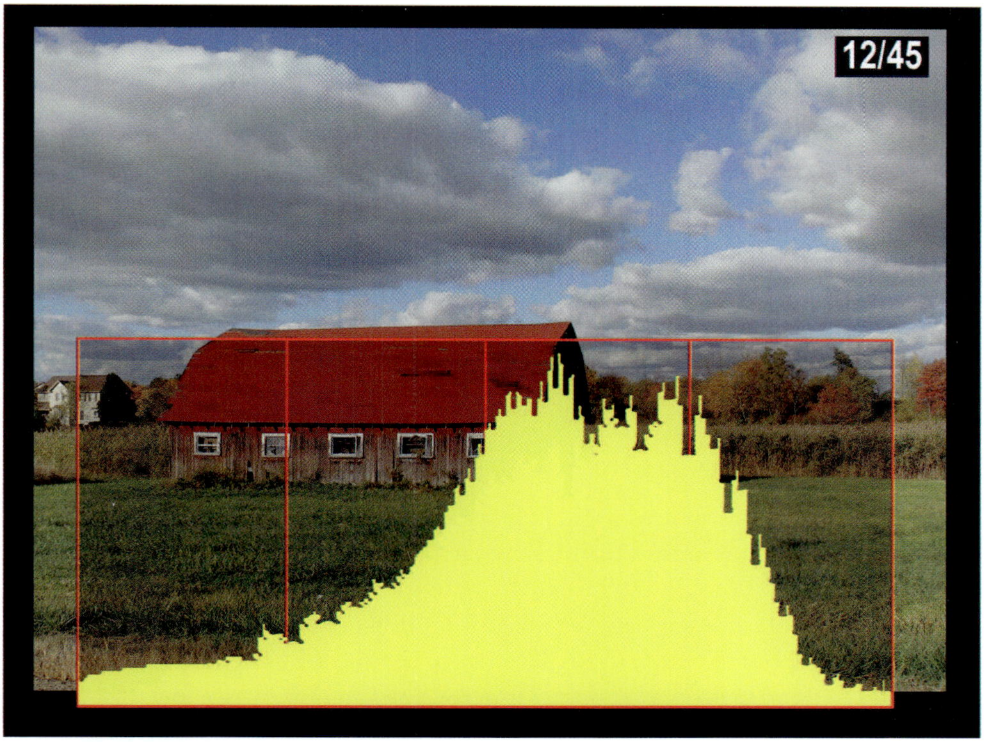


**Figure 6.23**
A large histogram can be overlaid on the image when you press the multi selector center button.

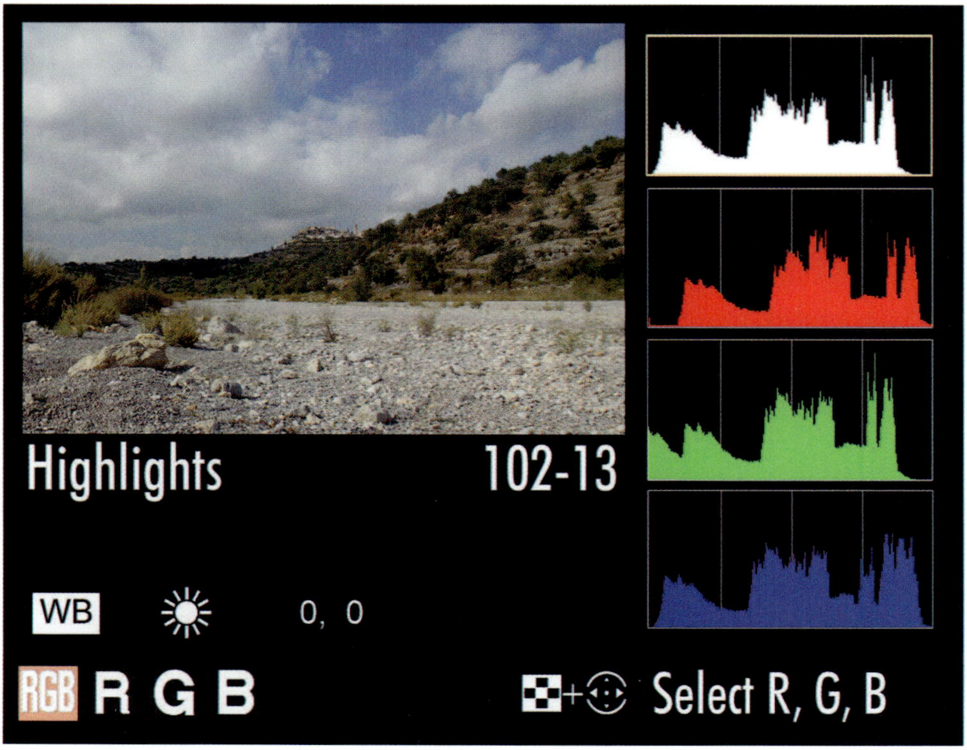


**Figure 6.24**
The D3s/D3x's most complete histogram screen shows both luminance and separate red, green, and blue histograms.

image has both a true black and a true white representing some details. Learn to spot histograms that represent over- and underexposure, and add or subtract exposure using an EV modification to compensate.

For example, Figure 6.25 shows the histogram for an image that is badly underexposed. You can guess from the shape of the histogram that many of the dark tones to the left of the graph have been clipped off. There's plenty of room on the right side for additional pixels to reside without having them become overexposed. Or, a histogram might look like Figure 6.26, which is overexposed. In either case, you can increase or decrease the exposure (either by changing the f/stop or shutter speed in manual mode or by adding or subtracting an EV value in A or S modes) to produce the corrected histogram shown in Figure 6.27, in which the tones "hug" the right side of the histogram to produce as many highlight details as possible. See "Making EV Changes," above for information on dialing in exposure compensation.

The histogram can also be used to aid in fixing the contrast of an image, although gauging incorrect contrast is more difficult. For example, if the histogram shows all the tones bunched up in one place in the image, the photo will be low in contrast. If the tones are spread out more or less evenly, the image is probably high in contrast. In either case, your best bet may be to switch to RAW (if you're not already using that format) so you can adjust contrast in post processing. However, you can also change to a user-defined Picture Control with contrast set lower (–1 to –3) or higher (+1 to +3) as required. You'll find instructions for creating Picture Controls in Chapter 3.

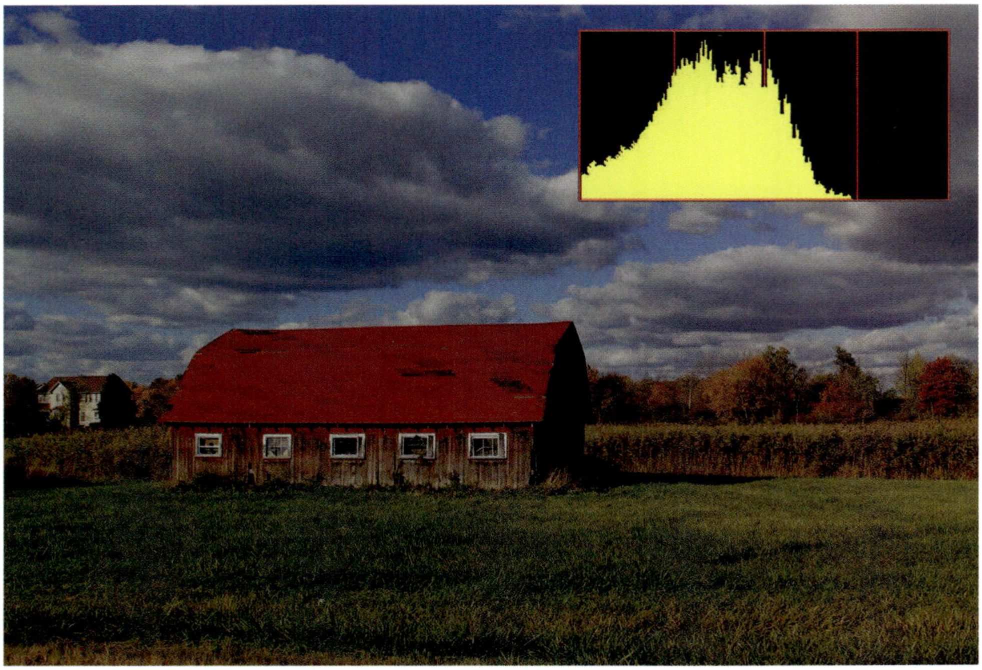

**Figure 6.25**
This histogram shows an underexposed image.

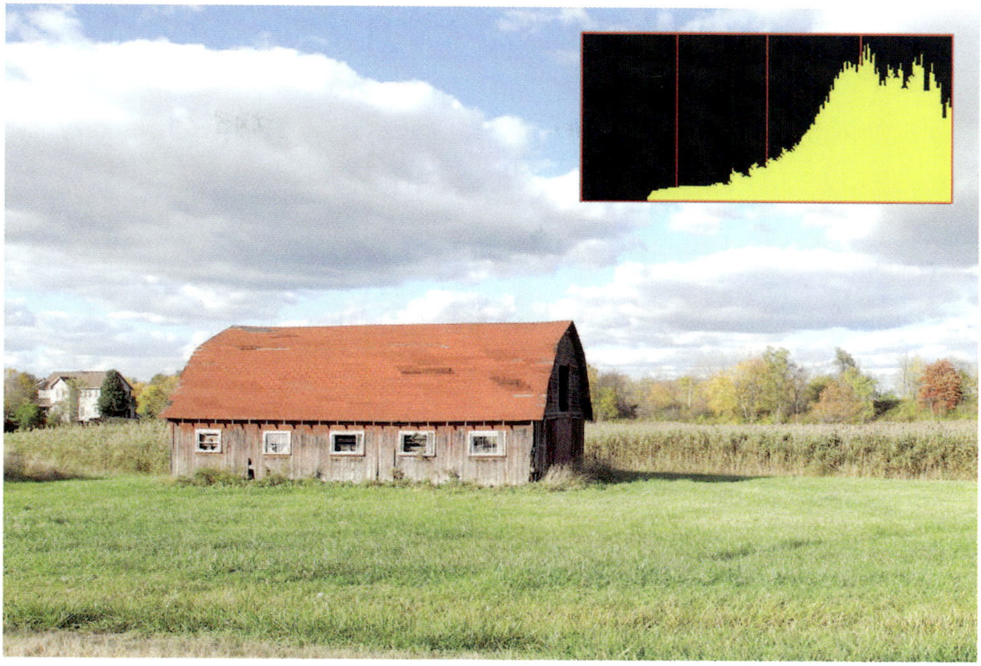

**Figure 6.26**
This histogram reveals that the image is overexposed.

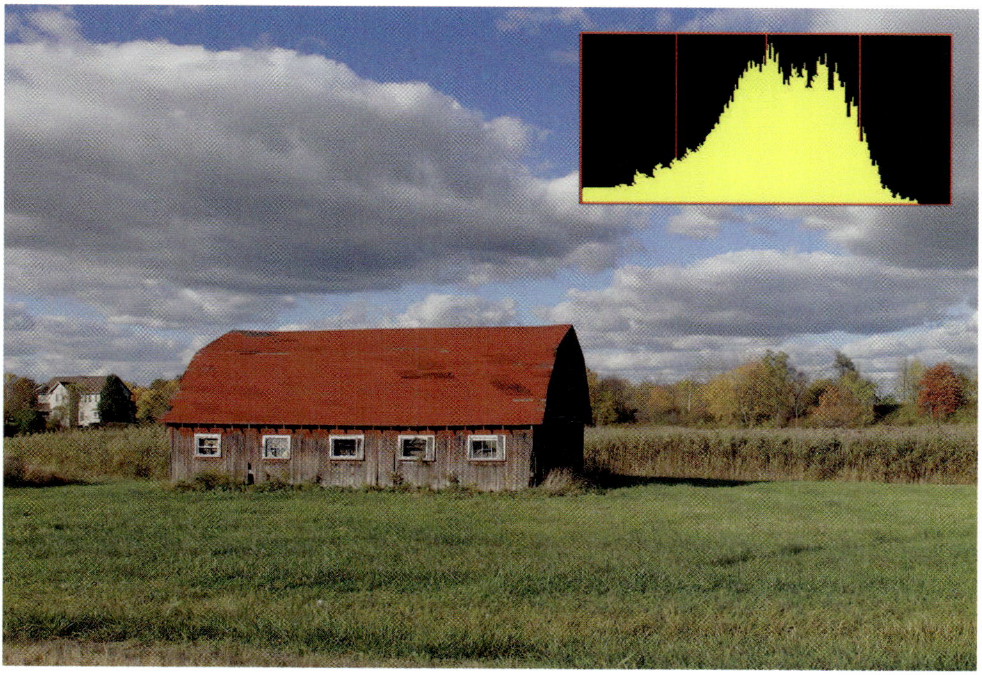

**Figure 6.27**
A histogram for a properly exposed image should look like this.

One useful, but often overlooked tool in evaluating histograms is the Highlights display, which shows blown out highlights in the thumbnail with a black blinking border. Highlights can give you a better picture of what information is being lost to overexposure. By default, the Highlights display shows "blinkies" for the luminance channel, but you can separately view highlights for the red, green, and blue channels. Just follow these steps:

1. With an image displayed, and the highlights/histogram screen shown, hold down the Thumbnail/Zoom button.
2. Press the multi selector left/right buttons to cycle among RGB (all channels), R, G, and B.
3. When a channel is framed in an orange outline, the Highlight information for that channel is shown in the thumbnail image in the upper-left corner. At the bottom left of the screen, RGB, R, G, or B will be highlighted to show the currently active channel.

In working with histograms, your goal should be to have all the tones in an image spread out between the edges, with none clipped off at the left and right sides. Underexposing (to preserve highlights) should be done only as a last resort, because retrieving the underexposed shadows in your image editor will frequently increase the noise, even if you're working with RAW files. A better course of action is to expose for the highlights, but, when the subject matter makes it practical, fill in the shadows with additional light, using reflectors, fill flash, or other techniques rather than allowing them to be seriously underexposed.

The more you work with histograms, the more useful they become. One of the first things that histogram veterans notice is that it's possible to overexpose one channel even if the overall exposure appears to be correct. For example, flower photographers soon discover that it's really, really difficult to get a good picture of a rose, like the one shown in Figure 6.28. The exposure looks okay—but there's no detail in the rose's petals. Looking at the histogram (see Figure 6.29) shows why: the red channel is blown out. If you look at the red histogram, there's a peak at the right edge that indicates that highlight information has been lost. In fact, the green channel has been blown, too, and so the green parts of the flower also lack detail. Only the blue channel's histogram is entirely contained within the boundaries of the chart, and, on first glance, the white luminance histogram at top of the column of graphs seems fairly normal.

Any of the primary channels, red, green, or blue, can blow out all by themselves, although bright reds seem to be the most common problem area. More difficult to diagnose are overexposed tones in one of the "in-between" hues on the color wheel. Overexposed yellows (which are very common) will be shown by blowouts in *both* the red and green channels. Too-bright cyans will manifest as excessive blue and green

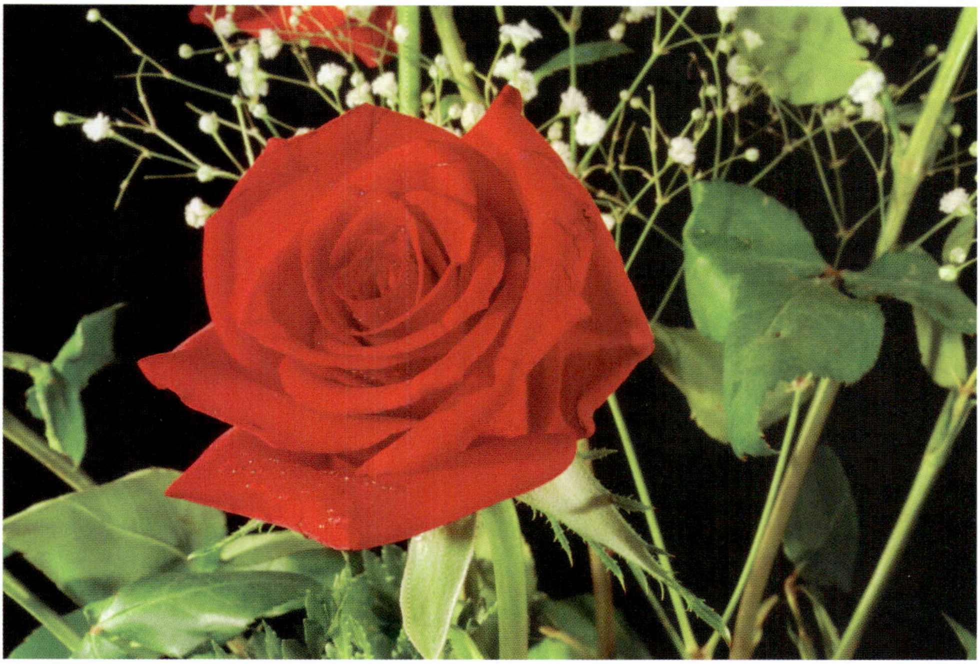

**Figure 6.28**
It's common to lose detail in bright red flowers because the red channel becomes overexposed even when the other channels are properly exposed.

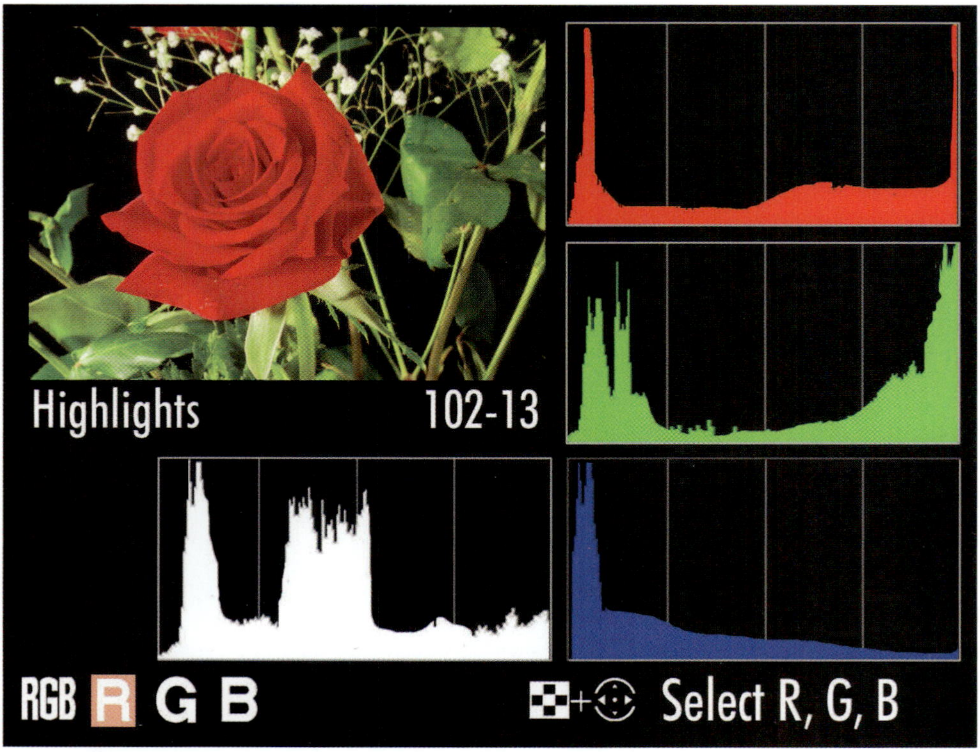


**Figure 6.29**
The RGB histograms show that both the red and green channels are overexposed.

highlights, while overexposure in the red and blue channels reduces detail in magenta colors. As you gain experience, you'll be able to see exactly how anomalies in the RGB channels translate into poor highlights and murky shadows.

The only way to correct for color channel blowouts is to reduce exposure. As I mentioned earlier, you might want to consider filling in the shadows with additional light to keep them from becoming too dark when you decrease exposure. In practice, you'll want to monitor the red channel most closely, followed by the blue channel, and slightly decrease exposure to see if that helps. Because of the way our eyes perceive color, we are more sensitive to variations in green, so green channel blowouts are less of a problem, unless your main subject is heavily colored in that hue. If you plan on photographing a frog hopping around on your front lawn, you'll want to be extra careful to preserve detail in the green channel, using bracketing or other exposure techniques outlined in this chapter.

# 7

# Mastering Autofocus Options

Fast autofocus is one of the reasons many shooters buy an upscale dSLR like the Nikon D3s/D3x. If you're shooting sports, the ability to lock in focus on a moving subject can mean the difference between missing a shot or grabbing a great action image. Candid photography, photojournalism, shots of active children or pets, and many other subjects can be captured more easily with modern digital SLR cameras that have the ability to lock in sharp focus faster than the blink of an eye.

Well, theoretically. Although autofocus has been with us for more than 20 years, it continues to be problematic. While vendors like Nikon are giving us faster and more precise autofocus systems, particularly in advanced cameras like the D3s/D3x, and offer many more focusing options, it's common for the sheer number of choices to confuse even the most advanced photographers.

One key problem is that the camera doesn't really know, for certain, what subject you want to be in sharp focus. It may select an object and lock in focus with lightning speed—even though the subject is not the one that's the center of interest of your photograph. Or, the camera may lock focus too soon, or too late. This chapter will help you choose the options available with your Nikon D3s/D3x that will help the camera understand what you want to focus, when, and maybe even why.

## How Focus Works

Although Nikon added autofocus capabilities in the 1980s, back in the day of film cameras, prior to that focusing was always done manually. Honest. Even though optical viewfinders were bigger and brighter than they are today, special focusing screens, magnifiers, and other gadgets were often used to help the photographer achieve correct focus. Imagine what it must have been like to focus manually under demanding, fast-moving conditions such as sports photography.

Focusing was problematic because our eyes and brains have poor memory for correct focus, which is why your eye doctor must shift back and forth between sets of lenses and ask "Does that look sharper—or was it sharper before?" in determining your correct prescription. Similarly, manual focusing involves jogging the focus ring back and forth as you go from almost in focus, to sharp focus, to almost focused again. The little clockwise and counterclockwise arcs decrease in size until you've zeroed in on the point of correct focus. What you're looking for is the image with the most contrast between the edges of elements in the image.

The camera also looks for these contrast differences among pixels to determine relative sharpness. There are two ways that sharp focus is determined: phase detection and contrast detection.

## Phase Detection

In this mode, the autofocus sampling area is divided into two halves by a lens in the sensor. The two halves are compared, much like (actually, *exactly* like) a two-window rangefinder used in surveying, weaponry—and non-SLR cameras like the venerable Leica M film models. The contrast between the two images changes as focus is moved in or out, until sharp focus is achieved when the images are "in phase," or lined up.

The 51 autofocus sensors of Nikon's Multi-CAM 3500FX autofocus module are located in the "floor" of the mirror box, just under the flip-up mirror, which is partially silvered so that most of the light reaching it from the lens is bounced upwards to the viewfinder, while some light is directed downward towards the focus sensors. If you lock up the mirror of your camera (using the Lock mirror up for cleaning option in the Setup menu), you can see where these sensors are located. The focus zones cover an area on the center of the viewing frame, as shown in Figure 7.1.

You can visualize how phase detection autofocus works if you look at Figures 7.2 and 7.3. (However, your camera's actual autofocus sensor layout doesn't look *anything* like this; I'm providing a greatly simplified view just for illustration.) In Figure 7.2, a typical horizontally oriented focus sensor is looking at a series of parallel vertical lines in a weathered piece of wood. The lines are broken into two halves by the sensor's rangefinder prism, and you can see that they don't line up exactly; the image is slightly out of focus.

Fortunately, the rangefinder approach of phase detection tells the D3s/D3x exactly how out of focus the image is, and in which direction (focus is too near, or too far) thanks to the amount and direction of the displacement of the split image. The camera can quickly and precisely snap the image into sharp focus and line up the vertical lines, as shown in Figure 7.3. Of course, this scenario—vertical lines being interpreted by a horizontally

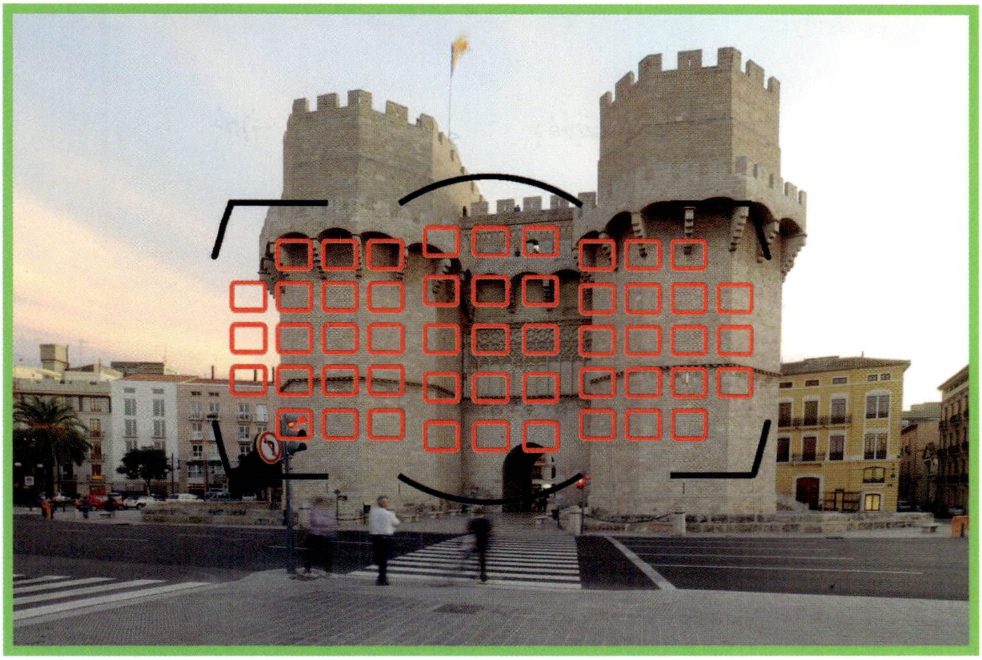

**Figure 7.1** The D3s/D3x's focus sensors cover an area in the center of the frame.

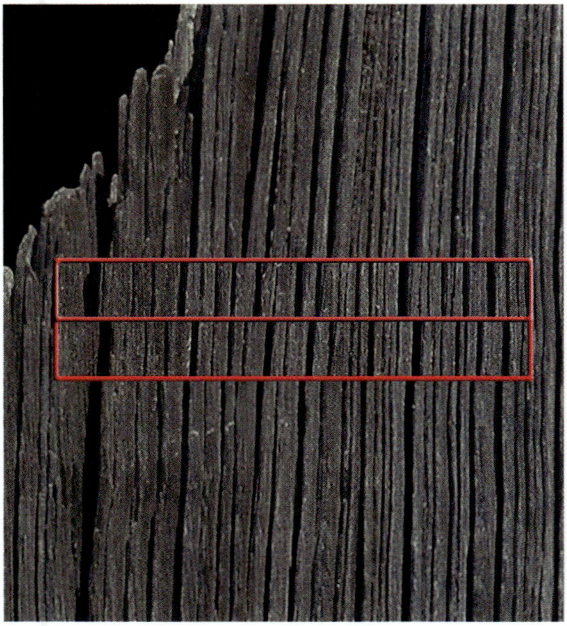

**Figure 7.2** When an image is out of focus, the split lines don't align precisely.

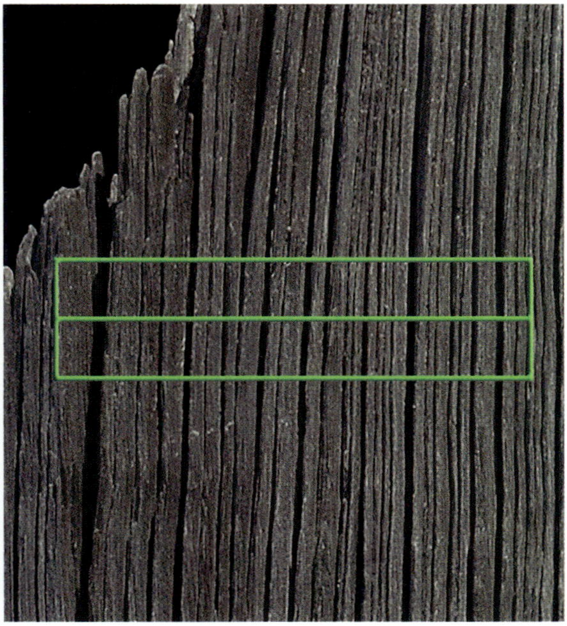

**Figure 7.3** Using phase detection, the D3s/D3x is able to align the features of the image and achieve sharp focus quickly.

oriented sensor—is ideal. When the same sensor is asked to measure focus for, say, horizontal lines that don't split up quite so conveniently, or, in the worst case, subjects such as the sky (which may have neither vertical nor horizontal lines), focus can slow down drastically, or even become impossible.

Phase detection is the normal mode used by the D3s/D3x (and is applied when using live view in hand-held mode). As with any rangefinder-like function, accuracy is better when the "base length" between the two images is larger. (Think back to your high school trigonometry; you could calculate a distance more accurately when the separation between the two points where the angles were measured was greater.) For that reason, phase detection autofocus is more accurate with larger (wider) lens openings—especially those with maximum f/stops of f/2.8 or better—than with smaller lens openings, and may not work at all when the f/stop is smaller than f/5.6. As I noted, the D3s/D3x is able to perform these comparisons very quickly.

## Improved Cross-Type Focus Point

One improvement that Nikon D3s/D3x owners sometimes overlook is the upgrade to a cross-type focus point at 15 of the 51 center positions. Why is this important? It helps to take a closer look at the phase detection system when presented with a non-ideal subject.

Figure 7.4 shows the same weathered wood pictured earlier, except in this case we've chosen to rotate the camera 90 degrees (say, because we want a vertically oriented composition). In the illustration, the image within the focus sensor's area is split in two and displaced slightly side-to-side, but the amount and direction of the misalignment is far from obvious. A horizontally oriented focus sensor will be forced to look for less obvious vertical lines to match up. Our best-case subject has been transformed into a *worst*-case subject for a horizontal focus sensor.

The value of the cross-type focus sensor, which can interpret contrast in both horizontal and vertical directions, can be seen in Figure 7.5. The horizontal lines are still giving the horizontal portion of the cross sensor fits, but the vertical bar can easily split and align the subject to achieve optimum focus. Cross-type sensors can handle horizontal and vertical lines with equal aplomb and, if you think about it, lines at any diagonal angle as well. In lower light levels, with subjects that were moving, or with subjects that have no pattern and less contrast to begin with, the cross-type sensor not only works faster but can focus subjects that a horizontal- or vertical-only sensor can't handle at all.

So, you can see that having a center cross-type focus sensor that is extra-sensitive with faster lenses is a definite advantage, and the total of 15 of these versatile focus sensors in the D3-series cameras is even better. The location of the D3s/D3x's cross-type focus sensors is shown in Figure 7.6.

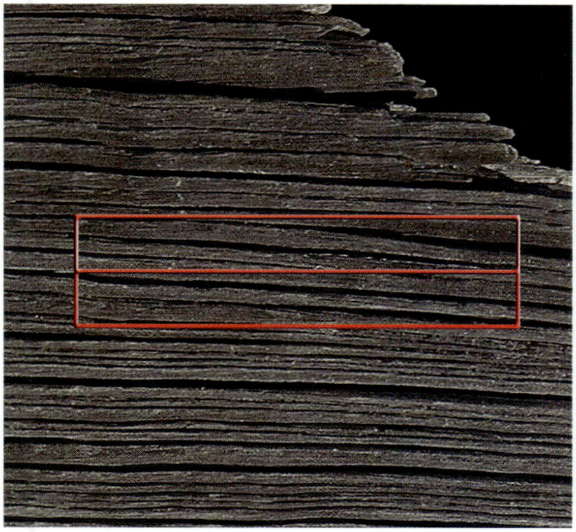

**Figure 7.4** A horizontal focus sensor doesn't handle horizontal lines very well.

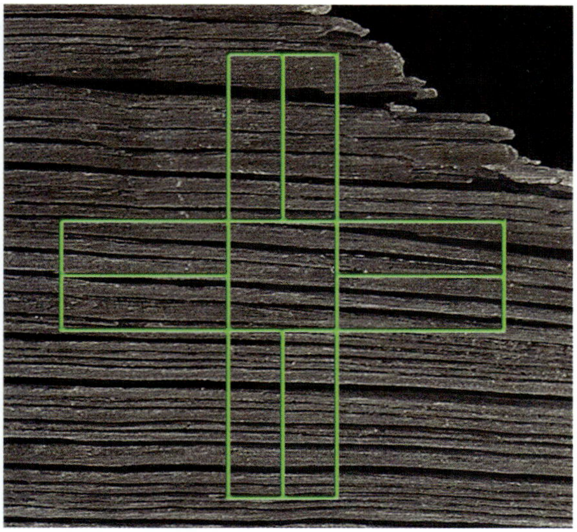

**Figure 7.5** Cross-type sensors can evaluate contrast in both horizontal and vertical directions, as well as diagonally.

**Figure 7.6** The D3s/D3x's cross-type sensors are located in the middle of the frame.

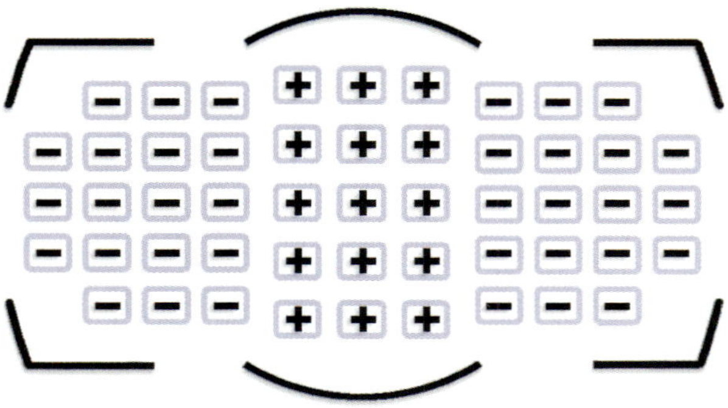

## Contrast Detection

This is a slower mode, suitable for static subjects, and used by the D3s/D3x with live view tripod mode. It's a bit easier to understand, and is illustrated by Figure 7.7. At top in the figure, the transitions between the edges found in the image are soft and blurred because of the low contrast between them. Although the illustration uses the same vertical lines used with the phase detection example, the orientation of the features doesn't matter. The focus system looks only for contrast between edges, and those edges can run in any direction.

At the bottom of Figure 7.7, the image has been brought into sharp focus, and the edges have much more contrast; the transitions are sharp and clear. Although this example is a bit exaggerated so you can see the results on the printed page, it's easy to understand

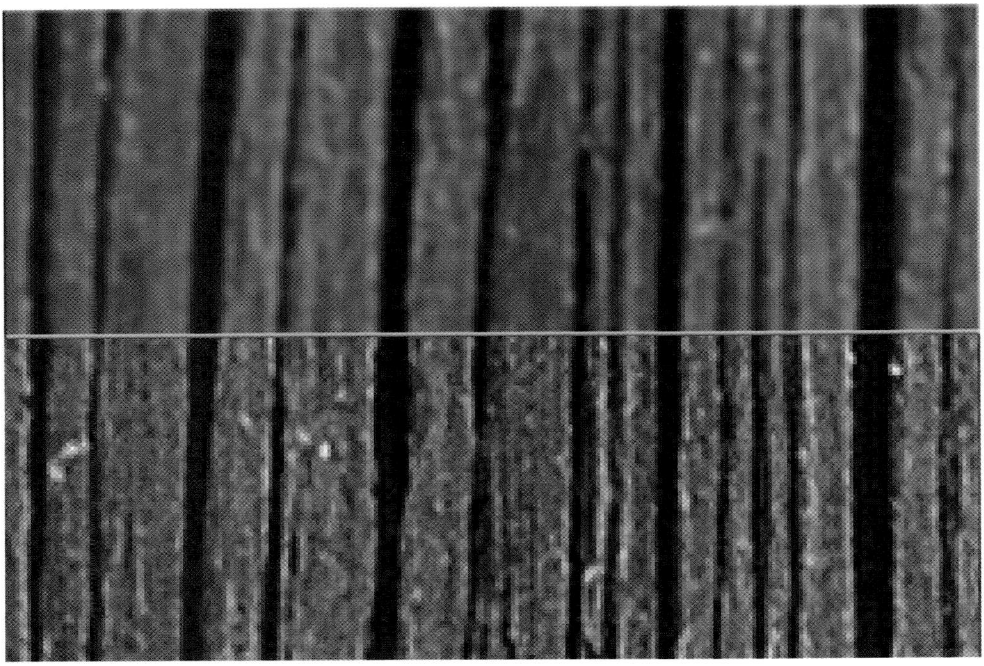

**Figure 7.7**
Focus in contrast detection mode evaluates the increase in contrast in the edges of subjects, starting with a blurry image (top) and producing a sharp, contrasty image (bottom).

that when maximum contrast in a subject is achieved, it can be deemed to be in sharp focus. Although achieving focus with contrast detection is generally quite a bit slower, there are several advantages to this method:

- **Works with more image types.** Contrast detection doesn't require subject matter rotated 90 degrees from the sensor's orientation to operate optimally. Any subject that has edges will work.
- **Focus on any point.** While phase detection focus can be achieved *only* at the points that fall under one of the nine autofocus sensors, with contrast detection, any portion of the image can be used. Focus is achieved with the actual sensor image, so focus point selection is simply a matter of choosing which part of the sensor image to use.
- **Potentially more accurate.** Phase detection can fall prey to the vagaries of uncooperative subject matter: if suitable lines aren't available, the system may have to hunt for focus or achieve less than optimal focus. Contrast detection is more clear-cut. The camera can clearly see when the highest contrast has been achieved.

The D3s/D3x's autofocus mechanism, like all such systems found in SLR cameras, evaluates the degree of focus, but, unlike the human eye, it is able to remember the progression perfectly, so that autofocus can lock in much more quickly and, with an image that has sufficient contrast, more precisely. Unfortunately, while the D3s/D3x's focus system finds it easy to measure degrees of apparent focus at each of the focus points in the viewfinder, it doesn't really know with any certainty *which* object should be in

## TAKING A DIM VIEW

One of the most common misconceptions about dSLR autofocus is that the systems "break" when the maximum aperture of a lens is smaller than f/5.6 because the illumination is too dim to tell whether a subject is in or out of focus. An alternate misunderstanding is that the increased depth-of-field at the smaller f/stop makes it more difficult to differentiate the actual plane of sharp focus. If you press the D3s/D3x's Depth-of-field preview (PV) button (the upper button mounted on the right side of the camera next to the lens), which stops down the lens to (picture) "taking" aperture, you'll see that the viewfinder image *does* become dimmer and the depth-of-field increases, which will, in fact, make the image more difficult to focus if we do so visually using manual focus.

But that's because the human eye focuses using contrast detection. The phase detection process that the D3s/D3x and other dSLRs use doesn't need to detect edge contrasts. The rangefinder system depends on that baseline separation of the two halves of the image. When a lens has a maximum f/stop smaller than f/5.6 (such as the f/6.3 aperture found in many zoom lenses), the smaller diameter of the lens opening produces a shorter baseline, and *that's* what causes the phase detection system to fail.

sharpest focus. Is it the closest object? The subject in the center? Something lurking *behind* the closest subject? A person standing over at the side of the picture? Many of the techniques for using autofocus effectively involve telling the Nikon D3s/D3x exactly what it should be focusing on, by choosing a focus zone or by allowing the camera to choose a focus zone for you. I'll address that topic shortly.

As the camera collects focus information from the sensors, it then evaluates it to determine whether the desired sharp focus has been achieved. The calculations may include whether the subject is moving, and whether the camera needs to "predict" where the subject will be when the shutter release button is fully depressed and the picture is taken. The speed with which the camera is able to evaluate focus and then move the lens elements into the proper position to achieve the sharpest focus determines how fast the autofocus mechanism is. Although your D3s/D3x will almost always focus more quickly than a human, there are types of shooting situations where that's not fast enough. For example, if you're having problems shooting sports because the D3s/D3x's autofocus system manically follows each moving subject, a better choice might be to switch autofocus modes or shift into manual and pre-focus on a spot where you anticipate the action will be, such as a goal line or soccer net.

## Adding Circles of Confusion

But there are other factors in play, as well. You know that increased depth-of-field brings more of your subject into focus. But more depth-of-field also makes autofocusing (or manual focusing) more difficult because the contrast is lower between objects at different distances. So, autofocus with a 200mm lens (or zoom setting) may be easier than at a 28mm focal length (or zoom setting) because the longer lens has less apparent depth-of-field. By the same token, a lens with a maximum aperture of f/1.8 will be easier to autofocus (or manually focus) than one of the same focal length with an f/4 maximum aperture, because the f/4 lens has more depth-of-field *and* a dimmer view. That's why lenses with a maximum aperture smaller than f/5.6 can give your D3s/D3x's autofocus system fits.

To make things even more complicated, many subjects aren't polite enough to remain still. They move around in the frame, so that even if the D3s/D3x is sharply focused on your main subject, it may change position and require refocusing. An intervening subject may pop into the frame and pass between you and the subject you meant to photograph. You (or the D3s/D3x) have to decide whether to lock focus on this new subject, or remain focused on the original subject. Finally, there are some kinds of subjects that are difficult to bring into sharp focus because they lack enough contrast to allow the D3s/D3x's AF system (or our eyes) to lock in. Blank walls, a clear blue sky, or other subject matter may make focusing difficult.

If you find all these focus factors confusing, you're on the right track. Focus is, in fact, measured using something called a *circle of confusion*. An ideal image consists of zillions of tiny little points, which, like all points, theoretically have no height or width. There is perfect contrast between the point and its surroundings. You can think of each point as a pinpoint of light in a darkened room. When a given point is out of focus, its edges decrease in contrast and it changes from a perfect point to a tiny disc with blurry edges (remember, blur is the lack of contrast between boundaries in an image). (See Figure 7.8.)

If this blurry disc—the circle of confusion—is small enough, our eye still perceives it as a point. It's only when the disc grows large enough that we can see it as a blur rather than a sharp point that a given point is viewed as out of focus. You can see, then, that enlarging an image, either by displaying it larger on your computer monitor or by making a large print, also enlarges the size of each circle of confusion. Moving closer to the

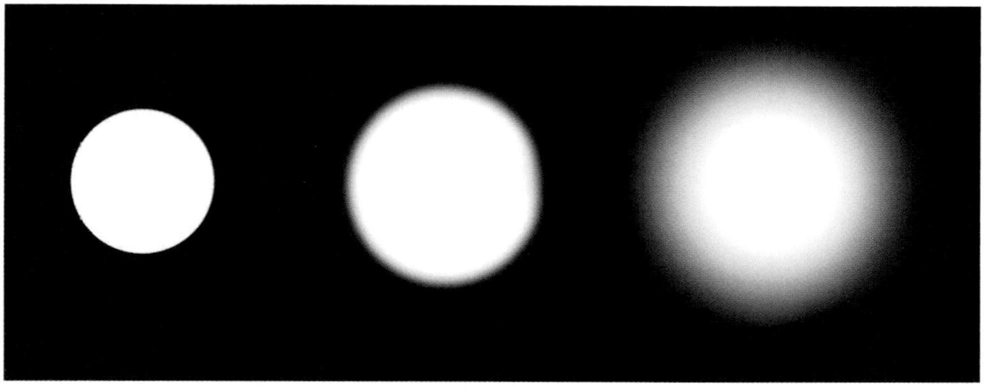

**Figure 7.8**
When a pinpoint of light (left) goes out of focus, its blurry edges form a circle of confusion (center and right).

image does the same thing. So, parts of an image that may look perfectly sharp in a 5 × 7-inch print viewed at arm's length, might appear blurry when blown up to 11 × 14 and examined at the same distance. Take a few steps back, however, and it may look sharp again.

To a lesser extent, the viewer also affects the apparent size of these circles of confusion. Some people see details better at a given distance and may perceive smaller circles of confusion than someone standing next to them. For the most part, however, such differences are small. Truly blurry images will look blurry to just about everyone under the same conditions.

Technically, there is just one plane within your picture area, parallel to the back of the camera (or sensor, in the case of a digital camera), that is in sharp focus. That's the plane in which the points of the image are rendered as precise points. At every other plane in front of or behind the focus plane, the points show up as discs that range from slightly blurry to extremely blurry (see Figure 7.9). In practice, the discs in many of these planes

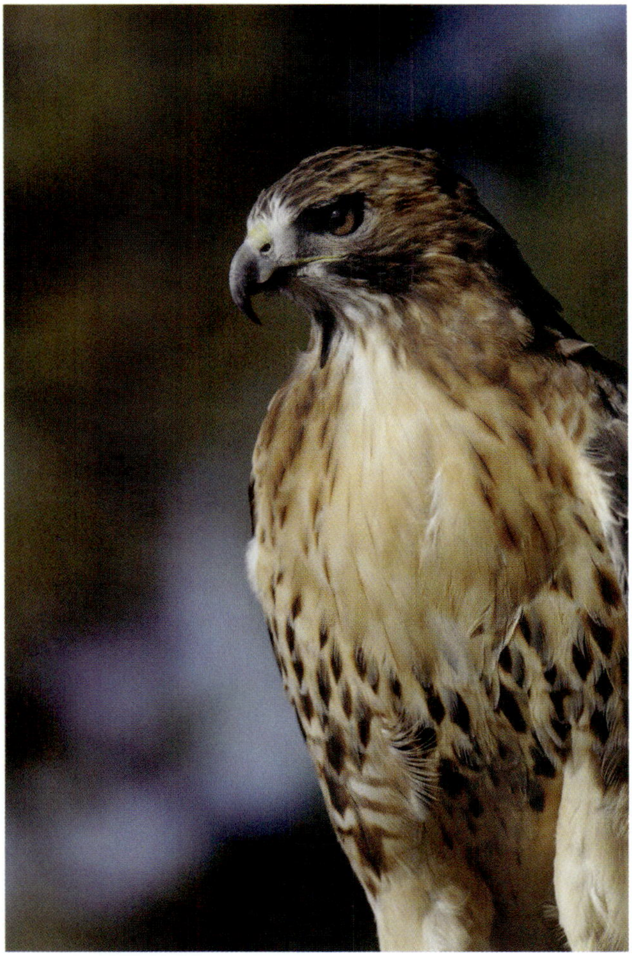

**Figure 7.9**
The bird is in focus—the area behind him appears blurry because the depth-of-field is limited.

will still be so small that we see them as points, and that's where we get depth-of-field. Depth-of-field is just the range of planes that include discs that we perceive as points rather than blurred splotches. The size of this range increases as the aperture is reduced in size and is allocated roughly one-third in front of the plane of sharpest focus, and two-thirds behind it. The range of sharp focus is always greater behind your subject than in front of it.

## Using Autofocus with the Nikon D3s/D3x

Autofocus can sometimes be frustrating for the new digital SLR photographer, especially those coming from the point-and-shoot world. That's because correct focus plays a greater role among your creative options with a dSLR, even when photographing the same subjects. Most non-dSLR digital cameras have sensors that are much tinier than the sensor in the D3s/D3x. Those smaller sensors require shorter focal length lenses, which have, effectively, more depth-of-field.

The bottom line is that with the average point-and-shoot camera, *everything* is in focus from about one foot to infinity and at virtually every f/stop. Unless you're shooting close-up photos a few inches from the camera, the depth-of-field is prodigious, and autofocus is almost a non-factor. The D3s/D3x, on the other hand, uses longer focal length lenses to achieve the same field of view with its larger sensor, so there is less depth-of-field. That's a *good* thing, creatively, because you have the choice to use selective focus to isolate subjects. But it does make the correct use of autofocus more critical. To maintain the most creative control, you have to choose three attributes:

- **How much is in focus.** Generally, by choosing the f/stop used, you'll determine the *range* of sharpness/amount of depth-of-field. The larger the DOF, the "easier" it is for the autofocus system's locked-in focus point to be appropriate (even though, strictly speaking, there is only one actual plane of sharp focus). With less depth-of-field, the accuracy of the focus point becomes more critical, because even a small error will result in an out-of-focus shot.
- **What subject is in focus.** The portion of your subject that is zeroed in for autofocus is determined by the autofocus zone that is active, and which is chosen either by you or by the Nikon D3s/D3x (as described next). For example, when shooting portraits, it's actually okay for part of the subject—or even part of the subject's face—to be slightly out of focus as long as the eyes (or even just the *nearest* eye) appear sharp.
- **When focus is applied.** For static shots of objects that aren't moving, *when* focus is applied doesn't matter much. But when you're shooting sports, or birds in flight, or children, the subject may move within the viewfinder as you're framing the image. Whether that movement is across the frame or headed right towards you, timing the instant when autofocus is applied can be critical.

## Autofocus Simplifies Our Lives... Doesn't It?

Manual focus is tricky, requires judgment, and fast reflexes. So, we're all better off now that autofocus has become almost universal, right? On the one hand, AF does save time and allows us to capture subjects (particularly fast-moving sports) that are difficult to image sharply using manual focusing (unless you have training and know certain techniques). On the other hand, learning to apply the Nikon D3s/D3x's autofocus system most effectively requires a bit of study and some practice. Then, once you're comfortable with autofocus, you'll know when it's appropriate to use the manual focus option, too.

The important thing to remember is that focus isn't absolute. For example, some things that look in sharp focus at a given viewing size and distance might not be in focus at a larger size and/or closer distance. In addition, the goal of optimum focus isn't always to make things look sharp. Not all of an image will be or should be sharp. Controlling exactly what is sharp and what is not is part of your creative palette. Use of depth-of-field characteristics to throw part of an image out of focus while other parts are sharply focused is one of the most valuable tools available to a photographer. But selective focus works only when the desired areas of an image are in focus properly. For the digital SLR photographer, correct focus can be one of the trickiest parts of the technical and creative process.

As you'll learn in the following sections, the autofocus system used in the Nikon D3s/D3x is considerably different from what you might have been accustomed to if you have migrated from an entry- or mid-level Nikon. Some earlier cameras used a system that let you choose various "patterns" for autofocus when using the multi-zone shifting AF mode ("Group Dynamic"). You could also select attributes like "Closest Subject" to help the camera decide what to focus on. With all the options available, autofocus was still not perfect. If anything, the camera (and photographer) had *too many* choices, which, if not selected appropriately, could lead to poor focus.

The D3s/D3x now uses Nikon's Multi-CAM 3500FX autofocus system that's very similar to the Multi-CAM 3500DX AF system used in the top-of-the-line DX camera, the Nikon D300s—with one key difference: how the "zones" used to evaluate focus are allocated. The D300s's DX AF sensor, although it's physically the same size as the D3s/D3x's FX AF sensor, covers a larger percentage of the cropped frame, as you can see at lower right in Figure 7.10. That's actually an advantage for D300s owners; there is less chance that an important subject will fall outside the larger focus area.

With the D3s/D3x, the same-size array of autofocus sensors are concentrated in the center of the 24 × 36mm frame, leaving the large areas you can see at upper left in the figure outside the autofocus coverage area. However, both systems deploy an intelligent array of 15 cross-type sensors and 36 horizontal sensors in the viewing system. All 51 autofocus sensors can be used individually or in groups of 9, 21, or all 51 focus zones.

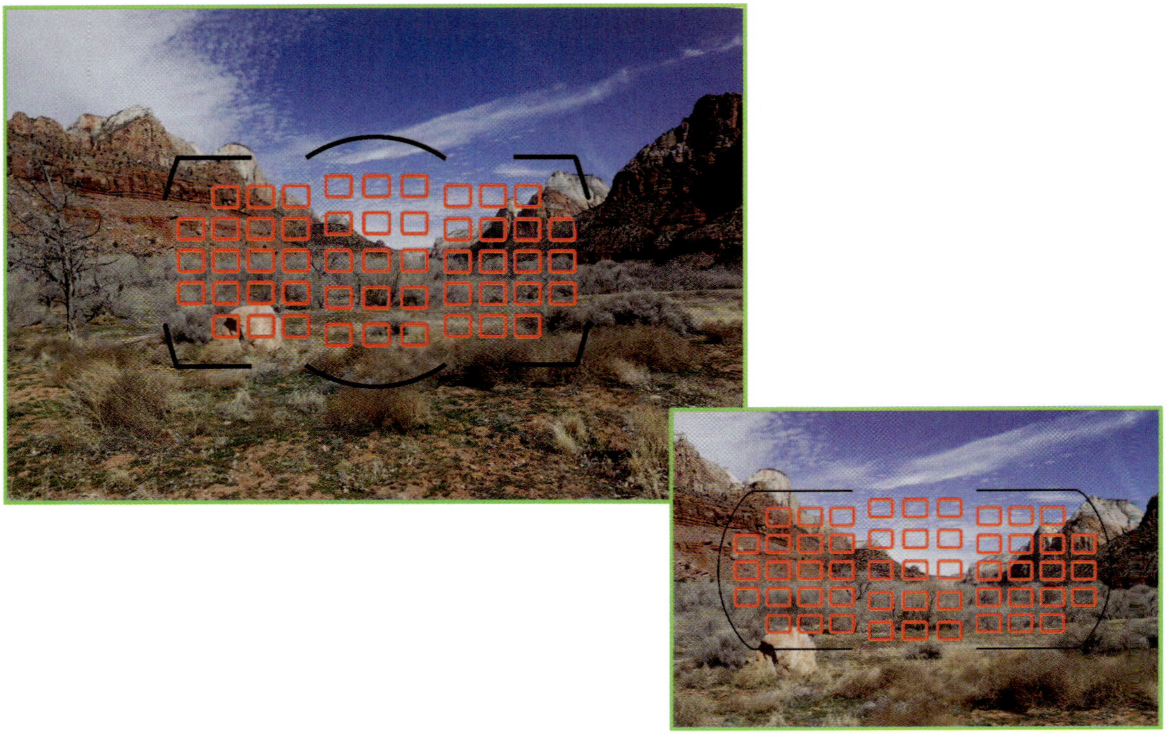

**Figure 7.10** The full-frame Nikon D3s/D3x's autofocus sensors (upper left) are spread out over a smaller percentage of the entire image compared to the Nikon D300s's layout (lower right).

The AF system uses the color and light values found in the focus zone array to accurately track moving objects, and to classify subjects into what Nikon calls a "scene recognition system." The autofocus system uses a separate sensor in the viewing system to measure the contrast of the image. That's Nikon's autofocus system in a nutshell.

As I noted in the sidebar, like all camera autofocus sensors, those in your D3s/D3x require a minimum amount of light as well as a minimum aperture size to operate, which, as I noted, is why autofocus capabilities are possible only with lenses having an f/5.6 or larger maximum aperture. While there's not a lot you can do to "fix" a lens that has a maximum aperture that's too small, if your subject's contrast is difficult to detect because of waning light levels, the AF assist beam built into the D3s/D3x and Nikon's dedicated flash units provide additional light that helps assure enough illumination for autofocus.

## ADJUSTING YOUR LENSES' AUTOFOCUS

If the focus of your lenses are consistently off by a wee smidge, you can adjust the point of focus for a lens using the AF Fine tune facility, found in the Setup menu. I'm providing complete instructions on how to do that, including a focus chart, in Chapter 9.

# Bringing the Multi-CAM 3500FX AF System into Focus

I've explained individual bits and pieces of the Nikon D3s/D3x's autofocus system earlier in this book, particularly in the "roadmap" sections that showed you where all the controls were located, and the "setup" chapters that explained the key autofocus options. Now it's time to round out the coverage as we tie everything together. There are three aspects of autofocus that you need to understand to use this essential feature productively:

- **Autofocus point selection.** This aspect controls how the D3s/D3x selects which areas of the frame are used to evaluate focus. Point selection allows the camera (or you) to specify a subject and lock focus in on that subject.
- **Autofocus mode and priority.** This governs *when* during the framing and shooting process autofocus is achieved. Should the camera focus once when activated, or continue to monitor your subject and refocus should the subject move? Is it okay to take a picture even if sharp focus isn't yet achieved, or should the camera lock out the shutter release until the image is sharp?
- **Autofocus activation.** When should the autofocus process begin, and when should it be locked? This aspect is related to the autofocus mode, but uses controls that you can specify to activate and/or lock the autofocus process.

## Autofocus Point Selection Overview

I'm discussing this aspect of autofocus first, because, in many ways, it is the most important. If your D3s/D3x isn't focusing on the correct subject, autofocus speed and activation are pretty much wasted effort. As you've learned, the D3s/D3x has up to 51 different points on the screen that can be individually selected by you or the camera as the active focus zone.

The number and type of autofocus sensors in use can affect how well the system operates. The focus sensors can consist of vertical or horizontal lines of pixels, cross-shapes, and/or a mixture of these types within a single camera, as with the D3s/D3x. The more AF points available, the more easily the camera can differentiate among areas of the frame, and the more precisely you can specify the area you want to be in focus if you're manually choosing a focus spot.

But, there's another side of the coin. There is such a thing as *too many* focus zones for some types of subjects. For example, when using 51 focus points to select a zone for large, evenly illuminated subjects, you can waste a lot of time thumbing the multi selector among the four-dozen (plus) focus points. That's why Custom Setting a8 lets you switch the D3s/D3x to a more widely spaced set of 11 focus zones that you can select quickly. (Flip back to Figure 4.4 for a comparison.)

As the camera collects contrast information from the sensors, it then evaluates the data to determine whether the desired sharp focus has been achieved. The calculations may include whether the subject is moving, and whether the camera needs to "predict" where the subject will be when the shutter release button is fully depressed and the picture is taken. The speed with which the camera is able to evaluate focus and then move the lens elements into the proper position to achieve the sharpest focus determines how fast the autofocus mechanism is.

Although your D3s/D3x will almost always focus more quickly than a human, there are types of shooting situations where that's not fast enough. For example, if you're having problems shooting sports because the D3s/D3x's autofocus system manically follows each moving subject, a better choice might be to switch autofocus modes or shift into manual and pre-focus on a spot where you anticipate the action will be, such as a goal line or soccer net. At night football games, for example, when I am shooting with a telephoto lens almost wide open, I often focus manually on one of the referees who happens to be standing where I expect the action to be taking place (say, a halfback run or a pass reception). I also use *trap focus*, which is a technique discussed in a sidebar later in this chapter.

## Choosing Autofocus Point Selection Mode

The D3s/D3x has only three different focus point selection modes. I'm going to describe each of the three modes, and explain how to use them. You can set any of the three modes using the AF-area mode selector switch, shown in Figure 7.11.

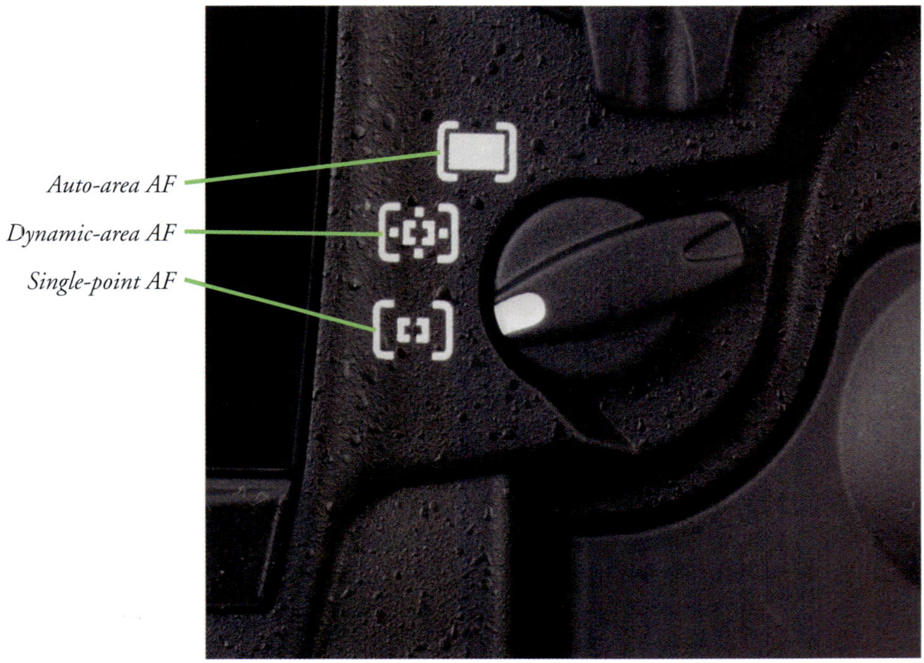


**Figure 7.11**
The autofocus mode selector switch is used to choose how autofocus points are allocated.

## Single-Point AF

In this mode, you always select the focus point manually, using the multi selector button (which, helpfully, will respond to your thumbpresses not only in the left/right and up/down directions, but diagonally, as well). The D3s/D3x evaluates focus based solely on the point you select, making this a good choice for subjects that don't move much. As I mentioned earlier, you can use Custom Setting a8 to choose whether the selected focus point resides in an 11-point widely spaced distribution, or within the full 51-point array. In either single-point AF or dynamic-area AF, if you want to lock the focus point you've selected for a series of shots, rotate the focus selector lock lever back to the L position. You can also temporarily lock the focus point by partially depressing the shutter release, or pressing the AE-L/AF-L button (unless you've redefined this behavior to some other controls in the Custom Setting menu).

## Dynamic-Area AF

In this mode, you still select the focus point yourself using the multi selector button, and when using single-servo autofocus (AF-S, discussed later), the D3s/D3x will evaluate focus solely based on that point. In that respect, the D3s/D3x behaves exactly as it does in single-point AF mode. However, if you have chosen continuous-servo autofocus (AF-C), the D3s/D3x's "smarts" spring to life if your subject leaves the selected focus zone. When that happens, the camera re-evaluates focus based on the other focus points surrounding the one you chose, as I originally described in Chapter 4 in the discussion of Custom Setting a3 (where you specify which points are used). To recap, you can set the D3s/D3x so that it will use 9, 21, 51 points, or 51 points with 3D tracking. You can view what pattern is currently being used by pressing the Info button and viewing the autofocus array representation in the screen that pops up.

- **9 points.** Only eight surrounding focus points will be used, allowing the D3s/D3x to respond quickly to subjects that are moving in a predictable way. (See Figure 7.12; the eight additional points are highlighted in green.) Use the 9-point setting when your subject will reside in a relatively small area of the frame, and won't be moving outside that area. Using just 9 points allows the D3s/D3x to ignore other objects outside the main subject's focus area, so focus can be acquired more quickly and with less confusion on the part of the focusing system.
- **21 points.** Should the subject leave the selected focus point, the D3s/D3x will refocus based on information from 20 surrounding focus points (highlighted in blue in Figure 7.12). This mode is best for subjects that are moving erratically. Autofocus may take slightly longer because more points are considered. I prefer this mode most of the time. It allows for subjects that roam around a slightly larger area of the frame, while still ignoring other objects. For example, I find the 21-point mode perfect for shooting basketball; I can concentrate on a player or two and not worry that the D3s/D3x will try to acquire focus of the other players on the court who aren't part of the immediate action.

**Note**

The active focus points surrounding the red highlighted focus zone will shift around the array as you move the manually chosen focus point. The highlighting shown in Figure 7.12 applies to the 9-point and 21-point options *only* when the center point is selected as the active focus point.

- **51 points.** Should the subject leave your selected focus point, the camera will refocus based on information from all 50 surrounding focus points, which may be best for fast moving subjects that may be located anywhere in the frame. If you don't know exactly where your main subject will be, this is your best choice.
- **51 points (3D tracking).** Should the subject leave your selected focus zone, the D3s/D3x uses distance information to calculate the path of the subject and select a new focus point. Nikon recommends using this setting to focus subjects that move erratically from side to side, because the camera can use the distance information to differentiate the original subject from objects that are closer or farther away. The D3s/D3x uses pattern recognition to keep track of your actual subject, based on information from multiple focus points—it knows the "shape" of your subject, and thus can follow it more reliably.

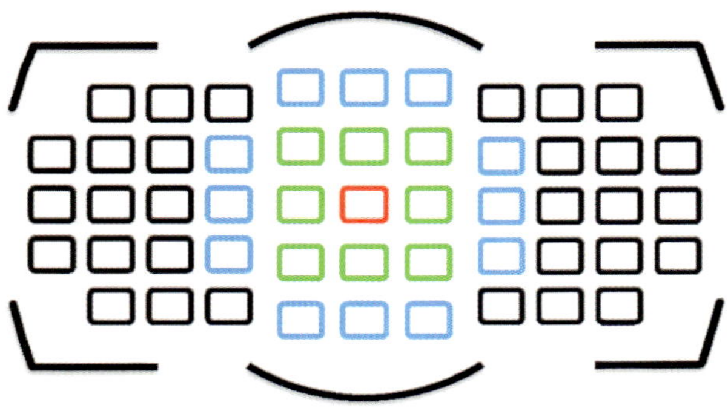

**Figure 7.12**
You can select from 9 (red/green), 21 (red/green/blue), or 51 (red/green/blue/black) active focus points.

## Auto-Area AF

In this mode, autofocus point selection is out of your hands; the D3s/D3x performs the task for you using its own intelligence. If you are using a type G or D lens, the camera can even work with the supplied distance information to distinguish humans from their background, so a person standing at the side of the frame will be detected and used to evaluate focus, while the camera ignores the background area in the frame. The autofocus system is integrated with the metering sensor, which detects color information, and so can read flesh tones to determine the location of people (which are likely to be your main subject).

The D3s/D3x tends to keep the active focus point somewhat of a mystery (although it will be displayed during picture review if you've activated that option). In AF-S mode, the active focus point is highlighted in the viewfinder for about one second after focus is achieved. In AF-C mode, the active focus point is not shown.

Auto-area and dynamic-area autofocus effectively replace two clumsier and confusing modes offered in earlier cameras, such as the D200 and D2xs: group dynamic and dynamic area (closest subject) options. In group dynamic mode you had to select from among two group patterns offered, with "center area" or "closest subject priority" options available for both. Dynamic area (closest subject) supposedly was the best choice if you always knew your subject would be the nearest object to the camera. I'm glad these two variations are gone.

# Autofocus Mode and Priority

Choosing the right autofocus mode (AF-S, AF-C, or manual) is another key to focusing success. To save battery power, your D3s/D3x doesn't start to focus the lens until you partially depress the shutter release or press the AF-ON button on the back of the camera or on the MB-D10 battery pack/grip (unless you've reprogrammed the AF-ON button for some other function or have specified another control to activate autofocus, as described in Chapter 4). But, autofocus isn't some mindless beast out there snapping your pictures in and out of focus with no feedback from you after you press that button. There are several settings you can modify that return at least a modicum of control to you. Your first decision should be whether you set the D3s/D3x to AF-S, AF-C, or manual. There's a switch on the side of the lens mount that allows you to do that.

## Autofocus Mode

This choice determines *when* your D3s/D3x starts to autofocus, and what it does when focus is achieved. Automatic focus is not something that happens all the time when your camera is turned on. (You can also use the AE/AL lock button to start autofocus, as described in Chapter 3.)

Your first decision should be whether you set the D3s/D3x to AF-S, AF-C, or manual. To change to any of the automatic modes, rotate the switch on the camera body next to the lens release button.

### Single-Servo Autofocus

In this mode, also called *AF-S*, focus is set once and remains at that setting until the button is fully depressed, taking the picture, or until you release the shutter button without taking a shot. For non-action photography, this setting is usually your best choice, as it minimizes out-of-focus pictures (at the expense of spontaneity). It's also a good choice when you want to know, as you shoot, what focus point has been selected when the camera is making the point selection in auto-area AF mode. That's common for new users of the D3s/D3x, until they become confident with the camera's ability to choose an appropriate focus point.

The drawback with AF-S is that you might not be able to take a picture at all while the camera is seeking focus; you're locked out until the autofocus mechanism is happy with the current setting. As described in Chapter 4, you can set AF-S mode to use either focus priority (the default) or release priority using Custom Setting a2.

When sharp focus is achieved, the selected focus point will flash red in the viewfinder, and the focus confirmation light at the lower left will flash green. If you're using matrix metering, the exposure will be locked at the same time. By keeping the shutter button depressed halfway, you'll find you can reframe the image while retaining the focus (and exposure) that's been set. You can also use the AE-L/AF-L button, as described in Chapter 4, if you've set that button to lock focus when pressed. Because of the small delay while the camera zeroes in on correct focus, you might experience slightly more shutter lag. This mode uses less battery power.

**NO MORE PREDICTIVE FOCUS IN AF-S**

Earlier Nikon cameras used a process called *predictive focus* when in AF-S mode to track moving objects, based on the direction of their motion while the focus process was underway. If a subject was racing toward the camera, for example, predictive focus would, in effect, focus where the subject was *going* to be, even before it got there. Nikon removed this feature from AF-S mode in the latest versions of its autofocus system, because the focus action (particularly with lenses having an internal autofocus motor) is fast enough that moving subjects can be focused in real time, without the need for prediction.

## Continuous-Servo Autofocus

This mode, also known as *AF-C* is the mode to use for sports and other fast-moving subjects. In this mode, once the shutter release is partially depressed, the camera sets the focus but continues to monitor the subject, so that if it moves or you move, the lens will be refocused to suit. Unlike AF-S, continuous-servo autofocus *does* use predictive autofocus techniques to track moving subjects. Focus and exposure aren't really locked until you press the shutter release down all the way to take the picture. You'll find that AF-C produces the least amount of shutter lag of any autofocus mode when set to release priority: press the button and the camera fires. It also uses the most battery power, because the autofocus system operates as long as the shutter release button is partially depressed.

Continuous-servo autofocus uses either the automatically selected AF point or the point you select manually to set focus. As described in Chapter 4, you can set AF-C mode to use release priority (the default), release priority + focus (which slows continuous shooting slightly to give the D3s/D3x additional time to focus), or focus priority using Custom Setting a1.

If you want to lock the focus point you've selected for a series of shots, rotate the focus selector lock lever up to the L position. You can also temporarily lock the focus point by partially depressing the shutter release, or pressing the AE-L/AF-L button (unless you've redefined this behavior to some other controls in the Custom Setting menu). You can disable manual focus point selection using the lock lever on the back of the camera concentric with the multi selector.

### Manual Focus

With manual focus activated by sliding the switch on the lens to the M position, or the rotating switch on the camera body near the lens mount set to M, your D3s/D3x lets you set the focus yourself. (Both the camera and lens settings must agree if you want to use an autofocus mode; when either is set to manual, then only manual focus is possible.) There are some advantages and disadvantages to this approach. While your batteries will last longer in manual focus mode, it will take you longer to focus the camera for each photo, a process that can be difficult. Modern digital cameras, even dSLRs, depend so much on autofocus that the viewfinders of models that have less than full-frame sized sensors are no longer designed for optimum manual focus. Pick up any film camera and you'll see a bigger, brighter viewfinder with a focusing screen that's a joy to focus on manually.

## Autofocus Activation... and More

The final considerations in using autofocus are the control or controls used to activate and lock autofocus, plus a few odds and ends. I've explained them in ample detail earlier in the book, but here are some cross-references if you feel you need some review.

- **Which controls activate/lock autofocus.** You can use a half-press of the shutter release or a press of the AF-ON button (or both). See the instructions for Custom Setting a5 in Chapter 4.
- **AF point illumination.** Do you want the active autofocus point illuminated when that is an option? Look up Custom Setting a6 in Chapter 4 to see how to adjust AF point illumination when using manual focus or continuous focus, and to adjust focus point brightness.
- **Focus tracking with lock-on.** Intervening subjects passing in front of your main area of interest can interfere with autofocus. Set a delay time before the camera refocuses using Custom Setting a4, as described in Chapter 4.

- **Focus point wrap-around.** Do you want the focus point to wrap around to the opposite side during manual selection? Use Custom Setting a7.
- **Center/show focus point.** You can program the multi selector center button to either jump the active focus point to the center or to highlight the active focus point, using Custom Setting f1, as described in Chapter 4.
- **Lock focus with Fn, DOF Preview, or AE-L/AF-L buttons.** Check out Custom Setting f4, Custom Setting f5, or Custom Setting f6, as outlined in Chapter 4.

## TRAP (AUTO) FOCUS

This technique comes in handy when you know where the action is going to take place (such as at the finish line of a horse race), but you don't know exactly *when.* The solution is to pre-focus on the point where the action will occur, and then tell your D3s/D3x not to actually take the photo until something moves into the pre-focus spot. That's not as difficult as you might think. The key is to decouple the focusing operation from the shutter release function. Just follow these steps:

1. Set Custom Setting a5 to AF-ON only. At that setting, pressing the shutter release halfway down does *not* activate autofocus. That happens only when you press the AF-ON button.
2. Set Custom Setting a2 to Focus priority.
3. Set your point selection mode to single-point .
4. Make sure your lens is set to autofocus (either A or M/A).
5. Pre-focus on the spot where the action will occur, or an equivalent distance.
6. Reframe your picture, if necessary, so that nothing is at the pre-focused distance. (If an object occupies that spot, the D3s/D3x will take the photo immediately when you press the shutter release.)
7. Press and hold down the shutter release. The camera will not refocus, because you've disconnected the autofocus function from the shutter release.
8. The picture will be taken when a subject moves into the pre-focused area.

# 8

# Live View, HDTV Movies, and Advanced Techniques

I've saved some advanced techniques for this chapter, which devotes a little extra space to some special features of the Nikon D3s/D3x. This chapter covers live view, GPS techniques, and special exposure options, including time-lapse photography, very long, and very short exposures. I wind up this section with a list of recommended settings for your Shooting menu and Custom Setting menu banks.

## The New Perspective of Live View

Live view is one of those features that experienced SLR users (especially those dating from the film era) sometimes think they don't need—until they try it. It's also one of those features (like truly "silent" shooting, without any shutter click) that point-and-shoot refugees are surprised that digital SLRs (until recently) have lacked. As I noted earlier, SLRs have actual, mechanical shutters that can't be completely silenced, as can be done with point-and-shoot cameras. I've fielded almost as many queries from those who want to know how to preview their images on the LCD—just as they did with their point-and-shoot cameras. Indeed, many P & S models don't even *have* optical viewfinders, engendering a whole generation of amateur photographers who think the only way to frame and compose an image is to hold the camera out at arm's length so the back-panel LCD can be viewed more easily.

While dSLR veterans didn't really miss what we've come to know as live view, it was at least, in part, because they didn't have it and couldn't miss what they never had. After all, why would you eschew a big, bright, magnified through-the-lens optical view that showed depth-of-field fairly well, and which was easily visible under virtually all ambient light conditions? LCD displays, after all, were small, tended to wash out in bright light, and didn't really provide you with an accurate view of what your picture was going to look like.

There were technical problems, as well. Real-time previews theoretically disabled a dSLR's autofocus system, as focus was achieved by measuring contrast through the optical viewfinder, which is blocked when the mirror is flipped up for a live view. Extensive previewing had the same effect on the sensor as long exposures: the sensor heated up, producing excess noise. Pointing the camera at a bright light source when using a real-time view could damage the sensor. The list of potential problems goes on and on.

That was then. This is now.

The Nikon D3s/D3x has a gorgeous three-inch LCD that can be viewed under a variety of lighting conditions and from wide-ranging angles, so you don't have to be exactly behind the display to see it clearly. It offers a 100-percent view of the sensor's capture area (the optical viewfinder shows just 95 percent of the sensor's field of view). It's large enough to allow manual focusing—but there is an automatic focus option, too. You still have to avoid pointing your D3s/D3x at bright light sources (especially the Sun) when using live view, but the real-time preview can be used for fairly long periods without frying the sensor.

Unlike some of the previous attempts at a live view-type mode by other vendors, the D3s/D3x's live view works. No beam-splitting prisms that divert some light to the sensor, no grainy black-and-white real-time preview, no need for a spare sensor to provide a simulated live view. Nikon's system works just like you'd want it to: the mirror flips up, the shutter opens, and what the sensor sees is displayed in full color on the LCD on the back of the camera, as shown in Figure 8.1, which pictures a typical live view screen found on the D3s. (The D3x and original D3 version lacks the four framing lines found near the corners of the image.)

Of course, live view (only), as found on the D3x, is just an interim step. The *full* implementation of live view didn't arrive in Nikon's pro-level cameras until HDTV movie making was introduced with the Nikon D3s. Live view, as useful as it may be, doesn't have quite the potential or the ability to make full-motion video clips with what is otherwise considered a still camera. I'll be covering both aspects—live view and movie making—in this chapter.

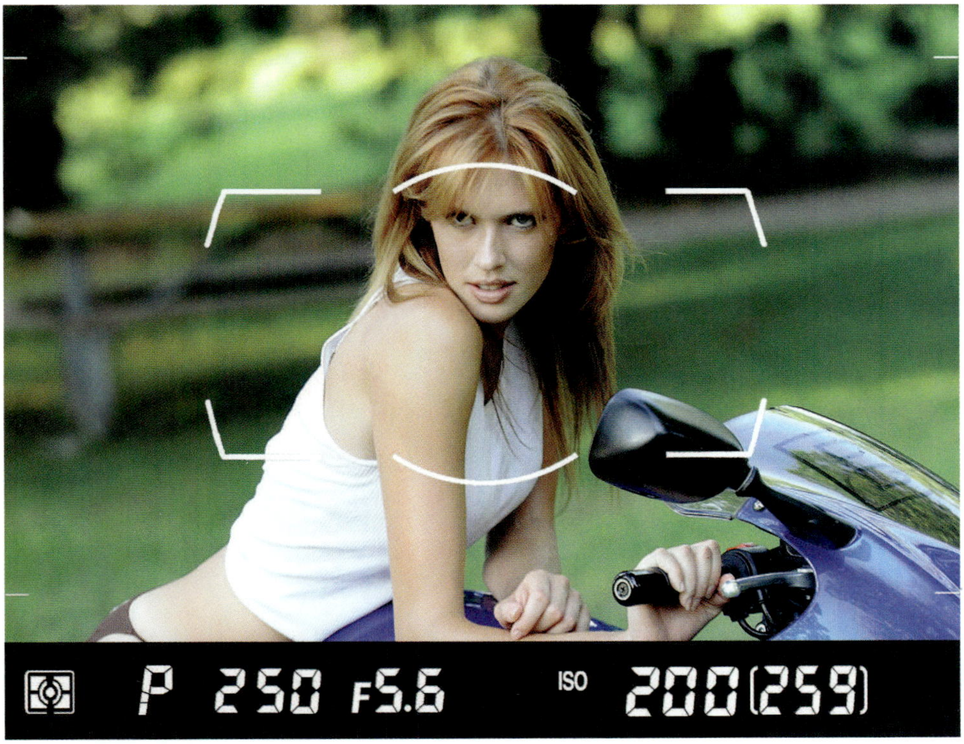


**Figure 8.1**
Live view really shines on the Nikon D3s/D3x's large three-inch LCD.

## What You Can Do with Live View

You may not have considered just what you can do with live view, because the capability is still relatively novel in a Nikon pro-level camera. But once you've played with it, you'll discover dozens of applications for this capability, as well as a few things that you can't do. Here's a list of live view Do's/Don'ts/Cans/Can'ts.

- **Preview your images on a TV.** Connect your D3s/D3x to a standard definition or high definition television using a video or HDMI cable, and you can preview your image on a large screen. Because you're viewing the actual image that will be captured, you can check things like focus or white balance in real time, on a larger display.
- **Preview exposure.** Unfortunately, one thing you can't preview with 100-percent accuracy is exposure. An exposure preview mode is offered, but it is available only in tripod mode. A live histogram can be viewed only in one display screen of tripod mode. At best, you can make some guesses about exposure.
- **Preview white balance.** Although live view provides only a rough estimation of the white balance delivered in your final image, the LCD image is close enough to allow you to do some rough tuning of your color balance.

- **Preview remotely.** Extend the cable between the camera and TV screen, and you can preview your images some distance away from the camera.
- **Improve your point of view.** If looking through the viewfinder to frame your subject is awkward (say, you have to hold the D3s/D3x over your head to clear obstructions such as a crowd of people), live view lets you see what you're going to shoot before you snap the shutter. (A remote release is a good idea in this mode.)
- **Shoot from your computer.** With Camera Control Pro 2, you can control your camera from your computer, so you can preview images and take pictures without physically touching the D3s/D3x. Prior to live view, you could *shoot* images with a tethered camera using Camera Control Pro, but you couldn't see the actual image on your computer until a picture had already been taken.
- **Continuous shooting.** You can shoot bursts of images using live view, but all shots will use the focus and exposure setting established for the first picture in the series.
- **Shoot from tripod or hand-held.** Of course, holding the camera out at arm's length to preview an image is poor technique, and will introduce a lot of camera shake. If you want to use live view for hand-held images, use an image-stabilized lens and/or a high shutter speed in hand-held mode. A tripod and tripod mode is a better choice if you can use one.
- **You can shoot movies (D3s only).** Live view makes movie shooting possible. I'll discuss that aspect later in the chapter.

But there are a few warnings you should keep in mind:

- **Caveat: Choose exposure mode before you start.** Metering mode can't be changed while live view is active. Select your metering method before you activate the feature.
- **Caveat: Watch your power.** Live view uses a lot of juice and will deplete your battery rapidly. The optional AC adapter is a useful accessory.
- **Caveat: Beware exposure snags.** If the camera is mounted on a tripod, you really should consider covering the viewfinder window to avoid light coming from the back affecting your meter reading in automatic exposure modes. Use the D3s/D3x's eyepiece shutter to block the light.
- **Caveat: Don't shoot the sun.** Very bright light sources can damage your sensor. Don't point the camera at the sun, or any excessively bright illumination.
- **Caveat: Watch your usage times.** Nikon says live view can be used continuously for as long as one hour, but notes that after periods of more than a few minutes, the sensor warms up and increases image noise and color artifacts. Your D3s/D3x will shut down before your camera seriously overheats, and will give you a warning on the monitor 30 seconds before shut-off.

- **Caveat: Eliminate flicker.** Certain types of fluorescent, sodium, or mercury vapor lamps pulsate, causing a flickering image during live view, and when recording movies a similar effect can be caused by panning the camera, or if a subject is moving horizontally through the frame at high speed. Try using Flicker reduction, available only with the D3s, and found in the Setup menu, as described in Chapter 5.
- **Caveat: Slower focus.** The contrast detection system used in tripod mode is slower than hand-held mode's phase detection, and may have difficulty if a subject lacks contrast, certain special filters are used, regular geometric patterns are present in the image which make determining contrast difficult, or there is either subject or camera movement (i.e., the D3s/D3x is not on a tripod).

# Enabling Live View

Activating live view is easy. All you need to do ahead of time is decide whether you want to use hand-held mode or tripod mode. Keep in mind that the names are only a suggestion, not a hard-and-fast requirement. You can use hand-held mode with the camera on a tripod, and tripod mode with the camera held in your hands.

The chief difference between the two (as I'll explain shortly) is the way in which the camera achieves focus. The default is hand-held mode, which gives you the most flexibility when photographing moving subjects and when composing images from angles that are difficult to achieve when looking through the optical viewfinder. (You don't need to hold the camera up to your eye; you can hold it away from your body, above you, below you, or at any angle that allows you to see the LCD.) The D3s/D3x flips the mirror back down to focus normally using the camera's phase detection system just before you take the picture.

Tripod mode is preferred for shooting non-moving subjects (especially macro shots), and focus is achieved by detecting the contrast of the image on the sensor, based on any point in the frame that you choose (not just the 51 autofocus points used with phase detection). (You'll find more on phase detection vs. contrast detection in Chapter 7.)

To start live view follow these steps:

1. **Set up live view.** Press the Menu button, and navigate through the Shooting menu to the Live view choice (D3x) or Live view mode entry (D3s). There, you'll be given several options: choice of Live view mode (D3s and D3x) and Release mode (D3x only).
2. **Select mode.** Highlight Live view mode and press the right cursor button.
3. **Choose Hand-held or Tripod mode.** I'll describe these modes later in this section.
4. **Activate choice.** Press OK to confirm your selection. You'll be returned to the main Live view screen. D3s owners can jump to step 6.

5. **Select Release mode (D3x only).** Because live view is activated using the release mode dial on the D3x (and original D3), you must specifically activate an additional release mode using the menu. Highlight Release mode and press the right cursor button. Choose Single frame, Continuous low speed, or Continuous high speed, and then press the OK button to confirm. (You can't select Self-timer or Mirror up.) You'll be returned to the main Live view screen again.
6. **Exit menus.** Press the Menu button twice to exit the menu system, or just tap the shutter release.
7. **Activate live view (D3x).** Hold down the release mode dial lock button and rotate the dial to the Live view (Lv) position. Press the shutter release down all the way. The mirror will flip up and the LCD will display the image that the sensor sees. You're in live view mode!
8. **Activate live view (D3s).** Press the Live view button on the back of the camera, just right of the Microphone button.
9. **Exit live view.** To exit live view mode, just press the Live view button again (D3s), or, with the D3x, press the Menu button, then hold down the release mode dial lock button and rotate the dial to some other position.

## Working with Live View—Hand-Held Mode

This mode turns your D3s/D3x into a point-and-shoot camera, at least from an image preview standpoint. You can see the exact image produced by the sensor, and take pictures using your camera's autofocus and autoexposure features. If you like, you can even hold the camera out at arm's length to compose a photo, just like the tourists you saw during your last visit to Niagara Falls. Despite the name, you can still use hand-held mode when the D3s/D3x is mounted on a tripod. It works fine in that mode, it's just that hand-held mode is better suited for taking pictures rapidly, compared to the slower tripod mode.

As I noted, hand-held mode is a good choice for photographing moving action from a variety of angles, because you can position the camera more quickly than if it were locked down on a tripod, and choose angles that lend themselves to odd positions and perspectives. If you can point the camera at something, you can use hand-held mode with it.

The drawback is that the D3s/D3x must use its normal phase detection autofocus mode, which requires that, just before exposure, the mirror flip down to allow focus, then flip back up to take the picture. Taking a photograph in this mode is easy. Just follow these steps:

1. **Turn on live view.** After you've activated Hand-held mode in the Shooting menu, turn on live view, as discussed in the last section, by pressing the Lv button (D3s) or setting the release mode dial to Lv and pressing the shutter release (D3x).
2. **Frame your photograph.** The optical viewfinder window goes blank (because the mirror is flipped up), so you can compose your image using the LCD.
3. **Zoom in.** Hold down the Zoom button and rotate the main command dial to zoom in on the live view image by up to 13x. A navigation window appears in the bottom-right corner. Use the multi selector keys to move the zoomed area around within the frame.
4. **Select an autofocus point.** Use the multi selector direction buttons to move the autofocus zone, highlighted on the screen with a red triangle, to an appropriate position. You can select only the normal 51 autofocus points within the focus brackets shown on the screen.
5. **Focus.** With the D3s/D3x set for single-servo autofocus (AF-S) or continuous-servo autofocus (AF-C), activate autofocus by pressing the shutter release button halfway, or by pressing the AF-ON button. The mirror will flip down and the camera will focus; the mirror will flip back up and restore the live view when you release the shutter release or AF-ON button.

   You can also focus manually by rotating the lens's focusing ring, if the camera focus mode lever on the front is set to M. You must do this through the optical viewfinder *before* activating live view, however. Because the position of the camera or your subject can change after you manually focus, you should use this option only with subjects that are not moving, and when parked in a stationary camera position.
6. **Take the picture.** Press the shutter release down all the way to lock in focus and exposure and take the picture. The live view image will vanish while the picture is being taken, and return once the shutter closes again.
7. **Exit live view.** Press the Lv button (D3s) or change the release mode dial to some other position to turn off live view.

Once you have live view displaying an image on your LCD screen, you can change the appearance and amount of shooting information displayed, just as you can with the shooting information screen. There are five different screen variations available in hand-held mode. The focus brackets in the center of the frame are displayed only when you're using hand-held mode. These display modes are available:

- **Information off.** Figure 8.1, shown earlier, illustrates the information off mode, which cancels the informational display overlay and shows only the basic information like you might see through the D3s/D3x's optical viewfinder.

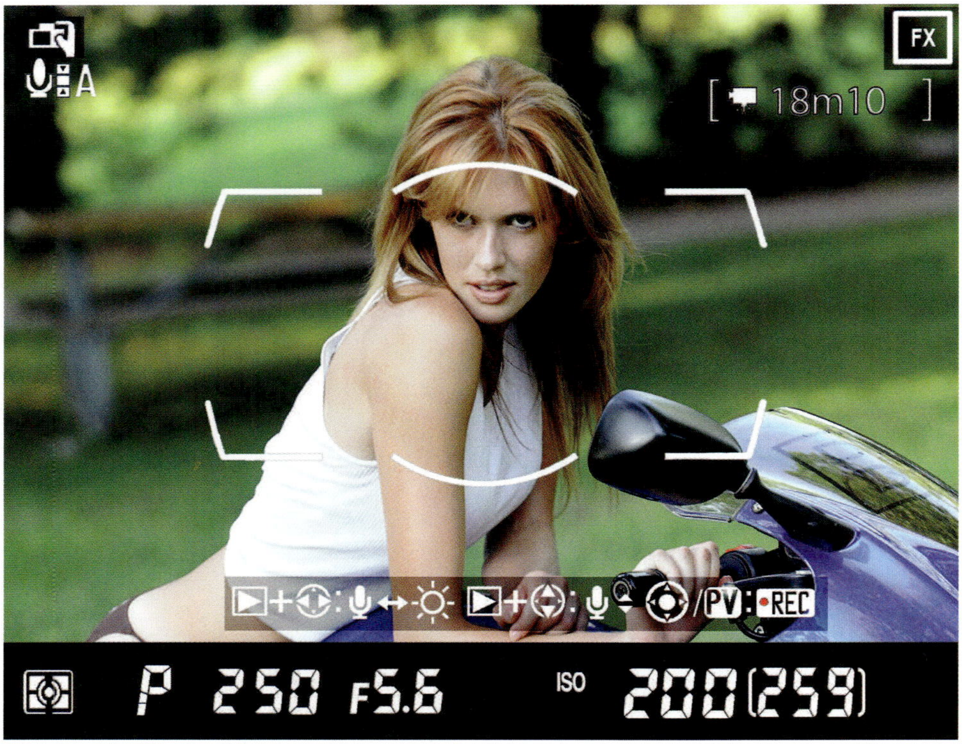


**Figure 8.2**
The information on live view display.

- **Information on.** In this mode, a full array of information is overlaid on the screen, as shown in Figure 8.2. The data shown includes image size, white balance, image area (such as FX or DX), and whether tripod or hand-held mode is active. Just above the information overlay is an action control reminder strip that doesn't show the status of anything: the icons show how to control the LCD brightness and activate recording.
- **Framing guides.** This mode shows framing lines, which vary depending on the shooting mode. If you're using hand-held mode, all you get is the plain grid shown in Figure 8.3.
- **Virtual horizon.** This mode activates the D3s/D3x's virtual horizon feature in its most useful incarnation, because you can actually line up the horizon at the same time you compose your image. (See Figure 8.4.)

## Working with Live View—Tripod Mode

Tripod mode is a good choice for photographing non-moving objects, particularly when you want to zoom in and focus precisely on a subject. This method uses contrast-detect focus (explained in Chapter 7) to choose the best focus based on the contrast between edges in an image.

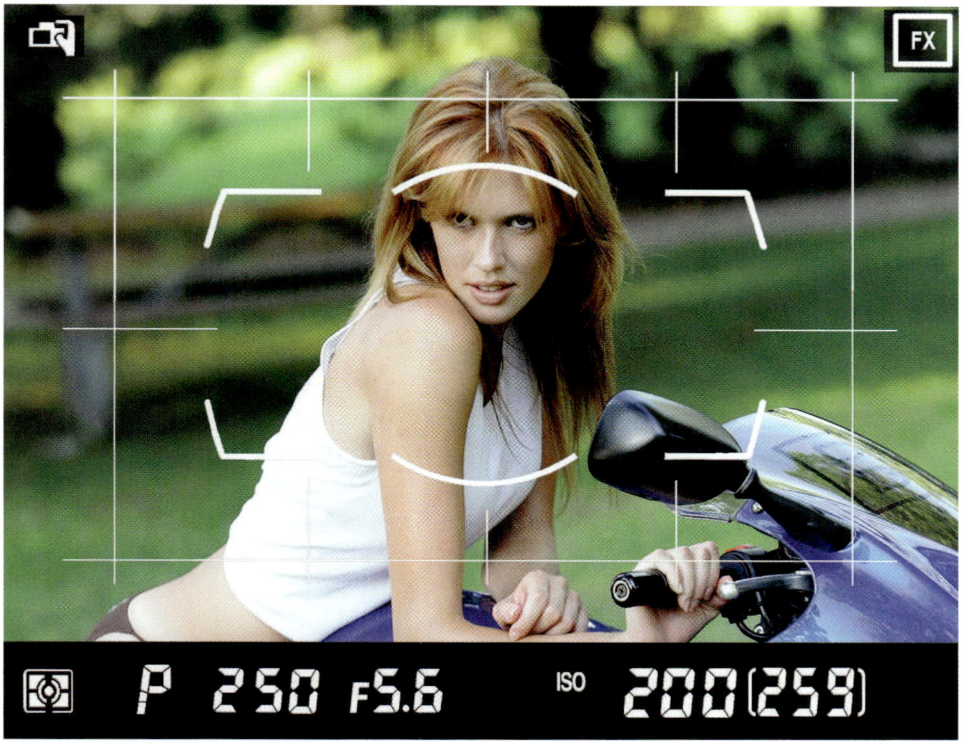


**Figure 8.3**
Framing guides as shown in hand-held mode.

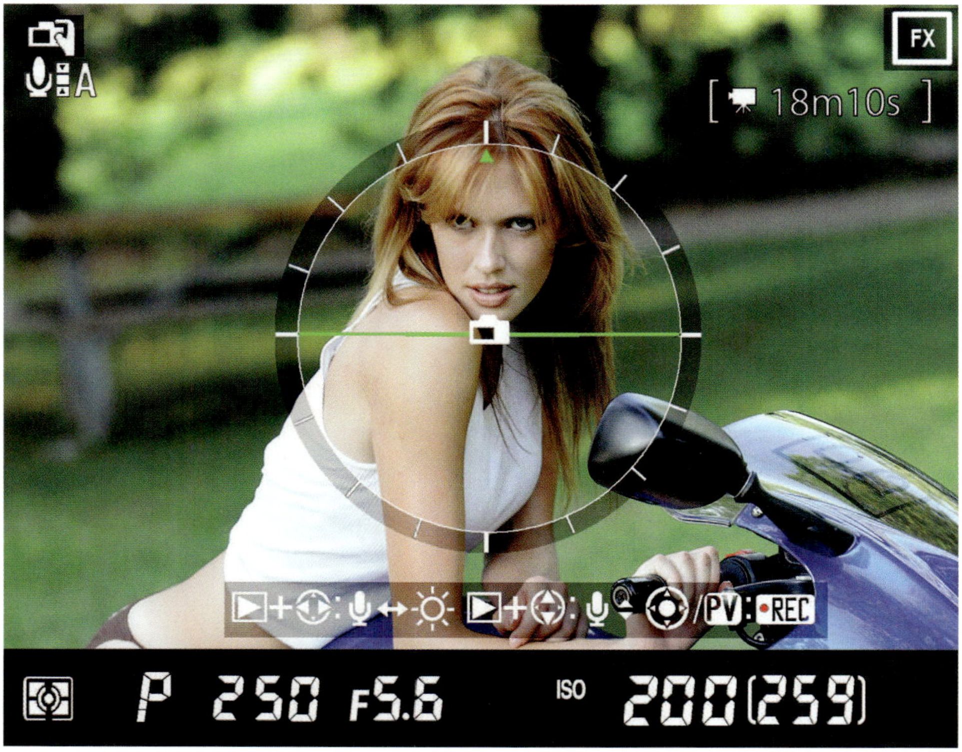


**Figure 8.4**
The virtual horizon display in live view.

The advantage is that you can specify focus from *anywhere* in the image frame, not just the 51 phase detect autofocus points. And, you can focus manually right on the LCD, using zoom, if necessary, to precisely evaluate your focus. To use tripod mode, just follow these steps:

1. **Turn on live view.** After you've activated tripod mode in the Shooting menu, turn on live view, as discussed in the last section, by pressing the Lv button (D3s) or setting the release mode dial to Lv and pressing the shutter release (D3x).
2. **Frame your photograph.** The optical viewfinder window goes blank (because the mirror is flipped up), so you can compose your image using the LCD.
3. **Zoom in.** Hold down the Zoom button and rotate the main command dial to zoom in on the live view image by up to 13x. Use the multi selector to change the area being zoomed. A navigation window appears in the bottom-right corner, and the focus point box enlarges to show the portion of the frame covered. (See Figure 8.5.)
4. **Select an autofocus point.** Use the multi selector direction buttons to move the autofocus zone, highlighted on the screen with a red triangle, to an appropriate position anywhere in the frame. If you move the focus point box to the center of the image, a red dot appears in the middle to show you've selected the center.

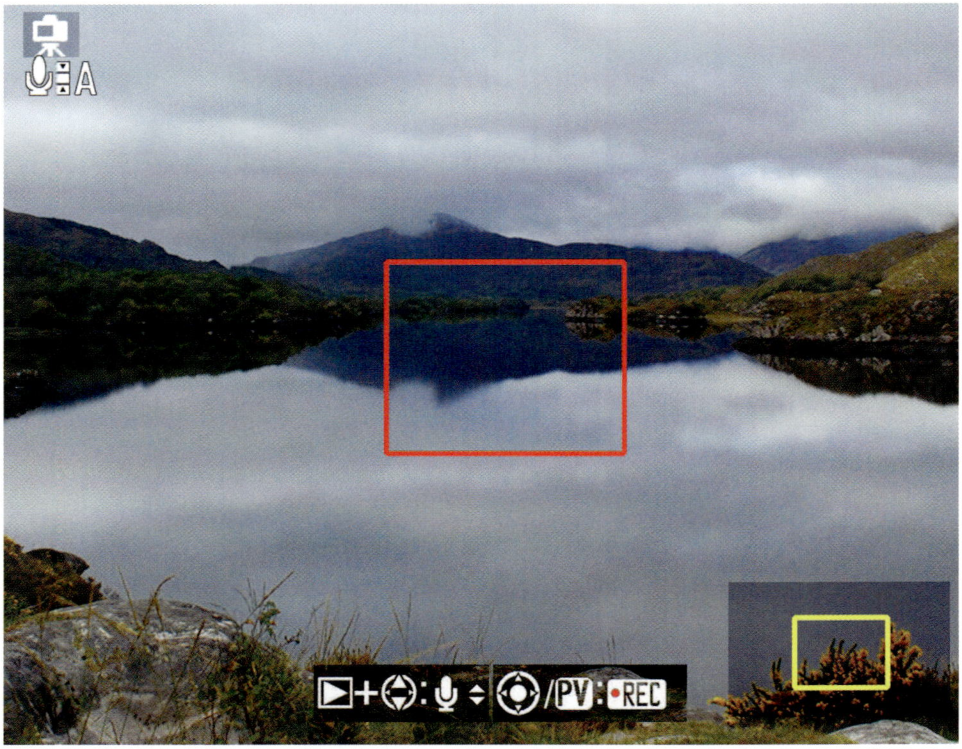


**Figure 8.5**
When you zoom in using live view, a navigation window appears.

5. **Focus.** With the D3s/D3x set for single-servo autofocus (AF-S) or continuous-servo autofocus (AF-C), activate autofocus by pressing the AF-ON button. The camera will autofocus using contrast detection. The selected focus point will blink green and stop blinking when correct focus is achieved. If the D3s/D3x is unable to focus, the point will blink red.

**Tip**

The camera focuses just once whether in AF-S or AF-C mode; it will not continue to focus if you hold down the AF-ON button while using AF-C. In both focus modes, the camera is set to *release priority* (discussed in Chapter 5). It's possible to take a picture even if the D3s/D3x has not locked in focus.

You can also focus manually by rotating the lens's focusing ring, if the camera focus mode lever on the front is set to M.

6. **Take the picture.** Press the shutter release down all the way to lock in focus and exposure and take the picture. The live view image will vanish while the picture is being taken, and return once the shutter closes again.
7. **Exit live view.** Press the Lv button (D3s) or change the release mode dial to some other position to turn off live view.

As with hand-held mode, once you have live view displaying an image on your LCD screen, you can change the shooting information displayed. Tripod mode has five different screen variations, one more than hand-held mode. These display modes are available:

- **Information off.** Figure 8.6 shows the Information off screen in tripod mode.
- **Information on.** In this mode, a full array of information is overlaid on the screen, as shown in Figure 8.7. The data shown includes image size, white balance, image area (such as FX or DX), and whether tripod or hand-held mode is active. Just above the information overlay is an action control reminder strip that doesn't show the status of anything: the icons show how to control the LCD brightness and activate recording.
- **Framing guides.** This mode shows framing lines, which vary depending on the shooting mode. The version that appears in tripod mode is shown in Figure 8.8.
- **Virtual horizon.** This mode activates the D3s/D3x's virtual horizon feature. (See Figure 8.9.)

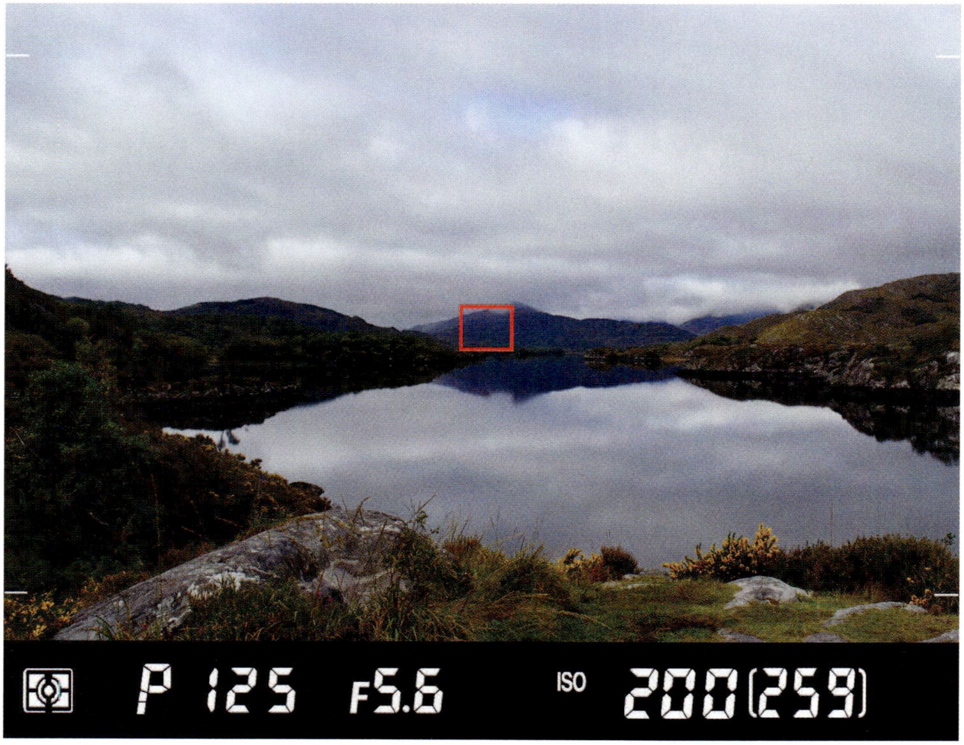


**Figure 8.6**
The Information off live view display in tripod mode.

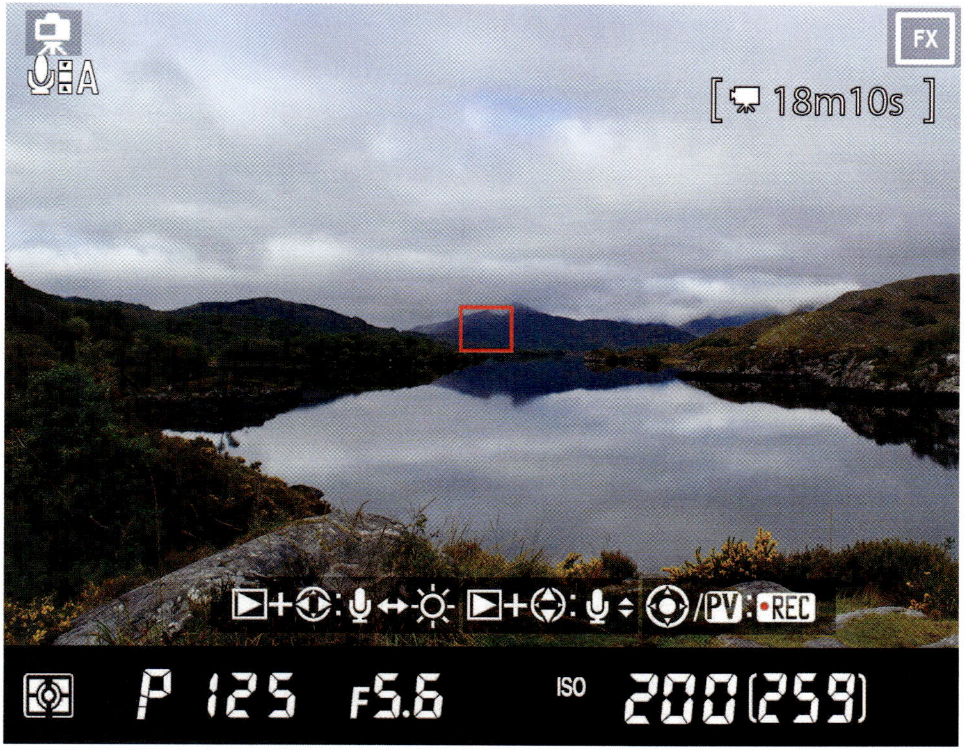


**Figure 8.7**
The Information on live view display.

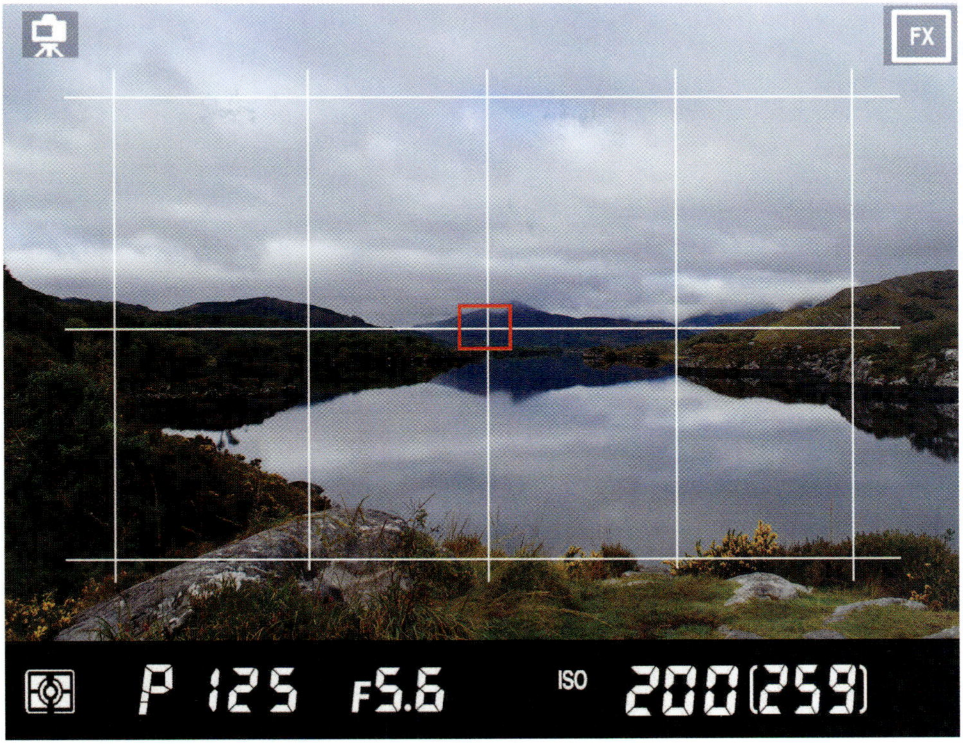


**Figure 8.8**
Framing guides as shown in hand-held mode.

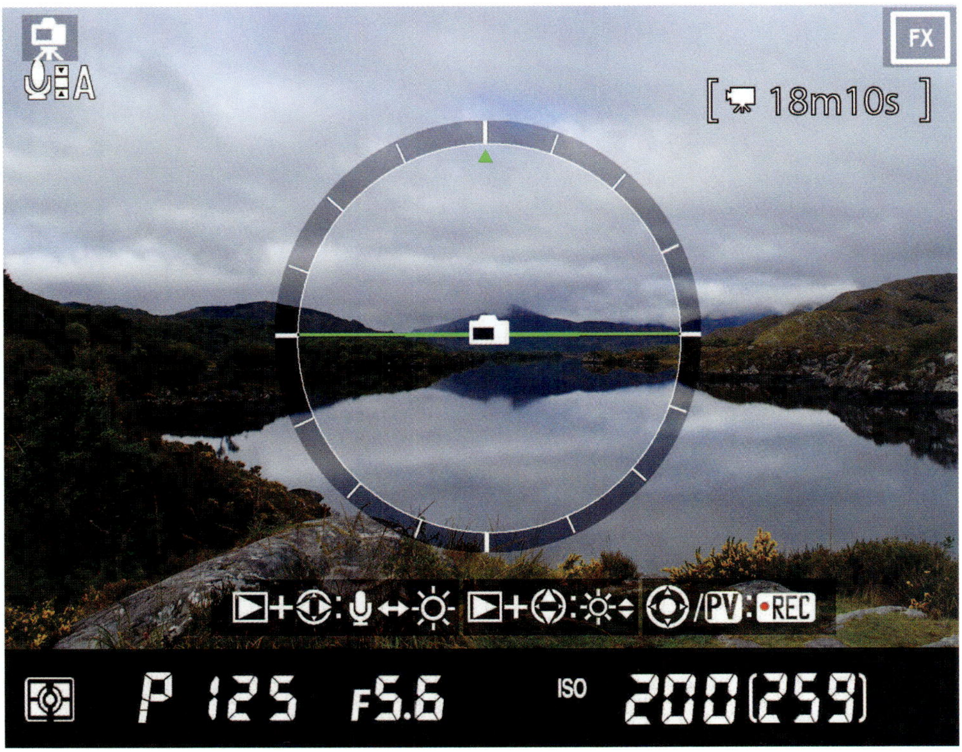


**Figure 8.9**
The Virtual horizon display in live view.

- **Exposure preview.** In hand-held mode only, you can see an exposure preview and view a histogram, in a variation of the Information on screen, shown in Figure 8.10. An exposure scale, visible at the right side of the frame, can be summoned for any of the five hand-held mode information displays. Use it to gauge the amount of under- or overexposure in the image. In the Exposure preview view, a live histogram appears. I explained how to use histograms in Chapter 6.

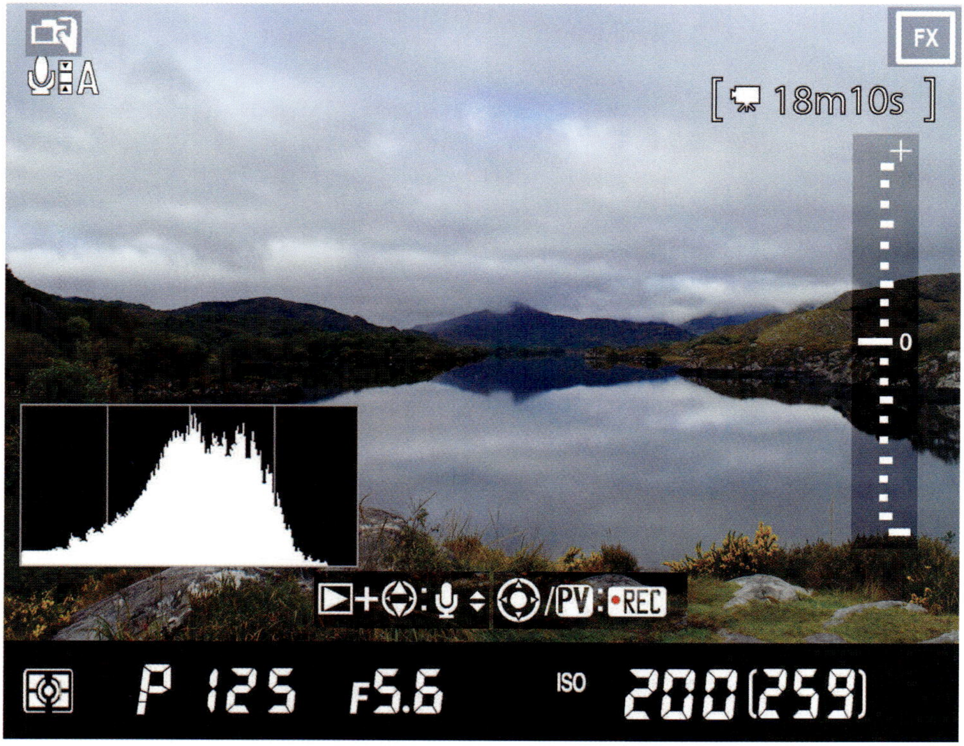


**Figure 8.10** Exposure preview with live histogram.

## USING EXPOSURE PREVIEW

When the exposure scale is visible, you can change the exposure by holding down the EV button and rotating the main command dial to add/subtract +/– 3EV. The amount of exposure compensation dialed in is shown on the scale (which actually displays +/– 5EV). If the histogram is shown, you'll see the effect your exposure compensation changes make on the image.

Exposure preview is not available if Active D-Lighting is activated (this is the most common culprit), but also cannot be displayed if you're doing bracketing or if you have selected x250 or bulb as a shutter speed (both are located at the far end of the shutter speed scale). The exposure preview may not be accurate if your subject is very dark or light, too.

## Adjusting Screen Brightness

The live view display is shown at an average brightness level that should work well under most lighting conditions. If you're shooting in very bright ambient lighting, you might want to pump the brightness up. If it's darker, you can dial the brightness down to avoid distracting glare (this is especially useful when shooting at concerts and other events where a bright LCD can annoy those behind you).

To adjust the LCD brightness, press the Playback button until a scale like the one shown in Figure 8.11 appears at the right side of the LCD. Press the multi selector up/down button to brighten or darken the display. To make changes, keep pressure on the Playback button as you adjust the brightness with the multi selector up/down buttons to brighten or darken the monitor. The scale automatically disappears when you remove your finger from the Playback button. Your changes affect only the live view display. When you turn live view off, the LCD returns to the setting you specified with the LCD brightness option in the Setup menu.

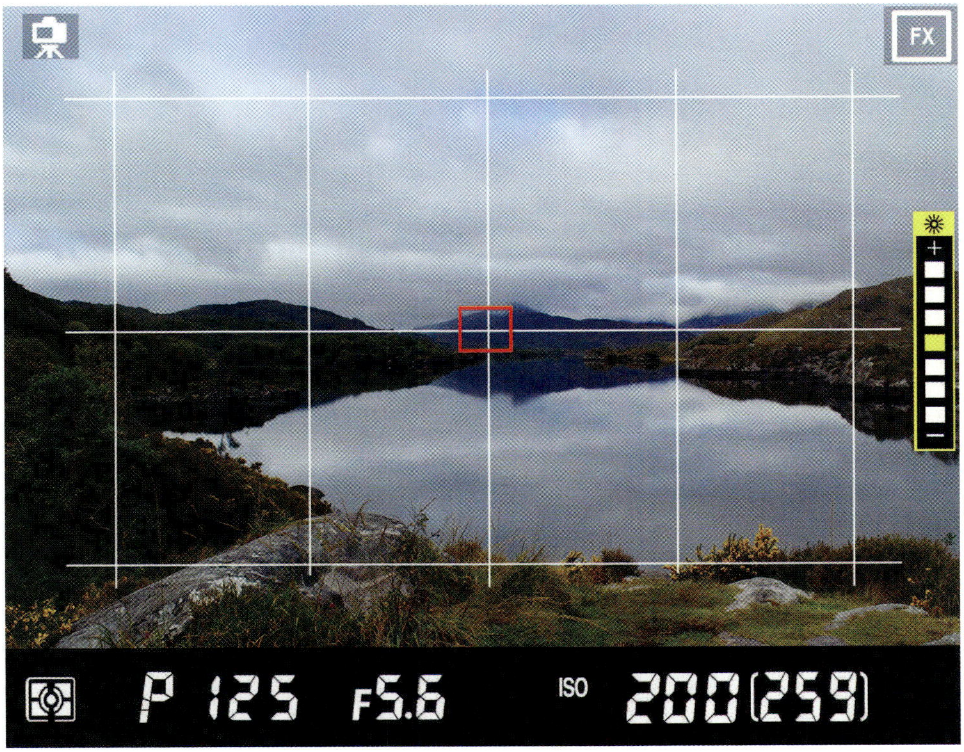


**Figure 8.11** Press the Playback button and the up/down keys to adjust LCD brightness.

## Using the Action Control Reminders

This strip of non-functioning icons at the bottom of the frame serves to remind you of the button combinations that activate various live view functions. The action control reminders differ between the D3s and D3x (and original D3). The D3s options are the most complicated:

- **Leftmost icon group.** Hold down the Playback button and press the left or right directional buttons to switch between microphone level setting (press left) and LCD screen brightness (press right). Depending on the direction you press, either the microphone icon in the upper-left corner or a pop-up screen brightness scale at the right edge of the screen will be activated.
- **Center icon group.** The icon to the right in this icon group will change from a microphone symbol to Sun symbol, depending on which mode you selected when the Playback button was pressed. Keep holding the Playback button down and press the up/down directional buttons to increase/decrease microphone sensitivity or screen brightness.
- **Right icon group.** Press the multi selector center button or the Depth-of-field preview (Pv) button to begin movie recording. Press again to stop recording.
- **D3x reminders.** Press the Playback button and the up/down directional buttons to change LCD screen brightness. Press the Menu button to exit live view (until you press the shutter release again).

# Shooting Movies with the D3s

Following a trend that Nikon started with the Nikon D90—the first ever digital SLR to include movie-making capabilities—the company has finally brought the feature to its latest pro dSLR. D3x owners may have the edge over the D3s in terms of resolution, but the youngest D3-series camera can stake a claim as the most expensive camcorder in the Nikon lineup.

As you've probably gathered, movie making is an extension of the live view concept. Once you've directed the output of the sensor to the LCD, capturing it as a video file—with audio—is relatively easy. With the D3s, you can shoot HDTV movies at resolutions up to 1280 × 720, at 24 frames per second, in either tripod mode or hand-held mode. The camera includes a built-in microphone mounted on the front surface to record rudimentary sound, and a tiny speaker tucked under the film card access button door, so you can shoot and review your clips immediately. But the D3s's movie-making capabilities really shine when you connect an external microphone and view your output on an HDTV monitor (if viewing directly from the camera) or through a high resolution TV or computer monitor after you've transferred your videos from the camera.

I have to point out that Nikon's movie-making capabilities are still a work in progress. The quality is not up to that produced by some Canon cameras (which can shoot full HDTV movies at 1920 × 1080 pixels, compared to Nikon's 1280 × 720 pixel maximum resolution—1080i vs. 720i). There have been some problems, such as an inability to focus or change apertures while filming (with some earlier Nikon implementations). But, as long as you consider the D3s to be a great still camera that can also capture video clips (rather than as a replacement for your camcorder), you can have a lot of fun with this feature.

Basic movie shooting is as easy as can be. While in live view mode, just press the center of the multi selector or the Depth-of-field (PV) button; press the button again to stop. The camera uses matrix metering, even if you've selected another metering method, and adjusts shutter speed and ISO sensitivity for you. If you use aperture priority or manual priority exposure in tripod mode, you can select aperture. In hand-held mode, the D3s always chooses the aperture for you. That's all you really need to know. But you'll get better results if you understand the process a little more through the information in this section.

## Reviewing Movie Settings

As you'll recall from Chapter 3, once you have chosen tripod or hand-held live view mode, the Movie settings entry in the Shooting menu allows you to choose three movie-making parameters for the D3s. To recap, the three are

- **Quality.** Choose from 1280 × 720 pixels (HDTV at 16:9 aspect ratio); 640 × 424 (3:2/VGA resolution); 320 × 216 (3:2 ratio for presentation on web pages and similar applications).
- **Microphone.** Select from low, medium, high-sensitivity microphones, auto sensitivity, or off.
- **Destination.** Choose the slot containing the Compact Flash card you want to store your movies on; generally, use the slot containing the fastest memory card.
- **High-sensitivity movie mode.** You can elect to shoot movies under the highest ISO settings (ISO 6400 to Hi 3) if you're willing to accept grain and some washed out highlights. Set to On to allow shooting movies at ISO 6400 to Hi 3. Switch to Off to limit movie making to ISO 200 to ISO 12800 (which is still fairly high, in my book).

### Choosing Movie Quality and Destination

Before you start shooting, you'll want to select the resolution of your video clip. Different recording quality settings are available from the Movie settings entry in the Shooting menu. Choose Quality, and then select from

- **1280 × 720 (16:9).** This setting gives you the 16:9 proportions displayed by high-definition television sets, and should be used when HDTV displays or high resolution monitors are your intended destination for your video. When you choose this mode, darkened bars appear at the top and bottom of the LCD screen to show you the approximate coverage area of a 16:9 aspect ratio video clip.
- **640 × 424 (3:2).** This is a standard definition television setting with a 3:2 aspect ratio. You can use this when you plan to show your videos on conventional television sets, or full-screen on a computer monitor. No crop marks are shown on the screen for this aspect ratio, or the next, as both correspond to the same proportions as the sensor.
- **320 × 216 (3:2).** This low-resolution option produces video clips suitable for display on web pages, iPods, and other smaller screens with a 3:2 aspect ratio.

You can also choose the destination for your film clip, either the Compact Flash card Slot 1 or Slot 2 using the Destination option in the Movie settings entry. Either will allow you to shoot a total of nearly 2 hours and 33 minutes of video with a 32GB card loaded in the D3s. Individual clips, however, can be no longer than 5 minutes for 1280 × 720-pixel movies, or 20 minutes for other resolutions. (See the sidebar on length limitation later in this chapter.)

I like to specify Slot 2 as my destination. There are several advantages to this approach. Sending all the video to Slot 2 separates it from the stills that are captured to the card in Slot 1 when I have the Slot 2 function set to Overflow. That keeps them separate. In addition, if I happen to have two cards of different write speeds, if I am not shooting sports I can go ahead and put the faster card in Slot 2, which can come in handy with continuous video capture.

## Using a Microphone

The D3s's built-in microphone is located on the front of the camera, just below the self-timer countdown lamp on the right side (as seen from your subject's point of view). It's handy, because you don't have to carry around a separate mic, but the location also means that the microphone will pick up all the noises you and the camera make, including the sounds emitted by the autofocus motor and vibration reduction system of your lenses.

You can plug in an external microphone that has a 3.5mm stereo mini-pin plug that fits into the jack on the side of the camera under the rubber port cover. Adjust the sensitivity of the mic by accessing the Movie settings entry in the Shooting menu, selecting Microphone, and choosing Automatic sensitivity, High sensitivity, Medium sensitivity, or Low sensitivity. If you want to shoot in Charlie Chaplin mode, you can also turn the external or internal mic off temporarily by selecting Microphone off. (Obviously, you could just unplug an external microphone to disable it, but that would leave the internal mic active.)

The sensitivity of your microphone can be adjusted while in live view. Before you begin filming, press and hold the Playback button and press the left multi selector button. A Microphone settings icon appears in the upper-left corner of the LCD. Continue holding down the Playback button and press the up/down multi selector buttons to adjust the microphone sensitivity. Release the Playback button when you're finished.

## Begin Filming

Just follow these steps to record your movie once you've switched to live view mode:

- **Focus the image before you begin shooting.** When using tripod mode, press the AF-ON button to initiate autofocus. The camera will refocus as required using contrast detection while you're shooting in tripod mode. If you choose hand-held mode, press the shutter release button halfway to focus using phase detection. The D3s will not refocus during shooting when using hand-held mode.
- **Begin shooting.** Press the center of the multi selector or Depth-of-field (PV) button to start recording. A recording indicator with the time available is shown overlaid on the LCD. The camera will adjust shutter speed and aperture automatically, always using matrix metering.
- **Lock exposure.** As you're shooting, you can change exposure by using EV compensation (press the EV button and rotate the main command dial). You can lock exposure at any time by pressing the AE-L/AF-L button.
- **Watch your ISO.** The D3s chooses an appropriate ISO setting for you. If you enabled High sensitivity mode in the Movie settings menu, a HiISO indicator will appear on the live view screen when it is being used. You may need to review your clips to make sure they don't have more noise than you find acceptable. Note that even if High sensitivity is enabled for movie shooting, any still photos you take during a session are taken at the ISO sensitivity you specify in the Shooting menu.
- **Refocus while shooting.** If you're using tripod mode, you can refocus while you're shooting by pressing the AF-ON button. Use this feature with caution when capturing sound with the built-in microphone, as any noises made by the lens during autofocus may be recorded. Note: Do not try to refocus when shooting in hand-held mode. Pressing the AF-ON button (or the shutter release) will not refocus, but will instead abort filming.
- **End recording.** When you're finished filming, you can stop recording in two ways. Press the shutter release all the way down to end recording and take a still photograph. Press the multi selector center button or Depth-of-field (PV) button to simply end filming.

### LENGTH LIMITATION—OR NOT?

Andy Warhol's first film, *Sleep*, was a 321-minute long epic consisting of interminably long takes of a friend asleep. The world is fortunate that your Nikon D3s won't allow you to duplicate this feat. Individual movie files can be only 2GB in size, which translates into about five minutes for 1,280 × 720-pixel clips, and about 20 minutes for other resolutions.

Unless you want to film a play or a concert from a fixed location for the duration of the entire event, this really isn't a limitation. In practice, movies with very long fixed sequences are incredibly boring. It's a better idea to cut a film up into sequences, varying the viewpoints, magnifications, and angles at intervals. Shoot establishing shots, medium shots, and close-ups. Change from eye-level to low or high angles. If you study movies on television or in theaters, you'll see that most scenes consist of sequences that are only a few seconds long. Break your mini-movies up into such sequences—either by stopping and starting the D3s's filming activities or by editing your scenes in the camera or your computer. Your audiences will love you for it, and you won't regret the "limitation" imposed by the camera on your maximum clip length at all.

## Manual Video in Tripod Mode

If you don't want your D3s to make all the exposure decisions for you, it's possible to take control of shutter speed, aperture, and ISO sensitivity while shooting in manual mode. For avid D3s cinematographers, going this route opens up some important options. Here are a few:

- **Depth-of-field control.** Compared to camcorders, your D3s has a much, much larger sensor, with much shallower depth-of-field. Selective focus such as we full-frame still photographers enjoy is highly prized by cinematographers. A combination of long lenses, short shooting distances, and wide apertures add up to *lots* of DOF control when shooting movies. In manual/tripod mode, you can choose any aperture you like.
- **Shutter speed control.** Creative cinematography often involves choosing a particular shutter speed to produce a specific effect. In manual/tripod mode you can choose any shutter speed from 1/25th to 1/8,000th second (the lower end is limited by the Nikon D3s's fixed 24 fps shooting speed). Use a slow shutter speed for creative blur in your movies, or a fast shutter speed to freeze action within each frame. Shutter speed (and aperture) control can be combined to allow the exact action-stopping and depth-of-field needed for a specific look.
- **ISO sensitivity.** In manual/tripod mode you can choose an ISO from 200 to 12800, which gives you lots of creative options in terms of low-light shooting, using noise for effect (or lack of it for creamy video).

To regain control of your exposure parameters, just follow these steps:

1. **Activate tripod mode.** Set the D3s to tripod mode for live view.
2. **Choose manual exposure.** Set the camera's exposure mode to M by holding down the Mode button on top of the camera and spinning the main command dial until M appears on the top-panel LCD.
3. **Start movie mode.** Press the multi selector center button or depth-of-field preview (PV) button to activate movie mode.
4. **Access exposure preview.** Press the OK button until exposure preview is visible.
5. **Make your settings.** Set shutter speed, aperture, and ISO sensitivity just as if you were shooting stills, using the main command dial, sub-command dial, and ISO button on the back of the D3s.
6. **Add/subtract EV or lock exposure.** In exposure preview mode, you can also use exposure compensation, as described earlier, and apply the AE lock button to lock in exposure (as long as you haven't redefined the button for some other task), as outlined in Chapter 4.

## Viewing Your Movies

Once you've finished recording your movies, they are available for review. Film clips show up during picture review, the same as still photos, but they are differentiated by a movie camera overlay (see Figure 8.12). Press the center button of the multi selector to start playback.

During playback, you can perform the following functions:

- **Pause.** Press the multi selector down button to pause the clip during playback. Press the multi selector center button to resume playback.
- **Rewind/Advance.** Press the left/right multi selector buttons to rewind or advance (respectively). Press once for 2X speed, twice for 8X speed, or three times for 16X speed. Hold down the left/right buttons to move to the end or beginning of the clip.
- **Single frame rewind/Advance.** Press the multi selector down key to pause the clip, then use the left/right buttons to rewind or advance one frame at a time.
- **Change volume.** Press the Zoom button and press the up/down buttons to increase/decrease volume.
- **Trim movie.** Press the OK button to edit the movie (as described next).
- **Exit playback.** Press the multi selector up button to exit playback.
- **View menus.** Press the Menu button to interrupt playback to access menus.

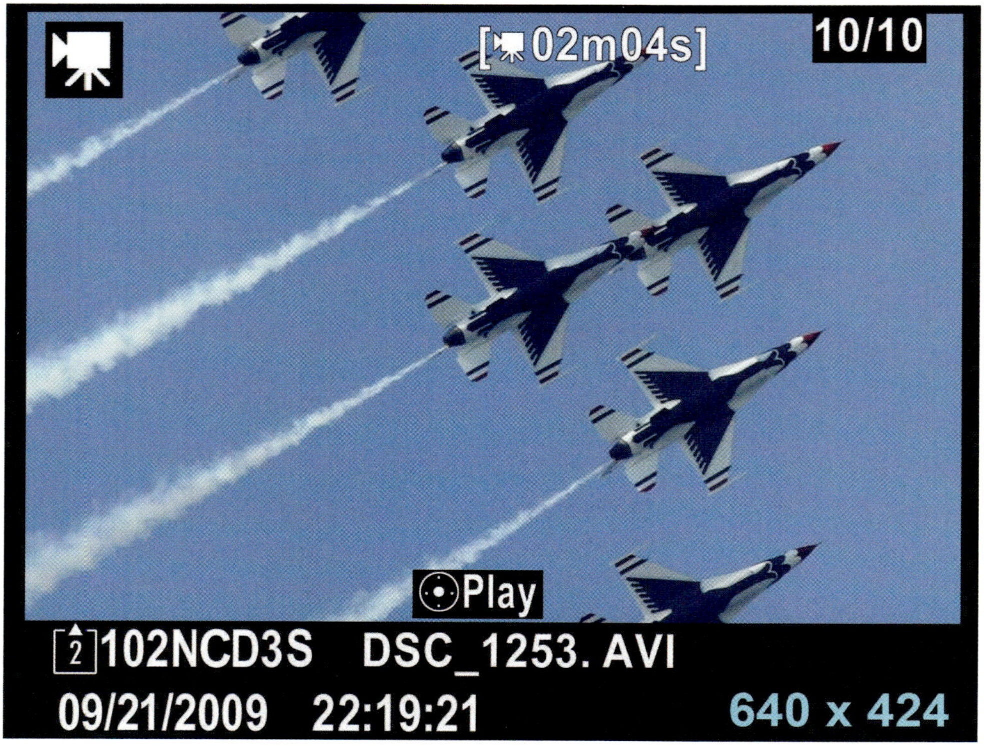


**Figure 8.12**
Movies are indicated by a movie camera icon during picture review.

## Editing Your Movies

In-camera editing is limited to trimming the beginning or end from a clip, and the clip must be at least two seconds long. For more advanced editing, you'll need an application capable of editing AVI movie clips. (Google "AVI Editor" to locate any of the hundreds of free video editors available, or use a commercial product like Corel Video Studio, Adobe Premiere Elements, or Pinnacle Studio.) These will let you combine several clips into one movie, add titles, special effects, and transitions between scenes.

To do in-camera editing/trimming, follow these steps:

1. **Activate edit.** While viewing a movie clip, press the OK button twice. The Edit movie prompt will appear. (See Figure 8.13.)
2. **Select start/end point.** Press the right multi selector button and highlight either Choose start point or Choose end point, and press OK.
3. **Resume playback.** Press the center button of the multi selector to start or resume playback. You can use the pause, rewind, advance, and single frame controls described previously to move around within your clip.
4. **Mark trim point.** When you reach the point where you want to trim, press the Pause button (if the movie is not already paused), and then press the multi selector up button. All frames prior to the pause will be deleted if you're in choose start point

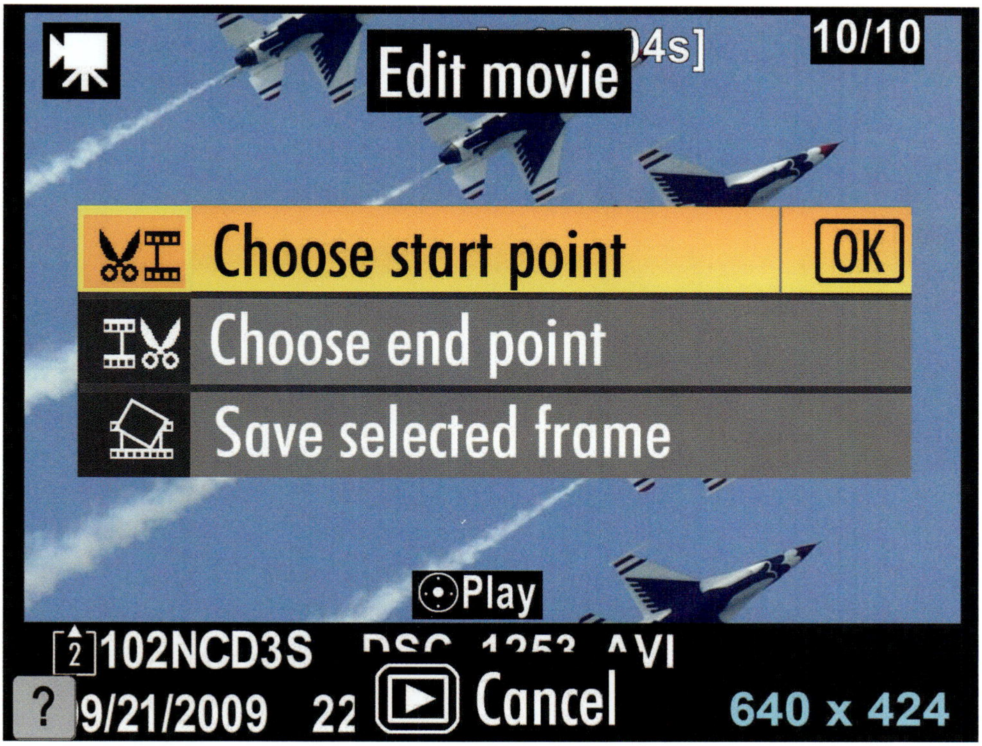


**Figure 8.13**
Choose editing options from this menu.

mode; all frames *after* the pause will be deleted if you're in choose end point mode. Your trimmed movie must be at least two seconds long.

5. **Confirm trim.** A Proceed? prompt appears. Choose Yes or No, and press OK.
6. **Save movie.** You'll see a message Saving movie and a green progress bar as the D3s stores the trimmed clip to your memory card. Storage takes some time, and you don't want to interrupt it to avoid losing your saved clip. So, make sure your D3s has a fully charged battery before you start to edit a clip.

## Saving a Frame

You can store any frame from one of your movies as a JPEG still, using the resolution of the video format (1280 × 720, 640 × 424, or 320 × 212 pixels). Just follow these steps:

1. Pause your movie at the frame you want to save. Press OK twice to access the Edit movie screen.
2. Choose Save selected frame and press OK.
3. Choose Proceed to confirm.
4. Your frame will be stored on the memory card, and will be marked with a scissors icon.

# Continuous Shooting

The Nikon D3s/D3x's pair of continuous shooting modes remind me how far digital photography has brought us. The first accessory I purchased when I worked as a sports photographer some years ago was a motor drive for my film SLR. It enabled me to snap off a series of shots in rapid succession, which came in very handy when a fullback broke through the line and headed for the end zone. Even a seasoned action photographer can miss the decisive instant when a crucial block is made, or a baseball superstar's bat shatters and pieces of cork fly out. Continuous shooting simplifies taking a series of pictures, either to ensure that one has more or less the exact moment you want to capture or to capture a sequence that is interesting as a collection of successive images.

The D3s/D3x's "motor drive" capabilities are, in many ways, much superior to what you get with a film camera. For one thing, a motor-driven film camera can eat up film at an incredible pace, which is why many of them are used with cassettes that hold hundreds of feet of film stock. At three frames per second (typical of film cameras), a short burst of a few seconds can burn up as much as half of an ordinary 36 exposure roll of film. Digital cameras, in contrast, have reusable "film," so if you waste a few dozen shots on non-decisive moments, you can erase them and shoot more.

The increased capacity of digital film cards gives you a prodigious number of frames to work with. At a baseball game I covered earlier this year, I took more than 1,000 images in a couple hours. Yet, even shooting RAW+JPEG Fine I could fit more than 200 images on a single 4GB Compact Flash card. If I'd switched to JPEG, I could have taken about 900 different images without switching cards. Even at the top speed of 9 frames per second that the D3s is capable of, that's a lot of shooting. Given an average burst of about eight frames per sequence (nobody really takes 15-20 shots or more of one play in a baseball game), I was able to capture 32 different sequences before I needed to swap cards. Even simple plays, like a lay-up on the basketball court, seemed more exciting when captured in a sequence of shots, as in Figure 8.14.

To use the D3s/D3x's continuous shooting modes, hold down the release mode dial's unlock button and rotate the dial until either $C_L$ or $C_H$ appear. When you partially depress the shutter button, the viewfinder will display at the right side a number representing the maximum number of shots you can take at the current quality settings. The extra large buffer in the D3s and more moderately sized internal memory of the D3x will generally allow you to take as many as 75 JPEG shots in a single burst, or 17 RAW photos.

To increase this number, reduce the image-quality setting by switching to JPEG only (from JPEG+RAW), to a lower JPEG quality setting, or by reducing the D3s/D3x's resolution from L to M or S. The reason the size of your bursts is limited is that continuous images are first shuttled into the D3s/D3x's internal memory buffer, then doled out to the Compact Flash card as quickly as they can be written to the card. Technically, the

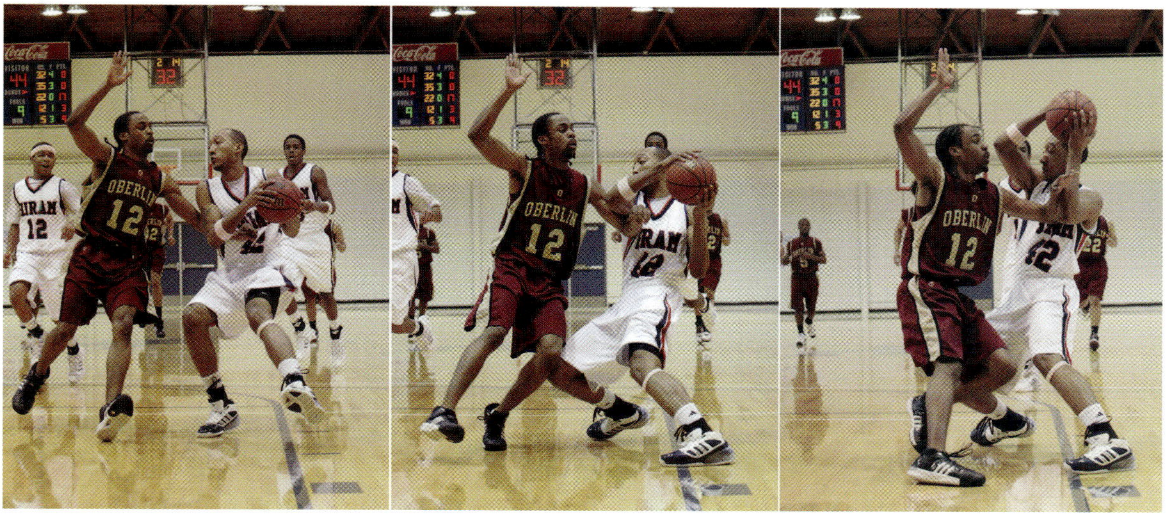


**Figure 8.14** Continuous shooting allows you to capture an entire sequence of exciting moments as they unfold.

D3s/D3x takes the RAW data received from the digital image processor and converts it to the output format you've selected—either .jpg or .nef (RAW)—and deposits it in the buffer ready to store on the card.

This internal "smart" buffer can suck up photos much more quickly than the CF card and, indeed, some memory cards are significantly faster or slower than others. When the buffer fills, you can't take any more continuous shots until the D3s/D3x has written some of them to the card, making more room in the buffer. (You should keep in mind that faster CF cards write images more quickly, freeing up buffer space faster.)

The frame rate you select will depend on the kind of shooting you want to do. Here are some guidelines:

- **7-9 fps.** The max rate of 9 fps is available when using continuous high speed mode on the D3s. Use this for sports and other subjects where you want to optimize your chances of capturing the decisive moment. Perhaps you're shooting some active kids and want to grab their most appealing expressions. This fast frame rate can improve the odds. However, there is no guarantee that even at 9 fps the crucial instant won't occur *between* frames. (A ball pitched at 90 miles per hour travels about 16 feet between each frame when you're shooting at 9 fps.) For example, when shooting major league baseball games, if I want to shoot a batter, I keep both eyes open, and keep one of them on the pitcher. Then, I start taking my sequence just as the pitcher releases the ball. My goal is to capture the batter making contact with the ball. But even at 9 fps, I find that a hitter connects between frames. I usually must take pictures of a couple dozen at-bats to get a shot of bat and ball connecting.

- **4.0-6.0 fps.** When using continuous low speed mode, you can choose the frame rate from 1 to 7 fps. A slower rate can be useful for activities that aren't quite so fast moving. But, there's another benefit. Using the fastest frame rate means that your camera may fill up its buffer and won't be ready for the next sequence. If you don't want to miss any sequences, using a slightly slower frame rate can help prevent buffer overload.
- **1.0-3.0 fps.** You can set continuous low speed mode to use a relatively pokey frame rate, too. Use these rates when you just want to be able to take pictures quickly, and aren't interested in filling up your memory card with mostly duplicated images. At 1 fps you can hold down the shutter release and fire away, or ease up when you want to pause. At higher frame rates, by the time you've decided to stop shooting, you may have taken an extra three or four shots that you really don't want. Slow frame rates are good for bracketing, too. Set the D3s/D3x to take a three-frame bracket burst, and you can take all three with one press of the shutter release. You'll find that slower frame rates also come in handy for subjects that are moving around in interesting ways (photographic models come to mind) but don't change their looks or poses quickly enough to merit a 9 fps burst.

## A Tiny Slice of Time

Exposures that seem impossibly brief can reveal a world we didn't know existed. In the 1930s, Dr. Harold Edgerton, a professor of electrical engineering at MIT, pioneered high-speed photography using a repeating electronic flash unit he patented called the *stroboscope.* As the inventor of the electronic flash, he popularized its use to freeze objects in motion, and you've probably seen his photographs of bullets piercing balloons and drops of milk forming a coronet-shaped splash.

Electronic flash freezes action by virtue of its extremely short duration—as brief as 1/50,000th second or less. An external flash, such as one of the Nikon Speedlights, offers such versatility. You can read more about using electronic flash to stop action in Chapter 10.

Of course, the D3s/D3x is fully capable of immobilizing all but the fastest movement using only its shutter speeds, which range all the way up to 1/8,000th second. Indeed, you'll rarely have need for such a brief shutter speed in ordinary shooting. If you wanted to use an aperture of f/1.8 at ISO 200 outdoors in bright sunlight, for some reason, a shutter speed of 1/8,000th second would more than do the job. You'd need a faster shutter speed only if you moved the ISO setting to a higher sensitivity (but why would you do that?). Under less than full sunlight, 1/8,000th second is more than fast enough for any conditions you're likely to encounter.

Most sports action can be frozen at 1/2,000th second or slower, and for many sports a slower shutter speed is actually preferable—for example, to allow the wheels of a racing automobile or motorcycle, or the propeller on a classic aircraft to blur realistically. Figure 8.15 is another example. The 1/500th second shutter speed effectively stopped the soccer players in mid-stride but allowed the fastest moving things, such as the players' feet, to blur slightly. The blur tells us that this shot is a true action picture.

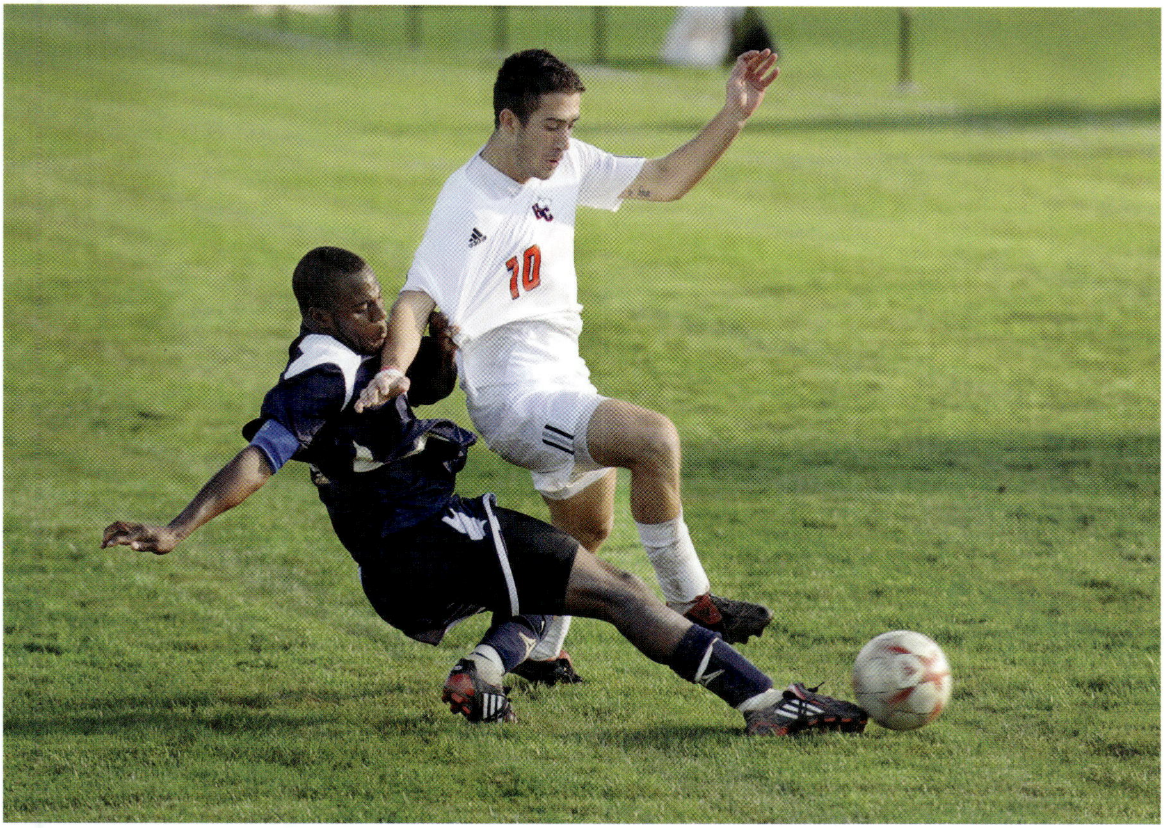

**Figure 8.15** A little blur can be a good thing, as the blurry feet and hands of the players add excitement to this action shot.

But if you want to do some exotic action-freezing photography without resorting to electronic flash, the D3s/D3x's top shutter speed is at your disposal. Here are some things to think about when exploring this type of high-speed photography:

- **You'll need a lot of light.** High shutter speeds cut very fine slices of time and sharply reduce the amount of illumination that reaches your sensor. To use 1/8,000th second at an aperture of f/6.3, you'd need an ISO setting of 1600—even in full daylight. To use an f/stop smaller than f/6.3 or an ISO setting lower than 1600, you'd need *more* light than full daylight provides. (That's why electronic flash units work so well for high-speed photography when used as the sole illumination; they provide both the effect of a brief shutter speed and the high levels of illumination needed.)

- **Forget about reciprocity failure.** If you're an old-time film shooter, you might recall that very brief shutter speeds (as well as very high light levels and very *long* exposures) produced an effect called *reciprocity failure,* in which given exposures ended up providing less than the calculated value because of the way film responded to very short, very intense, or very long exposures of light. Solid-state sensors don't suffer from this defect, so you don't need to make an adjustment when using high shutter speeds (or brief flash bursts).
- **No elongation effect.** This is another old bugaboo that has largely been solved through modern technology, but I wanted to bring it to your attention anyway. In olden times, cameras used shutters that traveled horizontally. To achieve faster shutter speeds, focal plane shutters (located just in front of the plane of the sensor) open only a smaller-than-frame-sized slit so that, even though the shutter is already traveling at its highest rate of speed, the film/sensor is exposed for a briefer period of time as the slit moves across the surface. At very short shutter speeds, and with subjects moving horizontally at very fast velocities, it was possible for the subject to partially "keep up" with the shutter if it were traveling in the same direction as the slit, producing an elongated or slanted effect. Conversely, subjects moving in the opposite direction of shutter motion could be compressed. Today, shutters like those in the D3s/D3x move vertically and at a higher maximum rate of speed. So, unless you're photographing a rocket blasting into space, and holding the camera horizontally to boot (or shooting a racing car in vertical orientation), it's almost impossible to produce unwanted elongation/compression.
- **High shutter speeds with electronic flash.** You might be tempted to use an electronic flash with a high shutter speed. Perhaps you want to stop some action in daylight with a brief shutter speed and use electronic flash only as supplemental illumination to fill in the shadows. Unfortunately, under most conditions you can't use flash in subdued illumination with your D3s/D3x at any shutter speed faster than 1/250th second. That's the fastest speed at which the camera's focal plane shutter is fully open: at shorter speeds, the "slit" described above comes into play, so that the flash will expose only the small portion of the sensor exposed by the slit during its duration. (Check out "High-Speed Sync" in Chapter 10 if you want to see how you *can* use shutter speeds shorter than 1/250th second, albeit at much-reduced effective power levels.)

## Working with Short Exposures

You can have a lot of fun exploring the kinds of pictures you can take using very brief exposure times, whether you decide to take advantage of the action-stopping capabilities of your built-in or external electronic flash or work with the Nikon D3s/D3x's faster shutter speeds. Here are a few ideas to get you started:

- **Take revealing images.** Fast shutter speeds can help you reveal the real subject behind the façade, by freezing constant motion to capture an enlightening moment in time. Legendary fashion/portrait photographer Philippe Halsman used leaping photos of famous people, such as the Duke and Duchess of Windsor, Richard Nixon, and Salvador Dali to illuminate their real selves. Halsman said, "*When you ask a person to jump, his attention is mostly directed toward the act of jumping and the mask falls so that the real person appears.*" Try some high-speed portraits of people you know in motion to see how they appear when concentrating on something other than the portrait.
- **Create unreal images.** High-speed photography can also produce photographs that show your subjects in ways that are quite unreal. A helicopter in mid-air with its rotors frozen or a motocross cyclist leaping over a ramp, but with all motion stopped so that the rider and machine look as if they were frozen in mid-air, make for an unusual picture. When we're accustomed to seeing subjects in motion, seeing them stopped in time can verge on the surreal.
- **Capture unseen perspectives.** Some things are *never* seen in real life, except when viewed in a stop-action photograph. Edgerton's balloon bursts were only a starting point. Freeze a hummingbird in flight for a view of wings that never seem to stop. Or, capture the splashes as liquid falls into a bowl, as shown in Figure 8.16. No electronic flash was required for this image (and wouldn't have illuminated the water in the bowl as evenly). Instead, a clutch of high-intensity lamps and an ISO setting of 1600 allowed the D3s/D3x to capture this image at 1/2,000th second.

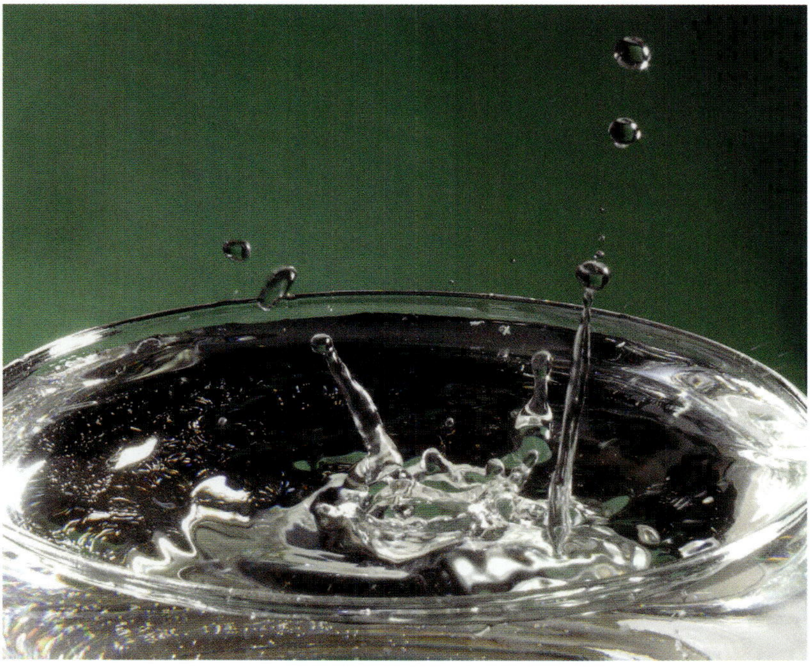

**Figure 8.16**
A large amount of artificial illumination and an ISO 1600 sensitivity setting allowed capturing this shot at 1/2,000th second without use of an electronic flash.

- **Vanquish camera shake and gain new angles.** Here's an idea that's so obvious it isn't always explored to its fullest extent. A high enough shutter speed can free you from the tyranny of a tripod, making it easier to capture new angles, or to shoot quickly while moving around, especially with longer lenses. I tend to use a monopod or tripod for almost everything when I'm not using an image-stabilized lens, and I end up missing some shots because of a reluctance to adjust my camera support to get a higher, lower, or different angle. If you have enough light and can use an f/stop wide enough to permit a high shutter speed, you'll find a new freedom to choose your shots (see Figure 8.17). I have a favored 170mm-500mm lens that I use for sports and wildlife photography, almost invariably with a tripod, as I don't find the "reciprocal of the focal length" rule particularly helpful in most cases. I would *not* hand-hold this hefty lens at its 500mm setting with a 1/500th second shutter speed under most circumstances. Nor, if you want to account for the crop factor, would I use 1/750th second. However, at 1/2,000th second or faster, it's entirely possible for a steady hand to use this lens without a tripod or monopod's extra support, and I've found that my whole approach to shooting animals and other elusive subjects changes in high-speed mode. Selective focus allows dramatically isolating my prey wide open at f/6.3, too.

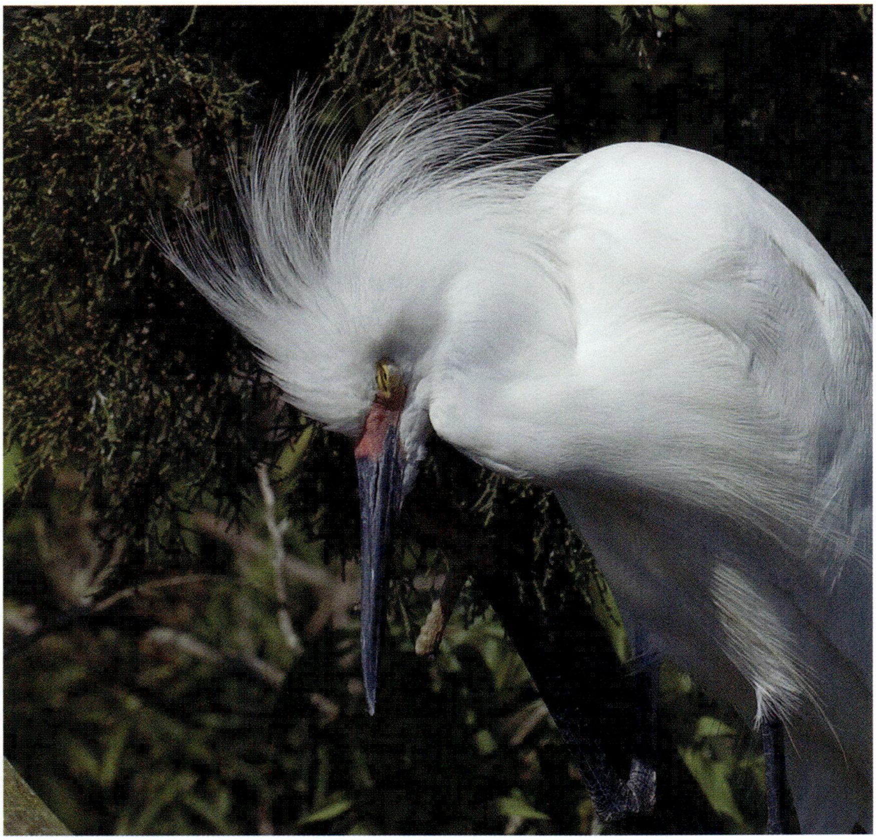

**Figure 8.17**
Outdoors, you may need a shutter speed of 1/2,000th second to hand-hold a 500mm lens to capture distant wildlife.

# Long Exposures

Longer exposures are a doorway into another world, showing us how even familiar scenes can look much different when photographed over periods measured in seconds. At night, long exposures produce streaks of light from moving, illuminated subjects like automobiles or amusement park rides. Extra-long exposures of seemingly pitch-dark subjects can reveal interesting views using light levels barely bright enough to see by. At any time of day, including daytime (in which case you'll often need the help of neutral-density filters to make the long exposure practical), long exposures can cause moving objects to vanish entirely, because they don't remain stationary long enough to register in a photograph.

## Three Ways to Take Long Exposures

There are actually three common types of lengthy exposures: *timed exposures, bulb exposures,* and *time exposures.* The D3s/D3x offers only the first two, but once you understand all three, you'll see why Nikon made the choices it did. Because of the length of the exposure, all of the following techniques should be used with a tripod to hold the camera steady.

- **Timed exposures.** These are long exposures from 1 second to 30 seconds, measured by the camera itself. To take a picture in this range, simply use manual or S modes and use the main command dial to set the shutter speed to the length of time you want, choosing from preset speeds of 1.0, 1.5, 2.0, 3.0, 4.0, 6.0, 8.0, 10.0, 15.0, 20.0, or 30.0 seconds (if you've specified 1/2 stop increments for exposure adjustments), or 1.0, 1.3, 1.6, 2.0, 2.5, 3.2, 4.0, 5.0, 6.0, 8.0, 10.0, 13.0, 15.0, 20.0, 25.0, and 30.0 seconds (if you're using 1/3 stop increments). The advantage of timed exposures is that the camera does all the calculating for you. There's no need for a stopwatch. If you review your image on the LCD and decide to try again with the exposure doubled or halved, you can dial in the correct exposure with precision. The disadvantage of timed exposures is that you can't take a photo for longer than 30 seconds.
- **Bulb exposures.** This type of exposure is so-called because in the olden days the photographer squeezed and held an air bulb attached to a tube that provided the force necessary to keep the shutter open. Traditionally, a bulb exposure is one that lasts as long as the shutter release button is pressed; when you release the button, the exposure ends. To make a bulb exposure with the D3s/D3x, set the camera on manual mode and use the main command dial to select the shutter speed immediately after 30 seconds—buLB. Then, press the shutter to start the exposure, and press it again to close the shutter. If you'd like to simulate a time exposure (described below), you can use the Nikon MC-30 remote control cable (about $60), MC-36 remote shutter release ($130), or ML-3 wireless remote control that attach to the 10-pin terminal on the left side of the camera under the rubber cover.

- **Time exposures.** This is a setting found on some cameras to produce longer exposures. With cameras that implement this option, the shutter opens when you press the shutter release button, and remains open until you press the button again. With the Nikon D3s/D3x, you can produce this effect with a locking cable release, like the Nikon MC-30 and other remote releases just mentioned. You can press the shutter release button, go off for a few minutes, and come back to close the shutter (assuming your camera is still there). The disadvantages of this mode are exposures must be timed manually, and with shorter exposures it's possible for the vibration of manually opening and closing the shutter to register in the photo. For longer exposures, the period of vibration is relatively brief and not usually a problem.

## Working with Long Exposures

Because the D3s/D3x produces such good images at longer exposures, and there are so many creative things you can do with long-exposure techniques, you'll want to do some experimenting. Get yourself a tripod or another firm support and take some test shots with long exposure noise reduction both enabled and disabled (to see whether you prefer low noise or high detail) and get started. Here are some things to try:

- **Make people invisible.** One very cool thing about long exposures is that objects that move rapidly enough won't register at all in a photograph, while the subjects that remain stationary are portrayed in the normal way. That makes it easy to produce people-free landscape photos and architectural photos at night or, even, in full daylight if you use a neutral-density filter (or two) (or three) to allow an exposure of at least a few seconds. At ISO 100 (actually LO 1.0 on the D3s), f/22, and with a pair of 8X (three-stop) neutral-density filters, you can use exposures of nearly two seconds; overcast days and/or even more neutral-density filtration would work even better if daylight people-vanishing is your goal. They'll have to be walking *very* briskly and across the field of view (rather than directly toward the camera) for this to work. At night, it's much easier to achieve this effect with the 20- to 30-second exposures that are possible, as you can see in Figure 8.18.
- **Create streaks.** If you aren't shooting for total invisibility, long exposures with the camera on a tripod can produce some interesting streaky effects. Even a single 8X ND filter will let you shoot at f/22 and 1/6th second in daylight.
- **Produce light trails.** At night, car headlights and taillights and other moving sources of illumination can generate interesting light trails, as shown in Figure 8.19. Your camera doesn't even need to be mounted on a tripod; hand-holding the D3s/D3x for longer exposures adds movement and patterns to your streaky trails. If you're shooting fireworks, a longer exposure may allow you to combine several bursts into one picture.

- **Blur waterfalls, etc.** You'll find that waterfalls and other sources of moving liquid produce a special type of long exposure blur, because the water merges into a fantasy-like veil that looks different at different exposure times, and with different waterfalls. Cascades with turbulent flow produce a rougher look at a given longer exposure than falls that flow smoothly. Although blurred waterfalls have become almost a cliché, there are still plenty of variations for a creative photographer to explore.
- **Show total darkness in new ways.** Even on the darkest, moonless nights, there is enough starlight or glow from distant illumination sources to see by, and, if you use a long exposure, there is enough light to take a picture, too. I was visiting a lakeside park about an hour after sunset and the sky was almost pitch black, with only a faint glow at the horizon. Yet, with a 20-second exposure the scene appears as if sunset were only minutes past, as you can see in Figure 8.20.

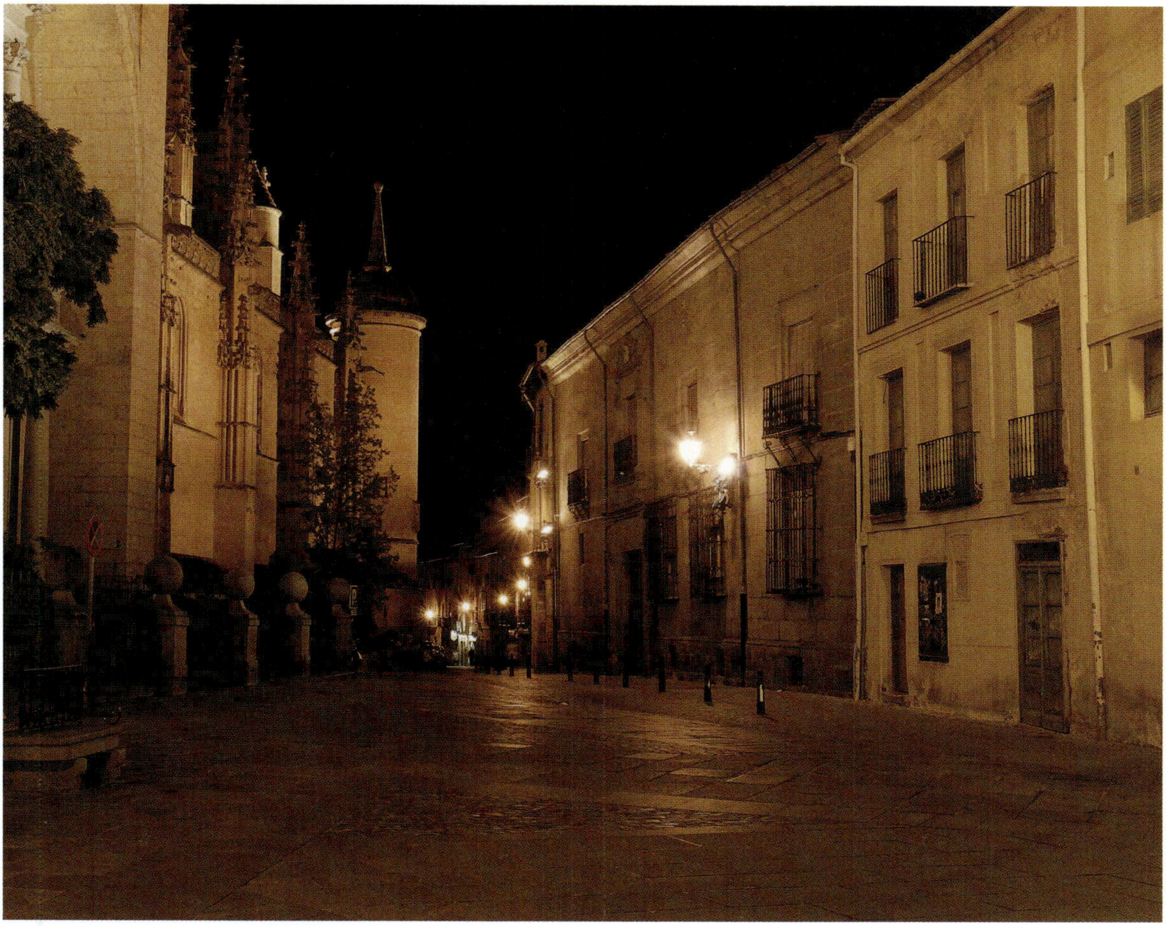

**Figure 8.18** This European alleyway is thronged with people, but with the camera on a tripod, a 30-second exposure rendered the passersby almost invisible.

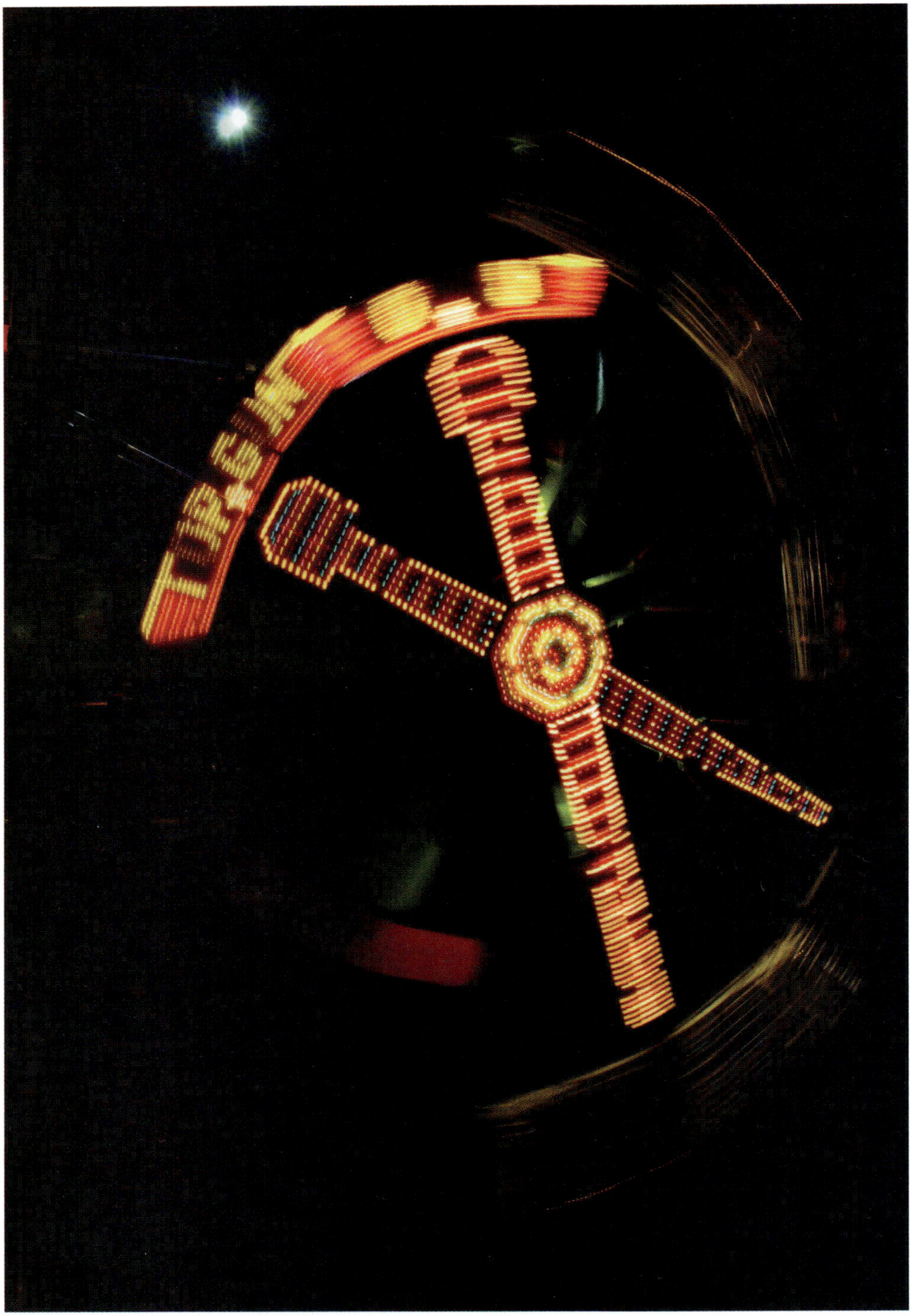

**Figure 8.19**
Long exposures can transform the most mundane nighttime subjects, such as this amusement park ride, into an interesting light-trails display.

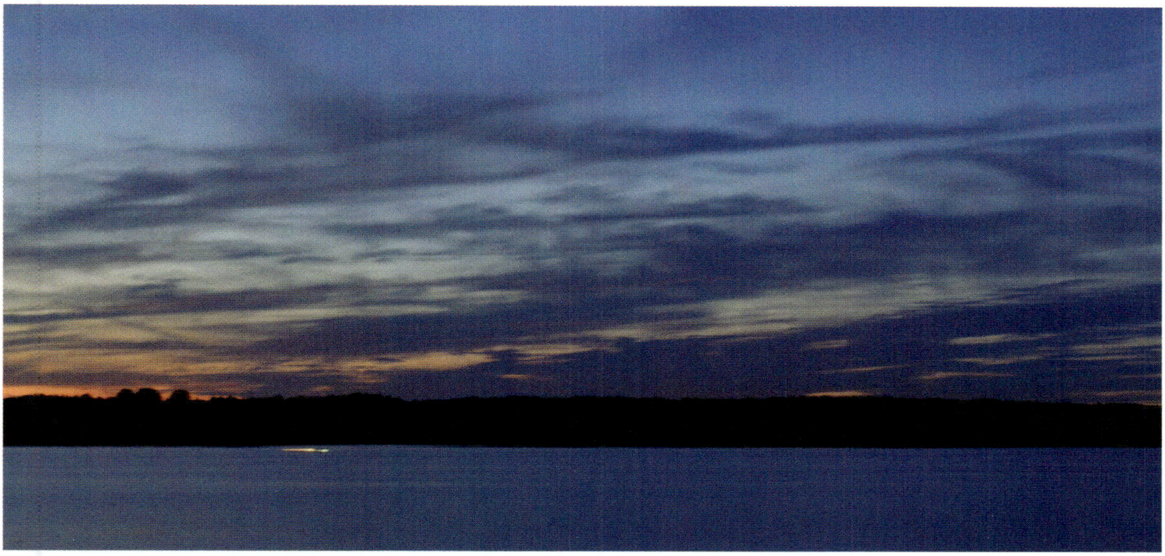

**Figure 8.20** A 20-second exposure on a dark night revealed this lakeside setting, illuminated only by starlight and a waning sunset that had taken place more than an hour ago.

# Delayed Exposures

Sometimes it's desirable to have a delay of some sort before a picture is actually taken. Perhaps you'd like to get in the picture yourself, and would appreciate it if the camera waited 10 seconds after you press the shutter release to actually take the picture. Maybe you want to give a tripod-mounted camera time to settle down and damp any residual vibration after the release is pressed to improve sharpness for an exposure with a relatively slow shutter speed. It's possible you want to explore the world of time-lapse photography. The next sections present your delayed exposure options.

## Self-Timer

The D3s/D3x has a built-in self-timer with a user-selectable delay. Activate the timer by rotating the release mode dial to the self-timer icon. Press the shutter release button halfway to lock in focus on your subjects (if you're taking a self-portrait, focus on an object at a similar distance and use focus lock). When you're ready to take the photo, continue pressing the shutter release the rest of the way. The lamp on the front of the camera will blink slowly for eight seconds (when using the 10-second timer) and the beeper will chirp (if you haven't disabled it in the Shooting menu, as described in Chapter 3). During the final two seconds, the beeper sounds more rapidly and the lamp remains on until the picture is taken. The top-panel LCD displays a countdown while all this is going on.

Another way to use the self-timer is with the Mup (mirror lockup) setting. This is something you might want to do if you're shooting close-ups, landscapes, or other types of pictures using the self-timer only to trip the shutter in the most vibration-free way possible. Forget to bring along your tripod, but still want to take a close-up picture with a precise focus setting? That happened to me when I encountered this colorful plant (see Figure 8.21) in a greenhouse when picking up some potted plants. I wheeled a planting cart over to the blossom, rested the D3s/D3x on a soft bag of potting soil (a beanbag would have been better!), carefully focused, and let the self-timer trip the shutter at the appropriate moment. In such situations, the camera might teeter back and forth for a second or two, but it will settle back to its original position before the self-timer activates the shutter. The self-timer remains the active mode until you turn it off—even if you power down the D3s/D3x—so remember to turn the release mode dial back to single frame mode when you're finished.

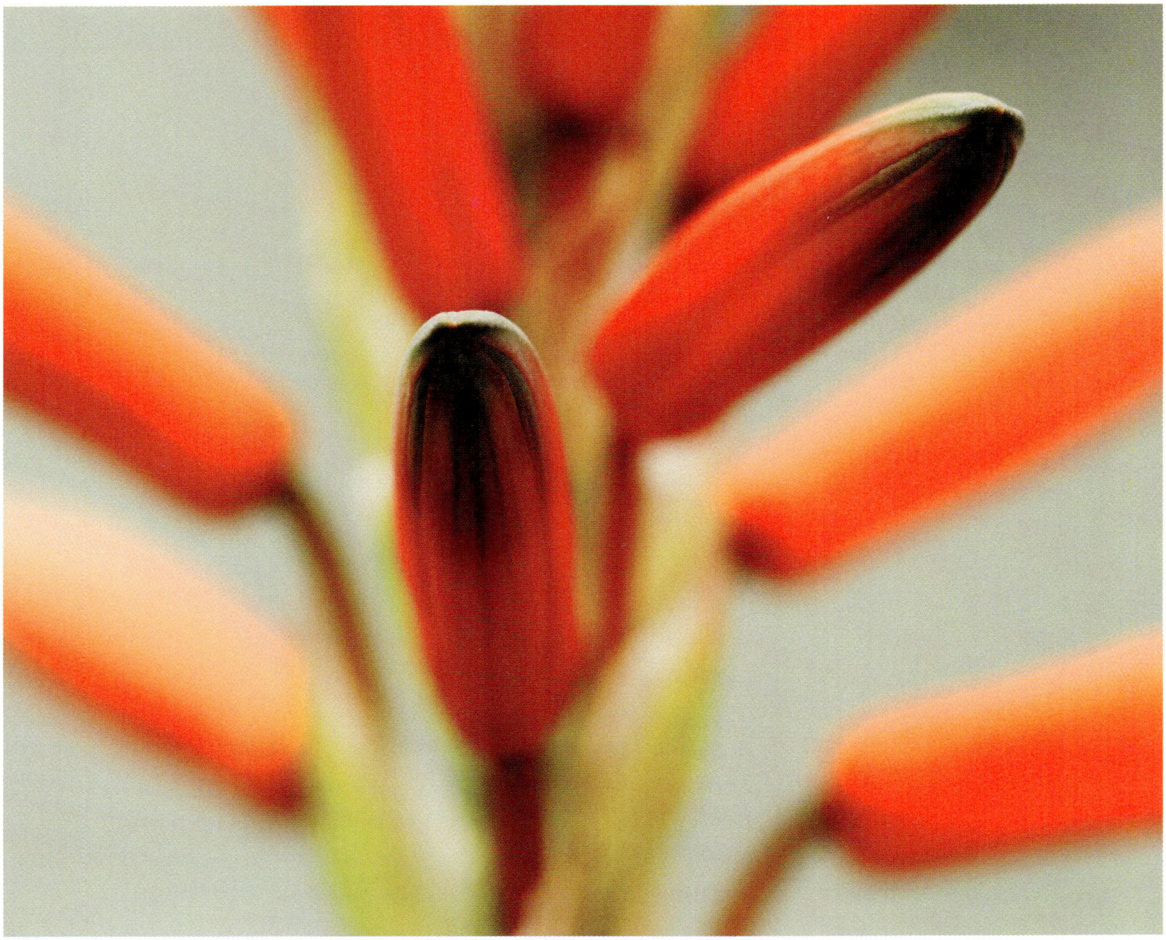

**Figure 8.21** With the camera resting on a bag of potting soil on a cart, the self-timer triggered this vibration-free image of a bud about to open.

## Remote Control

If you're not using the Interval timer as described next, your Nikon D3s/D3x can also be triggered using a plug-in remote control with an electronic or infrared connection. For example, Nikon MC-36 is a remote switch with a 2.6-foot cord (you can add a 33-foot extension cable) and includes a flexible self-timer that can be set to trip the camera after a delay of anywhere from 1 second to 99 hours, 59 minutes, and 59 seconds (in other words, one second less than 100 hours). It can be used for interval shooting (time-lapse photography) for up to 999 shots with up to 99 hours, 99 minutes, and 99 seconds between shots. (I'll describe applications for time-lapse photography in the next section.)

The ML-3 is a two-channel infrared remote for operating Nikon film and digital cameras that have a 10-pin terminal like the one found on the front of the D3s/D3x. Its features include automatic triggering, a three-second shutter release, and either single frame or continuous shooting modes that can be selected from the remote position.

Your final remote control option is the coolest of all: the WT-4a wireless transmitter. This is the gadget for wireless remote control operation with Nikon Camera Control Pro 2 software, which I'll describe in Chapter 10. It allows communications from your camera to your computer (to transmit photos to, say, a laptop as they are taken) or to let your computer have near-total control over your D3s/D3x's operation from a remote location. In photo-transmit mode, wedding and event photographers can get a lot of use out of this accessory, and studio photographers can benefit from it, too. Not only can you back up all your photos to a laptop or desktop computer as they are taken, you or an assistant can be viewing, editing, and displaying them virtually simultaneously to clients, art directors, or anyone else. When used to control the camera remotely with Camera Control Pro, the WT-4a is useful for photographing easily spooked wildlife, while the photographer remains hidden with a laptop.

## Time-Lapse/Interval Photography

Who hasn't marveled at a time-lapse photograph of a flower opening, a series of shots of the moon marching across the sky, or one of those extreme time-lapse picture sets showing something that takes a very, very long time, such as a building under construction.

You probably won't be shooting such construction shots, unless you have a spare D3s/D3x you don't need for a few months (or are willing to go through the rigmarole of figuring out how to set up your camera in precisely the same position using the same lens settings to shoot a series of pictures at intervals). However, other kinds of time-lapse photography are entirely within reach.

The D3s/D3x can take time-lapse/interval photographs all by itself, using the Interval timer shooting entry found in the Shooting menu. If you're willing to tether the camera to a computer (a laptop will do) using the USB cable, you can take time-lapse photos using the optional Nikon Camera Control Pro.

If you want freedom to shoot anywhere, the Nikon MC-36 is an affordable add-on (around $135) with much more than the self-timer and remote control features mentioned previously. In fact, it has many different modes with an interesting array of delay/interval combinations. For example, you can set the self-timer for a specific period of time, then take a specified number of exposures at one-second intervals. Or, you can set a delay period that must elapse before the D3s/D3x begins a long exposure. Finally, you can choose to shoot a set number of pictures at intervals from 1 second to 99 hours, 59 minutes, and 59 seconds.

Here is a recap of essential tips for effective time-lapse photography:

- **Use AC power.** If you're shooting a long sequence, consider connecting your camera to an AC adapter, as leaving the D3s/D3x on for long periods of time will rapidly deplete the battery.
- **Make sure you have enough storage space.** Unless your memory card has enough capacity to hold all the images you'll be taking, you might want to change to a higher compression rate or reduced resolution to maximize the image count.
- **Make a movie.** While time-lapse stills are interesting, you can increase your fun factor by compiling all your shots into a motion picture using your favorite desktop movie-making software.
- **Protect your camera.** If your camera will be set up for an extended period of time (longer than an hour or two), make sure it's protected from weather, earthquakes, animals, young children, innocent bystanders, and theft.
- **Vary intervals.** Experiment with different time intervals. You don't want to take pictures too often or less often than necessary to capture the changes you hope to image.

## Geotagging with the Nikon GP-1

The Nikon D3s/D3x gained a lot of credibility as a tool for serious photographers when Nikon introduced the compact Nikon GP-1 Global Positioning System device. The unit makes it easy to tag your images with the same kind of longitude, latitude, altitude, and time stamp information that is supplied by the GPS unit you use in your car. (Don't have a GPS? Photographers who get lost in the boonies as easily as I do *must* have one of these!) The geotagging information is stored in the metadata space within your image files, and can be accessed by Nikon View NX, or by online photo services such as mypicturetown.com and Flickr. Having this information available makes it easier to track where your pictures are taken. That can be essential, as I learned from a trip out West this Spring, where I found the red rocks, canyons, and arroyos of Nevada, Utah, Arizona, and Colorado all pretty much look alike to my untrained eye.

Like all GPS units, the Nikon GP-1 obtains its data by triangulating signals from satellites orbiting the Earth. It works with the Nikon D3s/D3x, as well as other Nikon cameras, such as the D90, D200, original D300, D3s/D3x, D3, and D700. It also works with the older Nikon D2x/D2xs and D2H/D2Hs. At about $225, it's not cheap, but those who need geotagging—especially for professional mapping or location applications—will find it to be a bargain.

The GP-1 (see Figure 8.22) slips onto the accessory shoe on top of the Nikon D3s/D3x. It connects to the GPS port on the camera using the Nikon GP1-CA10 cable, which plugs the 10-pin port on the front of the D200/D300/D3s/D3x/D3/D700.

A third connector connects the GP-1 to your computer using a USB cable. As I was writing this book, Nikon released a utility for Windows and Mac operating systems that allows you to read GPS data from the GP-1 directly in your computer—no camera required. I tried the new driver, and discovered that the GP-1 couldn't "see" any satellites from inside my office. I plan on trying it with my netbook outdoors, in a car, or in some other more satellite-accessible location. Once attached, the device is very easy

**Figure 8.22**
Nikon GP-1 geotagging unit.

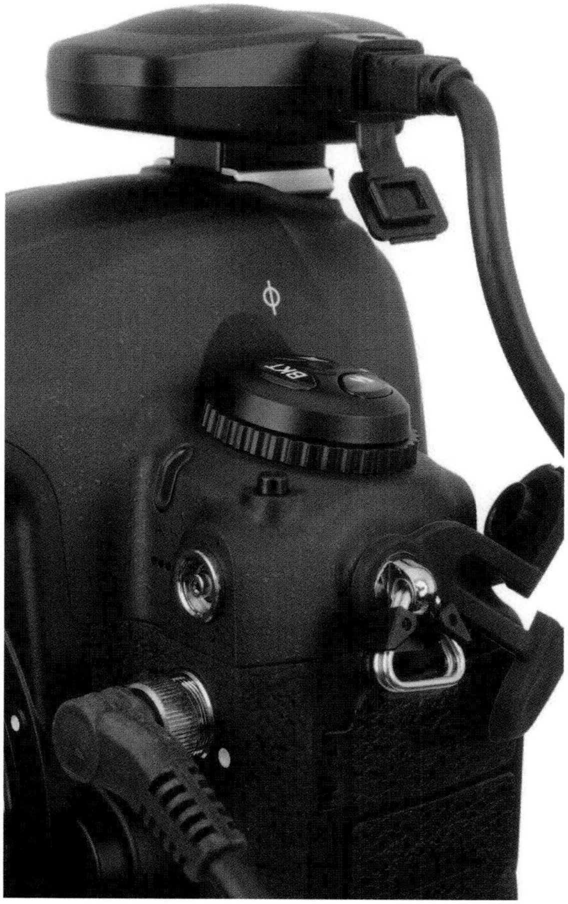

to use. You need to activate the Nikon D3s/D3x's GPS capabilities in the GPS choice within the Setup menu, as described in Chapter 5.

The first step is to allow the GP-1 to acquire signals from at least three satellites. If you've used a GPS in your car, you'll know that satellite acquisition works best outdoors under a clear sky and out of the "shadow" of tall buildings, and the Nikon unit is no exception. It takes about 40-60 seconds for the GP-1 to "connect." A red blinking LED means that GPS data is not being recorded; a green blinking LED signifies that the unit has acquired three satellites and is recording data. When the LED is solid green, the unit has connected to four or more satellites, and is recording data with optimum accuracy.

Next, set up the camera by selecting the GPS option found under the Setup menu on the Nikon D3s/D3x. Then, select Auto meter off to disable automatic shutoff of the D3s/D3x's exposure meters. That will assure that the camera doesn't go to sleep while you're using the GPS unit. Of course, in this mode the camera will use more power (the meters never go off, and the GPS draws power constantly), but you don't want to go through the 40-60-second satellite acquisition step each time you take a picture. Next, use the Position option in the GPS menu to activate the unit.

You're all set. Once the unit is up and running, you can view GPS information using photo information screens available on the color LCD (and described in Chapter 2). The GPS screen, which appears only when a photo has been taken using the GPS unit, looks something like Figure 8.23.

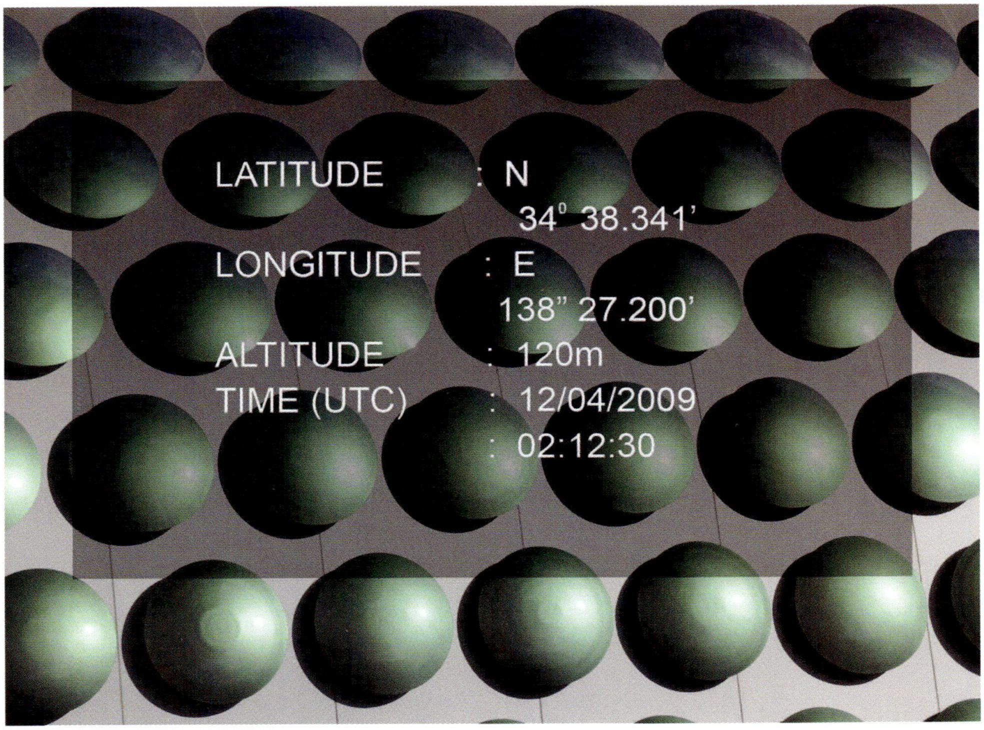


**Figure 8.23**
Captured GPS information can be displayed when you review the image.

# Recommended Customized Settings

I'm going to finish off this chapter with some tables listing recommended settings for your Shooting and Custom Setting banks. I outlined how to set the four Shooting menu banks, A, B, C, and D in Chapter 3, and showed you how to assign each of them a suitable name so you could more easily remember the shooting situations the customized settings were tailored for. In Chapter 4, I explained the four Custom Setting banks (also named A, B, C, and D by default), and some of the ways you could set up groups of settings for different kinds of picture-taking opportunities.

Because those two chapters had already ballooned to nearly 100 pages, it didn't really make sense to try to cram in some recommended settings there, as that level of detail would tend to confound those who were simply trying to get their cameras set up properly. So, I've deposited my recommended "starter" settings in this chapter, which has become something of a catch-all, anyway.

All the recommendations in this chapter are for the Nikon D3s. Virtually all of them apply to the Nikon D3x, too, although in the case of the older camera some of the menu entries are relocated. I'm sure you can locate them. In addition, settings in these tables for features that the D3x does not have obviously do not apply. I expect you won't waste a lot of time trying to figure out how to make movie settings with your D3x if you've spent any time at all with the rest of this book.

I've divided the recommended settings into a group of tables, rather than one or two huge tables that would be more difficult to read. The tables show the "default" settings for the Shooting menu banks and Custom Setting banks, as they come from the factory, plus eight groups intended for Basic, Studio flash, Portrait, Long exposure, Sports—Indoors, Sports—Outdoors, Landscapes, and Portraits. For the Custom Setting menu, I add one more group of settings, for exposure bracketing.

Each setting includes options that I consider best-suited for their particular shooting situations. For example, when I am bracketing exposures, I like to shoot off a single bracket burst fairly quickly, so I choose $C_L$ release mode, with the shooting speed set to 5 frames per second. When I press the shutter release, all the exposures are taken consecutively in a brief period of time. Similarly, when I am shooting indoor sports, I like to use ISO 3200 and set my autofocus priority to Release + Focus. That lets me shoot bursts of pictures with minimal shutter lag when I press the shutter release button, but still gives the camera a little extra time to get that first picture in sharp focus. I understand that the continuous shooting speed may be a little slower in that mode, but it works for me.

Now, obviously, your D3s/D3x has only four Shooting banks and four Custom Setting banks, plus the Extended banks to add additional parameters, so you'll have to choose which of my recommendations to "install" in the four available banks that reside in your camera. I also suggest further customizing these settings to best suit your own habits and needs. In addition, there are some settings that I do not suggest changes for, but which can easily be modified by you, if you like.

For example, you may not have known that you can select both a folder name and file naming scheme for *each* Shooting menu bank. So, you can deposit your image files in a different folder, if you like, based on which Shooting menu bank you've selected. Similarly, you could conceivably use different file name prefixes for each bank (say, to separate SPT_ [sports] shots from LND_ [landscape] pictures). That seems like a lot of trouble to me, but you can do it.

## Shooting Menu Bank Recommendations

I'll list my Shooting menu bank suggestions first. The Custom Setting menu bank recommendations are divided into the exact same categories but, of course, deal with different options. In the first table, the second column shows the default settings, as the D3s comes from the factory.

**Table 8.1 Shooting Menu Recommendations #1**

| Option | Camera Default | Basic Setting | Studio Flash | Portrait |
|---|---|---|---|---|
| **Extended menu banks** | Off | Off | Off | Off |
| **Active folder** | Default | Your choice | Your choice | Your choice |
| **File naming** | DSC/_DSC | Your choice | Your choice | Your choice |
| **Slot 2** | Overflow | Overflow | Backup | Backup |
| **Image format/ Quality** | JPEG Normal | NEF(RAW)+ JPEG Fine | NEF | NEF+ JPEG Fine |
| **Image size** | Large | Large | Large | Large |
| **Image area** | FX | FX | FX | FX |
| **JPEG compression** | Size priority | Optimal quality | Optimal quality | Optimal quality |
| **NEF (RAW) recording:** | | | | |
| **>Type** | Lossless compressed | Lossless compressed | Lossless compressed | Lossless compressed |
| **>NEF(RAW) bit depth** | 12-bit | 12-bit | 14-bit | 12-bit |
| **White balance** | Auto | Auto | Preset manual | Auto |
| **Set Picture Control** | Standard | C-1 (Standard+ Sharp 7) | Standard | C-3 (Neutral + Sharp -2) |

**Table 8.1 (Continued)**

| Option | Camera Default | Basic Setting | Studio Flash | Portrait |
|---|---|---|---|---|
| Color space | sRGB | Adobe RGB | Adobe RGB | Adobe RGB |
| Active D-Lighting | Off | Off | Off | Off |
| Vignette control | Off | Off | Off | Normal |
| Long exp. NR | Off | Off | Off | Off |
| High ISO NR | Normal | Low | Low | Low |
| ISO sensitivity settings: | | | | |
| >ISO sensitivity | 200 | 200 | 200 | 200 |
| >ISO sensitivity auto control: | Off | On | Off | Off |
| *Maximum sensitivity* | 3200 | 800 | 1600 | 1600 |
| *Minimum shutter speed* | 1/30 s | 1/60 s | 1/60 s | 1/60 s |
| Live view | | | | |
| >*Live view mode* | Hand-held | Hand-held | Hand-held | Hand-held |
| Multiple exposure: | | | | |
| >*Number of shots* | 2 | 2 | Applies to all banks | Applies to all banks |
| >*Auto gain* | On | Off | Applies to all banks | Applies to all banks |
| >*Series* | Off | Off | Off | Off |
| Movie settings | | | | |
| >Quality | 640 × 424 | 640 × 424 | NA | 1280 × 720 |
| >Microphone | Auto sensitivity | Auto sensitivity | Auto sensitivity | Auto sensitivity |
| >Destination | Slot 1 | Slot 1 | NA | Slot 2 |
| >High-sensitivity movie mode | Off | Off | NA | Off |

**Table 8.1 (Continued)**

| Option | Camera Default | Basic Setting | Studio Flash | Portrait |
|---|---|---|---|---|
| **Interval timer shooting:** | | | | |
| >***Start time*** | Now | Now/Set time | Applies to all banks | Applies to all banks |
| >***Interval*** | 00:00':00" | Select | Applies to all banks | Applies to all banks |
| >***No. of intervals*** | 1 | Select | Applies to all banks | Applies to all banks |
| >***No. of shots*** | 1 | Select | Applies to all banks | Applies to all banks |
| >***Start*** | Off | Turn On/Off | Applies to all banks | Applies to all banks |

**Table 8.2 Shooting Menu Recommendations #2**

| Option | Long Exposure | Sports Indoors | Sports Outdoors | Landscape |
|---|---|---|---|---|
| **Extended menu banks** | Off | Off | Off | Off |
| **Active folder** | Your choice | Your choice | Your choice | Your choice |
| **File naming** | Your choice | Your choice | Your choice | Your choice |
| **Slot 2** | Overflow | Overflow | Overflow | Backup |
| **Image format/ Quality** | NEF | JPEG Fine | JPEG Fine | NEF+ JPEG Fine |
| **Image size** | Large | Large | Large | Large |
| **Image area** | FX | FX | 1.2XCrop | FX |
| **JPEG compression** | Optimal quality | Optimal quality | Optimal quality | Optimal quality |
| **NEF (RAW) recording:** | | | | |
| >**Type** | Lossless compressed | Lossless compressed | Lossless compressed | Lossless compressed |
| >**NEF(RAW) bit depth** | 12-bit | 12-bit | 12-bit | 12-bit |
| **White balance** | Auto | Auto | Auto | Auto |

**Table 8.2 (Continued)**

| Option | Long Exposure | Sports Indoors | Sports Outdoors | Landscape |
|---|---|---|---|---|
| **Set Picture Control** | Standard | Standard | Standard | C-2 (Vivid+ Sharp 5) |
| **Color space** | Adobe RGB | Adobe RGB | Adobe RGB | Adobe RGB |
| **Active D-Lighting** | Off | Off | Off | Normal |
| **Vignette control** | Off | Off | Off | Normal |
| **Long exp. NR** | On | Off | Off | Off |
| **High ISO NR** | Low | Normal | Low | Low |
| **ISO sensitivity settings:** | | | | |
| **>ISO sensitivity** | 400 | 3200 | 800 | 200 |
| **>ISO sensitivity auto control:** | Off | Off | Off | Off |
| ***Maximum sensitivity*** | 1600 | 1600 | 1600 | 1600 |
| ***Minimum shutter speed*** | 1/60 s | 1/60 s | 1/60 s | 1/60 s |
| **Live view** | | | | |
| ***>Live view mode*** | Hand-held | Hand-held | Hand-held | Hand-held |
| **Multiple exposure:** | | | | |
| ***>Number of shots*** | Applies to all banks | Applies to all banks | Applies to all banks | Applies to all banks |
| ***>Auto gain*** | Applies to all banks | Applies to all banks | Applies to all banks | Applies to all banks |
| ***>Series*** | Off | Off | Off | Off |
| **Movie settings** | | | | |
| **>Quality** | 1280 × 720 | 1280 × 720 | 1280 × 720 | 1280 × 720 |
| **>Microphone** | Auto sensitivity | Auto sensitivity | Auto sensitivity | Auto sensitivity |
| **>Destination** | Slot 2 | Slot 2 | Slot 2 | Slot 2 |
| **>High-sensitivity movie mode** | On | Off | Off | Off |

**Table 8.2 (Continued)**

| Option | Long Exposure | Sports Indoors | Sports Outdoors | Landscape |
|---|---|---|---|---|
| **Interval timer shooting:** | | | | |
| >*Start time* | Applies to all banks | Applies to all banks | Applies to all banks | Applies to all banks |
| >*Interval* | Applies to all banks | Applies to all banks | Applies to all banks | Applies to all banks |
| >*No. of intervals* | Applies to all banks | Applies to all banks | Applies to all banks | Applies to all banks |
| >*No. of shots* | Applies to all banks | Applies to all banks | Applies to all banks | Applies to all banks |
| >*Start* | Applies to all banks | Applies to all banks | Applies to all banks | Applies to all banks |

## Custom Setting Menu Bank Recommendations

Next come the Custom Setting menu bank recommendations. They are divided into the exact same categories, but with the addition of a new category for bracketed shots. And, of course, they all deal with different options.

**Table 8.3 Custom Setting Menu Bank Recommendations #1**

| Item | Option | Camera Default | Basic Setting | Studio Flash | Portrait | Long Exposure |
|---|---|---|---|---|---|---|
| *Autofocus* | | | | | | |
| **a1** | AF-C priority selection | Release | Release | Release | Release | Release |
| **a2** | AF-S priority selection | Focus | Focus | Focus | Focus | Focus |
| **a3** | Dynamic AF area | 9 Points | 51 points 3D | 51 points 3D | 51 points 3D | 21 points |
| **a4** | Focus tracking with lock-on | Normal | Normal | Normal | Normal | Normal |
| **a5** | AF activation | Shutter/AF-ON (ON) | Shutter/AF-ON (ON) | Shutter/AF-ON (ON) | Shutter/AF-ON (ON) | Shutter/AF-ON (ON) |

**Table 8.3 (Continued)**

| Item | Option | Camera Default | Basic Setting | Studio Flash | Portrait | Long Exposure |
|---|---|---|---|---|---|---|
| **a6** | AF point illumination | Auto | Auto | Auto | Auto | Auto |
| **a7** | Focus point wrap-around | No wrap (OFF) | No wrap (OFF) | No wrap (OFF) | No wrap (OFF) | No wrap (OFF) |
| **a8** | AF point selection | 51 points | 51 points | 11 points | 51 points | 51 points |
| **a9** | AF-ON button | AF-ON | AF-ON | AF-ON | AF-ON | AF-ON |
| **a10** | Vertical AF-ON button | AF-ON | AF-ON | AF-ON | AF-ON | AF-ON |
| ***Metering/exposure*** | | | | | | |
| **b1** | ISO sensitivity step value | 1/3 step | 1/3 step | 1/3 step | 1/3 step | 1/3 step |
| **b2** | EV steps for exposure control | 1/3 step | 1/3 step | 1/3 step | 1/3 step | 1/3 step |
| **b3** | Exp comp/fine tune | 1/3 step | 1/3 step | 1/3 step | 1/3 step | 1/3 step |
| **b4** | Easy exposure compensation | Off | Off | Off | Off | Off |
| **b5** | Center-weighted area | 12mm | 12mm | 12mm | 8mm | 8mm |
| **b6** | Fine-tune optimal exposure: | | | | | |
| | *>Matrix metering* | 0 | 0 | 0 | 0 | 0 |
| | *>Center-weighted* | 0 | 0 | 0 | 0 | 0 |
| | *>Spot metering* | 0 | 0 | 0 | 0 | 0 |
| ***Timers/AE Lock*** | | | | | | |
| **c1** | Shutter-release button AE-L | Off | Off | Off | Off | Off |
| **c2** | Auto meter-off delay | 6 sec | 6 sec | 6 sec | 6 sec | 6 sec |
| **c3** | Self-timer delay | 10 sec | 20 sec | 10 sec | 10 sec | 2 sec |

**Table 8.3 (Continued)**

| Item | Option | Camera Default | Basic Setting | Studio Flash | Portrait | Long Exposure |
|---|---|---|---|---|---|---|
| c4 | Monitor off delay | | | | | |
| | ***>Playback*** | 10 sec | 10 sec | 10 sec | 10 sec | 20 sec |
| | ***>Menus*** | 20 sec | 20 sec | 20 sec | 20 sec | 20 sec |
| | ***>Information display*** | 10 sec | 10 sec | 20 sec | 20 sec | 20 sec |
| | ***>Image review*** | 4 sec | 10 sec | 4 sec | 4 sec | 4 sec |
| ***Shooting/display*** | | | | | | |
| **d1** | Beep | High | Off | Off | Off | High |
| **d2** | Shooting speed | Off | Off | Off | On | Off |
| | *>Continuous high speed* | 9 fps | 9 fps | 9 fps | 9 fps | 9 fps |
| | *>Continuous low speed* | 3 fps | 3 fps | 3 fps | 3 fps | 3 fps |
| **d3** | Max. continuous release | 130 | 20 | 20 | 20 | 20 |
| **d4** | File no. Sequence | On | On | On | On | On |
| **d5** | Control panel/Viewfinder | | | | | |
| | *>Rear control panel* | ISO sensitivity | ISO sensitivity | ISO sensitivity | ISO sensitivity | ISO sensitivity |
| | *>Viewfinder display* | Frame count | Frame count | Frame count | Frame count | Frame count |
| **d6** | Information display | Auto | Auto | Auto | Auto | Auto |
| **d7** | Screen tips | On | On | On | On | On |
| **d8** | LCD illumination | Off | Off | Off | Off | Off |
| **d9** | Exposure delay mode | Off | Off | Off | Off | Off |
| ***Bracketing/Flash*** | | | | | | |
| **e1** | Flash sync speed | 1/250 | 1/250 | 1/250 | 1/250 | 1/250 |
| **e2** | Flash shutter speed | 1/60 | 1/60 | 1/15 | 1/15 | 1/60 |
| **e3** | Modeling flash | ON | ON | ON | ON | ON |
| **e4** | Auto bracketing set | AE & Flash | AE & Flash | AE & Flash | AE & Flash | AE & Flash |

**Table 8.3 (Continued)**

| Item | Option | Camera Default | Basic Setting | Studio Flash | Portrait | Long Exposure |
|---|---|---|---|---|---|---|
| e5 | Auto bracketing (mode M) | Flash/Speed | Flash/Speed | Flash/Speed | Flash/Speed | Flash/Speed |
| e6 | Bracketing order | Meter> Under> Over | Meter> Under> Over | Meter> Under> Over | Meter> Under> Over | Meter> Under> Over |
| *Controls* | | | | | | |
| f1 | Multi selector center button | | | | | |
| | >*Shooting mode* | Select center focus point | Select center focus point | Select center focus point | Select center focus point | Select center focus point |
| | >*Playback mode* | Thumbnail On/Off | View histograms | View histograms | View histograms | View histograms |
| | >*Live view* | Rec | Rec | Rec | Rec | Rec |
| f2 | Multi selector | Do nothing (OFF) | Do nothing (OFF) | Do nothing (OFF) | Do nothing (OFF) | Do nothing (OFF) |
| f3 | Photo info/playback | Info __/ Playback__ | Info __/ Playback__ | Info __/ Playback__ | Info __/ Playback__ | Info __/ Playback__ |
| f4 | Assign Fn button | | | | | |
| | >*Fn button press* | None | Flash Off | FV Lock | FV Lock | None |
| | >*Fn button + dials* | Auto bracketing | Auto bracketing | Auto bracketing | None | Auto bracketing |
| f5 | Assign preview button | | | | | |
| | >*Preview button press* | Preview | Preview | Preview | Preview | Preview |
| | >*Preview button + dials* | None | None | None | None | None |
| f6 | Assign AE-L/AF-L button | | | | | |
| | >*AE-L/AF-L button press* | AE-AF lock | AE-AF lock | AE-AF lock | AE-AF lock | AE-AF lock |
| | >*AE-L/AF-L button + dials* | None | None | None | None | None |
| f7 | Assign BKT button | Auto bracketing | Auto bracketing | Auto bracketing | Auto bracketing | Auto bracketing |

**Table 8.3 (Continued)**

| Item | Option | Camera Default | Basic Setting | Studio Flash | Portrait | Long Exposure |
|---|---|---|---|---|---|---|
| **f8** | Customize command dials | | | | | |
| | >*Reverse rotation* | No (OFF) | No (OFF) | No (OFF) | No (OFF) | No (OFF) |
| | >*Change main/sub* | No (OFF) | No (OFF) | No (OFF) | No (OFF) | No (OFF) |
| | >*Aperture setting* | ON (Sub-command dial) | ON (Sub-command dial) | ON (Sub-command dial) | ON (Sub-command Dial) | ON (Sub-command dial) |
| | >*Menus and playback* | Off | Off | Off | Off | Off |
| **f9** | Release button to use dial | No (OFF) | No (OFF) | No (OFF) | No (OFF) | No (OFF) |
| **f10** | No memory card | Enable release (OK) | Release locked (LOCK) | Release locked (LOCK) | Release locked (LOCK) | Release locked (LOCK) |
| **f11** | Reverse indicators for exposure | + 0 - | + 0 - | + 0 - | + 0 - | + 0 - |

**Table 8.4 Custom Setting Menu Bank Recommendations #2**

| Item | Option | Sports Indoors | Sports Outdoors | Landscape | Bracketing |
|---|---|---|---|---|---|
| ***Autofocus*** | | | | | |
| **a1** | AF-C priority selection | Release + focus | Release + focus | Release | Release + focus |
| **a2** | AF-S priority selection | Focus | Focus | Focus | Focus |
| **a3** | Dynamic AF area | 21 points | 21 points | 21 points | 51 points |
| **a4** | Focus tracking with lock-on | Long | Long | Normal | Normal |
| **a5** | AF activation | Shutter/AF-ON (ON) | Shutter/AF-ON (ON) | Shutter/AF-ON (ON) | Shutter/AF-ON (ON) |

**Table 8.4 (Continued)**

| Item | Option | Sports Indoors | Sports Outdoors | Landscape | Bracketing |
|---|---|---|---|---|---|
| **a6** | AF point illumination | Auto | Auto | Auto | Auto |
| **a7** | Focus point wrap-around | No wrap (OFF) | No wrap (OFF) | No wrap (OFF) | No wrap (OFF) |
| **a8** | AF point selection | 51 points | 11 points | 51 points | 51 points |
| **a9** | AF-ON button | AF-ON | AF-ON | AF-ON | AF-ON |
| **a10** | Vertical AF-ON button | AF-ON | AF-ON | AF-ON | AF-ON |
| ***Metering/exposure*** | | | | | |
| **b1** | ISO sensitivity step value | 1/3 step | 1/3 step | 1/3 step | 1/3 step |
| **b2** | EV steps for exposure control | 1/3 step | 1/3 step | 1/3 step | 1/3 step |
| **b3** | Exp comp/fine tune | 1/3 step | 1/3 step | 1/3 step | 1/3 step |
| **b4** | Easy exposure compensation | Off | Off | Off | Off |
| **b5** | Center-weighted area | 8mm | 8mm | 12mm | 12mm |
| **b6** | Fine-tune optimal exposure: | | | | |
| | >*Matrix metering* | 0 | 0 | 0 | 0 |
| | >*Center-Weighted* | 0 | 0 | 0 | 0 |
| | >*Spot metering* | 0 | 0 | 0 | 0 |
| ***Timers/AE Lock*** | | | | | |
| **c1** | Shutter release button AE-L | Off | Off | Off | Off |
| **c2** | Auto meter-off delay | 6 sec | 6 sec | 6 sec | 6 sec |
| **c3** | Self-timer delay | 10 sec | 10 sec | 2 sec | 2 sec |

**Table 8.4 (Continued)**

| Item | Option | Sports Indoors | Sports Outdoors | Landscape | Bracketing |
|---|---|---|---|---|---|
| c4 | Monitor off delay | | | | |
| | ***>Playback*** | 4 sec | 4 sec | 4 sec | 4 sec |
| | ***>Menus*** | 10 sec | 10 sec | 10 sec | 10 sec |
| | ***>Information display*** | 4 sec | 4 sec | 4 sec | 4 sec |
| | ***>Image review*** | 4 sec | 4 sec | 10 sec | 10 sec |
| ***Shooting/display*** | | | | | |
| **d1** | Beep | Off | Off | High | High |
| **d2** | Shooting speed | Off | Off | On | Off |
| | *>Continuous high speed* | 9 fps | 9 fps | 9 fps | 9 fps |
| | *>Continuous low speed* | 4 fps | 4 fps | 3 fps | 5 fps |
| **d3** | Max. continuous release | 35 | 35 | 20 | 100 |
| **d4** | File No. Sequence | On | On | On | On |
| **d5** | Control panel/Viewfinder | | | | |
| | *>Rear control panel* | ISO sensitivity | ISO sensitivity | ISO sensitivity | ISO sensitivity |
| | *>Viewfinder display* | Exposures remaining | Exposures remaining | Frame count | Frame count |
| **d6** | Information display | Auto | Auto | Auto | Auto |
| **d7** | Screen Tips | On | On | On | On |
| **d8** | LCD Illumination | Off | Off | Off | Off |
| **d9** | Exposure delay mode | Off | Off | Off | Off |
| ***Bracketing/Flash*** | | | | | |
| **e1** | Flash sync speed | 1/250 | 1/250 | 1/250 | 1/250 |
| **e2** | Flash shutter speed | 1/30 | 1/30 | 1/60 | 1/60 |

**Table 8.4 (Continued)**

| Item | Option | Sports Indoors | Sports Outdoors | Landscape | Bracketing |
|---|---|---|---|---|---|
| e3 | Modeling flash | ON | ON | ON | ON |
| e4 | Auto bracketing set | AE & Flash | AE & Flash | AE & Flash | AE & Flash |
| e5 | Auto bracketing (mode M) | Flash/Speed | Flash/Speed | Flash/Speed | Flash/Speed |
| e6 | Bracketing order | Meter>Under >Over | Meter>Under >Over | Meter>Under >Over | Under>Meters >Over |
| *Controls* | | | | | |
| f1 | Multi selector center button | | | | |
| | >*Shooting mode* | Select center focus point | Select center focus point | Select center focus point | Select center focus point |
| | >*Playback mode* | View histograms | View histograms | View histograms | View histograms |
| | >*Live View* | Rec | Rec | Rec | Rec |
| f2 | Multi selector | Do nothing (OFF) | Do nothing (OFF) | Do nothing (OFF) | Do nothing (OFF) |
| f3 | Photo info/ playback | Info __/ Playback__ | Info __/ Playback__ | Info __/ Playback__ | Info __/ Playback__ |
| f4 | Assign Fn button | | | | |
| | >*Fn button press* | Spot metering | Spot metering | Bracketing burst | Bracketing burst |
| | >*Fn button + dials* | Auto bracketing | Auto bracketing | Auto bracketing | Auto bracketing |
| f5 | Assign Preview button | | | | |
| | >*Preview button press* | Preview | Preview | Preview | Preview |
| | >*Preview button + dials* | None | None | None | None |
| f6 | Assign AE-L/AF-L button | | | | |
| | >*AE-L/AF-L button press* | AE-AF lock (hold) | AE-AF lock (hold) | AE-AF lock | AE-AF lock |
| | >*AE-L/AF-L button + dials* | None | None | None | None |

**Table 8.4 (Continued)**

| Item | Option | Sports Indoors | Sports Outdoors | Landscape | Bracketing |
|---|---|---|---|---|---|
| f7 | Assign BKT button | Auto bracketing | Auto bracketing | Auto bracketing | Auto bracketing |
| f8 | Customize command dials | | | | |
| | >*Reverse rotation* | No (OFF) | No (OFF) | No (OFF) | No (OFF) |
| | >*Change main/sub* | No (OFF) | No (OFF) | No (OFF) | No (OFF) |
| | >*Aperture setting* | ON (Sub-command dial) | ON (Sub-command dial) | ON (Sub-command dial) | ON (Sub-command dial) |
| | >*Menus and playback* | Off | Off | Off | Off |
| f9 | Release button to use dial | No (OFF) | No (OFF) | No (OFF) | No (OFF) |
| f10 | No memory card | Release locked (LOCK) | Release locked (LOCK) | Release locked (LOCK) | Release locked (LOCK) |
| f11 | Reverse indicators for exposure | + 0 - | + 0 - | + 0 - | + 0 - |

# 9

# Working with Lenses

If Nikon has one advantage over many of the other vendors of digital SLRs (other than making great cameras), it's the mind-bending assortment of high-quality lenses available to enhance the capabilities of cameras like the Nikon D3s and D3x. You can use thousands of current and older lenses introduced by Nikon and third-party vendors since 1959 (although lenses made before 1977 may need an inexpensive modification). These can give you a wider view, bring distant subjects closer, let you focus closer, shoot under lower light conditions, or provide a more detailed, sharper image for critical work. Other than the sensor itself, the lens you choose for your dSLR is the most important component in determining image quality and perspective of your images.

This chapter explains how to select the best lenses for the kinds of photography you want to do.

## Sensor Sensibilities

If you've moved up to the full-frame Nikon D3s/D3x from one of Nikon's DX models specifically to escape from the effects of the "crop" factor, I have some bad news for you. In one sense, you're still at the mercy of the differences between full-frame (FX) and cropped-frame (DX) sensors. Whereas, owners of DX-format models, like the D300s can use virtually *any* Nikon lens ever produced, you can't—at least, not without some sacrifices. While lenses designed for DX use will *fit* on your D3s/D3x, the images they produce won't completely fill that precious full frame, at least, not at all focal lengths. To use these lenses in the way they were designed, you'll have to switch to the D3s/D3x's DX mode, which provides a cropped, 5-megapixel version on the D3s, and a more usable, but still cropped 10-megapixel version with the D3x. In either case, you're essentially wasting a lot of your sensor's photosites.

So, DX-to-FX upgraders have gone from near-universal lens compatibility—but with that crop factor reducing the field of view of some lenses (for better or for worse)—to a situation in which some lenses (perhaps, including a clutch of optics you already own) no longer are as usable as they once were for many applications.

The *crop factor*, also called a *lens multiplier factor* lives on. Both are misleading and inaccurate terms used to describe the same phenomenon: the fact that cameras like any of Nikon's DX models (D300s, D90, and others) provide a field of view that's smaller and narrower than that produced by full-frame, FX models like the D3s/D3x, D3, and D700.

Figure 9.1 quite clearly shows the phenomenon at work. The outer rectangle, marked 1X, shows the field of view you might expect with a 50mm lens mounted on a D3s/D3x or another one of Nikon's FX cameras. The area marked 1.5X shows the field of view you'd get with that 50mm lens installed on a D300s or other DX model. It's easy to see from the illustration that the 1X rendition provides a wider, more expansive view, while the inner field of view is, in comparison, *cropped.*

The cropping effect is produced because the sensors of DX cameras are smaller than the sensors of the D3s/D3x, D3, or D700. These "full-frame" cameras have a sensor that's the size of the standard 35mm film frame, 24mm × 36mm. Any DX sensor does *not* measure 24mm × 36mm; instead, it specs out at 23.6 × 15.8 mm, or about 66.7 percent of the area of a full-frame sensor, as shown by the yellow boxes in the figure. You

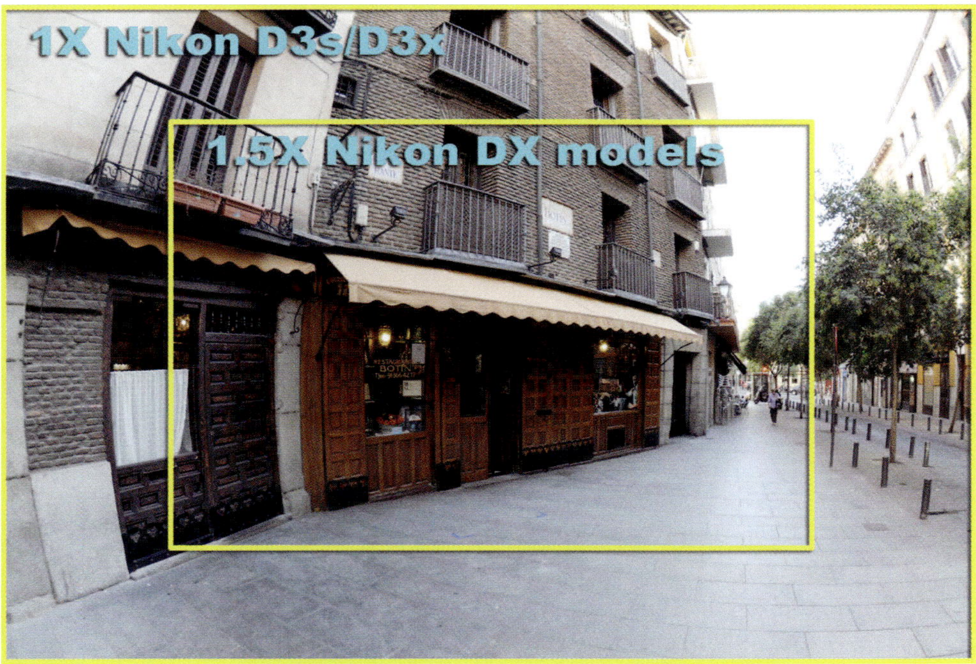


**Figure 9.1**
Nikon offers digital SLRs with full-frame (1X) crops, as well as 1.5X.

can calculate the relative field of view by dividing the focal length of the lens by .667. Thus, a 100mm lens mounted on a DX model has the same field of view as a 150mm lens on the Nikon D3s/D3x. We humans tend to perform multiplication operations in our heads more easily than division, so such field of view comparisons are usually calculated using the reciprocal of .667—1.5—so we can multiply instead. (100 / .667=150; 100 × 1.5=150)

This translation is generally necessary only if you're using your D3s/D3x accompanied by a DX model, and want to know how a familiar lens will perform on a particular digital camera. I strongly prefer *crop factor* over *lens multiplier*, because nothing is being multiplied; a 100mm lens doesn't "become" a 150mm lens—the depth-of-field and lens aperture remain the same. (I'll explain more about these later in this chapter.) Only the field of view is cropped. But *crop factor* isn't much better, as it implies that the 24 × 36mm frame is "full" and anything else is "less." I get e-mails all the time from photographers who point out that they own full-frame cameras with 36mm × 48mm sensors (like the Mamiya 645ZD or Hasselblad H3D-39 medium format digitals). By their reckoning, the "half-size" sensors found in cameras like the Nikon D3s/D3x and D700 are "cropped."

If you need to work with both types, you might find it helpful to use the crop factor "multiplier" to translate a lens's real focal length into the full-frame equivalent, even though, as I said, nothing is actually being multiplied. Throughout most of this book, I've been using actual focal lengths and not equivalents, except when referring to specific wide-angle or telephoto focal length ranges and their fields of view.

Lenses designed for the DX format may or may not be usable for full-frame images on your D3s/D3x. The image circle produced by a DX lens is generally smaller than the area of a full frame, at least at the widest focal length setting. Figure 9.2 shows the approximate coverage of a particular DX lens at a wide-angle setting. It covers the inner DX rectangle (just barely; some lenses exhibit darkening, or *vignetting* in the corners of the frame for this reason). But there is severe darkening at the corners of the full FX frame. Zoom the same lens in to a longer focal length setting, however, and the image coverage circle enlarges so that the lens is *almost* acceptable for full-frame use. (See Figure 9.3.)

Of course, even if there were no vignetting at a particular focal length, this DX lens might not be a great choice for full-frame photography; the image quality/sharpness at the very edges of the circle is likely to be deficient. Still, it's good to know that if you own, say, the Nikon 12-24mm f/4G ED IF Autofocus DX Nikkor Zoom Lens, and no other wide-angle lens, it can function as a perfectly good 18-24mm lens. All you must give up are the zoom settings between 12 and 18mm. (Whether the newer 10-24mm f/3.5-4.5G ED AF-S DX Nikkor Lens can be used in this mode, I don't know; I haven't tried it.)

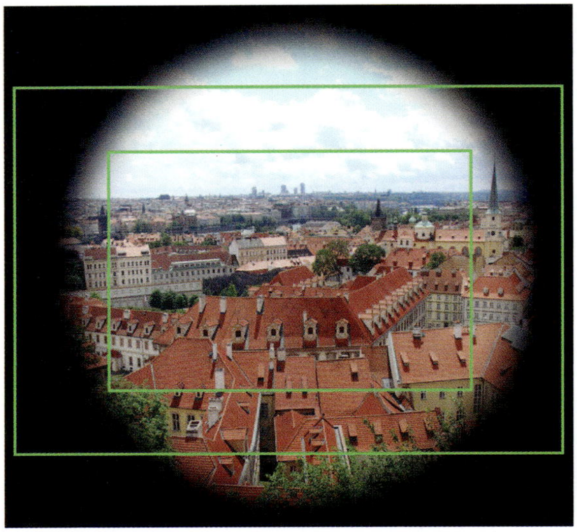

**Figure 9.2** At a wide-angle setting, the image circle of a typical lens won't cover the full D3s/D3x frame.

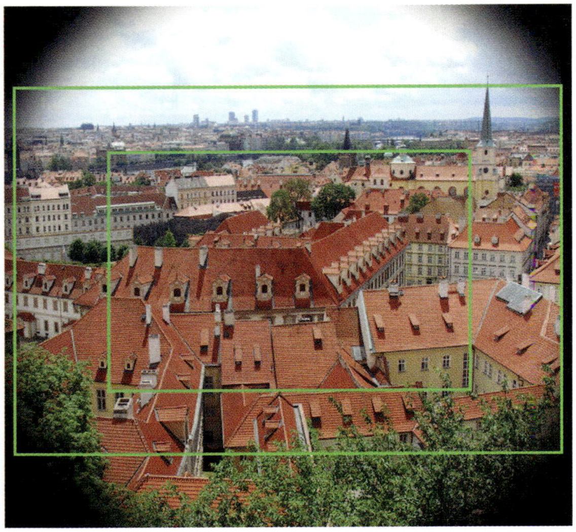

**Figure 9.3** Zoom in, and the image circle enlarges, making the lens acceptable for full-frame coverage.

If you do own a selection of DX lenses, you have several alternatives:

- **Give it a go.** Try them out on your D3s/D3x to see if they cover the full frame at various focal lengths.
- **Keep as DX/backup lens.** If you own a backup camera in the DX format, you can still use your old DX lenses on that camera. It may be a pain carrying around lenses that you can't use on all your cameras, but the pain will be less than if you must sell those lenses for hundreds of dollars less than you paid for them.
- **Use DX mode.** As I mentioned in Chapter 3, you can tell the D3s/D3x to automatically switch to DX crop mode when a DX lens is mounted and recognized, using the Auto DX crop option within the Image area entry of the Shooting menu. The camera may not identify non-Nikon DX lenses, but you can select the Choose image area entry and set either FX or DX mode manually, as I have to do when working with my Tokina 10-17mm fisheye zoom lens. In DX mode, your image will have only 5 megapixels with a D3s, but that might be enough for some uses, especially if you can get additional mileage out of your old DX-format lens (as I do with my Tokina fisheye). I've found that the D3x's DX mode, which provides a 10-megapixel cropped image, does an even better job.
- **Try one of the other cropped modes.** The D3s and D3x both have a 5:4 ratio crop mode (30 × 24mm) that is smaller than the full frame, and *may* provide enough of a crop to allow your DX lens to fill the remaining image area. In addition, the D3s has a 1.2x crop mode (30 × 20mm) that I've found works quite well with some DX format lenses. You'll find these options all tucked away in the Image area entry of the Shooting menu.

- **Retain for a future upgrade.** I sold my 12-24mm lens when I bought my Nikon 14-24mm full-frame optic. But, I kept other favored DX lenses, figuring that improvements in resolution that were coming down the road would make them viable again. Certainly, my remaining DX lenses are OK at 5MP on my D3s, but, as I said, when I mount them on my 24.5MP D3x, which has a 10MP DX/crop mode, they really rock. Your next camera will certainly have more megapixels, and you'll be glad you retained those old lenses.
- **Dump and replace.** Nikon has shown with its recent camera introductions that it won't be dumping the DX format anytime soon. So, your old DX lenses have retained a lot of their value on the used market. Instead of taking a bath when you sell them, you might have to endure little more than a splash in the face.

## Do You Need a DX Camera, Too?

For many photographers, the choice of an FX or DX camera is serious business. Wildlife and sports photographers appreciate having their longer lenses boosted 1.5X when using a DX model (as I discuss next), while landscape and architectural photographers need wide-angle optics that provide a truly wide field of view. There's a lot of debate over the "advantages" and "disadvantages" of using a camera with a "cropped" sensor, versus one with a "full-frame" sensor. The arguments go like these:

- **"Free" 1.5X teleconverter.** The Nikon D300s, which is very similar in operation to your D3s/D3x, along with other cameras with the 1.5X crop factor, magically transform any telephoto lens you have into a longer lens, which can be useful for sports, wildlife photography, and other endeavors that benefit from more reach. Yet, your f/stop remains the same (that is, a 300mm f/4 becomes a very fast 450mm f/4 lens). Some discount this advantage, pointing out that the exact same field of view can be had by taking a full-frame image, and trimming it to the 1.5X equivalent. While that is strictly true, it doesn't take into account a factor called *pixel density.* While both the Nikon D300s and the full-frame D3s have sensors with 12 megapixels of resolution, the D300s packs all those pixels together much more tightly, into that 23.6 × 15.8mm area. So, your 300mm f/4 lens delivers the same field of view as a 450mm optic at the D3s's full 12MP resolution. When you crop the D3s/D3x image to get the same FOV, you're using only 5 or 10 megapixels worth of resolution. So, while both images will be framed the same, the D300s version, with its higher pixel density, will be sharper. If you shoot a variety of different subject types, perhaps you need to own *both* a Nikon D300s and a D3s/D3x.
- **Dense pixels=more noise.** The other side of the pixel density coin is that the denser packing of pixels in a DX sensor means that each pixel must be smaller, and will have less light-gathering capabilities. Larger pixels capture light more efficiently,

reducing the need to amplify the signal when boosting ISO sensitivity, and, therefore, producing less noise. In an absolute sense, this is true, and cameras like the D3s/D3x and D3-series *do* have sensational high-ISO performance. However, the D300s's sensor is improved over earlier cameras (for one thing, it is a high-sensitivity CMOS sensor, rather than a noisier CCD sensor like that found in some earlier Nikon DX models), so you'll find it performs very well at higher ISOs. Indeed, its ISO sensitivity is more or less comparable to that of the Nikon D3x, which also relies on high-density pixel-packing to achieve its 24.5MP resolution. You needn't hesitate to use ISO 1600 (or even higher) with the latest DX models: just don't expect the same results at higher ISO settings that the typical D3s/D3x owner has come to expect.

- **Lack of wide-angle perspective.** Of course, the 1.5X "crop" factor applies to wide-angle lenses, too, so your 20mm ultrawide lens becomes a hum-drum 30mm near-wide angle, and a 35mm focal length is transformed into what photographers call a "normal" lens. Zoom lenses, like the 18-105mm lens that is often purchased with many DX models in a kit, have less wide-angle perspective at their minimum focal length. The 18-105mm optic, for example, is the equivalent of a 27mm moderate wide angle when zoomed to its widest setting. Nikon has "fixed" this problem by providing several different extra-wide zooms specifically for the DX format, including the (relatively) affordable 12-24mm f/4 DX Nikkor. Nikon D3s/D3x owners, on the other hand, can choose from a full range of FX-compatible optics, so you'll never really lack for wide-angle lenses.
- **Mixed body mix-up.** The Nikon D3s/D3x owners who also have a Nikon DX camera like the D300s can't ignore the focal length mix-up factor. If you own both FX and DX-format cameras (some D300s owners use them as a backup to a D3s/D3x, for example), it's vexing to have to adjust to the different fields of view that the cameras provide. If you remove a given lens from one camera and put it on the other, the effective focal length/field of view changes. That 17-35mm f/2.8 zoom works as an ultrawide to wide angle on a D3s/D3x, but functions more as a moderate wide-angle to normal lens on a D300s. To get the "look" on both cameras, you'd need to use a 12-24mm zoom on the D300s, and the 17-35mm zoom on the D3s/D3x. It's possible to become accustomed to this FOV shake-up and, indeed, some photographers put it to work by mounting their longest telephoto lens on the D300s and their wide-angle lenses on their full-frame camera. But, if you've never owned both an FX and DX camera, you should be aware of the possible confusion.

## Your First Lens

Some Nikon dSLRs are almost always purchased with a lens. The entry- and mid-level Nikon dSLRs, such as the Nikon D5000, D3000, or D90, are often bought by those new to digital photography, frequently by first-time SLR or dSLR owners who find the AF-S DX Nikkor 18-105mm f/3.5-5.6G ED VR or AF-S DX Zoom-Nikkor 18-55mm f/3.5-5.6G ED II, both with vibration reduction, irresistible bargains. But other Nikon models, including the Nikon D300s, D700, and D3-series, are most often purchased without a lens by veteran Nikon photographers who already have a complement of optics to use with their cameras.

Back in the film era, Nikon cameras were frequently sold with so-called "normal" lenses, which were fixed focal-length (non-zoom) lenses of about 50mm, with maximum apertures of f/1.2, f/1.4, f/1.8, or f/2. That explains how I happen to own eight 50mm f/1.4 lenses to the present day—they came with my camera bodies.

Today, fixed focal-length (*prime*) lenses have become a specialized tool for specific applications, such as sports photography (300mm and longer primes); close-up or macro photography; tilt/shift perspective control; and low-light capture. (I'll discuss lenses for these applications later in the chapter.) It's more common for photographers these days to work with zoom lenses, and a variety of zooms, at that. So, when you leave the DX world, with its panoply of 17-85mm, 18-105mm, or 18-200mm "do-everything" zoom lenses, you'll probably be purchasing a zoom lens with a more limited range, designed for a specific application. You may want a 14-24mm zoom for wide-angle work, a 24-70mm for street photography or indoor sports, a 70-200mm zoom for portraits or outdoor sports, or some other range. Nikon really figures that D3s/D3x's upscale market doesn't want a do-everything zoom lens for FX cameras, and doesn't offer one.

At least, not any more. My go-to lens when I am traveling light is the remarkable Nikon 28-200mm f/3.5-5.6G ED IF Autofocus Nikkor Zoom Lens. You can't buy one new, and may find it difficult to locate one of these highly prized lenses used. Although I originally purchased this lens for use with a Nikon D300, when I migrated to FX models, I found it even more useful. It was designed as a full-frame lens, has excellent image quality, and is the smallest lens of its range ever built. It's a compact tube measuring 4-inches in diameter, extends just 7 inches from the camera, and weighs a feather-light 12 ounces. (See Figure 9.4.) When I go wandering the backroads of Europe, I typically carry only one of my D3-series cameras (or a D700), this lens, and the Nikon 17-35mm f/2.8 zoom as my main kit (with a compact DX camera like the Nikon D60 as a backup).

So, why doesn't Nikon offer this gem any more? Unfortunately, there are a few things "wrong" with it. Many of the parts of the lens are tough plastic, instead of metal (including the lens mount), but with careful use, it is rugged enough to last a long, long time. It was introduced when even Nikon's professional cameras were DX models, so the

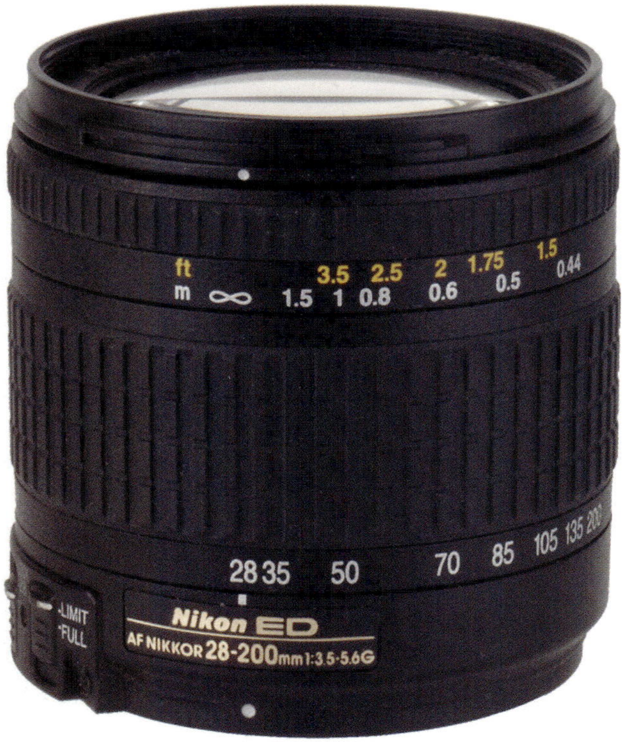


**Figure 9.4**
The Nikon 28-200mm f/3.5-5.6G ED IF Autofocus Nikkor Zoom Lens, although discontinued, ironically makes one of the best all-around basic lenses for the Nikon D3s or D3x.

28mm maximum wide-angle focal length had more of a "normal" 42mm (equivalent) perspective. Buyers were demanding at least 18mm wide angles, and it was easy to displace this 28-200mm lens with Nikon's 18-200mm VR lens that had only DX coverage. The 28-200mm G lens (as it's known) didn't have vibration reduction (VR), and was a slow f/5.6 at 200mm. Finally, because this lens doesn't have a built-in autofocus motor, it won't focus automatically on certain Nikon entry-level cameras, including the Nikon D40/D40x, D60, D3000, and D5000.

Yet, the problems are less problematic when you mount this lens on an FX camera like the D3s/D3x. It autofocuses just fine on the D3s/D3x, which can use lenses with or without built-in focus motors. The widest 28mm setting is a useful wide-angle view on a full-frame camera, and almost dovetails with even wider lenses (like the 14-24mm f/2.8, which I also own). I happen to find the slight overlap with my 17-35mm f/2.8 quite acceptable, too. Of course, the image quality of my D3s, in particular, at ISO 1600 is virtually as good as my D300 was at ISO 400, so that boost effectively makes the 28-200G two stops "faster" and perfectly usable, even indoors. (I am able to stop down to f/8 to get the best sharpness.) That two or three stops of speed granted by the D3s also means that I can use faster shutter speeds, reducing the need for VR. (Faster shutter speeds are actually *better* than VR, because they freeze subject movement in addition to camera motion.)

Let's hope Nikon introduces something similar to the 28-200G for full-frame cameras. The closest lens currently in the line is the AF-S VR Zoom-NIKKOR 24-120mm f/3.5-5.6G IF-ED, which to be charitable, is not the sharpest optic in the drawer. The AF-S NIKKOR 24-70mm f/2.8G ED is a useful (and fast) mid-range zoom, but not really long enough for all-purpose use. The AF Zoom-NIKKOR 24-85mm f/2.8-4D IF is slightly longer, and less expensive, but slower. So, rather than look for a do-everything walk-around lens for your D3s/D3x, you'll need to look at your favored types of photography, and purchase a first lens based on the kind of work you'll be doing.

- **Cost.** You might have stretched your budget a bit to purchase your Nikon D3s/D3x, so you might want to keep the cost of your first lens fairly low. Fortunately, there are excellent lenses available that will add from $300 to $400 to the price of your camera.
- **Zoom range.** If you have only one lens, you'll want a fairly long zoom range to provide as much flexibility as possible.
- **Adequate maximum aperture.** You'll want an f/stop of at least f/3.5 to f/4 for shooting under fairly low light conditions. The thing to watch for is the maximum aperture when the lens is zoomed to its telephoto end. You may end up with no better than an f/5.6 maximum aperture. That's not great, but you can often live with it, particularly with a lens having vibration reduction (VR) capabilities, because you can often shoot at lower shutter speeds to compensate for the limited maximum aperture.
- **Image quality.** Your starter lens should have good image quality, because that's one of the primary factors that will be used to judge your photos.
- **Size matters.** A good walking-around lens is compact in size and light in weight.
- **Fast/close focusing.** Your first lens should have a speedy autofocus system (which is where the Silent Wave motor found in all but the bargain basement lenses is an advantage). Close focusing (to 12 inches or closer) will let you use your basic lens for some types of macro photography.

## What Lenses Can You Use?

The previous section helped you sort out what basic lens you need to buy with your Nikon D3s/D3x. Now, you're probably wondering what lenses can be added to your growing collection (trust me, it will grow). You need to know which lenses are suitable and, most importantly, which lenses are fully compatible with your Nikon D3s/D3x.

With the Nikon D3-series, the compatibility issue is a simple one: It can use in full-frame format any modern-era non-DX Nikon lens with the AF-S or AF designation, with full availability of all autofocus, auto aperture, autoexposure, and image-stabilization features (if present). DX lenses must be used in cropped, 5MP/10MP DX mode. Spotting DX lenses is easy: Nikon's versions all have the letters DX in their names.

The process is a bit more complicated when it comes to third-party manufacturers. Tamron uses the Di (Digitally integrated) designation for its lenses that are compatible with full-frame digital (and film) cameras, and applies the Di II label to lenses suitable only for cropped-sensor models. With Sigma lenses, DG is used for lenses suitable for both FX and DX cameras, and DC indicates a DX-only model. Tokina seems to use the D (for FX) and DX (for DX) nomenclature. All three vendors have been making lenses for (full-frame) film cameras for many years, well before the digital/DX factor showed up, so when purchasing one of their lenses you may not see a special designation but, if the lens was introduced prior to about 2004, it's almost certainly a full-frame model.

That's the case with Nikon's older lenses, too, such as the Nikon AI, AI-S, or AI-P lens, which are manual focus lenses produced starting in 1977 and effectively through the present day, because Nikon continues to offer a limited number of manual focus lenses for those who need them. All are full-frame models.

Nikon lenses produced prior to 1977 must have a minor conversion done to be used safely, because cameras other than certain Nikon entry-level models (such as the D40/D40x, D60, D3000, and D5000) have a pin on the lens mount that can be damaged by an older, unmodified lens. John White at www.aiconversions.com will do the work for about $35 to allow these older lenses to be safely used on any Nikon digital camera.

## Ingredients of Nikon's Alphanumeric Soup

Nikon has always been fond of appending cryptic letters and descriptors onto the names of its lenses. Some of the first Nikon lenses I purchased had names like 35mm f/2 Auto Nikkor-O, 85mm f/1.8 Auto Nikkor-H, 105mm Auto Nikkor-P, and 200mm f/4 Auto Nikkor-Q. At the time, I didn't know what the funny letters represented, but I did know that the "Auto" portion of the name meant that, when you pressed the shutter release button, the lens would actually *stop down automatically* to the aperture you'd selected for the exposure. Don't laugh. Many lenses required rotating a ring manually after focusing and before taking the picture in order to close the lens down to the so-called *pre-set* aperture.

I actually still own all those lenses, because they work just fine on my Nikon digital camera bodies, including my beloved D3s and D3x. And I now know that the funny letters stood for the number of elements in the lens, which was apparently a more important attribute for a photographer to know than it is today. P stood for *penta* (five elements); H represented *hexa* (six elements); S stood for *septa* (seven elements), and so on through *octa*, *nona*, and *deca* (eight, nine, and ten). I'd finally found a use for my high-school

Latin, even though Nikon substituted *penta* for *quinta*, because Q was already taken by *quadra* (four elements).

In the years since, Nikon lens nomenclature has become considerably more complex. Even the basic name of the company's lenses can be a source of confusion. Back when Paul Simon wrote his hit *Kodachrome* it was always a "Nikon camera" and a "Nikkor lens." Today, *Nikkor* is still officially part of the name of each lens produced by Nikon, with the exception of the company's "budget" line of 30 years go, which were called *Nikon Lens Series E* to differentiate them from all the other "top of the line" lenses. But it's become more common to informally refer to a Nikon lens without fear of being corrected.

Here's an alphabetical list of lens terms you're likely to encounter, either as part of the lens name, or in reference to the lens's capabilities. Not all of these are used as parts of a lens's name, but you may come across some of these terms in discussions of particular Nikon optics:

- **AF, AF-D, AF-I, AF-S.** In all cases, AF stands for *autofocus* when appended to the name of a Nikon lens. An extra letter is added to provide additional information. A plain-old AF lens is an autofocus lens that uses a slot-drive motor in the camera body to provide autofocus functions (and so cannot be used in AF mode on the Nikon D40, D40x, D60, D3000, or D5000 which lack the camera body motor). The D means that it's a D-type lens (described later in this listing); the I indicates that focus is through a motor inside the lens; and the **S** means that a super-special (Silent Wave) motor in the lens provides focusing. (Don't confuse a Nikon AF-S lens with the AF-S [single-servo autofocus mode].) Nikon is currently upgrading its older AF lenses with AF-S versions, but it's not safe to assume that all newer Nikkors are AF-S, or even offer autofocus. For example, the PC-E Nikkor 24mm f/3.5D ED perspective control lens must be focused manually, and Nikon offers a surprising collection of other manual focus lenses to meet specialized needs.
- **AI, AI-S.** All Nikkor lenses produced after 1977 have either automatic aperture indexing (AI) or automatic indexing-shutter (AI-S) features that eliminate the previous requirement to manually align the aperture ring on the camera when mounting a lens. When AI/AI-S was introduced, Nikon included the designation in the lens name and offered a service to convert most older lenses to the new configuration. Within a few years, all Nikkors had this automatic aperture indexing feature (except for G-type lenses, which have no aperture ring at all), including Nikon's budget-priced Series E lenses, so the designation was dropped at the time the first autofocus (AF) lenses were introduced. The most important difference between AI and AI-S lenses is that the aperture action of the AI-S versions is *linear*, theoretically allowing for more efficient shutter-priority and programmed exposure metering on cameras of the time. Current models make no distinction between AI and AI-S lenses. These lenses can be used for aperture-priority and manual mode metering on the Nikon D3s/D3x and other Nikon "pro" bodies.

- **AI-P.** A lens with an AI-P designation is an AI lens that has the CPU chip included, which allows the transfer of basic lens information to the camera. It was possible to add an appropriate chip to most AI and AI-S lenses, upgrading them to AI-P status, but there are few companies offering this service anymore. "Chipped" AI/AI-S/AI-P lenses are manual focus optics that can be used with the full range of metering options, the same as with autofocus lenses.
- **CRC (Close Range Correction).** The so-called "floating element" system allowed lens elements to shift position to reduce curvature of field and spherical aberrations at close-focusing distances. Available with certain lenses, including the AF Micro-Nikkor 60mm f/2.8D, which was replaced by the AF-S Micro-Nikkor 60mm f/2.8G ED.
- **E.** The E designation was used for Nikon's budget-priced E Series optics, five prime and three zoom manual focus lenses built using aluminum or plastic parts rather than the preferred brass, so they were less rugged. All are effectively AI-S lenses. They do have good image quality, which makes them a bargain for those who treat their lenses gently and don't need the latest autofocus features. They were available in 28mm f/2.8, 35mm f/2.5, 50mm f/1.8, 100mm f/2.8, and 135mm f/2.8 focal lengths, plus 36-72mm f/3.5, 75mm-150mm f/3.5, and 70-210mm f/4 zooms. (All these would be considered fairly "fast" today.)
- **D.** Appended to the maximum f/stop of the lens (as in f/2.8D), a D Series lens is able to send focus distance data to the camera, which uses the information for flash exposure calculation and 3D color matrix II matrix metering.
- **DC.** The DC stands for defocus control, which allows managing the out-of-focus parts of an image to produce better looking portraits and close-ups.
- **DX.** The DX lenses are designed for use with digital cameras using the APS-C–sized sensor having the 1.5X crop factor. Their image circle isn't large enough to fill up a full 35mm frame at all focal lengths, but they can be used on Nikon's full-frame D3/D3x and D700 models using the automatic/manual DX crop mode. Theoretically, these lenses can be built smaller and lighter than their full-frame counterparts, but there are some hefty DX lenses available, including the AF-S DX Zoom-Nikkor 17-55mm f/2.8G IF-ED.
- **ED (or LD/UD).** The ED (extra low dispersion) designation indicates that some lens elements are made of a special hard and scratch-resistant glass that minimizes the divergence of the different colors of light as they pass through, thus reducing chromatic aberration (color "fringing") and other image defects. A gold band around the front of the lens indicates an optic with ED elements. You sometimes find LD (low dispersion) or UD (ultra-low dispersion) designations.

- **FX.** When Nikon introduced the Nikon D3 full-frame camera, it coined the term "FX," representing the 23.9 × 36mm sensor format as a counterpart to "DX," which was used for its 15.8 × 23.6mm APS-C-sized sensors. Although FX hasn't been officially applied to any Nikon lenses so far, expect to see the designation used more often to differentiate between lenses that are compatible with any Nikon digital SLR (FX) and those that operate only on DX-format cameras, or in DX mode when used on an FX camera like the D3s/D3x.
- **G.** G-type lenses have no aperture ring, and you can use them at other than the maximum aperture only with electronic cameras like the D3s/D3x that set the aperture automatically or by using the command dial while the Exposure compensation/Aperture button is depressed. This includes all Nikon digital dSLRs.
- **IF.** Nikon's *internal focusing* lenses change focus by shifting only small internal lens groups with no change required in the lens's physical length, unlike conventional double helicoid focusing systems that move all lens groups toward the front or rear during focusing. IF lenses are more compact and lighter in weight, provide better balance, focus more closely, and can be focused more quickly.
- **IX.** These lenses were produced for Nikon's long-discontinued Pronea 6i and S APS film cameras. While the Pronea could use many standard Nikon lenses, IX lenses cannot be mounted on any Nikon digital SLR.
- **Micro.** Nikon uses the term *micro* to designate its close-up lenses. Most other vendors use *macro* instead.
- **NAI.** This is not an official Nikon term, but it is widely used to indicate that a manual focus lens is *Not-AI*, which means that it was manufactured before 1977, and therefore cannot be used safely on modern digital Nikon SLRs without modification.
- **NOCT (Nocturnal).** Used primarily to refer to the prized Nikkor AI-S Noct 58mm f/1.2, a "fast" (wide-aperture) lens, with aspherical elements, capable of taking photographs in very low light.
- **PC (Perspective Control).** A PC lens is capable of shifting the lens from side to side (and up/down) to provide a more realistic perspective when photographing architecture and other subjects that otherwise require tilting the camera so that the sensor plane is not parallel to the subject. Older Nikkor PC lenses offered shifting only, but more modern models, such as the PC-E Nikkor 24mm f/3.5D ED lens introduced early in 2008 allow both shifting and tilting.
- **UV.** This term is applied to special (and expensive) lenses designed to pass ultraviolet light.

- **UW.** Lenses with this designation are designed for underwater photography with Nikonos camera bodies, and cannot be used with Nikon digital SLRs.
- **VR.** Nikon has an expanding line of vibration reduction (VR) lenses, including several very affordable models and the AF-S DX Nikkor 16-85mm f/3.5-5.6G ED VR lens, which shifts lens elements internally to counteract camera shake. The VR feature allows using a shutter speed up to four stops slower than would be possible without vibration reduction.

## What Lenses Can Do for You

I'm something of a lens nut. Because my work requires me to evaluate many different lenses and provide recommendations for specific lenses that may have overlapping focal lengths and features, I'm able to justify owning many more optics than the average person wants or needs. It probably wouldn't make sense for you to own 14-24mm, 17-35mm, 24-70mm, and 28-200mm zooms as I do. Indeed, a much saner approach to expanding your lens collection is to consider what each of your options can do for you and then choosing the type of lens and specific model that will really boost your creative opportunities.

So, in the sections that follow, I'm going to provide a general guide to the sort of capabilities you can gain for your D3s/D3x by adding a lens to your repertoire. Then, at the end of the chapter, I'll provide a more detailed discussion of some specific lenses and how they might fit into your camera bag toolkit.

- **Wider perspective.** Your mid-range zoom lens has served you well for moderate wide-angle shots. Now you find your back is up against a wall and you *can't* take a step backwards to take in more subject matter. Perhaps you're standing on the rim of the Grand Canyon, and you want to take in as much of the breathtaking view as you can. You might find yourself just behind the baseline at a high school basketball game and want an interesting shot with a little perspective distortion tossed in the mix. There's a lens out there that will provide you with what you need, such as the 14-24mm zoom I'll describe later in the chapter.
- **Bring objects closer.** A long lens brings distant subjects closer to you, offers better control over depth-of-field, and avoids the perspective distortion that wide-angle lenses provide. They compress the apparent distance between objects in your frame. The image shown in Figure 9.5 was taken using a wide 16mm lens, while the image in Figures 9.6 and 9.7 were taken from the same position as Figure 9.5, but with focal lengths of 70mm and 200mm, respectively.
- **Bring your camera closer.** Macro lenses allow you to focus to within an inch or two of your subject. Nikon's best close-up lenses are all fixed focal length optics in the 60mm to 200mm range. But you'll find good macro zooms available from Sigma and others. They don't tend to focus quite as close, but they provide a bit of

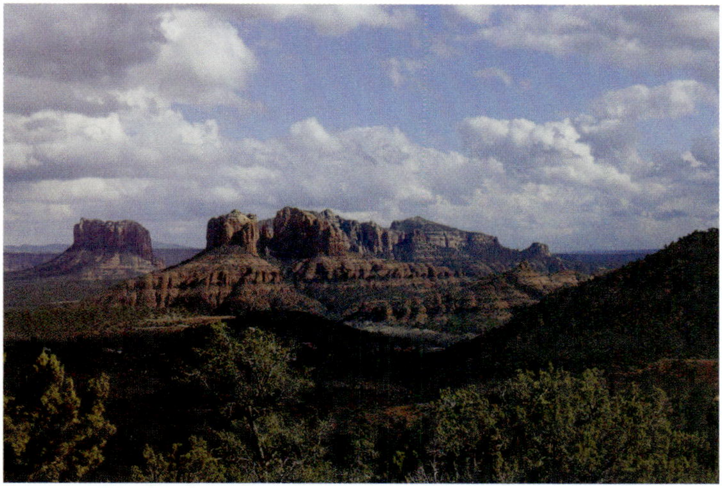

**Figure 9.5**
An ultrawide-angle lens provided this view of Sedona's Cathedral Rock.

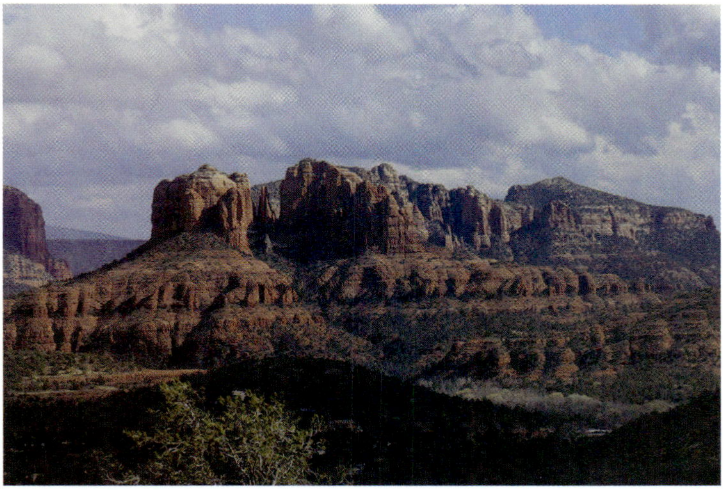

**Figure 9.6**
This photo, taken from roughly the same distance shows the view using a short telephoto lens.

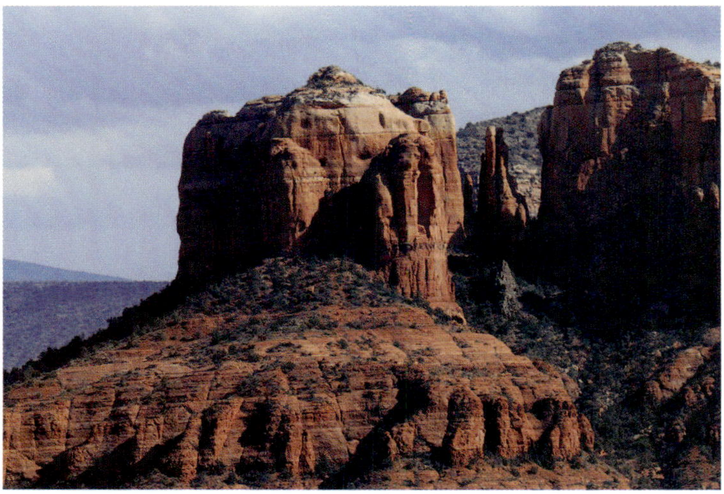

**Figure 9.7**
A long telephoto lens captured this close-up view of Cathedral Rock from approximately the same shooting position.

flexibility when you want to vary your subject distance (say, to avoid spooking a skittish creature).

- **Look sharp.** Many lenses are prized for their sharpness and overall image quality. While your run-of-the-mill lens is likely to be plenty sharp for most applications, the very best optics are even better over their entire field of view (which means no fuzzy corners), are sharper at a wider range of focal lengths (in the case of zooms), and have better correction for various types of distortion. You can read lens evaluations to help locate the sharpest lenses in online forums like www.popphoto.com and www.dpreview.com.
- **More speed.** Your Nikon 70-300mm f/4.5-5.6 telephoto zoom lens might have the perfect focal length and sharpness for sports photography, but the maximum aperture won't cut it for night baseball or football games, or, even, any sports shooting in daylight if the weather is cloudy or you need to use some ungodly fast shutter speed, such as 1/4,000th second. You might be happier to gain a full f/stop with an AF-S Nikkor 300mm f/4D IF-ED for a little more than $1,000, or even the pricier Nikon AF-S VR II Zoom-Nikkor 70-200mm f/2.8G IF-E mated to a 1.4x teleconverter (giving you a 98-280mm f/4 lens). If money is no object, you can spring for Nikon's superfast 400mm f/2.8 and 600mm f/4 (both with vibration reduction and priced in the $6,500-and-up stratosphere). Or, maybe you just need the speed and can benefit from an f/1.8 or f/1.4 prime lens. They're all available in Nikon mounts (there's even an 85mm f/1.4 and 50mm f/1.4 for the real speed demons). With any of these lenses you can continue photographing under the dimmest of lighting conditions without the need for a tripod or flash.
- **Special features.** Accessory lenses give you special features, such as tilt/shift capabilities to correct for perspective distortion in architectural shots. You'll also find macro lenses, including the new AF-S Micro-Nikkor 60mm f/2.8G ED, fisheye lenses like the AF DX Fisheye-Nikkor 10.5mm f/2.8G ED (which can be used on the D3s/D3x in crop mode), and all VR (vibration reduction) lenses also count as special-feature optics.

## Zoom or Prime?

Zoom lenses have changed the way serious photographers take pictures. One of the reasons that I own 12 SLR film bodies dating back to the pre-zoom days is that in ancient times it was common to mount a different fixed focal length prime lens on various cameras and take pictures with two or three cameras around your neck (or tucked in a camera case) so you'd be ready to take a long shot or an intimate close-up or wide-angle view on a moment's notice, without the need to switch lenses. It made sense (at the time) to have a half-dozen or so bodies (two to use, one in the shop, one in transit, and a couple backups). Zoom lenses of the time had a limited zoom range, were heavy, and not very sharp (especially when you tried to wield one of those monsters hand-held).

That's all changed today. Lenses like the razor-sharp AF-S VR II Zoom-Nikkor 70-200mm f/2.8G IF-ED boast longer zoom ranges, in a package that's about 8.5-inches long, and while not petite at 3.2 pounds, quite usable hand-held (especially with VR switched on). Although such a lens might seem expensive at $1,600-plus, it's actually much less costly than the six or so lenses it replaces. I'll explain more about this particular lens later in the chapter.

When selecting between zoom and prime lenses, there are several considerations to ponder. Here's a checklist of the most important factors. I already mentioned image quality and maximum aperture earlier, but those aspects take on additional meaning when comparing zooms and primes.

- **Logistics.** As prime lenses offer just a single focal length, you'll need more of them to encompass the full range offered by a single zoom. More lenses mean additional slots in your camera bag, and extra weight to carry. Just within Nikon's line alone you can choose from a good selection of general-purpose prime lenses in 28mm, 35mm, 50mm, 85mm, 100mm, 135mm, and 200mm focal lengths, all of which are overlapped by the 28-200mm zoom I mentioned earlier. Even so, you might be willing to carry an extra prime lens or two in order to gain the speed or image quality.
- **Image quality.** Prime lenses usually produce better image quality at their focal length than even the most sophisticated zoom lenses at the same magnification. Zoom lenses, with their shifting elements and f/stops that can vary from zoom position to zoom position, are in general more complex to design than fixed focal length lenses. That's not to say that the very best prime lenses can't be complicated as well. However, the exotic designs, aspheric elements, and low-dispersion glass can be applied to improving the quality of the lens, rather than wasting a lot of it on compensating for problems caused by the zoom process itself.
- **Maximum aperture.** Because of the same design constraints, zoom lenses usually have smaller maximum apertures than prime lenses, and the most affordable zooms have a lens opening that grows effectively smaller as you zoom in. The difference in lens speed verges on the ridiculous at some focal lengths. For example, an 18mm-55mm basic zoom gives you a 55mm f/5.6 lens when zoomed all the way out, while prime lenses in that focal length commonly have f/1.8 or faster maximum apertures. Indeed, the fastest f/2, f/1.8, f1/4, and f/1.2 lenses are all primes, and if you require speed, a fixed focal length lens, like the two shown in Figure 9.8, are what you should rely on. Figure 9.9 shows an image taken with a Nikon 85mm f /1.4 lens.
- **Speed.** Using prime lenses takes time and slows you down. It takes a few seconds to remove your current lens and mount a new one, and the more often you need to do that, the more time is wasted. If you choose not to swap lenses, when using a fixed focal length lens you'll still have to move closer or farther away from your subject to get the field of view you want. A zoom lens allows you to change magnifications and focal lengths with the twist of a ring and generally saves a great deal of time.

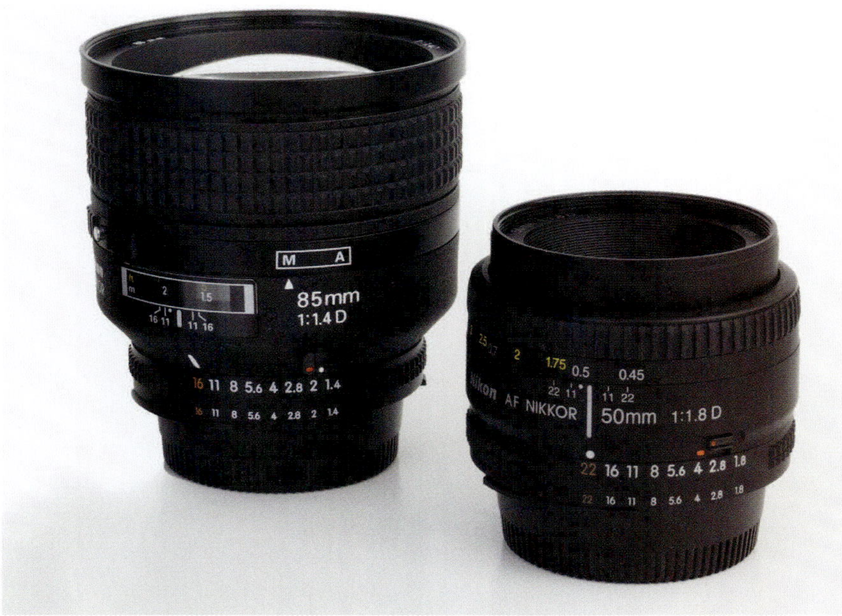


**Figure 9.8**
The 85mm f/1.4 and 50mm f/1.8 lenses shown are fast and can be used wide open.

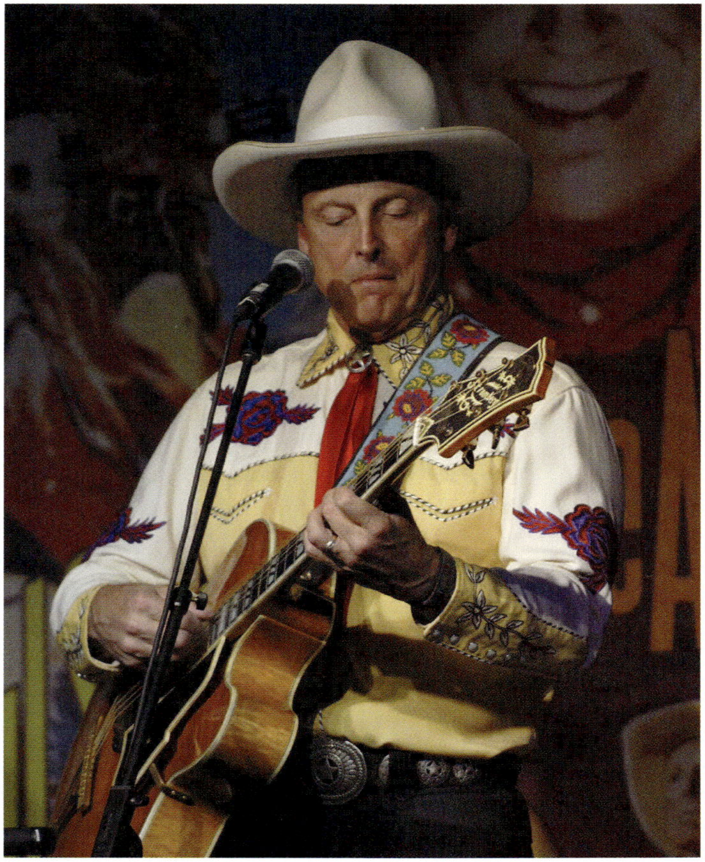

**Figure 9.9**
An 85mm f/1.4 lens was perfect for this hand-held photo.

## Categories of Lenses

Lenses can be categorized by their intended purpose—general photography, macro photography, and so forth—or by their focal length. The range of available focal lengths is usually divided into three main groups: wide-angle, normal, and telephoto. Prime lenses fall neatly into one of these classifications. Zooms can overlap designations, with a significant number falling into the catch-all wide-to-telephoto zoom range. This section provides more information about focal length ranges, and how they are used.

Without that pesky crop factor, any lens with a focal length of 10mm to 16mm is said to be an *ultrawide-angle lens*; from about 16mm to 30mm is said to be a *wide-angle lens. Normal lenses* have a focal length roughly equivalent to the diagonal of the film or sensor, in millimeters, and so fall into the range of about 40mm to 55mm on a D3s/D3x. *Short telephoto lenses* start at about 70mm to 85mm, with anything from 105mm to 300mm qualifying as a conventional *telephoto.* For the Nikon D3s/D3x, anything from about 300mm-400mm or longer can be considered a *super-telephoto.*

## Using Wide-Angle and Wide-Zoom Lenses

To use wide-angle prime lenses and wide zooms, you need to understand how they affect your photography. Here's a quick summary of the things you need to know.

- **More depth-of-field.** Practically speaking, wide-angle lenses offer more depth-of-field at a particular subject distance and aperture. (But see the sidebar below for an important note.) You'll find that helpful when you want to maximize sharpness of a large zone, but not very useful when you'd rather isolate your subject using selective focus (telephoto lenses are better for that).
- **Stepping back.** Wide-angle lenses have the effect of making it seem that you are standing farther from your subject than you really are. They're helpful when you don't want to back up, or can't because there are impediments in your way.
- **Wider field of view.** While making your subject seem farther away, as implied above, a wide-angle lens also provides a larger field of view, including more of the subject in your photos.
- **More foreground.** As background objects retreat, more of the foreground is brought into view by a wide-angle lens. That gives you extra emphasis on the area that's closest to the camera. Photograph your home with a normal lens/normal zoom setting, and the front yard probably looks fairly conventional in your photo (that's why they're called "normal" lenses). Switch to a wider lens and you'll discover that your lawn now makes up much more of the photo. So, wide-angle lenses are great when you want to emphasize that lake in the foreground, but problematic when your intended subject is located farther in the distance.

- **Super-sized subjects.** The tendency of a wide-angle lens to emphasize objects in the foreground, while de-emphasizing objects in the background, can lead to a kind of size distortion that may be more objectionable for some types of subjects than others. Shoot a bed of flowers up close with a wide angle, and you might like the distorted effect of the larger blossoms nearer the lens. Take a photo of a family member with the same lens from the same distance, and you're likely to get some complaints about that gigantic nose in the foreground.
- **Perspective distortion.** When you tilt the camera so the plane of the sensor is no longer perpendicular to the vertical plane of your subject, some parts of the subject are now closer to the sensor than they were before, while other parts are farther away. So, buildings, flagpoles, or NBA players appear to be falling backwards, as you can see in Figure 9.10. While this kind of apparent distortion (it's not caused by a defect in the lens) can happen with any lens, it's most apparent when a wide angle is used.

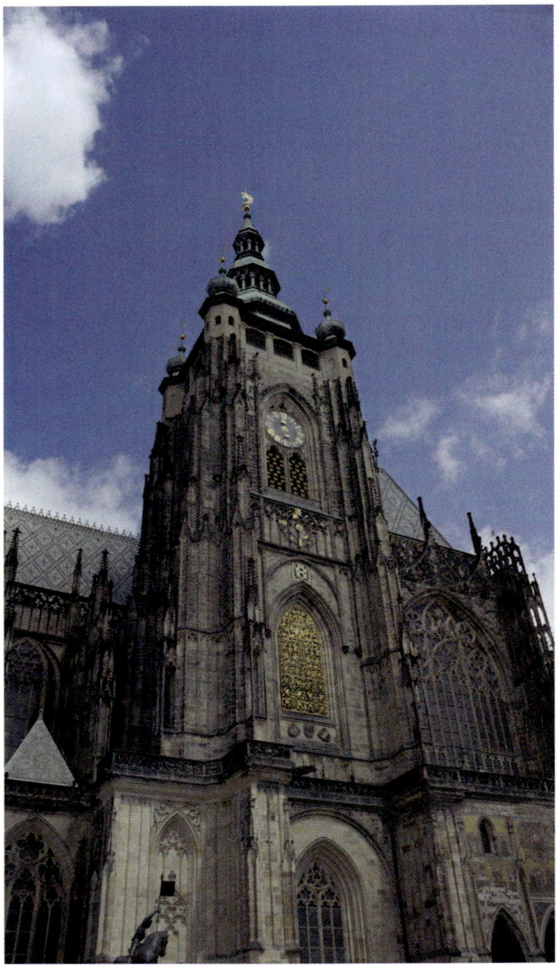

**Figure 9.10**
Tilting the camera back produces this "falling back" look in architectural photos.

- **Steady cam.** You'll find that you can hand-hold a wide-angle lens at slower shutter speeds, without need for vibration reduction, than you can with a telephoto lens. The reduced magnification of the wide-lens or wide-zoom setting doesn't emphasize camera shake like a telephoto lens does.
- **Interesting angles.** Many of the factors already listed combine to produce more interesting angles when shooting with wide-angle lenses. Raising or lowering a telephoto lens a few feet probably will have little effect on the appearance of the distant subjects you're shooting. The same change in elevation can produce a dramatic effect for the much closer subjects typically captured with a wide-angle lens or wide-zoom setting.

**DOF IN DEPTH**

The DOF advantage of wide-angle lenses is diminished when you enlarge your picture; believe it or not, a wide-angle image enlarged and cropped to provide the same subject size as a telephoto shot would have the *same* depth-of-field. Try it: take a wide-angle photo of a friend from a fair distance, and then zoom in to duplicate the picture in a telephoto image. Then, enlarge the wide shot so your friend is the same size in both. The wide photo will have the same depth-of-field (and will have much less detail, too).

## Avoiding Potential Wide-Angle Problems

Wide-angle lenses have a few quirks that you'll want to keep in mind when shooting so you can avoid falling into some common traps. Here's a checklist of tips for avoiding common problems:

- **Symptom: converging lines.** Unless you want to use wildly diverging lines as a creative effect, it's a good idea to keep horizontal and vertical lines in landscapes, architecture, and other subjects carefully aligned with the sides, top, and bottom of the frame. That will help you avoid undesired perspective distortion. Sometimes it helps to shoot from a slightly elevated position so you don't have to tilt the camera up or down.
- **Symptom: color fringes around objects.** Lenses are often plagued with fringes of color around backlit objects, produced by *chromatic aberration*, which comes in two forms: *longitudinal/axial*, in which all the colors of light don't focus in the same plane; and *lateral/transverse*, in which the colors are shifted to one side. Axial chromatic aberration can be reduced by stopping down the lens, but transverse CA cannot. Both can be reduced by using lenses with low diffraction index glass (or ED elements, in Nikon nomenclature) and by incorporating elements that cancel the chromatic aberration of other glass in the lens. For example, a strong positive lens

made of low-dispersion crown glass (made of a soda-lime-silica composite) may be mated with a weaker negative lens made of high-dispersion flint glass, which contains lead.

- **Symptom: lines that bow outward.** Some wide-angle lenses cause straight lines to bow outwards, with the strongest effect at the edges. In fisheye (or *curvilinear*) lenses, this defect is a feature, as you can see in Figure 9.11. When distortion is not desired, you'll need to use a lens that has corrected barrel distortion. Manufacturers like Nikon do their best to minimize or eliminate it (producing a *rectilinear* lens), often using *aspherical* lens elements (which are not cross-sections of a sphere). You can also minimize barrel distortion simply by framing your photo with some extra space all around, so the edges where the defect is most obvious can be cropped out of the picture. Some image editors, such as Photoshop and Photoshop Elements have a lens distortion correction feature.

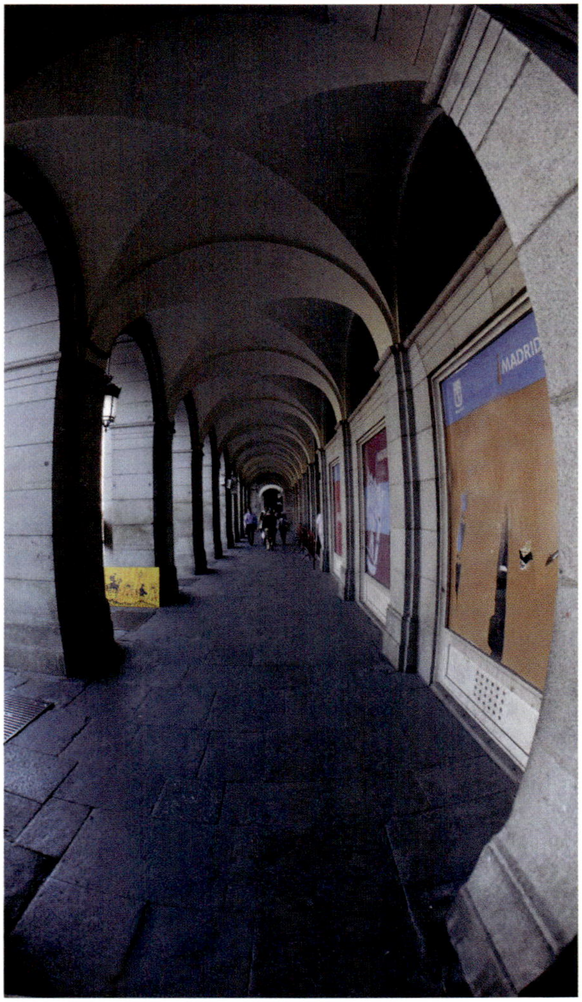

**Figure 9.11**
Many wide-angle lenses cause lines to bow outwards towards the edges of the image; with a fisheye lens, this tendency is considered an interesting feature.

- **Symptom: light and dark areas when using polarizing filter.** If you know that polarizers work best when the camera is pointed 90 degrees away from the sun and have the least effect when the camera is oriented 180 degrees from the sun, you know only half the story. With lenses having a focal length of 14mm-28mm, the angle of view is extensive enough to cause problems. Think about it: when a 14mm lens is pointed at the proper 90-degree angle from the sun, objects at the edges of the frame will be oriented at 135 to 41 degrees, with only the center at exactly 90 degrees. Either edge will have much less of a polarized effect. The solution is to avoid using a polarizing filter with lenses having an actual focal length of less than 28mm.

## Using Telephoto and Tele-Zoom Lenses

Telephoto lenses also can have a dramatic effect on your photography, and Nikon is especially strong in the long-lens arena, with lots of choices in many focal lengths and zoom ranges. You should be able to find an affordable telephoto or tele-zoom to enhance your photography in several different ways. Here are the most important things you need to know. In the next section, I'll concentrate on telephoto considerations that can be problematic—and how to avoid those problems.

- **Selective focus.** Long lenses have reduced depth-of-field within the frame, allowing you to use selective focus to isolate your subject. You can open the lens up wide to create shallow depth-of-field, or close it down a bit to allow more to be in focus. The flip side of the coin is that when you *want* to make a range of objects sharp, you'll need to use a smaller f/stop to get the depth-of-field you need. Like fire, the depth-of-field of a telephoto lens can be friend or foe. Figure 9.12 shows a photo of a meerkat, photographed using a telephoto lens and wider f/stop to de-emphasize a distracting background. The darkness of the background and backlighting didn't hurt, either!
- **Getting closer.** Telephoto lenses bring you closer to wildlife, sports action, and candid subjects. No one wants to get a reputation as a surreptitious or "sneaky" photographer (except for paparazzi), but when applied to candids in an open and honest way, a long lens can help you capture memorable moments while retaining enough distance to stay out of the way of events as they transpire.
- **Reduced foreground/increased compression.** Telephoto lenses have the opposite effect of wide angles: they reduce the importance of things in the foreground by squeezing everything together. This compression even makes distant objects appear to be closer to subjects in the foreground and middle ranges. You can use this effect as a creative tool to squeeze subjects together.

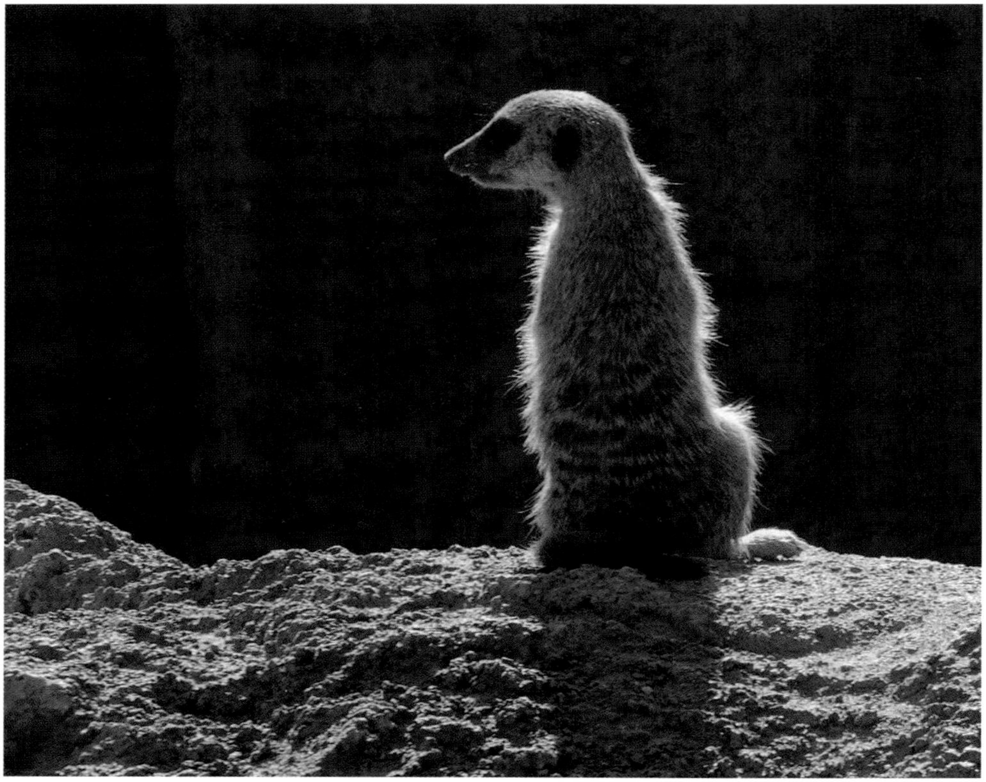

**Figure 9.12**
A wide f/stop and lighting helped isolate the meerkat from its background.

- **Accentuates camera shakiness.** Telephoto focal lengths hit you with a double whammy in terms of camera/photographer shake. The lenses themselves are bulkier, more difficult to hold steady, and may even produce a barely perceptible see-saw rocking effect when you support them with one hand halfway down the lens barrel. Telephotos also magnify any camera shake. It's no wonder that vibration reduction is popular in longer lenses.
- **Interesting angles require creativity.** Telephoto lenses require more imagination in selecting interesting angles, because the "angle" you do get on your subjects is so narrow. Moving from side to side or a bit higher or lower can make a dramatic difference in a wide-angle shot, but raising or lowering a telephoto lens a few feet probably will have little effect on the appearance of the distant subjects you're shooting.

## Avoiding Telephoto Lens Problems

Many of the "problems" that telephoto lenses pose are really just challenges and not that difficult to overcome. Here is a list of the seven most common picture maladies and suggested solutions.

- **Symptom: flat faces in portraits.** Head-and-shoulders portraits of humans tend to be more flattering when a focal length of 50mm to 85mm is used. Longer focal lengths compress the distance between features like noses and ears, making the face look wider and flat. A wide angle might make noses look huge and ears tiny when you fill the frame with a face. So stick with 50mm to 105mm focal lengths, going longer only when you're forced to shoot from a greater distance, and wider only when shooting three-quarters/full-length portraits, or group shots.

- **Symptom: blur due to camera shake.** Use a higher shutter speed (boosting ISO if necessary); consider an image-stabilized lens; or mount your camera on a tripod, monopod, or brace it with some other support. Of those three solutions, only the first will reduce blur caused by *subject* motion; a VR lens or tripod won't help you freeze a race car in mid-lap.
- **Symptom: color fringes.** Chromatic aberration is the most pernicious optical problem found in telephoto lenses. There are others, including spherical aberration, astigmatism, coma, curvature of field, and similarly scary-sounding phenomena. The best solution for any of these is to use a better lens that offers the proper degree of correction, or stop down the lens to minimize the problem. But that's not always possible. Your second-best choice may be to correct the fringing in your favorite RAW conversion tool or image editor. Photoshop CS4's Lens Correction filter (found in the Distort menu) offers sliders that minimize both red/cyan and blue/yellow fringing.
- **Symptom: lines that curve inwards.** Pincushion distortion is found in many telephoto lenses. You might find after a bit of testing that it is worse at certain focal lengths with your particular zoom lens. Like chromatic aberration, it can be partially corrected using tools like the correction tools built into Photoshop and Photoshop Elements. You can see an exaggerated example in Figure 9.13; pincushion distortion isn't always this obvious.
- **Symptom: low contrast from haze or fog.** When you're photographing distant objects, a long lens shoots through a lot more atmosphere, which generally is muddied up with extra haze and fog. That dirt or moisture in the atmosphere can reduce contrast and mute colors. Some feel that a skylight or UV filter can help, but this practice is mostly a holdover from the film days. Digital sensors are not sensitive enough to UV light for a UV filter to have much effect. So you should be prepared to boost contrast and color saturation in your Picture Controls menu or image editor if necessary.
- **Symptom: low contrast from flare.** Lenses are furnished with lens hoods for a good reason: to reduce flare from bright light sources at the periphery of the picture area, or completely outside it. Because telephoto lenses often create images that are lower in contrast in the first place, you'll want to be especially careful to use a lens hood to prevent further effects on your image (or shade the front of the lens with your hand).

- **Symptom: dark flash photos.** Edge-to-edge flash coverage isn't a problem with telephoto lenses as it is with wide angles. The shooting distance is. A long lens might make a subject that's 50 feet away look as if it's right next to you, but your camera's flash isn't fooled. You'll need extra power for distant flash shots. The Nikon SB-900 Speedlight, for example, can automatically zoom its coverage down to that of a 105mm medium telephoto lens, providing a theoretical full-power shooting aperture of about f/11 at 30 feet and ISO 400.

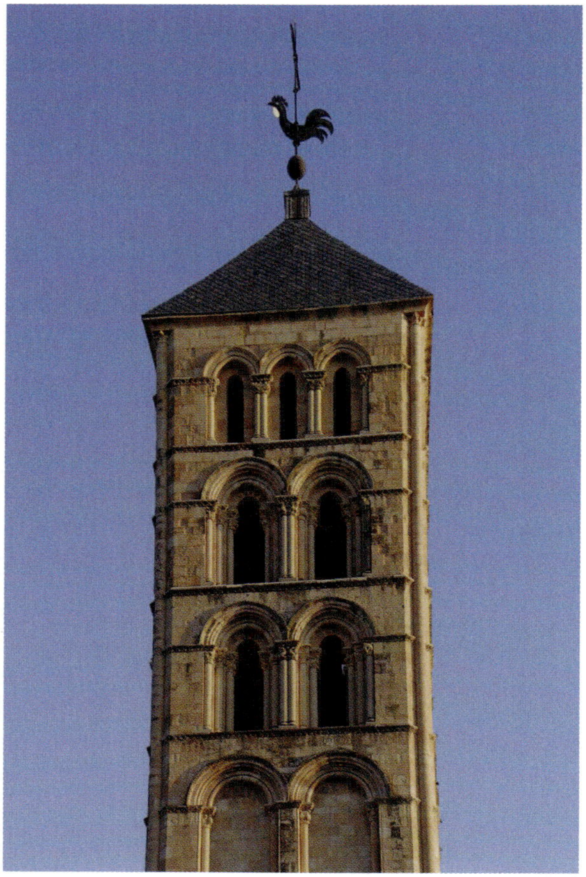

**Figure 9.13**
Pincushion distortion in telephoto lenses causes lines to bow inwards from the edges.

## Telephotos and Bokeh

*Bokeh* describes the aesthetic qualities of the out-of-focus parts of an image and whether out-of-focus points of light—circles of confusion—are rendered as distracting fuzzy discs or smoothly fade into the background. *Boke* is a Japanese word for "blur," and the h was added to keep English speakers from rendering it monosyllabically to rhyme with *broke.* Although bokeh is visible in blurry portions of any image, it's of particular concern with telephoto lenses, which, thanks to the magic of reduced depth-of-field, produce more obviously out-of-focus areas.

Bokeh can vary from lens to lens, or even within a given lens depending on the f/stop in use. Bokeh becomes objectionable when the circles of confusion are evenly illuminated, making them stand out as distinct discs, or, worse, when these circles are darker in the center, producing an ugly "doughnut" effect. A lens defect called spherical aberration may produce out-of-focus discs that are brighter on the edges and darker in the center, because the lens doesn't focus light passing through the edges of the lens exactly as it does light going through the center. (Mirror or *catadioptric* lenses also produce this effect.)

Other kinds of spherical aberration generate circles of confusion that are brightest in the center and fade out at the edges, producing a smooth blending effect, as you can see at right in Figure 9.14. Ironically, when no spherical aberration is present at all, the discs are a uniform shade, which, while better than the doughnut effect, is not as pleasing as the bright center/dark edge rendition. The shape of the disc also comes into play, with round smooth circles considered the best, and nonagonal or some other polygon (determined by the shape of the lens diaphragm) considered less desirable.

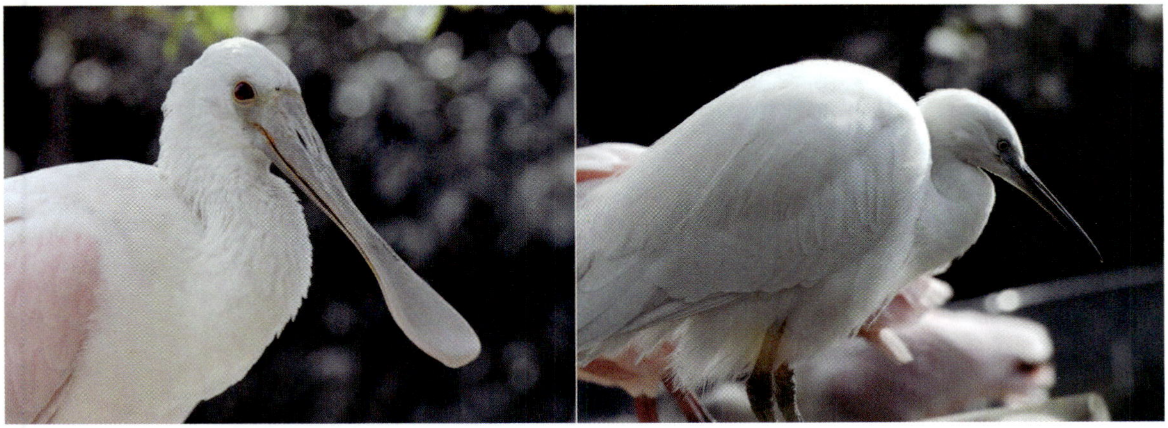

**Figure 9.14** Bokeh is less pleasing when the discs are prominent (left), and less obtrusive when they blend into the background (right).

If you plan to use selective focus a lot, you should investigate the bokeh characteristics of a particular lens before you buy. Nikon user groups and forums will usually be full of comments and questions about bokeh of particular lenses, so the research is fairly easy.

## Add-ons and Special Features

Once you've purchased your telephoto lens, you'll want to think about some appropriate accessories for it. There are some handy add-ons available that can be valuable. Here are a couple of them to think about.

## Lens Hoods

Lens hoods are an important accessory for all lenses, but they're especially valuable with telephotos. As I mentioned earlier, lens hoods do a good job of preserving image contrast by keeping bright light sources outside the field of view from striking the lens and, potentially, bouncing around inside that long tube to generate flare that, when coupled with atmospheric haze, can rob your image of detail and snap. In addition, lens hoods serve as valuable protection for that large, vulnerable, front lens element. It's easy to forget that you've got that long tube sticking out in front of your camera and accidentally whack the front of your lens into something. It's cheaper to replace a lens hood than it is to have a lens repaired, so you might find that a good hood is valuable protection for your prized optics.

When choosing a lens hood, it's important to have the right hood for the lens, usually the one offered for that lens by Nikon or the third-party manufacturer. You want a hood that blocks precisely the right amount of light: neither too much light nor too little. A hood with a front diameter that is too small can show up in your pictures as vignetting. A hood that has a front diameter that's too large isn't stopping all the light it should. Generic lens hoods may not do the job.

When your telephoto is a zoom lens, it's even more important to get the right hood, because you need one that does what it is supposed to at both the wide-angle and telephoto ends of the zoom range. Lens hoods may be cylindrical, rectangular (shaped like the image frame), or petal shaped (that is, cylindrical, but with cut-out areas at the corners which correspond to the actual image area). Lens hoods should be mounted in the correct orientation (a bayonet mount for the hood usually takes care of this).

## Telephoto Converters

Teleconverters (often called telephoto extenders outside the Nikon world) multiply the actual focal length of your lens, giving you a longer telephoto for much less than the price of a lens with that actual focal length. These converters fit between the lens and your camera and contain optical elements that magnify the image produced by the lens. Available in 1.4X, 1.7X, and 2.0X configurations from Nikon, a teleconverter transforms, say, a 200mm lens into a 280mm, 340mm, or 400mm optic, respectively. In effect, converters restore the "lens multiplier" factor you lost when you adopted the FX format. At around $300-$400 each, converters are quite a bargain, aren't they?

The only drawback is that Nikon's TC II and latest TC III teleconverters can be used only with a limited number of Nikkor AF-S lenses. The compatible models include the 200mm f/2G ED-IF AF-S VR Nikkor, 300mm f/2.8G ED-IF AF-S VR Nikkor, 400mm f/2.8D ED-IF AF-S II Nikkor, 80-200mm f/2.8D ED-IF AF-S, 70-200mm f/2.8G ED-IF AF-S VR Zoom-Nikkor, 200-400mm f/4G ED-IF AF-S VR Zoom-Nikkor, 300mm f/4D ED-IF AF-S Nikkor, 500mm f/4D ED-IF AF-S II Nikkor, and 600mm f/4D ED-IF AF-S II Nikkor. These tend to be pricey (or ultra-pricey) lenses. Teleconverters from Sigma, Kenko, Tamron, and others cost less, and may be compatible with a broader range of lenses. (They work especially well with lenses from the same vendor that produces the teleconverter.)

There are other downsides. While extenders retain the closest focusing distance of your original lens, autofocus is maintained only if the lens's original maximum aperture is f/4 or larger (for the 1.4X extender) or f/2.8 or larger (for the 2X extender). The components reduce the effective aperture of any lens they are used with, by one f/stop with the 1.4X converter, 1.5 f/stops with the 1.7X converter, and 2 f/stops with the 2X extender. So, your 200mm f/2.8 lens becomes a 280mm f/4 or 400mm f/5.6 lens. Although Nikon converters are precision optical devices, they do cost you a little sharpness, but that improves when you reduce the aperture by a stop or two. Each of the converters is compatible only with a particular set of lenses greater, so you'll want to check Nikon's compatibility chart to see if the component can be used with the lens you want to attach to it.

If your lenses are compatible and you're shooting under bright lighting conditions, the Nikon extenders make handy accessories. I recommend the 1.4X version because it robs you of very little sharpness and only one f/stop. The 1.7X version also works well, but I've found the original 2X teleconverter to exact too much of a sharpness and speed penalty to be of much use. I haven't had a chance to test the new TC-20E III converter to see if it offers improved sharpness (the speed penalty remains, alas). (See Figure 9.15.)

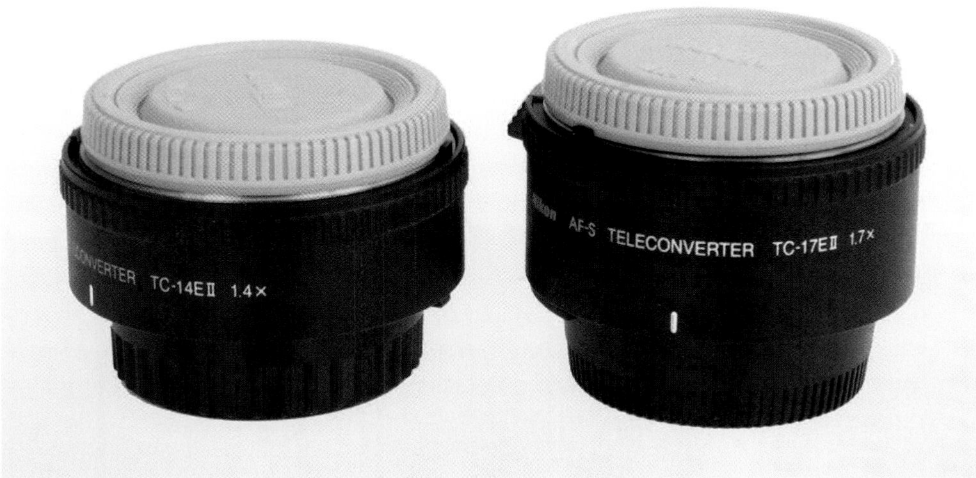


**Figure 9.15**
Telephoto converters increase the effective focal length of your lenses.

## Macro Focusing

Some telephotos and telephoto zooms available for the Nikon D3s/D3x have particularly close focusing capabilities, making them *macro* lenses. Of course, the object is not necessarily to get close (get too close and you'll find it difficult to light your subject). What you're really looking for in a macro lens is to magnify the apparent size of the subject in the final image. Camera-to-subject distance is most important when you want to back up farther from your subject (say, to avoid spooking skittish insects or small animals). In that case, you'll want a macro lens with a longer focal length to allow that distance while retaining the desired magnification.

Nikon makes five lenses that are officially designated as macro lenses for full frame use. They include

- **AF-S Micro-Nikkor 60mm f/2.8G ED.** This type G lens supposedly replaces the type D lens listed next, adding an internal Silent Wave autofocus motor that should operate faster, and which is also compatible with cameras lacking a body motor, such as the Nikon D40/D40x and D60. It also has ED lens elements for improved image quality. However, because it lacks an aperture ring, you can control the f/stop only when the lens is mounted directly on the camera or used with automatic extension tubes. Should you want to reverse a macro lens (which can improve image quality) or mount it on a bellows, you're better off with a lens having an aperture ring.
- **AF Micro-Nikkor 60mm f/2.8D.** This older lens's aperture ring gives it a little more versatility but, realistically, only fanatical close-up shooters actually use the Nikon BR-2a lens reversing ring (which can improve image quality) or mount the lens on a bellows. I happen to belong in that camp, so I am hanging onto mine.
- **AF-S VR Micro-Nikkor 105mm f/2.8G IF-ED.** This G-series lens did replace a similar D-type, non-AF-S version that also lacked VR. I own the older lens, too, and am keeping it for the same reasons described above—but also because I find VR a rather specialized tool for macro work. Some 99 percent of the time, I shoot close-ups with my D3s/D3x mounted on a tripod or, at the very least, on a monopod, so camera vibration is not much of a concern. Indeed, *subject* movement is a more serious problem, especially when shooting plant life outdoors on days plagued with even slight breezes. Because my outdoor subjects are likely to move while I am composing my photo, I find both VR and autofocus not very useful. I end up focusing manually most of the time, too. This lens provides a little extra camera-to-subject distance, so you'll find it very useful, but consider the older non-G, non-VR version, too, if you're in the market.
- **AF Micro-Nikkor 200mm f/4D IF-ED.** With a price tag of about $1,300, you'd probably want this lens only if you planned a great deal of close-up shooting at greater distances. It focuses down to 1.6 feet, but provides enough magnification to allow interesting close-ups of subjects that are farther away. A specialized tool for specialized shooting.

- **PC Micro-Nikkor 85mm f/2.8D.** Priced about the same as the 200mm Micro-Nikkor, this is a manual focus lens that offers both tilt and shift capabilities, so you can adjust the perspective of the subject as you shoot. The tilt feature lets you "tilt" the plane of focus, providing the illusion of greater depth-of-field (the actual DOF is just distributed differently), while the shift capabilities make it possible to shoot down on a subject from an angle and still maintain its correct proportions. If you need one of these, you already know it; if you're still wondering how you'd use one, you probably have no need for these specialized capabilities.

You'll also find macro lenses, macro zooms, and other close-focusing lenses available from Sigma, Tamron, and Tokina. If you want to focus closer with a macro lens, or any other lens, you can add an accessory called an *extension tube*, like the one shown in Figure 9.16, or a *bellows extension*. These add-ons move the lens farther from the focal plane, allowing it to focus more closely. Nikon also sells add-on close-up lenses, which look like filters, and allow lenses to focus more closely.

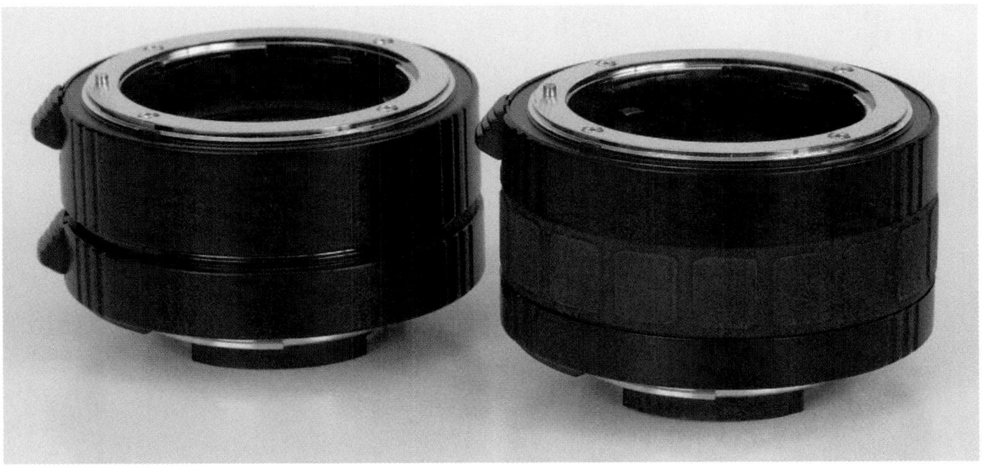

**Figure 9.16** Extension tubes enable any lens to focus more closely to the subject.

## Vibration Reduction

Nikon has a burgeoning line of about a dozen and a half lenses with built-in vibration reduction (VR) capabilities. I expect another half dozen or so new VR lenses to be introduced rather early in the life of this book.

The VR feature uses lens elements that are shifted internally in response to vertical or horizontal motion of the lens, which compensates for any camera shake in those directions. Vibration reduction is particularly effective when used with telephoto lenses, which magnify the effects of camera and photographer motion. However, VR can be useful for lenses of shorter focal lengths, such as Nikon's 24-120mm full-frame zoom.

Vibration reduction offers two to three shutter speed increments' worth of shake reduction. (Nikon claims a four-stop gain, which I feel may be optimistic.) This extra margin can be invaluable when you're shooting under dim lighting conditions or hand-holding a lens for, say, wildlife photography. Perhaps that shot of a foraging deer would require a shutter speed of 1/2,000th second at f/5.6 with your AF-S VR Zoom-Nikkor 200-400mm f/4G IF-ED lens. Relax. You can shoot at 1/250th second at f/11 and get a photo that is just as sharp, as long as the deer doesn't decide to bound off. Or, perhaps you're shooting indoors and would prefer to shoot at 1/15th second at f/4. However, consider these facts:

- **VR doesn't freeze subject motion.** Vibration reduction won't freeze moving subjects in their tracks, because it is effective only at compensating for *camera* motion. It's best used in reduced illumination, to steady the up-down swaying of telephoto lenses, and to improve close-up photography. If your subject is in motion, you'll still need a shutter speed that's fast enough to stop the action.
- **VR adds to shutter lag.** The process of adjusting the lens elements, like autofocus, takes time, so vibration reduction may contribute to a slight increase in shutter lag. If you're shooting sports, that delay may be annoying, but I still use my VR lenses for sports all the time!
- **Use when appropriate.** You may find that your results are worse when using VR while panning, although newer Nikon VR lenses work fine when the camera is deliberately moved from side to side during exposure. Older lenses can confuse the panning motion with camera wobble and provide too much compensation. You might want to switch off VR when panning or when your camera is mounted on a tripod.
- **Do you need VR at all?** Remember that an inexpensive monopod might be able to provide the same additional steadiness as a VR lens, at a much lower cost. If you're out in the field shooting wild animals or flowers and think a tripod isn't practical, try a monopod first. Or, with the Nikon D3s, you might be able to shift to a much higher ISO setting and use faster shutter speeds.

The original AF-S VR Zoom-Nikkor 70-200mm f/2.8G IF-ED, which I discuss next in terms of its role in the Nikon lens menagerie's ideal "Magic Three" (discussed below) is typical of the VR lenses Nikon offers. It has the basic controls shown in Figure 9.17, to adjust focus range (full, or limited to infinity down to 2.5 meters); VR On/Off; and Normal VR/Active VR (the latter an aggressive mode used in extreme situations, such as a moving car). Not visible (it's over the horizon, so to speak) is the M/A-M focus mode switch, which allows changing from autofocus (with manual override) to manual focus. There's also a focus lock button near the front of the lens (see Figure 9.18). I often use the rotating tripod mount collar as a grip for the lens when shooting hand-held, and, as you can see in Figure 9.19, I've replaced the factory tripod mounting foot with Kirk's Arca-Swiss-compatible quick release mount foot.

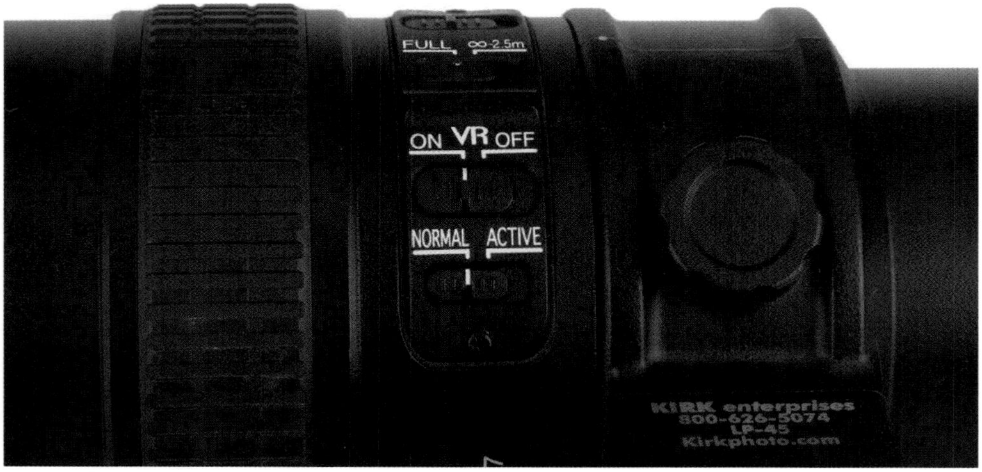


**Figure 9.17**
On the Nikon 70-200mm VR zoom you'll find (top to bottom): the focus limit switch, VR on/off switch, and Normal/Active VR adjustment.

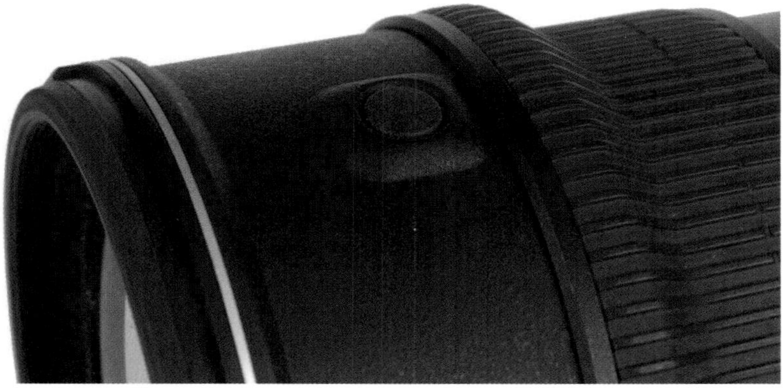

**Figure 9.18**
The lens also includes an autofocus lock button that can be activated while holding the lens.

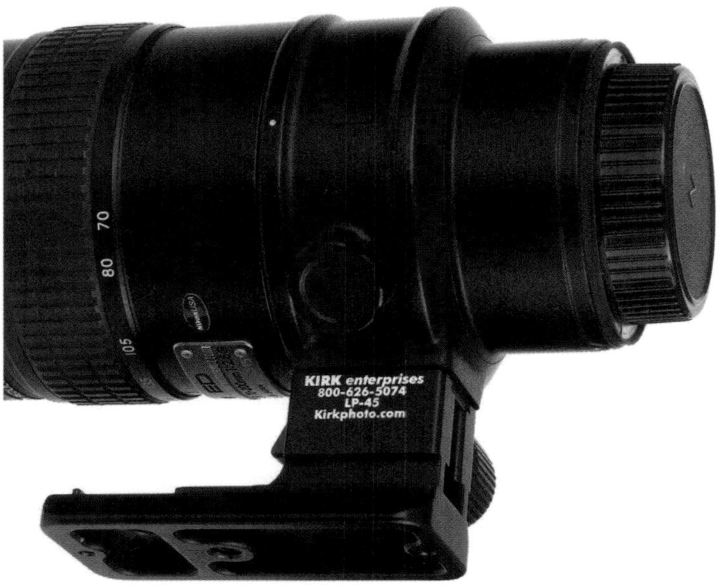


**Figure 9.19**
The rotating collar allows mounting the lens/camera to a tripod in vertical or horizontal orientations—or anything in-between.

## VIBRATION REDUCTION: IN THE CAMERA OR IN THE LENS?

Sony's acquisition of Konica Minolta's dSLR assets and the introduction of an improved in-camera image-stabilization system has revived an old debate about whether VR belongs in the camera or in the lens. Perhaps it's my Nikon bias showing, but I am quite happy not to have vibration reduction available in the body itself. Here are some reasons:

- Should in-camera VR fail, you have to send the whole camera in for repair, and camera repairs are generally more expensive than lens repairs. I like being able to simply switch to another lens if I have a VR problem.
- VR in the camera doesn't steady your view in the viewfinder, whereas a VR lens shows you a steadied image as you shoot.
- You're stuck with the VR system built into your camera. If an improved system is incorporated into a lens and the improvements are important to you, just trade in your old lens for the new one.
- VR in the body can't be easily optimized for a particular lens. Indeed, some vendors include a menu setup option you can use to tell the camera what lens is mounted, so the anti-shake properties can be adjusted to suit. That folderol isn't necessary when vibration reduction is built into each lens and tailored specifically for that lens.

# Your Second (and Third...) Lens

There are really only two advantages to using just a single lens. One of them is creative. Keeping one set of optics mounted on your D3s/D3x all the time forces you to be especially imaginative in your approach to your subjects. I once visited Europe with only a single camera body and a 35mm f/2 lens. The experience was actually quite exciting, because I had to use a variety of techniques to allow that one lens to serve for landscapes, available light photos, action, close-ups, portraits, and other kinds of images.

Of course, it's more likely that your "single" lens is actually a zoom, which is, in truth, many lenses in one, taking you from, say, 70mm to 200mm (or some other range) with a rapid twist of the zoom ring. You'll still find some creative challenges when you stick to a single zoom lens's focal lengths.

The second advantage of the unilens camera is only a marginal technical benefit since the introduction of the Nikon D3s. If you don't exchange lenses, the chances of dust and dirt getting inside your camera and settling on the sensor is reduced (but *not* eliminated entirely). Although I've known some photographers who minimized the number of lens changes they made for this very reason, reducing the number of lenses you work with is not a productive or rewarding approach for most of us. The D3s's automatic sensor cleaning feature has made this "advantage" much less significant than it was in the past.

It's more likely that you'll succumb to the malady known as *Lens Lust*, which is defined as an incurable disease marked by a significant yen for newer, better, longer, faster, sharper, anything-er optics for your camera. (And, it must be noted, this disease can *cost* you significant yen—or dollars, or whatever currency you use.) In its worst manifestations, sufferers find themselves with lenses that have overlapping zoom ranges or capabilities, because one or the other offers a slight margin in performance or suitability for specific tasks. When you find yourself already lusting after a new lens before you've really had a chance to put your latest purchase to the test, you'll know the disease has reached the terminal phase.

In this final part of the chapter, I'm going to discuss some specific Nikon lenses that I have experience with, and provide some recommendations. That's not to say that I use only Nikon lenses; as I mentioned multiple times already in this chapter, I absolutely love my 10-17mm Tokina fisheye zoom lens, and couldn't afford a zoom that reaches all the way out to 500mm if I hadn't been able to pick up my 170-500mm Sigma full-frame zoom lens second-hand for an excellent price. But there are so many lens options available that it makes more sense to confine my comments to the true-blue Nikkors that I've had experience with.

## The Magic Three

If you cruise the forums, you'll find the same three lenses mentioned over and over, often referred to as "The Trinity," "The Magic Three," or some other affectionate nickname. They are the three lenses you'll find in the kit of just about every serious Nikon photographer (including me). They're fast, expensive, heavier than you might expect, and provide such exquisite image quality that once you equip yourself with the Trinity, you'll never be happy with anything else.

Until, perhaps, now. Nikon has muddied the waters recently by introducing some new lenses that have displaced the original magic trio. Moreover, D3s/D3x owners just might be happier with a triad-plus-one that I'm going to describe.

### The Original Magic Three

For a significant number of years, the most commonly cited "ideal" lenses for "serious" Nikon digital SLRs (meaning the D200, D300, and D2xs) were the 17-35mm f/2.8, 28-70mm f/2.8, and 70-200 f/2.8 VR. The trio share a number of attributes. All three are non-DX lenses that (theoretically) work equally well on film cameras, the full-frame Nikon D3/D3s/D3x and D700, as well as DX cameras like the D300/D300s, making for a sound investment in optics that could be used on any Nikon SLR, past or future.

All three incorporate internal Silent Wave motors and focus incredibly fast. They all have f/2.8 maximum apertures that are *constant*; they don't change as the lens is zoomed in or out. All three are internal focusing (IF) models that don't change length as they focus, and include extra-low dispersion (ED) elements. And, all three are expensive, at

$1,400-$1,600. But, as I discovered when I added this set, once you have them, you don't need any other lenses unless you're doing field sports like football or soccer, extreme wide-angle, or close-up photography. I generally take these three lenses with me everywhere, adding another lens or two as required for specialized needs.

- **AF-S Zoom-Nikkor 17-35mm f/2.8D IF-ED.** When I am shooting landscapes, doing street photography, or some types of indoor sports, this lens goes on my D3s/D3x and never comes off. It was my main lens on my last trip to Europe; I was traveling light and took this one, a 10-17mm Tokina fisheye zoom, and my 28-200mm Nikkor G lens (in place of my humongous 70-200 VR lens), and didn't need anything else. It's one of the two or three sharpest lenses I own, and focuses down to about 1 foot, so I can use it for close-ups of flowers and other macro subjects.
- **AF-S Zoom-Nikkor 28-70mm f/2.8D IF-ED.** Nicknamed "The Beast" because of its size and weight, this lens, too, is wonderfully sharp, and well-suited for anything from sports to portraiture that falls within its focal length lens. I know many photographers who aren't heavily into landscapes who use this lens as their main lens. With its impressive lens hood mounted, The Beast is useful for terrifying small children, too.
- **AF-S VR Zoom-Nikkor 70-200mm f/2.8G IF-ED.** This legendary lens is perfect for some indoor and many outdoor sports, on a monopod, or hand-held, and can be used for portraiture, street photography, wildlife (especially with the 1.4X teleconverter), and even distant scenics. I use it for concerts, too, alternating between this lens and my 85mm f/1.4. It takes me in close to the performer, and can be used wide-open or at f/4 with good image quality. The only time I leave it behind is when I need to travel light (although it's not really that huge). This is the only lens of the magic trio that lacks an aperture ring, but you probably won't be using it with a bellows extension, anyway.

## FULL-FRAME FOLLY?

The only "problem" with the original 70-200mm lens is that it produces noticeable vignetting and reduced sharpness in the corners at many focal lengths when used on a full-frame camera like the Nikon D3/D3s/D3x, or D700. Many D3s/D3x owners might not notice any of these characteristics at all, if they operate in DX mode, because of the crop factor, and the vignetting and slight softness disappear on full-frame cameras when used with a 1.4X teleconverter. To be honest, I've had wonderful results with this lens with my full-frame cameras. I don't shoot landscapes or brick walls with 70 to 200mm focal lengths, and for the portrait and fashion work I do, the corners aren't important. You should keep this "shortcoming" of the original 70-200mm zoom in mind.

To the Original Magic Trio, I often recommend adding one more lens: the AF Nikkor 85mm f/1.4D IF. The nickname of this lens is "The Cream Machine" because of its remarkably smooth bokeh, which provides absolutely gorgeous out-of-focus backgrounds, especially when the lens is used with a wide aperture. It's incredibly sharp, and can definitely be used at f/1.4. The 85mm f/1.4 is the perfect portrait lens, and can be used wide-open without qualms. If you need this sort of lens, it's almost a bargain at its $1,000 price, and worth the extra $600 over its 85mm f/1.8 counterpart. Both Nikon 85mm lenses are D-series AF, rather than G-type AF-S lenses, and are becoming long in the tooth, so you might want to look for one now before they are replaced. I seriously doubt that the introduction of a newer lens will cause the used prices for this wonderful lens to plummet.

## The New Magic Three

When Nikon introduced the D3 and the original D300, it also debuted two new lenses, an AF-S Nikkor 14-24mm f/2.8G ED, and an AF-S Nikkor 24-70mm f/2.8G ED lens. Both are G-type lenses (they lack an aperture ring), have AF-S focusing, and have constant f/2.8 apertures. In 2009, Nikon announced a replacement for the 70-200mm VR lens, rounding out the Magic Trio with an all new lineup. Like the original big three, these are all full-frame lenses that work with any DX or FX-format Nikon camera.

The chief advantage of the new lineup (if you can call it that) is that there is no overlap. You can go from 14-24mm to 24-70mm to 70-200mm with no gaps in coverage. I don't find that an overwhelming advantage, because there are lots of situations in which the 17-35mm range of my existing lens is exactly what I need; if I used the "new" trio exclusively, I'd find myself swapping lenses whenever I needed more than a 24mm focal length.

So, I now own both the new 14-24mm f/2.8 zoom *and* the old 17-35mm f/2.8 lens—and I use them both about equally. The 14-24mm gives me a bit more wide-angle perspective than the 17-35mm lens, and it is fabulously sharp. I use the 17-35mm lens when I think I'll need the longer focal length, when I want to shoot semi-macro pictures of, say, flowers, and when I am traveling light. For example, when shooting in Europe I take along the 17-35mm lens (which is *much* smaller than the 14-24, and can be used with polarizing filters, to boot) and my 28-200mm zoom.

Carefully consider the focal lengths you need before deciding which "magic" triad is best for you. The new lineup looks like this:

- **AF-S Nikkor 14-24mm f/2.8G ED.** I own this lens, and its image quality is incredible, with very low barrel distortion (outward bowing at the edges) and very little of the chromatic aberrations common to lenses this wide. Because it has full-frame coverage, it's immune to obsolescence. It focuses down to 10.8 inches, allowing for some interesting close-up/wide-angle effects. The downside? The outward curving front element precludes the use of most filters, although I haven't tried this lens with add-on Cokin-style filter holders yet. Lack of filter compatibility isn't a fatal flaw for D3s/D3x users, as the use of polarizers would be problematic in any case. The polarizing effect would be highly variable because of this lens's extremely wide field of view.

- **AF-S Nikkor 24-70mm f/2.8G ED.** This lens seems to provide even better image quality than the legendary Beast, especially when used wide open or in flare-inducing environments. (You can credit the new internal Nano Crystal Coat treatment for that improvement.) My recommendation is that if you already own The Beast, or can get one used for a good price ($1,000 or less), you don't sacrifice much going with the older 28-70mm lens, and may find the overlap with the 14-24mm lens useful. But if you have the cash and opportunity to purchase this newer lens, you won't be making a mistake. Some were surprised when it was introduced without the VR feature, but Nikon has kept the size of this useful lens down, while maintaining a reasonable price for a "pro" level lens.
- **AF-S VR II Zoom-Nikkor 70-200mm f/2.8G IF-ED.** Not a lot to be added about the latest version of this lens, which is a worthy representative of the telephoto zoom range in this "ideal" trio of lenses. It does have better performance in the corners on full-frame cameras, but its other attributes remain the same.

## Fine-Tuning the Focus of Your Lenses

In Chapter 5, I introduced you to the D3s/D3x's AF Fine tune capability. In this section, I'll show you how to calibrate your lenses using this feature.

Why is the focus "off" for some lenses in the first place? There are lots of factors, including the age of the lens (an older lens may focus slightly differently), temperature effects on certain types of glass, humidity, and tolerances built into a lens's design that all add up to a slight misadjustment, even though the components themselves are, strictly speaking, within specs. A very slight variation in your lens's mount can cause focus to vary slightly. With any luck (if you can call it that) a lens that doesn't focus exactly right will at least be consistent. If a lens always focuses a bit behind the subject, the symptom is *back focus.* If it focuses in front of the subject, it's called *front focus.*

As I noted, you're almost always better off sending such a lens in to Nikon to have them make it right. But that's not always possible. Perhaps you need your lens recalibrated right now, or you purchased a gray market lens that Nikon isn't willing to fix. If you want to do it yourself, the first thing to do is determine whether or not your lens has a back focus or front focus problem.

For a quick-and-dirty diagnosis (*not* a calibration; you'll use a different target for that), lay down a piece of graph paper on a flat surface, and place an object on the line at the middle, which will represent the point of focus (we hope). Then, shoot the target at an angle using your lens's widest aperture and the autofocus mode you want to test. Mount the camera on a tripod so you can get accurate, repeatable results.

If your camera/lens combination doesn't suffer from front or back focus, the point of sharpest focus will be the center line of the chart, as you can see in Figure 9.20. If you do have a problem, one of the other lines will be sharply focused instead. Should you discover that your lens consistently front or back focuses, it needs to be recalibrated.

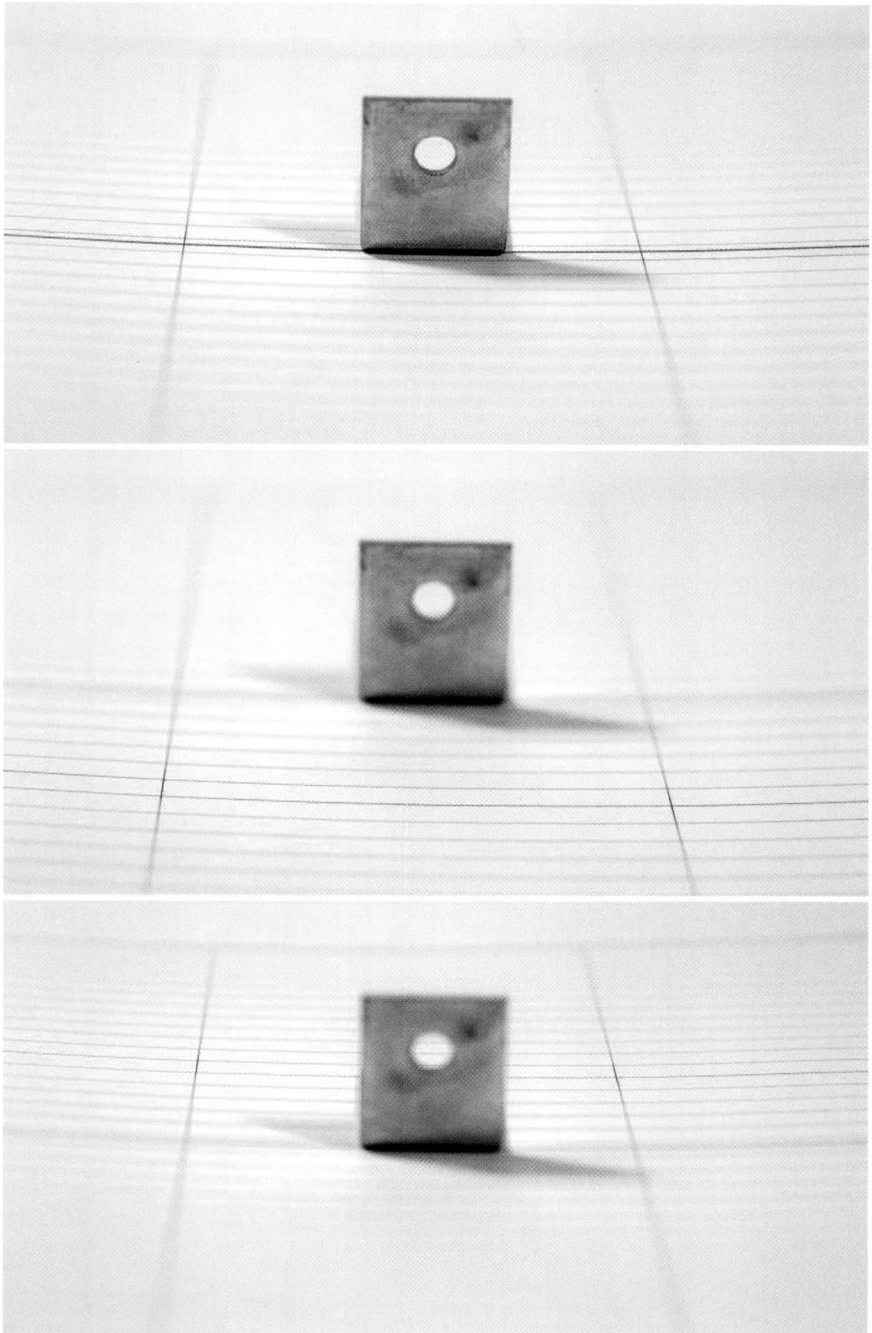

**Figure 9.20** Correct focus (top), front focus (middle), and back focus (bottom).

Unfortunately, it's only possible to calibrate a lens for a single focusing distance. So, if you use a particular lens (such as a macro lens) for close-focusing, calibrate for that. If you use a lens primarily for middle distances, calibrate for that. Close-to-middle distances are most likely to cause focus problems, anyway, because as you get closer to infinity, small changes in focus are less likely to have an effect.

## Lens Tune-up

The key tool you can use to fine-tune your lens is the AF fine tune entry in the Setup menu, shown in Figure 9.21. You'll find the process easier to understand if you first run through this quick overview of the menu options:

- **AF fine tune (On/Off).** This option enables/disables AF fine-tuning for all the lenses you've defined using the menu entry. If you discover you don't care for the calibrations you make in certain situations (say, it works better for the lens you have mounted at middle distances, but is less successful at correcting close-up focus errors), you can deactivate the feature as you require. You should set this to On when you're doing the actual fine-tuning.
- **Saved value.** This setting lets you tune the autofocus calibration for the current CPU-chipped lens (virtually all Nikon-brand autofocus lenses) mounted on the

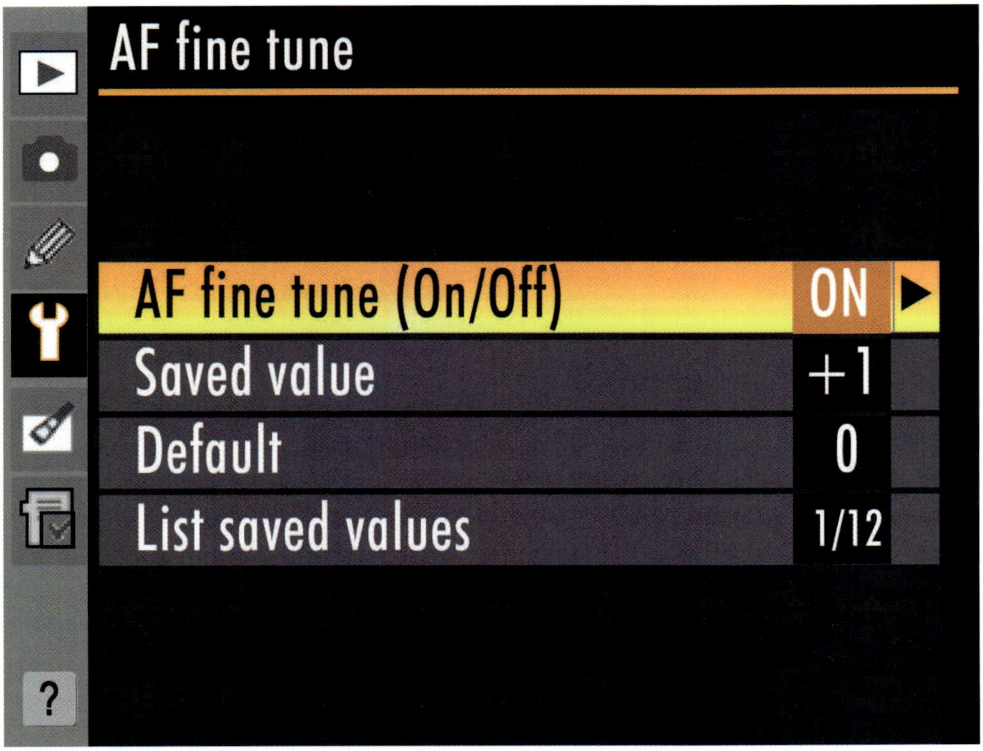


**Figure 9.21**
The AF fine tune menu.

D3s/D3x. When you first fine-tune a lens, the saved value will be 0 (zero). You can press the multi selector up/down buttons to choose a value between +20 and –20. Positive numbers move the focal point farther from the camera, and would be used if your lens consistently suffers from front focus problems. Negative numbers move the focal point closer to the camera, and would be used if your lens is plagued with consistent back focus. The value is relative, and doesn't correlate to any particular distance or percentage.

- **Default.** This entry often confuses. It is a value that is applied to *every* lens mounted on the camera that doesn't already have a customized saved value associated with it. That is, if your D3s/D3x has consistent front or back focus problems with *all* lenses, you can enter a value here, and the camera will apply the correction to each CPU lens you use. This default setting can be overridden by saved values you've stored for particular lenses. So, you can change the default focal plane for all lenses, and still further fine-tune specific lenses that need more autofocus correction. My recommendation is that if your camera and lenses are so out of whack that you need global correction and individual fine-tuning, you *really* ought to consider shipping the whole kit off to Nikon for proper calibration.
- **List saved values.** This screen shows you the saved fine-tuning values for all lenses. If the currently mounted lens has a stored value, it will be marked with a solid black box icon. You can delete lenses from this list by highlighting them and pressing the Trash button. You can also change the number (a two-digit number from 00-99) used to identify a particular lens.

## Evaluate Current Focus

The first step is to capture a baseline image that represents how the lens you want to fine-tune autofocuses at a particular distance. You'll often see advice for photographing a test chart with millimeter markings from an angle, and the suggestion that you autofocus on a particular point on the chart. Supposedly, the markings that actually *are* in focus will help you recalibrate your lens. The problem with this approach is that the information you get from photographing a test chart at an angle doesn't actually tell you what to do to make a precise correction. So, your lens back focuses three millimeters behind the target area on the chart. So what? Does that mean you change the Saved Value by –3 clicks? Or –15 clicks? Angled targets are a "shortcut" that don't save you time.

Instead, you'll want to photograph a target that represents what you're actually trying to achieve: a plane of focus locked in by your lens that represents the actual plane of focus of your subject. For that, you'll need a flat target, mounted precisely perpendicular to the sensor plane of the camera. Then, you can take a photo, see if the plane of focus is correct, and if not, dial in a bit of fine-tuning in the AF fine tuning menu, and shoot again. Lather, rinse, and repeat until the target is sharply focused.

You can use the focus target shown in Figure 9.22, or you can use a chart of your own, as long as it has contrasty areas that will be easily seen by the autofocus system, and without very small details that are likely to confuse the AF. Download your own copy of my chart from www.nikonguides.com/FocusChart.pdf. Then print out a copy on the largest paper your printer can handle. (I don't recommend just displaying the file on your monitor and focusing on that; it's unlikely you'll have the monitor screen lined up perfectly perpendicular to the camera sensor.)

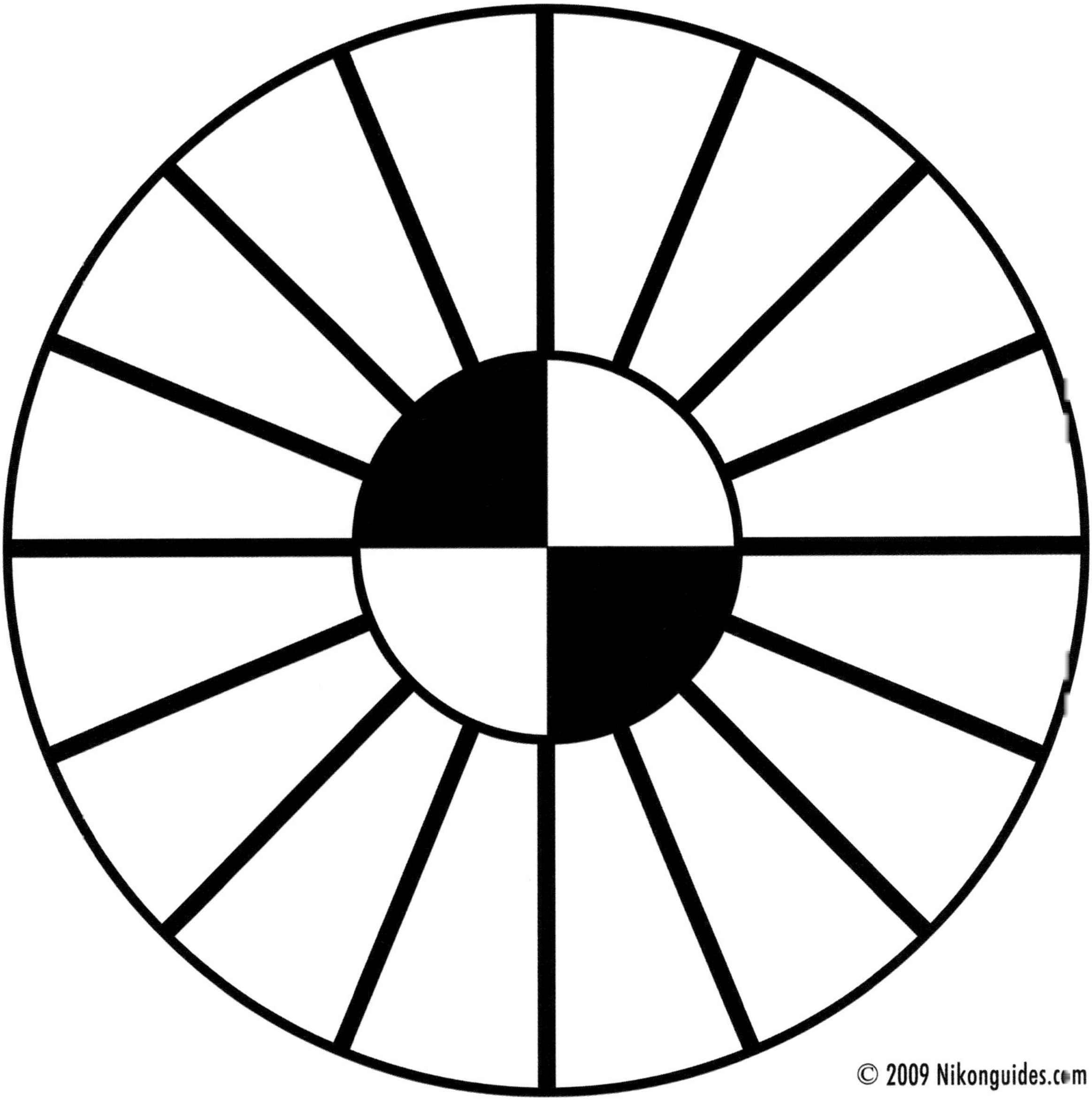


**Figure 9.22** Use this focus test chart, or create one of your own.

Then, follow these steps:

1. **Position the camera.** Place your Nikon D3s/D3x on a sturdy tripod with a remote release attached, positioned at roughly eye level at a distance from a wall that represents the distance you want to test for. Keep in mind that autofocus problems can be different at varying distances and lens focal lengths, and that you can enter only *one* correction value for a particular lens. So, choose a distance (close-up or mid range) and zoom setting with your shooting habits in mind.
2. **Set the autofocus mode.** Choose the autofocus mode (AF-C or AF-S) you want to test.
3. **Level the camera (in an ideal world).** If the wall happens to be perfectly perpendicular, you can use a bubble level, plumb bob, or other device of your choice to ensure that the camera is level to match. Many tripods and tripod heads have bubble levels built in. Avoid using the center column, if you can. When the camera is properly oriented, lock the legs and tripod head tightly.
4. **Level the camera (in the real world).** If your wall is not perfectly perpendicular, use this old trick. Tape a mirror to the wall, and then adjust the camera on the tripod so that when you look through the viewfinder at the mirror, you see directly into the reflection of the lens. Then, lock the tripod and remove the mirror.
5. **Mount the test chart.** Tape the test chart on the wall so it is centered in your camera's viewfinder.
6. **Photograph the test chart using AF.** Allow the camera to autofocus, and take a test photo, using the remote release to avoid shaking or moving the camera.
7. **Make an adjustment and rephotograph.** Make a fine-tuning adjustment and photograph the target again. Follow the instructions in the next section. I've separated the fine-tuning adjustments from these steps because some people may want to just tweak the focus at a later time without going through all these evaluation steps. Repeat steps 1-8 in the section that follows this one to make evaluation images at a range of corrections, say, –5 through +5.
8. **Evaluate the image.** If you have the camera connected to your computer with a USB cable and Camera Control Pro or other linkup software such as Nikon Transfer, or through a WiFi connection, so much the better. You can view the image after it's transferred to your computer. Otherwise, *carefully* open the camera card door and slip the memory card out and copy the images to your computer.
9. **Evaluate focus.** Which image is sharpest? That's the setting you need to use for this lens. If your initial range doesn't provide the correction you need, repeat the steps between –20 and +20 until you find the best fine-tuning.

## Changing the Fine-Tuning Setting

Adjust the fine-tuning for the lens you have mounted on the camera by following these steps:

1. If you haven't been running the test described previously, mount the CPU-equipped lens you want to fine-tune on the Nikon D3s/D3x. The camera will automatically recognize the lens you are using during the "calibration" process and display its name on the screen.
2. If you haven't already done so, choose AF fine tune (On/Off) and turn it ON.
3. Select Saved value.
4. Press the multi selector up/down buttons to tell the D3s/D3x to adjust the autofocus from +20 (move the focal point away from the camera to fix front focus problems) to –20 values (move the focal point toward the camera to fix back focus). (See Figure 9.23.)
5. Press OK when the value you want is entered. You may have to run the test described above several times and use some trial and error to determine the correct adjustment.
6. Choose List saved values to see the lenses you've fine-tuned. (See Figure 9.24.)

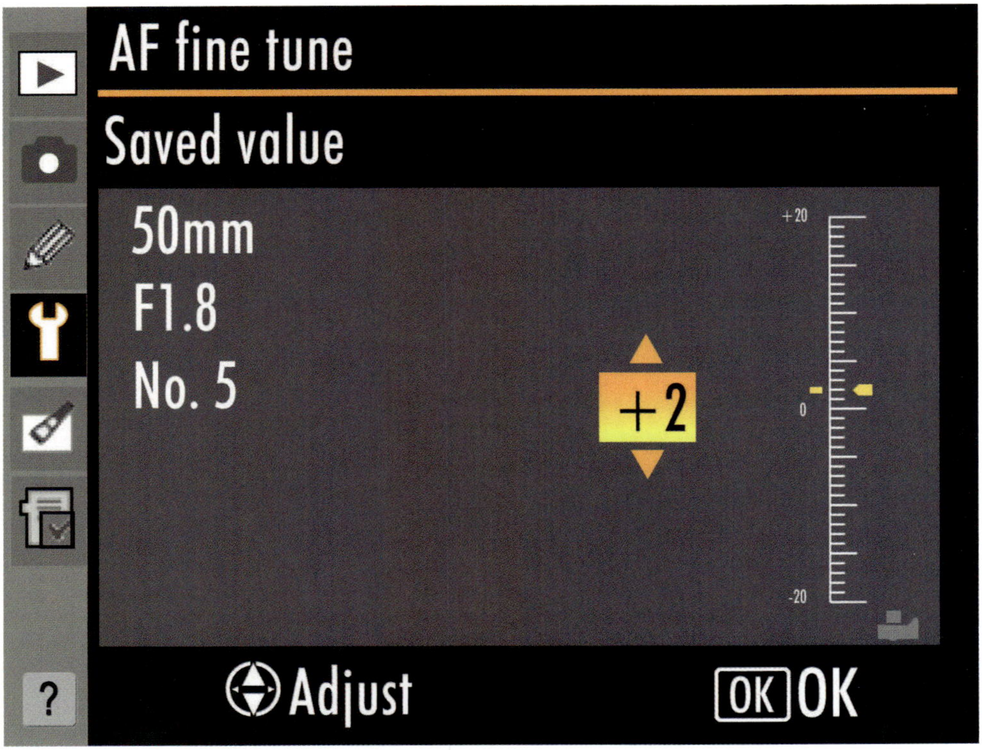


**Figure 9.23**
Change a Saved value for a particular lens.

**Figure 9.24**
List the Saved values you've stored.

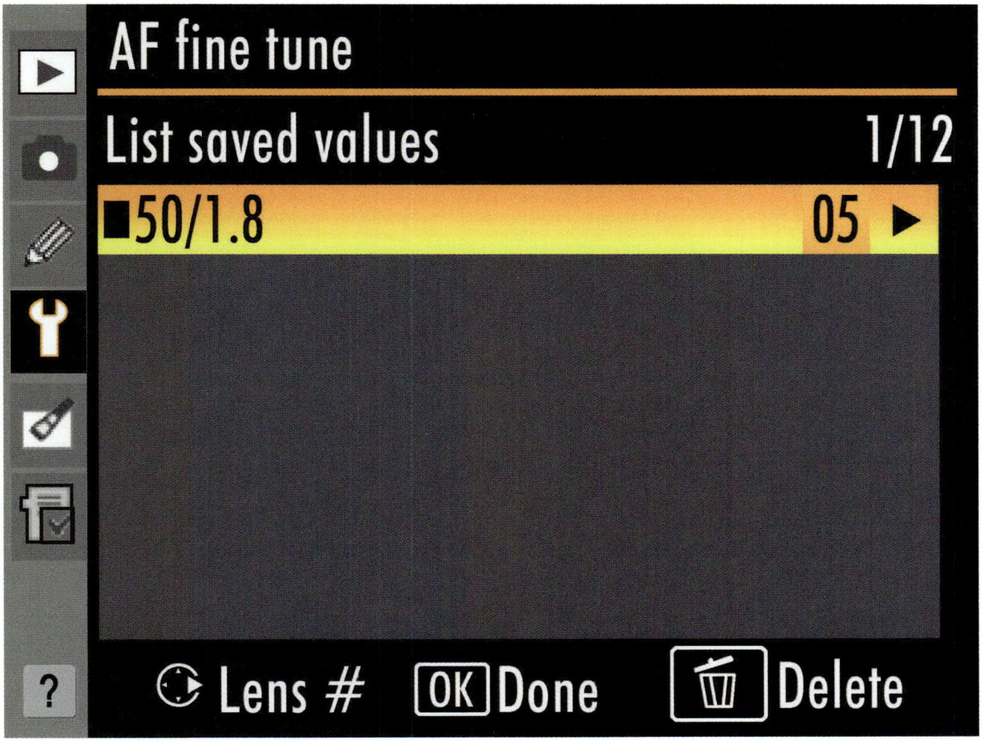


7. Assign a lens identifier from 00 to 99 to the lens you've just calibrated. This identifier can be used to differentiate a particular lens from other lenses of the same type, if you own, say, some duplicate lenses. That's not as far-fetched as you might think. Some organizations, such as newspapers, allow their photographers to use favorite lenses exclusively, but may need to share other optics among several photographers. If you don't know which of the pooled AF-S Nikkor 600mm f/4G ED VR lenses you'll be using on any particular day, you can calibrate your camera separately for each of them. (See Figure 9.25.)
8. Press Menu to exit.

## Set Default Value

If you want to set a default value for lenses that aren't in your Saved values list (say, because your camera always back or front focuses slightly), choose the Default setting from the AF fine tune menu, and adjust as shown in Figure 9.26.

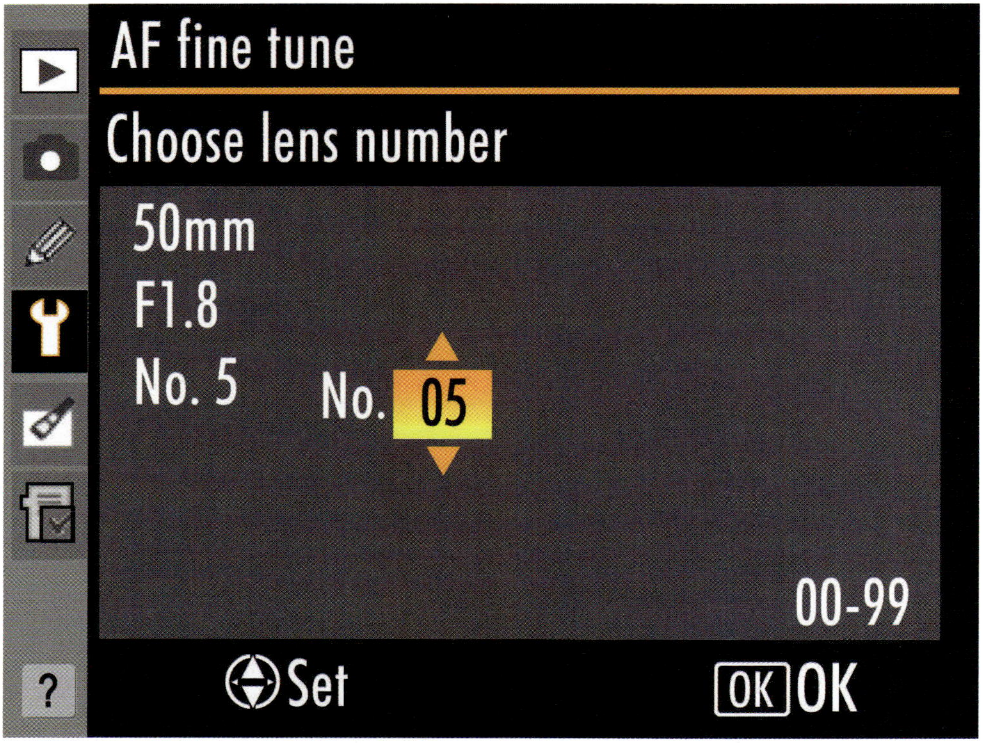


**Figure 9.25**
Assign a lens number, if necessary, to differentiate a particular lens from other lenses of the same type you may use.

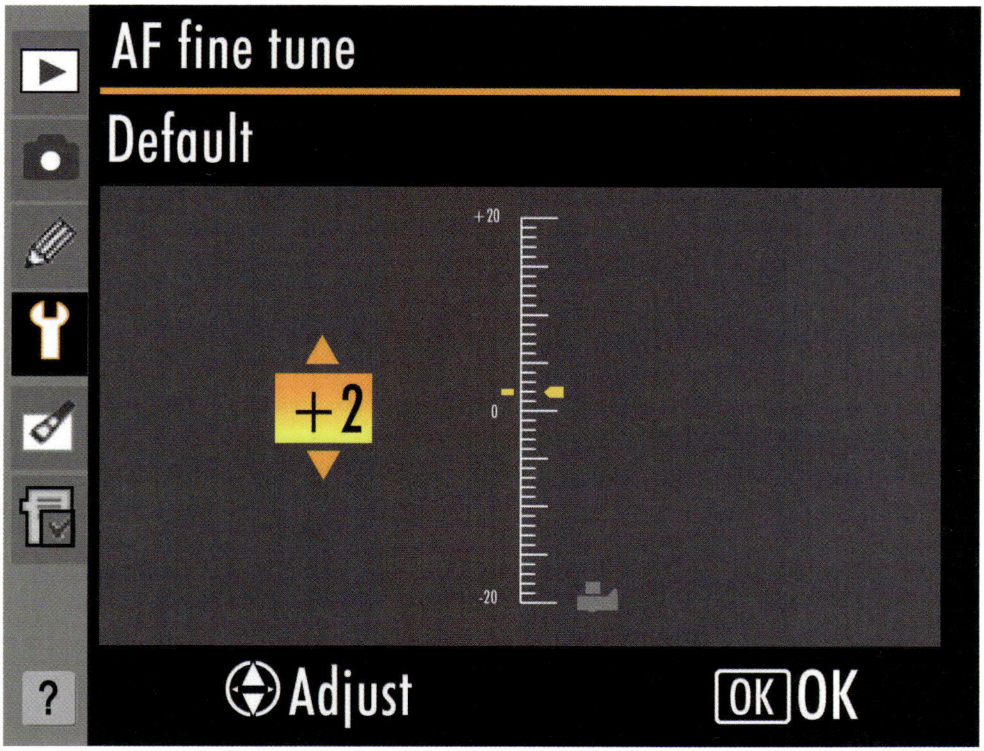


**Figure 9.26**
Choose a default value to be applied to all lenses not already fine-tuned.

# 10

# Making Light Work for You

If the sensor is the canvas on which you paint, light is your palette. Successful photographers and artists have an intimate understanding of the importance of light in shaping an image. Rembrandt was a master of using light to create moods and reveal the character of his subjects. Artist Thomas Kinkade's official tagline is "Painter of Light." The late Dean Collins, co-founder of Finelight Studios, revolutionized how a whole generation of photographers learned and used lighting. Photo guru Ed Pierce conducts seminars called "Captivated by the Light," that reveal his secrets for portrait lighting. It's impossible to underestimate how the use of light adds to—and how misuse can detract from—your photographs.

All forms of visual art use light to shape the finished product. Sculptors don't have control over the light used to illuminate their finished work, so they must create shapes using planes and curved surfaces so that the form envisioned by the artist comes to life from a variety of viewing and lighting angles. Painters, in contrast, have absolute control over both shape and light in their work, as well as the viewing angle, so they can use both the contours of their two-dimensional subjects and the qualities of the "light" they use to illuminate those subjects to evoke the image they want to produce.

Photography is a third form of art. The photographer may have little or no control over the subject (other than posing human subjects) but can often adjust both viewing angle *and* the nature of the light source to create a particular compelling image. The direction and intensity of the light sources create the shapes and textures that we see. The distribution and proportions determine the contrast and tonal values: whether the image is stark or high key, or muted and low in contrast. The colors of the light (because even "white" light has a color balance that the sensor can detect), and how much of those colors the subject reflects or absorbs, paint the hues visible in the image.

As a Nikon D3s/D3x photographer, you must learn to be a painter and sculptor of light if you want to move from *taking* a picture to *making* a photograph. This chapter provides an introduction to using the two main types of illumination: *continuous* lighting (such as daylight, incandescent, or fluorescent sources) and the brief, but brilliant snippets of light we call *electronic flash.*

## Your D3s/D3x and Continuous Illumination versus Electronic Flash

Continuous lighting is exactly what you might think: uninterrupted illumination that is available all the time during a shooting session. Daylight, moonlight, and the artificial lighting encountered both indoors and outdoors count as continuous light sources (although all of them can be "interrupted" by passing clouds, solar eclipses, a blown fuse, or simply by switching a lamp off). Indoor continuous illumination includes both the lights that are there already (such as incandescent lamps or overhead fluorescent lights indoors) and fixtures you supply yourself, including photoflood lamps or reflectors used to bounce existing light onto your subject.

Electronic flash, or "strobe," is notable because it can be much more intense than continuous lighting, lasts only a brief moment, and can be much more portable than supplementary incandescent sources. It's a light source you can carry with you and use anywhere.

Of course, your Nikon D3s/D3x does not have its own electronic flash unit built in. Cameras that are considered "pro" models (there's that dubious distinction cropping up again!) generally don't have a flash built in. Such models already boast a rather largish pentaprism "hump" on top, because they are designed to have optical viewfinders that are as big and bright as possible. A built-in flash would just add even more height and weight to a hefty camera body.

Even so, most owners of these cameras have an external unit tucked in their bag, such as the Nikon SB-900 shown in Figure 10.1. An external flash, either mounted on the D3s/D3x's accessory shoe or used off-camera is a useful supplement. Studio flash units are electronic flash, too, and aren't limited to "professional" shooters, as there are economical "monolight" (one-piece flash/power supply) units available in the $200 price range. Anyone can buy a couple to store in a closet and use to set up a home studio, or use as supplementary lighting when traveling away from home.

Until Joe McNally's *Hot Shoe Diaries* came along, and David Hobby started the Strobist movement (www.strobist.com), mundane electronic flash units were largely eschewed because they "encourage" direct flash, a form of illumination that's particularly unattractive when misused. Professional photographers, it is thought, would never stoop to using a simple strobe unit. But, that's not true. Need just a touch of fill-in flash to

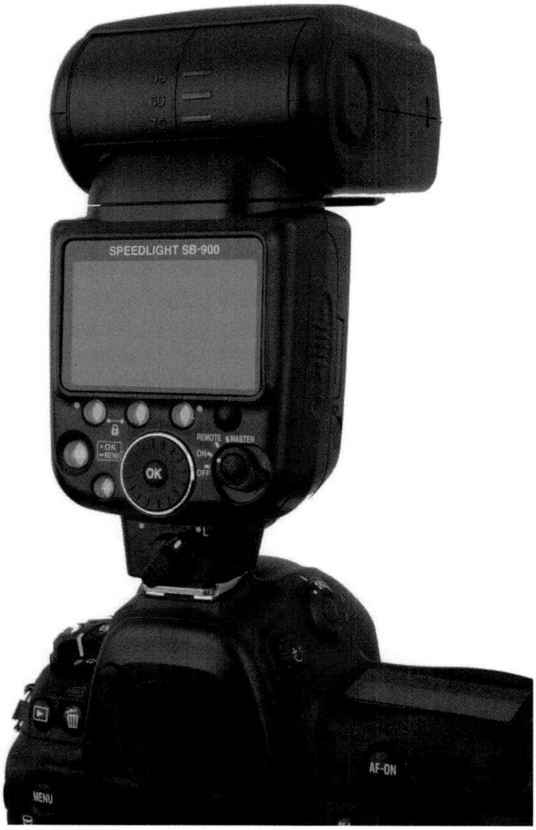


**Figure 10.1**
One form of light that can always be available is the electronic flash you keep in your camera bag.

brighten shadows under harsh sunlight? Want to add a little catchlight to bring a model's eyes to life? Forced to grab a quick-and-dirty shot of a breaking news event cloaked in the kind of available darkness that challenges even your D3s/D3x's ISO 6400 (and up) sensitivity settings? That compact flash just might be a lifesaver, especially under horrid uneven lighting conditions that are problematic even for high ISO photography.

So, whether you're using an add-on flash or continuous illumination, there are advantages and disadvantages to each type of lighting. Here's a quick checklist of pros and cons:

- **Lighting preview—Pro: continuous lighting.** With continuous lighting, you always know exactly what kind of lighting effect you're going to get and, if multiple lights are used, how they will interact with each other. (See Figure 10.2.)
- **Lighting preview—Con: electronic flash.** With flash, the general effect you're going to see may be a mystery until you've built some experience, and you may need to review a shot on the LCD, make some adjustments, and then reshoot to get the look you want. (In this sense, a digital camera's review capabilities replace the Polaroid test shots pro photographers relied on in decades past.)

- **Exposure calculation—Pro: continuous lighting.** Your D3s/D3x has no problem calculating exposure for continuous lighting, because it remains constant and can be measured through a sensor that interprets the light reaching the viewfinder. The amount of light available just before the exposure will, in almost all cases, be the same amount of light present when the shutter is released. The D3s/D3x's spot metering mode can be used to measure and compare the proportions of light in the highlights and shadows, so you can make an adjustment (such as using more or less fill light) if necessary. You can even use a hand-held light meter to measure the light yourself.

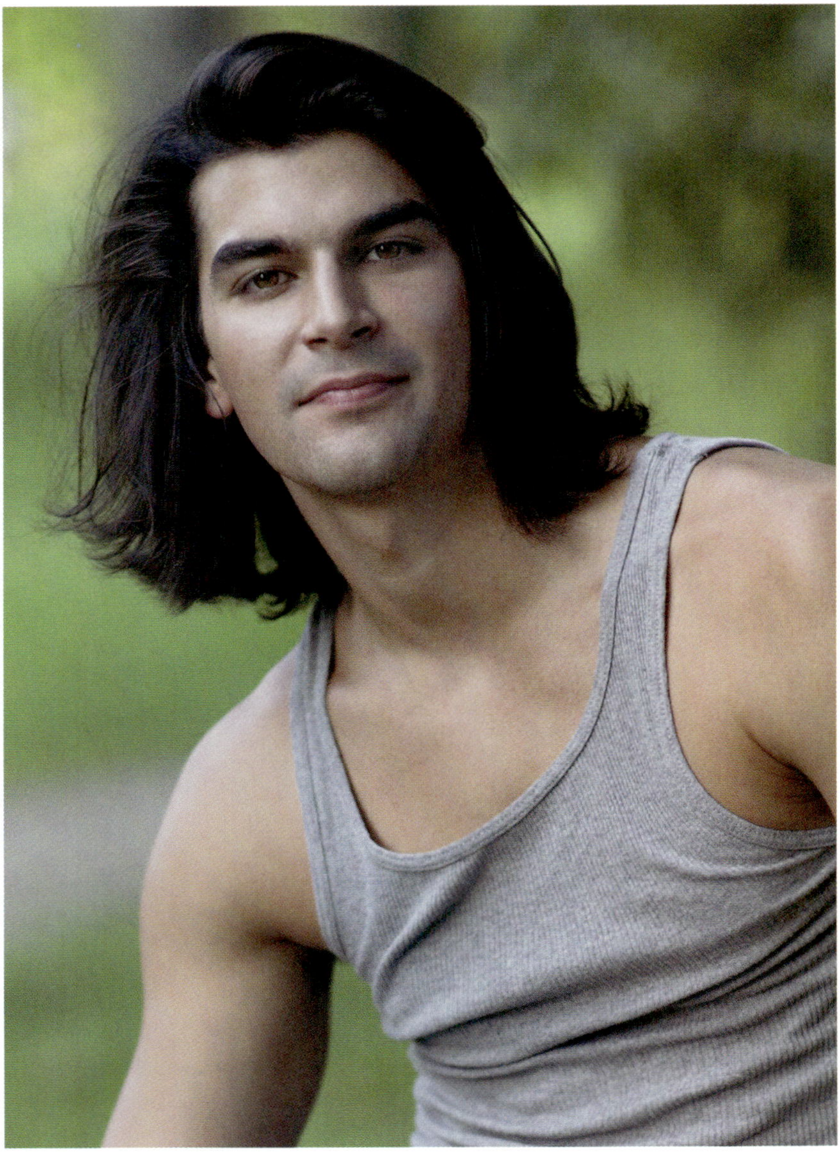

**Figure 10.2**
You always know how the lighting will look when using continuous illumination.

- **Exposure calculation—Con: electronic flash.** Electronic flash illumination doesn't exist until the flash fires, and so can't be measured by the D3s/D3x's exposure sensor when the mirror is flipped up during the exposure. Instead, the light must be measured by metering the intensity of a pre-flash triggered an instant before the main flash, as it is reflected back to the camera and through the lens. An alternative is to use a sensor built into the flash itself and measure reflected light that has not traveled through the lens. If you have a do-it-yourself bent, there are hand-held flash meters, too, including models that measure both flash and continuous light.
- **Evenness of illumination—Pro/con: continuous lighting.** Of continuous light sources, daylight, in particular, provides illumination that tends to fill an image completely, lighting up the foreground, background, and your subject almost equally. Shadows do come into play, of course, so you might need to use reflectors or fill-in light sources to even out the illumination further, but barring objects that block large sections of your image from daylight, the light is spread fairly evenly. Indoors, however, continuous lighting is commonly less evenly distributed. The average living room, for example, has hot spots and dark corners. But on the plus side, you can *see* this uneven illumination and compensate with additional lamps.
- **Evenness of illumination—Con: electronic flash.** Electronic flash units, like continuous light sources such as lamps that don't have the advantage of being located 93 million miles from the subject, suffer from the effects of their proximity. The *inverse square law*, first applied to both gravity and light by Sir Isaac Newton, dictates that as a light source's distance increases from the subject, the amount of light reaching the subject falls off proportionately to the square of the distance. In plain English, that means that a flash or lamp that's eight feet away from a subject provides only one-quarter as much illumination as a source that's four feet away (rather than half as much). (See Figure 10.3.) This translates into relatively shallow "depth-of-light."
- **Action stopping—Con: continuous lighting.** Action stopping with continuous light sources is completely dependent on the shutter speed you've dialed in on the camera. And the speeds that can be used are dependent on the amount of light available and your ISO sensitivity setting. Outdoors in daylight, there will probably be enough sunlight to let you shoot at 1/2,000th second and f/6.3 with a non-grainy sensitivity setting of ISO 400. That's a fairly useful combination of settings if you're not using a super-telephoto with a small maximum aperture. But inside, the reduced illumination quickly has you pushing your D3s/D3x to its limits. For example, if you're shooting indoor sports, there probably won't be enough available light to allow you to use a 1/2,000th second shutter speed (although I routinely shoot indoor basketball with my D3s at ISO 3200 and 1/1,000th second at f/4). In many indoor sports situations, you may find yourself limited to 1/500th second or slower.

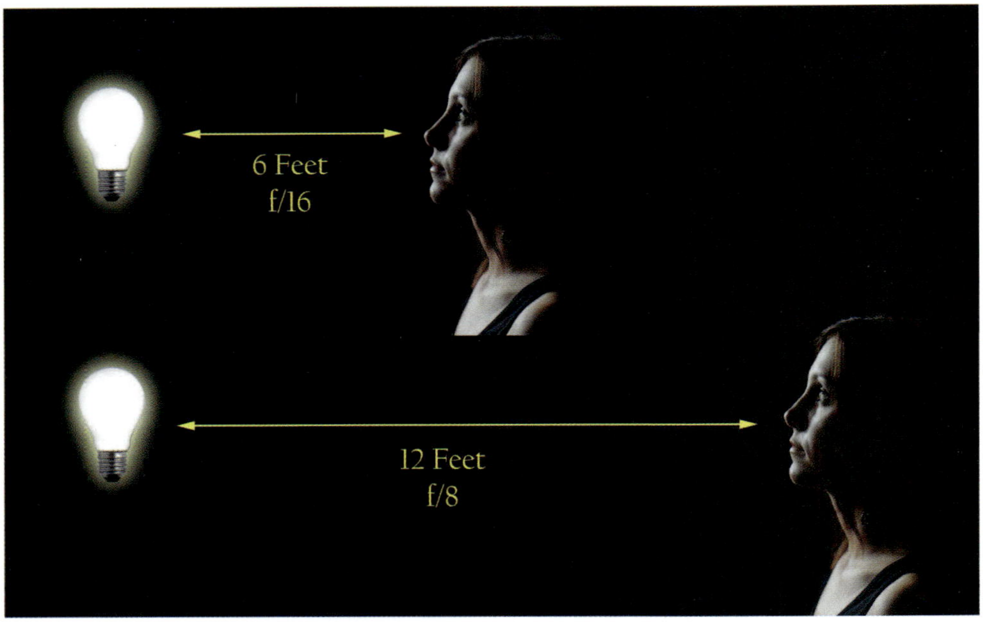


**Figure 10.3**
A light source that is twice as far away provides only one-quarter as much illumination.

- **Action stopping—Pro: electronic flash.** When it comes to the ability to freeze moving objects in their tracks, the advantage goes to electronic flash. The brief duration of electronic flash serves as a very high "shutter speed" when the flash is the main or only source of illumination for the photo. Your D3s/D3x's shutter speed may be set for 1/250th second during a flash exposure, but if the flash illumination predominates, the *effective* exposure time will be the 1/1,000th to 1/50,000th second or less duration of the flash, as you can see in Figure 10.4, because the flash unit reduces the amount of light released by cutting short the duration of the flash. The only fly in the ointment is that, if the ambient light is strong enough, it may produce a secondary, "ghost" exposure, as I'll explain later in this chapter.
- **Cost—Pro: continuous lighting.** Incandescent or fluorescent lamps are generally much less expensive than electronic flash units, which can easily cost several hundred dollars. I've used everything from desktop hi-intensity lamps to reflector flood lights for continuous illumination at very little cost. There are lamps made especially for photographic purposes, too, priced up to $50 or so. Maintenance is economical, too: many incandescent or fluorescents use bulbs that cost only a few dollars.
- **Cost—Con: electronic flash.** Electronic flash units aren't particularly cheap. The lowest-cost dedicated flash designed specifically for the Nikon dSLRs is about $110. Such units are limited in features, however, and intended for those with entry-level cameras. You probably wouldn't want to use a Nikon SB-400 on your D3s or D3x. For a $5,000-plus camera, that would be false economy. Plan on spending some money to get the features that a sophisticated electronic flash offers.

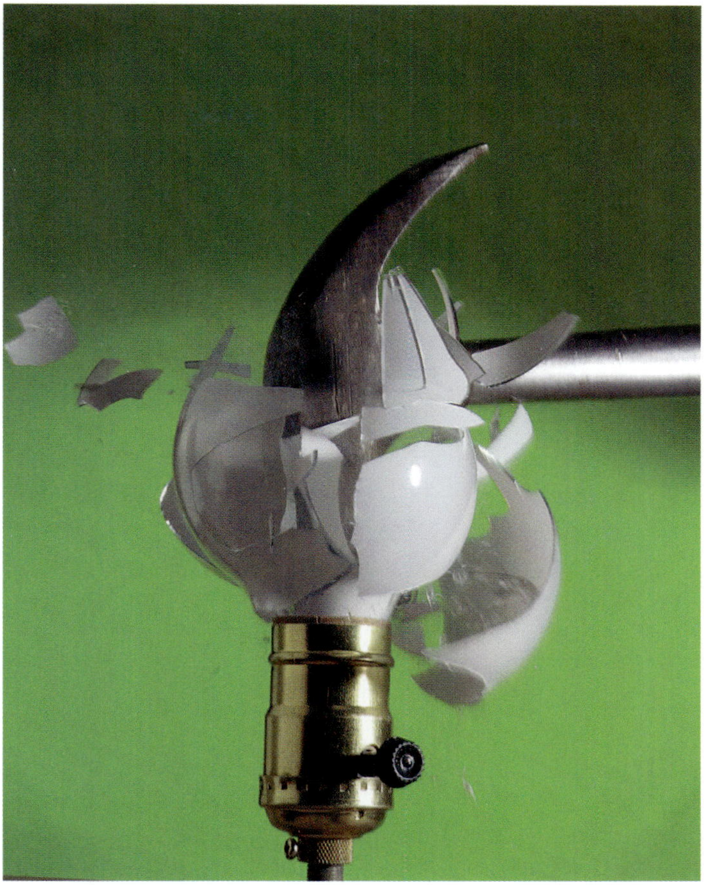

**Figure 10.4**
Electronic flash can freeze almost any action.

- **Flexibility—Con: continuous lighting.** Because incandescent and fluorescent lamps are not as bright as electronic flash, the slower shutter speeds required (see Action stopping, above) mean that you may have to use a tripod, especially when shooting portraits. The incandescent variety of continuous lighting gets hot, especially in the studio, and the side effects range from discomfort (for your human models) to disintegration (if you happen to be shooting perishable foods like ice cream). The heat also makes it more difficult to add filtration to incandescent sources.
- **Flexibility—Pro: electronic flash.** Electronic flash's action-freezing power allows you to work without a tripod in the studio (and elsewhere), adding flexibility and speed when choosing angles and positions. Flash units can be easily filtered, and, because the filtration is placed over the light source rather than the lens, you don't need to use high quality filter material. For example, a couple sheets of unexposed, processed Ektachrome film can make a dandy infrared-pass filter for your flash unit. Roscoe or Lee lighting gels, which may be too flimsy to use in front of the lens, can be mounted or taped in front of your flash with ease.

# Continuous Lighting Basics

While continuous lighting and its effects are generally much easier to visualize and use than electronic flash, there are some factors you need to take into account, particularly the color temperature of the light. (Color temperature concerns aren't exclusive to continuous light sources, of course, but the variations tend to be more extreme and less predictable than those of electronic flash, which output relatively consistent daylight-like illumination.)

Color temperature, in practical terms, is how "bluish" or how "reddish" the light appears to be to the digital camera's sensor. Indoor illumination is quite warm, comparatively, and appears reddish to the sensor. Daylight, in contrast, seems much bluer to the sensor. Our eyes (our brains, actually) are quite adaptable to these variations, so white objects don't appear to have an orange tinge when viewed indoors, nor do they seem excessively blue outdoors in full daylight. Yet, these color temperature variations are real and the sensor is not fooled. To capture the most accurate colors, we need to take the color temperature into account in setting the color balance (or *white balance*) of the D3s or D3x—either automatically using the camera's smarts or manually using our own knowledge and experience.

The only time you need to think in terms of actual color temperature is when you're making adjustments using the Choose color temp. setting in the White balance entry within the Shooting menu (which, as described in Chapter 3, allows you to dial in exact color temperatures, if known). So, those occasions are the only times you're likely to be confused by a seeming contradiction in how color temperatures are named: warmer (more reddish) color temperatures (measured in degrees Kelvin) are the *lower* numbers, while cooler (bluer) color temperatures are *higher* numbers. It might not make sense to say that 3,400K is warmer than 6,000K, but that's the way it is. If it helps, think of a glowing red ember contrasted with a white-hot welder's torch, rather than fire and ice.

The confusion comes from physics. Scientists calculate color temperature from the light emitted by a mythical object called a black body radiator, which absorbs all the radiant energy that strikes it, and reflects none at all. Such a black body not only *absorbs* light perfectly, but it *emits* it perfectly when heated (and since nothing in the universe is perfect, that makes it mythical).

At a particular physical temperature, this imaginary object always emits light of the same wavelength or color. That makes it possible to define color temperature in terms of actual temperature in degrees on the Kelvin scale that scientists use. Incandescent light, for example, typically has a color temperature of 3,200K to 3,400K. Daylight might range from 5,500K to 6,000K. Each type of illumination we use for photography has its own color temperature range—with some cautions. The next sections will summarize everything you need to know about the qualities of these light sources.

## Daylight

Daylight is produced by the sun, and so is moonlight (which is just reflected sunlight). Daylight is present, of course, even when you can't see the sun. When sunlight is direct, it can be bright and harsh. If daylight is diffused by clouds, softened by bouncing off objects such as walls or your photo reflectors, or filtered by shade, it can be much dimmer and less contrasty.

Daylight's color temperature can vary quite widely. It is highest in temperature (most blue) at noon when the sun is directly overhead, because the light is traveling through a minimum amount of the filtering layer we call the atmosphere. The color temperature at high noon may be 6,000K. At other times of day, the sun is lower in the sky and the particles in the air provide a filtering effect that warms the illumination to about 5,500K for most of the day. Starting an hour before dusk and for an hour after sunrise, the warm appearance of the sunlight is even visible to our eyes when the color temperature may dip to 5,000-4,500K, as shown in Figure 10.5.

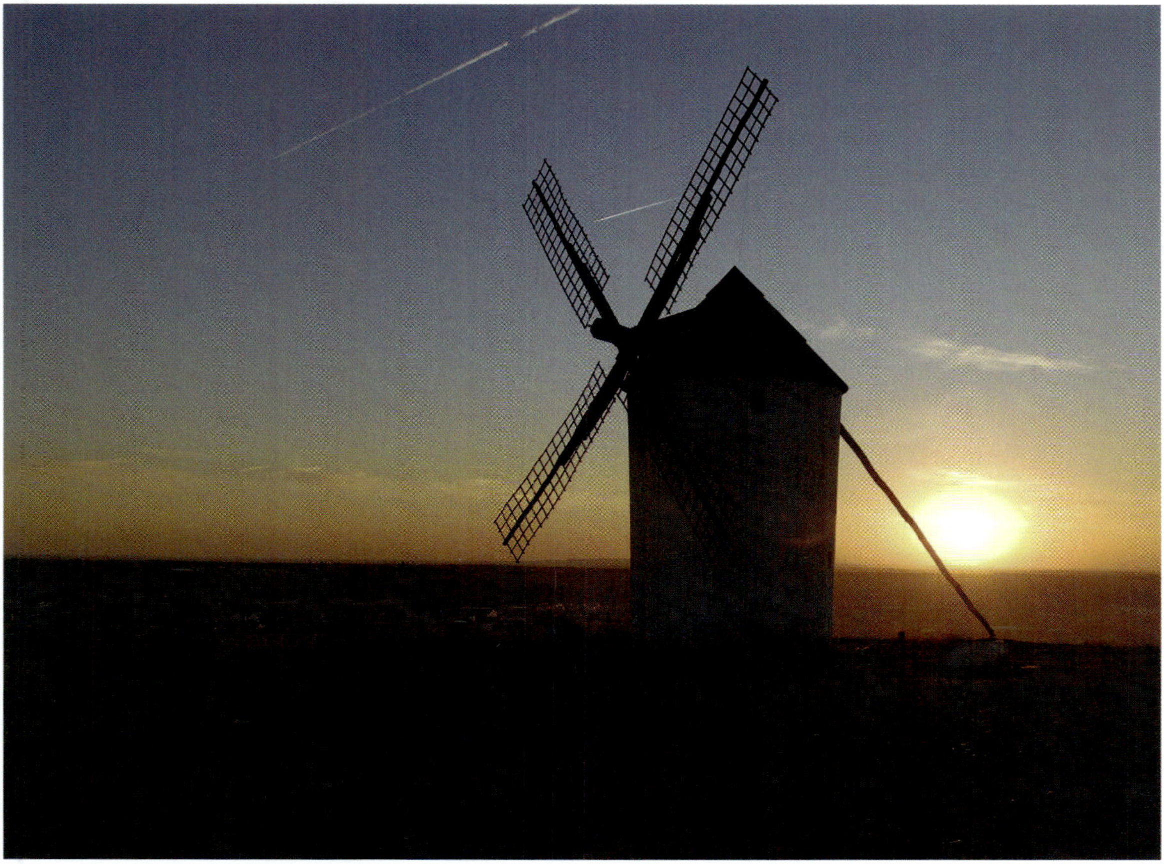

**Figure 10.5** At dawn and dusk, the color temperature of daylight may dip as low as 4,500K.

Because you'll be taking so many photos in daylight, you'll want to learn how to use or compensate for the brightness and contrast of sunlight, as well as how to deal with its color temperature. I'll provide some hints later in this chapter.

## Incandescent/Tungsten Light

The term incandescent or tungsten illumination is usually applied to the direct descendents of Thomas Edison's original electric lamp. Such lights consist of a glass bulb that contains a vacuum, or is filled with a halogen gas, and contains a tungsten filament that is heated by an electrical current, producing photons and heat. Tungsten-halogen lamps are a variation on the basic light bulb, using a more rugged (and longer-lasting) filament that can be heated to a higher temperature, housed in a thicker glass or quartz envelope, and filled with iodine or bromine ("halogen") gases. The higher temperature allows tungsten-halogen (or quartz-halogen/quartz-iodine, depending on their construction) lamps to burn "hotter" and whiter. Although popular for automobile headlamps today, they've also been used for photographic illumination.

Although incandescent illumination isn't a perfect black body radiator, it's close enough that the color temperature of such lamps can be precisely calculated and used for photography without concerns about color variation (at least, until the very end of the lamp's life).

The other qualities of this type of lighting, such as contrast, are dependent on the distance of the lamp from the subject, type of reflectors used, and other factors that I'll explain later in this chapter.

## Fluorescent Light/Other Light Sources

Fluorescent light has some advantages in terms of illumination, but some disadvantages from a photographic standpoint. This type of lamp generates light through an electrochemical reaction that emits most of its energy as visible light, rather than heat, which is why the bulbs don't get as hot. The type of light produced varies depending on the phosphor coatings and type of gas in the tube. So, the illumination fluorescent bulbs produce can vary widely in its characteristics.

That's not great news for photographers. Different types of lamps have different "color temperatures" that can't be precisely measured in degrees Kelvin, because the light isn't produced by heating. Worse, fluorescent lamps have a discontinuous spectrum of light that can have some colors missing entirely. A particular type of tube can lack certain shades of red or other colors (see Figure 10.6), which is why fluorescent lamps and other alternative technologies such as sodium-vapor illumination can produce ghastly looking human skin tones. Their spectra can lack the reddish tones we associate with healthy skin and emphasize the blues and greens popular in horror movies.

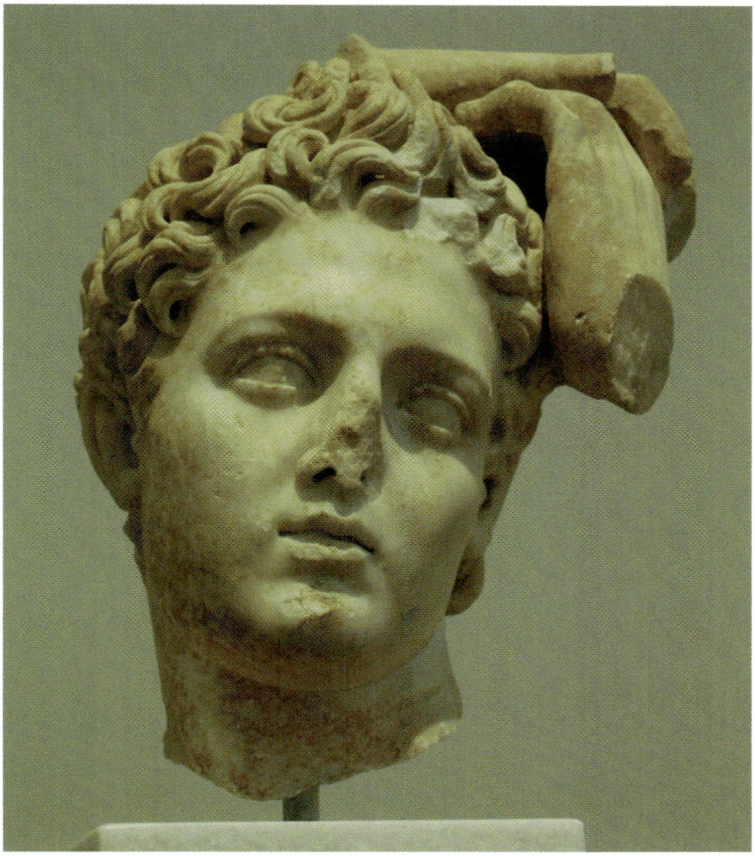

**Figure 10.6**
The uncorrected fluorescent lighting in the gallery added a distinct greenish cast to this image when exposed with a daylight white balance setting.

## Adjusting White Balance

I showed you how to adjust white balance in Chapter 3, using the D3s/D3x's built-in presets, white balance shift capabilities, setting exact color temperatures, and white balance bracketing (there's more on bracketing in Chapter 6, too).

In most cases, however, the Nikon D3s/D3x will do a good job of calculating white balance for you, so Auto can be used as your choice most of the time. Use the preset values or set a custom white balance that matches the current shooting conditions when you need to. The only really problematic light sources are likely to be fluorescents. Vendors, such as GE and Sylvania, may actually provide a figure known as the *color rendering index* (or CRI), which is a measure of how accurately a particular light source represents standard colors, using a scale of 0 (some sodium-vapor lamps) to 100 (daylight and most incandescent lamps). Daylight fluorescents and deluxe cool white fluorescents might have a CRI of about 79 to 95, which is perfectly acceptable for most photographic applications. Warm white fluorescents might have a CRI of 55. White deluxe mercury vapor lights are less suitable with a CRI of 45, while low-pressure sodium lamps can vary from CRI 0-18.

Remember that if you shoot RAW, you can specify the white balance of your image when you import it into Photoshop, Photoshop Elements, or another image editor using Nikon Capture NX, Adobe Camera Raw, or your preferred RAW converter. While color-balancing filters that fit on the front of the lens exist, they are primarily useful for film cameras, because film's color balance can't be tweaked as extensively as that of a sensor.

## Electronic Flash Basics

Until you delve into the situation deeply enough, it might appear that serious photographers have a love/hate relationship with electronic flash. You'll often hear that flash photography is less natural looking, and that the built-in flash in most cameras should never be used as the primary source of illumination because it provides a harsh, garish look. Indeed, the most advanced "pro" cameras like the previous Nikon D2xs and D3-series don't have a built-in flash at all. Available ("continuous") lighting is praised, and built-in flash photography seems to be roundly denounced.

In truth, however, the bias is against *bad* flash photography. Indeed, flash has become the studio light source of choice for pro photographers, because it's more intense (and its intensity can be varied to order by the photographer), freezes action, frees you from using a tripod (unless you want to use one to lock down a composition), and has a snappy, consistent light quality that matches daylight. (While color balance changes as the flash duration shortens, some Nikon flash units can communicate to the camera the exact white balance provided for that shot.) And even pros will cede that one of the add-on flash units available for the Nikon D3s/D3x has some important uses as an adjunct to existing light, particularly to fill in dark shadows.

But electronic flash isn't as inherently easy to use as continuous lighting. As I noted earlier, electronic flash units are more expensive, don't show you exactly what the lighting effect will be (unless you use a second source or mode called a *modeling light* for a preview), and the exposure of electronic flash units is more difficult to calculate accurately.

An electronic flash is triggered at the instant of exposure, during a period when the sensor is fully exposed by the shutter. As I mentioned earlier in this book, the D3s/D3x has a vertically traveling shutter that consists of two curtains. The first curtain opens and moves to the opposite side of the frame, at which point the shutter is completely open. The flash can be triggered at this point (so-called *front-curtain sync*), making the flash exposure. Then, after a delay that can vary from 30 seconds to 1/250th second (with the Nikon D3s/D3x; other cameras may sync at a faster or slower speed), a second curtain begins moving across the sensor plane, covering up the sensor again. If the flash is triggered just before the second curtain starts to close, then *second-curtain sync* is used. (I'll describe these in more detail later in this chapter.) In both cases, though, a shutter speed of 1/250th second is ordinarily the maximum that can be used to take a photo. If you use a faster shutter speed, you'll expose only the part of the sensor exposed by the gap between the shutter curtains when the flash fires.

## Determining Exposure

Calculating the proper exposure for an electronic flash photograph is a bit more complicated than determining the settings for continuous light. The right exposure isn't simply a function of how far away your subject is (which the D3s/D3x can figure out based on the autofocus distance that's locked in just prior to taking the picture). Various objects reflect more or less light at the same distance so, obviously, the camera needs to measure the amount of light reflected back and through the lens. Yet, as the flash itself isn't available for measuring until it's triggered, the D3s/D3x has nothing to measure.

The solution is to fire the flash twice. The initial shot is a *monitor pre-flash* that can be analyzed, then followed virtually instantaneously by a main flash (to the eye the bursts appear to be a single flash) that's given exactly the calculated intensity needed to provide a correct exposure. As a result, the primary flash may be longer in duration for distant objects and shorter in duration for closer subjects, depending on the required intensity for exposure. This through-the-lens evaluative flash exposure system is called i-TTL (intelligent Through The Lens), and it operates whenever you have attached a Nikon dedicated flash unit to the D3s/D3x.

## Guide Numbers

Guide numbers, usually abbreviated GN, are a way of specifying the power of an electronic flash in a way that can be used to determine the right f/stop to use at a particular shooting distance and ISO setting. In fact, before automatic flash units became prevalent, the GN was actually used to do just that. A GN is usually given as a pair of numbers for both feet and meters that represent the range at ISO 100. For example, the Nikon SB-900 has a GN in i-TTL mode of 48/157 (meters/feet) at ISO 200 when using the coverage needed for a 35mm lens (the flash has a *zoom head* to spread/narrow the light for a range of focal lengths). To calculate the right exposure at that ISO setting, you'd divide the guide number by the distance to arrive at the appropriate f/stop.

Using the SB-900 as an example, at ISO 200 with its GN of 157, if you wanted to shoot a subject at a distance of 10 feet, you'd use f/15.7 (or, f/16). At 5 feet, an f/stop of f/32 would be used. Some quick mental calculations with the GN will give you any particular electronic flash's range.

Today, guide numbers are most useful for comparing the power of various flash units, rather than actually calculating what exposure to use. You don't need to be a math genius to see that an electronic flash with a GN in feet of, say, 157 (like the SB-900) would be *a lot* more powerful than the built-in flash of a camera like the Nikon D700, which has a guide number of 56. At ISO 200, you could use f/8 instead of f/2.8 at 20 feet, an improvement of about 3.5 stops.

## How Electronic Flash Works

The bursts of light we call electronic flash are produced by a flash of photons generated by an electrical charge that is accumulated in a component called a *capacitor* and then directed through a glass tube containing xenon gas, which absorbs the energy and emits the brief flash. For most units, the full burst of light lasts about 1/1,000th of a second, and reduces in duration as the exposure system cuts back the amount of illumination to eliminate overexposure when the full power of the flash is not needed.

An electronic flash is triggered at the instant of exposure, during a period when the sensor is fully exposed by the shutter. As I mentioned earlier in this book, the D3s and D3x have a vertically traveling shutter that consists of two curtains. The first curtain opens and moves to the opposite side of the frame, at which point the shutter is completely open. The flash can be triggered at this point (so-called *first-curtain sync*), making the flash exposure. Then, after a delay that can vary from 30 seconds to 1/250th second (with the D3s/D3x; other cameras may sync at a faster or slower speed), a second curtain begins moving across the sensor plane, covering up the sensor again. If the flash is triggered just before the second curtain starts to close, then *second-curtain sync* is used.

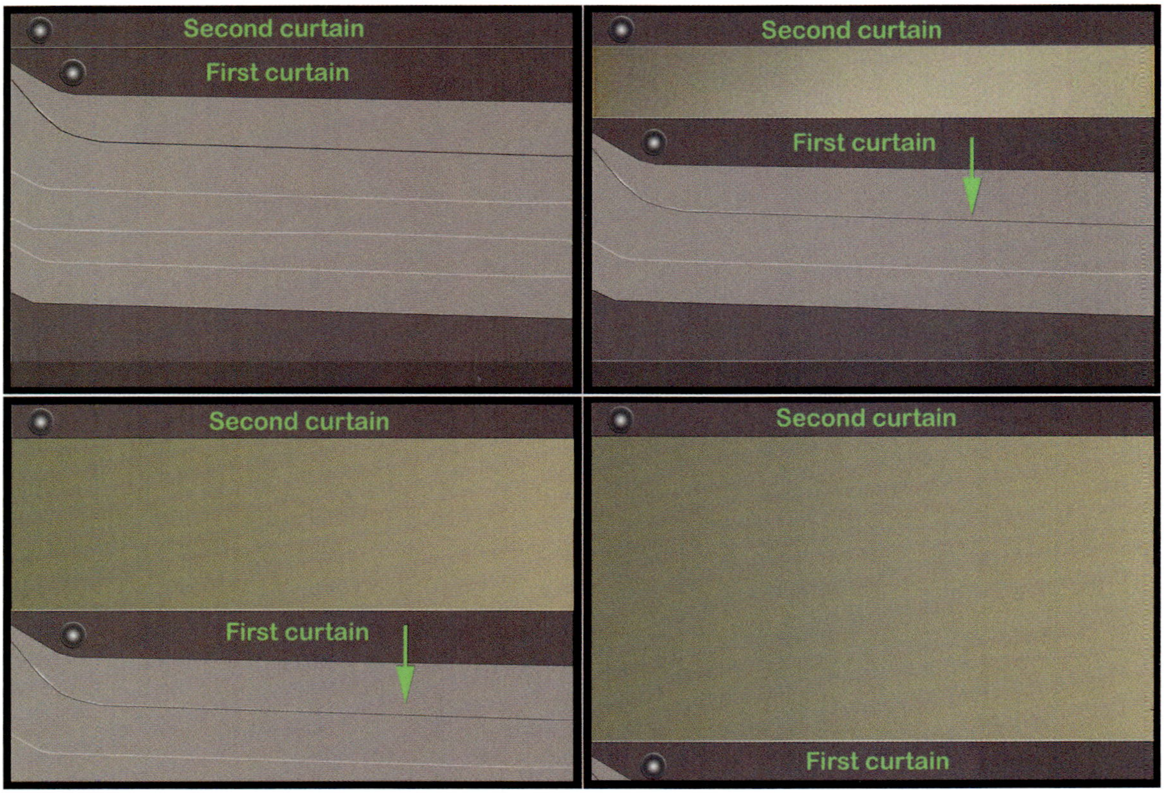


**Figure 10.7** A focal plane shutter has two curtains, the lower, or first curtain, and an upper, second curtain.

In both cases, though, a shutter speed of 1/250th second is the maximum that can be used to take a photo, unless you're using the high speed 1/320th second sync.

Figure 10.7 illustrates how this works, with a fanciful illustration of a generic shutter (your D3s/D3x's shutter does *not* look like this, and some vertically traveling shutters move bottom to top rather than the top-to-bottom motion shown). Both curtains are tightly closed at upper left. At upper right, the first curtain begins to move downwards, starting to expose a narrow slit that reveals the sensor behind the shutter. At lower left, the first curtain moves downwards farther until, as you can see at lower right in the figure, the sensor is fully exposed.

When first-curtain sync is used, the flash is triggered at the instant that the sensor is completely exposed. The shutter then remains open for an additional length of time (from 30 seconds to 1/250th second), and the second curtain begins to move downward, covering the sensor once more. When second-curtain sync is activated, the flash is triggered *after* the main exposure is over, just before the second curtain begins to move downward.

## A Typical Electronic Flash Sequence

Here's what happens when you take a photo using electronic flash:

1. **Sync mode.** Choose the flash sync mode by holding down the Flash button located on the release mode dial, and rotating the main command dial until the icon representing the choice you want is displayed in the top-panel monochrome LCD. (See Figure 10.8.)
2. **Metering method.** Choose the metering method you want, from matrix, center-weighted, or spot metering.
3. **Activate flash.** Mount (or connect with a cable) an external flash and turn it on. A ready light appears in the viewfinder and on the back of an external flash when the unit is ready to take a picture.

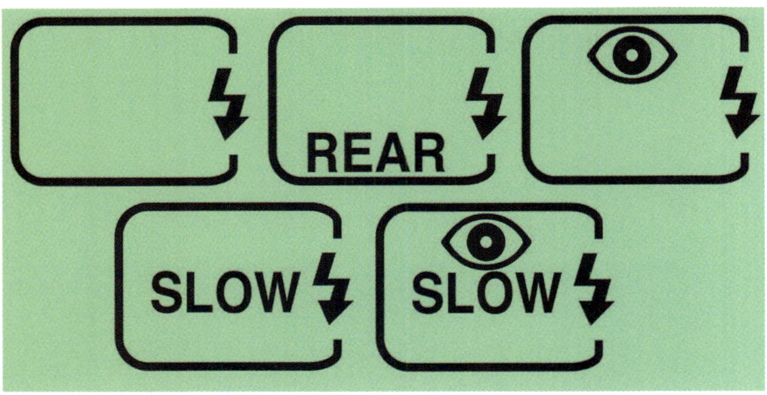


**Figure 10.8**
Icons for flash sync modes include front sync (top left), rear sync (top middle), red-eye reduction (top right), slow sync (lower left), and slow sync with red-eye reduction (lower right).

4. **Check exposure.** Select a shutter speed when using manual, programmed, or shutter-priority modes; select an aperture when using aperture-priority and manual exposure modes.
5. **Preview lighting.** If you want to preview the lighting effect, press the depth-of-field button to produce a modeling flash burst (unless you've redefined this control in the Custom Setting menu as described in Chapter 4).
6. **Lock flash setting (if desired).** Optionally, if the main subject is located significantly off-center, you can frame so the subject is centered, lock the flash at the exposure needed to illuminate that subject, and then reframe using the composition you want. Lock the flash level using the Flash value lock button (which can be assigned to the Fn, Preview, or AE-L/AF-L buttons in Custom Setting f4, Custom Setting f5, or Custom Setting f6). Press the FV lock button, and the flash will emit a pre-flash to determine the correct flash level, and then the D3s/D3x will lock the flash at that level until you press the FV lock button again to release it. FV lock icons appear in the monochrome LCD status panel and the viewfinder.
7. **Take photo.** Press the shutter release down all the way.
8. **D3s/D3x receives distance data.** A D- or G-series lens now supplies focus distance to the D3s/D3x.
9. **Pre-flash emitted.** The external flash sends out one or two pre-flash bursts. One burst can be used to control additional wireless flash units in commander mode, while the other burst is used to determine exposure.
10. **Exposure calculated.** The pre-flash bounces back and is measured by the 1,005-pixel RGB sensor in the viewfinder. It measures brightness and contrast of the image to calculate exposure. If you're using matrix metering, the D3s/D3x evaluates the scene to determine whether the subject may be backlit (for fill flash), a subject that requires extra ambient light exposure to balance the scene with the flash exposure, or classifies the scene in some other way. The camera to subject information as well as the degree of sharp focus of the subject matter is used to locate the subject within the frame. If you've selected spot metering, only standard i-TTL (without balanced fill-flash) is used.

### Tip

If you want to confirm that the pre-flash fires before the mirror flips up, set the D3s/D3x to Mup (Mirror Up) mode using the release mode dial (D3s, or using the menu with the D3x). (This separates the firing of the pre-flash from the flash used to make the exposure.) Press the shutter release as you look through the viewfinder. You'll see the pre-flash fire, and *then* the mirror will flip up, obscuring your view. Press the shutter release a second time to take the actual picture. Only *then* will the main flash fire.

11. **Mirror up.** The mirror flips up. At this point exposure and focus are locked in.
12. **Flash fired.** At the correct triggering moment (depending on whether front or rear sync is used), the camera sends a signal to one or more flashes to start flash discharge. The flash is quenched as soon as the correct exposure has been achieved.
13. **Shutter closes.** The shutter closes and the mirror flips down. You're ready to take another picture. Remember to press the FV lock button again to release the flash exposure if your next shot will use a different composition.
14. **Exposure confirmed.** Ordinarily, the full charge in the flash may not be required. If the flash indicator in the viewfinder blinks for about three seconds after the exposure, that means that the entire flash charge was required, and it *could* mean that the full charge wasn't enough for a proper exposure. Be sure to review your image on the LCD to make sure it's not underexposed, and, if it is, make adjustments (such as increasing the ISO setting of the D3s/D3x) to remedy the situation.

## Choosing a Flash Sync Mode

The Nikon D3s/D3x has five flash sync modes, selected by holding down the Flash button on the release mode dial while rotating the main command dial. (See Figure 10.8 for the icons.) Those modes (which I've listed in logical order, so the explanation will make more sense, rather than the order in which they appear during the selection cycle) are as follows:

- **Front-curtain sync.** This setting should be your default setting. In this mode, the flash fires as soon as the front curtain opens completely. The shutter then remains open for the duration of the exposure, until the rear curtain closes. If the subject is moving and ambient light levels are high enough, the movement will cause a secondary "ghost" exposure that appears in front of the flash exposure.
- **Rear-curtain sync.** With this setting, which can be used with shutter-priority, aperture-priority, programmed, or manual exposure modes, the front curtain opens completely and remains open for the duration of the exposure. Then, the flash is fired and the rear curtain closes. If the subject is moving and ambient light levels are high enough, the movement will cause a secondary "ghost" exposure that appears behind the flash exposure (trailing it). You'll find more on "ghost" exposures next. In programmed and aperture-priority modes, the D3s/D3x will combine rear-curtain sync with slow shutter speeds (just like slow sync, discussed below) to balance ambient light with flash illumination. (It's best to use a tripod to avoid blur at these slow shutter speeds.)
- **Red-eye reduction.** In this mode, there is a one-second lag after pressing the shutter release before the picture is actually taken, during which the electronic flash unit's red-eye reduction lamp lights, causing the subject's pupils to contract (assuming they are looking towards the camera), and thus reducing potential red-eye

effects. Don't try to use with moving subjects, non-Nikon dedicated flash units, or when you can't abide the delay.

- **Slow sync.** This setting allows the D3s/D3x in programmed and aperture-priority modes to use shutter speeds as slow as 30 seconds with the flash to help balance a background illuminated with ambient light with your main subject, which will be lit by the electronic flash. You'll want to use a tripod at slower shutter speeds, of course. As shown in Figure 10.9, it's common that the ambient light will be incandescent illumination that's much warmer than the electronic flash's "daylight" balance, so, if you want the two sources to match, you may want to use a warming

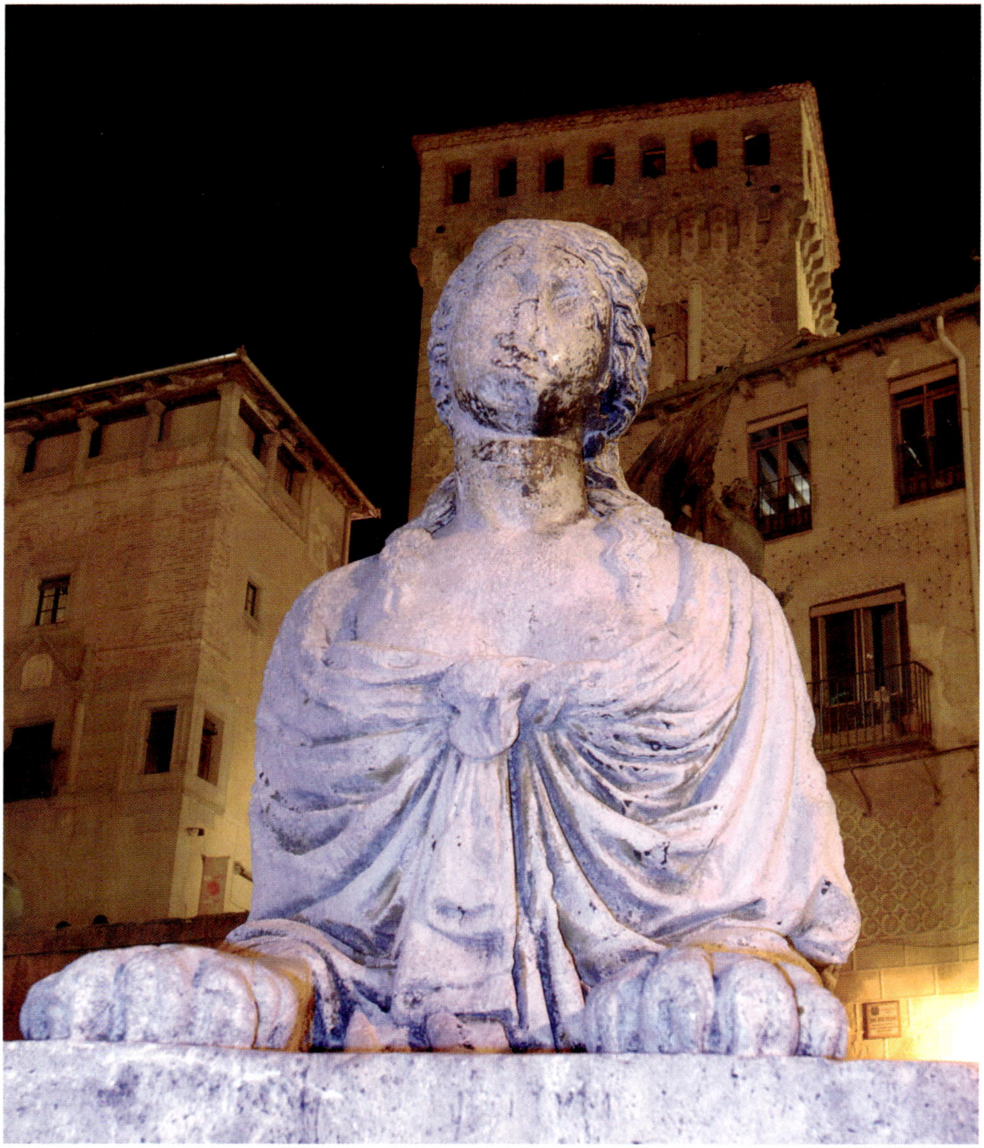

**Figure 10.9**
I deliberately used flash and slow sync to separate this Roman sphinx sculpture (limned in bluish light from the flash) from the background illuminated by warmer incandescents.

filter on the flash. That can be done with a gel if you're using an external flash like the SB-900, or by taping an appropriate warm filter over the D3s/D3x's built-in flash. (That's not a convenient approach, and many find the warm/cool mismatch unobjectionable and don't bother with filtration.)

- **Red-eye reduction with slow sync.** This mode combines slow sync with the D3s/D3x's red-eye reduction behavior when using programmed or aperture-priority modes.

In shutter-priority and manual exposure modes, you can select the following three flash synchronization settings:

- **Front-curtain sync/fill flash.** This setting should be your default setting. This mode is also available in programmed and aperture-priority mode, as described above, and, with high ambient light levels, can produce ghost images, discussed below.
- **Red-eye reduction.** This mode, with its one-second lag and red-eye lamp flash, is described above.
- **Rear-curtain sync.** As noted previously, in this sync mode, the front curtain opens completely and remains open for the duration of the exposure. Then, the flash is fired and the rear curtain closes. If the subject is moving and ambient light levels are high enough, the movement will cause that "ghost" exposure that appears to be trailing the flash exposure.

## Ghost Images

The difference might not seem like much, but whether you use first-curtain sync (the default setting) or rear-curtain sync (an optional setting) can make a significant difference to your photograph *if the ambient light in your scene also contributes to the image.* At faster shutter speeds, particularly 1/250th second, there isn't much time for the ambient light to register, unless it is very bright. It's likely that the electronic flash will provide almost all the illumination, so first-curtain sync or second-curtain sync isn't very important.

However, at slower shutter speeds, or with very bright ambient light levels, there is a significant difference, particularly if your subject is moving, or the camera isn't steady. In any of those situations, the ambient light will register as a second image accompanying the flash exposure, and if there is movement (camera or subject), that additional image will not be in the same place as the flash exposure. It will show as a ghost image and, if the movement is significant enough, as a blurred ghost image trailing in front of or behind your subject in the direction of the movement.

As I mentioned earlier, when you're using first-curtain sync, the flash goes off the instant the shutter opens, producing an image of the subject on the sensor. Then, the shutter remains open for an additional period (which can be from 30 seconds to 1/250th second). If your subject is moving, say, towards the right side of the frame, the ghost image produced by the ambient light will produce a blur on the right side of the original subject image, making it look as if your sharp (flash-produced) image is chasing the ghost. (See Figure 10.10, top.) For those of us who grew up with lightning-fast superheroes who always left a ghost trail *behind them*, that looks unnatural (see Figure 10.10, bottom).

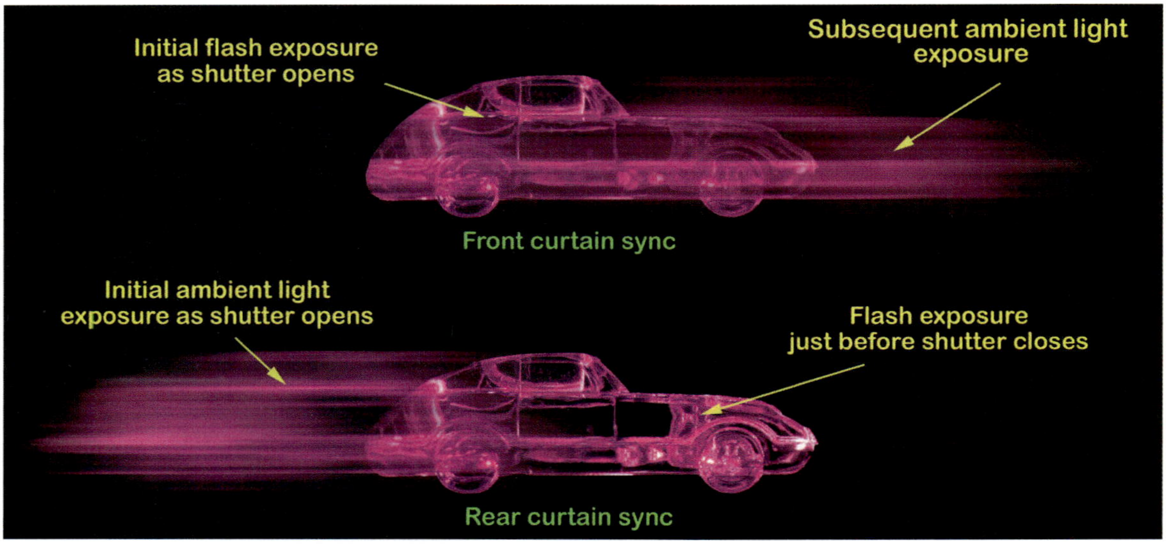


**Figure 10.10** Front-curtain sync produces an image that trails in front of the flash exposure (top), while rear-curtain sync creates a more "natural looking" trail behind the flash image (bottom).

So, Nikon provides rear (second) curtain sync to remedy the situation. In that mode, the shutter opens, as before. The shutter remains open for its designated duration, and the ghost image forms. If your subject moves from the left side of the frame to the right side, the ghost will move from left to right, too. *Then,* about 1.5 milliseconds before the second shutter curtain closes, the flash is triggered, producing a nice, sharp flash image *ahead* of the ghost image. Voilà! We have monsieur *le Flash* outrunning his own trailing image.

## EVERY WHICH WAY, INCLUDING UP

Note that, although I describe the ghost effect in terms of subject matter that is moving left to right in a horizontally oriented composition, it can occur in any orientation, and with the subject moving in *any* direction. (Try photographing a falling rock, if you can, and you'll see the same effect.) Nor are the ghost images affected by the fact that modern shutters travel vertically rather than horizontally. Secondary images are caused between the time the first curtain fully opens, and the second curtain begins to close. The direction of travel of the shutter curtains, or the direction of your subject does not matter.

## Avoiding Sync Speed Problems

Using a shutter speed faster than 1/250th second can cause problems. Triggering the electronic flash only when the shutter is completely open makes a lot of sense if you think about what's going on. To obtain shutter speeds faster than 1/250th second, the D3s/D3x exposes only part of the sensor at one time, by starting the second curtain on its journey before the first curtain has completely opened, as shown in Figure 10.11. That effectively provides a briefer exposure as a slit of the shutter passes over the surface of the sensor. If the flash were to fire during the time when the first and second curtains partially obscured the sensor, only the slit that was actually open would be exposed.

You'd end up with only a narrow band, representing the portion of the sensor that was exposed when the picture is taken. For shutter speeds *faster* than 1/250th second, the second curtain begins moving *before* the first curtain reaches the bottom of the frame. As a result, a moving slit, the distance between the first and second curtains, exposes one portion of the sensor at a time as it moves from the bottom to the top. Figure 10.11 shows three views of our typical (but imaginary) focal plane shutter. At left is pictured the closed shutter; in the middle version you can see the first curtain has moved up about 1/4 of the distance to the top; and in the right-hand version, the second curtain has started to "chase" the first curtain across the frame towards the top.

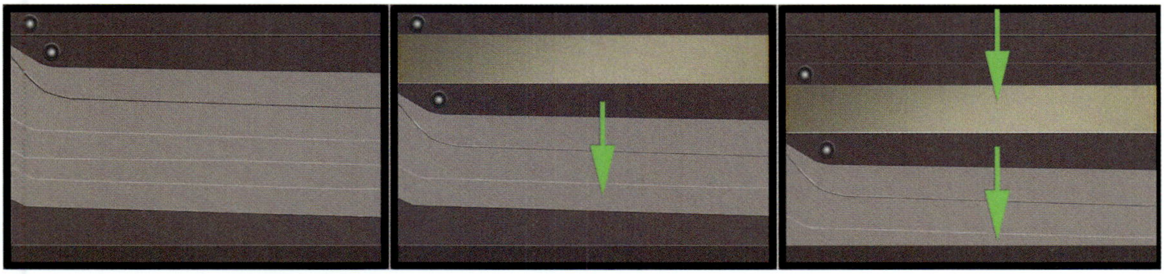

**Figure 10.11** A closed shutter (left); partially open shutter as the first curtain begins to move downwards (middle); only part of the sensor is exposed as the slit moves (right).

If the flash is triggered while this slit is moving, only the exposed portion of the sensor will receive any illumination. You end up with a photo like the one shown in Figure 10.12. Note that a band across the bottom of the image is black. That's a shadow of the second shutter curtain, which had started to move when the flash was triggered. Sharp-eyed readers will wonder why the black band is at the *bottom* of the frame rather than at the top, where the second curtain begins its journey. The answer is simple: your lens flips the image upside down and forms it on the sensor in a reversed position. You never notice that, because the camera is smart enough to show you the pixels that make up your photo in their proper orientation during picture review. But this image flip is why, if your sensor gets dirty and you detect a spot of dust in the upper half of a test photo, if cleaning manually, you need to look for the speck in the *bottom* half of the sensor.

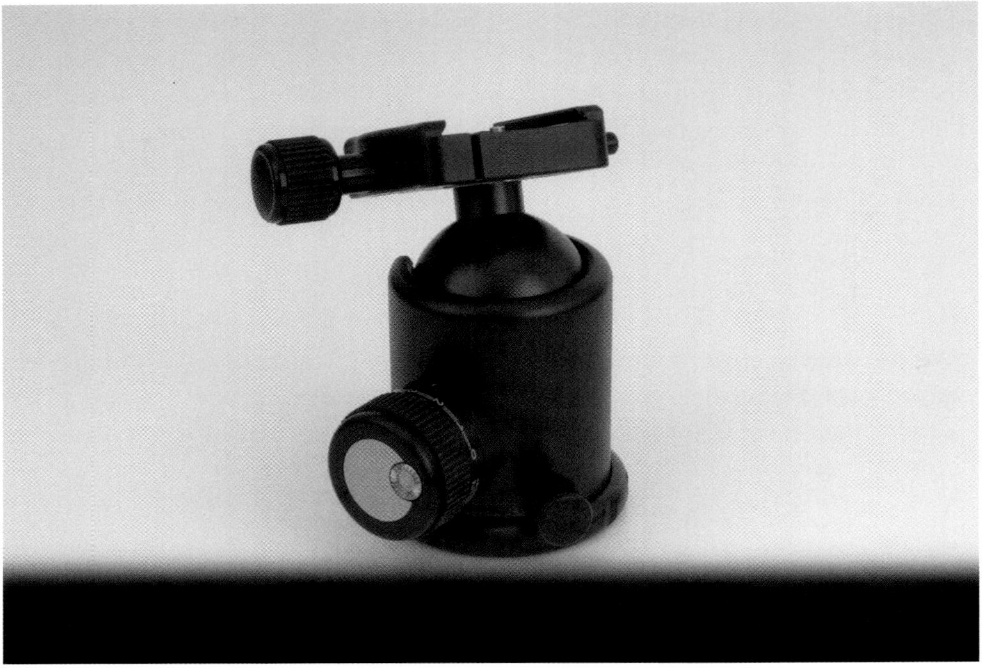

**Figure 10.12**
If a shutter speed faster than 1/250th second is used, you can end up photographing only a portion of the image.

I generally end up with sync speed problems only when shooting in the studio, using studio flash units rather than my Nikon dedicated Speedlight. That's because if you're using either type of "smart" flash, the camera knows that a strobe is attached, and remedies any unintentional goof in shutter speed settings. If you happen to set the D3s/D3x's shutter to a faster speed in S or M mode, the camera will automatically adjust the shutter speed down to 1/250th second as soon as you turn on an attached flash. In A or P, where the D3s/D3x selects the shutter speed, it will never choose a shutter speed higher than 1/250th second when using flash. In P mode, shutter speed is automatically set between 1/60th to 1/250th second when using flash.

But when using a non-dedicated flash, such as a studio unit plugged into the D3s/D3x's PC/X connector or through an adapter mounted on the hot shoe, the camera has no way of knowing that a flash is connected, so shutter speeds faster than 1/250th second can be set inadvertently. To avoid that problem with studio flash, I strongly recommend setting your camera to manual exposure, and using the x250 shutter speed, which is located *past* the Bulb speed when rotating the main command dial all the way to the left. You won't have to worry as much about accidentally changing the shutter speed to an unusable setting; there is no speed *beyond* x250th second, and if you nudge the main command dial to the right, you'll get a Bulb exposure, which will immediately become evident.

Note that the D3s/D3x can use a feature called *high-speed sync* that allows shutter speeds faster than 1/250th second with certain external dedicated Nikon flash units. When using high-speed sync, the flash fires a continuous series of bursts at reduced power for the entire duration of the exposure, so that the illumination is able to expose the sensor as the slit moves. HS sync is set using the controls that adjust the compatible external flash.

## High-Speed (FP) Sync

If you use certain external dedicated Nikon flash units, you have an additional option: high-speed (FP) sync. You don't need to make any special settings on the flash; the D3s/D3x takes care of the details for you, as I'll describe in this section.

As I said earlier, triggering the electronic flash only when the shutter is completely open makes a lot of sense if you think about what's going on. To obtain shutter speeds faster than 1/250th second, the D3s/D3x exposes only part of the sensor at one time, by starting the second curtain on its journey before the first curtain has completely opened. That effectively provides a briefer exposure as a slit of the shutter passes over the surface of the sensor. If the flash were to fire during the time when the first and second curtains partially obscured the sensor, only the area defined by the slit that was actually open would be exposed.

However, the D3s/D3x and certain Nikon flashes provide a partial solution, called *high-speed sync* or *FP sync* (focal plane sync). Those flash units can fire a series of flashes consecutively in rapid succession, producing the illusion of a longer continuous flash, although at reduced intensity. These multiple flashes have a duration long enough to allow exposing the area of the sensor revealed by the traveling slit as it makes its full pass. However, the reduced intensity means that your flash's range is greatly reduced.

This technique is most useful outdoors when you need fill-in flash, but find that 1/250th second is way too slow for the f/stop you want to use. For example, at ISO 200, an outdoors exposure is likely to be 1/250th second at, say, f/14, which is perfectly fine for an ambient/balanced fill-flash exposure if you don't mind the extreme depth-of-field offered by the small f/stop. But, what if you'd rather shoot at 1/1,600th second at f/5.6? High-speed sync will let you do that, and you probably won't mind the reduced flash power, because you're looking for fill flash, anyway. This sync mode offers more flexibility than, say, dropping down to L 1.0 (ISO 100 equivalent).

High-speed sync is also useful when you want to use a larger f/stop to limit the amount of depth-of-field. Select a shutter speed higher than 1/250th second, and the faster sync speed automatically reduces the effective light of the flash, without other intervention from you.

To use auto FP sync with units like the Nikon SB-900, SB-800, SB-600, and SB-R200 units, there is no setting to make on the flash itself. You need to use Custom Setting e1 to specify 1/250 s (Auto FP). When this setting is activated, when using P or A exposure modes, the shutter speed will be set to 1/250th second when a compatible external flash is attached. Higher shutter speeds than 1/250th second can then be used with full synchronization, at reduced flash output. (The D3-series does not have the 1/320 s [Auto FP] setting available with some other cameras, such as the Nikon D300s.)

# Working with Nikon Flash Units

If you want to work with dedicated Nikon flash units, at this time you have five choices, the Nikon SB-900, SB-800, SB-600, and SB-400 on-camera flash units, and the SB-R200 wireless remote flash. (The discontinued SB-800 can still be found on the used market.) These share certain features, which I'll discuss while pointing out differences among them. Nikon may introduce additional flash units during the life of this book, but the current batch and the Nikon Creative Lighting System ushered in with them were significant steps forward, so I don't expect any major changes in the near future. First, a quick introduction to the separate flash units currently available:

## Nikon SB-900

The Nikon SB-900 (see Figure 10.13) is currently the flagship of the Nikon flash line up, and has a guide number of 48/157 (meters/feet) at ISO 200 when the "zooming" flash head (which can be set to adjust the coverage angle of the lens) is set to the 35mm position. It has commander mode, repeating flash, modeling light, and selectable power output, along with some extra capabilities.

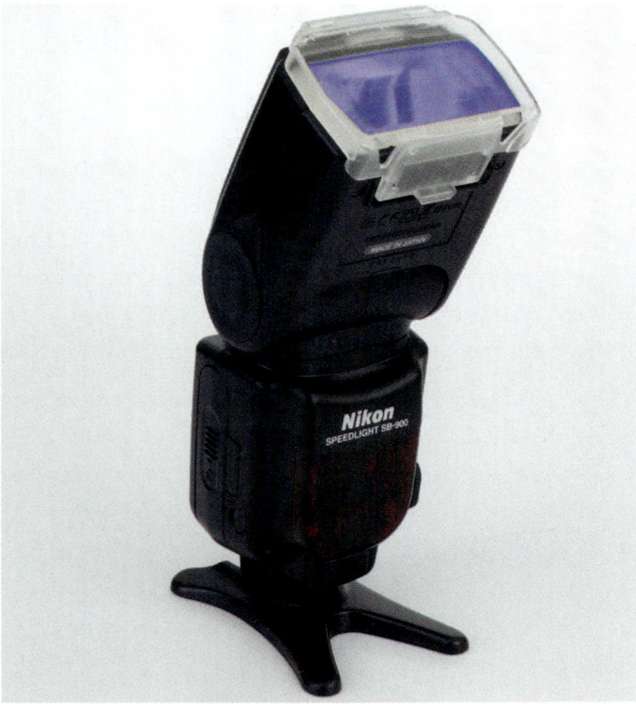


**Figure 10.13**
The Nikon SB-900, shown here with a blue filter attached, is currently the flagship of the Nikon electronic flash line up.

## OVERHEATING?

One of the new capabilities of the SB-900 is the ability to turn itself off when the flash is fired repeatedly over an interval that is short enough to cause the unit to overheat. Wedding photographers and others who shoot rapid-fire at full power or in manual mode are often outraged to find their SB-900's shutting down at the worst possible time, after what they consider only a moderate number of bursts. (Some report shut-down after only a dozen or so flashes, followed by a long wait while the unit cools off.) Consequently, SB-900 has achieved a bad rep as an "overheating" unit. In truth, the SB-900 may not overheat any more often than its predecessor, the SB-800, in many applications. The earlier flash didn't have the same auto shutoff features the SB-900 has, so overheating has become more visible and vexing. While you can shut off the automatic shut-down, I don't recommend it, as that step is a little like replacing a fuse with a penny: your device may operate until it melts. If lots of full-power flashes are among your requirements, especially if you shoot in manual mode a lot, you may want to consider a non-Nikon, non-dedicated flash designed to accommodate heavy-duty use.

Other features include the ability to angle the flash and rotate it to provide bounce flash. The SB-900 includes additional, non-through-the lens exposure modes, thanks to its built-in light sensor, and can "zoom" and diffuse its coverage angle to illuminate the field of view of lenses from 24mm to 105mm, plus 14mm with an included diffuser. The SB-900 also has its own powerful focus assist lamp to aid autofocus in dim lighting, and has reduced red-eye effects simply because the unit, when attached to the D3s/D3x, is mounted in a higher position that tends to eliminate reflections from the eye back to the camera lens. More detailed specifics include

- **Multiple flash exposure modes.** In addition to i-TTL mode, the SB-900 has AA (auto aperture) exposure mode, in which the flash unit reads the light reflected back from the subject to a sensor on the flash. There is a manual mode to allow you to set flash levels yourself. It also has D-TTL mode for use with older Nikon D1 and D100 cameras, a TTL Auto Flash mode for many Nikon film cameras, and an A (automatic) mode compatible with the Nikon N55/F55 and FM10 film cameras.
- **Flash groups.** In Advanced Wireless Lighting mode, you can use the SB-900 to control up to four groups of flash units (as you can with the built-in flash) and choose a flash exposure mode (i-TTL, AA, A, or M) individually for each of the four groups.
- **Bounce capability.** The SB-900's flash head tilts down –7 degrees or up 90 degrees, and rotates horizontally 180 degrees to the left and 90 degrees to the right for versatile bounce flash effects. There's a pop-up "white card" that reflects some fill light back to the subject to soften shadows or provide a catch light in the eye when the unit is bounced off the ceiling.

- **Distance priority manual mode.** Set the distance and aperture, and the SB-900 automatically adjusts the power output to a setting appropriate for that f/stop and subject distance.
- **Backlit illuminated LCD control panel.** Features of the SB-900 can be set using an array of buttons and a large, informative backlit LCD display.
- **Add Ons.** The SB-900 is furnished with a Sto-Fen-style clip-on diffuser dome, and several gel filters to adjust the flash color output for tungsten and fluorescent illumination (so you don't accidentally mix the flash's "blue" lighting with the ambient incandescent or fluorescent lighting).

## Nikon SB-800

This is a discontinued model with features in most respects similar to the SB-900. However, the SB-800 is less known for overheating (but that's not to say that it doesn't overheat; it just doesn't have the same auto-shutoff features of the newer unit) and it has a rather clumsy interface, compared to the SB-900, requiring much twiddling of dials and pressing of buttons to make even frequently used adjustments.

My recommendation is this: if you've learned the SB-800's Byzantine controls already and are reasonably happy with its performance, it makes sense to stick with it. Switch to the SB-900 only if you need a specific feature included in the newer flash. If you are trying to decide between the cheaper (discontinued) SB-800 and the SB-900, do yourself a favor and spend the extra money for the easier-to-use SB-900. Investigate the latest scuttlebutt about overheating (Nikon may be fixing the problem after I write this), and decide whether heat build-up is a problem for you. If the SB-900 meets your needs in all other respects, its easier interface should make deciding between it and the SB-800 fairly simple.

## Nikon SB-600

This lower-cost unit (see Figure 10.14) has a guide number of 30/98 (meters/feet) at ISO 200 when set to the 35mm zoom position. It has many of the SB-900's features, including zoomable flash coverage equal to the field of view of a 24-85mm lens on the D3s/D3x, and 14mm with a built-in diffuser panel. It has a built-in modeling flash feature, but lacks repeating flash, accessory filters, and an included flash diffuser dome, which can be purchased separately. Other differences include:

- **Multiple flash exposure modes.** The SB-600 does not offer AA or A automatic, non-TTL exposure modes, but does support i-TTL, D-TTL (for the Nikon D1 series and D100), TTL auto flash for many Nikon film cameras, and manual flash modes. (Output can be varied only from 1/1 to 1/64 power.)
- **Flash groups.** The SB-600 cannot function in commander mode to control other Nikon flash units, but it can serve as a slave unit triggered by a commander as part of a flash group.

- **Bounce capability.** The flash head tilts upwards up to 90 degrees, plus 180 degrees to the left or 90 degrees to the right.
- **No add-ons.** The SB-600 is not furnished with accessories, such as filters, a diffuser, or stand, but you can find these offered by third parties.

The SB-600 is long overdue for replacement. There's nothing in the works as I write this, other than rumors of a new SB-700 model, so you'd be smart to do some Googling before buying this unit.

## Nikon SB-400

The entry-level SB-400 (see Figure 10.15) really isn't suitable for most Nikon D3s/D3x applications, but I am including it to round out the discussion. It's intended for entry-level Nikon cameras like the D40 or D60, and has limited features. While it does offer i-TTL exposure functions, it can be used in manual mode only on the D40, and has a limited guide number of 30/98 at the 18mm zoom-head position. It tilts up for bounce flash to 90 degrees, with click detents at the 0, 60, 75, and 90 degree marks. Unless you feel the need for an emergency flash or fill-flash unit, you'll probably be happier with something more sophisticated.

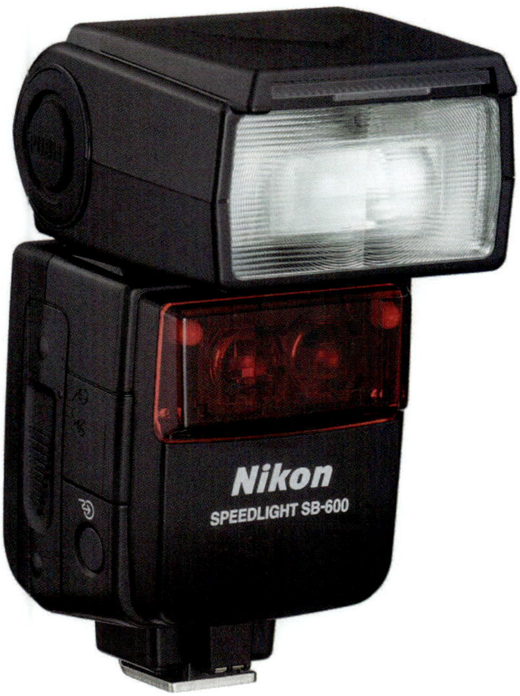


**Figure 10.14** The Nikon SB-600 is a popular medium-priced electronic flash with most of the features of the SB-900, except for commander mode to control remote units.

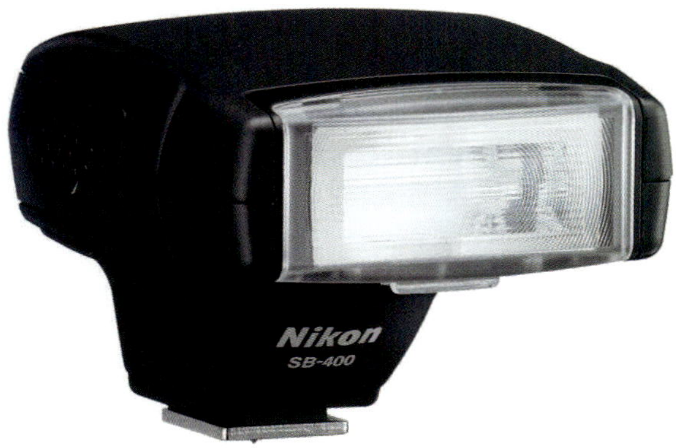


**Figure 10.15** The Nikon SB-400 is an entry-level flash best suited for Nikon's entry-level dSLRs.

## Nikon SB-R200

This is a specialized wireless-only flash (see Figure 10.16) that's especially useful for close-up photography, and is often purchased in pairs for use with the Nikon R1 and R1C1 Wireless Close-Up Speedlight systems. Its output power is low at 14/46 (meters/feet) as you might expect for a unit used to photograph subjects that are often inches from the camera. It has a fixed coverage angle of 78 degrees horizontal and 60 degrees vertical, but the flash head tilts down up to 60 degrees and up to 45 degrees (with detents every 15 degrees in both directions). In this case, "up" and "down" have a different meaning, because the SB-R200 can be mounted on the SX-1 Attachment Ring mounted around the lens, so the pair of flash units are on the sides and titled toward or away from the optical axis. It supports i-TTL, D-TTL, TTL (for film cameras), and manual modes.

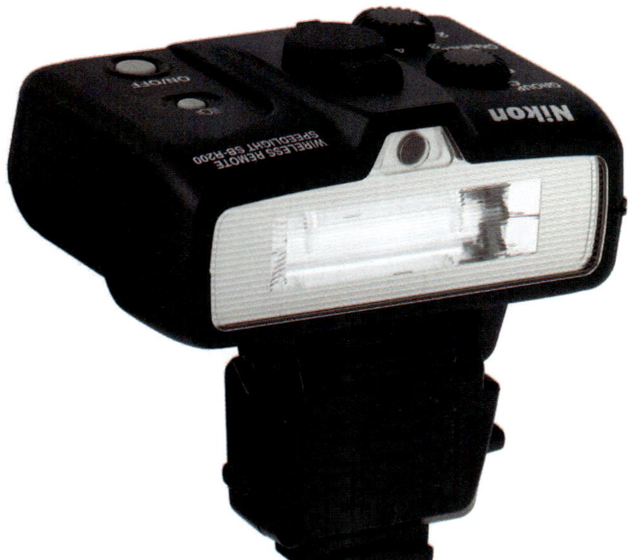


**Figure 10.16**
The Nikon SB-R200 is a wireless macro-only flash supplied with the Nikon R1 and R1C1 Wireless Close-Up Speedlight systems.

# Flash Techniques

Entire books have been written on using Nikon electronic flash units, and the Nikon Creative Lighting System (CLS). Even in a 500-plus page book like this one, I don't have room to show you how to use every feature of every flash unit. Instead, I'm going to use this next section to discuss key features of the Nikon dedicated external flash units. You'll find information on setting your Nikon D3s/D3x's flash options in Chapters 3, 4, and 5.

After reading this, you'll know more about what you can do, and will explore the controls and settings that will let you move beyond this overview. If you'd like an amazing practical guide to flash photography in general, I recommend Joe McNally's *Hot Shoe Diaries*. You can find basic information on flash photography and lighting techniques in my book *David Busch's Quick Snap Guide to Lighting*. Like Joe's book, it is non-Nikon-specific, but shows you tricks of studio lighting, and other techniques that you can easily apply to your D3s/D3x camera and its flash units.

## Using Zoom Heads

External flash zoom heads can adjust themselves automatically to match lens focal lengths in use reported by the D3s/D3x to the flash unit, or you can adjust the zoom head position manually if you want to use a setting that doesn't correspond to the automatic setting the flash will use. With older flash units, like the SB-600, automatic zoom adjustment wastes some of your flash's power, because the flash unit assumes that the focal length reported comes from a full-frame camera.

If you use both a full-frame FX camera like the D3s/D3x and a cropped-sensor DX model like the D300s, or you use the D3s or D3x in DX mode, you should know that, because of the 1.5X crop factor, the flash coverage when the flash is set to a particular focal length will be wider than is required by the DX cropped image.

In that case, you can manually adjust the zoom position yourself, using positions built into the flash unit that more closely correspond to your DX camera or DX mode's field of view when using a flash that does not, like the SB-900, automatically take into account the difference between FX (full-frame) and DX (APS-C) coverage. Table 10.1 shows the actual focal length of a lens (or focal length position of a zoom lens) in the left column, with the closest zoom head position on the flash unit in the right column. Note that only the SB-900 has 105mm zoom position, which is appropriate when using an 85mm lens on a Nikon D3s/D3x in DX mode.

**Table 10.1 Zoom Head Equivalents When Using DX Mode**

| Lens Focal Length | Zoom head position | Lens Focal Length | Zoom head position |
|---|---|---|---|
| 14mm | 20mm | 35mm | 50mm |
| 18mm | 24mm | 50mm | 70mm |
| 20mm | 28mm | 70mm | 85mm |
| 24mm | 35mm | 85mm | 105mm |
| 28mm | 50mm | | |

To set the zoom position manually, follow one of these steps:

- **SB-900.** Press the Zoom button (located southwest of the selector dial/OK button pad) once, release it, and then rotate the selector dial until the zoom setting you want appears on the LCD. An "M" appears on the LCD above the Zoom indicator to show that the zoom setting has been made manually. An FX or DX indicator appears to the left , just above the Zoom indicator to show that the SB-900 is set for FX or DX coverage. You can also change the zoom setting by pressing the Zoom button repeatedly, in which case the focal length setting will jump from one increment to the next, wrapping around at 200mm back to the 12mm setting. Figure 10.17 shows the controls on the back of the SB-900.
- **SB-800.** Press the Wide button on the selector pad (indicated by the "three trees" icon) to zoom wider, or the single tree icon to zoom to a more telephoto position. A small M appears above the Zoom indicator in the lower-left corner of the LCD. To cancel the manual zoom setting, press the buttons until the zoom setting corresponds to the actual focal length set on the lens.
- **SB-600.** Press the Zoom button and adjust zoom position manually. M appears above Zoom in the LCD. To cancel manual zoom, press the zoom button until it matches the focal length set on the lens.

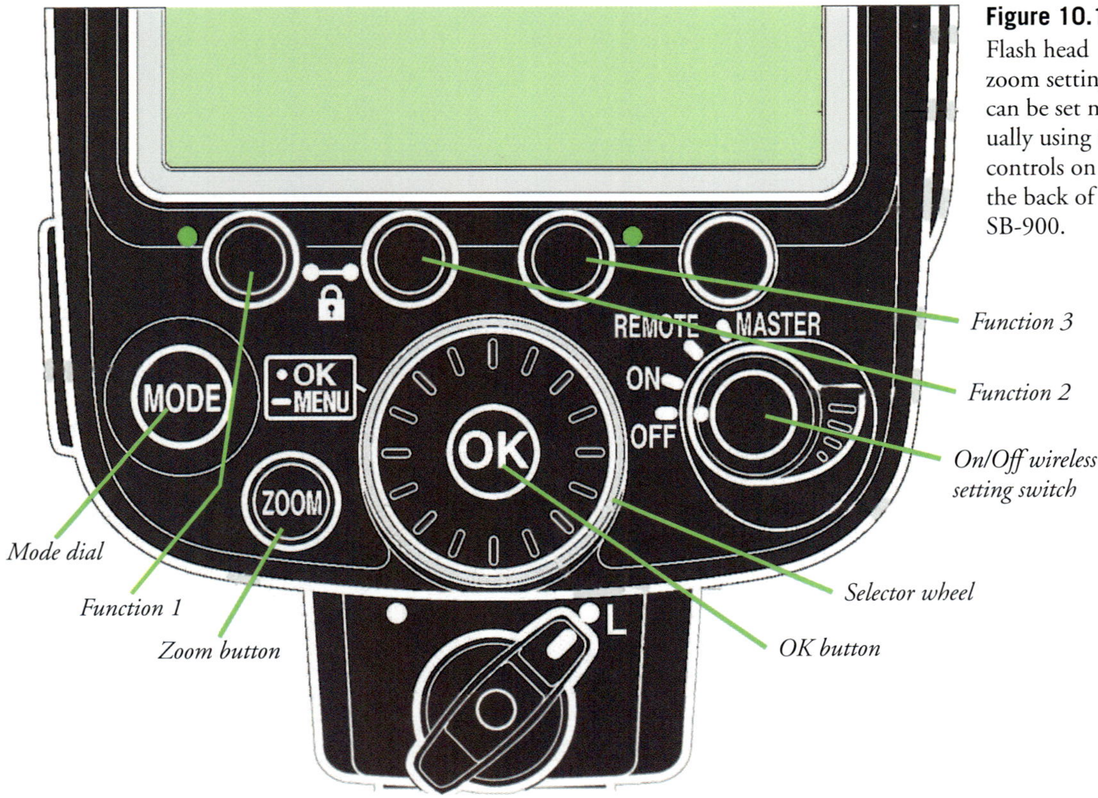


**Figure 10.17** Flash head zoom settings can be set manually using the controls on the back of the SB-900.

## Flash Modes

The external flash units have various flash modes included, which are available or not available with different camera models, categorized into nine different groups. A table showing most of the groups is included in the manuals for the external flash units, but the table is irrelevant for D3s/D3x users (unless you happen to own an older digital or film SLR, as well). For digital cameras, there are two main groups: digital cameras *not* compatible with the Nikon Creative Lighting System (Nikon D1-series cameras, and the Nikon D100), and digital cameras that *are* compatible with CLS (including the D3s/D3x). Groups I through VII, which support various combinations of features, consist of various film SLRs. You can ignore those options, unless you're using your external flash with an older film camera.

To change flash mode with the SB-900, press the Mode button on the back left edge, then release it and rotate the selector dial until the mode you want appears on the LCD. The TTL automatic flash modes available for the SB-900 are as follows:

- **iTTL automatic balanced fill flash.** In both matrix and center-weighted camera exposure modes, the camera and flash balance the exposure so that the main subject and background are well-exposed. A TTL BL indicator appears on the LCD. However, if you switch to spot metering, the flash switches to standard iTTL, described next.
- **Standard iTTL.** In this mode, the exposure is set for the main subject, and the background exposure is not taken into account. A TTL indicator appears on the LCD. In either iTTL automatic balanced fill flash or standard iTTL modes, if the full power of the flash is used, the ready-light indicator on the flash and in the camera viewfinder will blink for three seconds. This is your cue that perhaps even the full power of the flash might not have been enough for proper exposure. If that's the case, an EV indicator will display the amount of underexposure (–0.3 to –3.0 EV) on the LCD while the ready-light indicator flashes.
- **AA: Auto aperture flash.** An A indicator next to an icon representing a lens opening/aperture is shown on the LCD when this mode is selected. The SB-900 uses a built-in light sensor to measure the amount of flash illumination reflected back from the subject, and adjusts the output to produce an appropriate exposure based on the ISO, aperture, focal length, and flash compensation values set on the D3s/D3x. This setting on the flash can be used with the D3s/D3x in programmed or aperture-priority modes.
- **A: Non-TTL auto flash.** To work with this mode, you must set the SB-900 for its use using the flash's (not the camera's) Custom Setting menu. Press the OK button in the center of the flash unit's selector dial for about one second, and when the Custom Setting menu appears, rotate the selector dial to choose A. Press OK again, and you can choose from among four variations, Auto Aperture flash (described

above) with or without monitor pre-flash, or Non-TTL auto flash, with or without monitor pre-flash. (Note that the SB-900 manual calls these options "modeling illumination" instead.) In this mode, the SB-900's sensor measures the flash illumination reflected back from the subject, and adjusts the output to provide an appropriate exposure, without the feedback about the aperture setting of the camera that's used with AA mode. This setting on the flash can be used when the D3s/D3x is set to aperture-priority or manual modes. You can use this setting to manually "bracket" exposures, as adjusting the aperture value of the lens will produce more or less exposure; the flash has no idea what aperture you've changed to.

- **GN: Distance priority manual.** You enter a distance value, and the SB-900 adjusts light output based on distance, ISO, and aperture to produce the right exposure in either aperture-priority or manual exposure modes. Press the Mode button on the flash and rotate the selector dial until the GN indicator appears (the GN option appears only when the flash is pointed directly ahead, or is in the downward bounce position). Then press the OK button to confirm your choice. After that, you can specify a shooting distance by pressing Function Button 2, and then rotating the selector dial until the distance you want is indicated on the LCD. Press the OK button to confirm. The SB-900 will indicate a recommended aperture, which you then set on the lens mounted on the D3s/D3x in manual exposure mode.
- **M: manual flash.** The flash fires at a fixed output level. Press the Mode button and rotate the selector dial until M appears on the SB-900's LCD panel. Press the OK button to confirm your choice. Press the Function Button 1 and rotate the selector dial to dial in the power output level you want. Calculate the correct f/stop to use, either by taking a few test photos with a flash meter or by the seat of your pants. Then, set the D3s/D3x to aperture-priority or manual exposure and choose the f/stop you've decided on. (You can also use manual flash with the D3s/D3x's built-in unit by choosing a flash level in Custom Setting e3, as described in Chapter 4, and calculating the appropriate aperture.) (Good luck. I use test shots to calculate the f/stop, myself.)
- **RPT: repeating flash.** The flash fires repeatedly to produce a multiple flash strobing effect. To use this mode, set the D3s/D3x's exposure mode to manual. Then set up the number of repeating flashes per frame, frequency, and flash output level, as described in Chapter 4. When using the D3s/D3x's built-in flash, use Custom Setting e3; with the SB-900, press the Mode button and rotate the selector dial to display RPT. Set the flash output level with Function Button 1 and the selector dial, and choose the number of flashes with the Function Button 2 and the selector dial. Finally, press Function Button 3 and rotate the selector dial to choose the frequency. If you don't have a flash meter, the best way to decide what aperture to use on the camera in repeating mode is to take a few test shots.

## BURN OUT

Just to remind you again, when using repeating flash with the built-in flash or the SB-900, or *any* large number of consecutive flashes in any mode (more than about 15 shots at full power), allow the flash to cool off (Nikon recommends a 10-minute time out) to avoid overheating the flash. The SB-900 will signal you with a warning chime that rings when it's time for a cooling-off period. The flash will actually disable itself, if necessary, to prevent damage.

# Working with Wireless Commander Mode

Unlike most other Nikon dSLRs, the D3-series do not have a built-in flash that can be set to commander mode (as described in Chapter 4) and used to control other compatible flash units. Instead, you'll need to use the Nikon SB-900 as a flash "Commander" to communicate with and trigger other flash units. Nikon also offers a unit called the SU-800, which is a commander unit that has no built-in visible flash, and which controls other units using infrared signals.

The SU-800 has several advantages. It's useful for cameras like the D3 and D3x, which have no built-in flash to function in commander mode, and could also be used with other cameras like the D700 to function as a commander that doesn't have any effect on the exposure. However, you can achieve much the same effect by dialing down the SB-900/800 flash to 1/128 power, or by setting the flash to - - (flash cancelled) in commander mode to turn off the built-in flash during exposure. The real advantage the SU-800 has over the D3s/D3x's built-in flash is its "reach." Because it uses IR illumination rather than visible light to communicate with remote flashes, the infrared burst can be much stronger, doubling its effective control range to 66 feet.

Once you have set the SB-900 as the master or commander, you can specify a shooting mode, either manual with a power output setting you determine from 1/1 to 1/128, or for TTL automatic exposure. When using TTL, you can dial in from –1.0 to +3.0 flash exposure compensation for the master flash. You can also specify a channel (1, 2, 3, or 4) that all flashes will use to communicate among themselves. (If other Nikon photographers are present, choosing a different channel prevents your flash from triggering their remotes, and vice versa.)

Each remote flash unit can also be set to one of three groups (A, B, or C), so you can set the exposure compensation and exposure mode of each group separately. For example, one or more flashes in one group can be reduced in output compared to the flashes in the other group, to produce a particular lighting ratio effect. You'll find instructions for setting exposure mode, channel, and compensation next (for the built-in flash).

## Setting Commander and Remote Modes for the SB-900

Setting modes for the SB-900 has been greatly simplified, compared to the previous SB-900. Just rotate the On/Off/Wireless mode switch to the Remote or Master positions. In remote mode, the SB-900 will be triggered by the commander flash unit in its group. In master mode, the SB-900 will serve as the trigger for the other flash units in a group.

You'll want to tell the SB-900 which channel to use, and which group it belongs to so that it responds to/controls the other units in its group. You'll need to do this separately for each of the SB-900 units you are working with, if you're using more than one. Here are the (confusing) steps to follow (I recommend doing several dry runs to see how setting up multiple flashes works before trying it "live"):

1. On the master flash, press Function Button 1 to highlight M (Master).
2. Press the Mode button, then spin the selector dial to choose the flash mode you want to use for that flash unit, from among TTL, A (auto-aperture), M (manual), or - -. Then, press OK.

> **Tip**
>
> At the - - setting, the master flash is disabled; it will trigger the other units, but its flash won't contribute to the exposure—except if you're shooting very close to the subject using a high ISO setting. Tilt or rotate the flash head away from your subject to minimize this spill-over effect.

3. Press Function Button 2, and rotate the selector dial to choose the flash compensation level. The amount of EV correction appears at the right side, opposite the master flash's mode indicator.
4. Press Function Button 1 to move on to the Group Selection option. Press OK to choose Group A, or rotate the selector dial to choose Group B or C, then press OK to confirm the group you've chosen.
5. If you're using additional SB-900 flash units with this master flash, set their flash modes and exposure compensation individually by repeating Steps 2, 3, and 4 with the master flash.
6. If you'll be using even more SB-900 flash units, set up those groups as you did for Group A, but specify the group name you'll be using for the additional units (either B or C).
7. Once the modes for all the flash units have been set on the master flash, press Function Button 2 and rotate the selector dial to set a channel number that the master flash will use to control its groups.

8. Now take each of the remote flash units and set the correct group and channel number you want to use. Just press Function Button 1 on each remote flash, and rotate the selector dial to specify the group name. Press OK. Then press Function Button 2 and rotate the selector dial to choose the channel number, and then press the OK button. You're all set!

## Connecting External Flash

You have five basic choices for linking an external flash unit to your Nikon D3s/D3x. They are as follows:

- **Mount on the accessory shoe.** Sliding a compatible flash unit into the Nikon D3s/D3x's accessory shoe (see Figure 10.18) provides a direct connection. With a Nikon dedicated flash, all functions of the flash are supported.
- **Connect to the accessory shoe with a cable.** The Nikon SC-28 and SC-29 TTL coiled remote cords have an accessory shoe on one end of a nine-foot cable to accept a flash, and a foot that slides into the camera accessory shoe on the other end, providing a link that is the same as when the flash is mounted directly on the camera. The SC-29 version also includes a focus assist lamp, like that on the camera and SB-900. Figure 10.19 shows the SB-900 mounted on a Nikon SK-7 bracket and connected to a Nikon D700 camera with the SC-28 coiled cable.

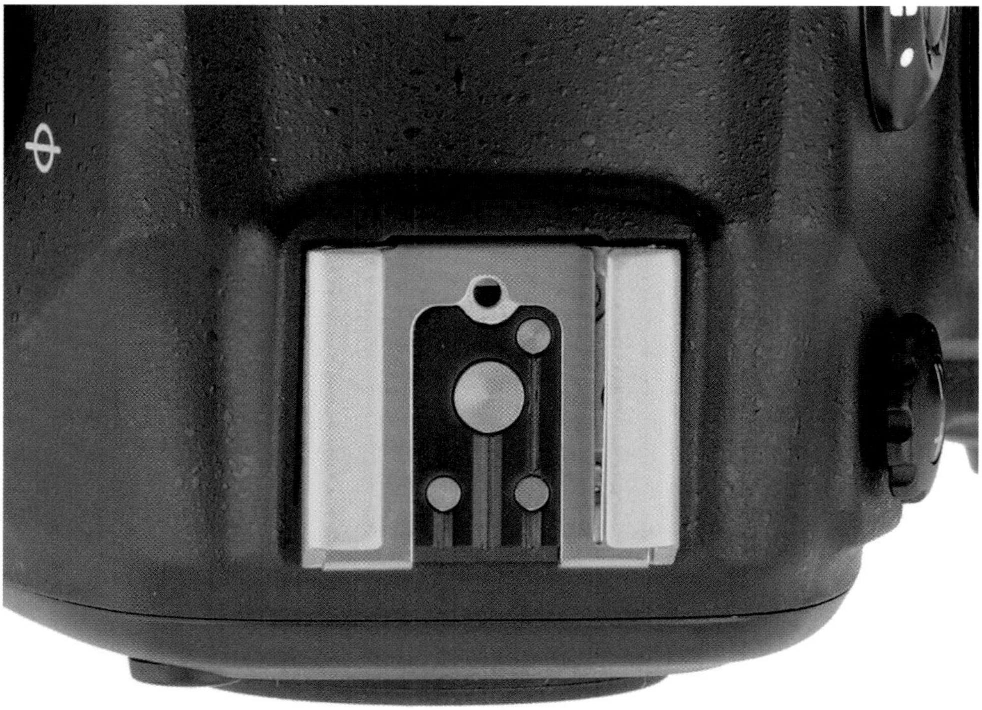

**Figure 10.18**
The D3-series accessory shoe has contacts that can communicate with dedicated flash units.

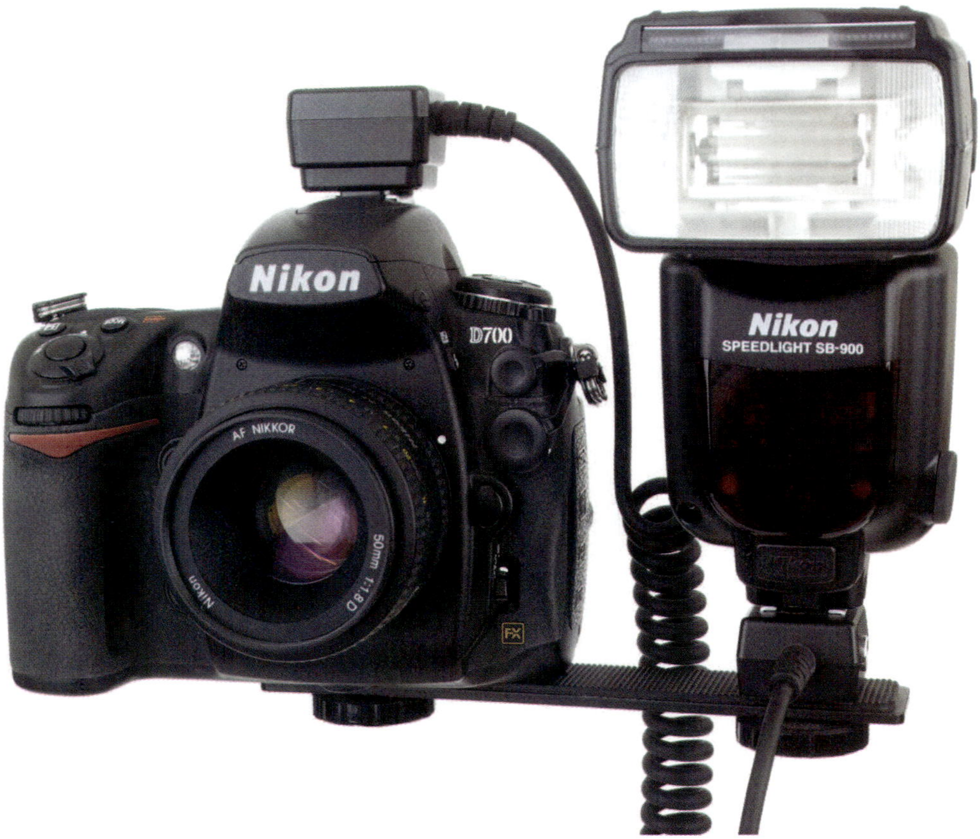


**Figure 10.19**
The Nikon SB-900 flash is connected for off-camera use with a Nikon SC-28 or SC-29 coiled cable.

- **Multi-flash cables.** The Nikon SC-27/SC-26 TTL Multi-Flash Sync Cords can be used to connect TTL flash units to each other or through the AS-10 TTL Multi-Flash Adapter or SC-28 TTL Remote Cord for multi-flash operation. However, this three-pin connector does not support i-TTL or D-TTL operation. You may wish to use it with older Nikon flash units.
- **Connect to the PC/X connector.** Some external flash units, including studio units, can connect to the Nikon D3s/D3x through the PC connector on the front of the camera, above the 10-pin terminal. You also may find accessory shoe adapters with a PC connector on them, which can be especially useful if they are combined with a voltage limiter so you needn't fear frying your camera with an older flash unit that has a triggering voltage that's too high. I sometimes use a wireless flash trigger that plugs into the PC connector, and sets off flash units through radio waves.
- **Wireless link.** As described earlier in this chapter, a Nikon electronic flash can be triggered by another master flash in commander mode or by the RU-800 infrared unit.

## Using Flash Exposure Compensation

You can manually add or subtract exposure to the flash exposure calculated by the D3s/D3x. Just press the same Exposure Compensation button on top of the camera that is used for non-flash photography. The D3-series camera will automatically apply EV changes to both the flash exposure and the background (ambient) illumination. The amount of exposure compensation you want appears on the monochrome LCD and in the viewfinder. You can make adjustments from –3EV to +1EV in 1/3 EV increments. As with ordinary exposure compensation, the adjustment you make remains in effect until you zero it out by pressing the Flash button and rotating the sub-command dial until 0 appears on the monochrome control panel and in the viewfinder.

To view the current flash exposure compensation setting, press the EV button. When compensation is being used, an icon will be displayed in the viewfinder and on the monochrome LCD.

## More Advanced Lighting Techniques

As you advance in your Nikon D3s/D3x photography, you'll want to learn more sophisticated lighting techniques, using more than just straight-on flash, or using just a single flash unit. Entire books have been written on lighting techniques, and I've written multiple chapters on them in books of my own, including *David Busch's Quick Snap Guide to Lighting*. I'm going to provide a quick introduction to some of the techniques you should be considering.

### Diffusing and Softening the Light

Direct light can be harsh and glaring, especially if you're using the flash built into your camera, or an auxiliary flash mounted in the hot shoe and pointed directly at your subject. The first thing you should do is stop using direct light (unless you're looking for a stark, contrasty appearance as a creative effect). There are a number of simple things you can do with both continuous and flash illumination.

- **Use window light.** Light coming in a window can be soft and flattering, and a good choice for human subjects. Move your subject close enough to the window that its light provides the primary source of illumination. You might want to turn off other lights in the room, particularly to avoid mixing daylight and incandescent light. (See Figure 10.20.)
- **Use fill light.** Your external flash makes a perfect fill-in light for the shadows, brightening inky depths with a kicker of illumination, as you can see in the outdoor shot shown in Figure 10.21.

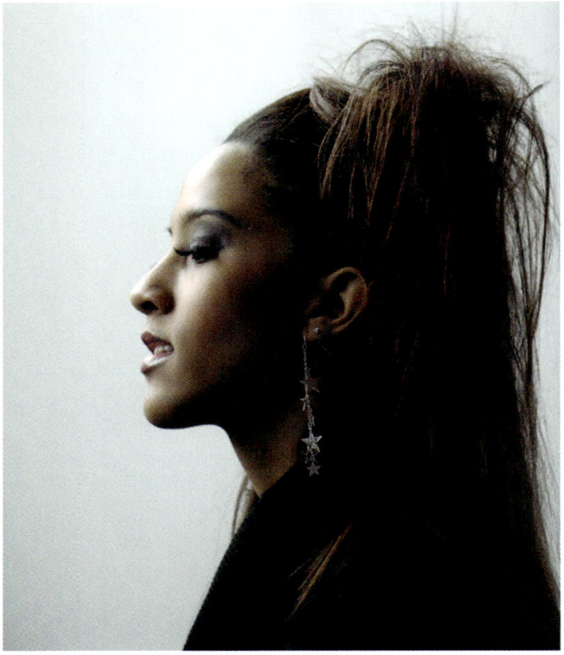

**Figure 10.20** Window light makes the perfect diffuse illumination for informal soft-focus portraits like this one.

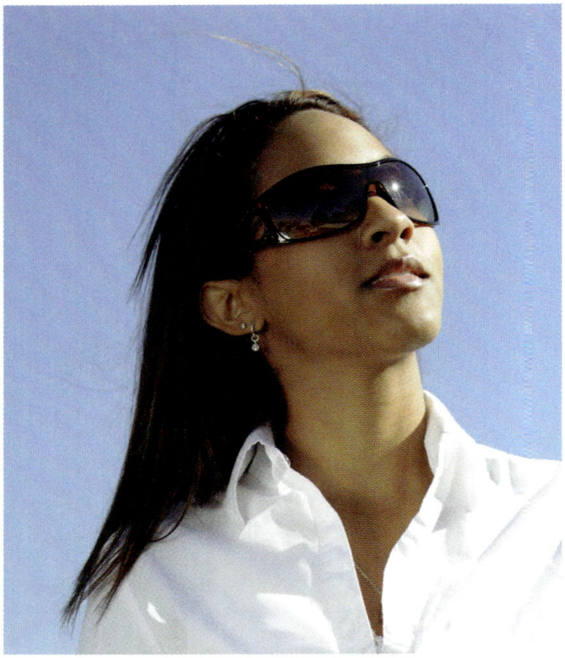

**Figure 10.21** Fill flash brightened up the shadows in this photo.

- **Bounce the light.** External electronic flash units mounted on the D3s/D3x usually have a swivel that allows them to be pointed up at a ceiling for a bounce light effect. You can also bounce the light off a wall. You'll want the ceiling or wall to be white or have a neutral gray color to avoid a color cast.
- **Use reflectors.** Another way to bounce the light is to use reflectors or umbrellas that you can position yourself to provide a greater degree of control over the quantity and direction of the bounced light. Good reflectors can be pieces of foamboard, Mylar, or a reflective disk held in place by a clamp and stand. Although some expensive umbrellas and reflectors are available, spending a lot isn't necessary. A simple piece of white foamboard does the job beautifully. Umbrellas have the advantage of being compact and foldable, while providing a soft, even kind of light. They're relatively cheap, too, with a good 40-inch umbrella available for as little as $20. I purchased some collapsible round aluminized reflectors used to block an automobile's windshield from the rays of the sun—at a remarkable two for $7.98.
- **Use diffusers.** Nikon supplies a Sto-Fen-style diffuser dome with the SB-900 flash. You can purchase a similar diffuser for the SB-600 from Nikon, Sto-Fen, and some other vendors that offer clip-on diffusers. The two examples shown in Figures 10.22 and 10.23 fit over your electronic flash head and provide a soft, flattering light. These add-ons are more portable than umbrellas and other reflectors, yet provide a nice diffuse lighting effect.

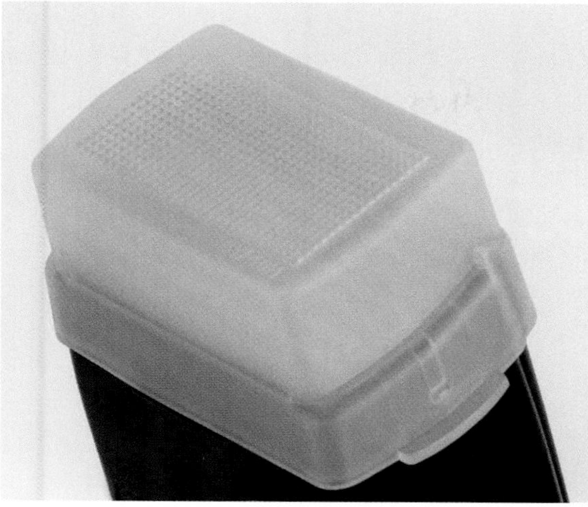

**Figure 10.22** This diffuser dome is provided by Nikon with the SB-900, and softens the light of an external flash unit.

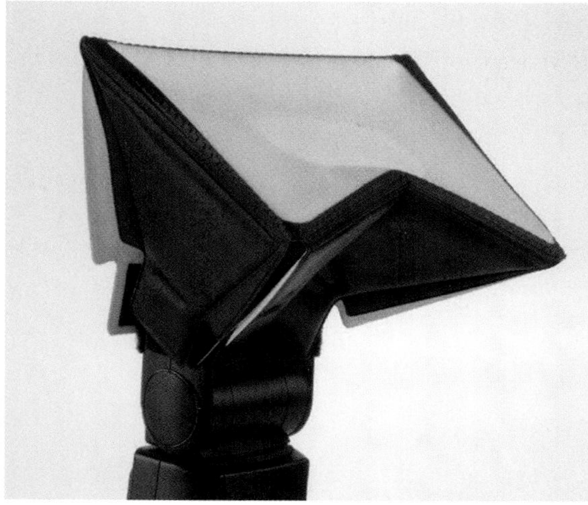

**Figure 10.23** Soft boxes use Velcro strips to attach them to just about any shoe-mount flash unit.

## Using Multiple Light Sources

Once you gain control over the qualities and effects you get with a single light source, you'll want to graduate to using multiple light sources. Using several lights allows you to shape and mold the illumination of your subjects to provide a variety of effects, from backlighting to side lighting to more formal portrait lighting. You can start simply with several incandescent light sources, bounced off umbrellas or reflectors that you construct. Or you can use more flexible multiple electronic flash setups.

Effective lighting is the one element that differentiates great photography from candid or snapshot shooting. Lighting can make a mundane subject look a little more glamorous. Make subjects appear to be soft when you want a soft look, or bright and sparkly when you want a vivid look, or strong and dramatic if that's what you desire. As you might guess, having control over your lighting means that you probably can't use the lights that are already in the room. You'll need separate, discrete lighting fixtures that can be moved, aimed, brightened, and dimmed on command.

Selecting your lighting gear will depend on the type of photography you do, and the budget you have to support it. It's entirely possible for a beginning D3s/D3x photographer to create a basic, inexpensive lighting system capable of delivering high-quality results for a few hundred dollars, just as you can spend megabucks ($1,000 and up) for a sophisticated lighting system.

## Basic Flash Setups

If you want to use multiple electronic flash units, the Nikon Speedlights described earlier will serve admirably. The higher-end models can be used with Nikon's wireless i-TTL features, which allow you to set up to three separate groups of flash units (several flashes can be included in each group) and trigger them using a master flash and the camera. Just set up one master unit, and arrange the compatible slave units around your subject. You can set the relative power of each unit separately, thereby controlling how much of the scene's illumination comes from the main flash, and how much from the auxiliary flash units, which can be used as fill flash, background lights, or, if you're careful, to illuminate the hair of portrait subjects.

## Studio Flash

If you're serious about using multiple flash units, a studio flash setup might be more practical. The traditional studio flash is a multi-part unit, consisting of a flash head that mounts on your light stand, and is tethered to an AC (or sometimes battery) power supply. A single power supply can feed two or more flash heads at a time, with separate control over the output of each head.

When they are operating off AC power, studio flash don't have to be frugal with the juice, and are often powerful enough to illuminate very large subjects or to supply lots and lots of light to smaller subjects. The output of such units is measured in watt seconds (ws), so you could purchase a 200ws, 400ws, or 800ws unit, and a power pack to match.

Their advantages include greater power output, much faster recycling, built-in modeling lamps, multiple power levels, and ruggedness that can stand up to transport, because many photographers pack up these kits and tote them around as location lighting rigs. Studio lighting kits can range in price from a few hundred dollars for a set of lights, stands, and reflectors, to thousands for a high-end lighting system complete with all the necessary accessories.

A more practical choice these days are *monolights* (see Figure 10.24), which are "all-in-one" studio lights that sell for about $200-$400. They have the flash tube, modeling light, and power supply built into a single unit that can be mounted on a light stand. Monolights are available in AC-only and battery-pack versions, although an external battery eliminates some of the advantages of having a flash with everything in one unit. They are very portable, because all you need is a case for the monolight itself, plus the stands and other accessories you want to carry along. Because these units are so popular with photographers who are not full-time professionals, the lower-cost monolights are often designed more for lighter duty than professional studio flash. That doesn't mean they aren't rugged; you'll just need to handle them with a little more care, and, perhaps, not expect them to be used eight hours a day for weeks on end. In most other respects, however, monolights are the equal of traditional studio flash units in terms of fast recycling, built-in modeling lamps, adjustable power, and so forth.

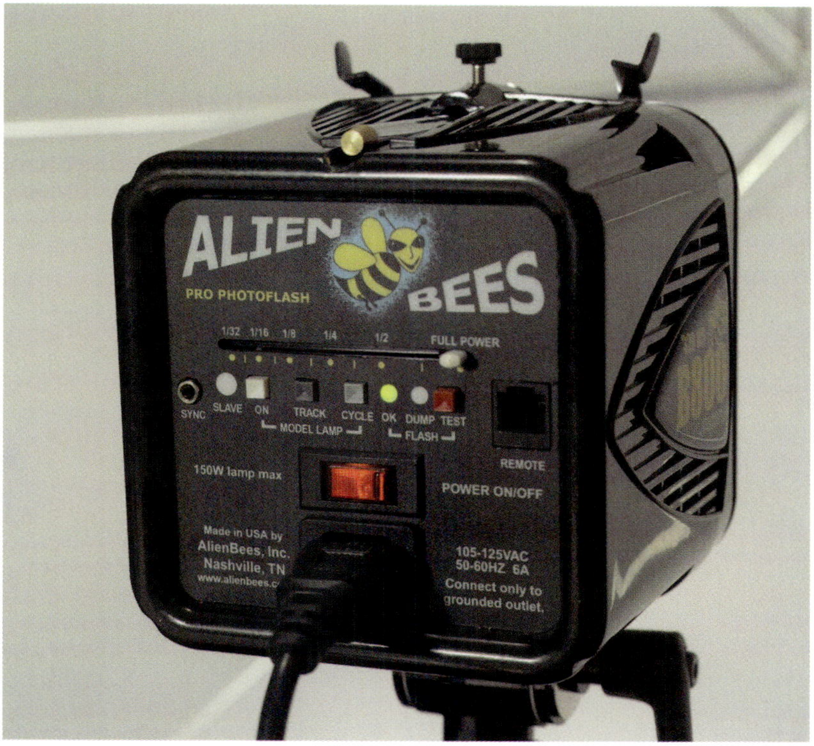


**Figure 10.24** All-in-one "monolights" contain flash, power supply, and a modeling light in one compact package (umbrella not included).

## Connecting Multiple Non-Dedicated Units to Your Nikon D3s/D3x

Non-dedicated electronic flash units can't use the automated i-TTL features of your Nikon D3s/D3x; you'll need to calculate exposure manually, through test shots evaluated on your camera's LCD, or by using an electronic flash meter. Moreover, you don't have to connect them to the accessory shoe on top of the camera. Instead, you can use the PC/X connector on the front of the camera under the rubber cover.

You should be aware that older electronic flash units sometimes use a triggering voltage that is too much for your D3s/D3x to handle. You can actually damage the camera's electronics if the voltage is too high. You won't need to worry about this if you purchase brand new units from Alien Bees, Adorama, or other vendors. But if you must connect an external flash with an unknown triggering voltage, I recommend using a Wein Safe Sync (see Figure 10.25), which isolates the flash's voltage from the camera triggering circuit.

Another safe way to connect external cameras is through a radio-control device, such as the transmitter/receiver set shown in Figure 10.26. It clips on the hot shoe and plugs into the D3s/D3x's PC/X connector (see Figure 10.27) and transmits a signal to a matching receiver that's connected to your flash unit. The receiver has both a PC connector of its own as well as a "monoplug" connector (it looks like a headphone plug) that links to a matching port on compatible flash units.

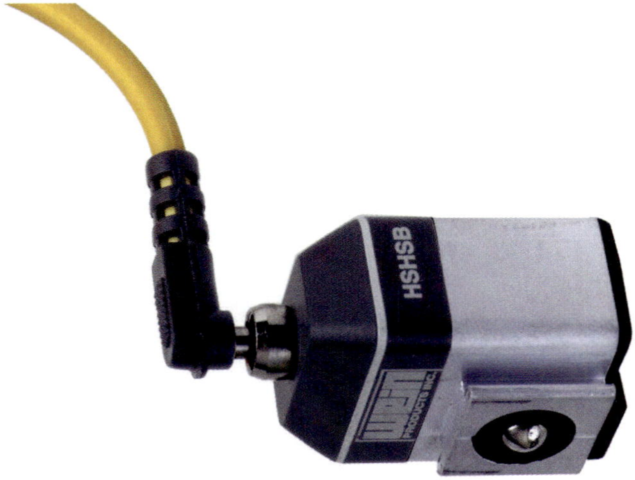


**Figure 10.25**
A voltage isolator can prevent frying your D3s/D3x's flash circuits if you use an older electronic flash.

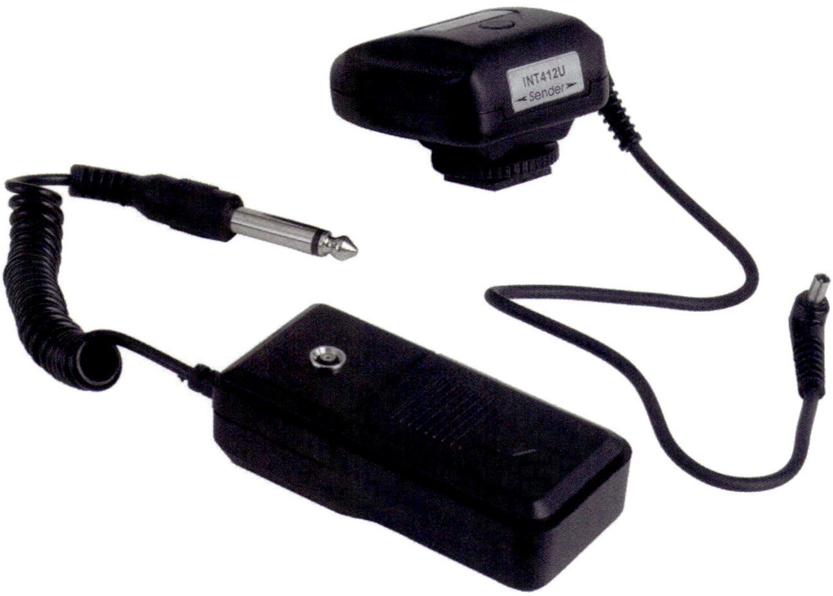


**Figure 10.26**
A radio-control device frees you from a sync cord tether between your flash and camera.

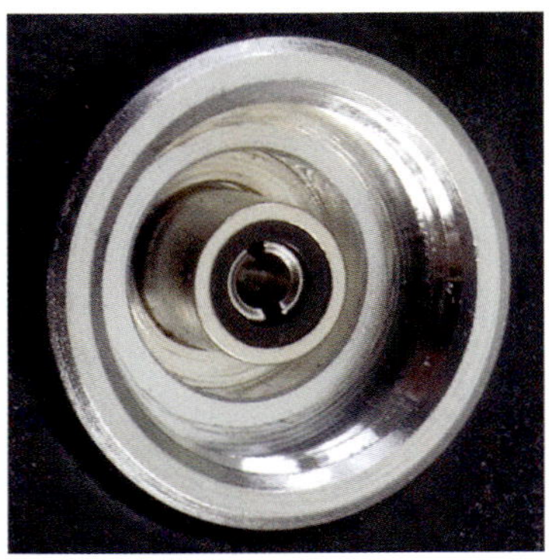

**Figure 10.27**
The PC/X connector allows attaching studio flash and non-dedicated flash units to the Nikon D3s/D3x.

Finally, some flash units have an optical slave trigger built in, or can be fitted with one, so that they fire automatically when another flash, including your camera's built-in unit, fires.

## Other Lighting Accessories

Once you start working with light, you'll find there are plenty of useful accessories that can help you. Here are some of the most popular that you might want to consider.

### Soft Boxes

Soft boxes are large square or rectangular devices that may resemble a square umbrella with a front cover, and produce a similar lighting effect. They can extend from a few feet square to massive boxes that stand five or six feet tall—virtually a wall of light. With a flash unit or two inside a soft box, you have a very large, semi-directional light source that's very diffuse and very flattering for portraiture and other people photography.

Soft boxes are also handy for photographing shiny objects. They not only provide a soft light, but if the box itself happens to reflect in the subject (say you're photographing a chromium toaster), the box will provide an interesting highlight that's indistinct and not distracting.

You can buy soft boxes or make your own. Some lengths of friction-fit plastic pipe and a lot of muslin cut and sewed just so may be all that you need. (See Figure 10.28.)

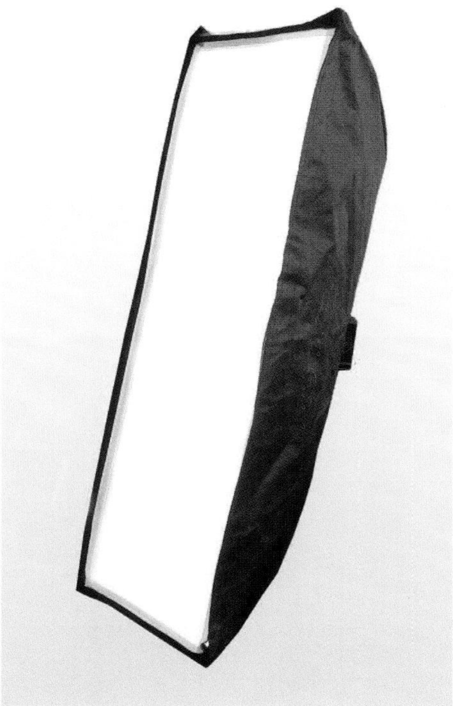

**Figure 10.28**
Soft boxes provide a diffuse light source.

## Light Stands

Both electronic flash and incandescent lamps can benefit from light stands. These are lightweight, tripod-like devices (but without a swiveling or tilting head) that can be set on the floor, tabletops, or other elevated surfaces and positioned as needed. Light stands should be strong enough to support an external lighting unit, up to and including a relatively heavy flash with soft box or umbrella reflectors. You want the supports to be capable of raising the lights high enough to be effective. Look for light stands capable of extending six to seven feet high. The nine-foot units usually have larger, steadier bases, and extend high enough that you can use them as background supports. You'll be using these stands for a lifetime, so invest in good ones. I bought my light stands when I was in college, and I have been using them for decades.

## Backgrounds

Backgrounds can be backdrops of cloth, sheets of muslin you've painted yourself using a sponge dipped in paint, rolls of seamless paper, or any other suitable surface your mind can dream up. Backgrounds provide a complementary and non-distracting area behind subjects (especially portraits) and can be lit separately to provide contrast and separation that outlines the subject, or which helps set a mood.

I like to use plain-colored backgrounds for portraits, and white or gray seamless backgrounds for product photography. You can usually construct these yourself from cheap materials and tape them up on the wall behind your subject, or mount them on a pole stretched between a pair of light stands.

## Snoots and Barn Doors

These fit over the flash unit and direct the light at your subject. Snoots are excellent for converting a flash unit into a hair light, while barn doors give you enough control over the illumination by opening and closing their flaps that you can use another flash as a background light, with the capability of feathering the light exactly where you want it on the background. (See Figure 10.29.)

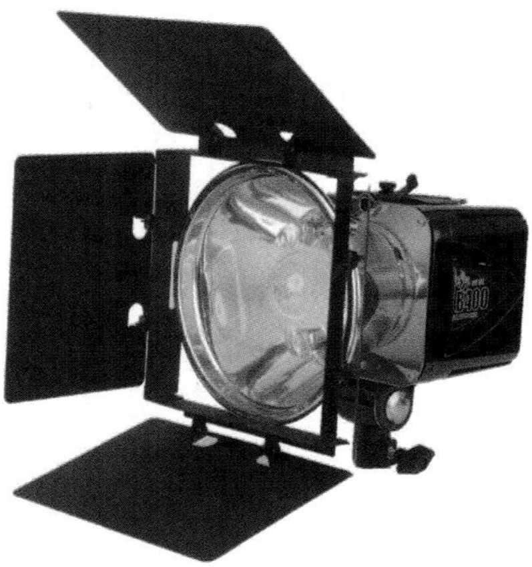

**Figure 10.29**
Barn doors allow you to modulate the light from a flash or lamp, and they are especially useful for hair lights and background lights.

# 11

# Useful Software for the Nikon D3s/D3x

Unless you only take pictures, and then immediately print them directly to a PictBridge-compatible printer, somewhere along the line you're going to need to make use of the broad array of software available for the Nikon D3s/D3x. The picture-fixing options in the retouch menu let you make only modest modifications to your carefully crafted photos. If your needs involve more than fixing red-eye, cropping and trimming, and maybe adjusting tonal values with D-Lighting, you're definitely going to want to use a utility or editor of some sort to perfect your images. After you've captured some great images and have them safely stored on your Nikon D3s/D3x's memory card, you'll need to transfer them from your camera and memory card to your computer, where they can be organized, fine-tuned in an image editor, and prepared for web display, printing, or some other final destination.

Fortunately, there are lots of software utilities and applications to help you do all these things. This chapter will introduce you to a few of them. Please note that this is *not* a "how-to-do-it" software chapter. This book has already expanded to more than twice the size of my previous camera guides, and I'm going to use every available page to offer advice on how to get the most from your D3s/D3x. There's no space to explain how to use all the features of Nikon Capture NX2, nor how to tweak RAW file settings in Adobe Camera Raw. Entire books have been written about both products. This chapter is intended solely to help you get your bearings among the large number of utilities and applications available, to help you better understand what each does, and how you might want to use them. At the very end of the chapter, however, I'm going to make an exception and provide some simple instructions for using Adobe Camera Raw, to help those who have been using Nikon's software exclusively get a feel for what you can do with the Adobe product.

The basic functions found in most of the programs discussed in this chapter include image transfer and management, camera control, and image editing. You'll find that many of the programs overlap several of these capabilities, so it's not always possible to categorize the discussions that follow by function. In fact, I'm going to start off by describing a few of the offerings available from Nikon.

## Nikon's Applications and Utilities

If nothing else, Nikon has made sorting through the software for its digital cameras an interesting pursuit. Through the years, we've had various incarnations of programs with names like PictureProject, NikonView, and Nikon Capture. Some have been compatible with both the Nikon dSLR and amateur Coolpix product lines. Many of them have been furnished on disk with the cameras. Others, most notoriously Nikon Capture, have been an extra-cost option, which particularly infuriated those of us who had paid several thousand dollars for a Nikon dSLR, and found that we'd need to pay more to get the software needed for the camera.

Recently, Nikon has begun splitting their software offerings into separate programs that are sort-of standalone products, but which integrate with the others. For example, if you bought the original Nikon Capture NX, you found that the program didn't really capture anything, as the previous Nikon Capture 4 did. If you wanted to operate the camera remotely, you needed to buy the offshoot program, Nikon Camera Control Pro, which cost even *more* money.

If Nikon software wasn't interesting enough already, some years back Nikon began *encrypting* the white balance information in image files, so that third-party utility programmers needed to use Nikon's software development kit or reverse-engineer the encryption to make their utilities work with Nikon NEF files. Even today, each time a new Nikon dSLR is introduced, you must upgrade your copy of most Nikon software products, as well as third-party products like Adobe Camera Raw, to ensure compatibility with the new camera's files. The fact that these upgrades often are not available until months after the camera is introduced is nothing short of frustrating.

The next few sections provide some descriptions of the Nikon software you'll want to use with your D3s/D3x.

### Nikon ViewNX

This latest incarnation of Nikon's basic file viewer is better than ever, making it easy to browse through images, convert RAW files to JPEG or TIFF, and make corrections to white balance and exposure, either on individual files or on batches of files. It works in tandem with Nikon Transfer and Nikon Capture NX, as you can open files inspected in ViewNX in one of the other programs—or within a third-party application you "register."

First and foremost, Nikon ViewNX is a great file viewer. There are three modes for looking at images: a thumbnail grid mode for checking out small previews of your images; an image viewer mode (see Figure 11.1) that shows a group of thumbnails along with an enlarged version of a selected image; and full screen mode, which allows you to examine an image in maximum detail.

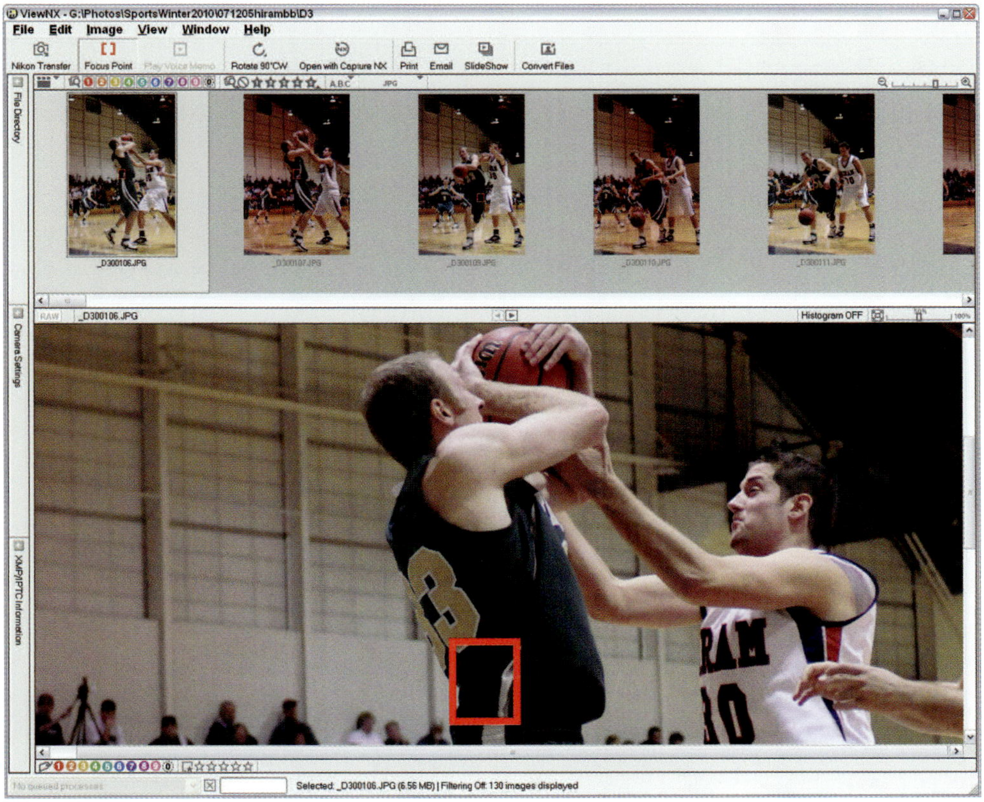


**Figure 11.1**
Nikon ViewNX is a great basic file viewing utility.

If you like to shoot RAW+JPEG, you can review image pairs as if they were a single image (rather than view the RAW and JPEG versions separately), and work with whichever version you need. The active focus area can be displayed in the image (see Figure 11.1 again), and there are histogram, highlight, and shadow displays (not shown in the figure) to help you evaluate an image.

Should you want to organize your images, there are 10 labels available to classify images by criteria such as images printed, images copied, or images sent as e-mail, and you can mark your best shots for easier retrieval with a rating system of one to five stars. ViewNX also allows you to edit embedded XMP/IPTC information in fields such as creator, origin, image title, and suitable keywords. The utility can be downloaded from the support/download pages of the Nikon website at www.nikonusa.com.

## Nikon Transfer

It seems like everyone offers some sort of image transfer system that automatically recognizes when a memory card is inserted in a reader, or a digital camera like the Nikon D3s/D3x is attached to a computer using a USB cable. The most popular operating systems, from Mac OS X to Windows XP, Vista, and Windows 7 have their own built-in transfer programs, and Adobe Photoshop Elements includes one in its suite of utilities.

Nikon Transfer is particularly well suited for D3s/D3x owners, because it integrates easily with other Nikon software products, including ViewNX and Nikon Capture NX2. You can download photos to your computer, and then continue to work on them in the Nikon application (or third-party utility) of your choice.

When a memory card is inserted into a card reader, or when the D3s/D3x is connected to your computer through a USB cable, Nikon Transfer recognizes the device, searches it for thumbnails, and provides a display like the one shown in Figure 11.2. You can

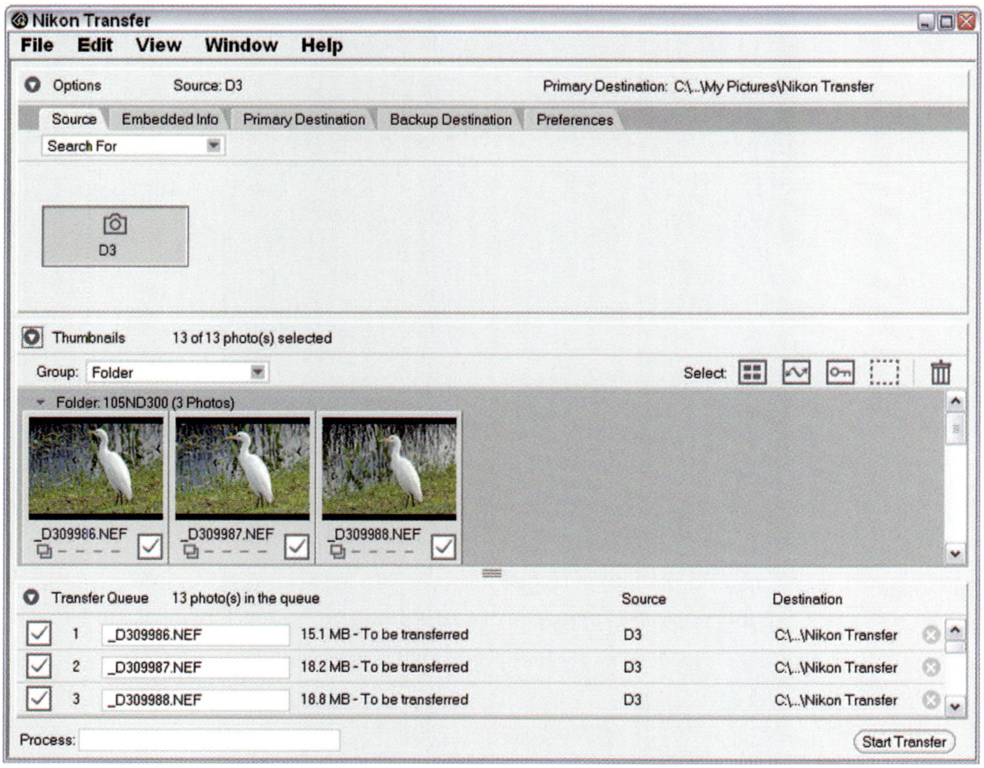


**Figure 11.2**
After Nikon Transfer displays thumbnails of the images on your memory card or camera, mark the ones you want to transfer.

preview the images and mark the ones you want to transfer with checks to create a transfer queue.

Then, click on the Primary Destination tab (see Figure 11.3) and choose a location for the photos that will be transferred. Nikon Transfer can create a new folder for each transfer based on a naming convention you set up (click the Edit button next to the box at top center in the figure), or copy to a folder named after the current folder in the D3s/D3x's memory card. You can keep the current filename as the files are transferred, or assign a new name with a prefix you designate, such as Spain09_ . The program will add a number from 001 to 999 to the filename prefix you specify.

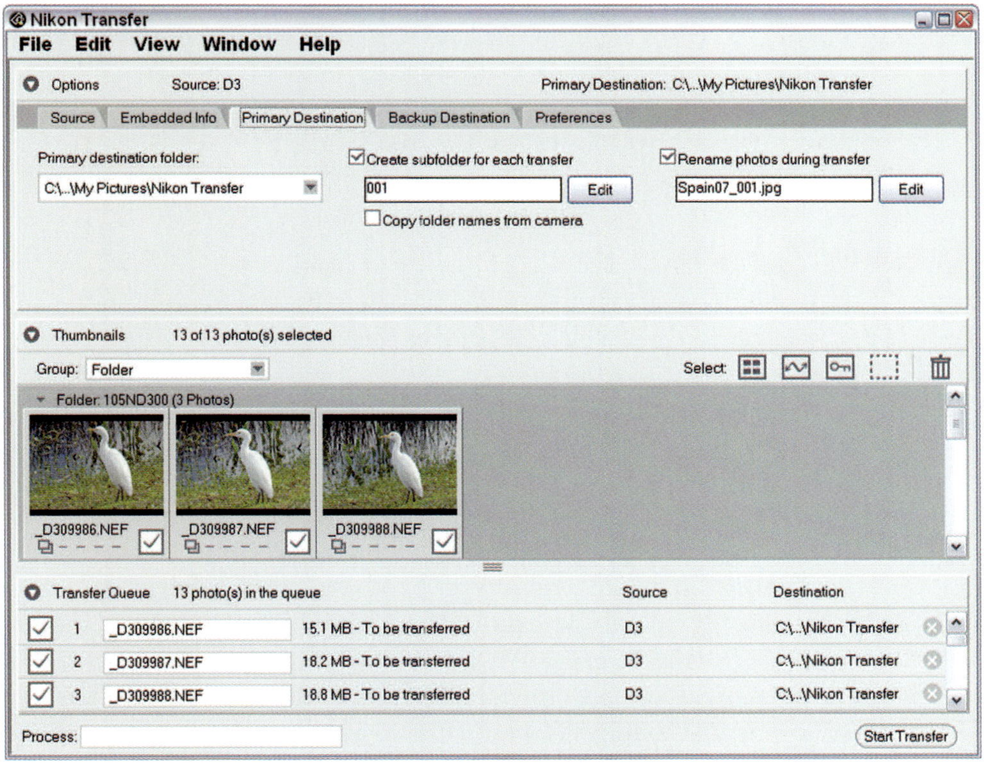


**Figure 11.3**
Copy files to a destination you specify using an optional filename template you can define.

One neat feature is the ability to name a Backup destination location, so that all transferred pictures can also be copied to a second folder, which can be located on a different hard disk drive or other media. You can embed information such as copyright data, star ratings, and labels in the images as they are transferred. When the file transfer is complete, Nikon Transfer can launch an application of your choice, set with a few clicks in the Preferences tab (see Figure 11.4).

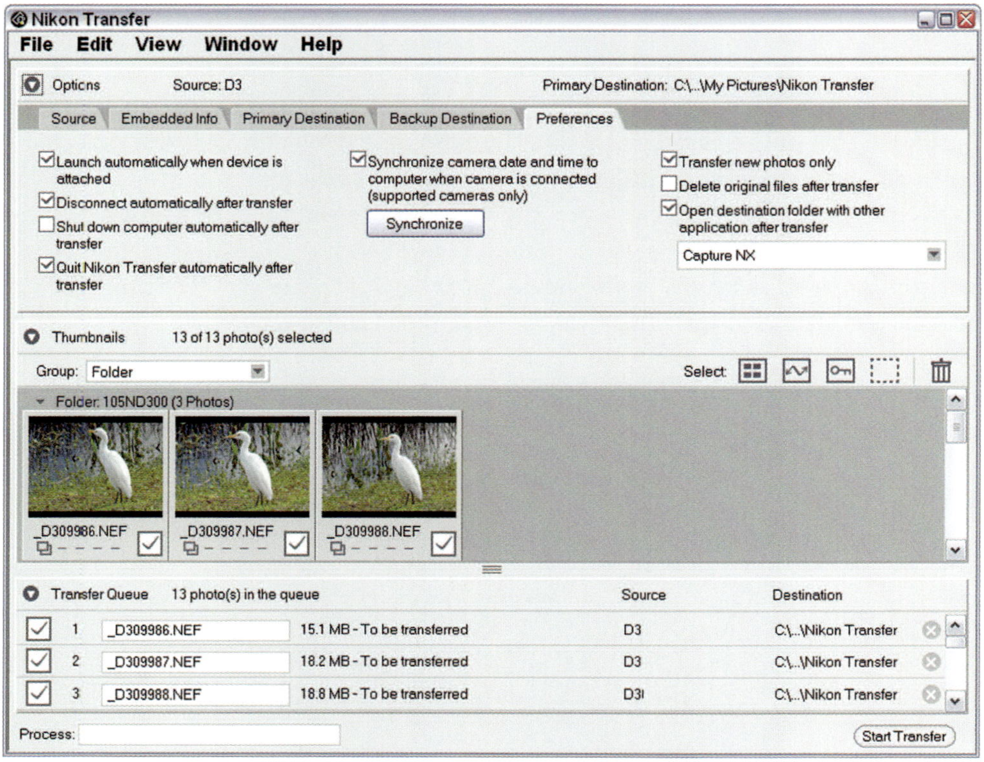


**Figure 11.4**
You can tell Nikon Transfer what to do after images are transferred in the Preferences tab.

## Nikon Capture NX

Capture NX (currently in version 2 as I write this) is a pretty hefty chunk of software for the typical Nikon D3s/D3x owner to tackle (and somewhat expensive at about $150), but if you're ambitious and willing to plant your pitons for a steep climb up the learning curve, the program is indeed a powerful image-editing utility. It's designed specifically to process Nikon's NEF-format RAW files (although this new edition has added the ability to manipulate JPEG and TIFF images as well). It includes an image browser (with labeling, sorting, and editing) that can be used to make many adjustments directly through the thumbnails. It also has advanced color management tools, impressive noise reduction capabilities, and batch processing features that allow you to apply sets of changes to collections of images. All the tools are arranged in dockable/expandable/collapsible palettes (see Figure 11.5) that tell you everything you need to know about an image, and provide the capabilities to push every pixel in interesting ways.

Photographers tend to love Capture NX or hate it, particularly in the NX2 version that was current when I wrote this book, and it's easy to separate the fans from the furious. Those who are enamored of the program have invested a great deal of time in learning

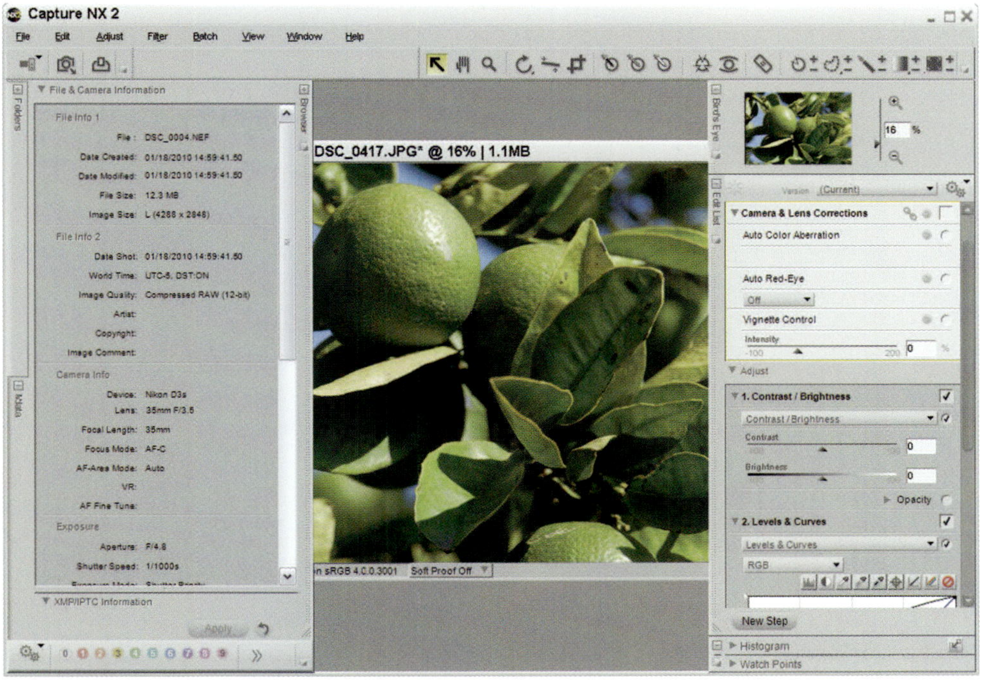


**Figure 11.5**
Capture NX's tools are arranged in dockable palettes.

its quirky paradigm and now appreciate just how powerful Capture NX is. The detractors are usually those who are comfortable with another program, such as Photoshop or even Capture 4, this program's predecessor, and are upset that even the simplest functions can be confoundingly difficult for a new user to figure out. Capture NX's murky Help system isn't a lot of help; there's room for a huge book (or two) to explain how to use this program.

For example, instead of masks, Capture NX uses Nik Software's U Point technology, which applies Control Points to select and isolate parts of an image for manipulation. There are Color Control Points, with up to nine different sliders for each selected area. (See Figure 11.6.) There are also Black and White Control points for setting dynamic range, Neutral Control Points for correcting color casts, and a Red-Eye Reduction Control Point that removes crimson glows from pupils.

The workflow revolves around an Edit List, which contains a list of enhancements, including Camera Adjustments, RAW Adjustments, Light & Color Adjustments, Detail Adjustments, and Lens Adjustments, which can each be controlled separately. You can add steps of your own, cancel adjustments individually, and store steps in the Edit List as Settings that can be applied to individual images or batches.

There are also Color Aberration Controls, D-Lighting, Image Dust Off, Vignette Control, Fisheye-to-Rectilinear Image Transformation ("de-fishing"), and a Distortion Control to reduce pincushion and barrel distortion.

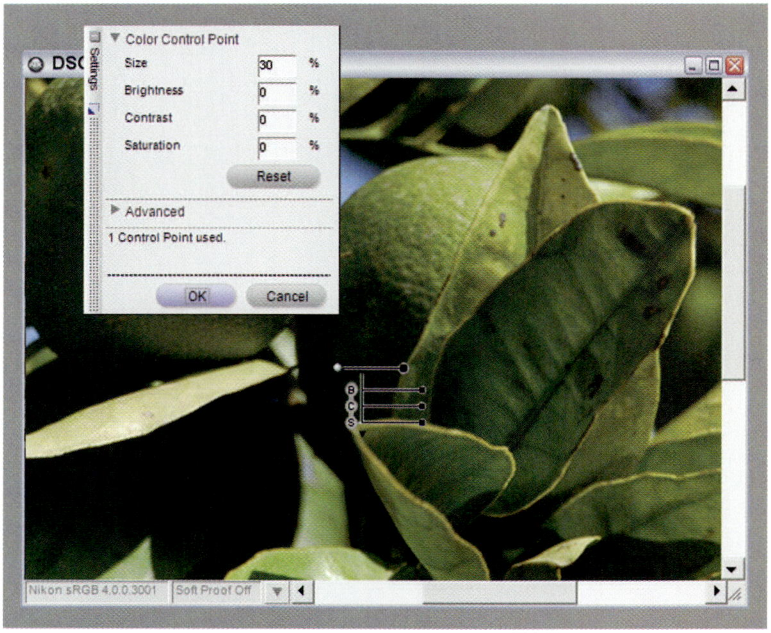


**Figure 11.6**
Control Points are used to make common adjustments

## Nikon Camera Control Pro

Nikon's Camera Control Pro (currently in version 2) is a versatile utility that allows you to communicate directly with your camera from your computer through a USB cable. Once the two are linked, you can perform a variety of functions:

- **Shoot remotely.** Just about any shooting function you can adjust on the camera can be performed remotely, as you can see from the cluster of tabbed dialog boxes shown at the top and right of Figure 11.7. Set exposure mode, adjust the aperture, add or subtract exposure compensation, choose a focus area, change ISO sensitivity or white balance—all are at your command through the software. You can even change Quality and Size settings, turn on auto bracketing, and change image optimization settings. You can optionally disable the controls on the camera, to prevent having settings you made at the computer changed accidentally.
- **Download directly to your computer.** When doing time-lapse photography, you can use Camera Control Pro to transfer the images you take directly to the computer.
- **Upload comments.** Frustrated by the Nikon D3s/D3x's text entry screen? Edit your Image Comment and upload it directly to the camera from your computer keyboard (lower left in Figure 11.7).

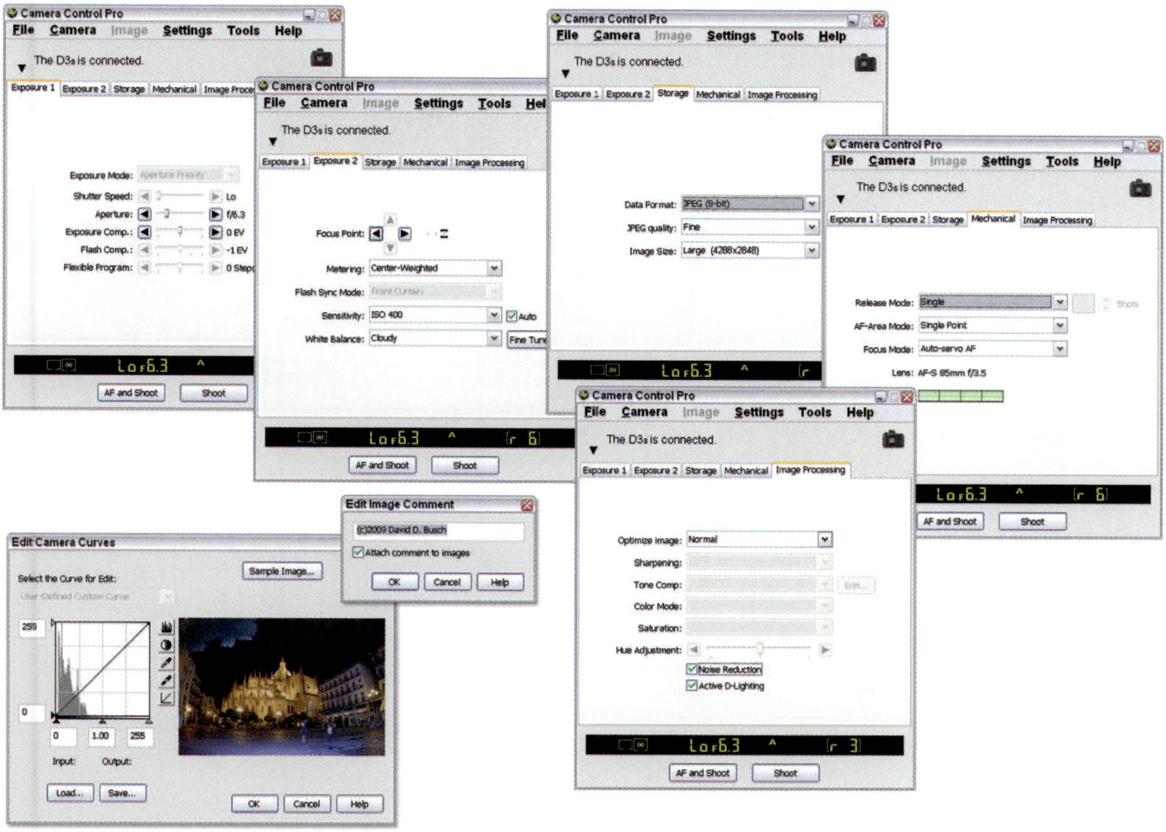


**Figure 11.7** You can operate the D3s/D3x from your computer using Camera Control Pro.

- **Create and save custom curves.** You can load a sample image and create a special tone compensation custom curve for that image using tools similar to those found in Photoshop.
- **View and change Custom Settings.** This is one of my favorite features. While changing the Custom Settings for any of the Custom Setting options using the D3s/D3x's menus isn't difficult (particularly after you've absorbed the information in Chapter 3), Camera Control Pro makes playing with these options a joy.

# Other Software

Other useful software for your Nikon D3s/D3x falls into several categories. You might want to fine-tune your images, retouch them, change color balance, composite several images together, and perform other tasks we know as image editing, with a program like Adobe Photoshop, Photoshop Elements, or Corel Photo Paint.

You might want to play with the settings in RAW files, too, as you import them into an image editor. There are specialized tools expressly for tweaking RAW files, ranging from Adobe Camera Raw to PhaseOne's Capture One Pro (C1 Pro). A third type of manipulation is the specialized task of noise reduction, which can be performed within Photoshop, Adobe Camera Raw, or tools like Bibble Professional. There are also specialized tools just for noise reduction, such as Noise Ninja (also included with Bibble) and Neat Image. Some programs, like the incomparable DxO Optics Pro, perform magical transformations that you can't achieve any other way.

Each of these utilities and applications deserves a chapter of its own, so I'm simply going to enumerate some of the most popular applications and utilities and tell you a little about what they do.

## DxO Optics Pro

DxO Labs (www.DxO.com) offers an incredibly useful program called Optics Pro ($170-$300) that is unique in the range of functions it provides. Figure 11.8 shows you DxO Optics Pro's clean user interface. Ostensibly an image quality enhancement utility that "cures" some of the ails that plague even the best lenses, the latest release also features a new RAW conversion engine that uses a new demosaicing algorithm to translate your NEF files into images with more detail, less noise, and fewer artifacts. These features meld well with the program's original mission: fixing the optical "geometry" of images, using settings custom-tailored for each individual lens. (I'm not kidding: when

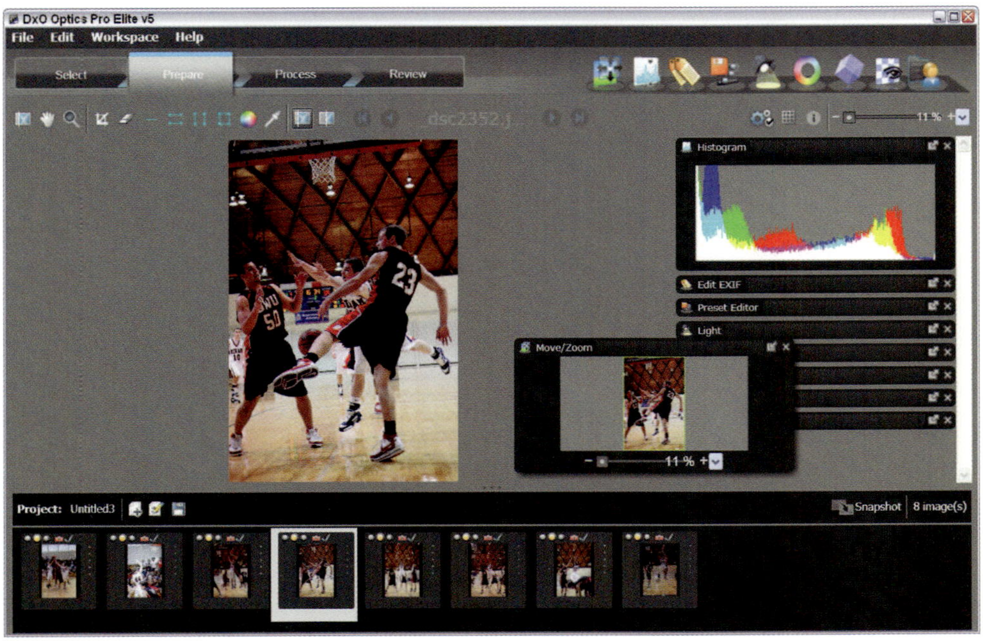


**Figure 11.8**
DxO Optics Pro fixes lens flaws, and functions as a high-tech RAW converter and noise reduction utility, too.

you "assemble" the program, you specify each and every camera body you want to use with Optics Pro, and designate exactly which lenses are included in your repertoire.)

Once an image has been imported into Optics Pro, it can be manipulated within one of four main sections: Light, Color, Geometry, and Details. It's especially useful for correcting optical flaws, color, exposure, and dynamic range, while adjusting perspective, distortion, and tilting. If you own a fish-eye lens, Optics Pro will "de-fish" your images to produce a passable rectilinear photo from your curved image. A new Dust/Blemish Removal tool operates something like a manual version of the D3s/D3x's Dust Off Reference Photo. The user creates a dust/blemish template, and the program removes dust from the marked area in multiple images.

## Phase One Capture One Pro (C1 Pro)

If there is a Cadillac of RAW converters for Nikon and Canon digital SLR cameras, C1 Pro has to be it. This premium-priced program from Phase One (www.phaseone.com) does everything, does it well, and does it quickly. If you can't justify the price tag of this professional-level software (as much as $500 for the top-of-the-line edition), there are "lite" versions for serious amateurs and cash-challenged professionals for as little as $130.

Aimed at photographers with high-volume needs (that would include school and portrait photographers, as well as busy commercial photographers), C1 Pro is available for both Windows and Mac OS X, and supports a broad range of digital cameras. Phase One is a leading supplier of megabucks digital camera backs for medium and larger format cameras, so they really understand the needs of photographers.

The latest features include individual noise reduction controls for each image, automatic levels adjustment, a "quick develop" option that allows speedy conversion from RAW to TIFF or JPEG formats, dual-image side-by-side views for comparison purposes, and helpful grids and guides that can be superimposed over an image. Photographers concerned about copyright protection will appreciate the ability to add watermarks to the output images.

## Bibble Pro

One of my personal favorites among third-party RAW converters is Bibble Pro. It supports one of the broadest ranges of RAW file formats available (which can be handy if you find yourself with the need to convert a file from a friend or colleague's non-Nikon camera), including NEF files from Nikon cameras dating as far back as the Nikon D1, D1x/h, D2H, and D100. The utility supports lots of different platforms, too. It's available for Windows, Mac OS X, and, believe it or not, Linux.

Bibble (www.bibblelabs.com) works fast, which is important when you have to convert many images in a short time (event photographers will know what I am talking about!). Bibble's batch-processing capabilities also let you convert large numbers of files using settings you specify without further intervention. Its customizable interface lets you organize and edit images quickly and then output them in a variety of formats, including 16-bit TIFF and PNG. You can even create a web gallery from within Bibble. I often find myself disliking the generic filenames applied to digital images by cameras, so I really like Bibble's ability to rename batches of files using new names that you specify.

Bibble is fully color managed, which means it can support all the popular color spaces (Adobe sRGB and so forth) and use custom profiles generated by third-party color-management software. There are two editions of Bibble, a Pro version and a Lite version. Because the Pro version is reasonably priced at $129, I don't really see the need to save $60 with the Lite edition, which lacks the top-line's options for tethered shooting, embedding IPTC-compatible captions in images, and can also be used as a Photoshop plug-in (if you prefer not to work with the application in its standalone mode). Bibble Pro now incorporates Noise Ninja technology, so you can get double-duty from this valuable application.

## BreezeBrowser Pro

A versatile program you'll want to consider is BreezeBrowser Pro, from Breeze Systems (www.breezesys.com), which performs several useful functions in addition to RAW file conversion and image browsing. It can produce contact sheets and proof images, generate nifty web pages with only a little input on your part, and, importantly in this GPS-crazy age, link geo-tagged images with Google Earth and online maps. Now that the Nikon D3s/D3x provides the compact Nikon GP-1 geo-tagging unit, which clips onto the camera's accessory shoe, software like BreezeBrowser provides an actual real-world application for this kind of data.

A real bargain at $69.95, BreezeBrowser Pro offers all the basic conversion, sharpening, resizing, and adjustments for your RAW images. You can create captioned web pages from within the program, and, if you want to sell your pictures, it will protect them with watermarking and provide a system for online ordering of images/prints. Batch rename features let you change the filename applied in the camera to something more useful, and edit the date/time stamps of your files. The Windows-only program is shown in Figure 11.9.

## BreezeSystems NKRemote

If you find Nikon Camera Control Pro too pricey, you may find BreezeSystems' NKRemote an attractive $95 alternative. It links to your camera through the USB cable, and offers direct control of virtually every camera control through a well-designed user interface, shown in Figure 11.10. It has a couple quirks—for example, you can discern the original Canon-oriented underpinnings of the program by the use of the label Tv (Time Value) for shutter-priority. But the features are solid.

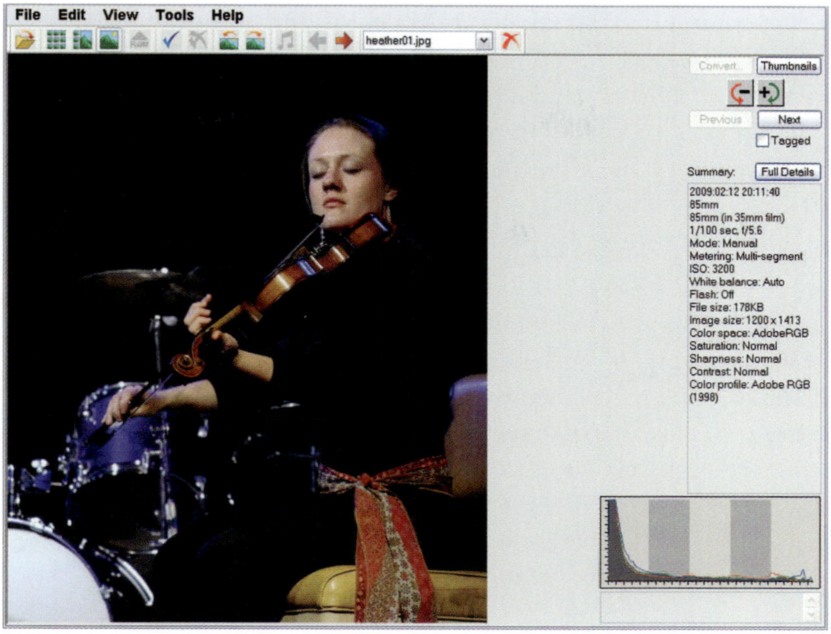


**Figure 11.9** BreezeBrowser Pro offers geo-tagging and support for web image sales among its innovative features.

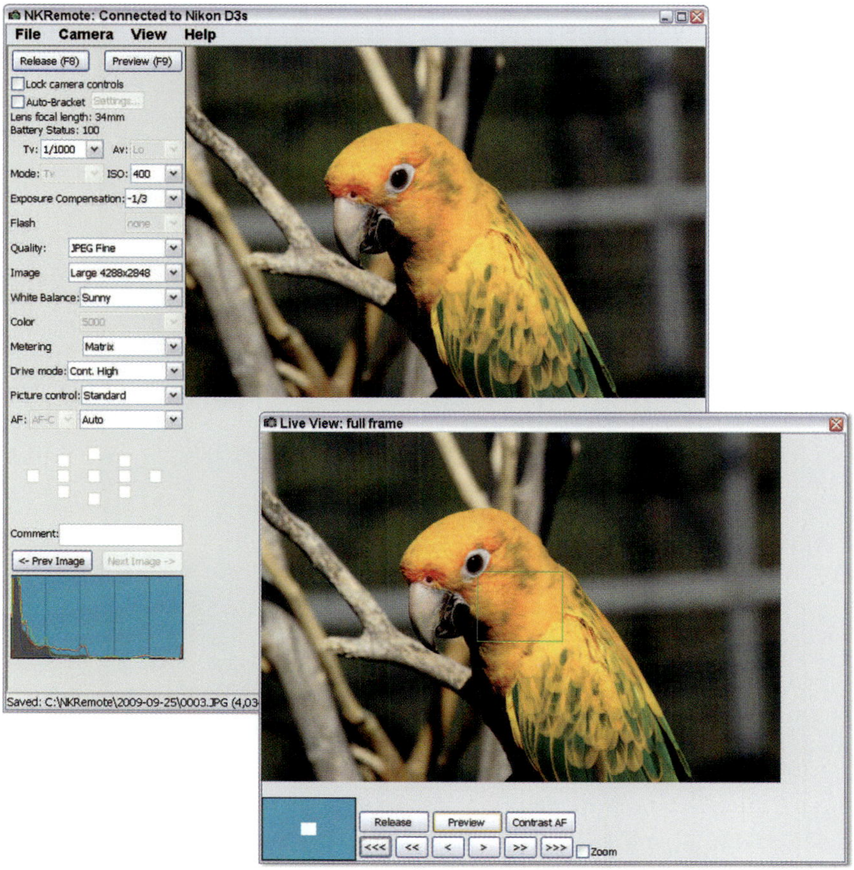


**Figure 11.10** BreezeSystems NKRemote offers an economical way to control your camera for direct shooting and time-lapse photography, especially in live view mode (lower right).

The program works not only with the Nikon D3s/D3x, but with the D300, D90, D700, and earlier D200 cameras, so if you add another model to your kit, you won't have to buy new software. NKRemote allows focusing automatically and manually from your PC (you can choose the focus point by checking one of boxes in the AF interface), thanks to its support for the live view feature available in all the cameras mentioned except the D200. You'll enjoy setting up your D3s/D3x on a long USB tether, and relaxing while you wait for that elusive plaid-bellied sapgrabber to perch within view of your lens.

You can shoot time-lapse photos to capture flowers blooming, construction sites constructing, or dawns breaking. It's easy to adjust Picture Controls from your PC, too. One of my favorite features (for Windows only) is the Photo Booth capability, which you can set up to operate like one of those three-shots-for-a-dollar photo booths at the County Fair. In this mode, the software automatically takes a series of photos in sequence, and then immediately prints them out. If you're a professional (or aspiring pro), you can set up your photo booth at an event; otherwise, the feature is great fun to use at home. The Photobooth options are shown in Figure 11.11.

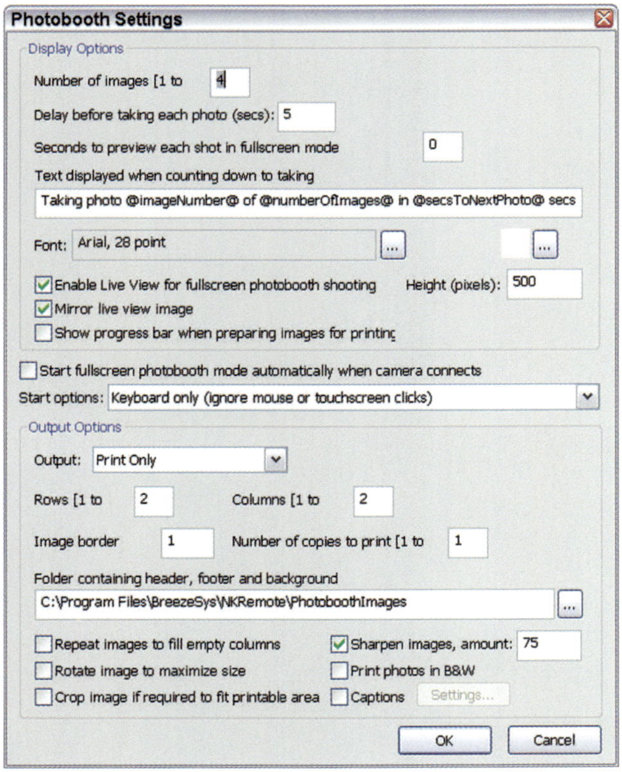


**Figure 11.11**
Set up your own automatic photo booth at an event, or at home, using NKRemote's options.

## Photoshop/Photoshop Elements

Photoshop is the high-end choice for image editing, and Photoshop Elements is a great alternative for those who need some of the features of Photoshop, but can do without the most sophisticated capabilities, including editing CMYK files. Both editors use the latest version of Adobe's Camera Raw plug-in, which makes it easy to adjust things like image resolution, white balance, exposure, shadows, brightness, sharpness, luminance, and noise reduction. One plus with the Adobe products is that they are available in identical versions for both Windows and Macs (eventually!).

The latest version of Photoshop includes a built-in RAW plug-in that is compatible with the proprietary formats of a growing number of digital cameras, both new and old, and which can perform a limited number of manipulations on JPEG and TIFF files, too. This plug-in also works with Photoshop Elements, but with fewer features. Here's how easy it is to manipulate a RAW file using the Adobe converter:

1. Transfer the RAW images from your camera to your computer's hard drive.
2. In Photoshop, choose Open from the File menu, or use Organizer or Bridge (depending on the version you have installed).
3. Select a RAW image file. The Adobe Camera Raw plug-in will pop up, showing a preview of the image, like the one shown in Figure 11.12.

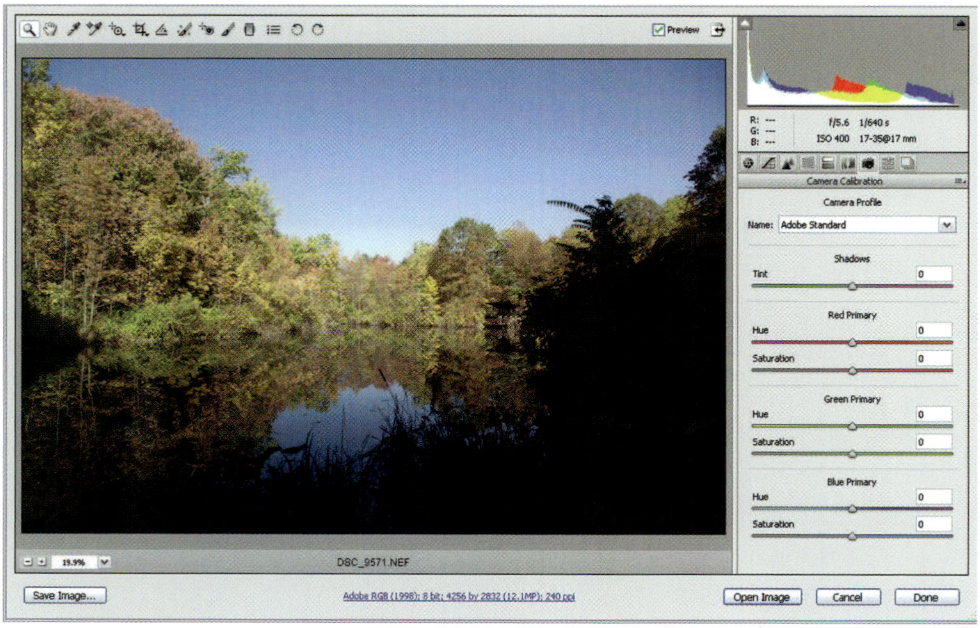


**Figure 11.12**
The basic ACR dialog box looks like this when processing a single image.

4. If you like, use one of the tools found in the toolbar at the top left of the dialog box. From left to right, they are
   - **Zoom.** Operates just like the Zoom tool in Photoshop.
   - **Hand.** Use like the Hand tool in Photoshop.
   - **White Balance.** Click an area in the image that should be neutral gray or white to set the white balance quickly.
   - **Color Sampler.** Use to determine the RGB values of areas you click with this eyedropper.
   - **Crop.** Pre-crops the image so that only the portion you specify is imported into Photoshop. This option saves time when you want to work on a section of a large image, and you don't need the entire file.
   - **Straighten.** Drag in the preview image to define what should be a horizontal or vertical line, and ACR will realign the image to straighten it.
   - **Retouch.** Used to heal or clone areas you define.
   - **Red-Eye Removal.** Quickly zap red pupils in your human subjects.
   - **ACR Preferences.** Produces a dialog box of Adobe Camera Raw preferences.
   - **Rotate Counterclockwise.** Rotates counterclockwise in 90-degree increments with a click.
   - **Rotate Clockwise.** Rotates clockwise in 90-degree increments with a click.
5. Using the Basic tab, you can have ACR show you red and blue highlights in the preview that indicate shadow areas that are clipped (too dark to show detail) and light areas that are blown out (too bright). Click the triangles in the upper-left corner of the histogram display (shadow clipping) and upper-right corner (highlight clipping) to toggle these indicators on or off.
6. Also in the Basic tab you can choose white balance, either from the drop-down list or by setting a color temperature and green/magenta color bias (tint) using the sliders.
7. Other sliders are available to control exposure, recovery, fill light, blacks, brightness, contrast, vibrance, and saturation. A checkbox can be marked to convert the image to grayscale.
8. Make other adjustments (described in more detail below).
9. ACR makes automatic adjustments for you. You can click Default and make the changes for yourself, or click the Auto link (located just above the Exposure slider) to reapply the automatic adjustments after you've made your own modifications.

10. If you've marked more than one image to be opened, the additional images appear in a "filmstrip" at the left side of the screen. You can click on each thumbnail in the filmstrip in turn and apply different settings to each.
11. Click Open Image/Open image(s) into Photoshop using the settings you've made.

The Basic tab is displayed by default when the ACR dialog box opens, and it includes most of the sliders and controls you'll need to fine-tune your image as you import it into Photoshop. These include:

- **White Balance.** Leave it As Shot or change to a value such as Daylight, Cloudy, Shade, Tungsten, Fluorescent, or Flash. If you like, you can set a custom white balance using the Temperature and Tint sliders.
- **Exposure.** This slider adjusts the overall brightness and darkness of the image.
- **Recovery.** Restores detail in the red, green, and blue color channels.
- **Fill Light.** Reconstructs detail in shadows.
- **Blacks.** Increases the number of tones represented as black in the final image, emphasizing tones in the shadow areas of the image.
- **Brightness.** This slider adjusts the brightness and darkness of an image.
- **Contrast.** Manipulates the contrast of the midtones of your image.
- **Convert to Grayscale.** Mark this box to convert the image to black-and-white.
- **Vibrance.** Prevents oversaturation when enriching the colors of an image.
- **Saturation.** Manipulates the richness of all colors equally, from zero saturation (gray/black, no color) at the –100 setting to double the usual saturation at the +100 setting.

Additional controls are available on the Tone curve, Detail, HSL/Grayscale, Split toning, Lens corrections, Camera calibration, and Presets tabs, shown in Figure 11.13. The Tone curve tab can change the tonal values of your image. The Detail tab lets you adjust sharpness, luminance smoothing, and apply color noise reduction. The HSL/Grayscale tab offers controls for adjusting hue, saturation, and lightness and converting an image to black-and-white. Split toning helps you colorize an image with sepia or cyanotype (blue) shades. The Lens corrections tab has sliders to adjust for chromatic aberrations and vignetting. The Camera calibration tab provides a way for calibrating the color corrections made in the Camera Raw plug-in. The Presets tab (not shown) is used to load settings you've stored for reuse.

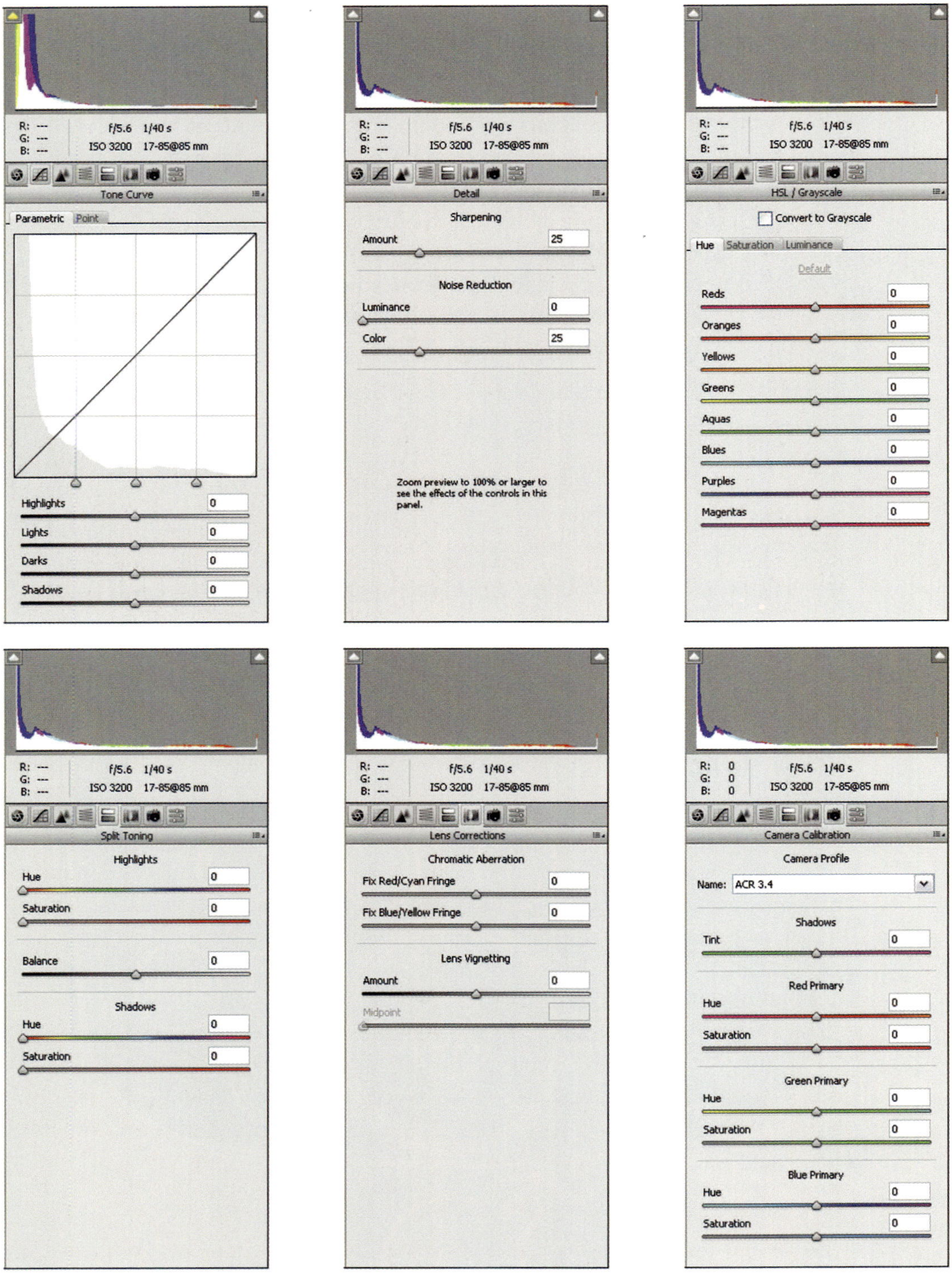


**Figure 11.13** More controls are available within the additional tabbed dialog boxes in Adobe Camera Raw.

# 12

# Nikon D3s/D3x: Troubleshooting and Prevention

If you've moved up to the Nikon D3s or D3x from one of Nikon's more consumer-oriented models, you'll be pleased to note their more rugged magnesium alloy bodies with weather sealing at all connections and buttons, and the Kevlar/carbon fiber shutter rated for a minimum of 300,000 shutter cycles or more. The camera's weight is comforting in the hand, and tends to help stabilize the D3s/D3x during hand-held exposures, when compared to lighter-weight models. Although the terms "pro" and "semi-pro" when applied to camera models are fairly useless in determining who uses what, the Nikon D3s/D3x is truly a camera that has both the features and construction designed to appeal to professional photographers—and avid amateurs who want to shoot like a pro.

But despite the reputation for tank-like robustness and reliability that "pro" class cameras boast, the Nikon D3s/D3x still requires a certain level of care and maintenance to keep it humming along click after click. One of the nice things about modern electronic cameras like the D3s/D3x is that they have fewer mechanical moving parts to fail, so they are less likely to "wear out." No film transport mechanism, no wind lever or motor drive, no complicated mechanical linkages from camera to lens to physically focus the elements (at least, that's true with modern AF-S optics). Instead, a tiny, reliable motor is built into each lens (and you lose the use of only that lens should something fail), and one of the few major moving parts in the camera itself is the lightweight mirror that flips up and down with each shot, and the shutter. Unless you're shooting sports in continuous mode day in and day out, the mirror and shutter on your D3s/D3x are likely to last as long as you expect to use the camera. Anecdotal reports from heavy shooters indicate that the D3s/D3x can weather many more than its rated 300,000 shutter actuations, with ease.

The only other vulnerable components on the camera that move are switches, dials, buttons, the flip-up electronic flash, and the door that slides open to allow you to remove and insert the Compact Flash card. Unless you're extraordinarily clumsy or unlucky and manage to bend the internal pins in the Compact Flash card slot, or give your built-in flash a good whack while it is in use, there's not a lot that can go wrong mechanically with your Nikon D3s/D3x.

On the other hand, one of the chief drawbacks of modern electronic cameras is that they are modern *electronic* cameras. Your D3s/D3x is fully dependent on two different batteries. Without them, the camera can't be used. There are numerous other electrical and electronic connections in the camera (many connected to those mechanical switches and dials), and components like the color LCD and top-panel status LCD that can potentially fail or suffer damage. The camera also relies on its "operating system," or *firmware*, which can be plagued by bugs that cause unexpected behavior. Luckily, electronic components are generally more reliable and trouble-free, especially when compared to their mechanical counterparts from the pre-electronic film camera days. (Film cameras of the last 10 to 20 years have had almost as many electronic features as digital cameras, but, believe it or not, there were whole generations of film cameras that had *no* electronics or batteries.)

Digital cameras have problems unique to their breed, too—the most troublesome being the need to clean the sensor of dust and grime periodically. This chapter will show you how to diagnose problems, fix some common ills, and, importantly, learn how to avoid them in the future.

## Battery Powered

I've grown to live with the need for batteries even though I shot for years using all-mechanical Nikon cameras that had no batteries. (Or even a built-in light meter! When I was a photojournalist, I used to travel around the country with three or four meterless Nikon film bodies, and a hand-held Sekonic or Weston light meter.) The need for electrical power is the price we pay for modern conveniences like autofocus, autoexposure, LCD image display, backlit menus, and, of course, digital images.

One of the batteries you rely on is the EN-EL4a battery installed in the grip. It's rechargeable, can last for several thousand shots, and is user-replaceable if you have a spare. It's a time-tested battery, used, not only in the D3s/D3x, but in the original Nikon D3, and earlier D2-series models like the D2x and D2xs.

The second power cell in your camera is a so-called *clock battery*, a CR1616 Lithium cell that stores settings such as the date and time. The clock battery retains the date and time settings of the camera when it's powered down, and, even, when the main battery is removed for charging. It should last about four years, and replacements can be found at Radio Shack and similar stores that stock button-cell batteries. To change the clock battery, follow these steps:

1. Remove the EN-EL4a battery.
2. Turn the camera upside down. Otherwise, the clock battery will fall into the innards of the battery chamber and anyone watching you perform this step will think you didn't know what you're doing.
3. Slide the small black cover in the floor (roof) of the battery chamber towards the outside of the camera.
4. Extract the old battery, and insert the new one with the side labeled + facing upwards towards the battery chamber. (See Figure 12.1.)
5. Replace the cover and reinsert the EN-EL4a battery.
6. Turn the camera on, go to the Setup menu, and re-enter the correct time (if you see the Clock indicator flashing on the top monochrome LCD control panel).

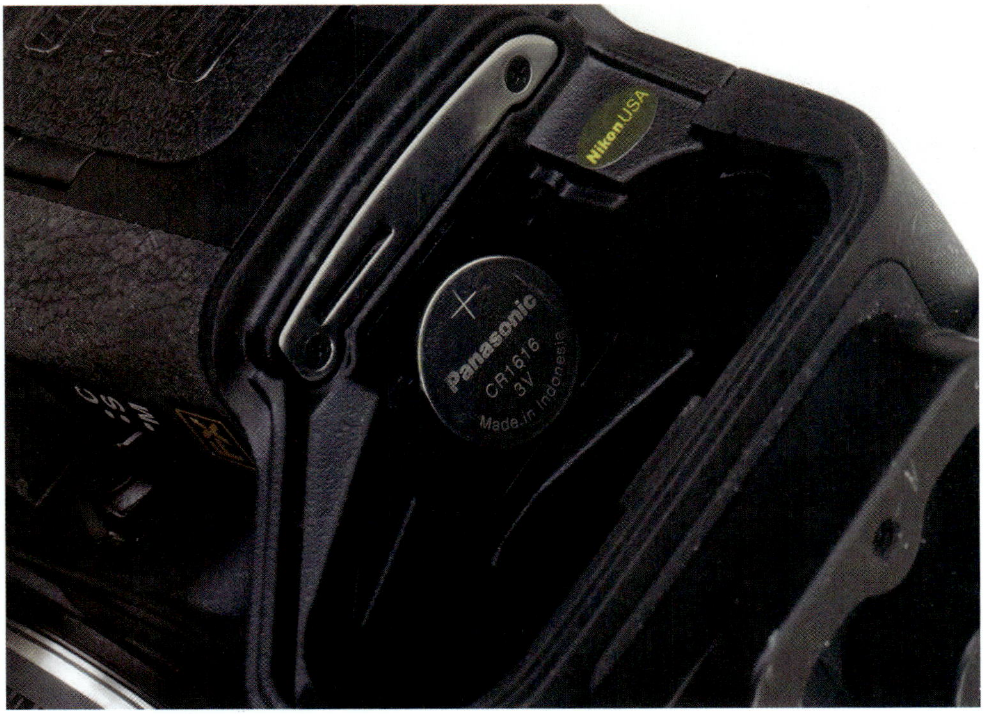


**Figure 12.1**
Replacing the clock battery.

Normally, your main concern will be to provide a continuous, reliable source of power for your D3s/D3x. As I noted in Chapter 1, you should always have a spare battery or two so you won't need to stop shooting when your internal battery dies. I recommend buying Nikon-brand batteries: saving $20 or so for an after-market battery may save you a few dollars, but can cost you much more than that if the battery malfunctions and damages your camera.

There are several techniques you can use to help you stretch the longevity of your D3s/D3x's battery. To get the most from each charge, consider these steps:

- **Playback menu: Image review.** Turn off automatic image review after each shot using this menu option. You can still review your images by pressing the Playback button. Or, leave image review on, but set the display for the minimum 4 seconds as described next.
- **Monitor off delay.** In Custom Setting c4, set for the minimum, 4 seconds, for playback, menus, shooting info display, and image review. That three-inch LCD uses a lot of juice, so reducing the amount of time it is active when you don't turn it off manually can boost the effectiveness of your battery.
- **Auto meter off delay.** Set to 4 seconds in Custom Setting c2 if you can tolerate such a brief active time.
- **Reduce LCD brightness.** In the Setup menu's LCD brightness option, select the lowest of the seven brightness settings that work for you under most conditions. If you're willing to shade the LCD with your hand, you can often get away with lower brightness settings outdoors, which will further increase the useful life of your battery.
- **Turn off the shooting information display.** Turn it on or off manually as needed by pressing the Info button.
- **Cancel VR.** Turn off vibration reduction if your lens (such as the 70-200mm VR lens) has that feature and you feel you don't need it.
- **Use a card reader.** When transferring pictures from your D3s/D3x to your computer, use a card reader instead of the USB cable. Linking your camera to your computer and transferring images using the cable takes longer and uses a lot more power.

## Upgrading Your Firmware

The camera relies on its "operating system," or *firmware,* which should be updated in a reasonable fashion as new releases become available. The firmware in your Nikon D3s/D3x handles everything from menu display (including fonts, colors, and the actual entries themselves), what languages are available, and even support for specific devices and features. Upgrading the firmware to a new version makes it possible to add or fine-tune features while fixing some of the bugs that sneak in.

Firmware upgrades are used most frequently to fix bugs in the software, and much less frequently to add or enhance features. The exact changes made to the firmware are generally spelled out in the firmware release announcement. You can examine the remedies provided and decide if a given firmware patch is important to you. If not, you can usually safely wait a while before going through the bother of upgrading your firmware—at least long enough for the early adopters (such as those who haunt the Digital Photography Review forums at www.dpreview.com) to report whether the bug fixes have introduced new bugs of their own. Each new firmware release incorporates the changes from previous releases, so if you skip a minor upgrade you should have no problems.

### WHEN TO UPGRADE YOUR FIRMWARE

I *always* recommend waiting at least two weeks after a firmware upgrade is announced before changing the software in your camera. This is often in direct contradiction to the online Nikon "gurus" who breathlessly announce each new firmware release on their web pages, usually with links to where you can download the latest software. *Don't do it!* Yet. Nikon has, in the past, introduced firmware upgrades that were buggy and added problems of their own. If you own a camera affected by a new round of firmware upgrades, I urge you to wait and let a few million over-eager fellow users "beta test" this upgrade for you. Within a few weeks, any problems (although I don't expect there will be any) will surface and you'll know whether the update is safe. Your camera is working fine right now, so why take the chance?

## How It Works

If you're computer savvy, you might wonder how your Nikon D3s/D3x is able to overwrite its own operating system—that is, how can the existing firmware be used to load the new version on top of itself? It's a little like lifting yourself by reaching down and pulling up on your bootstraps.

Not ironically, that's almost exactly what happens: At your command (when you start the upgrade process), the D3s/D3x shifts into a special mode in which it is no longer operating from its firmware but, rather, from a small piece of software called a *bootstrap loader*, a separate, protected software program that functions only at startup or when upgrading firmware. The loader's function is to look for firmware to launch or, when directed, to copy new firmware from a memory card to the internal memory space where the old firmware is located. Once the new firmware has replaced the old, you can "reboot" the camera using the new operating system.

## Why Two Firmware Modules?

Your Nikon D3s/D3x's firmware is divided into two parts (some models, like the Nikon D90, have three firmware components). Why chop the firmware up in the first place? There's a good reason why the firmware is divided in twain. Each of the two modules is "in charge" of particular parts of the camera's operating system. So, when a bug is found, or a new feature added, it is possible, in many cases, to offer only an upgrade for either Firmware A or Firmware B, depending on which module is affected. Although mistakes in upgrading firmware are rare, you cut the opportunities for user errors in half when only one of the modules needs to be replaced.

But there's a more important reason for having at least two firmware modules. If your camera had just one, and you had the misfortune to munge that firmware during an ill-fated upgrade, it's very likely your camera would be magically transformed into a digital doorstop. Part of the firmware is needed simply to install (or re-install) the firmware in the first place. With all Nikon cameras, Firmware A and Firmware B each has the capability of locating and installing replacement firmware. So, if A is ruined, you can use the routines in B to re-install a new copy of A. And vice versa. We can all agree that this is a wise move on Nikon's part.

**WARNING**

Use a fully charged EN-EL4a charged battery or a Nikon EH-6 AC adapter to ensure that you'll have enough power to operate the camera for the entire upgrade. Moreover, you should not turn off the camera while your old firmware is being overwritten. Don't open the memory card door or do anything else that might disrupt operation of the D3s/D3x while the firmware is being installed.

## Getting Ready

Before you get started, I have to emphasize that at the time this book was written, no single firmware upgrades have been made available for the Nikon D3s or D3x, so that I, personally, have not performed this task with these cameras. However, I have upgraded the firmware multiple times for most of my other Nikon dSLRs. The procedure I am going to describe is the recommended process Nikon has traditionally used for past upgrades. But when it comes time to do an actual firmware upgrade for your D3s/D3x, you should double-check the instructions below against the recommended procedure that Nikon implements at that time. It should be very close to the steps I outline, but there may be some small differences for later firmware updates.

The first thing to do is determine whether you need the current firmware update. First, confirm the version number of your Nikon D3s/D3x's current firmware:

1. Turn on the D3s/D3x.
2. Press the Menu button and select Firmware version from the Setup menu. The camera's firmware version will be displayed. (See Figure 12.2.)
3. Write down the Version number for Parts A and B.
4. Turn off the D3s/D3x.

Next, go to the Nikon support site, locate, and download the firmware update. In the USA, the place to go is http://support.nikontech.com/, which will offer a list of choices, including one that says Current Firmware Downloads available for Nikon Products. Click that link, then click the DSLR link on the page displayed next. Scroll down to the D3s/D3x row in the table, and review the version number for the current update.

If the version is later than the one you noted in your camera, click the firmware link in either the Windows or Macintosh column (depending on your computer) to download the file. It will have a name like D3s/D3xUpdate.zip (Windows) or D3s/D3xupdate.sitx (Macintosh). Extract the file to a folder on your computer using the unzipping or unstuffing software of your choice.

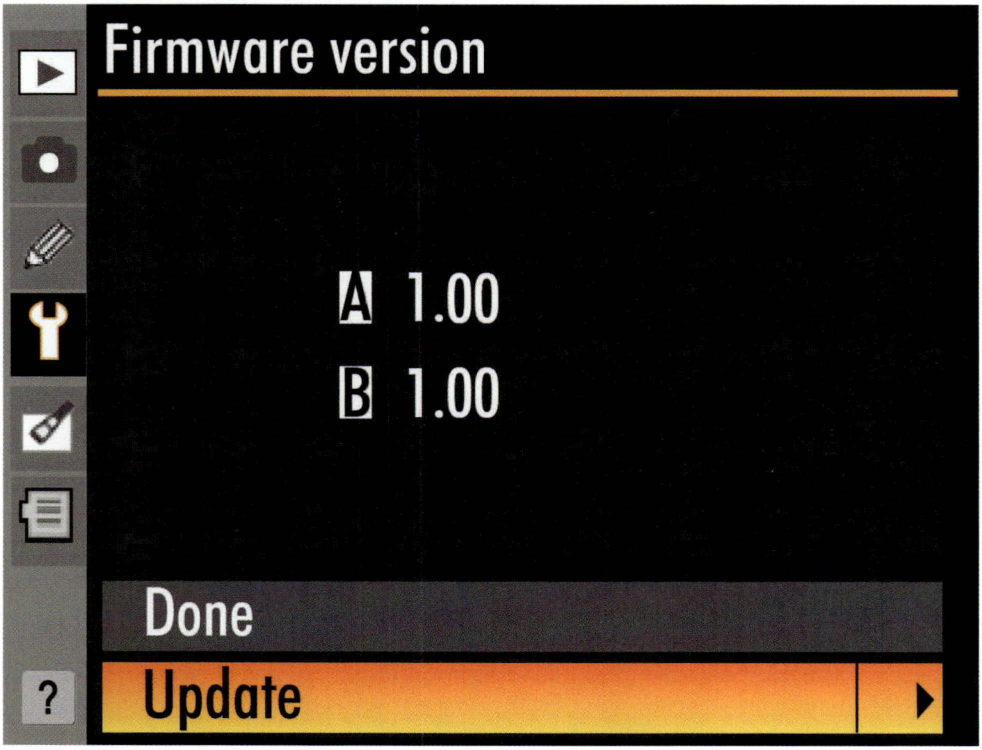


**Figure 12.2**
View your current firmware versions before upgrading.

The D3s/D3x's firmware comes in two parts, A and B, which can be updated individually. The actual update files will be named something like

**AD3S00101.bin**

**BD3S00101.bin**

The final preparation you need to make is to decide whether you'd like to upgrade your firmware using a memory card reader, or by transferring the software to the D3s/D3x using the UC-E4 USB cable. In either case, you'll need to format a memory card in the D3s/D3x. Then, perform one of the sets of steps in the sections that follow.

## Updating from a Card Reader

To update from a card reader, use a reader connected to your computer with a USB cable. Then, follow these steps:

1. Insert a formatted memory card into the card reader. If you have been using Nikon Transfer or the "autoplay" features of your operating system to transfer images from your memory card to the computer, the automated transfer dialog box may appear. Close it.
2. The memory card will appear on your Macintosh desktop, or in the Computer/My Computer folders under Windows 7/Windows Vista/Windows XP.
3. Drag one of the firmware files to the memory card. You can install "A" or "B" first (if both are provided); it doesn't matter. If your particular upgrade consists of only one of the two files, drag that to the memory card. Remember to copy the firmware to the *root* (top) directory of the memory card. The D3s/D3x will be unable to find it if you place it in a folder.

## Updating with a USB Connection

You can also copy the firmware to the D3s/D3x's memory card using a USB connection. Just follow these steps:

1. With the camera turned off, insert the formatted memory card. Then, turn the camera back on.
2. Press the Menu button and navigate to the Setup menu.
3. Choose USB and set the option to Mass storage, as described in Chapter 3.
4. Turn the D3s/D3x off and connect it to your computer using the UC-E4 USB cable.
5. Turn the camera back on. If you have been using Nikon Transfer or the "autoplay" features of your operating system to transfer images from your memory card to the computer, the automated transfer dialog box may appear. Close it.

6. The camera will appear on the Macintosh desktop, or in the Computer/My Computer folders under Windows 7/Windows Vista/Windows XP.
7. Drag one of the firmware files to the memory card. It doesn't matter whether you install "A" or "B". If your particular upgrade consists of only one .bin file, drag that to the memory card. Remember to copy the firmware to the *root* (top) directory of the memory card. The D3s/D3x will be unable to find it if you place it in a folder.
8. Disconnect the camera from the computer.

## Starting the Update

To perform the actual update, follow these steps:

1. With the memory card containing the firmware update software in the camera, turn the camera on.
2. Press the Menu button and select Firmware version in the Setup menu.
3. Select Update and press the multi selector button to the right. (See Figure 12.3.)
4. When the firmware update screen appears, highlight Yes and press OK to begin the update. (See Figure 12.4.)

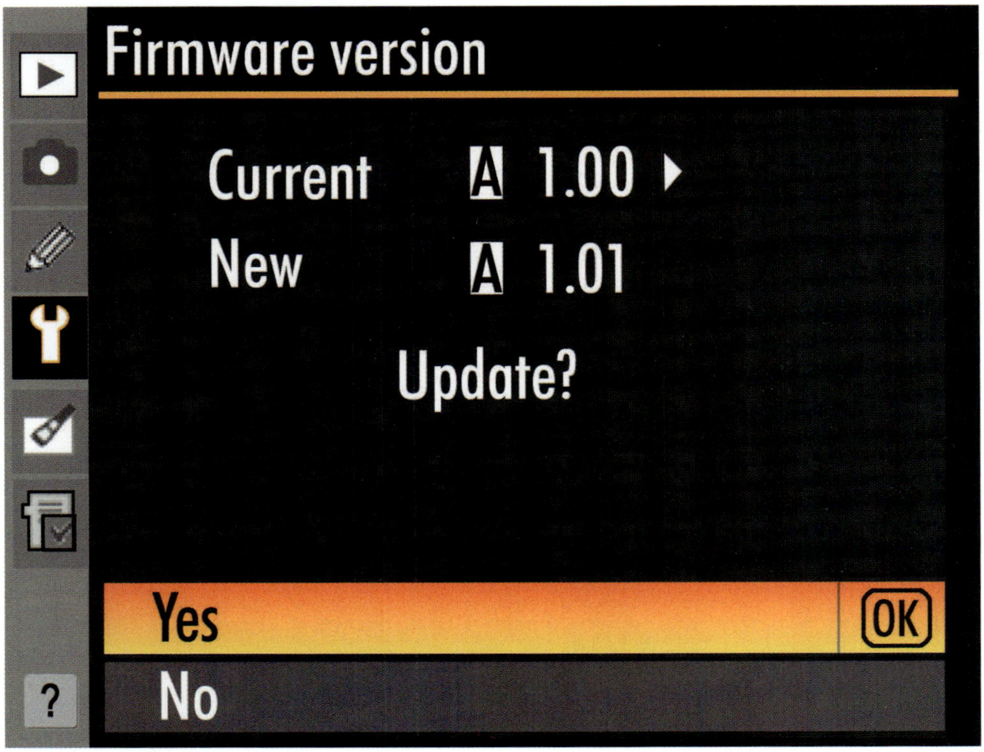


**Figure 12.3** Choose Update.

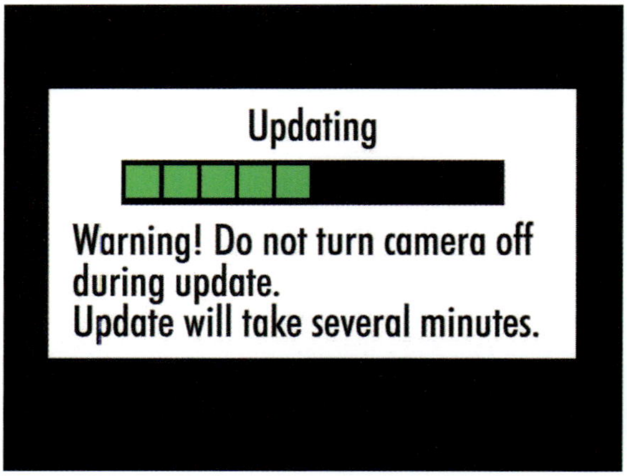


**Figure 12.4** Don't turn the camera off while updating is underway.

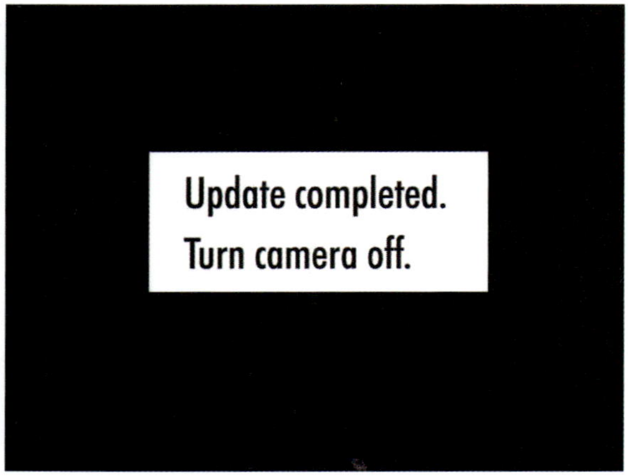


**Figure 12.5** Turn off the camera when update is finished.

5. The actual process may take a few minutes (from two to five). Be sure not to turn off the camera or perform any other operations while it is underway.
6. When the update is completed, the warning message will no longer be displayed on the screen. You can turn off the camera when the message disappears. (See Figure 12.5.)
7. Remove the memory card.
8. Turn the D3s/D3x back on to load the updated firmware.
9. Press the Menu button and select Firmware version in the Setup menu to view the current firmware number. If it matches the update, you've successfully upgraded that portion of the firmware.
10. Reformat the memory card.
11. If there is a second part to your firmware upgrade ("A" or "B"), then repeat all the steps for the additional firmware software.

# Protect Your LCD

The massive three-inch color LCD on the back of your Nikon D3s/D3x almost seems like a target for banging, scratching, and other abuse. The LCD itself is quite rugged, and a few errant knocks are unlikely to shatter the protective cover over the LCD, and scratches won't easily mar its tempered glass surface. However, if you want to be on the safe side, there are a number of protective products you can purchase to keep your LCD safe—and, in some cases, make it a little easier to view.

Here's a quick overview of your options.

- **Plastic overlays.** The simplest solution (although not always the cheapest), is to apply a plastic overlay sheet or "skin" cut to fit your LCD. These adhere either by static electricity or through a light adhesive coating that's even less clingy than stick-it notes. You can cut down overlays made for PDAs (although these can be pricey at up to $19.95 for a set of several sheets), or purchase overlays sold specifically for digital cameras. Vendors such as Hoodman (www.hoodmanusa.com) offer overlays of this type. These products will do a good job of shielding your D3s/D3x's LCD screen from scratches and minor impacts, but will not offer much protection from a good whack.
- **Acrylic/glass shields.** These scratch-resistant panels, laser cut to fit your camera perfectly, are my choice as the best protection solution, and what I use on my own D3s/D3x. At about $6-10 each, they also happen to be the least expensive option as well. I get thin glass GGS-brand shields from eBay or Amazon.com, shown in Figure 12.6. For acrylic shields, I use custom-sized versions from a company called

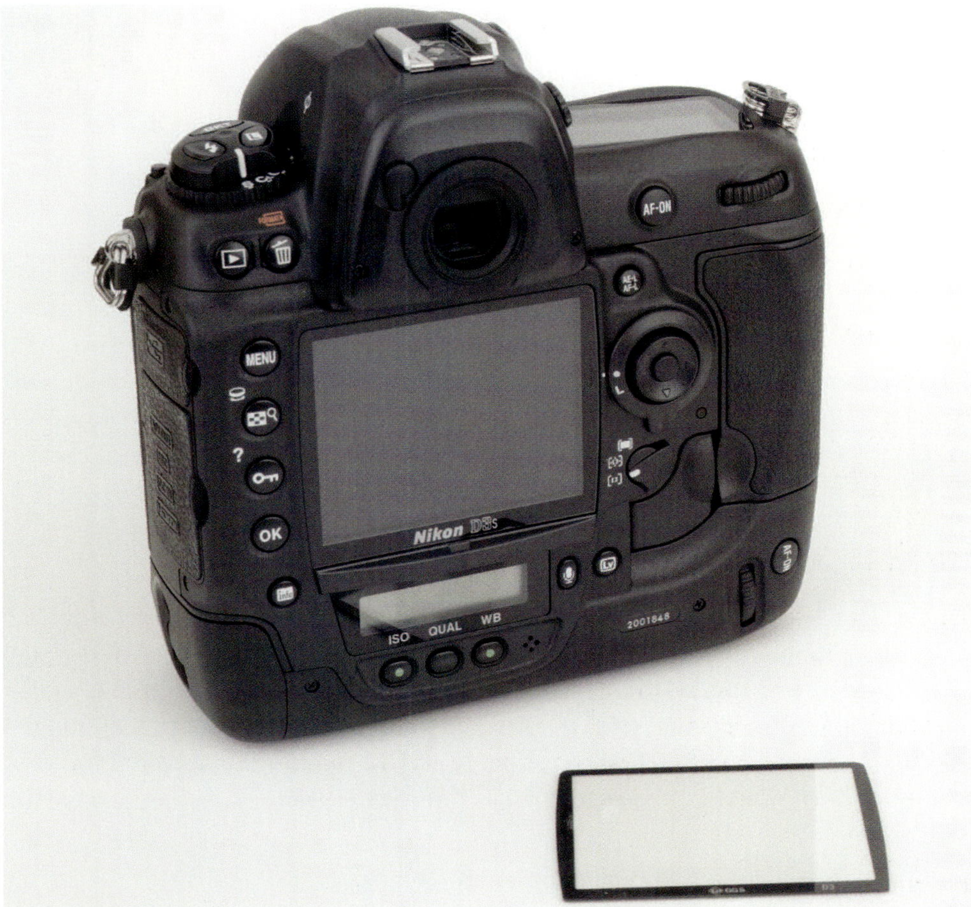


**Figure 12.6**
A tough acrylic or glass shield can protect your LCD from scratches.

'da Products (www.daproducts.com). They attach using strips of sticky adhesive that hold the panel flush and tight, but which allow the acrylic to be pried off and the adhesive removed easily if you want to remove or replace the shield. Neither type will attenuate your view of the LCD and are non-reflective enough for use under a variety of lighting conditions.

- **Flip-up hoods.** These protectors slip on and provide a cover that completely shields the LCD, but unfolds to provide a three-sided hood that allows viewing the LCD while minimizing the extraneous light falling on it and reducing contrast. They're sold for about $40 by Delkin (www.delkin.com) and Hoodman. If you want to completely protect your LCD from hard knocks and need to view the screen outdoors in bright sunlight, there is nothing better. However, I have a couple problems with these devices. First, with the cover closed, you can't peek down after taking a shot to see what your image looks like during picture review. You must open the cap each time you want to look at the LCD. Moreover, with the hood unfolded, it's difficult to look through the viewfinder: Don't count on being able to use the viewfinder *and* the LCD at the same time with one of these hoods in place.
- **Magnifiers.** If you look hard enough, you should be able to find an LCD magnifier that fits over the monitor panel and provides a 2X magnification. These often strap on clumsily, and serve better as a way to get an enlarged view of the LCD than as protection. Hoodman and other suppliers offer these specialized devices.

# Troubleshooting Memory Cards

Sometimes good memory cards go bad. Sometimes good photographers can treat their memory cards badly. It's possible that a memory card that works fine in one camera won't be recognized when inserted into another. In the worst case, you can have a card full of important photos and find that the card seems to be corrupted and you can't access any of them. Don't panic! If these scenarios sound horrific to you, there are lots of things you can do to prevent them from happening, and a variety of remedies available if they do occur. You'll want to take some time—before disaster strikes—to consider your options.

## All Your Eggs in One Basket?

The debate about whether it's better to use one large memory card or several smaller ones has been going on since even before there were memory cards. I can remember when computer users wondered whether it was smarter to install a pair of 200MB (not *gigabyte*) hard drives in their computer, or if they should go for one of those newfangled 500MB models. By the same token, a few years ago the user groups were full of proponents who insisted that you ought to use 128MB memory cards rather than the huge 512MB versions. Today, most of the arguments involve 8GB cards versus 4GB cards, and I expect that as prices for 16GB and 32GB memory cards continue to drop, they'll find their way into the debate as well.

Why all the fuss? Are 8GB memory cards more likely to fail than 4GB cards? Are you risking all your photos if you trust your images to a larger card? Isn't it better to use several smaller cards, so that if one fails you lose only half as many photos? Or, isn't it wiser to put all your photos onto one larger card, because the more cards you use, the better your odds of misplacing or damaging one and losing at least some pictures?

In the end, the "eggs in one basket" argument boils down to statistics, and how you happen to use your D3s/D3x. The rationales can go both ways. If you have multiple smaller cards, you do increase your chances of something happening to one of them, so, arguably, you might be boosting the odds of losing some pictures. If all your images are important, the fact that you've lost 100 rather than 200 pictures isn't very comforting.

After all, the myth assumes that a damaged card will always be full before it becomes corrupted. Fortunately, memory cards don't magically wait until they are full before they fail. In a typical shooting session, it doesn't matter whether you've shot 3.5GB worth of pictures on a 4GB card or 3.5GB worth of pictures on an 8GB card. If either card fails, you've lost the same number of images. Your risk increases *only* when you start shooting additional photos on the larger card. In the real world, most of us who use larger memory cards don't fill them up very often. We just like having the extra capacity there when we need it.

The myth also says that by using several smaller cards, you're spreading the risk around so that only some pictures will be lost in case of a failure. What is more important to you, your photographs or the members of your family? When going on vacation, do you insist on splitting your kin up and driving several smaller cars?

If you shoot photojournalist-type pictures, you probably change memory cards when they're less than completely full in order to avoid the need to do so at a crucial moment. (When I shoot sports, my cards rarely reach 80 to 90 percent of capacity before I change them.) Using multiple smaller cards means you have to change them that more often, which can be a real pain when you're taking a lot of photos. As an example, if you use 1GB memory cards with a Nikon D3s/D3x and shoot RAW+JPEG FINE, you may get only a few dozen pictures on the card. That's not even twice the capacity of a 36-exposure roll of film (remember those?). In my book, I prefer keeping all my eggs in one basket, and then making very sure that nothing happens to that basket.

## Preventive Measures

Here are some options for preventing loss of valuable images:

- **Interleaving.** One option is to *interleave* your shots. Say you don't shoot weddings, but you do go on vacation from time to time. Take 50 or so pictures on one card, or whatever number of images might fill about 25 percent of its capacity. Then, replace it with a different card and shoot about 25 percent of that card's available space. Repeat these steps with diligence (you'd have to be determined to go through this inconvenience), and, if you use four or more memory cards you'll find your pictures from each location scattered among the different memory cards. If you lose or damage one, you'll still have *some* pictures from all the various stops on your trip on the other cards. That's more work than I like to do (I usually tote around a portable hard disk and copy the files to the drive as I go), but it's an option.
- **Transmit your images.** Another option is to transmit your images, as they are shot, over a network to your laptop, assuming a network and a laptop are available. You can use Nikon's Wireless Transmitter WT-4a, and beam the images over to a computer as you shoot them using the gadget's Image Transfer mode. One inexpensive alternative denied to D3s owners, but available for the D3x is a Secure Digital card with wireless capabilities built-in from a company called Eye-Fi (www.eye.fi). The firm markets a clever Secure Digital card with wireless capabilities built-in. To use one with the D3x, you'll need a CF-to-SD card adapter like the one shown in Figure 12.7. Unfortunately, the D3s won't accept a Type II-form factor adapter, and so can't use the Eye-Fi card, until it becomes available in a Compact Flash Type I format. When it happens, snap one up! These innovative cards ($50-$150) can be used to transmit photos from an SD-compatible camera to a computer on your home network (or any other network you set up somewhere, say, at a family reunion) and to websites such as Flickr, Facebook, Shutterfly, Nikon's own My Picturetown, and digital printing services that include Walmart Digital Photo Center. The most sophisticated option is Eye-Fi Explore, which I use, a 4GB SDHC card that adds geographic location labels to your photo (so you'll know where you took it), and frees you from your own computer network by allowing uploads from more than 10,000 WiFi hotspots around the USA. Very cool, and the ultimate in picture backup.
- **External backup.** You can purchase external hard disk gadgets called Personal Storage Devices (see Figure 12.8), which can copy files from your memory cards automatically. More expensive models have color LCD screens so you can review your images. I tend to prefer using a netbook, like the one shown in Figure 12.9. I can store images on the netbook's internal hard disk, and make an extra backup copy to an external drive as well. Plus, I can access the Internet from WiFi hotspots, all using a very compact device.

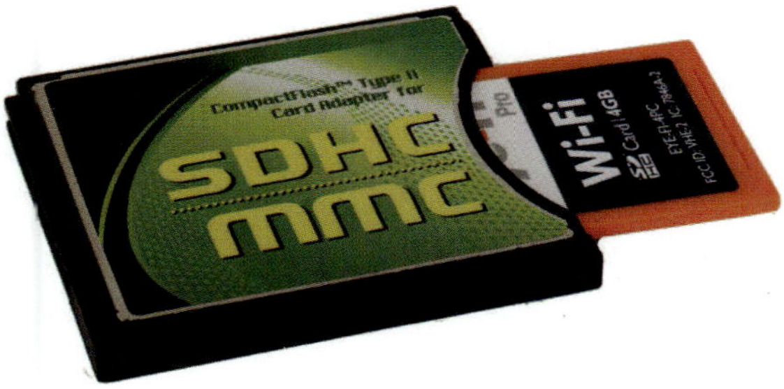


**Figure 12.7** Eye-Fi Secure Digital cards contain WiFi circuitry to connect to your network.

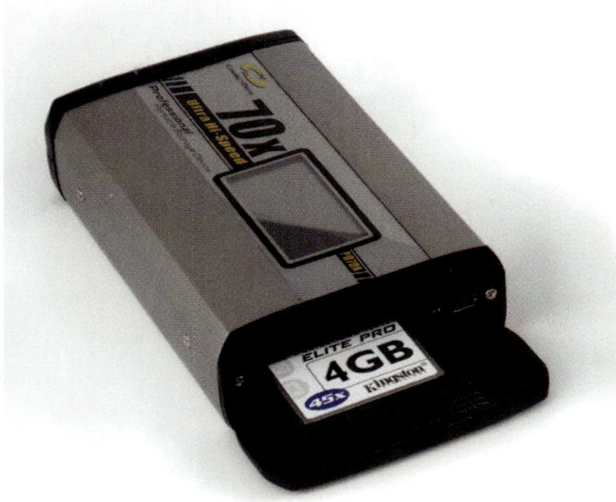


**Figure 12.8** Small battery-operated personal storage devices can back up your images.

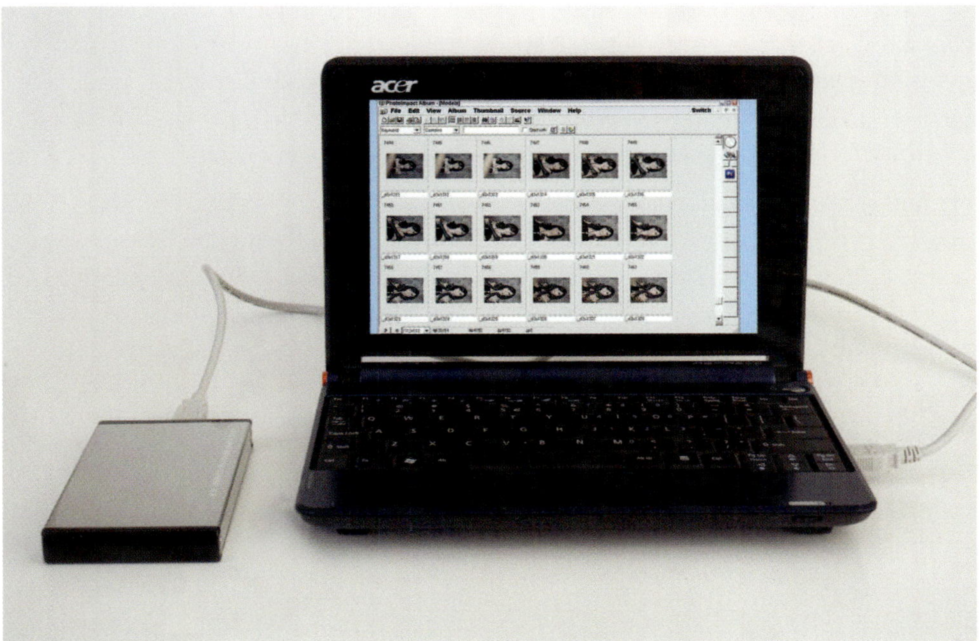


**Figure 12.9** A small netbook, linked to a card reader, and with or without an external hard drive, is another backup option.

## What Can Go Wrong?

There are lots of things that can go wrong with your memory card, but the ones that aren't caused by human stupidity are statistically very rare. Yes, a memory card's internal bit bin or controller can suddenly fail due to a manufacturing error or some inexplicable event caused by old age. However, if your card works for the first week or two that you own it, it should work forever. There's really not a lot that can wear out.

The typical memory card is rated for a Mean Time Between Failures of 1,000,000 hours of use. That's constant use 24/7 for more than 100 years! According to the manufacturers, they are good for 10,000 insertions in your camera, and should be able to retain their data (and that's without an external power source) for something on the order of 11 years. Of course, with the millions of cards in use, there are bound to be a few lemons here or there.

Given the reliability of solid-state memory compared to magnetic memory, though, it's more likely that your problems will stem from something that you do. Compact Flash cards are small and easy to misplace if you're not careful. For that reason, it's a good idea to keep them in their original cases or a "card safe" offered by Gepe (www.gepe .com), Pelican (www.pelican.com), and others. Always placing your memory card in a case can provide protection from the second-most common mishap that befalls memory cards: the common household laundry. If you slip a card in a pocket, rather than a case or your camera bag often enough, sooner or later it's going to end up in the washing machine and probably the clothes dryer, too. There are plenty of reports of relieved digital camera owners who've laundered their memory cards and found they still worked fine, but it's not uncommon for such mistreatment to do some damage.

Memory cards can also be stomped on, accidentally bent, dropped into the ocean, chewed by pets, and otherwise rendered unusable in myriad ways. It's also possible to force a Compact Flash card into your D3s/D3x's Compact Flash card slot incorrectly if you're diligent enough, doing little damage to the card itself, but bending the connector pins in the camera, eliminating its ability to read or write to any memory card.

Or, if the card is formatted in your computer with a memory card reader, your D3s/D3x may fail to recognize it. Occasionally, I've found that a memory card used in one camera would fail if used in a different camera (until I reformatted it in Windows, and then again in the camera). Every once in awhile, a card goes completely bad and—seemingly—can't be salvaged.

Another way to lose images is to do commonplace things with your card at an inopportune time. If you remove the card from the D3s/D3x while the camera is writing images to the card, you'll lose any photos in the buffer and may damage the file structure of the card, making it difficult or impossible to retrieve the other pictures you've taken. The same thing can happen if you remove the memory card from your computer's card reader while the computer is writing to the card (say, to erase files you've already moved to your computer). You can avoid this by *not* using your computer to erase files on a memory card but, instead, always reformatting the card in your D3s/D3x before you use it again.

## What Can You Do?

Pay attention: If you're having problems, the *first* thing you should do is *stop* using that memory card. Don't take any more pictures. Don't do anything with the card until you've figured out what's wrong. Your second line of defense (your first line is to be sufficiently careful with your cards that you avoid problems in the first place) is to *do no harm* that hasn't already been done. Read the rest of this section and then, if necessary, decide on a course of action (such as using a data recovery service or software described later) before you risk damaging the data on your card further.

Now that you've calmed down, the first thing to check is whether you've actually inserted a card in the camera. If you've set the camera so that shooting without a card has been turned on, it's entirely possible (although not particularly plausible) that you've been snapping away with no memory card to store the pictures to, which can lead to massive disappointment later on. Of course, the –E- warning appears on the LCD when the camera is powered up, and the Demo message is superimposed on the review image after every shot (assuming you've enabled the D3s/D3x to take photos when a card is not inserted), but maybe you're inattentive, aren't using picture review, or have purchased one of those LCD fold-up hoods mentioned earlier in this chapter. You can avoid all this by setting the No memory card? (Custom Setting f11) feature to Release locked, and leaving it there.

Things get more exciting when the card itself is put in jeopardy. If you lose a card, there's not a lot you can do other than take a picture of a similar card and print up some Have You Seen This Lost Flash Memory? flyers to post on utility poles all around town.

If all you care about is reusing the card, and have resigned yourself to losing the pictures, try reformatting the card in your camera. You may find that reformatting removes the corrupted data and restores your card to health. Sometimes I've had success reformatting a card in my computer using a memory card reader (this is normally a no-no because your operating system doesn't understand the needs of your D3s/D3x), and *then* reformatting again in the camera.

If your memory card is not behaving properly, and you *do* want to recover your images, things get a little more complicated. If your pictures are very valuable, either to you or to others (for example, a wedding), you can always turn to professional data recovery firms. Be prepared to pay hundreds of dollars to get your pictures back, but these pros

### THE ULTIMATE IRONY

I recently purchased an 8GB Kingston memory card that was furnished with some nifty OnTrack data recovery software. The first thing I did was format the card to make sure it was okay. Then I hunted around for the free software, only to discover it was preloaded onto the memory card. I was supposed to copy the software to my computer before using the memory card for the first time.

Fortunately, I had the OnTrack software that would reverse my dumb move, so I could retrieve the software. No, wait. I *didn't* have the software I needed to recover the software I erased. I'd reformatted it to oblivion. Chalk this one up as either the ultimate irony or Stupid Photographer Trick #523.

often do an amazing job. You wouldn't want them working on your memory card on behalf of the police if you'd tried to erase some incriminating pictures. There are many firms of this type, and I've never used them myself, so I can't offer a recommendation. Use a Google search to turn up a ton of them.

A more reasonable approach is to try special data recovery software you can install on your computer and use to attempt to resurrect your "lost" images yourself. They may not actually be gone completely. Perhaps your card's "table of contents" is jumbled, or only a few pictures are damaged in such a way that your camera and computer can't read some or any of the pictures on the card. Some of the available software was written specifically to reconstruct lost pictures, while other utilities are more general-purpose applications that can be used with any media, including floppy disks and hard disk drives. They have names like OnTrack, Photo Rescue 2, Digital Image Recovery, MediaRecover, Image Recall, and the aptly named Recover My Photos. You'll find a comprehensive list and links, as well as some picture-recovery tips at www.ultimateslr.com/memory-card-recovery.php. I like the RescuePro software that SanDisk supplies (see Figure 12.10), especially since it came on a mini-CD that I was totally unable to erase by mistake.

### DIMINISHING RETURNS

Usually, once you've recovered any images on a memory card, reformatted it, and returned it to service, it will function reliably for the rest of its useful life. However, if you find a particular card going bad more than once, you'll almost certainly want to stop using it forever. See if you can get it replaced by the manufacturer if you can, but, in the case of Compact Flash card failures, the third time is never the charm.

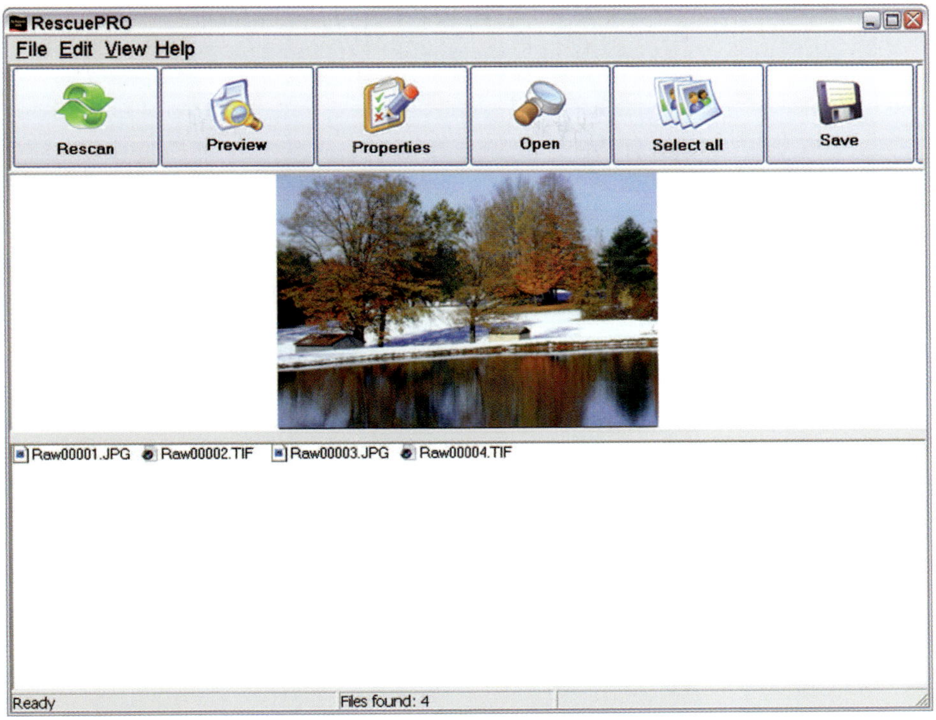


**Figure 12.10** SanDisk supplies RescuePro recovery software with some of its memory cards.

# Clean Your Sensor

Yes, the Nikon D3s (but not the D3x) has a two-pronged sensor dust prevention scheme: an innovative air control system that keeps dust away from the sensor in the first place, and a sensor-shaking cleaning mechanism. But no dust-busting technology is 100-percent effective.

Indeed, there's no avoiding dust. No matter how careful you are, some of it is going to settle on your camera and on the mounts of your lenses, eventually making its way inside your camera to settle in the mirror chamber. As you take photos, the mirror flipping up and down causes the dust to become airborne and eventually make its way past the shutter curtain to come to rest on the anti-aliasing filter atop your sensor. There, dust and particles can show up in every single picture you take at a small enough aperture to bring the foreign matter into sharp focus. No matter how careful you are and how cleanly you work, eventually you will get some of this dust on your camera's sensor. Some say that CMOS sensors, like the one found in the Nikon D3s/D3x, "attract" less dust than CCD sensors found in cameras from other vendors. But even the cleanest-working photographers using the Nikon D3s/D3x are far from immune.

Fortunately, one of the Nikon D3s's most useful features is the automatic sensor cleaning system that reduces or eliminates the need to clean your camera's sensor manually.

The sensor vibrates ultrasonically each time the D3s/D3x is powered either on or off (or both, at your option), shaking loose any dust.

Although the automatic sensor cleaning feature operates when you power the camera up or turn it off (depending on the behavior you specify in the Setup menu), you can activate it manually at any time. Choose Clean image sensor from the Setup menu, and select Clean now. If you'd rather specify when automatic cleaning occurs, choose On (clean at power up), Off (clean when the camera is switched off), On/Off (clean at both power up and power down), or Cleaning off (no automatic sensor cleaning will take place).

If some dust does collect on your sensor, you can often map it out of your images (making it invisible) using software techniques with the Dust off ref photo feature in the Shooting menu. Operation of this feature is described in Chapter 5.

Of course, even with the Nikon D3s's automatic sensor cleaning/dust resistance features, you may still be required to manually clean your sensor from time to time. This section explains the phenomenon and provides some tips on minimizing dust and eliminating it when it begins to affect your shots. I also cover this subject in my book, *Digital SLR Pro Secrets,* with complete instructions for constructing your own sensor cleaning tools. However, I'll provide a condensed version here of some of the information in that book, because sensor dust and sensor cleaning are two of the most contentious subjects Nikon D3s/D3x owners have to deal with.

## Dust the FAQs, Ma'am

Here are some of the most frequently asked questions about sensor dust issues.

**Q. I see tiny specks in my viewfinder. Do I have dust on my sensor?**

**A.** If you see sharp, well-defined specks, they are clinging to the underside of your focus screen and not on your sensor. They have absolutely no effect on your photographs, and are merely annoying or distracting.

**Q. I can see dust on my mirror. How can I remove it?**

**A.** Like focus screen dust, any artifacts that have settled on your mirror won't affect your photos. You can often remove dust on the mirror or focus screen with a bulb air blower, which will loosen it and whisk it away. Stubborn dust on the focus screen can sometimes be gently flicked away with a soft brush designed for cleaning lenses. I don't recommend brushing the mirror or touching it in any way. The mirror is a special front-surface-silvered optical device (unlike conventional mirrors, which are silvered on the back side of a piece of glass or plastic) and can be easily scratched. If you can't blow mirror dust off, it's best to just forget about it. You can't see it in the viewfinder, anyway.

**Q. I see a bright spot in the same place in all of my photos. Is that sensor dust?**

**A.** You've probably got either a "hot" pixel or one that is permanently "stuck" due to a defect in the sensor. A hot pixel is one that shows up as a bright spot only during long exposures as the sensor warms. A pixel stuck in the "on" position always appears in the image. Both show up as bright red, green, or blue pixels, usually surrounded by a small cluster of other improperly illuminated pixels, caused by the camera's interpolating the hot or stuck pixel into its surroundings, as shown in Figure 12.11. A stuck pixel can also be permanently dark. Either kind is likely to show up when they contrast with plain, evenly colored areas of your image.

Finding one or two hot or stuck pixels in your sensor is unfortunately fairly common. They can be "removed" by telling the D3s/D3x to ignore them through a simple process called *pixel mapping*. If the bad pixels become bothersome, Nikon can remap your sensor's pixels with a quick trip to a service center.

Bad pixels can also show up on your camera's color LCD panel, but, unless they are abundant, the wisest course is to just ignore them.

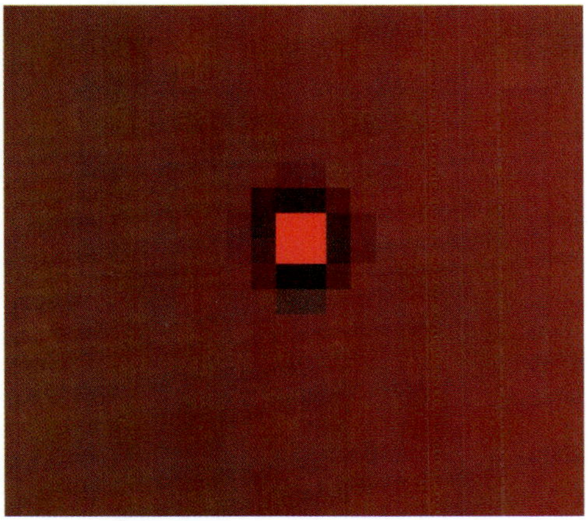

**Figure 12.11**
A stuck pixel is surrounded by improperly interpolated pixels created by the D3s/D3x's demosaicing algorithm.

**Q. I see an irregular out-of-focus blob in the same place in my photos. Is that sensor dust?**

**A.** Yes. Sensor contaminants can take the form of tiny spots, larger blobs, or even curvy lines if they are caused by minuscule fibers that have settled on the sensor. They'll appear out of focus because they aren't actually on the sensor surface but, rather, a fraction of a millimeter above it on the filter that covers the sensor. The smaller the f/stop used, the more in-focus the dust becomes. At large apertures, it may not be visible at all.

**Q. I never see any dust on my sensor. What's all the fuss about?**

**A.** Those who never have dust problems with their Nikon D3s/D3x fall into one of four categories: those for whom the camera's automatic dust removal features are working well; those who seldom change their lenses and have clean working habits that minimize the amount of dust that invades their cameras in the first place; those who simply don't notice the dust (often because they don't shoot many macro photos or other pictures using the small f/stops that makes dust evident in their images); and those who are very, very lucky.

## Identifying and Dealing with Dust

Sensor dust is less of a problem than it might be because it shows up only under certain circumstances. Indeed, you might have dust on your sensor right now and not be aware of it. The dust doesn't actually settle on the sensor itself, but, rather, on a protective filter a very tiny distance above the sensor, subjecting it to the phenomenon of *depth-of-focus.* Depth-of-focus is the distance the focal plane can be moved and still render an object in sharp focus. At f/2.8 to f/5.6 or even smaller, sensor dust, particularly if small, is likely to be outside the range of depth-of-focus and blur into an unnoticeable dot.

However, if you're shooting at f/16 to f/22 or smaller, those dust motes suddenly pop into focus. Forget about trying to spot them by peering directly at your sensor with the shutter open and the lens removed. The period at the end of this sentence, about .33mm in diameter, could block a group of hundreds of pixels. Dust spots that are even smaller than that can easily show up in your images if you're shooting large, empty areas that are light colored. Dust motes are most likely to show up in the sky, as in Figure 12.12, or in white backgrounds of your seamless product shots and are less likely to be a problem in images that contain lots of dark areas and detail.

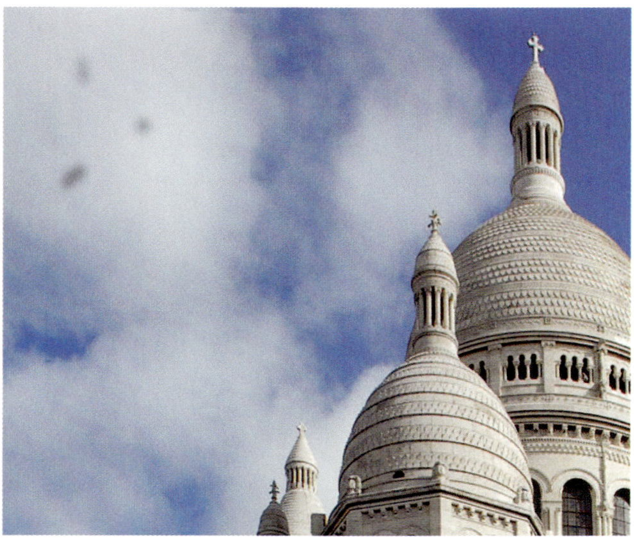

**Figure 12.12**
Only the dust spots in the sky are apparent in this shot.

To see if you have dust on your sensor, take a few test shots of a plain, blank surface (such as a piece of paper or a cloudless sky) at small f/stops, such as f/22, and a few wide open. Open Photoshop or another image editor, copy several shots into a single document in separate layers, then flip back and forth between layers to see if any spots you see are present in all layers. You may have to boost contrast and sharpness to make the dust easier to spot.

## Avoiding Dust

Of course, the easiest way to protect your sensor from dust is to prevent it from settling on the sensor in the first place. Here are my stock tips for eliminating the problem before it begins.

- **Clean environment.** Avoid working in dusty areas if you can do so. Hah! Serious photographers will take this one with a grain of salt, because it usually makes sense to go where the pictures are. Only a few of us are so paranoid about sensor dust (considering that it is so easily removed) that we'll avoid moderately grimy locations just to protect something that is, when you get down to it, just a tool. If you find a great picture opportunity at a raging fire, during a sandstorm, or while surrounded by dust clouds, you might hesitate to take the picture, but, with a little caution (don't remove your lens in these situations, and clean the camera afterwards!) you can still shoot. However, it still makes sense to store your camera in a clean environment. One place cameras and lenses pick up a lot of dust is inside a camera bag. Clean your bag from time to time, and you can avoid problems.
- **Clean lenses.** There are a few paranoid types that avoid swapping lenses in order to minimize the chance of dust getting inside their cameras. It makes more sense just to use a blower or brush to dust off the rear lens mount of the replacement lens first, so you won't be introducing dust into your camera simply by attaching a new, dusty lens. Do this before you remove the current lens from your camera, and then avoid stirring up dust before making the exchange.
- **Work fast.** Minimize the time your camera is lens-less and exposed to dust. That means having your replacement lens ready and dusted off, and a place to set down the old lens as soon as it is removed, so you can quickly attach the new lens.
- **Let gravity help you.** Face the camera downward when the lens is detached so any dust in the mirror box will tend to fall away from the sensor. Turn your back to any breezes, indoor forced air vents, fans, or other sources of dust to minimize infiltration.
- **Protect the lens you just removed.** Once you've attached the new lens, quickly put the end cap on the one you just removed to reduce the dust that might fall on it.

- **Clean out the vestibule.** From time to time, remove the lens while in a relatively dust-free environment and use a blower bulb like the one shown in Figure 12.13 (*not* compressed air or a vacuum hose) to clean out the mirror box area. A blower bulb is generally safer than a can of compressed air, or a strong positive/negative airflow, which can tend to drive dust further into nooks and crannies.

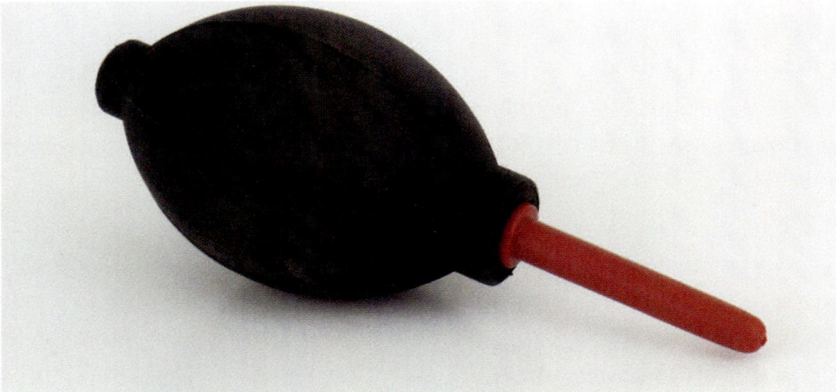

**Figure 12.13**
Use a robust air bulb for cleaning your sensor.

- **Be prepared.** If you're embarking on an important shooting session, it's a good idea to clean your sensor *now*, rather than come home with hundreds or thousands of images with dust spots caused by flecks that were sitting on your sensor before you even started.
- **Clone out existing spots in your image editor.** Photoshop and other editors have a clone tool or healing brush you can use to copy pixels from surrounding areas over the dust spot or dead pixel. This process can be tedious, especially if you have lots of dust spots and/or lots of images to be corrected. The advantage is that this sort of manual fix-it probably will do the least damage to the rest of your photo. Only the damaged pixels will be affected.
- **Use filtration in your image editor.** A semi-smart filter like Photoshop's Dust & Scratches filter can remove dust and other artifacts by selectively blurring areas that the plug-in decides represent dust spots. This method can work well if you have many dust spots, because you won't need to patch them manually. However, any automated method like this has the possibility of blurring areas of your image that you didn't intend to soften.

## Sensor Cleaning

Those new to the concept of sensor dust actually hesitate before deciding to clean their camera themselves. Isn't it a better idea to pack up your D3s/D3x and send it to a Nikon service center so their crack technical staff can do the job for you? Or, at the very least, shouldn't you let the friendly folks at your local camera store do it?

Of course, if you choose to let someone else clean your sensor, they will be using methods that are more or less identical to the techniques you would use yourself. None of these techniques are difficult, and the only difference between their cleaning and your cleaning is that they might have done it dozens or hundreds of times. If you're careful, you can do just as good a job.

Of course, vendors like Nikon won't tell you this, but it's not because they don't trust you. It's not that difficult for a real goofball to mess up his camera by hurrying or taking a shortcut. Perhaps the person uses the "Bulb" method of holding the shutter open and a finger slips, allowing the shutter curtain to close on top of a sensor cleaning brush. Or, someone tries to clean the sensor using masking tape, and ends up with goo all over its surface. If Nikon recommended *any* method that's mildly risky, someone would do it wrong, and then the company would face lawsuits from those who'd contend they did it exactly in the way the vendor suggested, so the ruined camera is not their fault.

You can see that vendors like Nikon tend to be conservative in their recommendations, and, in doing so, make it seem as if sensor cleaning is more daunting and dangerous than it really is. Some vendors recommend only dust-off cleaning, through the use of reasonably gentle blasts of air, while condemning more serious scrubbing with swabs and cleaning fluids. However, these cleaning kits for the exact types of cleaning they recommended against are for sale in Japan only, where, apparently, your average photographer is more dexterous than those of us in the rest of the world. These kits are similar to those used by official repair staff to clean your sensor if you decide to send your camera in for a dust-up.

As I noted, sensors can be affected by dust particles that are much smaller than you might be able to spot visually on the surface of your lens. The filters that cover sensors tend to be fairly hard compared to optical glass. Cleaning the 23.6mm × 15.8mm sensor in your Nikon D3s/D3x within the tight confines of the mirror box can call for a steady hand and careful touch. If your sensor's filter becomes scratched through inept cleaning, you can't simply remove it yourself and replace it with a new one.

There are four basic kinds of cleaning processes that can be used to remove dusty and sticky stuff that settles on your dSLR's sensor. All of these must be performed with the shutter locked open. I'll describe these methods and provide instructions for locking the shutter later in this section.

- **Air cleaning.** This process involves squirting blasts of air inside your camera with the shutter locked open. This works well for dust that's not clinging stubbornly to your sensor.
- **Brushing.** A soft, very fine brush is passed across the surface of the sensor's filter, dislodging mildly persistent dust particles and sweeping them off the imager.
- **Liquid cleaning.** A soft swab dipped in a cleaning solution such as ethanol is used to wipe the sensor filter, removing more obstinate particles.

- **Tape cleaning.** There are some who get good results by applying a special form of tape to the surface of their sensor. When the tape is peeled off, all the dust goes with it. Supposedly. I'd be remiss if I didn't point out right now that this form of cleaning is somewhat controversial; the other three methods are much more widely accepted.

## Placing the Mirror/Shutter in the Locked and Fully Upright Position for Landing

Make sure you're using a fully charged battery or the Nikon EH-6 AC adapter. Fortunately, the Nikon D3s/D3x is smart enough that it won't let you try to clean the sensor manually unless the battery has a sufficient charge.

1. Remove the lens from the camera and then turn on the camera.
2. You'll find the Lock mirror up for cleaning menu choice in the Setup menu. Select it.
3. Choose Start. The mirror will flip up and the shutter will open.
4. Use one of the methods described below to remove dust and grime from your sensor. Be careful not to accidentally switch the power off or open the Compact Flash card or battery compartment doors as you work. If that happens, the shutter may be damaged if it closes onto your cleaning tool.
5. When you're finished, turn off the power, replace your lens, and switch your camera back on.

## Air Cleaning

Your first attempts at cleaning your sensor should always involve gentle blasts of air. Many times, you'll be able to dislodge dust spots, which will fall off the sensor and, with luck, out of the mirror box. Attempt one of the other methods only when you've already tried air cleaning and it didn't remove all the dust.

Here are some tips for doing air cleaning:

- **Use a clean, powerful air bulb.** Your best bet is bulb cleaners designed for the job, like the Giottos Rocket. Smaller bulbs, like those air bulbs with a brush attached sometimes sold for lens cleaning or weak nasal aspirators may not provide sufficient air or a strong enough blast to do much good.
- **Hold the camera upside down.** Then look up into the mirror box as you squirt your air blasts, increasing the odds that gravity will help pull the expelled dust downward, away from the sensor. You may have to use some imagination in positioning yourself. (See Figure 12.14, which illustrates how I clean my Nikon D3s and D3x.)

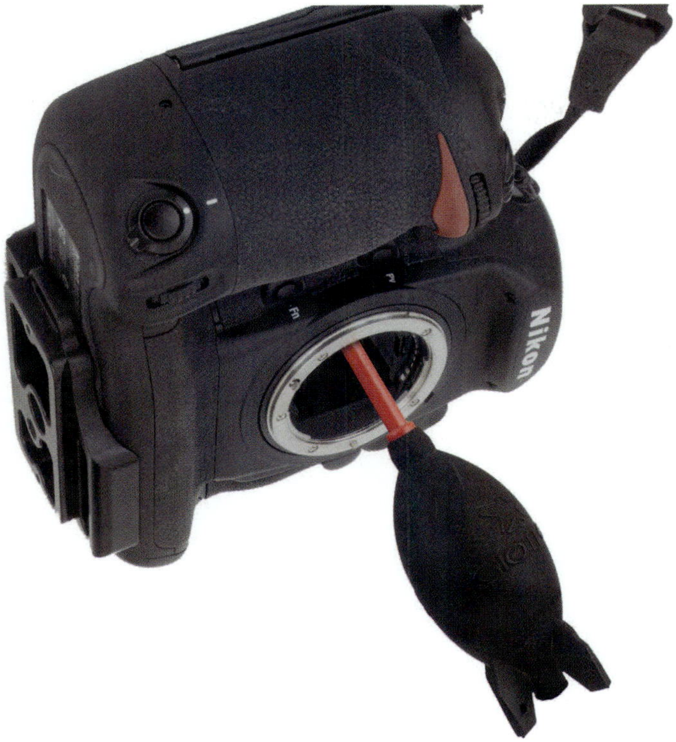


**Figure 12.14**
Hold the camera upside down and blow the dust off the sensor.

- **Never use air canisters.** The propellant inside these cans can permanently coat your sensor if you tilt the can while spraying. It's not worth taking a chance.
- **Avoid air compressors.** Super-strong blasts of air are likely to force dust under the sensor filter.

## Brush Cleaning

If your dust is a little more stubborn and can't be dislodged by air alone, you may want to try a brush, charged with static electricity, which can pick off dust spots by electrical attraction. One good, but expensive, option is the Sensor Brush sold at www.visibledust.com. A cheaper version can be purchased at www.copperhillimages.com. If you have one designed for a DX-format sensor, like the one shown in Figure 12.15, you can still use it, using two strokes across the long dimension of your sensor. However, you're better off if you can find a sensor brush that measures 24mm, the same width as your sensor.

Ordinary artist's brushes are much too coarse and stiff and have fibers that are tangled or can come loose and settle on your sensor. A good sensor brush's fibers are resilient and described as "thinner than a human hair." Moreover, the brush has a wooden handle that reduces the risk of static sparks. Check out my *Digital SLR Pro Secrets* book if you want to make a sensor brush (or sensor swabs) yourself.

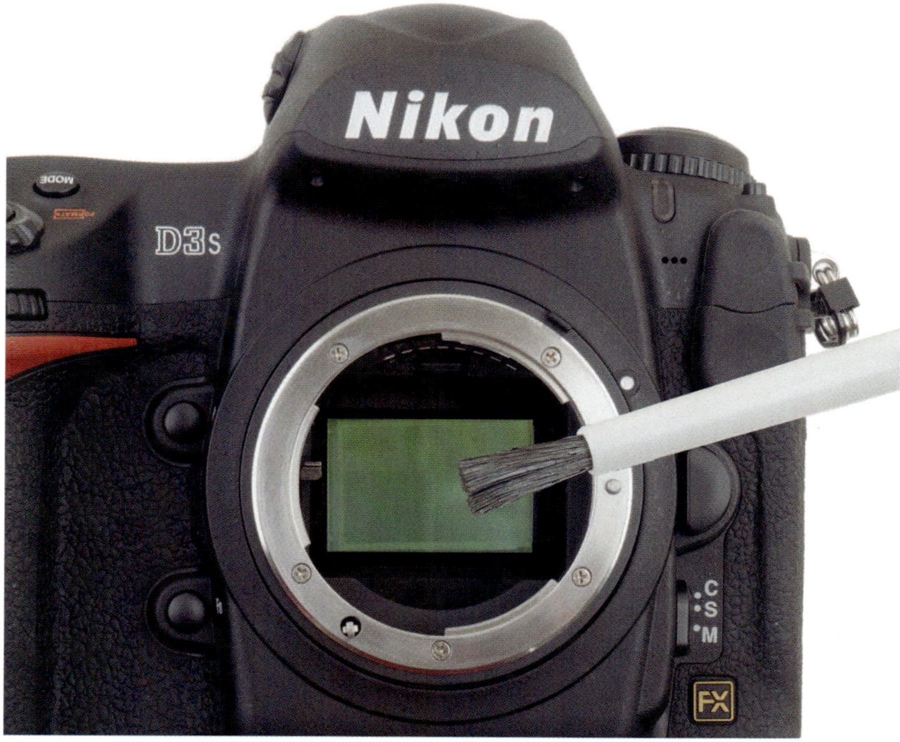


**Figure 12.15**
A special sensor brush is required for dusting off your sensor.

Brush cleaning is done with a dry brush by gently swiping the surface of the sensor filter with the tip. The dust particles are attracted to the brush fibers and cling to them. You should clean the brush with compressed air before and after each use, and store it in an appropriate air-tight container between applications to keep it clean and dust-free. Although these special brushes are expensive, one should last you a long time.

## Liquid Cleaning

Unfortunately, you'll often encounter really stubborn dust spots that can't be removed with a blast of air or flick of a brush. These spots may be combined with some grease or a liquid that causes them to stick to the sensor filter's surface. In such cases, liquid cleaning with a swab may be necessary. During my first clumsy attempts to clean my own sensor, I accidentally got my blower bulb tip too close to the sensor, and some sort of deposit from the tip of the bulb ended up on the sensor. I panicked until I discovered that liquid cleaning did a good job of removing whatever it was that took up residence on my sensor.

You want a sturdy swab that won't bend or break so you can apply gentle pressure to the swab as you wipe the sensor surface. Use the swab with methanol (as pure as you can get it, particularly medical grade; other ingredients can leave a residue), or the Eclipse solution also sold by Photographic Solutions. Eclipse is actually quite a bit purer than even medical-grade methanol. A couple drops of solution should be enough, unless you have a spot that's extremely difficult to remove. In that case, you may need to use extra solution on the swab to help "soak" the dirt off.

You can make your own swabs out of pieces of plastic (some use fast food restaurant knives, with the tip cut at an angle to the proper size) covered with a soft cloth or Pec-Pad, as shown in Figure 12.16. However, if you've got the bucks to spend, you can't go wrong with good quality commercial sensor cleaning swabs, such as those sold by Photographic Solutions, Inc. (www.photosol.com/swabproduct.htm). (See Figure 12.17.)

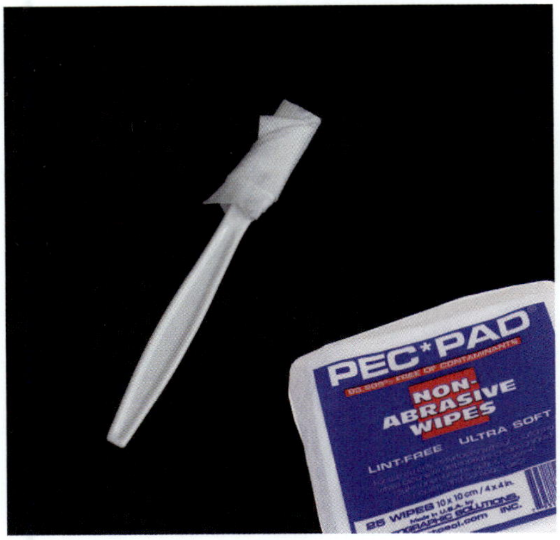


**Figure 12.16** Carefully wrap a Pec-Pad around a plastic knife that you've truncated.

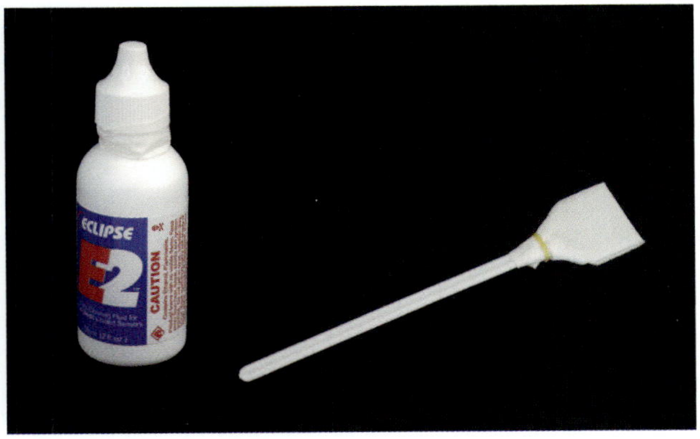


**Figure 12.17** Pure Eclipse solution makes the best sensor cleaning liquid.

Once you overcome your nervousness at touching your D3s/D3x's sensor, the process is easy. You'll wipe continuously with the swab in one direction, then flip it over and wipe in the other direction. You need to completely wipe the entire surface; otherwise, you may end up depositing the dust you collect at the far end of your stroke. Wipe; don't rub.

### THE ECLIPSE SAGA

If you read my advice in one of my earlier camera guides to use only Eclipse 2 cleaning solution (as recommended by Photographic Solutions) rather than the older Eclipse product, forget what I said—I was only repeating the manufacturer's advice, and the company has now reversed itself, discontinued Eclipse 2, and is recommending only the original solution once again. Wha' happen?

Photographic Solutions is fairly mum about the reversal. The original rationale for Eclipse 2 in the first place, as far as I've been able to piece together, was that the original Eclipse's methanol could change the properties of the indium tin oxide (ITO) coating on the glass anti-aliasing filter that covers the sensor. ITO is electrically conductive, and thus helps fend off the static electricity build-up that attracts dust to the sensor. Eclipse 2 was, presumably, more friendly to this coating. I suspect that the vendor discovered that the potential damage to ITO coatings by the original Eclipse was less than estimated, and that Eclipse 2 was not as effective in cleaning the sensor. So, New Eclipse was dumped and the recommendation is to use Eclipse Classic once again.

## Tape Cleaning

There are people who absolutely swear by the tape method of sensor cleaning. The concept seems totally wacky, and I have never tried it personally, so I can't say with certainty that it either does or does not work. In the interest of completeness, I'm including it here. I can't give you a recommendation, so if you have problems, please don't blame me. The Nikon D3s/D3x is still too new to have generated any reports of users accidentally damaging the anti-dust coating on the sensor filter using this method.

Tape cleaning works by applying a layer of Scotch Brand Magic Tape to the sensor. This is a minimally sticky tape that some of the tape cleaning proponents claim contains no adhesive. I did check this out with 3M, and can say that Magic Tape certainly *does* contain an adhesive. The question is whether the adhesive comes off when you peel back the tape, taking any dust spots on your sensor with it. The folks who love this method claim there is no residue. There have been reports from those who don't like the method that residue is left behind. This is all anecdotal evidence, so you're pretty much on your own in making the decision whether to try out the tape cleaning method.

## Magnifier Assisted Cleaning

Using a magnifier to view your sensor as you clean it is a good idea. I rely on two types. I have four Carson MiniBrite PO-25 magnifiers (see Figure 12.18), and keep one in each camera bag. So, no matter where I am shooting, I have one of these $8.95 gadgets with me. When I'm not traveling, I use a SensorKlear loupe. It's a magnifier with a built-in LED illuminator. There's an opening on one side that allows you to insert a SensorKlear cleaning wand, a lens pen-like stylus with a surface treated to capture dust particles. (See Figure 12.19.) Both the SensorKlear loupe and the SensorKlear wand are available from www.lenspen.com.

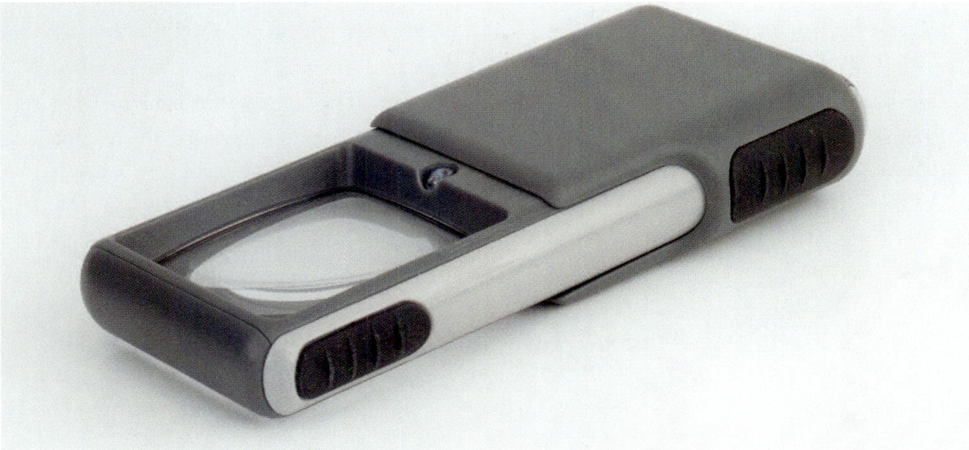

**Figure 12.18**
The Carson MiniBrite is a good value sensor magnifier.

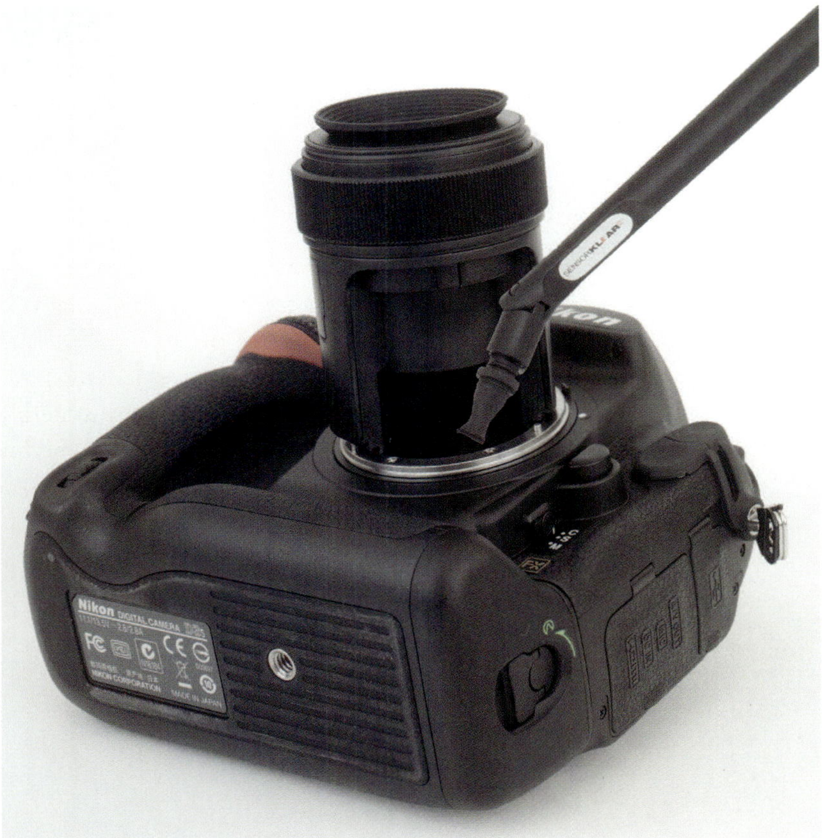


**Figure 12.19**
The SensorKlear Loupe and wand allow quickly removing multiple dust particles.

When I'm using the MiniBrite, I locate the dust on the sensor with the magnifier, remembering that the position of the dust will be *reversed* from what I might have seen on an image on the camera's LCD (because the camera lens flips the image when making the exposure). Then, I use the SensorKlear wand or the blower brush to remove the artifact.

The SensorKlear loupe actually allows you to keep your eye on the prize as you do the cleaning. You can peer through the viewer, rotate the opening to the side opposite the position of the dust, then insert the hinged wand to tap the dust while you're watching. This method allows removing a bunch of dust particles quickly, so it's my preferred procedure when I have the loupe with me.

# Appendix A

# A Tale of Two Cameras

## Overview of Nikon's D3-Class Models

This short appendix should provide you with everything you need to know to understand the differences between the Nikon D3s and D3x, and the kind of jobs each is best suited for. You'll learn that each model is versatile enough to handle many different types of photographic tasks that the other is traditionally associated with. For example, the D3x can be used as a nifty sports/photojournalism camera, and the D3s can work quite comfortably in the studio, for landscapes, or exterior architecture applications. However, you should have a better feeling for what kind of jobs each does better than virtually any other full-frame digital SLR in the world.

If you already understand certain topics—such as what a full-frame digital SLR is—feel free to skip ahead to the D3s/D3x comparisons later in this appendix. Or, if you are already comfortable in your understanding of how each of these cameras potentially fits in with your workflow, go ahead and start learning how to use your camera in Chapter 1. This overview is strictly optional and is provided at no extra cost to you.

## Migrating to the D3s

It was the best of times; it was the worst of times. It was the longest three weeks of my life. In late 2009, I sold the best and most versatile camera I'd ever owned—my Nikon D3—and its replacement, the new D3s, was little more than a promise of a post-Thanksgiving delivery from Nikon Professional Services. With the D3 shipped off to a new owner, for almost a month, I'd have to do all my full-frame digital shooting with my Nikon D700 and D3x. (My guess is that you're not exactly sympathetic with my "plight.")

I "unloaded" my beloved camera as soon as the D3s was announced because I had watched in horror in 2007, when my D2x plummeted in value from $2,000+ to less than $1,000 in the two-month period following the introduction of the D3, Nikon's first full-frame model. This time, I rushed to minimize my loss in order to fund the purchase of the sensational D3s, which Nikon demo'ed for me at Photo Plus Expo in New York City in late October. As good as the D3 was, I knew the D3s was going to be even better. It was going to raise the performance/image quality bar the same way the original D3 had in December 2007, and the way the 24.5-megapixel D3x had, in a different way, a year later.

Even though many of the controls and functions were almost identical, Nikon now had two very different "pro" class full-frame dSLRs—the D3x and D3s—each with its own strengths and weaknesses. I'd already seen raging debates in the online forums over the D3x and the original D3 for more than a year. Most of the postings missed the point. They concentrated on whether, say, the D3x was wildly overpriced, or whether the D3 was better enough than its stablemate (the Nikon D700) to be worth almost twice as much. There was even a lot of talk as to whether *other* full-frame cameras, from vendors like Canon and Sony, might be better choices.

In this overview, I'm going to try to clear up the confusion, a certain amount of bewilderment that you may still be feeling. And I do understand that many of you may be reading these pages, initially, not to learn how to use your Nikon D3x or D3s camera, but to help make a decision about which camera to buy. $5,000 and up is a lot of cash to expend on a digital camera, particularly at a time when technology is moving so fast that in 24 months (or less) you can fully expect to see even more amazing cameras on the market, possibly for less money. (Although the tendency at Nikon is to beef up the features in order to justify keeping the same price points with each new generation of camera.)

## What's a Full-Frame dSLR—and Why Should I Want One?

If you're old enough to remember film, you may recall a time when the most common type of single lens reflex (SLR) camera was the full-frame (24mm × 36mm) 35mm model, produced by Nikon, Canon, Minolta, Olympus, Pentax, and many other vendors. There were SLRs in other formats, too, ranging from the 24mm × 18mm "half-frame" compact cameras up through 60mm × 90mm/60mm × 70mm (or, more commonly 6cm × 9cm/6cm × 7cm) formats. These larger *medium format* SLRs and TLRs (twin-lens reflexes, like the famed Rollei, Yashica, and Mamiya shooters) could be called "full-frame" models, too (their full frames were simply larger than the 24mm × 36mm "full" frame).

But for the majority of amateur and professionals who wanted a portable, fast-working camera suitable for snapshots, candids, sports, and photojournalism, the 35mm full-frame models were the most popular standard format. Then, the introduction of digital cameras and (eventually) digital SLRs, deposited a fly into the ointment. Sensors were frightfully expensive to produce, even with the modest resolutions of the first digital cameras—often less (or much less) than 1.3 megapixels. Even with smaller sensor sizes, the first digital SLRs cost as much as $30,000, and remained in the $2,000-$5,000 price range until 2003-2004 (when the Canon EOS Digital Rebel and Nikon D70 first broke the sub-$1,000 barrier).

The first affordable dSLRs had sensors that were roughly 2/3 the size of the 35mm full frame, and were produced in that size not because there was a technological advantage to using smaller sensors (the first dSLRs were simply film cameras with a sensor and some electronics slapped into where the film plane formerly resided). The rationale was derived strictly from a cost standpoint: it was easier to reap acceptable yields of light-sensitive semiconductor chips (that is, produce CMOS or CCD sensors at a reasonable cost) by fabricating them in a smaller size.

Smaller sensor size has four major effects on your image, two of which are rather dramatic (the *crop factor* and *pixel density/sensitivity*), and the other two (*angle of incidence* and *diffraction*) a bit more subtle.

## Crop Factor

The *crop factor*, also called a *lens multiplier factor* is the most noticeable effect of smaller sensor size, and one of the primary reasons for desiring a full-frame camera like the Nikon D3s or D3x. Both terms are misleading and inaccurately used to describe the same phenomenon: the fact that cameras with a smaller than full-frame sensor (such as the Nikon D300s, D90, and other DX models) provide a field of view that's smaller and narrower than that produced by full-frame, FX models like the D3s/D3x, D3, and D700.

As I explain in Chapter 9, and recap here, the cropping effect is produced because the sensors of DX cameras are smaller than the sensors of the D3s, D3, D3x, or D700. These "full-frame" cameras have a sensor that's the size of the standard 35mm film frame, 24mm × 36mm. Any DX sensor does *not* measure 24mm × 36mm; instead, it specs out at 23.6 × 15.8 mm, or about 66.7 percent of the area of a full-frame sensor, as shown by the red boxes in the figure. You can calculate the relative field of view by dividing the focal length of the lens by .667, or by multiplying by 1.5. A 200mm lens mounted on a DX model has the same field of view as a 300mm lens on a Nikon D-series or D700 camera.

If you need to work with both DX and FX cameras, you might need to use the "multiplier" to calculate the equivalent field of view for each type of format. But the key thing to keep in mind is that the crop factor narrows the field of view of a particular lens. Lenses that have a wide angle when mounted on a D3s or D3x become less wide when used with a DX format camera like the D300s. If you're shooting landscapes, architecture, interiors, or other subjects that benefit from a wide-angle point of view, an FX-format camera definitely has an advantage over DX models, which need wider lenses just to achieve the same field of view.

On the other hand, the crop factor provides a "free" teleconverter that boosts the magnification of telephoto lenses. The 300mm f/4 lens you use on your D3-series model becomes the equivalent of a superfast 450mm f/4 prime lens on any DX camera, making it an excellent choice for sports or wildlife.

All else being equal, the bottom line seems to be that full-frame cameras like the D3-series have an advantage for those who need a wide-angle perspective, while DX-format cameras have an advantage if your needs call for telephoto reach. However, all other things are *not* equal. Another factor, the tradeoff between pixel density and sensitivity, comes into play.

## Pixel Density/Sensitivity

Smaller sensors have to use smaller pixels to squeeze the same resolution into the same area. For example, the D3s and earlier D3 have roughly 1.4 megapixels per square centimeter of sensor area in their 12 million pixel sensors. The Nikon D300s's smaller sensor also has 12 million pixels, but squeezes twice as many (3.3 million) into each square centimeter. Clearly, the pixel density is higher, and each individual pixel is smaller.

Higher pixel density is good when you're using the crop factor to increase the reach of a telephoto lens (a cropped Nikon D300s image has 12 megapixels; the same image area cropped out of the FX image of a D3 or D3s has only 5 megapixels). But there's a downside. The smaller DX pixels have less light-gathering power, so a DX sensor is less sensitive to light than an FX sensor of the exact same resolution. A DX sensor must amplify the photons it is able to capture more to match the sensitivity of the more light-hungry pixels of an FX sensor.

That's one of the reasons why a Nikon D3s produces an image with much less noise than a Nikon D300s at, say, ISO 1600. Indeed, the D3s at ISO 6400 frequently has less noise than a typical D300s image at ISO 1600. In fact, the D300s has a top sensitivity setting of ISO 3200, with a boost to the equivalent of ISO 6400. The D3s has conventional ISO settings all the way up to ISO 12800, with pushed sensitivity to the equivalent of 102400. Larger pixels have formidable light-gathering power.

Generally speaking, any FX-format camera will have more sensitivity, less noise, and improved dynamic range (the range of light-to-dark tones that can be captured) than a cropped sensor (DX) camera of the same resolution. This pixel density/sensitivity equation also explains why the 24.5-megapixel Nikon D3x, which has a higher pixel density than the D3s (2.8 megapixels per square centimeter) has more noise at equivalent ISO settings than the 12-megapixel D3s. Both are FX-format cameras, but the D3x has a higher pixel density (to achieve its 24.5 megapixel resolution), and smaller, less-sensitive pixels.

So, as you can see, the D3-series cameras have advantages over DX-series models that *don't* involve the crop factor.

## Angle of Incidence

A third factor that affects an image is the angle of incidence—the steepness of direction that the photons leaving the rear of the lens need to take to strike the sensor—which is also affected by sensor size. As you can imagine, lenses, especially optics created for full-frame cameras, "aim" the emerging light rays at a target that's 24mm × 36mm. Because the focal distance (from the rear of the lens to the sensor) is the same in both FX and DX models, converging those photons on a smaller DX-format sensor calls for a steeper approach angle. That may mean that some photons strike the "sides" of the individual photosite "wells" rather than impacting them head-on. It's a little like trying to toss marbles into a bucket from the side rather than dropping them in from overhead.

Film was less fussy about this angle of incidence of the light striking its surface, and FX sensors (which have larger pixels, too) have an easier time grabbing photons approaching from steeper angles. However, today, we have sensors with built-in microlenses that do a good job of focusing light onto individual photosites even if they approach from a steeper angle. In addition, lens manufacturers have developed new optical designs optimized for the DX format. These lenses take into account the needs of smaller sensors, and focus the light at more appropriate angles. So, problems caused by unfortunate angles of incidence are not as severe these days, and FX sensors have less of an advantage over DX sensors than they did in the past—as long as you are using only lenses designed for the DX format with your DX format camera.

That means that any lenses you accumulate for a camera like the Nikon D300s can't be used to their full potential if you migrate to an FX model. Because the typical lens collection totals several times what a typical dSLR body costs, and lenses can be used with multiple generations of camera bodies (which come and go), the potential obsolescence of DX-only lenses and partial incompatibility of lenses designed for FX format is a real problem for anyone with an eye to the future. That's why Nikon's full-frame cameras provide a DX mode so existing lenses can at least be used with a reduced resolution.

## Diffraction

Diffraction is a phenomenon that can cause a reduction in the apparent sharpness of your image due to scattering and interference of photons as they pass through smaller lens openings. In effect, the edges of your lens aperture affects proportionately more photons as the f/stop grows smaller. The relative amount of space available to pass freely decreases, and the amount of edge surface that can collide with incoming light increases.

So, an f/stop of f/11 may produce a slight loss of overall sharpness compared to an opening of f/8 (although depth of field will increase); and f/16 will be less sharp than f/11. Theoretically, this limit on sharpness should be independent of the resolution of the sensor, or the size of the sensor. The effects of diffraction *should* be the same at, say, f/11, regardless of what type of sensor is being used.

However, in practice, smaller pixels do show the effects of diffraction more readily. The diffraction produces a multi-ringed pattern called an *airy disk* (it has nothing to do with air; the phenomenon was named after scientist George Airy), and when the peak area of this disk is large enough, compared to the pixel size of the sensor, or if two disks overlap, an effect may be visible in the image. Typically, this happens at a particular f/stop with a particular pixel size, and that f/stop is said to be the diffraction limit for that camera/sensor. Point-and-shoot cameras, with their tiny sensors, may begin to show diffraction effects at f/5.6; a cropped-sensor camera at f/11; and a full-frame camera at f/16.

So, your Nikon D3s may be diffraction limited at a smaller f/stop than a D300s (*or* a D3x, which also has smaller pixels). As a result, you can effectively use smaller f/stops with a D3s than you can with a D300s or D3x. Is the sharpness lost to diffraction more objectionable than the reduced *range* of sharpness produced by less depth-of-field at wider apertures? That's up to you.

I've listed this effect fourth because the trade-offs may or may not be important to you. For example, most of the product shots in this book were taken with my Nikon D3x at f/22 or f/32. Given the size the images are reproduced in these pages, I felt that the increased depth-of-field of the smaller apertures was worth the possible loss of sharpness from diffraction. From an absolute standpoint, I would have noticed less image degradation if I'd used my D3s instead. But, in this case, better resolution trumped improved sharpness.

# The Nikon D3s vs. the Nikon D3x

Posters in the Nikon user forums often try to squeeze Nikon's FX-format cameras into a logical hierarchy. The Nikon D700 is the smaller, semi-pro full-frame camera, with fewer features, and best suited to the advanced amateur or a pro who wants to travel light or save some money. The original D3 was the "professional" camera, similar to the

D700 but with a more rugged body and higher shooting speed that lent itself to sports and action photography. The D3x was a step up from the D3, with more megapixels. The latest D3s is seen as a necessary improvement over the original D3, with improved high ISO performance and a few added features like automatic sensor cleaning and movie-making capabilities.

The implication is that there's a definite step-ladder from the D700 to the D3/D3s to the D3x, and that a reasonable Nikon shooter will select the model they can afford, assuming they have a need for the features that the next step up includes on its roster. The result has been some fiery debate over the D3s vs. D3x issue (the D3 vs. D700 contention has died down now that the D3s has some clear image quality advantages over the D700). My take is that all of Nikon's FX-format cameras are distinct models each best suited for a distinct set of tasks. None of them are *better* than the others. They are *different.* I've owned all four (because I can) and have found that I have had particular uses for each. I didn't dump my D3 when the D3x came out. And when I started using my D3s I found there were still many jobs that called for the extra resolution of my D3x.

It's likely that you won't be buying both cameras. Still, you should be interested in the following sections, which are task-oriented rather than focus on a comparison of each individual feature of the cameras.

## The Nikon D3s

The Nikon D3s, introduced at a price of $5,200, is Nikon's basic full-bore professional camera, stuffed full of features that pros and advanced amateurs need to shoot a very wide variety of jobs. It excels at sports and action photography, but has enough resolution and image quality to make it suitable for studio work and product photography. The D3s has some specific advantages when doing the following kinds of work:

- **Sports and action.** The D3s can capture 12 megapixel full-frame images of fast-moving sports at an astounding 9 frames per second. Use a crop mode, and the frame rate jumps to 11 fps. The D3s has a significantly larger buffer than its predecessor, the D3 (without an optional buffer upgrade), or the D3x, so it can suck up continuous shots at a much faster clip before slowing down to wait for images to offload to a memory card. Shooting JPEG Fine, the D3s's buffer can hold 82 images (typically four or more sequences in rapid succession), while the D3x's buffer tops out at 44 JPEG Fine images. (Of course, the D3x's files are 14MB each, versus 6MB for the D3s, which accounts for most of the disparity.)
- **Bad weather photography.** The D3s's weather sealing (the D3x has the same protection) makes it an excellent choice for photojournalism and sports under inclement conditions. I've shot football games in the pouring rain with no ill effects on the camera. (You do have to be careful of the lens-to-camera mount weakest link, which may not be as well sealed against the elements.)

- **Low light photography.** The D3s's superb image quality at high ISO settings makes it perfect for photojournalism, which usually calls for available light shooting, and for sports, which, unless you're a photographer from *Sports Illustrated* with the freedom to set up remote strobes, *always* calls for available light photography. Architectural photography, especially interiors, can also benefit from the D3s's low-light performance.
- **Fashion.** I shoot fashion outdoors and in the studio, and always prefer to shoot fast and with continuous lighting (if there's enough of it). The D3s's fast frame rates lend themselves to firing off shots quickly enough to capture a fleeting look or mood, and in the studio I can sometimes boost ISO settings and shoot using the modeling lights to keep up the pace, with a slight, but acceptable, increase in noise from the higher sensitivity settings.
- **Close-up photography.** Macro photography is often best done with the camera locked down on a tripod, but given Nikon's 105mm VR/autofocus Micro-Nikkor and a slight increase in ISO setting, it's actually possible to shoot close-ups hand-held. That extra flexibility can come in handy when shooting tiny fauna instead of flora.
- **Wildlife.** Shooting wild critters often calls for very long lenses and high ISO settings to allow shutter speeds that are fast enough to counter the inevitable camera shake that results—even with the camera mounted on a tripod. If you're shooting wildlife hand-held, the D3s has even more of an edge.
- **Landscapes.** Sometimes you don't have your tripod with you. In such cases, the D3s may give you the ability to use the fast shutter speeds you need to capture razor-sharp landscape images at an f/stop that provides reasonable depth-of-field. While the D3x may be the king of landscape photography, the D3s is the crown prince, especially when compared to wide-angle-challenged DX models.
- **Movies.** You can leave your camcorder at home if you have your D3s with you. Once you've mastered its movie-making capabilities you can shoot great clips seamlessly intermingled with stills.

## The Nikon D3x

The Nikon D3x, introduced at a price of $8,000, is Nikon's high-resolution camera, a rugged model that can shoot most of the kinds of jobs listed for the D3s previously, even if it isn't precisely suited for them. For example, its sports and low-light capabilities are limited by a 5 fps top shooting rate and ISO sensitivity settings that produce good image quality only up to ISO 1600, and which peter out completely at the equivalent of ISO 6400. However, the D3x does an especially good job at these kinds of tasks:

- **Product photography.** The D3x produces superb resolution, important for images of products that have fine details. The camera's 24.5-megapixel sensor creates images with a vast tonal range at ISO 100, and its files can be enlarged to billboard size and lend themselves to the kind of retouching and compositing that product photographs are often subjected to.
- **Fashion.** Although I love my D3s when I'm shooting fashion photojournalism-style using available lighting, I prefer the D3x for work that calls for high resolution images, superior color accuracy (a frequent need when photographing clothing), and lots of detail. But even for fast-moving work, the D3x's 5 fps shooting rate is no slouch.
- **Portraits.** Alas, even as digital cameras approach perfection, human beings still have defects that must be retouched to make us appear in prints as handsomely as we do in our minds. The D3x gives the digital photographer enough pixels to allow seamless retouching, and the resulting images have sufficient resolution to allow blowing them up to 30 × 40 inches for display over the fireplace in the manse. (Or next to the HDTV in the family room.)
- **Architecture.** The best images you see in *Architectural Digest* or *House Beautiful* probably weren't taken with a 12-megapixel camera. Indeed, many types of architectural photography is done using larger format cameras, and especially with lenses having perspective controlling swings and tilts. A Nikon D3x, mounted on a sturdy tripod, shooting at moderate ISO settings with carefully controlled lighting, is the Nikon photographer's best choice for this kind of shooting—especially interiors. Outdoors, the D3x is still formidable in daylight, with the D3s having an advantage only with scenes calling for higher ISO settings.
- **Close-up photography.** Some of the best close-up images have a stunning amount of detail, and high resolution is what the D3x does best. You haven't truly explored macro photography until you've tried it with the D3x.
- **Landscapes.** Photographers like Ansel Adams would set up their cameras (seemingly) according to the conjunction of the planets and stars, and then shoot exquisite images using large film formats that captured an amazing range of tones and astonishing detail. Of all of Nikon's cameras, only the D3x offers the highest resolution, the most accurate colors, and a dynamic range that's well-suited for landscapes and other pictorial work.

# Appendix B

## Glossary

It's always handy to have a single resource where you can look up various terms you'll encounter while working with your digital camera. Here is the latest update of a glossary I've compiled over the years, with some new additions specifically for the Nikon D3s/D3x.

**additive primary colors** The red, green, and blue hues, which can be used by themselves or in combinations to create all other colors that you capture with a digital camera, view on a computer monitor, or work with in an image-editing program, such as Photoshop. *See also* CMYK color model.

**Adobe RGB** One of two color space choices offered by the Nikon D3s/D3x. Adobe RGB is an expanded color space useful for commercial and professional printing, and it can reproduce a larger number of colors. Nikon recommends against using this color space if your images will be displayed primarily on your computer screen or output by your personal printer. *See also* sRGB.

**AE-L/AF-L** A button on the D3s/D3x that allows locking exposure and/or focus point prior to taking a photo.

**ambient lighting** Diffuse, nondirectional lighting that doesn't appear to come from a specific source but, rather, bounces off walls, ceilings, and other objects in the scene when a picture is taken.

**analog/digital converter** The module in a camera that electronically converts the analog information captured by the D3s/D3x's sensor into digital bits that can be stored as an image.

**angle of view** The area of a scene that a lens can capture, determined by the focal length of the lens. Lenses with a shorter focal length have a wider angle of view than lenses with a longer focal length.

**anti-alias** A process that smoothes the look of rough edges in images (called *jaggies* or *staircasing*) by adding partially transparent pixels along the boundaries of diagonal lines that are merged into a smoother line by our eyes. *See also* jaggies.

**aperture** The size of the opening in the iris or diaphragm of a lens, relative to the lens's focal length. Also called an *f/stop*. For example, with a lens having a focal length of 100mm, an f/stop with a diameter of 12.5mm would produce an aperture value of f/8.

**aperture-priority** A camera setting that allows you to specify the lens opening or f/stop that you want to use, with the camera selecting the required shutter speed automatically based on its light-meter reading and your ISO sensitivity setting. *See also* shutter-priority.

**artifact** A type of noise in an image, or an unintentional image component produced in error by a digital camera during processing, usually caused by the JPEG compression process in digital cameras.

**aspect ratio** The proportions of an image as printed, displayed on a monitor, or captured by a digital camera.

**autofocus** A camera setting that allows the Nikon D3s/D3x to choose the correct focus distance for you, based on the contrast of an image (the image will be at maximum contrast when in sharp focus). The camera can be set for *single-servo autofocus (AF-S)*, in which the lens is not focused until the shutter release is partially depressed, *continuous-servo autofocus (AF-C)*, in which the lens refocuses constantly as you frame and reframe the image, or *manual* focus.

**backlighting** A lighting effect produced when the main light source is located behind the subject. Backlighting can be used to create a silhouette effect, or to illuminate translucent objects. *See also* front lighting and sidelighting.

**barrel distortion** A lens defect that causes straight lines at the top or side edges of an image to bow outward into a barrel shape. *See also* pincushion distortion.

**blooming** An image distortion caused when a photosite in an image sensor has absorbed all the photons it can handle so that additional photons reaching that pixel overflow to affect surrounding pixels, producing unwanted brightness and overexposure around the edges of objects.

**blur** To soften an image or part of an image by throwing it out of focus, or by allowing it to become soft due to subject or camera motion. Blur can also be applied in an image-editing program.

**bokeh** A term derived from the Japanese word for blur, which describes the aesthetic qualities of the out-of-focus parts of an image. Some lenses produce "good" bokeh and others offer "bad" bokeh. Some lenses produce uniformly illuminated out-of-focus discs. Others produce a disc that has a bright edge and a dark center, producing a "doughnut" effect, which is the worst from a bokeh standpoint. Lenses that generate a bright center that fades to a darker edge are favored, because their bokeh allows the circle of confusion to blend more smoothly with the surroundings. The bokeh characteristics of a lens are most important when you're using selective focus (say, when shooting a portrait) to deemphasize the background, or when shallow depth-of-field is a given because you're working with a macro lens, with a long telephoto, or with a wide-open aperture. *See also* circle of confusion.

**bounce lighting** Light bounced off a reflector, including ceiling and walls, to provide a soft, natural-looking light.

**bracketing** Taking a series of photographs of the same subject at different settings, including exposure and white balance, to help ensure that one setting will be the correct one. The Nikon D3s/D3x allows you to choose the order in which bracketed settings are applied, or bracket sequence.

**buffer** The digital camera's internal memory where an image is stored immediately after it is taken until it can be written to the camera's non-volatile (semi-permanent) memory card.

**burst mode** The digital camera's equivalent of the film camera's motor drive, used to take multiple shots within a short period of time, each stored in a memory buffer temporarily before writing them to the media.

**calibration** A process used to correct for the differences in the output of a printer or monitor when compared to the original image. Once you've calibrated your scanner, monitor, and/or your image editor, the images you see on the screen more closely represent what you'll get from your printer, even though calibration is never perfect.

**Camera Raw** A plug-in included with Photoshop and Photoshop Elements that can manipulate the unprocessed images captured by digital cameras, such as the Nikon D3s/D3x's NEF files. The latest versions of this module can also work with JPEG and TIFF images.

**camera shake** Movement of the camera, aggravated by slower shutter speeds, which produces a blurred image.

**CCD** *See* charge-coupled device (CCD).

**center-weighted meter** A light-measuring device that emphasizes the area in the middle of the frame when calculating the correct exposure for an image. *See also* spot meter.

**channel** In an electronic flash, a channel is a protocol used to communicate between a master flash unit and the remote units slaved to that main flash. The ability to change channels allows several master flash units to operate in the same environment without interfering with each other.

**charge-coupled device (CCD)** A type of solid-state sensor that captures the image used in scanners and digital cameras.

**chromatic aberration** An image defect, often seen as green or purple fringing around the edges of an object, caused by a lens failing to focus all colors of a light source at the same point. *See also* fringing.

**circle of confusion** A term applied to the fuzzy discs produced when a point of light is out of focus. The circle of confusion is not a fixed size. The viewing distance and amount of enlargement of the image determine whether we see a particular spot on the image as a point or as a disc. *See also* bokeh.

**close-up lens** A lens add-on that allows you to take pictures at a distance that is less than the closest-focusing distance of the lens alone.

**CMOS** *See* complementary metal-oxide semiconductor (CMOS).

**CMYK color model** A way of defining all possible colors in percentages of cyan, magenta, yellow, and frequently, black. (K represents black, to differentiate it from blue in the RGB color model.) Black is added to improve rendition of shadow detail. CMYK is commonly used for printing (both on press and with your inkjet or laser color printer).

**color correction** Changing the relative amounts of color in an image to produce a desired effect, typically a more accurate representation of those colors. Color correction can fix faulty color balance in the original image, or compensate for the deficiencies of the inks used to reproduce the image.

**complementary metal-oxide semiconductor (CMOS)** A method for manufacturing a type of solid-state sensor that captures the image, used in scanners and digital cameras such as several of those from Nikon (including the Nikon D3, D3s/D3x, and D2xs).

**compression** Reducing the size of a file by encoding using fewer bits of information to represent the original. Some compression schemes, such as JPEG, operate by discarding some image information, while others, such as compressed RAW, preserve all the detail in the original.

**continuous-servo autofocus** An automatic focusing setting (AF-C) in which the camera constantly refocuses the image as you frame the picture. This setting is often the best choice for moving subjects. *See also* single-servo autofocus.

**contrast** The range between the lightest and darkest tones in an image. A high-contrast image is one in which the shades fall at the extremes of the range between white and black. In a low-contrast image, the tones are closer together.

**Creative Lighting System (CLS)** Nikon's electronic flash system used to coordinate exposure, camera information, and timing between a camera's built-in flash (if present) and external flash units, which can be linked through direct electrical connections or wirelessly.

**Custom Settings** A group of different settings you can make to specify how the Nikon D3s/D3x behaves, such as the function of certain controls, electronic flash features, and other customizable attributes.

**dedicated flash** An electronic flash unit, such as the Nikon SB-900 Speedlight, designed to work with the automatic exposure features of a specific camera.

**depth-of-field** A distance range in a photograph in which all included portions of an image are at least acceptably sharp. With the Nikon D3s/D3x, you can see the available depth-of-field at the taking aperture by pressing the Depth-of-field preview button, or estimate the range by viewing the depth-of-field scale found on some lenses.

**diaphragm** An adjustable component, similar to the iris in the human eye, which can open and close to provide specific-sized lens openings, or f/stops and thus control the amount of light reaching the sensor or film.

**diffuse lighting** Soft, low-contrast lighting.

**digital processing chip** A solid-state device found in digital cameras (such as the Nikon's EXSPEED module) that's in charge of applying the image algorithms to the raw picture data prior to storage on the memory card.

**diopter** A value used to represent the magnification power of a lens, calculated as the reciprocal of a lens's focal length (in meters). Diopters are most often used to represent the optical correction used in a viewfinder to adjust for limitations of the photographer's eyesight, and to describe the magnification of a close-up lens attachment.

**equivalent focal length** A digital camera's focal length translated into the corresponding values for a 35mm film camera. This value can be calculated for lenses used in DX mode with the Nikon D3s/D3x by multiplying by 1.5.

**exchangeable image file format (Exif)** Developed to standardize the exchange of image data between hardware devices and software. A variation on JPEG, Exif is used by most digital cameras, and includes information such as the date and time a photo was taken, the camera settings, resolution, amount of compression, and other data.

**Exif** *See* exchangeable image file format (Exif).

**exposure** The amount of light allowed to reach the film or sensor, determined by the intensity of the light, the amount admitted by the iris of the lens, the ISO sensitivity set in the camera, and the length of time determined by the shutter speed.

**exposure compensation** Exposure compensation, which uses exposure value (EV) settings, is a way of adding or decreasing exposure without the need to reference f/stops or shutter speeds. For example, if you tell your camera to add +1EV, it will provide twice as much exposure, either by using a larger f/stop or slower shutter speed, or both. The D3s/D3x offers both conventional exposure compensation and flash exposure compensation.

**fill lighting** In photography, lighting used to illuminate shadows. Reflectors or additional incandescent lighting or electronic flash can be used to brighten shadows. One common technique outdoors is to use the camera's flash as a fill.

**filter** In photography, a device that fits over the lens, changing the light in some way. In image editing, a feature that changes the pixels in an image to produce blurring, sharpening, and other special effects. Photoshop includes several interesting filter effects, including Lens Blur and Photo Filters.

**flash sync** The timing mechanism that ensures that an internal or external electronic flash fires at the correct time during the exposure cycle. A digital SLR's flash sync speed is the highest shutter speed that can be used with flash, ordinarily 1/250th of a second with the Nikon D3s/D3x. *See also* front-curtain sync and rear-curtain sync.

**focal length** The distance between the film and the optical center of the lens when the lens is focused on infinity, usually measured in millimeters.

**focal plane** A line, perpendicular to the optical axis, which passes through the focal point forming a plane of sharp focus when the lens is set at infinity. A focal plane indicator is etched into the Nikon D3s/D3x on the top panel.

**focus tracking** The ability of the automatic focus feature of a camera to change focus as the distance between the subject and the camera changes. One type of focus tracking is *predictive,* in which the mechanism anticipates the motion of the object being focused on, and adjusts the focus to suit.

**format** To erase a memory card and prepare it to accept files.

**fringing** A chromatic aberration that produces fringes of color around the edges of subjects, caused by a lens's inability to focus the various wavelengths of light onto the same spot. Purple fringing is especially troublesome with backlit images.

**front-curtain sync (first-curtain sync)** The default kind of electronic flash synchronization technique, originally associated with focal plane shutters, which consists of a traveling set of curtains, including a *front curtain*, which opens to reveal the film or sensor, and a *rear curtain*, which follows at a distance determined by shutter speed to conceal the film or sensor at the conclusion of the exposure. For a flash picture to be taken, the entire sensor must be exposed at one time to the brief flash exposure, so the image is exposed after the front curtain has reached the other side of the focal plane, but before the rear curtain begins to move. Front-curtain sync causes the flash to fire at the beginning of this period when the shutter is completely open, in the instant that the first curtain of the focal plane shutter finishes its movement across the film or sensor plane. With slow shutter speeds, this feature can create a blur effect from the ambient light, showing as patterns that follow a moving subject with the subject shown sharply frozen at the beginning of the blur trail. *See also* rear-curtain sync.

**front lighting** Illumination that comes from the direction of the camera. *See also* backlighting and sidelighting.

**f/stop** The relative size of the lens aperture, which helps determine both exposure and depth-of-field. The larger the f/stop number, the smaller the f/stop itself.

**graduated filter** A lens attachment with variable density or color from one edge to another. A graduated neutral-density filter, for example, can be oriented so the neutral-density portion is concentrated at the top of the lens's view with the less dense or clear portion at the bottom, thus reducing the amount of light from a very bright sky while not interfering with the exposure of the landscape in the foreground. Graduated filters can also be split into several color sections to provide a color gradient between portions of the image.

**gray card** A piece of cardboard or other material with a standardized 18-percent reflectance. Gray cards can be used as a reference for determining correct exposure or for setting white balance.

**group** A way of bundling more than one wireless flash unit into a single cluster that all share the same flash output setting, as controlled by the master flash unit.

**high contrast** A wide range of density in a print, negative, or other image.

**highlights** The brightest parts of an image containing detail.

**high-speed sync** A method for syncing Nikon external flashes, like the SB-900, at shutter speeds higher than 1/250th second by increasing the flash duration through multiple bursts to match the speed of the focal plane shutter.

**histogram** A kind of chart showing the relationship of tones in an image using a series of 256 vertical bars, one for each brightness level. A histogram chart, such as the ones the Nikon D3s/D3x can display during picture review, typically looks like a curve with one or more slopes and peaks, depending on how many highlight, midtone, and shadow tones are present in the image. The D3s/D3x can also display separate histograms for the red, green, and blue channels of an image.

**hot shoe** A mount on top of a camera used to hold an electronic flash, while providing an electrical connection between the flash and the camera. Also called an accessory shoe.

**hyperfocal distance** A point of focus where everything from half that distance to infinity appears to be acceptably sharp. For example, if your lens has a hyperfocal distance of four feet, everything from two feet to infinity would be sharp. The hyperfocal distance varies by the lens and the aperture in use. If you know you'll be making a grab shot without warning, sometimes it is useful to turn off your camera's automatic focus, and set the lens to infinity, or, better yet, the hyperfocal distance. Then, you can snap off a quick picture without having to wait for the lag that occurs with most digital cameras as their autofocus locks in.

**image rotation** A feature that senses whether a picture was taken in horizontal or vertical orientation. That information is embedded in the picture file so that the camera and compatible software applications can automatically display the image in the correct orientation.

**image stabilization** A technology that compensates for camera shake, usually by adjusting the position of the camera sensor (with some other camera types) or, with Nikon cameras, by shifting lens elements in response to movements of the camera.

**incident light** Light falling on a surface.

**International Organization for Standardization (ISO)** A governing body that provides standards used to represent film speed, or the equivalent sensitivity of a digital camera's sensor. Digital camera sensitivity is expressed in ISO settings.

**interpolation** A technique digital cameras, scanners, and image editors use to create new pixels required whenever you resize or change the resolution of an image based on the values of surrounding pixels. Devices such as scanners and digital cameras can also use interpolation to create pixels in addition to those actually captured, thereby increasing the apparent resolution or color information in an image.

**ISO** *See* International Organization for Standardization (ISO).

**i-TTL** Nikon's intelligent through the lens flash metering system, which uses pre-flashes to calculate exposure and to communicate between flash units, using the camera's 1,005-sensor viewfinder exposure meter.

**jaggies** Staircasing effect of lines that are not perfectly horizontal or vertical, caused by pixels that are too large to represent the line accurately. *See also* anti-alias.

**JPEG** A file "lossy" format (short for Joint Photographic Experts Group) that supports 24-bit color and reduces file sizes by selectively discarding image data. Digital cameras generally use JPEG compression to pack more images onto memory cards. You can select how much compression is used (and, therefore, how much information is thrown away) by selecting from among the other quality settings offered by your camera. (In the D3s/D3x's case, those are Fine, Standard, and Basic.) *See also* RAW.

**Kelvin (K)** A unit of measure based on the absolute temperature scale in which absolute zero is zero; it's used to describe the color of continuous-spectrum light sources and applied when setting white balance. For example, daylight has a color temperature of about 5,500K, and a tungsten lamp has a temperature of about 3,400K.

**lag time** The interval between when the shutter is pressed and when the picture is actually taken. During that span, the camera may be automatically focusing and calculating exposure. With digital SLRs like the Nikon D3s/D3x, lag time is generally very short; with non-dSLRs, the elapsed time easily can be one second or more under certain conditions.

**latitude** The range of camera exposures that produces acceptable images with a particular digital sensor or film.

**lens flare** A feature of conventional photography that is both a bane and a creative outlet. It is an effect produced by the reflection of light internally among elements of an optical lens. Bright light sources within or just outside the field of view cause lens flare.

Flare can be reduced by the use of coatings on the lens elements or with the use of lens hoods. Photographers sometimes use the effect as a creative technique, and Photoshop includes a filter that lets you add lens flare at your whim.

**lighting ratio** The proportional relationship between the amount of light falling on the subject from the main light and other lights, expressed in a ratio, such as 3:1.

**live view** The ability of recent Nikon cameras to provide a real-time preview image, as seen by the sensor, on the rear-panel color LCD, achieved by flipping up the mirror and opening the shutter.

**lossless compression** An image-compression scheme that preserves all image detail, while slightly increasing file size. When the image is decompressed, it is identical to the original version.

**lossy compression** An image-compression scheme, such as JPEG, that creates smaller files by discarding image information, which can affect image quality.

**macro lens** A lens that provides continuous focusing from infinity to extreme close-ups, often to a reproduction ratio of 1:2 (half life-size) or 1:1 (life-size).

**matrix metering** A system of exposure calculation that looks at many different segments of an image to determine the brightest and darkest portions, and base f/stop, and shutter speed on settings derived from a database of images stored in the camera's firmware. *See also* center-weighted meter and spot metering.

**maximum burst** The number of frames that can be exposed at the current settings until the buffer fills.

**midtones** Parts of an image with tones of an intermediate value, usually in the 25 to 75 percent brightness range. Many image-editing features allow you to manipulate midtones independently from the highlights and shadows.

**mirror lock-up** The ability of the D3s/D3x to retract its mirror to reduce vibration prior to taking the photo and to allow access to the sensor for cleaning.

**modeling light** A secondary light used to provide a preview of the lighting effects of an electronic flash unit. A modeling light can be an incandescent or fluorescent bulb, or may be simulated by a series of low-power bursts lasting a few seconds.

**neutral color** A color in which red, green, and blue are present in equal amounts, producing a gray.

**neutral-density filter** A gray camera filter that reduces the amount of light entering the camera without affecting the colors.

**noise** In an image, pixels with randomly distributed color values. Noise in digital photographs tends to be the product of low-light conditions and long exposures, particularly when you've set your camera to a higher ISO rating than normal.

**noise reduction** A technology used to cut down on the amount of random information in a digital picture, usually caused by long exposures at increased sensitivity ratings. In the Nikon D3s/D3x, noise reduction is automatically applied for long exposures, and it involves the camera automatically taking a second blank/dark exposure at the same settings that contain only noise, and then using the blank photo's information to cancel out the noise in the original picture. Although the process is very quick, it does double the amount of time required to take the photo.

**normal lens** A lens that makes the image in a photograph appear in a perspective that is like that of the original scene, typically with a field of view of roughly 45 degrees.

**overexposure** A condition in which too much light reaches the film or sensor, producing a dense negative or a very bright/light print, slide, or digital image.

**pincushion distortion** A type of lens distortion in which lines at the top and side edges of an image are bent inward, producing an effect that looks like a pincushion. *See also* barrel distortion.

**polarizing filter** A filter that forces light, which normally vibrates in all directions, to vibrate only in a single plane, reducing or removing the specular reflections from the surface of objects and effectively darkening the sky when shooting with the sun at an incident angle of 90 degrees from the axis of the lens.

**RAW** An image file format, such as the NEF format in the Nikon D3s/D3x, which includes all the unprocessed information captured by the camera after conversion to digital form. RAW files are very large compared to JPEG files and must be processed by a special program such as Nikon Capture NX or Adobe's Camera Raw filter after being downloaded from the camera.

**rear-curtain sync (second-curtain sync)** An optional kind of electronic flash synchronization technique, originally associated with focal plane shutters, which consists of a traveling set of curtains, including a *front (first) curtain* (which opens to reveal the film or sensor) and a *rear (second) curtain* (which follows at a distance determined by shutter speed to conceal the film or sensor at the conclusion of the exposure). For a flash picture to be taken, the entire sensor must be exposed at one time to the brief flash exposure, so the image is exposed after the front curtain has reached the other side of the focal plane, but before the rear curtain begins to move. Rear-curtain sync causes the flash to fire at the end of the exposure, an instant before the second or rear curtain of the focal plane shutter begins to move. With slow shutter speeds, this feature can create a blur effect from the ambient light, showing as patterns that follow a moving subject with the subject shown sharply frozen at the end of the blur trail. If you were shooting a photo of The Flash, the superhero would appear sharp, with a ghostly trail behind him. *See also* front-curtain sync (first-curtain sync).

**red-eye** An effect from flash photography that appears to make a person's eyes glow red, or an animal's yellow or green. It's caused by light bouncing from the retina of the eye and is most pronounced in dim illumination (when the irises are wide open) and when the electronic flash is close to the lens and, therefore, prone to reflect directly back. Image editors can fix red-eye through cloning other pixels over the offending red or orange ones.

**RGB color** A color model that represents the three colors—red, green, and blue—used by devices such as scanners or monitors to reproduce color. Photoshop works in RGB mode by default, and even displays CMYK images by converting them to RGB.

**saturation** The purity of color; the amount by which a pure color is diluted with white or gray.

**selective focus** Choosing a lens opening that produces a shallow depth-of-field. Usually this is used to isolate a subject in portraits, close-ups, and other types of images, by causing most other elements in the scene to be blurred.

**self-timer** A mechanism that delays the opening of the shutter for some seconds after the release has been operated.

**sensitivity** A measure of the degree of response of a film or sensor to light, measured using the ISO setting.

**shadow** The darkest part of an image, represented on a digital image by pixels with low numeric values.

**sharpening** Increasing the apparent sharpness of an image by boosting the contrast between adjacent pixels that form an edge.

**shutter** In a conventional film camera, the shutter is a mechanism consisting of blades, a curtain, a plate, or some other movable cover that controls the time during which light reaches the film. Digital cameras, including the Nikon D3s/D3x, use actual mechanical shutters for the slower shutter speeds (less than 1/250th second) and an electronic shutter for higher speeds.

**shutter-priority** An exposure mode in which you set the shutter speed and the camera determines the appropriate f/stop. *See also* aperture-priority.

**sidelighting** Applying illumination from the left or right sides of the camera. *See also* backlighting and front lighting.

**slave unit** An accessory flash unit that supplements the main flash, usually triggered electronically when the slave senses the light output by the main unit, or through radio waves.

**slow sync** An electronic flash synchronizing method that uses a slow shutter speed so that ambient light is recorded by the camera in addition to the electronic flash illumination. This allows the background to receive more exposure for a more realistic effect.

**specular highlight** Bright spots in an image, exhibiting no detail, caused by reflection of light sources.

**spot meter** An exposure system that concentrates its measurement on a small area in the image. *See also* center-weighted meter and matrix metering.

**sRGB** One of two color space choices available with the Nikon D3s/D3x. The sRGB setting is recommended for images that will be output locally on the user's own printer, as this color space matches that of the typical inkjet printer and a properly calibrated monitor fairly closely. *See also* Adobe RGB.

**subtractive primary colors** Cyan, magenta, and yellow, which are the printing inks that theoretically absorb all color and produce black. In practice, however, they generate a muddy brown, so black is added to preserve detail (especially in shadows). The combination of the three colors and black is referred to as CMYK. (K represents black, to differentiate it from blue in the RGB model.)

**through the lens (TTL)** A system of providing viewing and exposure calculation through the actual lens taking the picture.

**time exposure** A picture taken by leaving the shutter open for a long period, usually more than one second. The camera is generally locked down with a tripod to prevent blur during the long exposure.

**tungsten light** Light from ordinary room lamps and ceiling fixtures, as opposed to fluorescent illumination.

**underexposure** A condition in which too little light reaches the film or sensor, producing a thin negative, a dark slide, a muddy-looking print, or a dark digital image.

**unsharp masking** The process for increasing the contrast between adjacent pixels in an image, increasing sharpness, especially around edges.

**vignetting** Dark corners of an image, often produced by using a lens hood that is too small for the field of view, a lens that does not completely fill the image frame, or generated artificially using image-editing techniques (usually to enhance the appearance of certain kinds of images, such as portraits).

**white balance** The adjustment of a digital camera to the color temperature of the light source. Interior illumination is relatively red; outdoor light is relatively blue. Digital cameras like the Nikon D3s/D3x set correct white balance automatically or let you do it through menus. Image editors can often do some color correction of images that were exposed using the wrong white balance setting, especially when working with RAW files that contain the information originally captured by the camera before white balance was applied.

**zoom head** The capability of an electronic flash to change the area of its coverage to more closely match the focal length setting of a prime or zoom lens.

# Index

## A

## E

# F

## L

# M

## N

# T

# U



# V

# Y



# Z